AS S
for

wson

Hodder Arnold
A MEMBER OF THE HODDER HEADLINE GROUP

Orders: please contact Bookpoint Ltd, 130 Milton Park, Abingdon, Oxon OX14 4SB. Telephone: (44) 01235 827720. Fax: (44) 01235 400454. Lines are open from 9.00–6.00, Monday to Saturday, with a 24 hour message answering service. You can also order through our website www.hoddereducation.co.uk

If you have any comments to make about this, or any of our other titles, please send them to educationenquiries@hodder.co.uk

British Library Cataloguing in Publication Data
A catalogue record for this title is available from the British Library

ISBN-10: 0 340 88934 9
ISBN-13: 9 780340 88934 3

Published 2005
Impression number   10 9 8 7 6 5 4 3 2 1
Year   2009 2008 2007 2006 2005

Hodder Headline's policy is to use papers that are natural, renewable and recyclable products and made from wood grown in sustainable forests. The logging and manufacturing processes are expected to conform to the environmental regulations of the country of origin.

Cover photo by James Newell.
Typeset by Fakenham Photosetting Ltd, Fakenham, Norfolk.
Printed in Spain for Hodder Arnold, an imprint of Hodder Education, a member of the Hodder Headline Group, 338 Euston Road, London NW1 3BH.

Contents

Acknowledgements

The production of this book reflects, I think, one of the central concerns of sociology – it is at one and the same time both an individual and a social process; individual, in the sense of writing the text, but social in the sense that without the help, support and understanding of others the book itself would not exist.

I would like, therefore, to acknowledge the contributions made by the following people:

Firstly, and most importantly, my wife Julia, without whose intelligence, resourcefulness and patience none of this would have been possible.

Secondly, my parents – Ann and John – whose faith in education I hope I have, in some small way, started to repay.

Finally, although there has, no-doubt, been a small army of people working away behind-the-scenes to translate these words into something readable, I'd particularly like to thank Matthew Smith, for his faith and advice, Colin Goodlad for his patience and technical help and, of course, Tony Lawson for his overall contribution to the book.

Chris Livesey

The publisher's wish to thank the following for permission to use copyright material:

Nokia for photograph on p. 13.
Bettmann/CORBIS for A1 Gore photograph on p. 13, photograph of Karl Mark on p. 318, for photographs on pp. 104, and 195
Mark M. Lawrence/CORBIS for photograph on p. 31
Phil Backhouse, 2004, for photograph of three people on p. 33
Image Bank/Getty Images for man and woman at work photograph on p. 33
Stone/Getty Images for climbing wall photo on p. 33, young woman on p. 46, glamorous woman on p. 49
Hugh Threlfall – Alamy for photograph on p. 37
Rex Features for photograph of England fans on p. 42, photographs on pp. 83, 293
educationphotos.co.uk/walmsley for photograph of school children on p. 42, teenage boys on p. 69, public school on p. 234, comprehensive school on p. 234, modern classroom on p. 272, primary school science experiment, primary school home economics, secondary school science experiment on p. 277
Reuters/CORBIS for photographs on pp. 43, 289
Taxi/Getty Images for photograph of older woman on p. 46, woman in high paid job on 49, photograph on p. 95
Photofusion Picture Library – Alamy for photograph of housewife on p. 49
Rex/RICHARD JONES for photograph of woman in low paid job on p. 49
Rex/ISOPRESS for photograph of Madonna on p. 50, a cleaner at work on p. 64
The Guardian for 'Gender Stereotypes still hamper young' extract on p. 55

Rex/Caroline Woodham for photograph on p. 70

Rex/WOMANS OWN for photograph on p. 74

Mary Evans Picture Library for photograph on p. 78

Arnaldo Magnani/Getty for photograph on p. 90

Telegraph Group Limited 2003, for 'Housework is not the new sex' extract on p. 116

Rex/Ilyas J Dean for photograph on p. 146

News International 2004, for 'Now she's flabby Titmuss' extract on p. 149, 'Shame of our kids; extract on p. 158

Lindsay Parnaby/PA/Empics for photograph of Abi Titmuss 'flabby' on p. 149

Marc Gilliam for photograph of Abi Titmuss 'slim' on p. 149

Mirrorpix for front pages of *Mirror* 26/8/2004, 9/8/2004, 14/11/2003, 27/7/2004 on p. 152

2dtv Ltd for 2DTV advert on p. 160

The Advertising Archives for 'Club 18-30' and 'Wonderbra' advert on p. 160, photographs on p. 169, 174

ANDREW PARSONS/PA/EMPICS for photograph of strikers on p. 170

Rex/NILS JORGENSEN for photograph of *Coronation Street* on p. 170

Action Plus for photograph on p. 184

Rex/Sipa Press for photograph on p. 185, photograph of Tony Blair on p. 314, photograph on p. 389

Rex/TS/KEYSTONE USA for photograph on p. 201

Laurence Griffiths/Allsport/Getty for photograph on p. 223

JOHN STILLWELL/PA/EMPICS for photograph on p. 265

Hulton Archive/Getty Images for photograph of Edwardian classroom on p. 272

The BBC for 'Women on top?' extract on p. 297 and 'UK is "still a man's world"' extract on p. 325

PA/EMPICS for photograph of Margaret Thatcher on p. 314

Rex/Action Press for photograph of p. 316

Wesley Hitt/Alamy for photograph on p. 325

www.cartoonstock.com for cartoon on p. 337

Daily Mail for 'Year of the chav' extract on p. 346

HMSO for diagram on p. 349

Phil Cawley/Alamy for photograph on p. 370

Ken Light/Corbis for photograph of John Kerry on p. 375

Owen Franken/CORBIS for photograph of Jane Fonda on p. 375

Jean-Pierre Lescourret/CORBIS for photograph on p. 379

All other cartoons are by © Barking Dog Art

About this book

In writing this book, we had two main aims: firstly, to produce a text accessible to as wide a range of students as possible – from those coming to sociology with little or no previous knowledge of the subject, to those who, perhaps having studied sociology at GCSE, wanted to explore the subject further. Secondly, to create a text teachers – whatever their level of experience in terms of studying and teaching sociology – would feel comfortable using and, perhaps more importantly, be happy for their students to use. To fulfil these aims, we have developed a structure to the book that requires some initial explanation, so we have set out (briefly) below what we decided to do and, more importantly, how we decided to do it.

The structure of the book

Initially, we wanted to tie the information in the text closely to the 2005 AQA AS Sociology Specification, for two main reasons: firstly, to help students understand the overall requirements of the Specification (in basic terms, what they are required to know) and, secondly, to provide content that was clearly focused on these requirements. For better or worse, we decided that, for the majority of students (and teachers come to that), a primary consideration is both passing the AS exam and, of course, achieving as high a grade as possible. Each Module (such as Education) covered in the book, therefore, is divided into sections that reflect the demands of the Specification and, talking of modules, the book covers:

Module 1: Families and Households; Mass Media.

Module 2: Education; Wealth, Poverty and Welfare.

Module 3: Sociological Methods.

The *general structure* to the book is, in the above respect, fairly conventional; in terms of its *specific structure*, however, we have been a little more experimental in terms of our approach and, for this reason, it is worth briefly documenting our general strategy here.

Firstly, we have introduced an element of *differentiated learning* into the text, in the form of two types of section, namely:

- **Preparing the ground**, which introduces a basic level of information – enough to give the student an introduction to, and overview of, a particular issue or topic. This type of information is always followed by a second section:

- **Digging deeper** which, as the name suggests, involves looking in greater depth and detail into the issue or topic to provide more extensive information. In other words, if *Preparing the ground* provides an introduction to a topic, *Digging deeper* takes the student into areas and issues that extend their understanding and grasp of a topic.

The basic rationale for this structure is to allow students who are comfortable with the preparation work to concentrate on understanding this material, whereas students who need to be pushed a little further should find material in the *Digging deeper* section that will both challenge and extend their understanding.

Secondly, a conscious effort has been made to build the text around a *key word system* (as you will see if you have a quick flick through the various sections). This, we believe, helps students focus on the most significant ideas in a particular area; it will also, of course, help and encourage students to plan exam answers since these ideas, once grasped, can be used to unlock a wide range of sociological knowledge, understanding and interpretations. With exam preparation in mind, the focus on *key ideas* throughout the text means it can be used as either – or both – a conventional and revision textbook.

Exercises

The book contains three basic types of exercise, each of which is designed to achieve different things:

Warm Up exercises appear at the start of a section and, as the name suggests, are designed to ease students into a topic by requiring them to think about it in a way that builds on their existing knowledge. The basic idea here, therefore, is two-fold: firstly, to show students they already know something about a topic they are about to study and, secondly, to use prior knowledge as the basis for building a more sociological understanding of a topic (or issue within a topic). Warm up exercises are also, of course, just that – a whole-class activity that can be used to get things moving at the start of a topic.

Growing it yourself. These exercises are more focused than the general Warm Up type of exercise. In general, they are designed for small-group work within a topic, requiring students to talk about something and identify the key points surrounding an issue or topic. Many of these exercises are designed to introduce *evaluation skills* into the topic, mainly – but not exclusively – by asking students to think about the pros and cons of different arguments.

By design, the exercises appearing in this section develop naturally out of the text and can be completed as part of classwork rather than as an extension to that work. The majority require no prior preparation by the student or teacher (although there are a couple of exceptions in the Mass Media module, based on the analysis of newspapers and magazines which, if the exercise is to be completed, need to be provided).

Discussion points are the third type of exercise and these provide opportunities for students to discuss or debate different ideas – something we felt would be useful to build into the overall design because debate and discussion helps students to clarify and express their thinking in a relatively structured way. Some of the discussion points are tightly constructed around a particular issue, while others are more loosely constructed to allow students greater scope for discussion and debate.

Key Skills

If students are doing Level 2 or 3 Key Skills (in areas such as Communication or Working with Others) the exercises we have included provide opportunities for discussions, presentations, planning and extended pieces of work. They are not, it should be noted, primarily designed as Key Skills exercises – but many can, with a little forward-thinking and planning, be used as the basis for evidence collection in this particular area of the post-16 curriculum.

Finally . . .

Although it might seem a bit odd to draw your attention to things 'missing' from the book, we have decided, as part of the overall thinking behind the text, not to include the following:

Aims and objectives. We decided *not* to include these for a couple of reasons: firstly, there is what we might term the *Official* (or *OfSted*) reason: rather than be prescriptive in how the book is used by students and teachers, we decided to leave this particular issue open, partly because the book will invariably be used in a variety of different ways. Some students, for example, will follow the text from start to finish, whereas others will dip into and out of it at various points to supplement other forms of classroom material. In this respect, we felt it a little presumptive to impose our particular ideas about what students should/should not take from the text.

Secondly, there is the *Unofficial* (or *Bitter Experience*) reason: very few students ever seem to bother reading these things and, consequently, no-one ever uses them to check what has been learned or – more usually perhaps – what has not been learned.

Web links. Unusually for a contemporary textbook, we've decided *not* to include web links in the text (with one important exception explained in a moment). The reason for this is deceptively simple: the printed word is static and, once printed it is difficult to change. Websites, on the other hand, are dynamic; sites come and go (or, in some cases, they change their URL, which in this instance is just as bad) and there is nothing worse than being a given a website URL that does not work (okay, there are actually plenty of things worse than this, but you probably get the point).

Having said this, there *are* a few web links dotted throughout the book but all point to a single site (www.sociology.org.uk/as4aqa.htm in case you're wondering) – one we can be sure exists and whose URL will not change. Ever. When – or if – you find your way to the site we've set up to support the book, you'll find a wide range of 'good things' there to enhance your teaching and learning (and if you want to know what they are, you'll have to visit the site to find out).

Exam questions. Rather than hide them at the end of each chapter, waiting to snare the unwary and hogging valuable print space, if you need them (and, let's be honest, who doesn't?) you can find them on the website (www.sociology.org.uk/as4aqa.htm, in case the URL has unaccountably slipped from your consciousness).

1. Introduction to sociology

INTRODUCTION

For most students reading this book, AS level is probably a first introduction to sociology in any serious way. This is not to say you do not have some idea about the subject, but it is probably true that the extent of your knowledge is somewhat limited. In the normal course of events this is not a problem although, as with any new subject, you will have to become familiar with the particular ways in which sociologists like to look at things and the 'technical language' they use.

Leaving aside any positive or negative preconceptions you have, the idea of 'learning a new language' is actually a useful way of starting to think about sociology, since it involves approaching things that are familiar to us – people and their behaviour – and looking at them in a new and different way. As **Peter Berger** (*An Invitation to Sociology*, 1962) puts it: 'The fascination of sociology lies in the fact that its perspective makes us see in a new light the very world in which we have lived all our lives . . . '.

This idea is both *important* (if sociologists had nothing new to say about the social world there would not be much point to the subject) and, I think, *interesting*, mainly because it suggests there are different ways of looking at and understanding human behaviour.

We need to do some initial preparation work as a way of sensitising you to the idea of looking at human behaviour sociologically. This introduction, therefore, is designed to help you identify the subject matter of sociology and to do this we will be looking at three main ideas:

- an initial definition of sociology
- the difference between facts and opinions
- the sociological perspective – how sociologists look at the social world.

WARM UP: ASKING QUESTIONS

Sociology, at its most basic, is the study of people, their life and their relationships, and you can find out a great deal about people if you ask them the right questions. In pairs, therefore, discover as much as you can about your neighbour by asking them about their life. You might, for example, try asking them about their:

- family relationships (do they have brothers and sisters?)

- education (what subjects are they studying and why?)
- work (what they do, what they hope to do in the future).

You could develop this questioning by asking them what they feel about the people and relationships in their life (how do they get on with brothers, sisters, work colleagues and so forth?).

Defining sociology

⚠ Preparing the ground

In basic terms, sociology is the study of human societies. In other words, its subject matter is both human behaviour and, most importantly, human relationships. It is usually, as you may be aware, classed as one of the social sciences along with subjects like psychology. It was largely established as a discipline in the late eighteenth century through the work of writers such as **Auguste Comte**.

As an academic *subject*, sociology developed in the late nineteenth to early twentieth centuries through the work of writers such as **Emile Durkheim**, **Max Weber** and **Talcott Parsons** (all names that, for the present, probably mean nothing to you). One name you may have heard – **Karl Marx** (1818–84) – has probably done more to stimulate interest in the subject than anyone else, even though he wrote in a period before sociology became fully established as a discipline. Sociology, therefore, has a reasonably long history of development (150–200 years), although in Britain it has only achieved prominence as an examined subject in the last 30 to 40 years.

Definitions of the subject are not hard to come by, although for our purposes we can restrict ourselves to just a couple to give you some idea about what sociologists study and, equally importantly, how they study it.

- **What sociologists study**: A useful starting point is **George Ritzer's** (*Sociology:*

Experiencing a Changing Society, 1979) observation that: 'Sociology is the study of individuals in a social setting that includes groups, organisations, cultures and societies. Sociologists study the interrelationships between individuals, organisations, cultures and societies'.

In this respect, sociology involves studying human beings (which you probably knew) and, perhaps more importantly, their *patterns of behaviour* (which you may not have thought about). To do this, we focus on the relationships people form and how these connect to each other. In other words, the focus of the sociologist's attention is group behaviour and, more specifically, how our membership of social groups (such as families, friends and schools) impacts on individual behaviour.

- **How sociologists study behaviour: Barry Sugarman** (*Sociology*, 1968) suggests: 'Sociology is the *objective* study of human behaviour in so far as it is affected by the fact that people live in groups.'

For the moment, the idea of **objectivity** can be taken to mean that sociologists try to create factual knowledge, rather than knowledge based on opinion and, in this respect, sociologists – as they study group behaviour and relationships – try to avoid personal bias intruding into their research. To achieve this, they try to be *systematic* in their study of people's behaviour. This means that when collecting information about behaviour, sociologists use research methods (questionnaires, observations, experiments etc.) governed by certain **rules of evidence** – rules which tell sociologists how to go about the task of collecting and making sense of evidence. One example of this is that a sociologist will try to *test* their ideas in some way, rather than simply assuming something is either true or false.

Concepts of 'truth' and 'falsity' are always significant for many reasons, not the least being that sociologists – like most people – want the information they produce to be considered true. Assessing these concepts is, as we will consider at various points in this course, not always simple and straightforward, but for the moment we just need to consider the distinction between two types of information closely related to these ideas, namely **facts** and **opinions**.

- **Facts** are things that are true, regardless of whether or not we would like them to be true. For example, it is a fact that AS Sociology courses currently involve public examinations; you may not like this fact but if you want to achieve an AS Sociology qualification you will have to sit exams to determine your final grade.

  One major characteristic of factual knowledge, as I have suggested, is that it is considered true because we have tried to test it in some way (for example, through observing something over time) and found we cannot prove it false. This is a nice though initially somewhat confusing distinction that will be increasingly useful as your course develops. For example, I have observed various Advanced Level Sociology courses over time and found it to be true that there is always an examination of some kind involved. This is not to say facts are true for all time (in the future, sociology grades may not be awarded on the bases of tests) but, given certain

specified conditions, a fact is a statement that is true while those conditions apply.

- **Opinions** on the other hand can be generally defined as ideas that may or may not be factual or true. An opinion, in this respect, is simply a statement we make that we believe to be true (or not as the case may be), regardless of whether or not we have any evidence to support it. For example, I may hold the opinion that I am the most intelligent person in the world, but the only way to assess the truth or falsity of this opinion is to test it.

The main purpose of this little detour from the path of sociological enlightenment is to suggest sociologists try to create factual knowledge about human behaviour. That is, we try (not always successfully it has to be said) to produce statements about human relationships that are not only true, but demonstrably true – in other words, we are able to demonstrate such statements are not false on the basis of testing and evidence.

At A-level it is necessary – but unfortunately not sufficient – for students to both separate facts from opinions and be able to demonstrate a sound knowledge of these facts. Sociology, at this level, is not a simple memory test ('If I can memorise enough facts I will pass the course'), but clearly factual knowledge is very important.

Sociologists, however, are not simply interested in facts for their own sake; rather, we are (possibly more) interested in how facts are produced. In other words, how is factual knowledge created? The deceptively simple answer is that factual sociological knowledge is created by asking **theoretical questions**. Theory, for our purpose here, is something that explains the relationship between two or more things. For example, it is a fact that in 1995 approximately 160,000 marriages in Britain ended in divorce. Sociologically, we would like to know why this happens – what are the causes of divorce?

We can only explain facts by constructing possible explanations (theories) and then testing our theory against other, known, facts (or 'reality' as we sometimes like to call it). For example, a very basic theory in this instance might be that 'If a man and a woman are both in their teens when they marry, they are more likely to divorce' (something that, statistically, happens to be true).

 Digging deeper

So far we have looked at a couple of basic definitions of sociology, in terms of what sociologists study and how they study it. Before we move on to look at some important introductory sociological concepts, we need to step back for a moment to consider some of the basic beliefs shared by most sociologists.

Basic beliefs

Sociologists, like any social group, share a number of beliefs about the enterprise in which they are engaged (which, for those of you with very short memories, is to understand human behaviour). This is not to say sociologists are a group of like-minded individuals, always in complete agreement with each other; on the contrary, sociologists rarely agree with each other – but that is a story we will develop throughout this book. However, it is true that to be a sociologist means to subscribe to a set of principles that govern our basic outlook on 'Life, the Universe and, indeed,

almost Everything' to paraphrase **Douglas Adams** (*The Hitchhiker's Guide to the Galaxy*, 1979). In other words, if you do not or cannot agree with any of the following then, at best, you are going to find sociology difficult and, at worst, very frustrating indeed. Let us begin, therefore, by noting the following basic beliefs.

- **Human beings are social animals**: Not a particularly controversial opening statement, but one that needs to be noted. Sociology stems from the idea that 'the human animal' lives, works and plays in groups and this group behaviour involves the requirement to cooperate with others to produce the social world in which we live.

- **Human beings belong to social groups**: To understand human behaviour we focus on the groups to which people belong. This follows from the above in the sense that, if people form social groups (such as a family), it makes sense to examine and try to understand how these groups influence our behaviour. You might, for example, like to briefly reflect on how your family or friends have influenced your personal development (or, then again, you might not – we will need, at various points, to think about how the choices we make affect both our own behaviour and that of the people around us).

- **Human beings learn**: A fundamental idea for sociologists is that social behaviour is learned, not instinctive. This, of course, is a rather more controversial statement (for reasons we will develop in a moment), but it expresses the basic sociological belief that there is nothing in our biological or genetic make-up that forces us to behave in particular ways (to be, for example, selfish, aggressive or caring – to mention just three of my many human characteristics).

This is not to say human biology and genes are unimportant; you only have to look around to see they are – as a species, human beings are, for example, genetically different from cats and we are all, in various significant and insignificant ways, biologically different from each other. However, in terms of the relative influence on our behaviour, 'learning' is considered the most important for sociologists.

It is important you understand and, to some extent, accept these ideas and, in order to encourage such acceptance, we can briefly outline some of the reasons why sociologists see social behaviour as **learned behaviour.** Although it is not a particularly hard concept to grasp, one difficulty students tend to have at the start of a course is overcoming a lurking belief that, deep down, human behaviour really does have some sort of instinctive basis. This is not too surprising (and is really nothing to be ashamed about) given two things.

- **Teaching**: Firstly, we tend to be taught that animal behaviour is guided by instinct (by which, for the moment, we generally mean to be some sort of genetic programming that tells animals how to behave without them having to think about such behaviour). Since people are essentially animals too, it is only a short step to believe that some – if not necessarily all – of our behaviour has a similar instinctive basis.

- **Language**: Secondly, the concept of

instinct is frequently used in everyday language. For example, we hear or use phrases like 'The striker's instinct for goal' or 'She seemed to instinctively know they were talking about her'. This everyday usage gives the impression that instinct commonly influences behaviour and enters the realm of 'what everybody knows'. It becomes, in effect, part of our common sense store of knowledge.

Instinct

To understand why sociologists often question the usefulness of thinking about human behaviour in terms of instincts, we need to be clear about its meaning. Instincts have three main features: they tell an animal, for example, *what* to do, *when* to do it and, finally, *how* to do it. To clarify these ideas, consider this example from the bird world.

- **What**: Every year for as long as I can remember, blue tits have nested in the bird box I have so thoughtfully provided for them in my garden (except, I should add, when my garden was being redesigned and I took the box down – they nested in my barbeque instead). This is evidence of instinctive behaviour because the adult blue tits know what they have got to do each year.

- **When**: Aside from nesting every year, the blue tits also know at what point in the year to start nest-building, egg-laying and chick-rearing. Again, this is instinctive behaviour because it does not have to be taught or learned – they just seem to know when to start nesting.

- **How**: Without fail, these birds build exactly the same sort of nest each year (a single-storey 'everyone-in-it-together' affair). This, yet again, is instinctive behaviour because the adult birds have no choice in the matter – they build the type of nest they have been genetically programmed to build.

In terms of the above, human beings do not behave instinctively in the way we understand some animals or birds to. However, we can qualify this slightly by noting a further concept, frequently confused with the idea of instinct, namely **biological drives**. These are things that are biologically desirable or necessary, examples of which might include eating and sleeping. We should note that even though such drives are part of our biological make-up, they can be regulated though our social experiences (in other words, we may exercise some degree of choice about when and how we do them). Eating, for example, can be regulated through dieting, and sleep patterns can be fairly easily adjusted, depending on social circumstances.

WARM UP: INSTINCTIVE BEHAVIOUR?

In the following exercise we are going to test whether or not it is possible to identify human instincts. As you may imagine (given what you have just read), this is not very likely; nevertheless, it is a useful exercise, not simply to test this idea, but also because it leads into the main part of this chapter, a discussion of learned behaviour.

Firstly, make sure you understand the concepts of *instinct* and *biological drives* and the difference between them.

Secondly, make a list of anything you think could conceivably be instinctive human behaviour (for example eating or sleeping, crime, looking after children).

Next, remove from your list any biological drives.

Finally, for each of the remaining things on your list, remove it if we have a *choice* about whether or not to do it – which will put paid to things like crime (many people never break the law) and looking after children (many people choose to remain childless, or they employ other people to look after their children).

You should be left with a suspiciously blank list – and if it is not blank then you have either cheated, have a chronic inability to follow simple instructions or have listed things that are too trivial to have any real impact on people's behaviour).

Before we start to look at sociological ideas about learned behaviour, we can note that sociologists are sceptical about the idea of instinct as the basis for human behaviour, for three main reasons.

- **Choice**: Instincts, by definition, involve a lack of choice (their purpose, after all, is to create order by explicitly removing choice from the agenda). Human behaviour, on the other hand, involves an almost limitless set of choices, some of which are fairly banal ('Should I do my sociology homework or watch TV?') and some of which are not ('Should I buy this very interesting book or steal it from the bookshop?').

- **Diversity** of our behaviour: One of the fascinations of sociology is the fact different people develop different (or diverse) ways of doing things. If human behaviour was simply based on instinct, we would expect to see much the same sort of behaviour wherever we were in the world – and while there are, as we will see, many similarities and continuities in human behaviour, there is also a vast range of differences that stem from our ability to make choices.

- **Adaptation**: We live in a vast and complex world, one that seems to change increasingly rapidly. People have to be able to adapt to changes in their world and instinctive behaviour is, by its very nature, not well-suited to change.

Having suggested our behaviour is based on experience rather than instinct, what we need to do next is look at how sociologists consider social behaviour to be a learned process.

Learned behaviour

Preparing the ground

The first point to note is that if behaviour is learned, it follows it must also be taught – which leads to the idea that our membership of social groups is the initial key to understanding behaviour sociologically. We need, therefore, to understand the concept of a social group and how belonging to groups affects our behaviour. As you probably appreciate, there are various types of social group we can identify, such as:

- **Family groups**, consisting of people related to each other through **kinship** (a direct biological relationship – such as mother and daughter) or **affinity** (their relationship is by marriage or some other living arrangement).
- **Educational groups**, which could include people studying together in the same school/college or class.
- **Work groups** – people who do the same type of job, for example.
- **Peer groups**, consisting of people of roughly the same age (teenagers, for example) who share a number of common interests, such as music and fashion.

Our individual lives, therefore, are surrounded by social groups – some of which we actively join and others which we may

 Growing it yourself: social groups and their effects

Identify a group to which you belong (if done as a class, split into small groups, and each group identify a different social group). Examples of groups you could use are: family, education, work, friends and peers. Draw a table such as the one below and provide examples that answer the two questions (I've given you a couple of examples to get you started).

Group	How has my behaviour been shaped by this group?	How has the behaviour of group members been shaped by my behaviour?
School class	I sit quietly and listen	I am a style icon – they look to me for fashion advice

merely observe. Their significance to us, however, needs to be considered in terms of how membership of these groups affects two things:

- how we think about the social world (our personal 'sociological perspective')
- how we behave – in other words, how our behaviour is both learned from and shaped by the behaviour of others.

This exercise will have demonstrated two things: firstly, that we all belong to a wide variety of social groups and these groups shape our behaviour in some way; and secondly, as a member of these groups we are involved in shaping the behaviour of others.

In other words, this is a two-way process – my behaviour towards you affects your behaviour towards me which, in turn, affects how I behave towards you. The significance of this idea, if it is not immediately apparent, will be made clear in a moment. However, rather than explore these ideas further now, what we need to do is to briefly examine one of the largest groups to which we all belong, namely a **society**. This is useful for a couple reasons.

- **Common behaviour**: Membership of a society is something we have in common – we are all aware (because we have been taught such awareness) that we live in a particular society. Since it is a familiar concept to us, we should already have some basic idea about what it involves.
- **Sociological problems**: Examining this idea will help us understand some of the problems sociologists face in their study of social behaviour, mainly because, as we will see, it is not easy to pin down exactly what we mean by the 'thing' (society) we are supposed to be studying.

When we think about the concept of a 'society' we tend to characterise it in terms of ideas like:

- **Geographical area**, which is marked by either a physical border (such as a river), or a symbolic border (for example, an imaginary line marking where one society ends and another begins).
- **System of government**, which may involve things like a monarchy, parliament and civil service, for example.
- **Language**, **customs** and **traditions** which people within a society share (speaking the same language, for example, or celebrating a particular religious festival).
- **Identity**: we develop an awareness that 'our society' is different from other societies and 'We', in turn, consider ourselves different from 'Them' (for example, the English may see themselves as different from French or American people).
- **Culture**: What we are starting to develop, in very general terms, are ideas about distinctive 'way of life' characteristics of different societies. This concept is one to which we will necessarily return in a moment, since it involves the need to learn certain things.

Digging deeper

One of the problems sociologists have is that the 'thing' we want to study doesn't have a physical existence. 'Society', in other words, cannot be sensed – seen, smelt, touched, tasted or heard. This, as you might expect, creates a couple of immediate problems.

- **Arguments**: Our inability to point to something solid and say, 'This is society' means sociologists have developed different opinions about the nature of society – how it's organised or how it affects our behaviour, for example. In addition, not all sociologists agree about how to define 'society' or, indeed, how it can be studied.

- **Knowledge**: Sociologists are often accused of not being 'real' scientists (such as physicists, for example). Whether this matters probably depends on how important you consider this status to be. However, it does tend to mean the value of sociological knowledge is generally downgraded, mainly because sociologists seem incapable of *predicting* human behaviour. Whether this 'unpredictability' is a quality of sociology or of human behaviour is a matter for debate.

For the moment, we can note that there are plenty of things in the natural world that can be studied without the scientist being able to see them. Gravity, electricity, radiation and oxygen, for example, are all things we know exist, but they are not things you could easily pick up and physically examine.

The important point here, therefore, is that we know these things exist (or, if you prefer, we can *theorise* their existence) not because we can physically sense them but because we can feel their effects. This is an important idea because it gets us thinking about something like society in terms of it being a *force*, rather than a physical object – in the same way that gravity is a force rather than an 'object'. We can't see it, but we know it's there because we feel its effect. In a similar way, if we think about society as an invisible force, it should be possible to study its effects and, by so doing, demonstrate its existence.

If we view society in this way, it would be helpful to think about how this force is created and, to do this, we can use the idea of society as an **imagined community**. **Benedict Anderson** (*Imagined Communities: Reflections on the Origin and Spread of Nationalism*, 1983), for example, argues that society 'is imagined because the members of even the smallest nation will never know most of their fellow-members, meet them, or even hear of them, yet in the minds of each lives the image of their communion.'

In other words, society exists for us in our thoughts – each of us, in some way, imagines we belong to that community we call 'our society', just as we imagine we belong to social groups (such as a family) within that society. This may seem a complex idea to grasp (especially this early in the course), but we can simplify it by thinking about how and why we imagine ourselves to be part of a community, based on the idea of relationships.

Relationships

Whenever we enter into a relationship with someone – either through choice or necessity – we create an invisible *bond*. For example, when you say something like, 'That person is my friend', you recognise some kind of special relationship between the two of you. This relationship is different from the one created when you say something like, 'That person is my mother'.

There are hundreds (probably, I haven't counted them) of different social relationships we could identify. Some of these relationships are *personal* ('This is my lover') and some are *impersonal* (such as when you watch television), but the important thing is they all affect your behaviour in some way. You might like to think about this in terms of the way you classify the people around you – and how this classification system affects your respective behaviours.

Growing it yourself: classifying people

Next time you walk around your school or college, think about the different ways you classify people and how this classification affects your behaviour towards them. To help you, think about the following classes of people and how you're expected to behave towards them:

- strangers (people you don't know)
- acquaintances (people you recognise, but don't really know very well)
- friends
- close friends
- best friends.

If you think about this exercise, the relationships we form are significant to us because of the **meanings** we give to them. In a way, it is as if we are involved in an elaborate game, where we convince ourselves that the relationships we form are real, in the sense of having some sort of physical existence. We can think about this in terms of **behaviour.** How would a stranger be able to identify the different types of relationship in your life? How, for example, would they know which person was your father or sister, employer or lover? The simple answer is that, merely by looking, they wouldn't. They could only guess at these relationships by the way both you and these people behave towards each other.

Discussion point: using your imagination

What would happen if you imagine a relationship exists and the people around you deny that it does?

What would happen, for example, if you went up to a complete stranger and started behaving towards them as if they were your boy/girlfriend?

What should be clear from the above is that relationships and their meanings are important to us – not just on an individual level, but also in terms of the various ways we imagine our connections to other people. What we need to do next, therefore, is to explore in more detail the various ways we construct our social relationships.

Culture and socialisation

Preparing the ground

In this section we can develop some of the ideas we have touched upon in relation to the idea that social behaviour is learned. In particular, we can look more closely at two central ideas, namely, *what* we learn and *how* we learn it.

As we have just seen, the idea of being born into – and living in – a society is an important one, not simply because this happens to be true (everyone is born into an existing society), but also because it suggests 'a society' involves some sort of organisation. In other words, for a society to exist it must have *order* and *stability* and for these to exist people's behaviour must display *patterns* and *regularities* – ideas we can initially understand in terms of **culture**. At its most basic, a culture is, as I have already noted, a 'way of life'. It consists, in other words, of the behaviour and beliefs that characterise people of a particular society, and we can start to explore this idea in the following exercise.

WARM UP: BEHAVIOUR AND BELIEFS

This exercise involves identifying behaviours and beliefs characteristic of British culture. It can be done individually, but it is more fun if you do it as a class.

I have provided one example of behaviour and beliefs in each section to get you started. What further examples could you add to each of the categories?

In this exercise we have identified three main aspects of culture we can develop in the following way:

- **Social institutions**: We can think about 'our culture' (or indeed any culture) in terms of general patterns of behaviour based around four different categories: politics, economics, family life and culture (which includes areas like education and religion). The technical term for these large-scale, persistent (long-term) patterns of behaviour is 'social institution' – an idea we will develop in more detail in a moment.
- **Norms**: When we think about 'typical' forms of behaviour (such as going to school or working) we are referring to *norms* (short for 'normative' or 'normal') These can be defined as expected forms of behaviour in a given situation. For example, it might be a norm in our education system for students to sit quietly and listen when their teacher is talking to the class.
- **Values**: When we think about beliefs associated with institutions and norms (such as the belief someone is 'innocent until proven guilty') we are expressing a *value* – a belief about the way something should be. Thus, when you catch yourself saying what you believe someone should or should not do, you are expressing your values.

Aspect of Culture	Behaviour typical of British culture	Typical beliefs of British culture
Politics	Legal system – law abiding	Fair trial
Family	Marriage/cohabitation	Romantic love
Economic (Work)	Employer/employee	Work for money
Education	Attending school (5–16)	Qualifications important
Media	Watching TV	Private/public ownership
Religion	Prayer	Christianity/Islam
Science	Medical surgery	Keeping people alive as long as possible

⚠ Digging deeper

So far we have seen that a society has a culture that consists of a combination of social institutions, norms of behaviour and values. Before we examine these ideas in more detail, however, we can dig a little deeper around the concept of culture to identify some of its most important aspects and suggest why culture (rather than instinct) is the basis for human behaviour. Let's begin, therefore, by noting that culture consists of two basic elements, **material culture** and **non-material culture**.

Material culture

This aspect of culture consists of the physical objects (cars, telephones, computers, etc.) a society produces to reflect their knowledge, skills, interests and preoccupations. These objects do, of course, have meaning for the people who produce and use them, adding a further dimension to the concept of culture which we can illustrate in the following way.

If you think about a mobile phone it is fairly easy to see these two dimensions of material culture:

- **Technology**: On the one hand, the mobile phone is an object that allows you to communicate with anyone who has access to a telephone, wherever you may be.
- **Meaning**: On the other hand, your mobile has certain cultural meanings; it says something, in other words, about who you are.

For example, your ringtone, the functions your mobile can perform and so forth, all say something about you. Whether or not it's

Discussion point: cultural meaning

Look at the picture and describe what it means to you.

These are two of the very latest mobile phones

Now look at the following picture and describe what it means to you.

This picture of Alan Gore shows him using an early mobile (a word I use loosely) phone

What do the two pictures tell us about:
- how meanings change
- how changes in technology may change the meaning of something?

what you intend them to mean is, of course, something other people will decide – perhaps that Cliff Richard ringtone you intend to be an ironic comment on popular culture is just seen as totally naff by people who have to listen to it.

The Discussion Point has started you thinking about the idea of **social status**, which involves ideas about how you are viewed by others and, most importantly, the level of respect they give you on the basis of their understanding of your status. Another aspect to status, in this particular context, is that a mobile phone is an example of a *status symbol* – an object that partly functions to tell other people something about you (which, in terms of the second picture at least, may or may not be what you intended). This, in turn, leads us to think about the concept of **function**: **Robert Merton** (*Social Theory and Social Structure*, 1957) argued that the purpose of something (its *function*) can always be considered on two levels, namely in terms of:

- **Manifest function**, which relates to an apparent or obvious purpose (the manifest function of a mobile phone, for example, is to communicate with people)

- **Latent function**, which involves the idea something may have a hidden or obscured purpose (for example, the idea of a mobile phone being used as a status symbol).

A further example of manifest and latent functions might be when a teacher takes the register at the start of a class. The *manifest* function of this behaviour is to see who is present and who is absent. However, this behaviour also serves a latent or hidden function – one that demonstrates to students who is in charge of the class (since only the teacher is allowed to mark the register).

Growing it yourself: finding functions

In the following table I have identified some examples of behaviour in our society. In small groups, reproduce the table and suggest manifest and latent functions for the actions I have left blank.

As a class, if you have the time (and the inclination), suggest some further actions and their associated manifest and latent functions.

Action	Manifest function(s)	Latent function(s)
Taking the register	To see who is present or absent	To establish authority of the teacher
A teacher standing at the front of the class		
Going to school		
A school assembly		
Wearing an engage-ment ring		
A wedding		

Non-material culture

The second aspect of culture we can usefully note is non-material culture, which consists of the knowledge and beliefs that influence people's behaviour. For example, in our culture, behaviour may be influenced by religious beliefs (if you are a Christian or a Muslim, for example, the teachings of these religions may exert a powerful influence over your behaviour) and/or scientific beliefs – your view of human biological development, for example, has probably been influenced by **Charles Darwin's** 'Theory of Evolution'.

Having outlined these two basic dimensions of culture, we can develop the concept of non-material culture further by examining a number of related ideas.

Roles, status, values, norms

⚠ Preparing the ground

So far we have touched on the idea of societies and cultures being characterised by certain behavioural patterns or regularities. The main question to address next, therefore, is that if we are all individuals, unique in our own small ways, and without instincts to guide us, how is it possible for these patterns of behaviour to exist?

For sociologists, the answer to this question is behaviour patterns are culturally created; that is, individual behaviours are shaped by the groups – and culture – to which we belong and with which we identify. To understand this idea, we need to introduce a couple of new concepts and revisit some we have already (briefly) met.

Social roles

These are one of the main ways the 'invisible hand' of culture reaches out to influence people's behaviour. Roles are the

parts we play in our relationships with others – an idea similar to that of an actor in a play. Just as an actor may play many parts during their career, each of us plays many roles during our lifetime; teacher, student, mother, son, employer and employee are just a few examples we can identify.

Roles are an important part of culture because they are the basic foundations for behaviour; without instincts to guide us we are forced to develop a sense of how we are expected to behave in particular social situations. This means that roles have some interesting features worth noting.

- **Sharing**: A role is always played in relation to other roles. My role of teacher, for example, would be meaningless if it wasn't played out in relation to students (standing at the front of an empty classroom patiently explaining the concept of social roles would probably be interpreted as a sign of insanity).

- **Expectations**: Because roles always involve certain expectations (I expect to teach, you expect to learn) they create a sense of order and predictability in our relationships. This is because role-play is governed by certain rules of behaviour (sometimes termed a *prescribed aspect* of a role – expectations about how you *should* behave when playing a particular role), which links to the concept of:

- **Norms**: As I have suggested earlier, these are expected, socially acceptable ways of behaving when playing a role. For example, as a teacher, it's a norm for me to arrive on time for my classes, mainly because my students expect their classes to start on time and it would be unacceptable for me to turn-up an hour late.

Similarly, there are a variety of norms associated with the student role; I expect my students to listen to my words of wisdom, ask intelligent questions, pretend to look interested, laugh at my 'jokes' and so forth. Norms, in this respect, are *specific guidelines*, designed to govern our behaviour in various situations; they are, if you like, the basic rules of behaviour we develop and use to perform roles predictably and acceptably.

One further point to note is that norms are frequently open to negotiation; it may be possible to play the same role (such as a student) differently in different situations. For example, when attending one class the teacher may interpret their role narrowly, enforcing all kinds of rules and restrictions (working in silence, for example). However, in a different class the teacher may interpret their role very broadly, allowing their students to behave in ways unacceptable to the first teacher. This idea leads us neatly into a discussion of a related concept, that of values.

Values

As we have briefly seen, values are beliefs about what is important, both to us and to society as a whole. We can, however, develop this idea by noting three further points.

- **Interpretations**: Our values influence how we interpret and play a particular role and, in turn, influence the norms we associate with that role. For example, if, when playing the role of 'father', you believe 'Children should be seen but not heard', you're not likely to bother asking your kids about where to go on holiday.

- **General Guidelines**: If norms are specific behavioural guidelines, values provide very general behavioural guidelines. As **Thio** (*Sociology: A Brief Introduction*, 1991) puts it: 'While norms are specific rules dictating how people should act in a particular situation, values are general ideas that support the norm'.

- **Judgements**: Values, by definition, always involve judgements about behaviour; whenever we think about – or express – the values we hold we are choosing to believe one thing rather than another.

Social roles

 Digging deeper

The different roles we play can be neatly grouped into two main categories.

- **Achieved**: These are roles we choose – or are allowed – to play and they are 'achieved' because we have to do something to earn the right to play them (a doctor, for example, will have worked to gain the qualifications necessary to play this role). The majority of roles in our society are achieved.

- **Ascribed**: These roles are ones we're forced to play by other, more powerful, people. For example, between the ages of 5 and 16 in Britain, the government gives everyone the *ascribed role* of 'schoolchild'. Although, in our society at least, ascribed roles tend to be in the minority, they are nevertheless still significant – think, for example, about the possible consequences of being male or female, young or old, rich or poor.

As I have suggested, role-play is a source of order and predictability in both our individual and institutional relationships – which is one of the reasons we develop and play roles. Without them the social world would be a very confusing place – imagine, for example, a situation in which you could not remember what your relationship to everyone around you was supposed to be.

One benefit of role-play, therefore, is that once we've learned what's expected of us, we use that knowledge whenever we play that role – it helps us accomplish certain tasks. The teaching and learning process, for example, is made easier if both teacher and student behave towards each other in ways considered appropriate for their roles (think how difficult it is to learn if the teacher is unclear about what they're teaching or if students misbehave in the classroom).

Another aspect of social order, therefore, is that role-play helps us regulate both our behaviour and that of others. Role-playing is a way of controlling people's behaviour, for example, because the norms associated with each role give us *boundary markers* against which to judge acceptable and unacceptable behaviour. This idea of *social control* is important enough for us to consider in more detail in a moment.

One feature of role-play, as we've seen, is each role is played out in relation to other roles; a group of roles relating specifically to the role we're playing is called a **role-set** and an example of a student's role set might be:

- other students
- your class teacher
- other teachers
- caretaking staff
- administration staff
- your parent(s)/guardian(s).

This idea leads us inexorably to a further concept related to roles and role-sets, called **social status**. As I have suggested, social status involves the 'level of respect we're expected to give someone playing a particular role'. Every role has an associated status and we can, for example, measure the status of a student against the status of a teacher. Alternatively, we could measure the status of a teacher against the status of the Queen. As with the concept of role, social status has two basic forms.

- **Achieved** status involves doing something to earn that status – a teacher's status is earned, for example, because they have achieved the level of qualification and training necessary to play this role.

- **Ascribed** status, on the other hand, is given to you, whether or not you want it. You may not, for example, have wanted the status of 'pupil', but you were given it regardless.

The way we feel about our status in relation to others affects the way we behave in certain situations. This is because status is closely related to a further concept, that of **power**. This involves the ability to force people to do something, regardless of their ability to resist. A teacher, for example, probably believes that, because their status is greater than that of their students, they are justified in:

- setting students work do outside their class
- telling a noisy student to be quiet
- making an unruly student leave the class.

One final idea to note here is that, for all the advantages they give us in the organisation of our lives, the wide number and variety of roles we play occasionally causes us problems, one aspect of which we can note in terms of **role conflict**, which occurs when the norms consistent with one role prevent us from behaving in accordance with the norms consistent with another role. Imagine, for example, you play two different roles in your life:

- **Student** role: For this, one norm is you have to be in class at 3 pm on a Friday.
- **Part-time employee role**: When a crisis occurs at work your employer demands you start work 3 hours earlier than usual on a Friday. Instead of starting at 5 pm, they ask you to start at 2 pm.

This is a no-win situation for you. If you follow the norms associated with one role (student), you break the norms associated with the other (employee). The fact that it's not your fault and that whatever you choose will mean getting into trouble, merely makes you an innocent victim of role conflict.

Norms

 Digging deeper

Although you're probably not aware of it (and why should you be?), norms come in a variety of shapes and sizes which we can note as follows.

- **Folkways** (or informal norms) are a weak kind of norm; if you break them, the sanctions (penalties) involved are fairly minor. Folkways relate mainly to social politeness and customs. For example, when you meet someone you know it's polite to greet them ('Hello') and expect them to respond in kind. Similarly, it's customary in our culture to send people birthday cards. In many ways folkways are examples of *situational* norms – they only apply in specific situations. Your failure to send me a birthday card is unlikely to worry me unduly, for the deceptively simple reason that I don't know you (it might have been nice if you'd made the effort, however); your failure to remember a loved one's birthday, on the other hand, is likely to result in some sort of penalty . . .

- **Mores** (pronounced 'more-rays') are stronger norms and a failure to conform to them will result in a consequently stronger social response from whoever resents your failure to behave appropriately. In some ways it's useful to think of them as rules relating to particular situations – for example, a no-smoking policy in an office. Another example might be a rule that bans cheating in an exam.

- **Laws** (legal or formal norms) are the strongest norms in any society. They are expressions of moral feelings and exist to explicitly control people's behaviour. Punishment for breaking legal norms varies in terms of their perceived seriousness. In our society, punishments vary from things like community orders and fines to life imprisonment (although in some societies, such as the USA or Saudi Arabia, capital punishment may be the most extreme sanction for breaking this type of norm).

Discussion point: exploring norms

Exploring personal and cultural norms can be an interesting and sociologically rewarding experience because it helps us understand the nuts-and-bolts of cultural life.

In small groups, or as a class if you wish, choose one of the following to think about and discuss:

- the norms of window shopping
- when and how to kiss
- the gender norms of public lavatories
- personal space.

So far we have talked in general terms about the concept of culture, outlined in terms of a society having general beliefs that apply to the majority of its members. While this is both true and useful, it is interesting to note how this sense of belonging to the same culture can be broken down into more specific values and norms since, although we share many things with others, not every group has exactly the same values and norms – and this is where the concept of **sub-cultures** comes into its own. This concept refers to the idea of some (smaller) groups within a general culture sharing a particular way of life. Some examples that show the wide range of sub-cultural groups in our society might be:

- football supporters
- train-spotters
- orthodox jews
- travellers
- A-level students.

We can use the last example – being part of a student sub-culture – to illustrate the possible relationship between cultural and sub-cultural groups.

A student is part of a sub-cultural group with its own particular 'way of life' (attending classes, and doing all the things students are supposed to do.). However, just because they are part of this sub-culture doesn't mean they can't be part of other sub-cultural groups or, indeed, the culture of society as a whole.

While some of the values of a student sub-culture (wanting to get an A-level qualification, for example) and the norms associated with these values (such as gaining a qualification by passing examinations) may be different from the values and norms of other sub-cultures, they can still be part of the wider culture of society. Indeed, the reason you might value an educational qualification is precisely because it has a value in wider society. A prospective employer, for example, might offer you a job on the basis of your qualifications.

So far we have looked at the things we need to learn (roles, values, norms and so forth) in order to take our place in society. What we need to do next, therefore, is to look at how we learn these things – through a process called socialisation.

The socialisation process

⚠ Preparing the ground

Learning how to behave in ways that accord with the general expectations of others (in short, to be socialised) is a process that begins at birth and continues throughout our life. We never stop learning how to behave, mainly because society is always changing and we are continually faced with learning how to behave in new and different situations (especially in terms our individual relationships). When we start to look at socialisation as a process, therefore, we can begin by identifying two basic types.

- **Primary socialisation** occurs between the individual and those people in their life with whom they have *primary relationships*; that is a relationship involving close, personal and face-to-face interaction with the people responsible for doing the socialising. For most of us, the first primary relationship we form is with our parent(s); as we grow older, we form primary attachments with people we call friends and, eventually, perhaps, with other adults.

- **Secondary socialisation**, on the other hand, occurs, as you can probably guess, between the individual and those people with whom they have secondary relationships – situations where the individual doesn't necessarily have close, personal and/or face-to-face contacts with the people responsible for the socialisation process. This form of socialisation represents the way we learn about the nature of the social world beyond our primary contacts, mainly because in our society we have to learn to deal with people we meet, the majority of whom are not emotionally close to us.

Given that the socialisation process – whether primary or secondary – involves both teaching and learning, we can talk about those responsible for teaching us roles, norms, values and so forth as **agents of socialisation**. For most of us, the first *agency* responsible for primary socialisation is our family, and the main agents of socialisation are a child's parents (although brothers, sisters and wider relations – such as aunts, uncles and grandparents – may also be involved). The family group initially takes responsibility for teaching the basic things we need to learn as part of growing-up – how to walk, talk and use culture-appropriate tools (such as knives and forks), among other things.

Parents don't just teach the basics of 'becoming human', however. They are also influential in teaching basic values, such as their perception of right and wrong behaviour, how to relate appropriately to other people such as family, friends, strangers and so forth.

Although this socialisation process is lengthy and complicated (there's a great deal to learn), it is important not to see it as a situation where a socialising agent, such as a parent, simply teaches behaviour that is then copied without question. Although part of a child's socialisation does involve copying the behaviour they see around them (children frequently copy adult roles through their play, using games such as 'Mothers and Fathers' or 'Doctors and Nurses' to both mimic and practise behaviour), the child is also actively involved in the socialisation process.

Children, for example, don't always obey their parents and even at an early age, conflicts occur – the socialising efforts of parents, relatives and friends, for example, don't always neatly coincide. In addition, while the child is learning how to adapt to their environment they are changing the way the people around them behave (think, for example, about how parental attitudes to your behaviour have changed as you have grown older).

Finally, perhaps, as we get a little older we start to make decisions for ourselves, based upon our experience; we learn, in effect, how to deal with other people by understanding the behaviour they expect of us.

Many of the things we learn during our initial, family-based, primary socialisation stay with us for life. This is because we learn the basic principles of 'being human', rather than simply a set of things we must or must not do. This is important because it means we can apply these principles to new and different situations. For example, we don't just learn how to relate to adults, we learn how to distinguish between different types of adult on the basis of their status and relationship to us – we don't, for example, behave towards a parent in the same way we behave towards a teacher or a complete stranger.

Young children, when introduced to unfamiliar adults, frequently become quiet and shy. This is because they are unsure about how they are expected to behave towards the stranger. The same process happens in any new situation. Teenage males and females, for example, may be initially shy and awkward in each other's company (for about 30 seconds, anyway). One of the main things socialised into us during this particular period of primary socialisation is a knowledge of *gender roles*; that is, what it means, in our society to be either masculine or feminine – something we will return to at a later point.

In terms of secondary socialising agencies, these may include schools, religious organisations, the mass media and so forth.

Associated agents of socialisation here would, therefore, include people like teachers, priests, television personalities and pop stars. In some cases, such as in school, we are in daily, face-to-face contact with the people socialising us without ever developing a primary attachment to them. In other cases, such as when admiring a particular film star, we may never meet them, yet we can still be influenced by what they look like, what they do and how they do it.

⚠ Digging deeper

Before we examine examples of socialising agencies in more detail, we need to say a couple of things about the purpose of socialisation.

Firstly, primary socialisation is necessary because human infants require the assistance of other members of society to develop as both human beings (the walking, talking bit) and as members of a culture (the learning roles, norms and values bit). In terms of secondary socialisation, this is also necessary because, as **Talcott Parsons** (*The Social System*, 1951) argued, its main purpose (or function) is to 'Liberate the individual from a dependence upon the primary attachments and relationships formed within the family group.'

What Parsons meant by this is that, in modern societies, the vast majority of the people we meet are strangers and it would be both impossible and undesirable to relate to them in the same way we relate to people for whom we have great affection. We have, therefore, to learn **instrumental relationships**, or how to deal with people in terms of what they can do for us and what we can do for them in particular situations.

For example, think about what life would be like if we only knew how to deal with people on the basis of primary social attachments (love, trust, affection and so forth). Whenever we went shopping, the assistant would deal with us as if we were a long lost and very dear friend. We might find this quite nice at first, but imagine having to deal with this sort of behaviour *every* time you passed someone in the street.

Secondly, although one purpose of socialisation is clearly to teach, it also has a further purpose, namely **social control**. The ideas we have examined so far have been largely concerned with the various ways people attempt to create order, stability and predictability in their own and other people's behaviour. In this respect, we have been indirectly talking about the way any society attempts to control the behaviour of its members. These controls affect not just the way people actually behave, but also the way they think about the nature of the world (both social and natural) in which they live. We can start to bring these ideas together under the general heading of social control and look a little more closely at the various forms of control in any society.

At its most basic, social control involves all of the things we do or have done to us that are designed to maintain or change behaviour. The primary socialisation process, for example, involves social control because it attempts to shape the way a child is raised. When we develop certain values and adopt particular norms, this too is a form of control since we are placing limits on what we consider to be acceptable (or normal) behaviour. Role-play is another a form of control because we are acting in ways people consider appropriate in certain situations. We can think about social control, at least

initially, in terms of **rules**. Social life, in this respect, is a life-long process of rule-learning. We may not always agree with those rules (nor do we always obey them, come to that), but the fact remains they exist and we have to take note of their existence. People, therefore, create behavioural rules as the basis for social organisation and since we always have a choice as to whether or not we obey these rules, they are supported by **sanctions** – things we do to make people conform to our expectations and which can be one of two types.

- **Positive sanctions** (or rewards) are the nice things we do to make people behave in routine, predictable, ways. Examples here might be things like buying a child an ice cream to make it stop crying (an odd example of the way breaking a norm can actually bring a reward) or awarding a student a valuable qualification if they pass an AS-level exam.

- **Negative sanctions** (or punishments) are the not-very-nice things we do to try to make people conform. There are a vast range of negative sanctions in our society, from not talking to people if they annoy us to putting them in prison. The ultimate negative sanction, perhaps, is to kill someone.

Social controls are, as I have suggested, closely related to norms and just as there are two basic types of norm (informal and formal), we can talk about there two basic types of social control.

- **Formal social controls** may be based on the idea of legal norms (laws). That is, written rules of behaviour that, theoretically, apply equally to everyone (although not all societies apply formal rules equally). Where laws are involved we usually find people (normally employed by the government), whose job involves enforcing such laws. In our society, the main agencies of formal social control are the police and the judiciary (the legal system), although the armed forces can, on occasions, be used to perform this role.

Not all formal norms are laws, however. In a workplace, for example, there are formal rules governing behaviour while at work – if you are repeatedly late for work you may be punished in some way. In general terms, formal rules and social controls exist to tell everyone within a social group what is – and is not – acceptable behaviour. Such formal controls usually exist where a group is very large and its members are not necessarily all in day-to-day contact with each other.

- **Informal social controls**, like their formal counterpart, exist to reward or punish people for acceptable or unacceptable behaviour ('deviance') and cover a vast array of possible sanctions that may differ from individual to individual, group to group and society to society. Such controls apply to informal norms and include things like ridicule, sarcasm, disapproving looks, punching people in the face and so forth.

As an example, at a Women's Institute gathering a disapproving look may be enough to tell you people think it's inappropriate to flirt with the vicar. Among members of a criminal gang, however, it's unlikely a disapproving look would be used as a means of informal social control should you tell them you intend to inform on their activities to the police.

To complete this section on socialisation, it might be helpful to look a little more closely at some examples of agencies of socialisation, partly to provide a flavour of the wide range of actions and behaviours involved and partly to firm-up the work we've done previously. In this respect, we can identify a range of significant agencies and outline selected roles, values, norms and social controls (both positive and negative) involved in each.

WARM UP: AGENCIES OF SOCIALISATION

Either individually or in groups (each group can look at one agency), and using the following table as a guide, identify examples of the roles people play, values they might develop and norms they are expected to obey for your chosen agency. In addition, identify examples of positive and negative sanctions employed by agents of socialisation within each agency.

Agency of socialisation	Roles	Values	Norms	Positive sanctions	Negative sanctions
Family					
Peers					
School					
Work					
Media					
Religion					

The family

The family is the first agency we can examine since, for many of us, our family is one of the most significant socialising agencies in our life. However, it's arguably in the early years that it has the most important socialising influence on us, in terms of things like:

- **Roles**: Although there are only a limited number of roles to learn within the family (both for adults and children), this hides a certain complexity of role development (how roles change depending on how the group develops). Adults within the family may learn roles ranging from husband and wife to parent, mother, father and, increasingly in our society, single-parent and step-parent. For children, there is a complex learning process as we come to terms with being a baby, toddler, child, teenager, young adult and, eventually perhaps, an adult with children of our own.

- **Values**: Parents are influential in shaping our basic values. For example, our family may teach us manners, moral values (such as the difference between right and wrong) and the importance of family members as what **Geroge Herbert Mead** (*Mind, Self and Society*, 1934) called 'significant others' – people whose opinions we respect and value deeply.

- **Norms**: Although these may differ from family to family, basic norms such as how to address family members ('Mum', 'Dad'), when, where and how to eat, the meaning of 'good' and 'bad' behaviour and the like are normally part of the primary socialisation process.

- **Sanctions**: Most, if not all, sanctions

within the family are informal (although, in some instances, it is possible for formal rules to be applied – setting times by which children have to be home, for example). Positive sanctions are many and varied, ranging from things like facial expressions (smiling), through verbal approval/reinforcement ('You are such a good boy/girl') to physical rewards (toys, money and so forth). Negative sanctions are similarly wide-ranging – from showing disapproval through language (shouting for example) to things like physical punishment.

Module link: These basic ideas are a useful starting point for an exploration of the Family Life module

Peer groups

Peer groups are defined in terms of people of a similar age, but the concept can be widened to refer to friends of a similar age (most children, for example, develop friendships with some of their peers). Their socialising efforts and influence can be considered in areas like:

- **Behaviour**: Peers are influential on both a primary level (close friends, for example) and secondary level (as a general *reference group* – people whose approval we seek and value and against whom we check the appropriateness of our behaviour). We may, for example, use our knowledge of peers against which to check our fashion sense. In this respect we can also note the idea of *peer pressure* as a form of social control.

- **Roles**: We play a range of peer-related roles, depending on our age group and situation. 'Friend', for example, expresses very personal role-play, whereas at school or work we may have a variety of *acquaintances*. In the workplace too, we are likely to play the role of colleague to at least some of our peers.

- **Values**: As with roles, the values we are taught within a friendship or peer group vary with age and circumstances. However, something like the value of friendship itself will probably be carried with us throughout our life.

- **Norms** relating to peer group behaviour might, for example, relate to ideas about age-appropriate behaviour; young children, for example, are not allowed to smoke or buy alcoholic drinks in a pub. Conversely, it is generally not considered age-appropriate for the elderly to take part in extreme or dangerous sports.

- **Sanctions**: As with family, positive and negative sanctions applied within a peer group are rarely formal. This means norms for one group may differ widely from those for another group. The same behaviour – in different situations – may also produce different responses. Swearing at your grandmother, for example, will probably be met with disapproval, whereas swearing in the company of friends may actually be a norm. Approving gestures and language, laughing at your jokes and seeking out your company may represent positive sanctions; refusing to speak to you, rejecting your friendship and physical violence are negative sanctions.

Education

School is one of the first times a child, in our society, is separated from their parent(s) for any length of time and, as a socialising experience, provides both opportunities (to

make new and different friends or demonstrate your skills and abilities to a wider, non-family, audience) and new traumas – you need to learn, for example, how to deal with authority figures (otherwise known as teachers) as well as how to deal regularly with people who are not family.

- **Behaviour**: The education system is designed to teach the skills and knowledge required for adult life within our culture. This includes specific knowledge (such as history, which gives us a sense of our society's past, and geography, which confers a knowledge of both our own and other societies) and particular skills (such as learning to read and write or solve mathematical problems). This *manifest function* of education, however, is counterbalanced by certain *latent functions*, such as learning how to deal with strangers, respect for authority figures, the need for punctuality, attendance and the like.

  The school is also a place where we 'learn to limit our individual desires', which is a way of saying the requirements of the group (such as sitting quietly, listening and responding to questions) takes precedence over our individual needs or preferences (such as wanting desperately to be somewhere – anywhere – else).

- **Roles**: A limited number of roles are played within the school (teacher and pupil, for example), although at different stages of the education system the names, perceptions and content of these roles tends to change. In post-16 (further and higher) education, for example, lecturer and student labels reflect the changing nature of roles and relationships.

- **Values**: Schools project a range of values,

some technical (pupils should work hard to achieve qualifications) and some social, in the sense of schools teaching things like individual competition for academic rewards, teamwork (especially, but not exclusively, in sports and games), conformity to authority (not questioning what is being learned and why it is necessary to learn it) and achievement on the basis of merit – the idea pupils should receive rewards based on their abilities and efforts. In some respects, our education system generally values 'academic ability' (such as the ability to write essays on Chaucer) more highly than practical ability (such as being able to paint or draw).

- **Norms**: A range of norms apply specifically within the school and classroom, although, as writers such as **Bowles** and **Gintis** (*Schooling in Capitalist America*, 1973) have suggested, there may be a correspondence between school norms and workplace norms. The daily need to attend and register, for example, the right of those in authority to give orders and expect them to be obeyed and the wearing of uniforms might be examples here.

  Module link: The work of Bowles and Gintis is discussed in more depth in the Education module.

- **Sanctions**: Positive sanctions include the gaining of grades, qualifications and prizes, as well as more personal things like praise and encouragement. On the negative side, teachers use sanctions like detentions, suspensions and exclusions; failure to achieve qualifications or gaining a reputation for 'stupidity' also function as negative sanctions in this context (at least from the viewpoint of teachers, if not always from that of the pupil).

Work

Work is a place many of us spend a great deal of our lives and, for this reason if no other, it deserves consideration as a socialising agency in terms of:

- **Roles**: Two main workplace roles, in our society, are those of employer and employee. This, however, hides a range of differences in terms of how such roles are performed; an employee may be a professional worker (such as a lawyer) with an associated high status or, alternatively, they may perform a low-skill, poorly-paid role (flipping burgers, for example). Differences in the employee role relate to different experiences in the workplace and not simply to differences in the terms and conditions of employment. A professional employee, for example, as well as enjoying a higher status may occupy a position of trust and responsibility that involves controlling the behaviour of other employees, whereas a casual manual labourer or shop assistant may experience high levels of boredom, frustration and control by others.

- **Values**: One obvious value in relation to work is payment – we believe we should get money in exchange for working. However, less obvious values, such as competition and the belief that hard work and competence should be rewarded by things like promotion (and more money of course), increased responsibility (even more money) and control over the working environment are also apparent here.

- **Norms**: Continuing the money theme, we expect to be paid for working (although many types of work in our society, such as housework and voluntary work to name but two, don't involve money). Similar norms (attendance, obeying those in authority, etc.) to those we have seen in relation to the school as a socialising agency apply in this context.

- **Sanctions**: Employers have a range of positive sanctions at their disposal; the aforementioned pay increases, more responsibility, freedom (to work at your own pace, for example) and control over both your working day and the work of others might be considered to be rewards. On the negative side, disciplining someone, demoting them or, in the worst case, sacking them, constitute the main negative sanctions available.

Mass media

The media is a slightly unusual secondary socialising agency in that our relationship with it is *impersonal*; it doesn't involve face-to-face contact with those doing the socialising – even when you press your nose to the TV screen and shout really loudly at people, they can't hear or react to you. However, this does not mean the media doesn't socialise us – we rely, for example, on the media for information about what's happening in both our own and other societies.

- **Behaviour**: Surprisingly, perhaps, there is very little evidence the media has a direct, long-term effect on our behaviour (although if you have ever become angry about what you have seen, heard or read in the media you will be aware there are limited short-term effects), but there do seem to be a number of *indirect* long-term effects (of which we may not always be fully aware).

We see examples of this in areas such as male and female sexuality – magazines aimed directly at teenagers, for example, perform (at least partially) a socialising role in terms of understanding sexual relationships. In addition, some sociologists argue the media 'sets the agenda' for debates (that is, decides for us the terms under which something will be debated) – think about arguments about immigration, the European Community and crime, for example. An interesting examination of the role of television in this respect is the **Glasgow Media Group's** *Really Bad News* (1982), in which they note the role of agenda-setting in the media:

It is sometimes argued that people simply make up their own minds and are not influenced very much by what they read or see . . . television cannot exclusively shape people's thoughts or actions. Nonetheless it has a profound effect, because it has the power to tell people the *order* in which to think about events and issues. In other words it 'sets the agenda', decides what is important and what will be featured. More crucially it very largely decides what people will think *with*; television controls the crucial information with which we make up our minds about the world.

Module link: Questions relating to the extent to which the media affects our behaviour are considered in more detail in the Media module.

- **Values**: Questions about the extent to which the media can impose its values on our behaviour remain largely unresolved, but it does represent a

<table>
<tr><td>

**INFANTS SUFFER
IF MUM WORKS**

Mothers of under-fives who work full time damage their children's future academic success, according to a study

</td><td>

**TOLERANCE FOR MENTALLY
ILL IS NOT ENOUGH**

Discrimination against people with mental health needs is a human rights issue, writes Lynne Friedli

</td></tr>
</table>

Preserving traditional behaviour? (*The Sun* 14/03/01)

Promoting social change? (*The Guardian* 01/12/00)

potentially powerful force in terms of supporting or marginalising certain values. For example, the media has a (loud) voice in debates over nationality (what it means to be 'English', 'British' or 'French', for example). It also has the ability to promote certain values and devalue others – think about the way newspapers in Britain tend to take an 'anti-European Community' stance, for example. The following quote is from Sir Paul lever, British ambassador to Germany (http://news.bbc.co.uk 3 January, 2002).

In *The Sun* or *The Times* you see a portrayal of Germany that is rather dominated by a vocabulary from the war . . . that's partly because these papers are foreign owned and their underlying political philosophy is anti-European . . .

- **Norms**: The media has what **Durkheim**, when talking about crime, called a *boundary marking* function. In other words, it publicises acceptable and unacceptable forms of behaviour to reinforce perceptions of expected behaviours. This idea does, of course, work both ways – it can act as a way of trying to *preserve* particular ways of behaving and as a way of *promoting changes* in behaviour (as the following demonstrates):

- **Sanctions**: In terms of sanctions, the most obvious way the media exercises social

control is through the publicity given to behaviour of which it approves or disapproves (see above). Positive sanctions may involve the use of approving language, praise and so forth, whereas negative sanctions involve the opposite – such as being pictured in an unflattering pose or being harshly criticised.

The England goalkeeper David James, for example, was heavily criticised for his performance in an international match in 2004 and *The Sun* newspaper ran a poll for its readers asking whether they would 'prefer a donkey or James in goal after his error had presented Austria with the equaliser in Saturday's 2–2 draw'. James came second in this particular poll and – coincidence or not – he was subsequently dropped from the team for the following game.

Religion

Whether or not we classify ourselves as 'religious' (in the sense of attending services, praying or 'believing in God'), religious institutions (such as the Church of England) have played – and continue to play – a significant role in the general socialisation process in our society.

- **Behaviour**: In terms of directly influencing our behaviour (unless we are a member of a religious group), religion seems to play an increasingly peripheral role in our lives (that is, religious beliefs do not seem central to most people's lives). However, indirectly, religions play an important socialising role in terms of both influencing general social values (think of the Ten Commandments in Christian religions) and performing certain ceremonial functions (think, for example, about the significance of marriage, christenings and funerals).

- **Values**: Many of our most important moral values (fundamental beliefs about right and wrong) have been influenced in some way by religious values. Once again, Christianity's Ten Commandments, for example (and many other religions have developed their own moral codes) are reflected in our moral beliefs; few, for example, would argue you should be allowed to kill people or that theft is desirable (unless, of course, you happen to be a thief – which raises a whole bundle of sub-cultural issues I don't propose to delve deeper into here).

- **Sanctions**: The power of positive and negative sanctions for religions probably turns, in our society, on the extent to which you are a believer in the god – or gods – being promoted. In Christian religions, for example, the belief in an 'afterlife' is a powerful religious sanction, both positive – in the sense that if you do good deeds in life you will get your reward in Heaven – and negative, in the sense that bad behaviour in life is punished by an eternity in Hell. Other religions, such as Hinduism, which involves a belief in *reincarnation* (the idea that once you die you are reborn into a new life), have similar social control measures; in the example of Hinduism, the reward for good deeds in one lifetime is being reborn into a higher social position – with the reverse being the case for bad behaviour.

At the start of this chapter I introduced the idea of a 'sociological perspective', involving a set of beliefs to which the majority of sociologists subscribed. I also suggested that, once we moved beyond these basic beliefs, disagreements developed about how best to study and understand people's behaviour. In the next section, therefore, we can develop this idea by looking at a couple of basic differences of interpretation within the general sociological perspective.

Sociological perspectives

Introduction

In this section we can build on the work we've done by developing a couple of ideas. Firstly, the relationship between 'the individual' (as a thinking, acting, being) and 'society' (considered in terms of rules designed to guide people's behaviour). Secondly, the different ways sociologists see and study social behaviour. In other words, the different sociological perspectives associated with different groups of sociologists in their attempts to understand and explain people's behaviour.

Structure and action

⚠ Preparing the ground

The first of these ideas – the relationship between individuals and the social world we both create and inhabit – is frequently described as a debate between 'social structure' and 'social action'. This is an important, if sometimes complex, debate focusing on a central problem for sociologists – the relationship, as I have suggested, between the individual and society:

- **The individual**: On the one hand, we are all individuals, each with our particular histories, hopes, fears and aspirations. We are all uniquely different, not just from our fellow human beings, but also, as a species, from all other animals – and the thing we each possess that confers this uniqueness is *consciousness* – our ability to think (both about ourselves and our relationship to others) in ways more highly developed than in any other animal.

  The ability to think, if you think about it, is both a blessing and a curse; the former because it enables us to create complex technologies (the microwave oven!) and relationships (my father's brother's sister's child, to name a simple one) and the latter because, in a sense, we are all prisoners of our own individuality – however much I may want to, I can never really know what you're thinking. I can make educated guesses based on how you talk to me, your body language and so forth, but I can never know for sure.

- **The group**: On the other hand, we all live in a large social group we call a society. Although all societies are different, one of the striking things about human behaviour is that, for all our unique individuality, we do a surprising number of things with a regularity and general predictability that can't be accidental. In other words, something forces us to behave in routinely predictable ways and, while for some social scientists that 'thing' is instinct (or 'genetic imperatives' – an imperative is simply a command we are forced to obey), for sociologists that 'thing' is social structure.

What sociologists have to do, therefore, is to note the fact of human individuality (and our ability to act in almost any way we care to imagine) and square it with human predictability (the fact that, generally, our behaviour is characterised by almost mundane similarities) – and this is where the concept of *structure* and *action* come into the equation.

- **Social structure**: It sometimes helps to visualise social structure as a 'framework of rules' – a rule being something you are supposed to obey and a framework being the way rules are created, maintained and policed. For example, think about how your behaviour is governed by laws – we can talk about a *legal framework* (or structure, if you prefer) involving: governments making laws (formal, legal rules), a police force enforcing these rules, a judicial system deciding whether or not you've broken the law and prisons in which to lock you up if you're judged to be guilty.

Keeping this idea in mind, if you think about the variety of ways your behaviour is governed by informal rules (norms), the idea of a social structure surrounding you and your behaviour should become a little clearer. Every relationship you enter into (such as with family, school, work and friends) involves playing a role, which in turn involves values relating to the role and, of course, norms associated with the role; every time you play a role, therefore, you are experiencing (however unwittingly) the effect of social structures – rules which shape your potential behavioural choices.

• **Social action**: If the concept of social structures focuses on how behaviour is governed by rules designed to constrain (limit) and control, the associated concept of social action focuses on our ability to make choices about how to behave. Just as, for example, we make choices about such things as who will be our friends, so too, ultimately we can make choices about the rules we obey or disobey – although, because we're talking about social structures, there may well be consequences in the form of negative social sanctions (punishments), for choosing to disobey.

Be that as it may, the important point to note – regardless of how 'society' or people try to influence our behaviour – is we always have a choice about how to behave. To put this another way, in terms of social action our choices are potentially unlimited – we are free to act in whatever way we choose. However, our actual choices about how to behave are limited by the effects of social structures – by the framework of rules that characterise our relationships, our culture and our society.

Synoptic link: The relationship between structure and action is clearly demonstrated in Robert Merton's 'Strain Theory' of deviance discussed in the A2 Crime and Deviance module.

WARM UP: CAN YOU FEEL THE FORCE?

If you are at school or college, an easy initial way to grasp ideas about structure and action is to think about the following:

Things I'm supposed to do	How I express my individuality
Have to attend classes	Pretend to be ill

Either individually or as a class, what ideas can you add to the two columns?

This early in the course the introduction of these quite complex ideas can be a

Society is like a game of chess

little daunting, but we can make things a little clearer by using an *analogy* (identifying and comparing the features of something we know a lot about to something we know little or nothing about).

If, therefore, we liken society to a game such as chess – although you could use any game with which you're familiar (football, battleships, Connect 4, Twister …) – it can help us understand the relationship between structure and action in the following way:

- **Structure**: Thinking about chess, for example, we know it has certain physical boundaries (the playing area). It also has rules governing how the game is played: these are both technical (relating to the basic mechanics of the game – the starting position of each playing piece, how different pieces are allowed to move, taking it in turn to move and so forth) and cultural (it's a competitive situation, for example, with the main objective being to beat your opponent). This represents the basic structure of the game – or, if you prefer, the basic *framework of rules* within which the game should be played.

- **Action**: Each player is free to choose their own particular strategies and moves within the game, based on their particular assessment of how to successfully play the game. In chess, therefore, structure and action come together, in the sense each player's behaviour (action) is limited, in some ways by:
  - **Rules**: If one player decides to change or break the rules, their opponent will react to this deviant

act in some way (by protesting or refusing to continue playing, for example).

- **Players**: Each player must, in this competitive environment, take note of how their opponent is playing – by responding to certain moves or moving in ways that produce particular responses from their opponent.

⚠ Digging deeper

We can dig deeper into concepts of structure and action by both developing them in more detail and exploring the relationship between the two ideas.

Social action

Max Weber (*Economy and Society*, 1922) drew an important distinction between the concepts of *behaviour* and *action* on the basis that behaviour becomes action when it is directed towards other people in such a way that it takes account of how others act. If this is a little unclear, think about the following ideas.

- **Behaviour**: Weber argued the animal world was governed by behaviour, rather than action. That is, animal behaviour is not based on any understanding of how their behaviour might affect other animals. When a dog barks, for example, it does not understand how this behaviour affects other dogs or indeed other animals.

- **Action**: The social world, on the other hand is, for Weber, governed by action. Whenever we act, we do so in the knowledge of how our behaviour might impact on people at whom the action is directed. For example, whenever you have a conversation you are engaging in social action because you are interacting – how you behave is influenced by how the other person behaves and vice versa.

In this respect, social action involves a range of things that simple behaviour excludes. For example, it involves:

- **Meanings**: Whatever we say or do means something to both ourselves and others. For example, when I'm getting ready to go to the local disco on a Friday night after a hard week teaching, I choose what clothes to wear carefully. This is because I aim to make an impression on my disco buddies – my choice of clothes has meaning to both me ('How cool do I look!') and the people I interact with ('Why would anyone think they looked good in those clothes?').

  This is not, of course, to say we always fully understand what our actions mean to other people (as my disco example probably demonstrates), nor that our actions will mean the same things to others as they mean to us. This, however, leads to the idea of:

- **Interpretations**: Our behaviour is constantly open to interpretation, both by ourselves ('Why did I wear that tie with that shirt?') and others ('What a mess he looks!'). In addition, interpretation reflects back on meaning since, as I've suggested, how I interpret the behaviour of others is going to depend on what it means to me.

- **Negotiations**: When we think about how people interact, this involves a

certain level of negotiation; we are able to 'discuss' (in the widest sense) the meaning of our actions and how others should interpret them. Social life does not simply involve obeying rules – the meaning of our behaviour to others can change, depending on the circumstances surrounding our behaviour.

For example, whenever I start to teach a new class we lay down some basic rules of behaviour, one of which is that when I set homework I specify the date for its completion. The first piece of homework is, normally, dutifully completed on time by all my students (they're new and unsure about how I'll act if they try to hand the work in late). By the next piece of work, there's usually one student who asks if they can hand the work in after the deadline. This is an example of how rules are negotiated, since the student is asking the lecturer to renegotiate the established rule.

This is a crucial point in my teaching since how I respond to this deviant (norm-breaking) behaviour sets the tone for all future homework deadlines – if I extend the deadline for this student then I send a signal to my students that deadlines are negotiable and rules are flexible. If, however, I say the student must hand in the work on time or leave the course I've sent a different message – one that says 'Don't mess with me'.

Introduction to sociology

Discussion point:
understanding meaning

In small groups, have a look at the following pictures and, for each in turn, think about:

1. what they mean to you
2. can they have more than one meaning? If so, which interpretation is correct? (You need to think about and explain how you know which is correct).

Discuss the pictures with the rest of the class.

1. What similarities in interpretation/meaning are there between you?
2. What differences in interpretation/meaning are there?
3. Why do you think there are similarities/differences in interpretation?

Social structure

The concept of social structure, as I've suggested, focuses on group behaviour (usually, but not exclusively, on very large groups – social *institutions* such as education) and how social life is *patterned* (in terms of regularities in group behaviour).

An easy way to develop our thoughts about social structures is to illustrate this idea using the concept of **haunting** suggested by **Roland Meighan** (*A Sociology of Education*, 1981), when he argues social actions are always surrounded by the ghosts of social structures. We are all, he argues, haunted by things we cannot see but which nevertheless affect our behaviour.

The Ghost of Social Structure (whoooooo).

For example, when teachers and students enter a classroom (for the purpose of education), the interaction between them is haunted by things like:

- **Physical environment**: Whether the room is warm and inviting or, alternatively, cold, dark and off-putting; whether the classroom resembles a prison cell or a bright, modern, learning lab – such things affect the teaching and learning process.

- **Knowledge** being taught: Classroom teaching reflects what our culture values (or doesn't value, as the case may be). What and how you are taught and the ways you are allowed, as students, to demonstrate knowledge are all evidence of the impact of social structures. Is, for example, theoretical knowledge, such as the ability to write essays about Shakespeare more valued than practical knowledge, such as the ability to build a brick wall?

- **Language** of education: The language we speak is structured in terms of both grammatical rules and in terms of how it can be used to communicate ideas. At A-level, for example, you are expected to learn the technical language of sociology, physics or media studies if you want to do well in your exams.

- **Demands** of employers: If employers require qualifications from their workforce, teachers are haunted (in terms of what they teach, when they teach it and so forth) by the ghost of examinations. Students have to be taught against a background of preparation for formal examinations – they have to learn the techniques involved, what constitutes knowledge acceptable to an examiner and so forth.

Module link: Meighan's concept of 'haunting' can be applied to our understanding of the role and purpose of the education system.

Social structure and social action

The concepts of structure and action are both important – in terms of understanding the relationship between society and the individual – and complementary. Although we are all individuals, our behavioural choices are influenced, limited and enhanced by the framework of rules and responsibilities (social structures) that surround us as we go about our daily lives. Just as we cannot conceive of society without individuals (who, after all, but people can create society?) it is very difficult to think about people without needing to refer to the various ways our behaviour is structured.

Ideas about structure and action, therefore, are fundamental to sociologists (just as they are, probably unwittingly, to us all) because they reflect two important ideas about social behaviour.

- **Cultural diversity**: On the one hand, people are free to make choices about their behaviour and this results in cultural diversity (or difference) over the way they organise their society and relationships. We can demonstrate this idea by looking at examples of how different cultures view the same behaviour.

  - In Britain, it is legal for an 18 year old to go into a pub and order a pint of beer. In most states in the USA, an 18 year old trying to order a pint in a bar is committing a criminal offence (you have to be at least 21 in most states for this behaviour to be legal).

  - In Britain, when you meet someone, it is acceptable to shake their hand. In Japan, it is more usual – and socially acceptable – to bow when greeting someone. The depth of the bow is important – if greeting someone of a higher social status you should bow lower than they do. In India, shaking hands with someone of the opposite sex is unacceptable.

- In the USA, to beckon someone with the palm facing upwards and waggling your index finger is an acceptable way of calling someone towards you. In India, the same action is viewed as an insult (the palm should always face downward, in case you were wondering).

Acceptable behaviour in one culture but unacceptable in another . . .

- **Culture**: On the other hand, our behavioural choices are influenced by both the society/culture into which we are born and our relationship to other people (whether as family, friends and work colleagues or simply on the basis of our awareness of sharing things – like a common nationality – with others in our society).

A key idea to understand, therefore, is that in order to engage in social action there must exist some sort of framework (or structure) within which that action can take place. For example, in terms of the cultural diversity examples I've just noted, the framework might include things like:

- **Verbal communication**: It is difficult to communicate with someone if you don't share a language.

- **Non-verbal communication**, which may involve the ability to understand gestures, body language, roles being played and the respective statuses of the social actors.

The next question to consider, therefore, is which is most important in the explanation of human behaviour – structure or agency? The answer depends, as you probably deep-down and very secretly thought it might, on your viewpoint.

Flippant as this answer may seem, it is actually very important when we look at the final section of this chapter dealing with the idea of different sociological perspectives; that is, the idea different sociologists lean towards either structure, action or a mix of both interpretations of social behaviour which, in turn, leads them to develop different ways of looking at and explaining social behaviour.

Sociological perspectives

⚠ Preparing the ground

A perspective, as I have suggested, is a way of seeing, thinking about and understanding the social world. Everyone has a perspective on things and sociologists are no different in this respect. However, when we start to think about the way the views of different sociologists can be broadly grouped into

sociological perspectives, we need to note two things: firstly, the idea that it's possible for different people to view the same behaviour yet see it from a different perspective and, consequently, interpret its meaning and significance differently.

WARM UP: DIFFERENT PERSPECTIVES

To illustrate the idea that it's possible to look at something yet see different things, take a look at each of the following pictures.

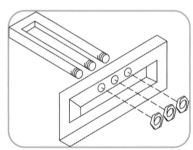

Secondly, some sociologists view social structures as the most important factor in understanding people's behaviour while other sociologists see social action as the key factor. A third group argue structure and action should be given equal prominence in any explanation of behaviour.

What we need to do next, therefore, is examine perspectives within these three general categories.

Structuralist perspectives

For Structuralist sociologists, the key idea, as you might have guessed, is the way social structures shape and, possibly, determine people's behaviour. Structuralist perspectives (which, as we will see, can be sub-divided into two further categories – *consensus* and *conflict* structuralism) focus on the following ideas.

- **Roles**, **routines** and **responsibilities**: In other words, understanding how the relationships we form 'lock us into' orderly and broadly predictable behaviour.

- **Group**, rather than individual, behaviour: The interest here is looking at how cultural rules limit our behavioural choices through the social pressures they exert. Just as our behaviour is constrained by physical objects (walls and tables for example), it is also constrained by social objects (such as roles, norms and values).

- **Institutions** not individuals: Developing from the above, structuralists argue we should examine large social groups (families, for example) if we are to understand how society works and, for this reason, you sometimes see this perspective called *macro* (or 'large-scale') sociology.

- **Objectivity**: This relates to the idea of people being *objects* (in the same way as we refer to things like tables as objects). For structuralists, people are often portrayed as 'puppets', their behaviour determined by the 'invisible hand' of society.

Structuralist Perspectives
Are people puppets, controlled by society?

Action perspectives

In some ways social action perspectives are the opposite to structural perspectives and, for action sociologists, the emphasis is on the way people create the social world through their relationships and actions. These sociologists, therefore, tend to focus on ideas like:

- **Individual behaviour**: In some ways, action sociology is a type of social psychological perspective, one that tries to understand social behaviour (or action) from the individual's point of view – understanding, for example, the different ways people see the social world, their place in it and their relationship to others.

- **People create society**: An obvious point, perhaps, but a significant one nonetheless. For action theorists it's important to remember that 'society' is not a thing; rather it consists of people going about their lives on a daily basis, creating and recreating a 'sense of society' as they do so. In this respect, social action perspectives are often called *micro* (or 'small-scale') sociology.

- **Meanings**: To explain behaviour we must understand what the social world means to people. We have, in short, to understand how people 'define situations' because how we define a situation determines how we will behave in that situation.

- **Subjectivity** relates to the idea of people being able to think about both their own behaviour and that of others – to make decisions and choices, for example. Rather than being puppets, people are seen more as actors on the 'stage' of society.

Structure and action perspectives

Sometimes referred to as 'structuration', this perspective aims to combine the ideas of structure and action to arrive at a sociological perspective that expresses two main ideas.

- **People make society**: As we have already seen, the idea of a society (or, indeed, any social group) is nonsensical without people. Only people can create societies (which reflects the action approach noted above).

- **Society makes people**: On the other hand, the idea of social action can only have meaning when we place it in a structural context. For example, the only reason these words have meaning to you is because they exist within a structure of language (rules we need to obey in order to communicate effectively).

Growing it yourself: the meaning of language

The idea of language as a form of both structure and of action can be demonstrated as follows.

Read the following and see if it makes sense to you:

'Aoccdrnig to a rscheearch at an Elingsh uinervtisy, it deosn't mttaer in waht oredr the ltteers in a wrod are palecd, the olny iprmoetnt tihng is taht the frist and lsat ltteer is in the rghit pclae. The rset can be a toatl mses and you can sitll raed it wouthit porbelm. Tihs is bcuseae we do not raed ervey lteter by itslef but the wrod as a wlohe.'

You can, if you wish, try writing a paragraph of your own to test the above idea.

Although there is a clear structure to our language (based on grammatical norms), we can be actively creative in the way we use it – not just through the ideas and emotions we can express, but also in our ability to adapt the structure of language itself – as these two examples of text messaging demonstrate.

Four quotes from Shakespeare:

To be or not to be, that is the question

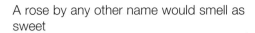

A rose by any other name would smell as sweet

Romeo, Romeo, wherefore art thou Romeo?

Once more unto the breech, dear friends, once more

Written as txt messages:

2b or not 2b thats ?

a @(—-`—-`—- by any otha name wd sml swEt

rm rm w4Ru rm?

1nc mr un2 T brech dr frnds 1nc mr

When a 13-year-old Scottish girl handed in an essay written in text message shorthand, she explained to her flabbergasted teacher that it was easier than standard English. She wrote:

My smmr hols wr CWOT. B4, we used 2go2 NY 2C my bro, his GF & thr 3 :- kids FTF. ILNY, it's a gr8 plc.

Translation

My summer holidays were a complete waste of time. Before, we used to go to New York to see my brother, his girlfriend and their three screaming kids face to face. I love New York. It's a great place.

Source: http://www.bbc.co.uk

 # Digging deeper

Having identified some features of different sociological approaches, we can break these large categories down to look in more detail at a number of specific sociological perspectives.

WARM UP: SOCIETY IS LIKE …

One way of grasping the basic ideas involved in different sociological perspectives is to use an analogy. In this exercise, therefore, we can outline the following perspectives using their associated analogies:

- **functionalism** (human body)
- **Marxism** (league table – e.g. football)
- **feminism** (league table – e.g. football)
- **interactionism** (a play)
- **postmodernism** (a theme park)

If possible, split the class into five groups, each looking at a different perspective. Each group should copy the table overleaf onto a piece of paper.

In column A (Features of …) you need to list up to five characteristics of the specified analogy. For example, for functionalism, the analogy is 'The human body', so you need to list five characteristics of a human body – e.g. bones, organs (such as the heart and brain), etc.

In column B (Features of society) you need to say how the ideas you've listed relate to society. In the example below, I've identified 'Bones' as a feature of a human body. In column B I've argued the 'bones of society' is the way different parts of society link together (because, in the human body, bones are linked to form the body's skeleton or basic structure).

The same analogy (a league table) is used for both Marxism and feminism. For the latter you need to keep in mind that feminist perspectives argue society is characterised by conflict between men and women.

Society is like: [a human body]	
A. Features of [human body]	B. Features of society
1. Bones	Link parts of the body together just as all parts of society link together.
2.	
3.	
4.	
5.	

Structuralist perspectives

For structuralist sociologists society, as **Philip Jones** (*Theory and Method in Sociology*, 1987) argues, is seen as, 'A structure of (cultural) rules', guiding our behaviour and telling us:

- how to behave appropriately in any given situation
- what to expect in terms of the behaviour of others.

From this perspective, individual behaviour is considered both uninteresting (structuralists don't want to know why I didn't like going to school) and relatively unimportant. The fact I didn't like going to school (and managed not to go for a year or so) is what **C. Wright Mills** (*The Sociological Imagination*, 1959) has called a:

- **Private problem**: It is an issue for a small number of people and not very interesting to the majority. If, however, everyone

stopped going to school this would represent a:

- **Public issue** – something of concern to everyone. Structural sociologists, therefore, start to get interested at the point where *private problems* become *public issues*. Attention, in this respect, is focused on how society pressurises individuals to perform roles, for example, so social life can continue on an orderly, predictable, basis.

This general idea – that sociologists should study the way society impacts on individual behaviour – represents the main way structuralist sociologists differ from action sociologists. However, just to complicate matters we can, as I noted earlier, sub-divide structural perspectives into two further categories, consensus structuralism and conflict structuralism.

Consensus structuralism

These sociologists focus on the way social order is created and maintained through agreement ('consensus') – through, for example, the development of shared norms and values. In this respect, one of the main consensus perspectives we can examine is **functionalism** – a perspective that involves a number of key ideas.

- **Social system**: Functionalists use this idea rather than 'society' because systems involve the idea of things working together – harmoniously – and, consequently, being dependent on each other. The human body, for example, is a system in which the various parts (heart, lungs, brain and so forth) work together to form a living thing. In a similar way, all the different parts of a social system (family, school and so forth) are interconnected and work together to form a society.

This, therefore, is a perspective that focuses on *consensus*, which in turn is characterised by the idea that everything in society has both a *purpose* (what it exists to do) and *needs* (things it requires from other parts of the system in order to function).

- **Sub-systems**: **Talcott Parsons** (*The Structure of Social Action*, 1937) argues that every social system consists of four very large institutions (or, as he puts it, 'functional sub-systems'), each of which performs a different, but related, set of functions based on certain 'problems' faced by every known society. These sub-systems (and the problem they exist to solve) are as follows:
  - **Economic** sub-systems exist to solve the problem of *survival*; that is, how to organise people into economic (work) relationships to produce the things (food, shelter, etc.) necessary for human survival.
  - **Political** sub-systems exist to solve the problem of *order*, which involves finding ways of governing and controlling people (political parties, the police and so forth). In other words, the political sub-system exists to ensure the 'rules and values of society' are maintained.
  - **Family** sub-systems exist to solve the problem of *socialisation* – how to ensure children are socialised in ways that allow them to grow into functioning adult members of society.
  - **Cultural** sub-systems exist to solve the problem of *social integration*; that is,

how to make people feel they have things in common (belonging to a society, sharing a common culture, etc.). Cultural institutions (schools, religious organisations, the mass media and so forth) exist to develop and foster cultural values.

- **Organismic analogy**: As we have seen in the exercise you did earlier, an easy way to visualise this perspective is to think in terms of society being like a human body – the organismic analogy. Social systems, as we have noted, consist of interconnected parts, in much the same basic way as a human body consists of interconnected parts.

- **Purpose** and **needs**: Social systems fit together on the basis of institutional purposes and needs. For example, in order for a family to exist (and perform its functions) it needs to be able to survive. The work institution performs this survival function in our society by allowing family members to earn the money they need to buy the food they consume (among other things); in order to fulfil its purpose, work needs the family group to produce socialised human beings.

- **Social solidarity** relates to the idea of social systems as *imagined communities* – a society cannot exist without its members working together and feeling they have things in common with each other (for example, a sense of 'being British'). To promote social solidarity, people have to be socially integrated into the institutions and culture of their society and, for functionalists, every society (or, indeed, every social group) develops *integrating mechanisms* (such as a common language) to achieve this.

Discussion point: social integration

1. How do events like football World Cups and international competitions encourage social solidarity?

2. What 'integrating mechanisms and devices' do schools use to create a sense of identity and belonging among their members? For example, how do school uniforms help to integrate pupils?

- **Dysfunctions**: Although functionalists focus (not too surprisingly perhaps) on the idea of function, consensus and harmony, they do recognise some things can be dysfunctional (dangerous or damaging). Too much (or not enough) of something may be harmful to society. For example, although something like crime can have a social solidarity function – if it unites people against a common (criminal) enemy – too much crime can leave people feeling uncertain about the rule of law and their own safety (and hence it would be dysfunctional).

Key criticisms: Functionalism, like any sociological perspective, has its critics, and we can identify three key criticisms in terms of:

- **Social change**: It is sometimes difficult to explain why anything in a society should change if it performs an essential function. In this respect, functionalism is often seen as a politically conservative perspective that lends its support to the *status quo* (that is, the desire to 'keep things as they are').

- **Dysfunction**: Do functionalists place too much emphasis on the 'beneficial aspects' of social institutions and groups? Schools, for example, may be places where children learn many useful things – but they are also places where bullying, sexism and racism may exist.

- **Tautology**: This a statement that contains its own proof and functionalists are sometimes accused of producing such arguments to justify their ideas. For example, the claim that, 'If something exists in society, it has a function' is supported by the argument that, 'It has a function because it exists … '. A tautological statement (such as the one I've just noted), in other words, cannot be disproved.

Conflict structuralism

The key idea for this type of perspective is that societies are generally orderly because of the ability of powerful groups to impose their ideas on other groups (the powerless). Unlike consensus theorists who see society as being broadly beneficial, in some way, to all its members, conflict theorists argue some groups benefit far more than others.

Two types of conflict structuralism we can examine in more detail are *Marxism* (where the basis of conflict is economic – different social classes constantly battling against each other) and *feminism*, where the basis of conflict is gender – men and women battling it out with each other).

Marxism: The key ideas of this perspective are:

- **Work**: For Marxists, the most important form of activity in any society is work, for the deceptively important reason that all other forms of social activity (politics, family, culture and the like) cannot exist without people first having secured the means to their survival (if you don't have enough to eat then the lack of anything interesting to watch on TV is probably not going to be your most pressing concern). Thus, how work is socially organised (who does it, what they do and who benefits from it) is seen as the key to understanding how all other relationships are organised.

- **Conflict**: The workplace is a key area of conflict in any society because of the way it is organised. Marxists argue that, in our

society (called 'capitalist' for reasons that will be clear in a moment) the 'means of economic production' (things like factories, machinery and land) are owned by one *class* of people (the *bourgeoisie* or ruling class). The vast majority of people, on the other hand, own little or nothing and so are forced to sell the one thing they do own – their ability to work. For Marxists, therefore, we have a situation in which:

- a small number of people own the means of production – they become very rich because they keep profits made from producing goods and services

- a large number of people own nothing but their ability to work for wages – these people (the working class or *proletariat*) are relatively poor (when compared to their Bourgeois employers).

Conflict potentially occurs, because:

- **owners** want to keep as much of their profit as possible (the less you pay in

Roman Abramovich – estimated wealth: £8 billion.

wages, the greater the amount you can keep to buy desirable things – like Chelsea Football Club, for example)

- **non-owners** want a larger slice of the economic pie. The working class also want the desirable things society has to offer – it is in their interests, therefore, to demand more from employers.

- **Competition** (and therefore conflict) is inevitable. Competition is not merely encouraged in capitalist societies; it is also viewed as desirable since it is through competition, the argument goes, that wealth is created and progress made (through the constant invention and reinvention of new ways of doing things, for example). Although, for Marxists, economic forms of competition and conflict are, as I have noted, most significant, competition occurs throughout society – between businesses, between different groups of workers, between men and women and so forth.

- **Social class**: This involves grouping people in terms of their 'relationship to the means of production'. For Marxists, two basic classes exist in any capitalist society:

  - the **bourgeoisie** (sometimes called the ruling or upper class): those who own the means of production

  - the **proletariat** (sometimes called the lower or working class): people who own nothing but their ability to work.

The picture is not quite as simple as this, of course; there may be many different relationships to the means of production – managers, for example, may not own a business but they can be considered to be a different social class to non-managers – but you get the basic idea.

As you might expect, because of their view of work as the most important social activity, class conflict is considered more significant than other types (such as male–female conflict).

- **Power**: Amidst all this emphasis on conflict, you could be forgiven for thinking our society is engaged in a war of all against all; this, however, is clearly not the case and Marxists explain this by noting that those at the top of society (the ruling class) are not only economically powerful, they are also politically powerful. This means they control how laws are made (through politicians identifying with the interests of a ruling class) and, of course, they can use force (the police and the army for example) to try to minimise conflict. **Louis Althusser** (*Lenin and Philosophy*, 1968) calls these 'Repressive State Apparatuses'. They are also able to influence how people generally think through political control/ownership of ideological institutions, such as the media and the education system, that deal in ideas (what Althusser calls 'Ideological State Apparatuses').

Key criticisms: Marxism, as you might expect, has its critics, and we can identify three key criticisms as follows.

- **Conflict**: Marxism over-emphasises the level of conflict in society and underplays the significance of non-economic types of conflict (gender or ethnic conflicts, for example). Some feminists are especially critical of the emphasis on work-based conflicts.

- **Communism**: For Marxists, class conflict will only end once the economic system on which it's based (capitalism) is replaced by a communist form of society – a type of society where work is not organised around private profit. Whatever the short-comings of capitalist societies, communism does not appear imminent.

- **Economic determinism**: Marxism assumes work is the most important institution in any society. While this may have (arguably) been true in Britain in the past, some writers (especially, as we will see, *postmodernists*) argue this is no longer the case and, consequently, question the significance of social class as a source of people's identity.

Feminism: Like people, 'feminism' comes in a variety of different shapes and sizes – too many to properly consider here. Instead we can examine four varieties – the *classical feminist perspectives* (the ones every textbook, including, of course, this one includes): **liberal**, **Marxist** and **radical** feminism as well as a newer variety, sometimes called **post-feminism**. You will sometimes see the classical forms of feminism called 'second-wave feminism', whereas post-feminism ('post' meaning 'after') is sometimes called 'third-wave feminism' to indicate its – quite radical – break with classical feminisms.

Despite their many differences, one theme common to all varieties of classical feminism (post-feminism has a rather different take on the matter) is the belief our society is *male-dominated*; that the interests of men have always been – and continue to be – considered more important than the interests of women. We can see how this idea influences the basic beliefs of different forms of classical feminism in the following terms:

Liberal feminism has a number of key ideas:

- **Equality of opportunity**: Liberal feminists are mainly concerned with *equal opportunities* for men and women (not 'equality', as such, but rather the chance to compete equally with men); they want to end the *sexual discrimination* which denies women the opportunity to compete on equal terms with men. One way to establish equality of opportunity is through the:

- **Legal system**: Liberal feminists have been active, in Britain and America, for example, in promoting a range of *anti-discriminatory* laws which, they argue, are needed to redress the historical gender imbalance. In the UK, legislation such as the *Sex Discrimination Act* (1975), which made discrimination in the workplace illegal and the *Equal Pay Act* (1970) are examples of this approach to gender inequality.

- **Dual role**: The idea that women increasingly play a dual role (as both carers within the family and paid employees) is, according to liberal feminists, a major area of inequality that needs to be addressed – both in terms of changing male attitudes to family life and through the continued development of anti-discriminatory laws and practices (for example, the introduction of child-care facilities for working women, maternity and paternity leave and so forth).

Key criticisms of this perspective are:

- **Status inequality**: Critics (not the least being other feminist perspectives) argue that *legal equality* is not the same as *status equality* (the idea of women having equal status to men). In other words, women are still treated in ways that assume they are inferior to men; women in the UK, for example, can expect to earn, on average during their working lifetime, 80 per cent of male income – even when they are doing work that's roughly comparable.

- **Class differences**: By lumping all women together as a 'class', liberal feminism ignores differences in the life experiences of different women; working-class women, for example, do not have the same advantages as upper-class women – they face, for example, far greater difficulties in securing equal opportunities. In addition, black women, in general, have different life experiences and chances from white women.

Marxist feminism: The key ideas here are:

- **Class inequality**: Marxist feminists see class inequality as the main cause of female oppression, exploitation and discrimination in our society. In a competitive, capitalist, society, men are encouraged to exploit any 'weaknesses' in women's market position (for example, the fact women may be out of the workforce during pregnancy) to their own advantage.

- **Patriarchal ideology** (ideas that support male domination of women): Although patriarchy is an important concept, Marxist feminists use it to show how the social and economic exploitation of women is justified (by both men and women) through powerful ideas about masculinity and femininity. For example,

 Growing it yourself: life experiences

As a class, make two lists identifying the **similarities** and **differences** between the life experiences and chances of the two types of women pictured below.

Young black woman

Old white woman

ideas that men are 'natural breadwinners' and women 'natural homemakers' can be strong influences on people's behaviour.

- **Social class**: Marxist feminists argue men and women are not separate (sex-based) classes because higher-class women have very little in common with working-class women except their biology – the fact they are all physically women. Men and women, the argument goes, both have an interest in creating a communist society in which men and women are treated equally.

- **Domestic labour** is viewed as exploitation (because it is unpaid labour). Women are also sometimes seen as what **Barrett** and **McIntosh** (*The Anti-Social*, 1982) call a 'reserve army of labour' – people who are called into the workforce when the economy expands and 'dumped' – encouraged to return to domestic labour – when the economy contracts.

- **Gender socialisation**: The development of patriarchal ideas, attitudes and practices (such as sexual discrimination) are seen as the product of differences in the way men and women are socialised – men are not naturally exploitative of women; rather, it is the economic system (capitalism) that encourages and rewards sexist attitudes and behaviour.

Key criticisms of this perspective are:

- **Patriarchy**: Male domination of women seems to be a feature of all known human societies, not just class-based (capitalist) societies. For some feminists, this means patriarchal relationships should be given more emphasis than economic (class) relationships.

- **Patriarchal exploitation**: Marxist feminism assumes (rightly or wrongly) men and women have similar 'long-term' interests (the replacement of an unequal, patriarchal, capitalist society with an equal, non-patriarchal, communist society). Whether or not this is true, the development of a communist form of society (as I have noted earlier) doesn't look a very likely prospect, in our society at least, for the foreseeable future.

- **Social change**: A major criticism of Marxist feminism is it ignores the extent to which society – and the position of men and women – has changed and continues to change. Female lives, for example, have changed dramatically over the past 50 years in terms of family responsibilities, educational achievements (where women now out-perform men at just about every level) and work opportunities.

In the light of these ideas, therefore, we can consider a third form of classical feminism, namely **radical feminism**, which involves a number of key ideas:

- **Patriarchy/patriarchal ideology**: These are two key ideas for radical feminists, mainly because, they argue, all known human societies have been – and remain – male dominated (a situation these feminists want to change). Given this idea, improvements in women's lives can only come about through the overthrow of patriarchal ideas and practices. This follows because radical feminists see men and women as having basic psychological differences – in crude terms, men are seen to be naturally aggressive and confrontational whereas women have qualities of cooperation, caring (nurturing) and so forth. Given these basic differences, therefore, men and women are seen in terms of the concept of:

- **Sex class**: This type of feminism sees women as a class (based on a common gender) with its own experiences and interests different from those of men. Just as Marxist perspectives see the overthrow of the ruling (economic) class as the way to achieve human liberation, radical feminists argue it's necessary for women to overthrow the ruling sex class (men) if they are to achieve liberation – an idea based on the concept of:

- **Matriarchy** (female domination of men): Men are the enemy of women because, throughout history, they have exploited women for their own gain. For this situation to end, women have to establish a *matriarchal society* – one in which women dominate men. Radical feminists often advocate lesbian relationships and the development of women-only support groups as a way of developing matriarchal ideas and practices. **Adrienne Rich** ('Compulsory Heterosexuality and Lesbian Existence', 1980) developed the term '*compulsory heterosexuality*' to express the idea that male–female relationships are the basis of patriarchy (and therefore the source of male domination).

- **Public and private spheres**: Discrimination against women takes place in two main areas: the public (for example, the workplace where women are paid less and have lower status) and the private (the home, where women carry out the majority of unpaid domestic work) – a dual form of female exploitation not experienced by men.

Key criticisms of this perspective involve the following ideas.

- **Sex class**: As we have noted, female life chances are not necessarily very similar; differences clearly exist, for example, in terms of:
  - **Social class**: The life chances of upper-class women are significantly different from those of working-class women.
  - **Ethnicity**: The life chances of black women are different from those of white women.

  The question, therefore, is do all women share the same interests – are they, in short, a sex class or does radical feminism downplay the importance of class, age and ethnic differences in the exploitation of women?

- **Psychologies**: Differences in male and female psychologies can be seen as the product of *gender socialisation* rather than being *innate* (fixed and unchanging) differences. Given the opportunity, women seem just as capable as men of aggressive behaviour, for example.

- **Relationships**: Not all gender relationships are characterised by oppression and exploitation and the general position of women in society has improved and changed over the past 50 years.

The criticisms of classical feminist perspectives have, in part, led to the development of a further form of feminist perspective we can briefly examine.

Post-feminism is a perspective covering many different viewpoints, making it difficult to capture the flavour of all its varieties in a few short paragraphs. As the 'Feminism with a Difference' website puts it: 'The term "post-feminism" has had popular usage in Western society since the late 1980s. It refers to a belief that gender equality has been successfully achieved, while simultaneously castigating the feminist movement for making women frustrated and unhappy.' (www.difference-feminism.com)

We can identify some of the key ideas of this perspective in terms of:

- **Anti-essentialism**: The concept of *essentialism* relates to the idea that 'deep down' there are fundamental ('essential') differences between males and females. These relate not simply to biological differences but, most importantly, to psychological differences in the way men and women think, act and feel. **Judith Butler** (*Gender Trouble*, 1990) argues that this is mistaken, for two main reasons; firstly, she rejects the claim that women are a sex class. Secondly, and more controversially perhaps, she questions the usefulness of categories such as 'man' and 'woman' since, in our society today, they probably involve more differences than similarities. For example, think about the different forms of male and female identities that exist in our society – from homophobic men to transsexual women.

  Gender, for Butler, is considered as a 'performance' – things we do at different times, rather than something we 'always are'. Butler's solution to gender essentialism is the subversion of separate 'male' and 'female' gender identities. That is, she believes we should no longer see men and women as two distinctive sexes; rather, we should see gender as a range of social processes, some of which are similar (such as some gay men who display traditional female traits and women who display traditional masculine traits) and some of which are different.

- **Choice**: This idea – central to postmodernist perspectives (see below) – reflects the idea that in contemporary ('present day') society, men and women have a range of choices open to them that were denied to all but the rich few in the past. One choice is how we define ourselves (our personal identity) – men and women have the freedom to construct gender identity in any way they choose. For post-feminists, this personal construction of femininity often involves what they see as 'reclaiming femininity' in the sense women can be both feminine (whatever that may mean) and able to pursue their education, career and so forth.

Madonna: post-feminist icon or just rich enough not to care?

- **Transgression**: This idea means cutting across categories or boundaries and can be used in two ways here. Firstly, it relates to (traditional) ideas about masculinity and femininity – the idea, in short, that you

Discussion point: is gender dead?

Have a look at the following examples of different types of female gender identity.

Do you think the wide range of different identities in our society makes the concepts of 'male' and 'female' redundant?

are either 'a man' or 'a woman'. In this respect, post-feminism argues that *identity transgression* occurs when women, for example, choose to adopt ways of thinking and behaving traditionally seen as masculine.

Examples here range from 'ladettes' (young women who mirror the often

outrageous behaviour of young males –
'booze, bonking and the beautiful game')
to transgendered individuals who define
themselves as neither male nor female.

Secondly, it relates to the argument that
the traditional concerns of feminism
(patriarchy, equality and so forth) are
now redundant – they are concerns
related to a type of society that has
disappeared. As society has changed,
therefore, so too have notions about
gender, and it is becoming increasingly
meaningless to talk about men and
women as if they were two separate and
unrelated ideas.

Key criticisms of this perspective include:

- **Choice**: For critics of post-feminism, the
  idea of women in general being able to
  exercise choice in their lives is doubtful.
  For those with enough money (whether
  they are male or female) a massive range
  of behavioural choices exist. For those
  with little or no money, behavioural
  choices are far more restricted.

- **Class**: Leading on from the above, it is
  clear that concepts such as social class,
  age and ethnicity impact on the range
  of choices open to both men and
  women.

- **Individualism**: Post-feminism has been
  accused of downplaying the problems
  faced by the majority of women, in the
  sense that most women's lives are not
  characterised by unlimited choice,
  freedom and individual self-expression
  (just as the same is probably true for most
  male lives).

As **Vicki Coppock** (*The Illusions of 'Post-
Feminism': New Women, Old Myths*, 1995)
notes:

The irony is . . . that the proclamation of
'post-feminism' has occurred at precisely
the same moment as acclaimed feminist
studies demonstrate that not only have
women's real advancements been limited,
but also there has been a backlash against
feminism of international significance.

Action perspectives

For action sociologists, the emphasis is on
how we construct the social world through
our relationships and actions. From this
perspective, society is something created and
recreated on a daily basis by people going
about their lives. In other words, unlike
structural sociologists, who focus on the way
society pushes and pulls the individual in
various directions – 'making' us form family
groups or develop educational systems –
action sociologists want to reverse this
picture. Their interest lies in the way
thinking, conscious, human beings
constantly produce and reproduce the social
world through their behaviour.

From this perspective, society is little
more than a label or name – an 'elaborate
fiction' we create to explain to ourselves and
others the reasons for the limits we
consciously and unconsciously place on our
behaviour. Social life, therefore, is a series of
encounters – separate, but linked, episodes
that give the appearance of order and
stability, not something imposed on us from
above by society. Order and predictability
exist, therefore, for as long as we *act* in ways
that serve to maintain them.

Although there are, like feminist
perspectives, a number of competing social
action perspectives (*ethnomethodology,
phenomenology* and *symbolic interactionism* to
name but three), for our purposes we can
consider this perspective in terms of the
catch-all category *interactionism*.

Interactionism's key ideas are:

- **Social interaction:** The social world is created by the meaningful interactions between people, a process that involves:

- **Meanings:** In terms of social interaction, this perspective stresses the importance of meanings (what we each understand by something) that work on two levels. Firstly, to interact socially we must develop shared definitions of any situation (if your teacher, for example, defines a situation as 'education' and you define it as 'a skateboard park', a free and frank exchange of views might develop). Secondly, if the meaning of something is only developed through interaction then meanings can change fairly easily. For example, in terms of gender, the meaning of being masculine or feminine in our society has changed quite dramatically over the past few years.

If this idea is valid, it means the social world always involves:

- **Negotiated realities:** This idea follows from the above since, for interactionists, society and culture are not things that are fixed or slow to change. On the contrary, because meanings are *negotiated* (or argued over) the social world is a very fluid place that can rapidly change. Unlike structural perspectives, therefore, Interactionists don't see society as a 'thing' acting on our behaviour (since it has no objective reality outside of social interaction); rather, society, as I have suggested, is just a convenient label we give to the pressures, rules and responsibilities that arise out of our social relationships.

- **Labels:** The idea of labelling (or naming)

is an important one since it suggests how interactionists view social structures as forms of social interaction. *Labelling theory*, for example, argues that when we name something (such as categorising people as 'young' or 'elderly') we associate the name with a set of characteristics, our knowledge of which is used to guide our behaviour (which, in a roundabout way, brings us back to the idea of a *definition of a situation*). For example, the characteristics I assign to the label 'student' lead me to expect certain things from a person so labelled.

Key criticisms of this perspective are:

- **Over-emphasis on 'the individual':** The emphasis on individuals, meanings and interaction ignores the idea that social structures do seem to impact on our lives (as we saw when we looked at Meighan's idea of haunting). In another respect, by focusing on the social-psychological aspects of social life, interactionists fail to explain adequately how and why people seem to behave in broadly similar ways.

- **Social structures:** A major criticism of interactionism is that it doesn't explain how individual meanings, definitions and interpretations are affected by social structures. For example, if I define a situation as one thing (a fancy dress party, for example) and others define it as something else (a game of cricket), this will have serious consequences for me (and not just because I can't bowl properly in my chicken outfit) – which introduces the idea of *power* as an important concept. We are not equal in our ability to define situations – some groups (or classes) have greater power than others when it comes to defining a

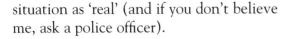

situation as 'real' (and if you don't believe me, ask a police officer).

Postmodernism

This is a relatively new type of sociological perspective, one developed over the past 15 or so years. Although I have characterised it as an action approach, you need to be careful with such a characterisation (as with any attempt to categorise sociological perspectives) since postmodernism does not fit neatly into any particular theoretical category. Be that as it may, there are a number of key ideas related to this perspective we can note.

- **Narratives**: Postmodernists refer to *narratives* (or stories) when talking about people's lives and their experiences, mainly because our lives are viewed as a seamless web of interlocking narratives which we define and move between at will.

  For example, when I'm with my wife, the narrative I construct is one of a loving, helpful, dutiful, husband, alert to her every need, whim and desire. However, when I'm in the pub with my mates the narrative I construct is somewhat different. I have no problem moving between these narratives and I am always the person I believe myself to be in each (which means I'm either a fantastic person or a consummate liar).

- **Metanarratives**: These are 'big stories' we construct either individually or, more usually, as a culture to explain something about the nature of the social and natural worlds. Examples of metanarratives might include religions (such as Christianity or Islam) and political philosophies (socialism or conservativism, for example).

For the French writer **Jean-Francois Lyotard** (*The Postmodern Condition*, 1986) postmodernism is characterised by an 'incredulity towards metanarratives'. In other words, he argues big stories about the world are not believable or sustainable since, at some point their claims to explain 'everything about something' are challenged, breakdown or co-exist in an uneasy ignorance of each other. If you think about it, Christianity or Islam can't both be right since they explain the same thing (religion) in almost completely different ways.

- **Globalisation**: The idea we now live in a *global society* (we no longer think or behave in terms of national boundaries) means the way we think about, communicate and interact with people is changing rapidly; think, for example, about how easily email lets you communicate with people around the globe.

- **Identity** refers to 'who we believe ourselves to be' or how we define ourselves. In past societies, identities were more likely to be **centred** – that is, clear, relatively fixed and certain. For example, in the past people in our society had a much clearer ('centred') idea about what it meant to be a man or a woman because there were relatively few choices available to them in terms of the meaning of these categories.

In postmodern society, however, things have changed to such an extent we now have a wide range of possible choices about 'how to be a man' or 'how to be feminine' which leads to the concept of **de-centred identity**. This means that as the range of possible meanings expand (in terms of sexuality, for example, I can choose to be heterosexual, homosexual, bisexual, asexual, trans-sexual ...) people become less certain ('de-centred') about how they are supposed to behave, (think, for example, about the many possible ways you can play the role of student). Under the influence of globalisation, categories such as class, gender, age and ethnicity are easily combined to create a whole new range of identities (such as some young British Asians defining themselves as *Brasian* – a mix of both British and Asian cultures and identities).

If identities are changing, under the influence of choice, we need to consider the idea of:

- **Uncertainty**: The downside to almost unlimited choice from which we pick-and-mix our identities is uncertainty and confusion about who we are and how we're supposed to behave. The old certainties of class, gender, age and ethnicity no longer have much currency in terms of telling us how to behave appropriately.

To investigate postmodernism further, go to:

http://www.sociology.org.uk/kc1_home.htm

Key criticisms of this perspective are many and varied, but we can note some of the major ones as follows.

- **Choice**: One criticism of this idea, as we have seen previously, is that for the vast majority of people, choice is pretty much an illusion – they simply do not have the money, power or resources to exercise

choice. In this respect, postmodernism ignores the various ways in which choice is socially created, produced and available to all.

- **Identity**: Despite the claims of postmodernists, a large number of people in our society still define themselves (or an defined by others) in fairly traditional ways when it comes to categories such as class, gender, age and ethnicity.

Growing it yourself: the limits of choice?

To test the idea of 'unlimited choice', go into a supermarket and look down the rows. If you are doing this as a class, split into groups, each group taking responsibility for a particular type of product (washing powders, tea and coffee, etc.).

For your chosen product, count/record the number of different types available (there will be a lot in most cases).

Finally, for each different type you have identified, check the packaging and record the name of the manufacturer.

Each group should then report their findings to the class.

- **Disputes**: Some sociologists have argued (*Sociology Review*, 1998) the concept of postmodernism is not a particularly useful one when applied to the analysis of social behaviour. **Jonathon Gershuny** for example, argues: 'Postmodernists conclude that we have reached the end of the grand theory and that now we must retreat to something altogether less ambitious in our attempts to understand society. My conclusion, by contrast, is that we must search for new theories.'

Discussion point

Read the following report:

Gender stereotypes still hamper young

Will Woodward, Education editor: *The Guardian*, 20/09/00

Adolescents are still unable to shake off gender stereotypes that appear as entrenched as ever . . . . Inside, outside and beyond school, young men and women are under continuing pressure to conform to traditional behaviour.

At school, women avoid physics and information technology and choose English, biology, history and modern languages. 'Young women find it easier to ask for help than young men, who find it harder to admit a lack of knowledge,' the report, 'Young People and Gender' says. Boys are more likely to break the law – a gap which extends after the age of 14 – or be involved in crime, alcohol abuse and illegal drugs.

Girls, who are more likely to be concerned about their body image and weight, are much more likely to start smoking. Suicide rates are higher for men and double the number of boys die at 17. Boys are less likely to visit their GP or to use other health services. Girls are more at risk of depression, eating disorders and self-harm.

Boys 'take greater risks and feel greater pressure' to be sexually active and find it harder to admit inexperience. But 'in spite of the notion of "girl power", young women still find it problematic to say no to sex and negotiate the use of contraception'.

At work, young men are more likely to want managerial or professional jobs – 75% compared with 25% for women, who are concentrated in personal service industries with part-time jobs and lower wages. 'The need to conform to masculine stereotypes prevents young men from joining traditionally female careers.' Although more young men are officially unemployed, a large group of young women remains outside employment, education and training opportunities because of caring responsibilities.

To what extent does the report support or reject ideas about centred and de-centred gender identities put forward by postmodernists?

Anthony Giddens, on the other hand, disputes the very use of the term 'postmodern' when he argues: 'I believe we still live in an era of modernity and modernisation', and **John Westergaard** offers the following (somewhat scathing) assessment of the idea: 'In my view, postmodernist approaches constitute neither a theoretical advance – on the contrary – nor even a backward step, but rather a declaration of intellectual bankruptcy.'

Structuration perspectives

As I have noted, this relates to the possibility of combining structural and action perspectives in the following ways:

- **Structure and action**: Unlike the previous perspectives (with the possible exception of postmodernism, since this, by and large, rejects the idea we can think in these terms), *structuration* argues that both structure and action are equally significant in terms of our ability to understand human behaviour.

- **Practices**: The key to understanding this perspective is, according to **Anthony Giddens**, the idea of *practices* (in simple terms, the things people do). As he explains it: 'The theory of structuration states that the basic domain of social science study is neither the experience of the individual nor the existence of any form of societal totality, but social practices. Through social activities people reproduce the actions that make these practices possible' (www.sociology.org.uk/as4aqu.htm).

  In other words, as people develop relationships, the rules they use to govern their respective behaviours are *formalised* (as norms, for example) into *practices* – in effect, routine ways of behaving towards each other. Once we start to think of the huge range of practices surrounding our lives we start to develop a sense of structure to the social world, which necessarily involves:

- **Rules**: This concept is important here since it suggests both the way our actions create behavioural rules and the idea that such rules become *externalised* (they seem to take on a life of their own, separate from our individual behaviours). In effect, therefore, although we may be involved in rule-making behaviour, such rules 'reflect back' on our behaviour in ways that suggest or demand conformity.

- **Resources**: This idea refers to concepts such as power and relates to how and why rules are created. Some rules, for example, are negotiated between individuals (your relationship with your friends, for example, is based on a series of unwritten and unspoken rules you've worked out between yourselves), but others – such as laws governing things like the definition of murder – are, in some respects, non-

negotiable; that is, some rules are created by powerful groups and are simply imposed on people. For example, whatever your opinion about the European Community, many of its rules apply to the United Kingdom.

Key criticisms of this perspective are:

- **Power**: One possible criticism of structuration is it doesn't sufficiently take account of the way power in society is unequally distributed (for example, the rich have more power than the poor, men have more power than women). The practices of the powerful may become entrenched, in the sense they are beyond the ability of the powerless to change. In other words, the relatively powerless do not, through their everyday practices, 'create society'; rather, it is through everyday practice that people experience the power of 'society'.

- **Structure or action**: A number of criticisms have been aimed at the (plausible, it has to be admitted) notion we can easily combine these two very different types of idea.

  Clegg (*Frameworks of Power*, 1989), for example, argues that although structuration theory talks about structure and action being equally significant, Giddens, in effect, considers human action as being considerably more significant. Similarly, **Layder** (*Key issues in Structuration Theory*, 1987) argues structuration gives very little attention to the concept of social structures as 'determinants of action'. In other words, there is little sense that social structures (as opposed to human practices) can have very much affect on people's behaviour.

INTRODUCTION

As you have probably guessed, this chapter deals with family life in all its many forms, and the main aim of this opening section is to explore 'different conceptions of the relationships of the family to the social structure, with particular reference to the economy and to state policies'. To do this successfully we need to:

- outline different perspectives on family life
- examine how these perspectives see the role of the family in society
- explore how economic and social policies impact on family structures and relationships.

Defining the family group

⚠ Preparing the ground

The first thing we need to do is define 'a family' given that, in order to relate the family to social structure and social policy, it would be useful to know what it involves.

WARM UP: FAMILY DEFINITIONS

To get you started, in small groups, think about and discuss among the group what a family means to you. Make a note of the kinds of things you believe it involves.

Once you have done this, as a class, compare your notes and identify the common features (if any) of a family.

At a guess, I'd say your definition of a family will probably involve two basic ideas, considered in terms of family.

- **Characteristics**: You will have identified certain features of a family (such as different generations sharing a common residence) that make it different to other social groups.

- **Relationships**: This involves the idea families share particular social relationships (for example, that someone is a mother or grandfather to a child) that clearly mark them out as a distinctive group in society.

As I am sure you have discovered, however, defining a family is not quite as easy as you might have first thought, for a couple of reasons.

- Is there such an institution as 'the family' in any society? In other words, is there only one family type or is it possible to talk about many different types?

- If there are a variety of types, are they

really different or are they simply variations on a basic theme? For example, if our definition of a family involved the idea of 'two adults and their children', is a family consisting of 'one adult and their children' a different form of family?

Although they may not seem too important at the moment, how we answer these questions is going to be central to our initial exploration of family life.

If we look at some sociological definitions of families, we can begin with a classic one provided by **George Murdock** (*Social Structure*, 1949):

> The family is a social group characterised by common residence, economic cooperation and reproduction. It includes adults of both sexes, at least two of whom maintain a socially-approved sexual relationship, and one or more children, own or adopted, of the sexually cohabiting adults

As an initial definition, it is useful for a couple of reasons: firstly, it is both a starting-point (we have to begin somewhere) and, speaking personally, a definition most of us would recognise as being 'a family'. Secondly, whether we go with it or not, it is useful for highlighting a couple of general points about families. It tells us, for example:

- **Social relationships** are a key concept to consider (families are not necessarily linked to the concept of marriage, for example).
- **Functions**: Family groups seem to exist to fulfil a number of purposes, the main ones being reproduction and the raising/socialisation of children.

There are, however, a few debatable areas to consider.

- **Adults** and **children**: This definition

suggests families do not have to be *monogamous* (for example, one man married to one women), they can also be *polygamous* – where one man is married to a number of women (*polygny*) or one woman married to a number of men (*polyandry*). However, it also suggests a family involves children – which raises the question, how do we classify a childless couple? Are they a family (and if not, what are they)?

- **Sexuality**: Does this definition allow for the possibility of homosexual families?
- **Common residence**: Do family members have to live together to consider themselves a family?

Discussion point: classic or outdated?

Is Murdock's definition too restrictive in the way it defines the family?

Can you identify any groups that might constitute a 'family' without conforming to his definition?

Murdock's definition was originally produced in the USA in the 1940s.

Do you think the world has changed and, if so, what implications does this have for the way we can define a family?

If Murdock's definition raises more questions than it answers, perhaps we need to investigate a slightly different way of defining the family group – and one way involves introducing the concept of **kinship**. This involves relationships based on biology (so-called blood relationships – such as between a mother and her child – where there's a genetic link between the two) or *affinity* (relationships created through custom – such as two adults living together – or relationships created by law, marriage being an obvious example here).

Weiss ('Family support and education programs', 1988) uses this concept to define the family group as, 'A small kinship structured group with the key function of . . . socialisation of the newborn'. **Giddens** (*Sociology*, 1993) suggests family groups can be defined as, 'A group of persons directly linked by kin connections, the adult members of which assume responsibility of caring for the children.'

However we decide to define a family, it is clear we need to distinguish this group from a concept used with increasing frequency, namely a **household**. This, at its most basic, involves a single person or group living together in the same location (such as friends sharing accommodation). In this respect, we can note most families are households, but not all households are families.

⚠ Digging deeper

So far we have seen that defining a family is not unproblematic (that is, there are arguments over how best to define it), which should alert us to a key characteristic of family life in our society, namely its *diversity* (considered in terms of both different family structures and relationships). We will develop these ideas in a moment, but for now we can note we have identified a distinction between two types of definition:

- **Exclusive** definitions (such as that produced by Murdock) where the focus is on the specific characteristics of a family that make it different to other social groups (such as a household or a school class). This type has the advantage of being clear about what is – and is not – a family group but, as we have seen, it is perhaps difficult to produce a definition that applies to all possible types of family.

- **Inclusive** definitions (such as those of Weiss or Giddens) where the focus is on defining a family group in terms of the general relationships (such as kinship or

❀ Growing it yourself: families or households?

Using the following table as a template (and working individually, in small groups or as a class) what advantages and disadvantages can you identify to the use of concepts like families and households?

Families		Households	
Advantages of this concept	Disadvantages of this concept	Advantages of this concept	Disadvantages of this concept
Identifies kinship as significant	Difficult to define	Includes all groups who live together	A household can be different to a family
Further advantages and disadvantages?			

affinity) that make it different from other social groups. One advantage to this definition is that it covers a variety of different family forms, but if the definition is drawn too broadly it may include family-type groups (such as households) that are significantly different to families in terms of their relationships.

Each type of definition has, therefore, certain advantages and disadvantages for the sociological researcher and, whichever definition you choose to use, it is ultimately just that – a choice reflecting your personal ideas, interests and preoccupations; there is, in effect, no correct way of defining a family group.

Thus, rather than see families as a particular type of social group it might be better to think about them in terms of what **John Goldthorpe** (*Family Life in Western Societies*, 1987) calls 'a network of related kin'; in other words, as a *social process* based on relationships involving a particular set of:

- **labels** – such as mother, father, son and daughter
- **values** – such as the belief parents should raise their own children
- **norms** – such as living together (through marriage or cohabitation)
- **functions** – such as primary socialisation.

By adopting this view we start to capture the potential richness of family relationships and, by extension, reflect the diversity of family experiences in our society.

However we eventually decide to define 'the family' (something, as I've suggested above, that is actually quite difficult to do) it is probably safe to say that family groups are important to us – the majority of us, after all, spend at least some of our lives

surrounded in various ways by 'family' of some description. This being the case, therefore, it would be useful to examine how different sociologists have explained the social significance of these groups.

Family perspectives

⚠ Preparing the ground

Family groups, considered mainly in term of what they exist to do, are generally considered by sociologists to be important institutions in any society. However, as you might expect, there are disagreements over how we interpret the role of the family group and, in this section we can introduce some different perspectives on the relationships of families to social structure. **Functionalist perspectives** start from the observation the family group has existed – in one form or another – in all known societies (in other words, the family is considered to be a 'cultural universal' because it has existed in all known cultures in one form or another). For this reason, families are seen as crucial to the functioning of any social system (you will recall, no doubt, functionalists consider the family to be one of the four major *functional sub-systems* in any society). To put this another way, the family group is considered functional – and therefore essential – for any social system because it has a couple of vital purposes, namely:

- **Socialisation**: Families are the main institution for the initial socialisation of children and any institution charged with this responsibility plays a significant part in the reproduction of cultural norms and values.

- **Social order**: The family acts as a stabilising force in society. Great stress is placed by functionalists on things like emotional and sexual stability, economic co-operation and so forth.

New Right perspectives, although closely related to functionalism, involve more directly political (rather than sociological) ideas about the significance of families. For New Right theorists, whether we define them in terms of personalities (politicians such as Margaret Thatcher in the UK, Ronald Reagan and George W. Bush in the USA) or practices (issues such as anti-abortion, anti-immigration, anti-Europe and liberal economic policies), the family group is the cornerstone of any society.

The New Right particularly like to promote the idea of 'traditional family relationships' – families should consist of two, heterosexual, adults, preferably married (to each other) with clearly defined gender

The New Right view of a traditional family

roles and relationships (which normally means men as family breadwinners and women as domestic workers).

Marxist perspectives on family life reflect their conflict view of society, where they relate what the family group does (socialisation, for example) to how it benefits powerful groups, whether this be on a group level – how a ruling class benefits from various 'free family services', such as raising children to be future employees – or a personal level, such as how men dominate and exploit women.

For Marxists, it is not what the family does that's important, but *why* it does it. One argument here is the family helps to maintain and reproduce inequalities by presenting them as 'normal' and 'natural' within the socialisation process.

Feminist perspectives have, traditionally, focused on the role of the family group in the exploitation of women. In this respect, attention has mainly been given to identifying how traditional gender roles within the family have been enforced and reinforced, mainly for the benefit of men. The family group, therefore, has tended to be seen as oppressive of women, trapping them in a fairly narrow range of roles and responsibilities (domestic labour and child care, for example) that defines female roles in terms of the kind of *service functions* just noted.

In modern families, the notion of women's *dual role* or *double shift* (women as both paid workers *and* unpaid housewives) has been emphasised as has, more-recently, the idea of women performing, according to **Duncombe** and **Marsden** ('Love and intimacy: The Gender Division of Emotion and "Emotion Work"', 1993) a *triple shift* – the third element being the idea of *emotional labour* (that is, investing time and effort in the psychological well-being of family members).

Postmodern perspectives reject the kinds of views we have just noted (since they all, in their different ways, are seen as putting forward narrow (or prescriptive) views about what families *are* and how they *should be*). The key ideas of this perspective in relation to family life and relationships are *diversity* and *choice*, two concepts that reflect postmodern ideas about behaviour and lifestyles.

From this viewpoint, sociological perspectives such as functionalism, Marxism or feminism are hopelessly outdated in their view of societies and individuals. A family – in short – is whatever people want it to be (whether it involves adults of the opposite sex, the same sex, own children, adopted children or whatever). From this perspective, therefore, the relationship between families and the social structure is a largely meaningless question for two reasons. Firstly, they reject the idea of social structures – which makes trying to identify and isolate any relationship between family groups and something that doesn't exist (social structures) a fairly pointless exercise. Secondly, they reject the idea we can talk, in any useful way, about 'the family'; all we have, in effect, is a variety of people living out their lives and lifestyles in ways they believe are acceptable and appropriate to how they want to live.

 # Digging deeper

In thinking about families and their relationships to social structure we have two distinct viewpoints to consider; on the one hand, we have traditional sociological perspectives (such as functionalism) that emphasise how the structure of society impacts (for good or bad) on family forms and relationships. On the other, we have postmodern perspectives that suggest the question of any relationship (of whatever type) between families and social structures is not worth posing (let alone trying to answer).

Whatever your position in relation to the above, we need to dig a little deeper into the different perspectives we have just outlined, if for no better reason than this is an AS textbook designed to provide a range of views for you to personally evaluate, accept or reject. In this respect, therefore, **functionalist** sociology has tended to look at the family as the initial, essential, bedrock of social integration in any given society. This involves the idea that ways have to be found to make people feel they belong to the society into which they were born – to believe they have something in common with the people around them. **Ronald Fletcher** (*The Family and Marriage in Britain*, 1973), in this respect, has identified the *core functions* of the family as being:

- **procreation** and **child-rearing** (the 'having sex and its consequences' bit – which includes, of course, the initial, general, socialisation process)

- **regulation of sexual behaviour** (between adults, for example, by defining the limits of sexual freedom)

- **provision of a home** (in the widest sense of the word).

In addition, Fletcher argues families perform certain non-essential functions, many of which provide linkages with the wider social structure. These include:

- **consumption** of goods and services
- **basic education**

- **health care** (both physical and psychological)
- **recreation**.

For **Talcott Parsons**, on the other hand, the modern family has become increasingly specialised. He argues it performs only two essential functions:

- **Primary socialisation**: Families are 'factories whose product is the development of human personalities.'
- **Stabilisation of adult personalities**, which involves adult family members providing things like physical and emotional support for each other.

Marxist perspectives have been generally more critical of the role of the family group, seeing it in terms of:

- A **safety valve** for (male) frustrations: The majority of men are relatively powerless in the workplace and this condition is disguised by allowing males to be powerful figures within the family group. This serves as a safety value for the build-up of tension and frustration at work and directs frustration away from criticism of employers, workplace conditions and so forth. In this respect, we could also note the family is a fairly violent institution in our society: The Home Office, for example, through its Crime Reduction Service ('Domestic Violence', 2004) documents the range, risk and consistency of family-related violence in terms of the fact that: 'Every year, around 150 people are killed by a current or former partner. One in four women and one in six men will suffer from domestic violence at some point in their lives.'
- **Channelling** and **legitimising** the exploitation of women. Within the

family, for example, many women are still generally expected to do the majority of domestic labour tasks (a situation that mirrors, the exploitative work relationships experienced by many men). This situation is, to some extent, considered right and proper or, at least, legitimate by many men and women because it is seen as being part of the female role in (patriarchal) society.

- **Free services**: The basic idea here is that the majority of children raised within a family group will grow-up to be future workers who will, according to this perspective, be taking their place amongst those exploited by capitalist owners. The costs of replacing 'dead labour' (a concept that includes both those who literally die and those who become too old or sick to work anymore) are, in the main taken on by the family group in a couple of ways.

  - **Economic costs** involved in raising children to adulthood fall on the family group. Employers make little or no contribution to these general family costs.
  - **Psychological costs** are also involved since the family group is an important socialising agency. If children are to be future workers they need to be socialised in ways that orientate them towards seeing their future in such terms.

Complementing the idea of free services, we can note how Marxists relate such ideas to that of the family group as a:

- **Stabilising force** in capitalist society. This idea reflects the argument that the responsibilities people take on when they create family groups locks them into capitalist economic relationships. In other words, family members have to work to provide both the basic necessities of life – food, clothing and shelter – and the range of consumer goods that goes with modern lifestyles (Personal computers, DVDs, the family car and so forth). The requirement to take responsibility for family members (both adults and children) also acts as an emotionally stabilising force in society.

Finally, in this respect, we can note the idea of the family group as:

- **Consumers** of products: Marxists note how the family group has, historically, moved from being active producers of goods and services to passive consumers of these things – someone, after all, has to buy the things that make profits for a ruling class and the family, with all its expenses and expectations represent an increasingly important source of consumption.

Feminist perspectives on family life tend to stress things like:

- **Service roles**: Women, by and large, take on the role of 'unpaid servants' to their partner and children. This is sometimes done willingly – because they see it as part of the female role – and sometimes unwillingly because their partner will not, or is unable, to take it on. This type of role – especially when it's part of a female double shift involving both paid and unpaid work – contributes, according to feminists, to:

- **Exploitation**: In this respect, feminists point to the idea women in our society increasingly suffer from dual forms of exploitation:

  - **patriarchal** exploitation as domestic labourers within the home

  - **capitalist** exploitation as employees in the workplace.

- **Reserve army of labour**: **Mary Macintosh** ('The State Oppression of Women') argues that women are called into the workforce at various times when there is a shortage of male labour and forced back into the family when there is a surplus. Women are a marginalised workforce, forced into low pay, low status, employment on the basis of sexual discrimination.

- **Oppression**: Feminists also point to the idea that women's lives within the family are oppressive when considered in a couple of ways. Firstly, in terms of the 'housewife role' effectively forced on women. Even though many women seem to perform this role willingly it could be argued this willingness to identify domestic labour with femininity is a result of both socialisation and patriarchal ideologies. Secondly, in terms of violence within the family. **Dodd** et al ('Crime in England and Wales 2003/2004'), for

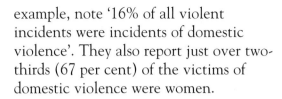

example, note '16% of all violent incidents were incidents of domestic violence'. They also report just over two-thirds (67 per cent) of the victims of domestic violence were women.

Postmodern perspectives, on the other hand, tend to view family groups in **individualistic** terms – as arenas in which people play out their personal narratives, as it were. In this sense, we can identify two basic forms of individualistic experience:

- **Choice**, in the individual sense of the word, whereby people are increasingly able to make decisions about their behaviour – from the basic choice of whether or not to form a family group to the variety of extended choices now available in terms of how people express their 'lived experiences' in family relationships. Think, for example, about the multitude of different family forms and relationships in our society – from childless couples, through step-families, to gay couples with children and beyond. This notion of choice links into the idea of:

- **Pluralism** as the defining feature of postmodern societies. In other words, such societies are increasingly characterised by a plurality of family forms and groups which coexist – sometimes happily and sometimes uneasily. Within this context of family pluralism, therefore, Postmodernists argue it's pointless to make judgements about family forms (in the way we've seen other sociological perspectives make such judgements about the form and function of family groups). From this perspective therefore, each family unit is, in its own way unique and involves people working out their personal choices and lifestyles in the best ways they can.

As **Judith Stacey** ('Fellow Families?', 2002) puts it when discussing same-sex relationships, 'Under the postmodern family condition, every family is an alternative family.' Because of this uniqueness, as we have seen in the previous section, one of the problems we encounter when discussing families is the difficulty involved in trying to precisely define this group; exclusive definitions appear much too narrow and restrictive, in the sense they generally fail to account for all types of family structures, whereas inclusive definitions may be so widely drawn in terms of what they include as a family as to be somewhat less than useful for students of AS Sociology (and their teachers, come to that). In this respect, **David Elkind** ('Waaah, Why Kids Have a Lot to Cry About', 1992) has suggested the transition from modern to postmodern society has produced what he terms the **permeable family** which, he notes, 'encompasses many different family forms: traditional or nuclear, two-parent working, single-parent, blended, adopted child, test-tube, surrogate mother, and co-parent families. Each of these is valuable and a potentially successful family form'. In this respect he argues: 'The Modern Family spoke to our need to belong at the expense, particularly for women, of the need to become. The Permeable Family, in contrast, celebrates the need to become at the expense of the need to belong.'

While Elkind doesn't necessarily see this latter state – the idea individual needs and desires override our sense of responsibility to others (and, in some respects, the 'denial of self' in favour of one's children and their needs) – as generally desirable **Dyske Suematsu** ('Postmodern Family', 2004) is not so sure: 'A family is essentially a unit of support. There were days when human beings could not survive without it. Those days are over.'

Discussion point: is the family dead?

Do you agree or disagree with the argument Suematsu puts forward that, in some respects, families have outlived their usefulness?

What arguments could you put forward to either support or reject this idea?

Whatever your personal perspective on family life, whether you see yourself as a family traditionalist, looking forward to producing 1.6 children – the current average family size in the UK – in a loving, heterosexual, relationship or as a postmodern free-spirit ready-and-willing to indulge whatever sexual craving takes your fancy, with whoever takes your fancy, in a loose-knit family-style relationship, it remains true that governments – the makers of social policy – tend to have quite specific views about what constitutes a family.

The technical term for this idea is an **ideology** (a set of related beliefs about something) and, in the next section, we can examine some ways social and economic ideologies and policies impact on family structures and relationships.

Family and social policy

⚠ Preparing the ground

We can begin this section by defining social policy which, according to **Susan** and **Peter Calvert** (*Sociology Today*, 1992) refers to: the main principles under which the government of the day directs economic resources to meet specific social needs.'

We can add some flesh to the bare bones of this definition by noting **Susannah Morris**'s observations (*Social Policy: From the Victorians to the Present Day*, 2004) that social policy involves the government identifying and regulating:

- **social problems** – such as an increase in the level of crime
- **social needs** – such as those of the unemployed
- **social conditions** – such as the provision of health care through something like a National Health Service.

Once you have done the warm up exercise opposite, it should be apparent that social and economic policy is a potentially vast area to cover (even if we restrict ourselves to considering only those polices directly affecting families), since it involves both a:

- **Historical perspective**: identifying, for example, polices from both the distant past – such as the various *Factory and Child Labour Acts* of the nineteenth century – and the recent past – such as the *Child Support Agency*, created in 1993 to ensure parents living apart met 'their

WARM UP: SOCIAL POLICIES

Although you may not be aware of it, you already know a great deal about how social and economic policies impact on family life.

Using the following table as a starting point (and working initially in small groups, adding any further family areas as required),

identify as many things as you can that impact on what you're allowed/not allowed to do in the context of family life.

Once you have done this, get together as a class to combine the things you have identified.

Some of the areas we're going to look at later (such as divorce) may also provide examples of policies.

Family Area	What can you do?	What can't you do?
Marriage	Marry someone of the opposite sex	Marry someone of same sex Marry a close relative (brother or sister) Marry someone under 16
Divorce	You can get divorced	Marry someone else while already married
Sexuality	Have a sexual relationship	Have a sexual relationship with someone under 16
Children (0–12)		Paid employment
Teenagers (13–16)	Paid employment: a limited number of hours each day	
Adults	Cohabit (with people of same/different sex)	

financial responsibilities to their children'.

- **Future perspective**: thinking about polices now being proposed – such as limits on the smacking of children – and polices whose impact cannot be adequately judged, as yet.

Rather than trawl through this vast sea of policy, therefore, this section focuses on two main areas, namely:

- **identifying** a selection of government policies that impact on family life
- **reviewing** a sample of recent social and economic policies to give you a flavour for this area (and your further research if so desired).

Before we look at these ideas, don't forget family life is also covered by general social policies relating to the criminal law; although we tend to talk about things like domestic violence as if they were somehow a special legal category, it is actually a form of criminal assault. Areas such as child abuse and bigamy are also covered by crime policies.

 Digging deeper

Rather than simply list a selection of recent social and economic policies that have impacted on family life, a more interesting way to think about this information might be to use a biographical approach. This involves creating an imaginary individual and showing some of the ways social policies impact on their life – from birth to retirement. You should also remember what follows is just an illustration – it is designed to give you a general overview of how social policy impacts on family life. Having duly noted this proviso, we can begin our biological approach with:

- **Conception**: Until recently, contraceptive devices were available 'free' (paid for out of general taxation) from the National Health Service (NHS); however IVF (fertility treatments) are now available for those unable to conceive 'naturally'.

Here's one I made earlier.

- **Abortion** is also available for a period of 24 weeks (under the *Abortion Act*, 1967) after conception. Whether or not you are conceived will depend upon a range of family circumstances governed by government policy (child care facilities, employment prospects for your parents and so forth).

- **Pregnancy**: Working women are entitled to maternity leave, *statutory maternity pay* and, once they have given birth, they have a right to resume their former job. From 2003, fathers also have the right to a period of paternity leave (up to two weeks), during which they can claim statutory paternity pay from their employer (currently £100 a week or 90% of average weekly earnings if this is less than £100).

- **Birth/infancy**: The NHS provides free medical services, the level and range of which depends on government funding policies and decisions made by Regional Health Authorities. In general, the lower the social class of your parents, the greater the chance of you not surviving childbirth (child mortality) or the first few years of life (infant mortality), as the following table illustrates:

Higher managerial (non-manual)	Semi-skilled manual
2.7 per 1,000 live births	7.5 per 1,000 live births

Table 2.1 Infant Mortality rate 2002 (for babies born inside marriage) by father's occupation (Standard Occupational Classification 2000)

If, for whatever reason, your parents can't care for you, the government (through local councils) makes provision for fostering/adoption.

- **Pre-school**: Nursery facilities are not provided by the government (although tax credits are available for nursery places), which restricts the ability of one parent to work and affects family living standards. If your mother works, you are most likely to be looked after by a grandparent (one-third of children under 15 in 2002). If you are abused or neglected, you may be taken into local authority care – something that happened to 40,000 children in 2002.

- **Education**: Between the ages of 5 and 16 you must, by law, receive formal tuition, either through attending a state (free)/private school or by a private tutor (who can be your parents). The education you receive may depend on your parents' income (if they can afford to send you to a private school) or where they live (children who attend schools in inner city areas achieve fewer GCSE and A-level exam passes than those who attend schools in suburban areas). Such things may affect your future employment prospects and may affect the decision about whether or not you remain within the family home.

  - You may be eligible for free school meals and there is the possibility you could be suspended or excluded from school.

  - A range of health/welfare services and benefits are provided by the state, but these no longer include things like free prescriptions or dental and eye care.

- **Early adulthood** (16–18): Once you reach the minimum school-leaving age, a range of government policies come into effect. You can legally marry (as long as your parents agree) and you can have sexual intercourse (as long as your partner – of whatever sex – is at least 16). If you get a job, you have to be paid the legal *minimum wage* for your age. Your

earnings, however, will be subject to Income Tax and National Insurance deductions.

- **Adulthood** (18+): Adult family members are affected in numerous ways by social and economic policies.

  - You can get married (subject to various restrictions – incest, bigamy, age of prospective partner and so forth), cohabit (live with someone) and divorce.

  - If you start your own family, your housing options may be limited. In the past 20 years the government has discouraged the building of low-rent (subsidised) housing and local authority ('council') housing has been progressively sold to private owners and housing associations.

  - Your ability to afford a mortgage is affected by your employment prospects, which relate to things like your level of education and where you live (the South East has lower rates of unemployment than the north of England, Scotland and Wales).

- In 2002, the average house price was £128,000 (although regional differences apply; living in London, for example, is more expensive – a detached house, on average, will set you back £385,000 in 2004). These factors may result in children continuing to live within the family home (see above).

- Mortgage tax relief was abolished in 2002.

- Between the ages of 18 and 24, if you claim the Job Seeker's Allowance continuously for six months you will have to enter the New Deal scheme; if you can't find a job through this scheme you will be required to do one of the following: subsidised employment; work experience with a voluntary organisation/environmental task force or full-time education. If you refuse to do one of these options your Job Seeker's Allowance will be stopped.

- The government provides a range of (means tested – they depend on your level of income) social security benefits for adults and families. These include working families' tax credit/income support; council tax benefit; incapacity or disability benefits and housing benefit. In addition, child benefit is paid to all families with eligible children, regardless of income.

- **Old age/retirement**: State pensions currently start at 65 for men and 60 for women (although this may change by 2010 with the retirement age for all set at 65). Pension payments depend on the

National Insurance contributions you have – or have not – paid throughout your working life (many women in our society, for example, have not paid enough contributions to qualify for a full state pension).

- Pensioners who rely solely on a state pension are one of the most likely groups to experience poverty (roughly 20% of all pensioners are classed as poor). Means-tested income support is available for pensioners who, at 52%, are the largest recipient group of social security expenditure (the next largest group – 26% – are the sick and disabled).

- As a pensioner, you may receive some free services (the bus pass!), but you have to pay VAT (at 17.5%) on heating costs (although the government does make provision for 'bad weather payments'). Hypothermia (death through lack of heat) is one of the greatest causes of premature death

Old age – the happiest days of your life?

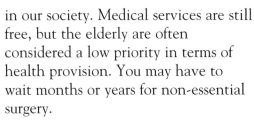

in our society. Medical services are still free, but the elderly are often considered a low priority in terms of health provision. You may have to wait months or years for non-essential surgery.

- Services such as home helps, district nurse/health visitor, day centre care, social workers and meals-on-wheels are also provided for those aged 65 and over.

- If you reach a stage where you are unable to adequately care for yourself, you will be faced with the choice of entering a private nursing home (which will be expensive and largely unsubsidised – which may affect any inheritance for your children) or, more likely, you will be forced to rely on your children for care and accommodation ('care in the community'). If you have no children or no means of support you will receive some form of state care.

In this section we have looked at a range of social policies affecting family life and experiences in our society which, as I indicated earlier, involves a sense of historical development and continuity. Continuing this general theme, therefore, we can turn next to an examination of changes to family and household structures and their relationship to processes of industrialisation and urbanisation.

Family and household changes

Introduction

As I have just noted, the focus of this section is an examination of changes in family and household structure and their relationship to industrialisation and urbanisation. To understand the nature and extent of such changes we need to do two main things: firstly, we have to outline what we mean by:

- family and household structure
- industrialisation
- urbanisation.

Secondly, we need to examine how family and household structures have changed historically in our society and how such changes can be related to processes of industrialisation and urbanisation.

WARM UP: FAMILY GENOGRAMS

A genogram originally developed by **McGoldrick** and **Gerson** (*Genograms in Family Assessment*, 1985) is a way of describing family relationships and their structure. It is similar to a family tree, but a little more sophisticated in terms of the information it contains.

Draw a genogram for your family (using the examples of McGoldrick and Gerson's notation, overleaf).

Start by identifying your immediate family and work outwards from there . . .

Males are indicated by squares, females by

circles. Marriage/cohabitation is shown by an unbroken line.

The person drawing the genogram is indicated by a double box. Put the birth date of each family member at the top left.

Links between living family members can be indicated as a broken line. Indicate the relationship (uncle, for example) beneath the line.

Marriage dates are recorded above the link line.

A separation is recorded by a slash (with date) along the line.

Divorce is recorded as above, except two lines are used.

Remarriage (or ex-marriage) is indicated to one side with a smaller shape.

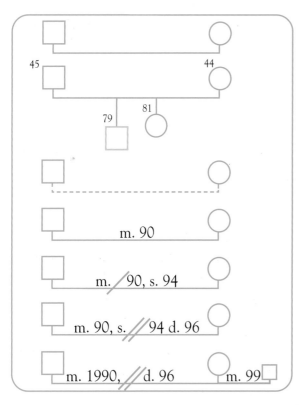

Preparing the ground

Family/household structure is based on the idea we can identify differences in the way people relate to each other; in other words (going back to the work we did on the concept of structure in Chapter 1) family and household structures are *differentiated* (or different) from each other on the basis of the different lifestyles, values and norms surrounding people's relationships. The following examples of different family and household structures make this a little more understandable:

- **Nuclear** families consist of two generations of family members (parents and children) living in the same household. Contacts with wider kin (aunts and cousins, for example) are usually infrequent and more likely to involve 'impersonal contacts' such as the telephone or email. For this reason, this family structure is sometimes called an *isolated nuclear* (reflecting its isolation from wider kin and it's 'economic isolation' from the rest of society) or *conjugal* family – a self-contained unit where family members are expected to support each other socially, economically and psychologically.

- **Extended** families, as the name suggests, involve additional family members. This structure comes in three basic flavours:

  - **Vertically extended** consists of three or more generations (grandparents, parents and children) living in the same household (or very close to each other). *Matrifocal* families are a variation on this type of family structure in that they involve (or are focused on) women (a female grandparent, female parent and children). Conversely, *patrifocal* families (quite rare in our society) are focused on men.

- **Horizontally extended** involves relations such as aunts, uncles, cousins, etc. (relations of the same generation as the parents). These 'extensions' to the basic family group branch out within generations – a wife's sister and her partner, for example, living with the family group. *Polygamous* families (where one man lives with many women or vice versa) sometimes take this form – the parents may, for example, be drawn from the same generation.

- **Modified-extended** refers, according to **Michael Gordon** (*The Nuclear Family in Crisis: The Search for an Alternative*, 1972) to the idea that wider family members keep in regular touch with each other. This may be both physically (in the sense of visiting or exchanging help and services) and emotionally (contacts by telephone, email and the like). Related to this idea is a distinction drawn by **Peter Wilmott** ('Urban Kinship Past and Present', 1988) when he talks about **local extended** families, involving 'two or three nuclear families in separate households' living close together and providing mutual help and assistance; **dispersed extended** families, involving less frequent personal contacts; and **attenuated extended** families involving, for example, 'young couples before they have children', gradually separating from their original families.

- **Single-parent** families involve a single adult plus their dependent children. Although this is more likely to be a female parent, a significant proportion involve a male parent. This type of family is sometimes called a *broken nuclear* family, because it often – but not always – arises from the break-up of a two-parent family.

- **Reconstituted** (or 'step') families (usually nuclear in form) result from the break-up of one family (through things like death or divorce) and its reconstitution as a unique family by remarriage or cohabitation. It may, therefore, involve children from a previous family as well as the new family.

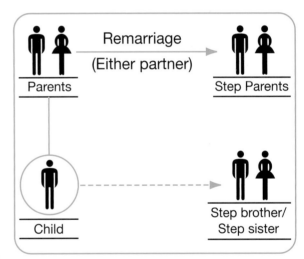

A reconstituted (step) family

- **Homosexual** families: Usually nuclear in form, this type of family involves adults of the same sex plus children (own or adopted). Homosexual couples cannot currently legally marry in the UK (a Labour Government Bill to recognise 'Civil Partnerships' – giving each partner legal rights similar to married heterosexual couples – was rejected by the House of Lords in June 2004). Gay couples can, however, legally cohabit.

Tony Barlow and Barrie Drewitt, who have lived together since 1988, paid an American surrogate mother to carry twins artificially conceived using one of the partner's sperm.

Household structures in our society, involve the following:

- **Single households** consist (as you might have guessed) of an adult living alone. Traditionally, death and relationship breakdown have been the main reasons for this type of household, although there is increasing evidence people are choosing to live this way (in 2003, for example, 13% of all households consisted of a single person).

- **Couple households** consist of two people living without children. In 2003, 25% of all households were of this type, making it the second most common household type after couples with dependent children (38% of all households).

- **Shared households** are not particularly common and involve, for whatever

reason, a group of people living together. This may be a temporary arrangement (such as students sharing a flat) or a permanent arrangement whereby families/individuals live together as a *commune*.

We can complete the first part of this section by briefly outlining what we mean by the concepts of:

- **Industrialisation** – a process whereby machines are extensively applied to the production of goods in society (*mechanisation*). One result of this process is the development of factories and the ability to mass produce consumer goods (clothes, cars, mobile phones). Related to this process is the concept of:

- **Urbanisation**, which involves the idea of population movement away from rural (village) living to larger communities based in towns and cities. This is sometimes called social migration from the countryside (rural areas) to towns – urban areas which developed as industrialisation and factory production developed.

Digging deeper

Having familiarised ourselves with some basic concepts about family and household structures, industrialisation and urbanisation, we need to explore the relationship between these ideas. To do this, we need to frame debates about possible changes in this relationship within a sociological context, one that involves thinking about the relationship between *social change* and *social behaviour* in a historical context – and to explore possible historical changes within both society and family structures, we need to do two things: firstly, establish a framework for our analysis of social change and secondly examine historical changes in society and how they link to economic changes over time. Since we want to look at the effects of industrialisation, we can organise the framework in terms of the characteristics of three 'historical types' of society, namely:

- **pre-industrial** (or *pre-modern*)
- **industrial** (or *modern*) and
- **post-industrial** (or *postmodern*).

The table below identifies a range of significant social and economic features of each of these basic types. When referring to this table, keep the following in mind:

- **Types of society**: These are not 'hard-and-fast' categories – pre-modern society didn't end abruptly, to be replaced by modern society. The table simply helps you identify some possible differences between different types of society.

- **Post-modernity**: There are arguments within sociology about whether we now live in a postmodern/post-industrial society. I have included it as a type here mainly because it's easy to make the mistake of thinking 'industrialisation' is something that happened a long time ago. Whatever we want to call present day society (postmodern or *late modern*, for example) the important thing is to relate family and household change to both an understanding of the past *and* the present.

- **Mass production** refers to the idea that machines were used to produce goods to a standard design, cheaply enough to make them available to large numbers of people.

- **Service production** refers to the idea that providing services to people (either physically – as in McDonald's – or through things like banking, insurance and knowledge-based systems) is the dominant form of economic activity in postmodern society.

- **Feudal** refers to a political system involving a major social distinction between the Nobility (large

	Pre-modern	Modern	Post-modern
Time	Pre-18th century	18th-late 20th century	Late-20th century to present
Features of economic production	Pre-industrial Agriculture Tools	Industrial Mass production Mechanisation	Post-industrial Service production Automation
Scale	Local	National	Global
Political system	Feudal	Capitalist	Late capitalist

Table 2.2 Selected characteristics of types of society in Britain

landowners) and the Peasantry (largely landless).

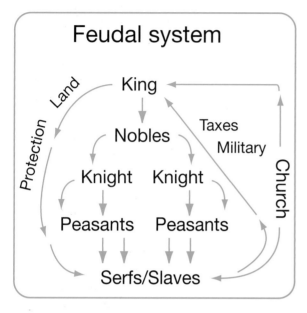

Feudal system

- **Capitalist** refers to a political system based on a class distinction between owners (employers) and workers (employees).

In the table I have suggested significant historical changes in our society based on the idea of economic changes to the way goods are made and services provided. There is, in this respect, little doubt Britain today is a very different place to Britain 500 years ago and it would not be difficult to establish changes in, for example, personal relationships (family or otherwise) between these two periods. However, the crucial question we need to explore next is the extent to which the social changes created by industrialisation and urbanisation produced changes in family and household structures.

Family and household changes

⚠ Preparing the ground

In terms of the question just posed, there are two basic positions we need to examine. The first argument suggests **industrialisation** and **urbanisation** were important factors in the promotion of family and household change. These processes, as they developed over a couple of hundred years between the late seventeenth and late nineteenth centuries, radically changed the nature of work and economic production as Britain gradually moved from an *agrarian* (agricultural) to an *industrial* (factory-based) society. This change in the nature and organisation of work – from the land-based, rural, agricultural, family-centred, organisation of pre-industrial society to the capital-intensive, urban, industrial, factory-centred, organisation of industrial society – produced, from this viewpoint, radical **family and household changes**. The basic argument here is that family structures changed from the predominantly extended-family organisation of pre-industrial society to the predominantly nuclear family organisation of industrial society. The main reason for this was that industrialisation saw the development of factories and, in turn, the rapid growth of large urban centres (towns and cities) to support and supply labour for factory-based production.

To accommodate such changes, the old extended families of pre-industrial society (ideally suited to the demands of a family-based, subsistence form of farming) were broken down into nuclear families that fitted the economic requirements of:

- **geographic mobility** – the need for families to move to towns and factories
- **labour flexibility** – the need to move to where jobs were located.

Industrialisation, therefore, was seen as the motor for family change – people were forced to change the way they lived to accommodate new forms of economic production.

If we trace this idea into the late twentieth/early twenty-first century, a similar pattern emerges, but this time the emphasis is on family **fragmentation and diversity**. The nuclear family structures created by industrialisation and urbanisation are disrupted by the needs of global economic systems and work processes, processes of de-industrialisation (a decline in the economic importance of manufacturing) and of de-urbanisation (a move away from towns and cities to the countryside).

The second, alternative, argument also involves thinking, initially, about **industrialisation and urbanisation**. The argument here is that these occurred in Britain (the first country to industrialise) *because* pre-industrial family structures were mainly nuclear and thus ideally positioned to take advantage of new economic opportunities requiring family mobility and flexibility; in other words, pre-industrial family structures – with few unbreakable physical or emotional ties with extended kin – are seen as the motor for subsequent industrial development.

In addition, the relatively large number of extended households in pre-industrial times (which included, for example, servants who had few, if any, emotional or economic ties with their employers) also represented flexible structures that could adapt relatively easily to the changed economic world. This idea of flexibility translates relatively easily to **post-modern society**, which, so this argument goes, requires highly flexible family and household structures if new economic opportunities are to be grasped and exploited. Our society, it is suggested, has already evolved fragmentary family and household structures (through industrialisation and changes to legal relationships – the easy availability of divorce, the growth of single-parent families and single-person households etc.) that are well-suited to taking on board globalised forms of work (living and working in different countries, working at home using computer technology and so forth).

Having identified two opposing sides to the debate, therefore, we need to examine the historical evidence to help us decide which, if any, of these two arguments best describes the relationship between changes in family and household structures, industrialisation and urbanisation.

⚠ Digging deeper

Evidence for the first argument (generally known as the 'Fit Thesis' because it proposed a close fit between changes in family structures, industrialisation and urbanisation) has been put forward by Functionalist writers such as **Parsons** ('The Social Structure of the Family', 1959) and **Goode** (*World Revolution and Family Patterns*, 1963) as well as, in a slightly different way, the social action theorist **Max Weber** (*The Protestant Ethic and Spirit of Capitalism*, 1904).

In basic terms, extended family structures were seen as the norm for pre-industrial society because they were:

- **Multi-functional**: A wide family network performed a range of different functions related to the economic and social well-being of family members.

- **Kinship-based**: Members of the extended family group shared not only a household, but a common economic position that involved working together as a social group (mainly as subsistence farmers but also in various craft trades – brewing and baking, for example – within the home).

- **Economically productive**: People lived and worked within a family group that provided the only viable means for their physical survival.

This situation arose, according to this argument, for three main reasons.

- **Agriculture**: Labour-intensive farm work required as many people as possible to work the land.

- **Geographic mobility**: The ability to move away from the family group was severely limited by poor communications (no railways or cars, basic road systems and so forth). This meant, in effect, family members – even if they had wanted to – were physically unable to move far from the family home.

- **Society**: In pre-industrial society there was no well-developed welfare system (few hospitals existed, for example) which meant family members relied on their own resources when it came to looking after and caring for the sick, the elderly and so forth.

The development of industrial society produced, according to this view, a structural family change – nuclear families became dominant because of the demands of factory forms of production and the opportunities this system created.

- **Geographic mobility**: People had to be mobile to find and keep work in the new industrial processes. There was a huge – if gradual – movement away from rural areas to the developing towns and, in such a situation, the extended family of pre-industrial society gradually broke down.

- **Social mobility**: New opportunities arose for social mobility and economic advancement as different types of work developed – people were no longer simply subsistence farmers. However, to seize these new opportunities, families had to be ready and willing to move to those areas where the chances of economic advancement were greatest.

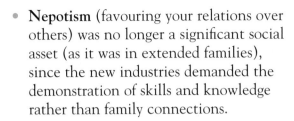

- **Nepotism** (favouring your relations over others) was no longer a significant social asset (as it was in extended families), since the new industries demanded the demonstration of skills and knowledge rather than family connections.

If we extend this argument to post-industrial society we can identify significant changes to both family and household structures.

- **Family structures**: One feature of post-industrial society is the increasing *diversity* and *fragmentation* of family life – notwithstanding **Chester**'s observation (*The Rise of the Neo-conventional Family*, 1985) that the majority of people in Britain still live at least part of their life within some form of nuclear family structure. Just as, in the industrial period, family structures changed to accommodate new forms of economic organisation, so too, in the post-industrial period, further changes have occurred.

  New forms of working (especially through computer technology and networking) open up opportunities for homeworking which, in turn, means single-parent families are, potentially, no longer excluded from the workforce. The relatively small size of nuclear families and improved communications (such as the ability to stay in close contact with extended family members relatively easy) makes this family group increasingly mobile – both in terms of national and international movement.

- **Households**: One of the features of post-industrial society is the increase in the number of single-person households, indicative, according to this argument, of the way economic changes have impacted on people's behaviour. The single-person household is, of course, potentially the most geographically mobile of all family/household structures and reflects the changing (increasingly global) nature of work.

Having outlined the evidence for the first argument, we can turn to an alternative interpretation of the relationship between family and household structures and industrialisation.

Pre-industrial society

Carlin ('Family, Society and Popular Culture in Western Europe c. 1500–1700', 2002) argues, 'most households in early modern Western Europe were nuclear family households, i.e. all the blood relations they contained were one couple and their children'. Although extended families existed, the main reasons for this type of family not being more common seem to be:

- **Life expectancy**: Average life expectancy was low (around 35–40 years) and, consequently, parents didn't always live long enough to become grandparents. Although this may have been a reason for many families remaining nuclear, we should note calculations of *average* life expectancies in pre-modern societies may be biased by high rates of infant and child mortality (large numbers of children dying drags the average down).

- **Choice: Carlin** (2002) notes that some parts of Western Europe, with similar birth and death rates to Britain, contained more vertically extended (sometimes called *stem*) families. This suggests, at least in part, people in Britain were choosing not to live in extended family structures.

- **Retirement**: Demographic evidence (information about how people live) from areas where people did survive into old age suggests they were expected to retire into households separated from their children.

- **Extended households**: **Peter Laslett** (*The World We Have Lost*, 1965 and *Household and Family in Past Time*, 1972) notes that upper-class households frequently included both wider kin and servants (mainly because there was sufficient room for them to live within the household). Lower-class households, although frequently nuclear because of high mortality rates among the elderly, probably contained 'lodgers' (who are likely to have been kin) staying temporarily within the family group. Laslett, however, estimates only 10% of pre-industrial households contained more than two generations of kin.

- **Modified extended structures**: **Michael Gordon** (1972) suggests arguments that the extended family was dominant in pre-industrial society confuse *temporary extensions* to a family (such as a relative living within a nuclear family for a short period) with the idea of a *permanent extended family* structure which, he argues, 'is seldom actually encountered in any society, pre-industrial or industrial'.

According to this argument, therefore, the mainly nuclear pre-industrial family was actually necessary for industrialisation.

Industrialisation

Harris ('The Family and Industrial Society', 1983) argues nuclear family structures dominated pre-industrial society because industrialisation required:

- An **inheritance system** that concentrated wealth, making capital (investment money) available to relatively small numbers of people. A close-knit, nuclear structure allied to a system of *primogeniture* (inheritance, by the first-born son, of a family's total wealth) made this possible. In addition, it forced those who didn't inherit to move away from the family home. **Wegge's** (really quite fascinating) research into peasant population movements in Germany ('To Part or Not to Part', 1999) supports this idea when she notes, 'it is the primogeniture institution which better promotes emigration'.

- **Population growth**: According to the Office for National Statistics, the population of England and Wales trebled between 1700 (6 million) and 1851 (18 million), indicating the existence of a large, landless, potential workforce. This is significant because it suggests geographic mobility wasn't a requirement for the development of industrialisation since what we see here is a population explosion in urban areas, rather than migration from the countryside to towns.

- **Migration**: If ideas about population growth are valid, it suggests urbanisation didn't result from the break-up and migration of extended rural families; rather, it occurred as the result of the population growing rapidly during the early industrial period.

Rosemary O'Day (*Women in Early Modern Britain*, 2000), for example, notes that a large rural class of agricultural labourers existed in the seventeenth century. They owned no land and lived by selling their labour outside the family group.

In terms of this argument, therefore, **Michael Anderson** (*Approaches to the History of the Western Family*, 1995) points out there were 'many continuities' of family structure during the change from agricultural to industrial forms of production, during which no single family or household structure was wholly dominant. Thus, although we have focused on extended/nuclear family and household structures, this doesn't mean other types (with the possible exception of gay families) were not in evidence. Both reconstituted and single-parent family structures, for example, existed in pre-industrial societies, mainly because of high adult death rates, especially among the lower classes.

However, the historical evidence does suggest that, at least during some part of the industrialisation/urbanisation process, changes to family and household structures did occur, especially in relation to social class and the increasing diversity of family and household structures. **Anderson** (1995), for example, notes the working classes, during the process of industrialisation, developed a broadly extended family structure which resulted from:

- **Urbanisation**: As towns rapidly developed around factories, pressure on living space (and the relative underdevelopment of communications) resulted in extended family living arrangements.
- **Mutual aid:** The lack of state welfare provision meant working class families relied on a strong kinship network for their survival. During periods of sickness and unemployment, for example, family members could provide for each other.

- **Employment**: Where the vast majority could barely read or write, an 'unofficial' kinship network played a vital part in securing employment for family members through the process of 'speaking out' (suggesting to an employer) for relatives when employers needed to recruit more workers.
- **Child care**: Where both parents worked, for example, relatives played a vital part in child care. In addition, high death rates meant the children of dead relatives could be brought into the family structure. In an age of what we would now call child labour, young relatives could be used to supplement family income.

Middle-class family structures tended to be nuclear, mainly because of:

- **Education**: The increasing importance of education (for male children) and its cost meant middle class families were relatively smaller than their working class counterparts.
- **Geographic mobility** among the class from which the managers of the new industrial enterprises were recruited weakened extended family ties.

Upper-class family structures, according to **Roger Gomm** (*The Uses of Kinship*, 1989) have historically been a mixture of nuclear and extended types, although extended family networks, even up to the present day, are used to maintain property relations and for mutual economic aid amongst kin.

In addition, wealth meant extended kin (such as elderly grandparents) could be relatively easily accommodated within the family home and the evidence suggests it was – and still is to some degree – relatively common for the vertically-extended family to exist among the upper classes.

Post-industrial society

Family and households structures in the late twentieth/early twenty-first centuries are, arguably, more complex, fragmented and diverse than at any time in our history, ideas we can briefly examine in the following terms.

- **Diversity**: As we have seen earlier, our society is characterised by a wide range of different family and household structures (nuclear, reconstituted, single-parent, gay and extended) apparently co-existing. It is, however, difficult to disentangle this diverse range of family structures, for two reasons.

  - Nuclear family structures seem to be the dominant family form, although they clearly involve a range of different family relationships; a single-parent family contains a different set of relationships to those in a reconstituted family, for example. The question here, therefore, is the extent to which either or both these family structures can be characterised as nuclear families.

  - Definitions of nuclear and extended family structures determine, to some degree, your view of their relationship. For example, **Willmott**'s (1988) concept of a dispersed extended family appears to plausibly characterise many types of family relationship in our society – what we have here, therefore, is a basic nuclear family structure surrounded and supported by extended family networks (and whether or not you count this structure as nuclear or

extended depends, as I have suggested, on how you define such things).

- **Social changes**: Relatively easy access to divorce (resulting from legal changes over the past 50 years) has led to greater numbers of reconstituted/single-parent families and single-person households.

- **Social attitudes**: Whatever the origins of such changes, it is clear lifestyle factors, in terms of greater social acceptance of single-parent and homosexual family structures, has played some part in creating family structural diversity. The Office for National Statistics (2000), for example, recorded 26% of all families with dependent children as containing a single adult parent.

- **Life expectancy**: Increased life expectancy, a more active lifestyle and changes to the welfare system (which in recent years has encouraged the de-institutionalisation of the elderly) has created changes within family structures, giving rise to the concept of a *new grandparenting* (grandparents play a greater role in the care of grandchildren, for example, than in the recent past). These trends have led to what **Julia Brannen** ('The age of beanpole families', 2003) calls the *beanpole family structure* – a form of inter-generational (different generations of family members), vertically-extended family structure with very weak intra-generational (people of the same generation – brothers and sisters, for example) links.

Similarly, **Bengston** ('Beyond the nuclear family', 2001) speculates about the extent to which the phenomenon of increasing bonds between different generations of family members (as represented, for

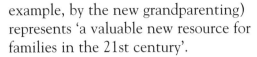

example, by the new grandparenting) represents 'a valuable new resource for families in the 21st century'.

- **Ambivalence**: **Luscher**, ('Ambivalence: A key concept for the study of intergenerational relations', 2000) on the other hand, suggests that people are becoming increasingly uncertain (ambivalent) about family structures and relationships in the light of family changes. Increases in divorce, for example, have led to the widespread creation of single-parent and reconstituted families. These may have resulted in a weakening of family relationships as family members seek to create new social spaces for themselves and their (new) families away from the relationships that previously existed in their lives. One result of these changes, perhaps, is families seeking 'to put geographical distance between different family generations'.

- **Households**: Finally, one of the most striking features of our society is the growth of lone person households. In 2003, for example, this household type was the single most common family or household structure in our society – according to the Office for National Statistics (Social Trends 34, 2004), 29% of families and households in the UK now involve a single person, marginally outstripping 'couples with no children' (28% of all family and household structures).

In turn, on current projections ('Complicated Lives II – the Price of Complexity', Abbey, 2002), the 'Couple with no children' household will soon be more common in our society than the 'Couple with children' family – at present, according to the Office for National Statistics (Social Trends 34, 2004), each of these types constitutes 28% of all family and household structures.

🌱 Growing it yourself

Having looked at the two arguments about the relationship between family and household structures, industrialisation and urbanisation:

1. Create a list (based on the following table) of what you think are the **three** most important strengths and weaknesses of each argument.

Argument 1		Argument 2	
Strengths	Weaknesses	Strengths	Weaknesses
1.			
2.			
3.			

2. Based on the strengths and weaknesses you've identified, write a brief (500–600 words) comparison of the two arguments.

In this section we have looked at the debate surrounding the significance of historical family and household changes and, in the next section we can bring things a little more up to date by looking more closely at both the diversity of contemporary family structures and changing patterns of family relationships.

Family and household diversity and change

Introduction

In the two previous sections we have looked at the complexities of family life by considering, firstly, how this social group can be defined and, secondly, how different family structures have developed in our society across the centuries. We can build on this work in two main ways. Firstly, by investigating in more detail 'the diversity of contemporary family and household structure' (in other words, the differences within and between family and household groups). Once we've done this we can then examine 'changing patterns of marriage, cohabitation, separation, divorce and child bearing'.

Preparing the ground

The previous exercise will have sensitised you to a range of differences – some minor and others quite major – between the family/household groups in which we

WARM UP: DISCUSSING FAMILY DIFFERENCES

One way of thinking about diversity is to discuss your family experiences with others. I have identified some questions to get you started in the table below. In small groups, discuss and record your answers to these questions – and any others that spring to mind during the discussion.

Your plans?	Division of labour	Rules	Parents and children	Structure
Do you plan to marry, have children, a career?	Who does what in your family – paid work, domestic work, child care, etc.?	Who makes the rules, what are they, how are they enforced (and by whom)?	What's the relationship between you and your parents? Do you have brothers and sisters? Natural or step-parents?	Is your family nuclear, extended, single-parent, etc.?

live. We can develop this 'sense of difference' by identifying five main types of family and household diversity in contemporary Britain, using a general framework suggested by **Rhona** and **Robert Rappoport** (*Families in Britain*, 1982):

Organisational diversity

This refers to differences in family life and experiences both within and between family groups. In this respect we could think, for example, about differences in:

- **family structures**: nuclear and extended, for example
- **roles**: in terms of things like the household division of labour – who does what within the group?
- **status** of the family members: married or cohabiting, natural or step-parents etc.
- **relationships**: in terms of things like contact with extended kin, the extent to which the group is *patriarchal* (male dominated) or *matriarchal* (female dominated).

Cultural diversity

This refers to differences within and between different cultural (or *ethnic*) groups in terms of things like:

- **size**: the number of children within the family
- **marriage**: for example, whether the marriage is arranged by the parents or 'freely chosen' by the participants
- **division of labour**: considered in terms of whether family roles are patriarchal (for example, the male in paid employment

and the female as housewife) or symmetrical (where roles and responsibilities are shared equally among family members).

Richard Berthoud's analysis of diversity amongst White British, Black Caribbean and South Asian families (*Family formation in multi-cultural Britain*, 2004) highlights a number of key differences within and between these broad ethnic groups. For example:

- **Black Caribbean** families are characterised by:
  - Low rates of marriage.
  - High levels of single parenthood. In 2001, 43% of Black or Black British families with dependent children were headed by a lone parent (Social Trends 34).
  - High rates of separation and divorce.
  - Relatively high levels of mixed partnerships (living with someone from a different (usually white) ethnic group).
  - Absent fathers (not living within the family home but maintaining family contacts).
- **South Asian** (Indian, Pakistani and Bangladeshi) families are characterised by:
  - High rates of marriage.
  - Low rates of separation/divorce/single-parenthood. In 2001, 11% of Asian/Asian British families were headed by a lone parent (Social Trends 34).
  - Lower rates of mixed partnerships.
  - Greater likelihood (especially among Muslims and Sikhs) of arranged marriage.

- Majority of Pakistani and Bangladeshi women look after home and family full time.

- High fertility rates among Pakistani and Bangladeshi women.

- Larger family size (four or more children).

- Grandparents more likely to live with son's family.

- Patriarchy – power and authority more likely to reside with men.

If you want to review Berthoud's research, you can find a more detailed description at:
www.sociology.org.uk/as4aqa.htm

Class diversity

This refers to divisions between social classes (upper, middle and working, for example) and within these broad groupings. For example, a distinction (identified originally by **Goldthorpe** et al's 'Affluent Worker' (1965) study) is sometimes made within working class families between the:

- **traditional family**, characterised by *segregated conjugal roles* (family members have different household and work roles, develop different leisure and friendship patterns and so forth) and the

- **privatised family**, which involves a 'home and child-centred' focus, characterised by the family partners having *joint conjugal roles* (where both partners may work and take responsibility for domestic labour tasks such as childcare) and common leisure and friendship networks (which is a

sociologist's way of saying they do things together and have friends in common).

Diversity between social classes involves things like:

- **Relationships** between the sexes (whether the family group is patriarchal or symmetrical, for example). Middle-class families are more likely to be the latter.

- **Socialisation** of children (upper- and middle-class families, for example, tend to stress the significance of education and the importance of qualifications).

  Diane Reay ('Activating Participation', 2004) has also highlighted the importance of middle-class women's *emotional labour*, which is invested in their children's education; she notes, for example, the active educational involvement of many middle-class women in terms of helping their children, monitoring school progress, questioning teachers about their children's school performance and so forth.

- **Kinship networks** and their importance, considered in terms of the different level and type of help (financial, practical and the like) family members can provide.

Life-cycle

This refers to differences occurring at different stages of a family's lifetime. This may include factors such as:

- **Age:** The family experience of a young couple with infant children is quite different from that of an elderly couple with adult children who may have left home and started a families of their own.

- **Attachment**: For example, families with children of school age may become dual-income families, with both partners working for at least part of the day. This family's experience will be very different to that of a single-parent family.

Generational differences

These may be in evidence in terms of how people of similar generations have broadly shared experiences. For example, family members who were raised during the 1940s have the experience of war and post-war austerity (hardship – things like the experience of rationing, for example); family members who grew up during the 1980s, on the other hand, may well have developed very different attitudes and lifestyles.

The extent to which the generations are linked (such as the relationship between parents and children, grandparents and grandchildren) is also relevant here.

Although *family diversity* is clearly important, we also need to keep in mind the increasing significance of *household diversity* in our society. We can, for example, develop some ideas about the 'non-family' households we identified earlier in this chapter.

Single person households have some interesting features:

- **Proportion**: One-person households in our society have doubled in the past 40 years (from 14% in 1961 to 29% in 2003).
- **Age**: Within this group, an important demographic change is the proportion of people under retirement age living in single person households – just over 50% in 2003, up from 33% in 1961.
- **Region**: This type of household is more likely to be found in urban areas, especially large cities such as London and Glasgow.

Discussion point: single people

Brighton and Manchester are two areas in the UK that have the highest proportion of single households, whereas Northern Ireland has the lowest.

What single factor might explain this difference? (For the answer, see below under Region.)

Couples with no children are a significant household type, although over the past 40 years their proportion has remained largely unchanged (at 30–35% of all households and 28% of all families and households). Within single-person/couple households we could note differences in:

- **Economics**: Important distinctions can be made between employed and unemployed single people, for example, as well as between dual and single-income couples. Each group's economic situation will impact on their lifestyles and relationships.
- **Age and lifestyle**: a young single person, for example, is likely to have a very different lifestyle from an elderly single person.
- **Region**: Urban areas such as Brighton, Manchester and London have large gay communities which contributes to their high percentage of single-person households.

Shared households cover a range of differences, from the not uncommon (a group of friends living together – short or long term – to share rent and living costs) to the less common communal living arrangements we find in some societies (the *kibbutzim* of Israel, for example). Again, the lifestyles and experiences of these diverse groups are likely to be very different.

⚠ Digging deeper

When we start to think about the extent of family and household diversity – and its possible social implications – there are a number of observations and explanations we need to consider. Before we do so, however, it is important to note that when thinking about the extent of such diversity in our society a pertinent question might be 'How deep do you want to go to discover diversity?'

In other words, if you drill down deeply enough you'll find differences between every family or household relating to how they're structured and organised in terms of roles and relationships. There comes a point when sociologists have to draw some sort of line about diversity – but, unfortunately, there are no guidelines to tell us where to draw such a line. Keeping this idea in mind, however, we can make the following observations about diversity in terms of:

- **Family structures**: Although we have identified a range of diversity here, we can note that, depending on how you draw your definition, nuclear family structures are the general norm in our society (if you assume the majority of single-parent families were originally nuclear and would like – given suitable opportunities – to be nuclear or will, at some point in the future, become nuclear).

On the other hand, we could probably make a convincing argument that some type of modified extended *family* is the norm, given many families enjoy some form of contact with extended kin.

- **Family processes**: The idea of diversity in family relationships may be overstated. The 'cereal packet family' (consisting of married adults with one male and one female child living in a loving relationship where dad earns the money and mum does the housework) beloved of media and advertising may not be a realistic representation of family life, but, following **Chester**'s (1985) argument, most people are, at some point in their life, either living in nuclear-type arrangements or, perhaps more significantly, wanting to live in that type of arrangement.

Explanations

It is one thing to observe the idea of family and household diversity (however we choose to define it), but it is quite another to explain it. It is possible, though, to identify factors that contribute to diversity, in terms of **demographic changes**, that relate to things like:

- **Life expectancy**: As the following table illustrates, people in our society are generally living longer.

Average Life expectancy (years)	1926	2001
Women	59.3	80.4
Men	55.4	75.7

Table 2.3

In addition, the overall population is generally ageing; that is, there are proportionately more elderly than young people in the population (a consequence of longer life expectancy and a declining birth rate). These ideas are significant for family diversity in a couple of ways. Firstly, couples are potentially living together for longer (especially after their children have left home) and the longer a relationship has to last, the more likely it is, statistically, to end in separation or divorce. Secondly, it raises the increased possibility of grandparents becoming involved in the raising of their grandchildren (allowing both parents to have paid work, for example).

- **Relationships**: Apart from things like a relative decline in the number of people marrying, an increase in the number cohabiting and an increasing likelihood of people choosing to remain single/unattached throughout their lifetime, the average age at which men and women marry is increasing, as the following table demonstrates:

Average age at first marriage	1971	2001
Men	24.6	30.6
Women	22.6	28.4

Table 2.4

Some consequences of this particular trend include smaller families and increased opportunities for women to establish a career before marrying and then returning to that career after completing a family.

- **Immigration**: Diversity has been increased by different forms of family organisation and relationships among immigrant groups.
- **Family size**: The trend towards smaller

families (the average size is now 1.6 children, compared with 2.3 in 1950 and 4 in 1900) releases adults from childcare responsibilities and increase the opportunities for both partners to have paid work outside the home.

Economic changes include ideas like:

- **Female independence**: According to **Abercrombie** and **Warde** (*Contemporary British Society*, 1992), 'One of the most significant changes in the labour market in the 20th century is the rising proportion of married women returning to work after completing their families ... Greater participation by women in paid work and changes in family structure thus seem to be closely related'.
- **Affluence**: The relationship between poverty and family size is well documented (poorer families tend to have more children), so it is little surprise to find a relationship between increasing affluence and smaller families.
- **Globalisation**: As our society becomes ever more open to influences from other cultures, we're presented with a greater range of choices about how to behave. This has a couple of dimensions: firstly, family and household arrangements from one society may be introduced into another (different ideas about male and female roles, for example) and, secondly, it opens up the potential for a *hybridisation* of family and household cultures – that is, a situation in which two different cultural family forms combine to produce a new and slightly different form.

Attitude and lifestyle changes involve a range of different factors:

- **Sexuality**: Increasing tolerance of 'alternative sexualities' (homosexuality, bisexuality, transsexuality and the like) and lifestyles (such as transvesticism) serves to increase household diversity.

The popular comedian Eddie Izzard. Are we, as a society, more tolerant of alternative lifestyles such as transvesticism than in the past?

- **Religion**: The decline in the power of organised religion amongst some ethnic groups – known as *secularisation* – may account for increases in cohabitation, the decline of marriage, the availability of remarriage after divorce and so forth. Conversely, among some ethnic groups the reverse may be true – their religion may put great emphasis on marriage and disallow divorce.

- **Femininity and masculinity**: Changes in the way we view our bodies (and our sexuality) create changing meanings for male and female lives. Women in the twenty-first century are less likely to define their femininity in terms of child-rearing and domestic labour than their grandmothers, for example. Similarly, changing perceptions of masculinity have resulted in changes to how some men view family roles and relationships.

Legal/technological changes make important contributions to diversity in terms of:

- **Divorce**: Legal changes relating to both the availability and cost of divorce encourage diversity through the development of different family structures. Similarly, changes in attitudes to divorce, step- and single-parenting have resulted in less stigma (social disapproval) being attached to these statuses.

- **Medical**: The availability of contraception (enabling couples to plan their families) and abortion change the way people relate to each other in terms of starting and continuing families.

In this section we have outlined a number of observations about family and household diversity and suggested a range of social and economic factors contributing to this process. As you should be aware however, the concept of diversity does not simply involve listing examples and offering general explanations; sociologically, it has a moral dimension, in the sense it would be useful to understand the social and psychological implications of family diversity.

In this respect, **Bren Neale** ('Theorising Family, Kinship and Social Change', 2000), poses the question, 'How are we to view the diversity and fluidity of contemporary patterns of partnering, parenting and kinship?', and answers it in terms of two further questions: 'Should we view these transformations with optimism or, at least, accept the reality of them and attempt to work with them, or should we view them as a cause for concern?'

To complete this section, therefore, it would be useful to outline some of the views associated with these two basic perspectives on diversity, beginning with a perspective that generally views family diversity as a 'cause for concern'.

New Right perspectives

These perspectives on family diversity can be summarised in terms of how they view **family structures**. The traditional (heterosexual) nuclear family is seen as more desirable than other family structures – such as single-parent families, for example – because it provides a sense of social, economic and psychological stability, family continuity and primary socialisation. It is, for New Right theorists, an arena in which, according to **Neale**'s (2000) characterisation, 'traditional family values' are emphasised and reinforced, thereby creating a sense of individual and social responsibility that forms a barrier against 'rampant, selfish, individualism'. In other words, within the traditional family children and adults learn certain moral values that are continually reinforced through their relationship with family members. In this respect, **family relationships** are seen as a crucial source of both individual happiness and, perhaps more importantly, social stability because of the moral core at the heart of such relationships – a sense of morality that includes things like:

- caring for family members
- taking responsibility for the behaviour of children
- economic provision for both partners and children

- developing successful interpersonal relationships.

Patricia Morgan (*Marriage-Lite*, 2000), for example, argues a marriage – rather than cohabiting – is a more desirable relationship state for both individuals and societies. For Morgan, this is not just a moral argument but also one based on the notion that cohabitation is not simply, to paraphrase **Penelope Leach** (*Children First*, 1994), 'Marriage without a piece of paper'. On the contrary, Morgan asserts cohabitation is:

- **Unstable**: She notes, for example, the fragility of cohabiting relationships in terms of the idea that they 'are always more likely to fracture than marriages entered into at the same time, regardless of age and income'. In addition, cohabiting couples tend to behave in a more sexually promiscuous way than married couples ('Cohabitants behave more like single people than married people', as she puts it) – another reason, she argues, for the instability of this type of family relationship.

- **Fragmentary**, in the sense that their instability means cohabitating couples with children who marry are statistically more likely to divorce. Of those who never marry, '50% of the women will be lone unmarried mothers by the time the child is ten'. One reason for this, Morgan argues, is that, unlike marriage, cohabitation for women is 'not so much an ideal lifestyle choice as the best arrangement they can make at the time'.

- **Abusive**: both women and children, Morgan notes, are at greater risk of physical and sexual abuse 'than they would be in married relationships'.

Neale summarises the general New Right position on family and household diversity in terms of:

- **Community**: Stable family relationships – such as those created within married, heterosexual, dual-parent nuclear families – provide significant emotional and psychological benefits to family members that override any possible dysfunctional aspects. In addition, a sense of personal and social responsibility is created which is translated into benefits for the community in general, for example, children being given clear moral and behavioural guidance within traditional family structures.

- **Commitment** to others, both in terms of family and the community, is encouraged by the sense of moral duty created through stable family relationships. Within the traditional family, for example, each adult partner plays a role – such as breadwinner or domestic worker – that involves a sense of personal sacrifice and commitment to other family members.

- **Morality**: Developing from the above, the notion that any type of family structure is just as good – or bad – as any other (what New Right theorists call 'moral relativism') is not only mistaken but dangerous since it questions the concept of moral commitment to others – both family and community – which, for the New Right, sits at the heart of social responsibility. They emphasise, in this respect, the need for a moral consensus that encourages 'beneficial' forms of family structure and 'discourages' forms – such as single-parenthood – that are seen as damaging to both individuals and communities.

An alternative interpretation of family diversity suggests it should be embraced, either because it points the way forward to an optimistic realignment of family roles and relationships or, not to put too fine a point on it, because it is going to happen whether we want it to or not.

Postmodern perspectives

This view of the world is neatly summarised by **Zeitlin** et al (*Strengthening the Family: Implications for International Development*, 1998) when they note: 'The post-modern world is shaped by pluralism, democracy, religious freedom, consumerism, mobility, and increasing access to news and entertainment. Residents of this post-modern world are able to see that there are many beliefs, multiple realities, and an exhilarating but daunting profusion of world views – a society that has lost its faith in absolute truth and in which people have to choose what to believe'.

As you might expect, a number of ideas about family diversity follow from this type of view, which we can identify and summarise in the following terms.

- **Economic changes**: Global economic changes impact on national and local economies in numerous ways, one of which, according to Zeitlin et al, is the breakdown of 'economic forces underlying social conformity'. For example, in the past women generally needed to marry (as advantageously as they could) because they were either barred from the workplace or consigned to low-pay forms of work which made their financial survival problematic without male support. In addition, inheritance laws focused on the need to produce children

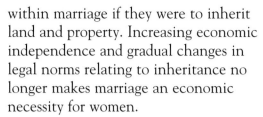

within marriage if they were to inherit land and property. Increasing economic independence and gradual changes in legal norms relating to inheritance no longer makes marriage an economic necessity for women.

- **Political changes**: One feature of globalisation – as it relates to political ideas – is the 'questioning of the old order' as people are increasingly exposed to new and different ways of doing things. In situations where the possibility of choice develops, it is hardly surprising to find people exercising such choices in their personal relationships and lifestyles – which, as the established political and legal order changes, results in family and relationship diversity.

- **Cultural changes**: Related to the above changes, the media contributes to relationship diversity by both exposing people to new ideas and, in some ways, endorsing or failing to condemn new types of family relationship. People become, in this respect, generally more accepting of single parents, surrogate mothers and gay and lesbian families.

For writers such as **Jagger** and **Wright** ('End of Century, End of Family?', 1999) attempts to 'turn back the tide of family diversity' and 'recapture an idealised "nuclear" version of family life where time stands still and traditional values are re-vitalised' is no longer a possibility or an option (presupposing, of course, it ever was). Family relationships reflect the wider economic, political and cultural changes in our society that have, according to different postmodernist writers, become characterised by things like:

- **Choice**: Just as when we go to the supermarket we expect a choice of things to buy, so too do we increasingly expect our personal relationships to be governed by choice.

- **Uncertainty**: **Smart** and **Neale** ('Good enough morality? Divorce and Postmodernity', 1997) draw our attention to the idea that, although the downside of increased choice is uncertainty ('Have I made the right choice?') we should not simply assume marriage, as opposed to cohabitation for example, involves greater personal certainty because it is legally sanctioned (it is legally more difficult to break away from a marriage than from a cohabiting relationship). On the contrary, perhaps, it is our knowledge of uncertainty – that a family relationship is not backed up by legal responsibilities and sanctions – that makes people work harder within such relationships to make them work.

Finally, we can note how **Neale** (2000) summarises the general postmodern position, in terms of a 'relational approach' to understanding family and household diversity that involves:

- **Commitment**: Family (and other personal) relationships are increasingly played out in *micro networks*. That is, people are increasingly likely to negotiate their relationships with other individuals in ways that take more account of personal needs and responsibilities, rather than, perhaps, worrying about what 'others in the community might think'.

- **Morality**: In situations where a wide diversity of family roles, relationships and structures exist, notions of social morality (that one way of living is better than any other) become much weaker. In this respect, society in general becomes 'less judgemental' about how others choose to form family relationships (the idea of gay family structures, for example, being a case in point).

Family and household changes

Introduction

This section examines 'changing patterns of marriage, cohabitation, separation, divorce and child bearing' and this involves, firstly, establishing what these respective patterns are (using a variety of statistical material) and, secondly, offering a range of explanations for why these patterns exist.

Marriage

 Preparing the ground

When examining changing patterns of marriage we have to keep in mind that the picture is complicated by serial monogamy (in our society people can marry, divorce and remarry), which makes simple comparisons between past and present difficult. However, this doesn't mean marriage statistics tell us nothing of importance.

Look at 'Growing it yourself', below. From this we can note a number of broad changes:

- **First marriage**: A steady and absolute decline in the number of people marrying over the past 50 years.

- **Second marriage**: Conversely, remarriage (which includes second and subsequent marriages) peaked in the 1980s and has

 Growing it yourself: thinking about marriage

What changing patterns of marriage can you identify in the following table?

Year	All marriages (000s)	First marriage (000s)	Remarriage (000s)	Remarriage as % of all marriages	UK population (Millions)
1901	360	–	–	–	38
1950	408	330	78	19	49
1960	394	336	58	15	51
1970	471	389	82	17	53
1980	418	279	139	33	53
1990	375	241	134	36	55
1999	301	180	128	43	56
2000	306	180	126	41	57
2001	286	180	106	37	58

Table 2.5 UK patterns of marriage
Source: Social Trends 34: 2004

since slowly declined. Remarriage, as a percentage of all marriages, has doubled in the past 50 years.

- **Marriage** was most popular just after the Second World War and during the 1970s, since when it has rapidly declined.

Digging deeper

There are a number reasons we can consider for changes in the popularity of marriage.

- **Alternatives**: In contemporary society the main alternative option is cohabitation (see below); this has increased in popularity in recent years and, although many cohabiting couples eventually marry, many do not.

- **Social pressures**: There is less stigma attached to both being unmarried and bearing/raising children outside marriage. These ideas, coupled with the easy availability of contraception (allowing sexual relationships outside marriage to be relatively free from the risk of conception) mean social pressures to marry have declined.

- **Secularisation**: For some (but by no means all) ethnic groups, the influence of religious beliefs and organisations has declined (secularisation), leading to changes in the meaning and significance of marriage. If people fail to see marriage as special or important, this opens the way to the development of other forms of partnership (such as cohabitation).

In addition, if some men and women are increasingly choosing to remain childless, the legal and moral aspect of marriage may lose its significance, making it less likely for people to marry.

Does the increasing popularity of non-Church weddings indicate a decline in the religious significance of marriage?

- **Lifestyle**: The decision not to marry may have become something of a lifestyle choice. Among women especially, increased financial, career and personal independence may be reflected in decisions about alternative relationships – something related to both male and female expectations of marriage (questions of who, for example, is expected to perform child care and domestic labour roles).

The argument here is that women are increasingly less likely, for a range of reasons, to enter into a relationship (such as marriage) that restricts their ability to work and develop a career. As **Andrew Oswald** ('Homes, Sex and the Asymmetry Hypothesis', 2002) argues:

Women are now more highly educated and can look after themselves financially. They do better at school than boys. They go to university in equal proportions to men and often go into better jobs. Their skills are in demand in the workforce. Nobody needs brute strength any more, and certainly having brutes in a high-powered white-collar office, where teamwork matters, is worse than useless. In a sense, the modern world of work is better suited to females. In 2002 a lot of women do not depend on men.

- **Risk: Ulrich Beck** (*The Risk Society: Towards a New Modernity*, 1992) has argued that, in contemporary society, people's behaviour is conditioned by their knowledge of risk – in other words, we increasingly reflect on and assess the likely consequences of our actions. In this respect, knowledge about the statistical likelihood of divorce – with all its emotional, legal and economic consequences – may lead people to the simple step of avoiding the risk by not marrying.

- **State support**: Until recently, the state offered a range of tax incentives (Married Man's (sic) Tax Allowance and Mortgage Interest Relief, for example) for couples to marry; these are no longer available.

Although the type of explanations for the decline in the popularity of marriage just noted are significant – either alone or in combination – we need to consider data reliability and validity. In terms of the reliability of contemporary (or recent) data, we can note two things.

- **Internal reliability**: All marriages are recorded by law and the definition of a marriage hasn't changed over the past 50 or so years, so we can be reasonably confident that marriage statistics accurately measure what they claim to measure.

- **Longitudinal changes** (changes over time) in marriage can be accurately tracked using official statistical data – but only up to a point.

The historical picture of marriage in our society is, however, complicated by:

- **divorce** – it wasn't, for example, available to most people 150 years ago

- **data availability** – marriage statistics were not collected as accurately in the nineteenth century, for example, as they are now.

These two factors make tracking long-term historical changes in the popularity of marriage both difficult and potentially unreliable.

When assessing the validity of marriage statistics, we need to keep in mind how population changes may affect their validity. To understand the significance of this idea we need to note two main ways in which marriage is measured.

- **Raw number** measures involve a simple counting of the number of people marrying in any given year. For example, in the previous table (UK Patterns of Marriage) we saw there were 286,000 recorded marriages in the UK in 2001. This type of measure, however, creates problems when we take into account differences in population size (in terms of both historical and cross-cultural comparisons). An obvious example here is any attempt to validly measure the relative popularity of marriage between the UK and the USA, using a 'raw number' measure, would have to take into account the large difference in population size (in 2001, for example, the UK population was approximately 58 million, while that of America was approximately 275 million).

- **Marriage rates** (as in the following table) can be both a more valid way of

	1981	1989	1993	2001	2002
UK	7.1	6.8	5.9	5.1	4.8
France	5.8	5.0	4.4	5.1	4.7
Ireland	6.0	5.0	4.4	5.1	5.1
Germany	5.8	6.4	5.5	4.7	4.7
Denmark	5.0	6.0	6.1	6.6	6.9
Spain	–	–	–	5.2	5.1

Table 2.6 Marriage rates (per 1000 population): Selected European countries
Source: Social Trends 30–34

measuring marriage and used as the basis for comparing both *historical* and *cross-cultural changes* in the popularity of marriage.

However, we need to keep in mind both these forms of measurement are sensitive to population changes, which we can illustrate in two ways.

Firstly, in terms of the overall number of people living in a particular society at a particular time, which we can illustrate by using the concept of a '**babyboom**'. During the Second World War in Britain people, for various reasons, delayed starting a family. In 1950, the average span for family completion (from the birth of the first to the last child) was 10 years and this compression of family formation is important because it produces a *population bulge* – a rapid, if temporary, increase in the number of children in society (a so-called *baby boom*). As these children reached adulthood in the 1970s and 1980s we saw an increase in the number of people marrying. For this reason, we shouldn't simply assume a rise in the number of people marrying means marriage has become more popular.

Having said that, the fact there are more people in a particular society doesn't necessarily mean there will be more marriages. For example, in the UK in 1901,

there were 360,000 marriages for a total population of 38 million; in 2001, in a population of 58 million, there were 286,000 marriages. This would indicate a significant decline in the popularity of marriage, something seemingly confirmed by looking at marriage rates over the past 20 years – a near 32% decline in the UK.

Secondly, therefore, we need to understand how the validity of marriage statistics can be sensitive to changes in the *characteristics* of a population, which we can illustrate in terms of **marriageable cohorts**. This is the idea that, in any given population, some age groups (cohorts) are more likely than others to marry. We can see the significance of this idea – in relation to questions of whether or not marriage has declined in popularity – in a couple of ways.

Firstly, in any population there are 'peak periods' for marriage (the age range at which marriage is more likely – in 2001, for example, the average age at first marriage for men was 30 and for women 28). The more people there are in this age range (as a result of baby booms, for example) the greater the number of likely marriages (and vice versa, of course).

Secondly, the relationship between this marriageable cohort and other age-related cohorts in a population is also significant. For example, if there are large numbers of children or elderly people in a population, this will affect both raw marriage numbers and, most importantly, marriage rates; in the case of children, for example, they are not legally allowed to marry and, in the case of the elderly, they are less likely to marry. The size of these cohorts (both in absolute terms in the case of raw marriage numbers and in relative terms for marriage rates) does, however, affect the validity of marriage statistics.

If, however, we control for these groups and focus our attention on the 'marriageable population' rate we can note that, for this cohort, there was a decline from 7.1 marriages to 6.8 marriages between 1981 and 1989 – a decline in the popularity of marriage on a much smaller scale than that suggested by either raw marriage numbers or rates.

Cohabitation

⚠ Preparing the ground

Unlike marriage and divorce data, information about cohabitation is not legally recorded, so anything we say about the number of couples 'living together' outside marriage in contemporary Britain will always be limited by data reliability. As **Gillis** (*For Better, For Worse: British Marriages, 1600 to the Present*, 1985) notes:

> Couples living together 'as husband and wife' have always been difficult to identify and quantify. Informal marriage, however, is not a new practice; it is estimated that between the mid-eighteenth and mid-

nineteenth centuries as many as one-fifth of the population of England and Wales may have cohabited.

Keeping this in mind, we can note trends about cohabitation in our society in terms of:

- **Gender**: **Haskey** ('Trends in marriage and cohabitation', 1995) notes that in the mid-1960s, approximately 5% of single women cohabited. By the 1990s, this had risen to 70%, a figure confirmed by **Ermisch** and **Francesconi** ('Patterns of household and family formation', 2000). However, they observed that, on average, such partnerships lasted only two years, were largely 'experimental' and not intended to develop into long-term relationships.

  Haskey ('Cohabitation in Great Britain', 2002) also notes that, of women marrying in the late 1960s, 2% had previously cohabited with their partner. By the late 1990s, this had risen to 80% of all women marrying. According to the General Household Survey (2004), cohabitation among women aged 18–49 rose from 11% in 1979 to 32% in 2001.

- **Age**: According to Social Trends (2004), 13% of adults aged 16–59 reported living in a cohabiting relationship that had since dissolved. Twenty-five per cent of the 25–39 age group reported cohabiting at some point, compared with 5% of those aged 50–54. In 2002, 25% of unmarried adults aged 16–59 reported living in a cohabiting relationship.

  Ferri et al (*Changing Britain, Changing Lives*, 2003) noted a trend for younger people to cohabit, not simply as a prelude to marriage (approximately 60% of cohabiting couples subsequently marry) but also as a possible alternative. The General Household Survey (2004) confirmed that 25–29 year olds represent the main age group for cohabitation in our society.

Among older age groups, **Berrington** and **Diamond** ('Marriage or Cohabitation', 2000) found cohabitation was most likely in situations where one or both partners had been married before. The likelihood of cohabitation is also increased in situations where one or both partners had parents who cohabited.

⚠ Digging deeper

Given that cohabitation (or *consensual union* as it is often termed) is a similar form of living arrangement to marriage (and the only form currently available – until or if civil partnerships are recognised in law – to same-sex partners) it is not too surprising to find the reasons we have examined in relation to changing patterns of marriage (lack of stigma, secularisation, lifestyle choice, risk avoidance and lack of incentives to marry) all apply to cohabitation. Having noted this, however, we can briefly explore reasons for cohabitation in a little more depth **Smart** and **Stevens** ('Cohabitation Breakdown', 2000) interviewed 40 separated parents and identified the following reasons for cohabitation.

- **Attitudes to marriage**: These ranged from indifference to marriage to being unsure about the suitability for marriage of the person with whom they were cohabiting.

- **Trial marriage**: For some of the mothers involved, cohabitation represented a trial for their partner to prove they could settle down, gain and keep paid work and interact successfully with the mother's children.

- **Legal factors**: Many cohabiting parents were either unwilling to enter into a legal relationship with their partner (often because they were suspicious of the legal system) or they believed it easier to back away from a cohabiting relationship if it didn't work out as they had hoped.

- **Opposition** to marriage as an institution was also a factor, with some parents believing cohabitation led to a more equal form of relationship.

Table 2.7 summarises the different 'commitments to cohabitation' identified by Smart and Stevens.

Finally, we can note **Lewis** et al ('Cohabitation, Separation and Fatherhood', 2002) found three distinct orientations to cohabitation in their sample of 50 parents who had cohabited, had a child and then separated.

- **Indistinguishable**: Marriage and cohabitation were equally preferable.

- **Marriage preference**: One or both partners viewed cohabitation as a temporary prelude to what they had hoped would be marriage.

- **Cohabitation preference**: Each partner saw their relationship in terms of a moral commitment on a par with marriage.

Contingent commitment involved couples cohabiting 'until they were sure it was safe or sensible to become permanently committed or married'.	Mutual commitment involved the couple feeling as committed to each other and their children as married couples.
Characteristics of contingent commitment • the couple have not known each other for long • legal and/or financial agreements are absent • the children are not planned (although they may be wanted) • pregnancy predates the cohabitation • there is a requirement for significant personal change if the relationship is to work • there is no presumption that the relationship will last – only a hope	**Characteristics of mutual commitment** • the relationship is established before cohabiting • there are some legal and financial agreements • children are planned and/or wanted by both parents • both parents are involved in childcare • there are mutually agreed expectations of the relationship • there is a presumption that the relationship will last

Table 2.7

 Growing it yourself: marriage and cohabitation

Copy the following table and then individually, in small groups or as a class, identify as many advantages and disadvantages of marriage and cohabitation as possible.

The following statements from Lewis et al's respondents might help get you started:

- 'My commitment to a relationship is the same, regardless of the piece of paper.' (Father)

- 'I don't honestly see a lot of difference between marriage and cohabitation ... what matters is the relationship and whether it works or not.' (Mother)

Marriage		Cohabitation	
Advantages	Disadvantages	Advantages	Disadvantages

Divorce

⚠ Preparing the ground

In 'A Brief History of Marriage' (2002), **Samantha Callan** notes: 'The first divorce [in Britain] took place in 1551 and, over the next 187 years, 300 marriages were dissolved by private acts of parliament . . . '.

In 1857, the *Divorce Act* allowed divorce for adultery (but only for men – and rich men at that). It wasn't until the mid-twentieth century that divorce (as opposed to separation) became a possibility for both men and women, rich or poor.

This brief – and highly selective – overview tells us that, for most of our history, divorce has been beyond the reach of most people. However, as 'Growing it yourself', on page 102 shows, once it was available, people seem to have taken advantage of it in ever increasing numbers.

In terms of the trends illustrated by these tables, over the past:

- 40 years divorce has become increasingly popular and rates for both sexes have increased
- 30 years divorcees, both male and female, have been getting older (reflecting, perhaps, the later average age of modern marriage partners)
- 20 years divorce peaked and then returned to its previous level (a result of the baby boom bulge)
- 10 years we have witnessed a slight decline (and flattening out) in the numbers divorcing.

⚠ Digging deeper

We can start by noting that the same population changes affecting the validity of marriage statistics also apply to divorce statistics. If more people marry, for example, this increases the chances of a rise in the numbers of people divorcing. We can however suggest some reasons for changes in *patterns* of divorce.

- **Legal changes**: Whenever we examine historical changes to the number of people divorcing in our society, we always need to be aware of potential *reliability* problems with divorce statistics. The legal definition of divorce, for example, has changed many times over the past century (as Table 2.10 shows) and, each time divorce is made easier, the number of people divorcing increases.

  Legal changes, although significant, are not necessarily a *cause* of higher divorce; rather, an increase in divorce after legal changes probably indicates the number of people who *would* have divorced – given the opportunity – before the change. This includes, for example, couples who had separated prior to a change in the law and those living in *empty-shell marriages* – couples whose marriage had effectively ended but were still living together because they could not legally divorce.

- **Economic changes**: for example, in 1949, Legal Aid was made available for divorcing couples for the first time. This created opportunities to divorce for those other than the well off.

- **Social changes** cover a range of possible reasons.

⚠️ Growing it yourself: reasons for divorce

In small groups, identify as many reasons as possible why people may want to divorce.

Once you have done this, look at the following tables and cross off any reason on your list that would have applied equally to the dates in the table (for example, 'not being in love any more' or 'adultery' would have applied equally in 1921 and 2001).

As a class, write any remaining reasons for divorce on a white board/flipchart.

Read the 'Digging deeper' section and match your reasons to those I have provided.

Year	No. of divorces (000s)	Average age at divorce	
		Males	Females
1921	3	–	–
1941	7.5	–	–
1947	47	–	–
1951	29	–	–
1961	20	–	–
1971	80	39.4	36.8
1981	160	37.7	35.2
1991	180	38.6	36.0
1999	170	–	–
2000	155	38.6	36.0
2001	157	41.5	39.1

Table 2.8 Divorce in the UK
Source: Social Trends 30–34

	1961		1981		1999	
	Male	Female	Male	Female	Male	Female
16–24	1.4	2.4	17.7	22.3	29.0	30.3
25–29	3.9	4.5	27.6	26.7	31.5	32.3
45 and over	1.1	0.9	4.8	3.9	6.3	5.1
All 16 and over	2.1	2.1	11.9	11.9	13.0	12.9

Table 2.9 Divorce by gender and age per 1000 of population
Source: Social Trends 30–34

Year	Main Change
Pre-1857	Only by Act of Parliament
1857: Matrimonial Causes Act	Available through Law Courts for first time (but expensive to pursue). 'Fault' had to be proven. Men could divorce because of adultery, women had to show both cruelty and adultery.
1923: Matrimonial Causes Act	Grounds for divorce made the same for men and women.
1937: Herbert Act	Added range of new grounds for divorce (desertion, cruelty etc.) and no divorce petition was allowed for the first three years of marriage.
1969–1971: Divorce Reform Act	Abolished idea of 'matrimonial offence' (adultery, etc.) as grounds for divorce. 'Irretrievable breakdown of marriage' became the only requirement. Divorce could be obtained within two years if both partners consented and five years if one partner contested the divorce.
1985: Matrimonial and Family Proceedings Act	Time limit on divorce reduced from three years of marriage to one.
1996 – 2000: Family Law Act	Introduced range of ideas ('no-fault' divorce, counselling, cooling-off period to reflect on application for divorce – not all of which have been applied). Idea was to make divorce a less confrontational process.

Table 2.10 Divorce: selected legal changes in the UK

- **War-time marriages**, for example, have a high probability of ending in divorce.
- **Attitudes to marriage**: The weakening of the religious significance of marriage (people probably no longer view it as 'until death do us part') also goes some way to explaining attitudes to divorce – there is little moral stigma attached to it anymore (or, if you prefer, less stigma attached now than in the past).
- **Lifestyle choices**: Some couples see marriage as a search for personal happiness, rather than a moral commitment to each other (which , as an aside, may also explain the increase in *remarriages*; divorcees (90% of whom remarry) are not unhappy with marriage as an institution, just the person they married).
- **Social position**: As women have experienced increased financial opportunities and independence they have become more willing to end an unsatisfactory marriage.
- **Romantic individualism**: The arguments here are two-fold: firstly, that family relationships have, over the years, become stripped of all but their individual/personal functions – if people 'fall out of love', therefore, there is nothing to hold their marriage together. Secondly, that we increasingly have (media-fuelled) illusions about love, romance and family life and once the reality hits home, many people opt for divorce as a way out of an unhappy marriage experience.

'At risk' relationships

Statistically, those marriages most at risk of ending in divorce involve:

- Different social backgrounds: Pressure from family and friends can create conflict within the marriage that makes divorce statistically more likely. Differences in class, religion and ethnic background also lead to a higher risk of divorce.
- Short acquaintance before marriage.
- Separation for long periods.
- Teenagers: A range of reasons apply here (length of potential marriage, low incomes, shared accommodation with parents and so forth).
- Remarriage: Divorcees are twice as likely to divorce again.

Strange reasons for divorce

Anita Davis, a family law solicitor has identified some odd reasons for divorce:

- a husband was divorced because he made irritating noises with Sellotape
- a wife divorced her partner because he crept into bed for sex during her hospital treatment for sexual exhaustion
- a woman divorced her partner for refusing to let her buy her own underwear
- a man sued for divorce because his wife used their Pekingese dog as a hot water bottle.

Separation

⚠ Preparing the ground

Our ability to understand changing patterns of separation are complicated by two factors, divorce and cohabitation.

Divorce

In the past – before divorce was either available or affordable – it was not uncommon for married couples to end their relationship by separation. However, we have no reliable data about those who separated (or those who would have separated had divorce been possible). The best we can do is make educated guesses – based on the number who currently divorce and the fact that, every time it is made easier more people divorce – about the prevalence of separation. Once divorce became readily available, of course,

Charles and Diana – one of the most famous separated couples of recent times.

Year of marriage	Males	Females
1965–1969	7	7
1970–1974	10	10
1975–1979	14	13
1980–1984	10	14
1985–1989	13	16

Table 2.11 Percentage of first marriages in Great Britain ending in separation within five years: by year of marrige and gender
[Source: Social Trends 34]

separation as a way of ending a relationship became much less common – couples divorced (which allowed them to remarry) without the need to separate.

The *1969 Divorce Reform Act*, however, introduced the concept of separation into the divorce process itself; a divorce could be granted after two years of separation if both partners consented and five years if only one partner consented.

In terms of married couples therefore, separation is, as Table 2.11 suggests, likely to be a *prelude* to divorce rather than, as in the past, an *alternative*.

Cohabitation

To further complicate matters, do we include in our analysis figures for cohabiting couples who separate? Numbers here are difficult to estimate and data reliability is low because this information is not legally recorded.

However, one area in which we do have reliable data for contemporary separation is for marriages that breakdown within the first 12 months. This is because of **judicial separation** decrees. Although couples cannot divorce – and they remain legally married – they can apply to the family courts for a legal separation. All marital obligations are ended and it can be granted for things like adultery or unreasonable behaviour, although it is not actually necessary to show the marriage has irretrievably broken down. Table 2.12 gives some idea of the (relatively small) number of such separations.

Year	Petitions	Decrees granted
1980	5423	2560
1983	7430	4854
1990	2874	1794
1997	1078	589
1998	1374	518

Table 2.12 Judicial Separation: 1980–1998. Source: Office for National Statistics 2000. A 'petition' is an application for separation. The separation is confirmed when a decree is granted by the Courts. The difference between the two figures results from couples deciding to stay together following the petition but before any decree.

⚠ Digging deeper

When thinking about separation, we can note two points. Firstly, we can't reliably establish comparative historical patterns of separation and secondly, the concept itself is largely redundant in our society given the easy availability of divorce.

What we can usefully do, however, is change the focus slightly to briefly examine the possible *consequences* of separation for the breakdown of marital or cohabiting relationships. **Rodgers** and **Pryor**'s review, for example, of over 200 research reports in this general area ('Divorce and Separation', 1998) showed children of separated families had a higher probability of:

- poverty and poor housing
- poverty during adulthood
- behavioural problems
- school underachievement
- needing medical treatment
- leaving school/home when young
- pregnancy at an early age.

They also identified a range of factors that influenced these probabilities:

- financial hardship

- family conflict
- parental ability to recover from stress of separation
- multiple changes in family structure
- quality of contact with the non-resident parent.

Lewis et al (2002) noted in their sample of 50 parents who had cohabited, had a child and then separated:

- 40% gave 'irresponsibility of their partner' as the main cause of separation
- 70% of separations were started by the woman
- Mothers initially took primary responsibility for the child (which is similar to the pattern for marriage breakdown).

Child-bearing

⚠ Preparing the ground

Changing patterns of fertility and child-bearing involves looking at the behaviour of those who decide, for whatever reason, to have children and the following table identifies some key recent changes.

Year	Number of live births (000s)	Births per 1000 women aged 15–44	Average age of mother (1st child)	% of births outside marriage
1964	876	93	–	7.2
1971	–	–	23.7	–
1991	699	64	25.6	30.2
2003	621	54	26.7	41.4

Table 2.13 Live birth statistics: England and Wales
Source: Office for National Statistics

Over the past 40 years, changing patterns of child-bearing in our society can be summarised in terms of the following:

- general fertility has substantially declined, in terms of both the number of live births and the birth rate
- family size has declined from an average of 3 to 1.6 children
- the average age at which women have their first child is increasing
- births outside marriage now account for nearly half of all births – a substantial increase over 40 years ago.

 Digging deeper

When we think about reasons for changing patterns of fertility, a number of factors spring to mind.

Contraception

The development and widespread use of the contraceptive pill, for example, has allowed people to plan their fertility more easily than in the past.

Childlessness

An interesting feature of modern households is the number of people who choose to remain childless (who, as we have seen, form the majority of UK households). The Office for National Statistics (Social Trends 34, 2004), has noted: 'Related to the trend of delaying childbirth, is the growth in the number of women remaining childless':

Year of birth	% childless at age 35
1960	11
2000	25

Table 2.14

One reason for this situation is **later marriage**. As we have seen, men and women are increasingly choosing to marry later and, consequently, start a family later. This has led to an increase in child-bearing among women aged 30 and over.

McAllister and **Clarke** ('Choosing childlessness', 1988) noted the following points about childless households:

- **Rates**: The UK has one of highest European levels of childlessness.
- **Decisions** to remain childless are affected by a range of life events.
- **Education**: Highly qualified women are more likely to remain childless.
- **Security**: Parenthood was identified with disruption, change and poverty; the childless chose independence over the constraints of childcare and material security over financial risk.

Technology

Improvements in both child and mother care, IVF treatments and so forth have extended fertility into age groups which, in the past, would have been too old to safely bear children.

Financial costs

One factor in decisions about the number of children produced within families is likely to be the cost of raising them.

The **Family Expenditure Survey** (Office for National Statistics, 2000) estimated the average spend on each child (for both single- and two-adult households) as £52 per week. *Pregnancy & Birth* **magazine** (March 2001) estimated having a baby 'costs parents £20,315 for the first five years alone' (although this rises to £36,000 for more affluent households).

First child		Subsequent children	
Typical spend	Less Child Benefit	Typical spend	Less Child Benefit
About £67 pw	About £52 pw	About £56 pw	About £46 pw

Table 2.15 Middleton et al ('Small Fortunes: Spending on children, childhood poverty and parental sacrifice', 2002) estimate of the cost of children in 1995

In this section we have looked at areas such as family diversity and changing patterns of family life (in terms of things like marriage, divorce and cohabitation). In the next section we can continue the general theme of family and social change by looking more closely at possible changes in family relationships.

Family and social change

Introduction

The focus in previous sections has been on the family group as an institution – although we have, at times, touched on relationships within this group. In this section, the focus changes to the family group itself in order to examine 'the nature and extent of changes within the family'. To do this we can look at evidence relating to 'gender roles, domestic labour and power relationships'. The section is completed by looking at 'changes in the status of children and childhood'.

Gender roles

Preparing the ground

The first thing we can usefully do is to outline the distinction sociologists generally make between 'sex' and 'gender'.

- **Sex**: **Anthony Giddens**, (*Sociology*, 1989) notes, 'sex' refers to the physical characteristics that lead to people being labelled 'male' or 'female'. Sex characteristics are, in a sense, biologically determined and 'fixed' (although it is, of course, now possible to change your biological sex).

- **Gender**, on the other hand, refers to the social characteristics assigned by any given society to each biological sex (whatever these may actually turn out to be). In other words, *gender* represents the things we, as a society, associate with being biologically male or female.

The classic expression of these ideas is **Robert Stoller**'s argument (*Sex and Gender: on the Development of Masculinity and Femininity*, 1968): 'Gender is a term that has psychological and cultural connotations; if the proper terms for sex are "male" and "female", the corresponding terms for gender are "masculine" and "feminine"; these latter may be quite independent of (biological) sex'.

WARM UP: WHAT DOES IT MEAN?

To get you thinking about gender, consider the following categories of masculinity and femininity. In small groups, think about what the two concepts mean to you and also how you think our society views them (make a table like the one I've started and add your ideas to it). As a class, bring your ideas together.

Masculinity		Femininity	
What does 'masculinity' mean to you?	What do you think masculinity means in our society?	What does femininity mean to you?	What do you think femininity means in our society?
Men should be strong and protective.	Men are expected to be unemotional ('boys don't cry').	Women should make themselves attractive to men.	Women should be in touch with their 'caring side'.
Further Meanings			

While all societies (considered both in historical and comparative terms) have 'men and women', the *meaning* of gender can vary considerably in the same society over time and, of course, between different societies.

Masculinity (what it means to be 'a man'), for example, is a concept that has a different general meaning in our society than it does in Australia or Peru. In addition, its meaning changes to reflect different stages in our physical development – 'boy', for example, is a different gender category from 'man'.

Femininity (what it means to be 'a woman') similarly has different meanings at different times and in different places although, as **Beattie** ('Who Was That Lady?', 1981) notes, there are significant differences in the way we use language to describe gender:

> ... 'girl' like 'lady' is often used for 'woman' in contexts where 'boy' or 'gentleman' would not appear for 'man'. We find Page Three 'girls' (not women) in *The Sun*. Calling a nude male pin-up a 'boy' would be derogatory. Our tendency to call all women 'girls' is enormously significant. We stress their positive evaluative properties (especially the physical ones) and suggest a lack of power. We are to some extent creating immaturity and dependence through linguistic devices [language].

When we start to think about gender roles within the family group, therefore, we must understand their content (what people do and how do they do it, for example) and, by extension, how such roles have changed.

Gender perspectives: Traditionally, sociological perspectives on *conjugal roles* (the roles played by men and women within a marriage or cohabiting relationship) have fallen into two (opposed) camps characterised by their different views on the essential nature of family roles. We can, for example note the concept of:

- **Patriarchy**: This view, mainly associated with feminist and conflict perspectives, generally sees the family group as male dominated, oppressive and exploitative of women. Over the past few hundred years the form of patriarchy may have changed (it no longer, perhaps, takes the aggressive form of the Victorian family, with the father ruling the family roost through a mixture of violence and economic threats), but both violence and more subtle forms of male control (in relation to who does housework, controls decision making and so forth) are still characteristic of family life from this perspective.

- **Symmetry** is the other side of this coin, and is associated (mainly) with functionalist perspectives, such as **Willmott** and **Young** (*The Symmetrical Family*, 1973), who argued it was possible to track historical changes in family relationships in the following way.

- **Pre-industrial family** (pre-1750), an economically productive unit with the father as patriarch (head of household), exercising complete physical and economic control over his family.

- **Asymmetrical family** (1750–1900), characterised in terms of segregated conjugal roles involving a separation between home and work – both for the husband, who spent long periods away from the home and the wife, whose role as mother and domestic labourer started to become established.

- **Symmetrical family** (twentieth century), which they characterised as involving joint conjugal roles that demonstrate greater levels of equality between males and females in terms of both paid and domestic (unpaid) work.

Whatever the reality of the situation, as I've briefly characterised it, a third way of looking at gender roles within the home is one that straddles the two.

New Right perspectives argue family relationships should be 'symmetrical' in the sense of husband and wife (this perspective doesn't particularly like non-marriage family relationships) performing 'different but complementary' roles within the family; these roles are, supposedly, tuned to male and female biological capabilities – men as the traditional family breadwinner and women as the family carer and domestic labourer. In other words, a patriarchal form of family relationship based around a biological (as opposed to social) symmetry.

 Digging deeper

If we move away from these types of 'standard' arguments about gender roles within the family, the first thing to note is families are potentially confusing and contradictory institutions, an idea neatly expressed by **Decca Aitkenhead** ('When Home's a Prison', *The Guardian*, 24/07/04): '"What about Dad?" Eileen demanded "He used to hit you". "Your father never laid a finger on me! Not once!" flamed Kathleen Ward. Eileen knew her father had once been to prison for beating her mother – yet … nobody bothered to correct the discrepancy'.

An alternative way of thinking about gender roles (which we can relate to ideas about domestic labour and power), therefore, is to think about them in terms of *identities*. That is, how family members organise their relationships on the basis of two concepts noted by **Hogg** and **Vaughan** (*Social Psychology*, 2002), namely:

- **Social identity** – which represents how our membership of social groups influences our perception of certain roles. For example, in our culture, the roles 'male' and 'female' carry general social characteristics that define the meaning of 'being a man or a woman'. These ideas are important because they represent a *structural* aspect to our relationships – I know how men and women are expected to behave, for example, because my cultural (gender) socialisation has taught me the general characteristics of such roles.

- **Personal identity**, on the other hand, works at the level of social *action*. How I actually play (in my case) 'the male role' is open, to apply **Goffman**'s ideas ('The

Presentation of Self in Everyday Life', 1959), to *interpretation* and *negotiation* within, for example, my family.

Thus, how I interpret and play the role of 'husband' is conditioned by my perception of what this role means in general cultural terms (what husbands are expected to do) and in the more specific, personal, context of my family relationships – which probably goes some way to explaining why, in my household, I have to iron my own clothes and mow the lawn (although not, of course, at the same time).

In this respect, as **Alison James** ('Imaging Children "At Home", "In the Family" and "at School"', 1998), argues, 'The home is a spatial context where identities are worked on' – which, in plain English, means family identities are not fixed, but, on the contrary, fluid. They are, as **Anne-Marie Fortier** ('Making home: queer migrations and motions of attachment', 2003) puts it, 'continuously re-imagined and redefined'.

⚠🌷 Growing it yourself: social and personal identities.

In pairs, identify ten words commonly used to describe adult men and women. Enter the most popular words identified by the whole class in the table below.

Men					Women		
+	−	+/−			−	+	+/−
			1				
			2				
			3				
			4				
			5				
			6				
			7				
			8				
			9				
			10				

For each male and each female 'describing word', decide as a group whether you think they are used positively (+), negatively (−) or neither (+/−) in our culture.

Discussion point: take my wife

Use the table on page 111 as the basis for a discussion about how language can be used as a means of social control. You might want to think about the following:

How do you feel about being described in certain ways (such as being called 'boy' or 'girl')? My wife, for example, dislikes being called 'dear' (she also dislikes being called 'my wife', but that's another story).

How does the language used to describe the sexes impact on how we see ourselves (our masculinity and femininity) and on our behaviour (you could, if you wish, explore some of the derogatory (insulting) ways males and females are described)?

If we think of gender roles in terms of *identity*, therefore, we can note two things:

- **Changing gender roles**: In the past, social identities relating to gender roles were dominant; they provided clear, unshakeable, guidelines for roles within the family (the classic idea of husband as breadwinner and wife as domestic labourer/carer, for example). There were few opportunities to develop *personal identities* that differed from the social norm – and the penalties for trying were severe (in terms of, for example, male violence against women who attempted to reject or renegotiate personal identity within the family).

In contemporary families, although we are aware of social expectations about gender behaviour, we have far more sources of reference for our personal identities – and far more opportunities for the successful renegotiation and

reinterpretation of our roles within the family.

- **Diversity** of gender roles within contemporary families is, consequently, much more apparent – family groups with very similar social and economic circumstances may display marked differences in the way gender roles are allocated and performed.

Allan and **Crow** (*Home and Family: Creating the Domestic Space*, 1989) reinforce this idea when they note: 'The creation of the home is an active process which is an integral part of people's family projects'. **Stacey** (*Brave New Families*, 1998) observes that in 'postmodern society' both the *public domain* (the workplace) and the *private domain* (the home) have undergone radical changes in recent times to become 'diverse, fluid and unresolved, with a broad range of gender and kinship relations'. **Reich** (2001) argues the 'incredible shrinking family' is one where: 'People spend less time together, couples are having fewer children, financial support between spouses is eroding, and care and attention are being subcontracted … living together remains a conjugal norm, but there is no longer adherence to permanent monogamous family units as the basis for family life, or of heterosexual relationships composed of male breadwinner and female homemaker'.

Finally, **Michael Willmott** (*Complicated Lives*, 2000) argues:

It no longer makes sense to rely on traditional roles when dividing up tasks in the home. Instead, new roles must be negotiated by every couple depending on their individual circumstances. In the future, the important thing will be who has the time or the inclination to do the housework, and not whether they are a man or a women.

Which is as good a reason as any turn to an examination of domestic labour.

Domestic labour

Preparing the ground

Like it or not (and, on the whole, I don't), housework is something that has to be done – and, to explore who does it (and why), we need to think about what counts as housework (or 'domestic labour' if you prefer).

For our purposes, domestic labour refers to *anything* that needs to be accomplished in order to ensure the running of a home and family; it includes the standard stuff like cooking, cleaning and shopping as well as things like household repairs (mending the microwave!) and chores; it may also include things like care of children, the sick and the elderly.

Complete the 'Growing it yourself' exercise below. Having done this exercise, we can summarise recent evidence about domestic labour in our society.

Amount and type

As Table 2.16 (Office for National Statistics, 2002) demonstrates, on average women spend twice as long on housework each day as men. It also suggests that men and women do different tasks within the household – women spend more time on routine domestic tasks (cooking, cleaning, etc.),

Growing it yourself: who does what?

A relatively simple piece of social research you can carry out is to establish who does what around your home, using a content analysis grid to record your observations.

As a class, identify as many aspects of housework as you can (don't go into too much detail, except where it's necessary to distinguish things like general care of children (washing, feeding, dressing and so forth) as against things like playing with children).

Once you've agreed this, draw and complete the following grid for your family.

Household task	Task usually performed by?				
	Male parent	Female parent	Both parents	Children (male or female?)	Other relative (e.g. grand-parent)
Cooking					
Laundry					
Shopping					
Playing with children					
Further tasks . . .					

men spend more time on repair work and playing with children). **Ramos** ('Domestic Work', 2003) noted how women's share of domestic labour increased with children in the household.

Men	Women
(2 hrs 20 mins.)	(4 hrs)
Cooking	Cooking
Childcare	Childcare
Gardening	Cleaning house
Pet care	laundry

Table 2.16 UK 2000 Time Use Survey: average daily housework and main chores

- **Age**: Ramos (2003) notes how the amount of female housework increases with age – younger women do less housework than older women.

- **Comparative**: According to the Future Foundation ('Complicated Lives', 2000) there has been a slight decline in the amount of housework done by women and an increase in male housework. They estimate 60% of men do more housework than their father, while 75% of women do less housework than their mother.

- **Employment**: Although **Man-yee Kan** ('Gender Asymmetry in the Division of Domestic Labour', 2001) found levels of female housework were marginally reduced by paid employment, unemployment or retirement increased female housework hours and reduced those of her partner. Throughout the

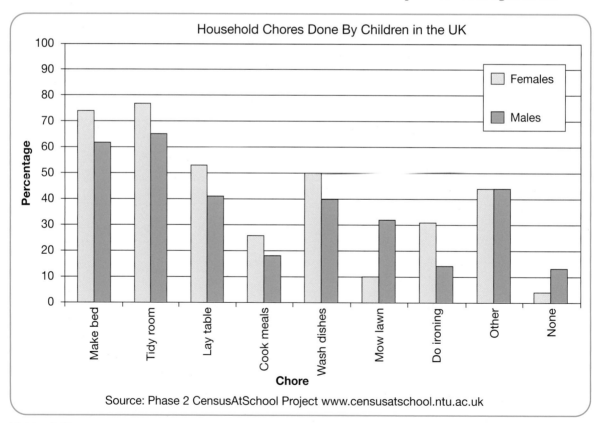

Table 2.17

1990s, *total family workload* (paid and domestic labour) stayed roughly constant for men, whereas for women it decreased (an increase in paid work was off-set by a decrease in domestic work). However, Ramos (2003) noted that, where the man is unemployed and his partner works full time, domestic labour is equally distributed.

- **Income and Education**: Man-yee Kan (2001) noted how levels of both male and female housework decreased by income and level of education.

- **Gender Beliefs**: Ramos (2003) found that, in families with 'traditional gender beliefs', women do more housework than in families where beliefs reflect sexual equality. In households where partners hold conflicting beliefs, men do less domestic work.

- **Children**: One area of domestic labour often overlooked is that performed by children. However, as table 2.17 demonstrates, they contribute to housework in a number of ways.

  Jens Bonke ('Children's household work', 1999) notes that children generally make a relatively small contribution to domestic labour – contributions peak at age 20 (approximately 2½ hours a week) and boys contribute less than girls. In lone children families, girls averaged five times as much housework as boys (2½ hours/week as against 30 minutes).

- **Grandparenting**: A final area we should note is the role played by grandparents in the care of children. **Tunaley** et al ('Relatively Speaking', 1999), for example, suggested almost 50% of working parents in the UK rely on grandparents for child care, for any of four main reasons:

- more working women
- long and unsociable working hours
- more active grandparents
- high cost of child care.

A more detailed set of statistics on domestic labour can be found at:
www.sociology.org.uk/as4aqa.htm

 # Digging deeper

Debates over domestic labour can be a methodological minefield in terms of:

- **Reliability**: There is no clear definition of housework – some researchers focus on domestic tasks, whereas others, such as **Duncombe** and **Marsden** (1993) have included 'emotion work' (the work women do to 'make their partners and children feel good') as part of the definition.

- **Validity**: We need to be aware of *observer effects* (when housework is recorded in diaries by respondents) and *interviewer effects* (when people are questioned about their housework chores). A general problem here is men overestimate – and women underestimate – the amount of time spent on domestic labour.

In order to interpret the data, however, we can return to the distinction, noted earlier, between social and personal identities.

Social identities

It is clear that, in some respects, cultural beliefs about male and female abilities and roles are significant in terms of explaining differences in domestic labour. Evidence drawn from a range of studies suggests domestic labour is both overwhelmingly performed by women and that, to some extent, this is tied up with notions of:

- **Patriarchy**: Ideas about gender roles and behaviour reflect patriarchal attitudes mainly – but not exclusively – amongst older age groups in the population. **Pleck** ('Working Wives. Working Husbands', 1985), for example, noted the 'more traditional' the views held by couples about gender roles, the greater the level of domestic labour inequality.

  Pilcher ('Gender Matters?', 1998) found similar views. Older respondents – unlike their younger counterparts – didn't talk about equality but thought instead in traditional ways about gender roles, responsibilities and relationships which reflected their socialisation and life experiences – where 'men undertook limited household work, married women had limited involvement in paid work and where a marked gendered division of labour was the norm'.

- **Femininity**: Although changing, notions of what it means to be a woman are still, to some extent, tied up with ideas about caring and nurture (and, as **Ramos** (2003) suggests, responsibility for child care still falls mainly on the female partner).

- **Masculinity**: Conversely, traditional notions of masculinity are still, to some extent, bound up with ideas about

Discussion point: is housework the new sex?

Housework is not the new sex. It's the same old dreary chore

Rachel Johnson: *Daily Telegraph*: 23/05/2003

You know that thing when you have your hands in the kitchen sink, and your beloved comes up behind you and wraps his arms around you. 'Mmm, I love it when you're doing the washing-up,' he says. The whole point of this manoeuvre, as we all know, is to signal the attractiveness of women pinned, like butterflies, in the middle of committing an act of domesticity.

As Pat Mainardi wrote in *The Politics of Housework*, women are conditioned to want to live in a clean, sweet-smelling home, with piles of folded laundry in drawers, plumped cushions and gleaming surfaces. Men are quite happy to do some light carpentry, moving furniture around, some weekend DIY, to help live this dream. 'But men recognise the essential fact of housework right from the very beginning. Which is that it stinks,' says Mainardi. That was in 1970. Three decades later, housework – which is unrewarding, unrecognised, unpaid work that never ends – is being sold back to women, who do most of it anyway, as sexy and glamorous. Marigolds the new Manolos? Phwoar! We've come a long way, baby'.

To help you discuss this (frankly quite scary idea), think about:

What does the phrase 'women are conditioned to want ... ' mean?

How do you think men and women are conditioned in relation to housework?

How is 'housework being sold back to women'?

What does the article tell us about changes in gender roles over the past 30 years?

providing for a family by taking on the main economic role. **Linda McDowe** ('Young men leaving school', 2001), for example, noted the 'continued dominance of a "traditional" masculinity' in her study.

Personal identities

Although social identities are clearly important, personal identities give us a sense of the way gender roles are interpreted and negotiated according to the specific family circumstances of those involved; this is especially clear when we consider class differences (although in some ways this represents a *displacement* of domestic responsibilities – high income families can pay others to do their housework), age and educational differences.

Callaghan ('The Interaction of Gender, Class and Place in Women's Experience', 1998), for example, highlights the importance of considering these factors when thinking about how gender roles are created and performed within the family and **Dench** ('The place of men in changing family cultures', 1996) argues that younger men, as a group, believed 'couples should share or negotiate family roles' and resist conventional ideas that men should be the main breadwinners.

Speakman and **Marchington** ('Ambivalent patriarchs, shift workers, breadwinners and housework', 1999) however, noted how some men used *learned helplessness* when trying to avoid domestic tasks – their 'inability' to work domestic machinery served to throw domestic tasks back into the hands of their partners.

To sum up the ideas at which we have just looked, we can identify three main reasons for the generally unequal distribution of domestic labour in our society.

- **Social identities**, relating to deep-seated cultural beliefs about male and female 'natures' exert a powerful pull, through the socialisation process, that leads to the reproduction of traditional forms of gender relationship (women as 'carers' for example).

- **Socio-personal identities** involving the way the latter are *pragmatically* ('reasonably') shaped by the former. For example, in a family where the man is the main breadwinner, decisions about who will give up work to care for children may be guided by the reality of differences in earning power.

- **Personal identities** involve looking at quite specific relationships between the family partners and may be played out against a background of complex personal and cultural histories. For example, a man may be able to get away with doing little in the household; on the other hand, his relationship with his partner may not allow him to shirk his share of family responsibilities. Gender roles and relationships are shaped, to some extent, by how partners personally relate to one another.

Power relationships

Preparing the ground

Like any social institution, family groups involve power relationships. In other words, they involve 'struggles' between family members – both adults and children – in areas like:

- **Physical** resources – things like food, clothing and shelter – considered in terms of who provides and consumes these things.
- **Social** resources – things like decision making, control over family resources (such as money) and so forth.
- **Psychological** resources – things like love, trust, affection and care – in short, the range of emotional securities (and insecurities) that surround our relationships.

In this section, therefore, we need to explore this aspect of family life in more detail and to do this it would be helpful to define **power**. According to **Anthony Giddens** (1989) power involves 'the ability of individuals or groups to make their own concerns or interests count, even where others resist. Power sometimes involves the direct use of force, but is almost always also accompanied by the development of ideas (ideology) which justify the actions of the powerful.'

In terms of this type of definition, therefore, power has two dimensions we need to note:

- **Force**: This aspect is probably the one that springs most readily to mind because it involves making someone do something against their will – usually through the act or threat of violence.
- **Authority**, however, is an important aspect because it suggests we can get people to do what we want because they think it's right – or they feel they want – to obey us.

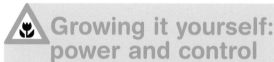

Growing it yourself: power and control

Copy and complete the following table to identify how power/authority is exercised in your school or college.

Examples of situations which use:	
Power	Authority
Detentions Attendance	Taking notes in class

Having outlined the concept of power, we can examine some examples of how it is exercised within families.

Domestic violence

This covers a range of behaviours (physical and emotional), the aim of which is to aggressively control the behaviour of a family member (adult and/or child). It can involve physical violence (assault), sexual violence (rape) and economic sanctions (denying a family member something they need, for example). The one common thread linking these examples is the desire for power and control on the part of the perpetrator.

The extent of domestic violence is difficult to estimate reliably since it generally happens behind closed doors within the privacy of the family group and victims may be reluctant to admit or acknowledge their victimisation. Keeping this in mind, **Hilary Abrahams** (Domestic Violence Research Group, University of Bristol) has identified some significant facts about domestic violence:

- **British Crime Survey** (2000): 20% of all crimes and 23% of all violent crimes were classified as domestic violence (more recent figures from **Dodd** et al ('Crime in England and Wales 2003/2004') suggest this percentage has recently fallen – they report 16% of all violent incidents were incidents of domestic violence).

In 1995, 10% of 16–29 year old disabled women were assaulted within the home. Women are most likely to be sexually assaulted by men they know, and 45% of reported rapes were carried out by a current partner.

- **Repeat victimisation**: Nearly 50% of all victims experience more than one violent attack by their partner.
- **Gender**: The majority of victims (81% according to the 2002 British Crime Survey) are female.
- **Reported crime**: In 1999, nearly 40% of female murder victims (92 women) were killed by present or former partners. The comparable figure for men was 6%.

Kirkwood (*Leaving Abusive Partners*, 1993) notes that domestic violence has psychological consequences, including low self-esteem, dependence on the perpetrator and a tendency to minimise or deny the violence. In addition, a Zero Tolerance Charitable Trust report (1998) found 20% of young men and 10% of young women agreed abuse or violence against women was acceptable in some circumstances.

Child abuse

This is a further aspect of power within family groups, with writers such as **Humphreys** and **Thiara** ('Routes to Safety', 2002) claiming a strong link to domestic violence. In terms of statistical evidence:

- One child dies each week from adult cruelty. Roughly 80 children are killed each year, mainly by parents and carers – a level that has remained constant for almost 30 years (Office of National Statistics: 1998–2001).
- Twenty-five per cent of all *recorded* rape victims are children (Home Office Statistical Findings 1996).
- The most likely abuser is someone known to the child (National Commission of Inquiry into the Prevention of Child Abuse, 1996).
- According to the NSPCC, around 30,000 children are currently on child protection registers for being at risk of abuse.

Decision making

Power relationships are not always played out in terms of violence or abuse – the majority of family groups experience neither of these things (the rate of child deaths from abuse/neglect each year is less than 1 in 100,000, for example). Power relationships, therefore, can take other forms within the home.

- **Financial** decision making is a significant indicator of where power lies within a family, since these types of decision – buying a house, a car or a holiday for example – involve concepts of authority. **Edgell**'s influential study (*Middle-Class Couples*, 1980) suggested men made the most important financial decisions within the family, whereas women made decisions about everyday domestic spending (food, clothing and the like).

Although Edgell's study is nearly 25 years old, **Pahl** and **Vogler** ('Money, power and inequality within marriage', 1994) broadly confirmed his argument, although they found the 102 couples in their sample could be grouped into four main categories:

- **Wife-controlled pooling** (27% of couples) involved joint bank accounts with female control of finances.

- **Husband-controlled pooling** (37% of couples) involved a joint bank account with the husband controlling financial decisions.

- **Husband-controlled** (22%), where the husband had his own bank account and took responsibility for all major family bills. This type was most commonly found in higher income families.

- **Wife-controlled** (14%) included couples with no bank accounts where the wife controlled the family finances. This type was common in low-income families.

As the above suggests, financial decision making can be a complex issue, not simply in terms of 'who makes decisions' but, most significantly perhaps, in terms of the type of decisions made; men, it seems, generally take the most important (macro) decisions whereas women are given a degree of financial *autonomy* (freedom) to micro-manage household accounts. This, in part, reflects traditional gender roles in terms of household management being seen as part of the female role.

A further aspect to financial decision making is added by the existence of **secret economies**: In a small proportion of families, one or both partners have access to bank accounts of which their partner has no knowledge. **Jayatilaka** and **Rake** (Fawcett Society Report, 2002), for example, noted that in 5% of families men had secret accounts and in 10% of families women kept such accounts. Most families in their study reported a strong belief financial decisions should be shared, but this didn't seem to be the case in reality – particularly for women with low personal incomes (less than £400 a month). Twenty-five per cent of these women said their husband controlled family financial decisions.

In general, the study suggested women believed they either had some control over or input into financial decisions that, according to Rake, were objectively taken by the male partner. As she notes: 'Bringing money into the household brings with it a sense of entitlement to decide how it is spent. Because men earn more than women they have greater control of how money is spent or shared, and more access to personal spending.'

- **Work and relocation**: Other areas of major decision making in dual-earner families include those relating to work, and includes things like whose work has the greatest priority when, for example, the family is forced to move because of a change in employment. **Irene Hardill** ('A tale of two nations? Juggling work and home in the new economy', 2003) found women were more likely to be the 'trailing spouse' – male occupations had greatest priority and the family relocated mainly to follow male employment patterns.

- **Status enhancement** is an interesting – and little-discussed – aspect of authority within families. It involves, according to **Coverman** ('Women's Work Is Never

Done', 1989), 'work done by one partner (typically the woman) to aggrandize the other partner's career' (dinner parties, attending work functions and so forth). In extreme cases, status enhancement can take the form of a 'trophy wife' – a marriage pattern used by some powerful (mainly, but not necessarily, older) men as a form of status symbol, used to demonstrate their wealth and power.

 Digging deeper

There are a number of different aspects to power relationships within the family. Some – domestic violence and abuse, for example – rest on the expression of physical force as a form of power that creates control through fear and intimidation; others – probably the majority – rest on concepts of authority (who has the right to make decisions, for example).

When we think about the patterns of domestic labour and power relationships we have previously examined, we can see decision making (in its widest sense to include things like how family life is organised) involves a complex interplay between the *private domain* (the domestic arena of relationships within a family) and the *public domain* (work, for example). This distinction is useful because:

- **Exercising power** involves access to sources of power. The greater the access to (and control over) a variety of sources, the greater your level of power.
- **Major sources of power** in our society originate in the public domain, mainly because it's where family income is earned.

We can explore the theoretical side of these ideas by applying **Stephen Lukes'** (*Power*,

1990) argument that power has three main dimensions.

- **The ability to make decisions**: Although women exercise power within families, it's mainly in areas where they're traditionally seen to have greater expertise (the micro-management of family resources to which we have previously referred). Major decisions tend to be monopolised by men, mainly because men tend to earn more money and this 'public domain resource' gives them power within the family.

  Where both partners work, women have more control over the wider decision making process (which supports the idea power is substantially dependent on control over a wide range of social resources). Having said this, female power depends on such things as the status of female work, relative level of income, domestic responsibilities and so forth.

- **The ability to prevent others making decisions** involves the 'ability to manipulate any debate over the kinds of decisions that actually reach the stage of "being made"'. In terms of gender roles, the personal identities of family members are important (for example, how each partner sees their role within the family).

  Gender socialisation is significant also, since if males and females are raised to have certain expectations of both their own social role and that of their partner then the ability to make decisions affecting the family group takes on a 'natural' quality. It appears 'right, proper and natural' for women to raise children and men to have paid employment, for example. In this instance, decisions about family roles never reach the stage of actually having to be made, simply because the stronger partner makes the decisions.

- **The ability to remove decision making from the agenda** involves the idea that who does what inside and outside the family group is conditioned by various social factors (gender socialisation, male and female social identities, the realities of power distributions in society and so forth) that reflect our personal experiences.

For example, decisions about paid employment, domestic labour and the like may be removed from the decision making agenda (the respective partners don't actually have to make conscious decisions about them) for a variety of reasons: they may, for example, share the belief women are better child-rearers than men. Alternatively, where one partner earns more than the other, has higher career expectations and so forth, this partner may remain in work while the other cares for the children.

Childhood

⚠ Preparing the ground

In this final section we are going to examine the changing status of children and childhood, which involves two things: defining what we mean by 'children' and exploring historical differences in perceptions of childhood. These tasks are not unconnected, since our ability to identify and explain changes will depend, to some extent, on how childhood is defined.

WARM UP: DEFINING CHILDHOOD

To get us started, we can think about two broad indicators of childhood:

- **biological** (how people physically and mentally develop) and
- **cultural** (the characteristics people give to the label 'child').

Using the following table as a starting point, what characteristics of childhood can you identify?

Indicators of childhood	
Biological	Cultural
Age at which childhood begins and ends	Innocence? Immaturity?

It is not always easy – either biologically or culturally – to precisely identify an agreed set of characteristics about childhood (in this respect we sometimes refer to the idea as a 'contested concept' because there are always arguments about how to define it).

Biologically, we are all young once and, with the passage of time, we all become old – but this simple statement hides a much wider and more complex set of ideas.

Culturally, two ideas are significant:

- **Duration**: It is difficult to say precisely when child status ends (or even when it begins, come to that). In my lifetime, the age when people are officially classified as 'adults' has changed from 21 to 18 (although, just to confuse things further, at 16 you can legally do some of the things 'children' can't do – work full time, marry, join the army and so forth). This simple cultural change alters the way we define childhood and, of course, children.

- **Social categories**: 'Childhood' actually hides a range of different categorisations of people who are 'not adults' (babies, toddlers, infants, teenagers, youth …). The status and experience of being a teenager is very different to being an infant – so should we classify them all as children?

    Come to that, the status of 'teenager' – as **Thomas Hine** (*The Rise And Fall of the American Teenager*, 2000) demonstrates – is a relatively modern invention (the word was apparently first used in the USA during the Second World War – 'teenagers' didn't make much of an appearance in Britain until the mid to late 1950s).

What this shows is that societies develop beliefs about age categories and our understanding of their meaning helps us to interpret not only age differences, but also concepts of *age-appropriate behaviour*. For example, while it may be considered appropriate for a male child to cry, crying may be considered inappropriate for an adult male – although, just to confuse things further, there are times – at a funeral for example – when it isn't inappropriate for a man to cry. Although this makes tracking changes in our general perception of childhood a little difficult, we can begin by looking at a **historical dimension**. The work of **Philip Aries** (*Centuries of Childhood*, 1962) stimulated debate about the changing status of childhood and children and, although it has been extensively criticised in recent times (for example, **Martin Shipman**'s, 'When Childhood Was Discovered'), it is useful for our purpose

because it helps us focus on a number of questions relating to the historical analysis of childhood.

- **Recent construction**: Aries argues that in Western Europe the idea of childhood is a relatively modern one that developed over the past 300 or so years – effectively with the change from pre-industrial to industrial society. While there were (obviously) 'non-adults' in pre-industrial society, Aries argues they were neither called 'children', nor treated in ways we, nowadays, would recognise as 'childhood'.

- **Religious beliefs**: Changing beliefs about children developed as the Christian Church popularised the idea of children as 'fragile creatures of God' – in effect, childhood became defined as a phase of 'uncorrupted innocence', to be nurtured and encouraged. Children were not to be seen as little adults, but as something different and perhaps highly vulnerable – human beings who needed the protection of adults.

- **Physical and cultural separation**: Gradually, children started to live in a separate sphere from adults. As the education system developed (from the mid-nineteenth century onwards) children were treated differently to adults. As Aries puts it, they were 'progressively removed from adult society'.

Whether or not we agree with Aries' argument about the 'invention of childhood' – **Linda Pollack** (*Forgotten Children: Parent–Child Relations from 1500 to 1900*, 1983) suggests the view there was no conception of childhood in pre-industrial society was mistaken – there seems little reason to doubt that, over the past few hundred years, the status of children has changed in a number of ways. As **Archard** (*Children: Rights and Childhood*, 1993) helpfully notes, 'Aries claims to disclose an *absence* of the idea of childhood, whereas he should only claim to find a *dissimilarity* in ideas about childhood between past and present'.

We can, therefore, identify a number of historical changes in the status of children.

Attitudes

If we accept (and as sociologists I think we should) that, according to **Chris Jenks** (*Childhood*, 1996), 'childhood is not a natural but a social construct', it follows that its status is, to a large degree, determined by adults. Jenks notes two basic historical statuses of children that have existed, in one form or another, over the past 300 years.

- The **Dionysian child** is one constructed as 'a wilful material force ... impish and harbouring a potential evil'. This view suggests adults must control children in ways that prevent them falling victim to their essential 'badness'.

- The **Apollonian child**, on the other hand, is constructed as 'angelic, innocent, untainted by the world it has recently entered. It has a natural goodness and a clarity of vision that must be encouraged, enabled, facilitated, not crushed or beaten into submission'. This view suggests the role of adults is to create the conditions under which children can develop their essential 'goodness'.

These ideas reflect a basic uncertainty, as a society, about how to understand the status of children – at one and the same time we feel they need to be both controlled by adults and given the freedom to develop 'naturally', away from the corrupting influence of adult society. As **Hendrick** ('Constructions and Reconstructions of British Childhood', 1990) suggests, the status of children has undergone a number of radical transformations since 1800.

- The **delinquent child** started to appear in the mid-nineteenth century, reflecting concerns about how to deal with law-breaking children and provide protection and care. One solution was:

- The **schooled child**, involving ideas about the need for education (moral and spiritual as well as technical – the skills of literacy and numeracy required for the newly-emerging industrial culture).

- The **psycho-medical child** was constructed towards the end of the nineteenth century with the development of psychological theories and techniques. This perception stressed the uniqueness of childhood status and constructed childhood as a time of biological and emotional 'stress and turmoil'. At this time the concept of *adolescence* as a distinctive phase of childhood started to develop, through the work of writers like **G. Stanley Hall** (*Adolescence*, 1904).

- The **welfare child** emerged in the twentieth century, stressing both the vulnerability of children and ideas about delinquent behaviour being shaped by neglect, poverty and so forth.

- The **psychological child** has emerged in the late twentieth century and focuses on the idea of children having their own needs which, in turn, should be protected and encouraged.

Legal protections

The changing status of children has been reflected in their changing legal status – not simply in terms of legal definitions of 'children' (an 1833 Royal Commission, for example, decided childhood officially ended at 13) but also through laws designed to either protect children or control their behaviour. The nineteenth century, for example, saw the introduction of *Factory Acts* designed to limit the type and length of work done by children as well as laws governing a child's education.

The regulation of childhood has, of course, continued throughout the last and into the present century – in 1972, for example, the minimum school leaving age was raised to 16 (with a suggestion it may soon be raised to 18 or even 19). Children aged 13 to 16 can legally work 12 hours a week during school terms and not after 7 pm. Sexual behaviour is also regulated by law and the table below demonstrates cultural variations (even within the UK) in the age of consent.

Children's Rights: The latter part of the twentieth century has witnessed moves – both official and unofficial – to develop concepts of 'Children's Rights' – the idea that children, like adults, have fundamental human rights that should be both stated and protected.

The United Nations 'Declaration on the Rights of the Child' (1959), for example, defined the minimum rights a child should expect and in 1989 the Convention on the Rights of the Child laid down rights that included:

Article 6: All children have the right to life. Governments should ensure children survive and develop healthily.

Article 16: Children have a right to privacy. The law should protect them from attacks against their way of life, their good name, their families and their homes.

Age of consent: selected countries			
Country	Male–Female	Male–Male	Female–Female
Canada	14	18	14
Chile	12	18	18
France	15	15	15
Guyana	13	Illegal	Illegal
Iran	Must be married	Illegal	Illegal
Korea	13	13	13
Saudi Arabia	Must be married	Illegal	Illegal
Spain	13	13	13
Tunisia	20	Illegal	Illegal
G. Britain	16	16	16
N. Ireland	17	17	17

Article 31: All children have a right to relax and play, and to join in a range of activities.

Article 34: The Government should protect children from sexual abuse.
(Source: www.un.org)

Growing it yourself: children's rights

A simple and satisfying task is to design and create a poster, illustrating 'changing constructions of childhood', based on the ideas of **Jenks** and **Hendrick**.

Digging deeper

To complete this section we can look at reasons for the changing status of children and childhood. In the early industrial period (seventeenth and eighteenth centuries), for example, we can note:

- **Economic roles**: As the family group stopped producing things (and turned into consumers), children lost their economic role.

- **Separation of home and workplace**: 'The home' became a place different to 'the workplace' and, with the loss of their economic role, women and children developed new and different statuses.

- **The sexual division of labour**: The removal of women's economic role led to an increasing focus on their 'natural' role as mother and child-rearer, responsible for primary childcare within the family.

- **Changing perceptions of children**: Hand-in-hand with altered adult statuses, the social identities and status of children changed – they became people in need of

'care, attention and nurture' (something which, rather conveniently, fitted the new role assigned to women).

Governments in the nineteenth century also took an interest in the status of children, for a number of reasons.

- **Education** was needed to establish basic levels of literacy and numeracy for the new industrial enterprises. Since families were largely unable to perform this task, separate institutions (schools) developed which served to define and prolong childhood.

- **Moral conformity**: Education was also seen as a way of socialising the unruly working classes.

- **Economic productivity**: The use of machinery in factories made adult workers more productive and reduced the need for (unskilled) child labour.

- **Moral entrepreneurs** (people and organisations who take it on themselves to 'protect the morals' of others) protested about the exploitation of children. This, coupled with ideas about the 'uncorrupted innocence' of childhood, led to legal and social changes to their status.

In the twentieth century:

- **Social science** developed to underline the concept of childhood as involving various stages of social, psychological and biological development. This hardened the division between full adult membership of society and the period in which the child 'learns how to achieve full adulthood'.

- **Attitudes**: In some ways, contemporary attitudes to childhood reflect an extreme reversal of pre-industrial concepts; moral concerns about the 'increasing corruption of childhood innocence', through such things as child abuse and exposure to sex and violence in the media, reflect how childhood is seen as a somewhat idyllic period before the cares and responsibilities of adulthood.

- **Education**: This is increasingly promoted – especially at the post-16 level. The 2004 Labour Government has set a target of 50% of all 18 year olds attending University (compared with approximately 15% in 1974). This, again, serves to redefine notions of

childhood, based on the dependent status of children.

Contemporary trends: Disappearing Childhood? Two (opposed) contemporary perceptions of children and childhood can be summarised by, firstly, looking briefly at the work of those (*liberationalists*) who argue children should not be seen as a separate, segregated, category of human beings; rather, they argue children should be given the same rights as adults.

A second position in this debate is characterised by writers such as **Neil Postman** (*The Disappearance of Childhood*, 1985) who argues:

Discussion point: children's liberation

In the 1960s and 1970s, the debate over 'children's rights' developed into calls for children's liberation. The following table lists a number of rights put forward by John Holt (*Escape From Childhood*, 1974) and Richard Farson (*Birthrights*, 1974)

Tick those you agree/disagree with and compare your views with those of the rest of your class (be prepared to argue your case).

A child has a right to:	Agree	Disagree
Exercise choice in their own living arrangements		
Information that is accessible to adults		
Choose belief systems including to educate oneself		
Sexual freedom		
Work		
Vote		
Freedom from physical punishment		
Justice		
Own property		
Travel independently		
Whatever drugs their elders use		

Modern communications (**Postman** cites television, but recent developments in mobile phone technology and the Internet would also apply here) are blurring the distinction between childhood and adult, changing the status of children, as he describes it, to one where 'adults have a different conception of what sort of person a child is, a conception not unlike that which prevailed in the 14th century: that they are miniature adults'. **Television**, for example, represents 'open admission technology' – it cannot differentiate between adults and children; the latter, therefore, are exposed to images of adulthood (sex, violence, news and so forth) that, according to Postman, diminish both adult and child abilities to decide where childhood ends and adulthood begins. Children, in this respect, become more like adults in terms of their criminality, sexuality and dress, and adults, in our culture at least, become more like 'children' in their equation of 'youthfulness' with health, vitality and excitement. Will a point be reached when the distinction between them disappears?

Internet technology has arguably closed this gap further since it effectively allows children access to information and images that, in former times, were denied until adulthood.

Finally, one area in which the status of children is becoming increasingly blurred is in the workplace. The growth of **service sector industries** (such as fast-food outlets) has created a growth in (illegal) child labour.

Child labour crackdown: Sean Coughlan: April, 2002
Source: http://news.bbc.co.uk/2/hi/uk_news/education/1949145.stm

When you hear of illegal child labour, the leafy suburbs of Surrey might not be the first place that springs to mind. But in recent months, the county has seen some of the highest-profile prosecutions for child labour offences so far seen in the United Kingdom.

A McDonald's restaurant, Woolworths, Tesco, Safeway, Burger King, Odeon Cinemas, Heritage Hotels, Fourbuoys and Thorpe Park amusement park have all been successfully prosecuted.

What is believed to be the biggest ever fine for such offences was imposed on a McDonalds' franchise holder in Camberley. The £12,400 penalty followed an investigation that found school pupils working up to 16 hours a day, in what was described as a 'fast-food sweatshop'.

 Growing it yourself: child status

Make a list of possible reasons why the status of children has changed in the past 100 years.

Select four reasons from your list and write 100 words on each explaining how they illustrate the changing position of children in our society.

INTRODUCTION

The focus of this opening section is an examination of different explanations of the relationship between ownership and control of the mass media and, in order to do this, we need to begin by thinking about how the mass media can be defined.

Defining mass media

⚠ Preparing the ground

We can start by breaking down the concept of a 'mass media' into its constituent parts. A **medium**, is a 'channel of communication' – a means through which people send and receive information. The printed word, for example, is a medium; when we read a newspaper or magazine, something is communicated to us in some way. Similarly, electronic forms of communication – television, telephones, film and such like – are **media** (the plural of medium). **Mass** means 'many' and what we are interested in here is how and why different forms of media are used to transmit to – and be received by – large numbers of people (the audience).

Mass media, therefore, refers to channels involving communication with large numbers of people. This is traditionally seen as 'one-to-many' communication – 'one' person (the author of a book, for example), communicates to many people (their readers) at the same time. This deceptively simple definition does, of course, hide a number of complexities – such as, how large does an audience have to be before it qualifies as 'mass'?

In addition to thinking about a basic definition of the term, we can note how **Dutton** et al (*Studying the Media*, 1998) suggests that, *traditionally* (an important qualification I will develop in a moment), the mass media has been **differentiated** from other types of communication (such as interpersonal communication that occurs on a one-to-one basis) in terms of four essential characteristics.

- **Distance**: Communication between those who send and receive messages (media-speak for information) is impersonal, lacks immediacy and is one way (from the producer/creator of the information to the consumer/audience). When I watch a film, for example, no matter how emotionally involved I become in the action, I can't directly affect what's unfolding on the screen.

- **Technology**: Mass communication requires a vehicle, such as a television receiver, a method of printing and so forth, that allows messages to be sent and received.

- **Scale**: One feature of a mass medium, as we've noted, is it involves *simultaneous* communication with many people; for example, as I sit in my living room watching Chelsea play Manchester United on TV, the same behaviour is being reproduced in thousands of other living rooms across the country.

- **Commodity**: An interesting feature of mass communication – in our society at least – is that it comes at a price. I can watch football on TV, for example, if I can afford a television, a license fee (to watch BBC or ITV) or a subscription to something like Sky Sports if it's on satellite or cable.

WARM UP: IDENTIFYING MASS MEDIA

Using the following table as a guide, in pairs or small groups, identify as many media as possible and decide (by ticking (✓) or crossing (✗) the appropriate box) whether or not they qualify as a *mass medium* (of the ones I have identified, television does qualify but the telephone, for example, doesn't).

Digging deeper

In the above exercise, you will have found it reasonably easy to identify a range of mass media. However, I suspect you will have identified some forms of communication (such as mobile phones and email) that don't fit easily (if at all) into traditional definitions, mainly because they have the capacity to be both:

- **interpersonal** ('one-to-one') communication and

- **mass** ('one-to-many') communication.

Depending on how it is used, for example, email can involve exchanging interpersonal messages with friends and family ('Hi, how are you?') or sending one message to many thousands – potentially millions – of people; customers of on-line retailers, such as Amazon (www.amazon.co.uk), for example, can request email notification of special offers and so forth. Unrequested mass emails – commonly known as 'Spam' – also come into this category.

In defining the mass media, therefore, we have hit upon something that, as recently as 25 years ago, wouldn't have been a problem; namely, the development of *computer networks*. The ability to link computer technology (to create something like the

Medium	Distance	Technology	Scale	Commodity
Television	✓	✓	✓	✓
Telephone	✗	✓	✗	✓
Daily newspaper	✓			✓
Mobile telephone		✓		✓
Further media?				

Internet or mobile phone networks) has created a subtle – but incredibly important – change in the way we both define and conceptualise the mass media. To make matters even more complicated, computer networks open up the potential for '**many-to-many**' communication, where a mass audience can, simultaneously, interact and communicate with each other. In other words, a mass medium based on interpersonal communication.

To clarify this idea, think about things like:

- **Internet chatrooms**. These conform to three of the components of a 'mass medium' identified above (technology, scale and commodity). However, the 'distance' component is a problem. This is because, rather confusingly, a chatroom can, simultaneously, involve one-to-one, one-to-many and many-to-many communication.

- **Peer-to-peer** networks involve using software to link individual computers, such that anyone connected to the network can exchange information directly with anyone else. In the workplace, for example, this can mean any number of people can contribute to the same piece of work at the same time. We can also note, however, this type of network can also be used to breech copyright laws through the (illegal) sharing of music and films.

In the light of these developments, therefore, we need to redefine the concept of mass media by creating a distinction between:

- **old mass media**, such as television, books and magazines, that involve 'one-to-many' communication, based on a one-

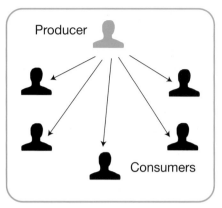

'Old' forms of mass media involve one-way communication between a producer and a mass audience.

way process of producers creating information that is transmitted to large numbers of consumers, and

- **new mass media**, such as peer-to-peer networks, involving 'many-to-many' communication based on two-way communication with participants as both producers and consumers of information.

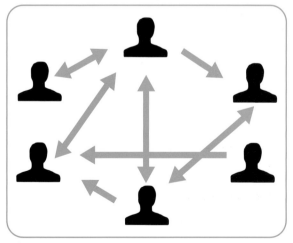

'New' forms of mass media can involve two-way communication within a mass audience who are both producers and consumers.

Crosbie ('What Is New Media?', 2002) argues that new (mass) media have characteristics that, when combined, make them very different to other forms of mass media. These include:

- **Technology**: They cannot exist without the appropriate (computer) technology.

- **Personalisation**: Individualised messages (either tailored to the particular needs of those receiving them or having the appearance of being so constructed) can be simultaneously delivered to vast numbers of people.

- **Collective control**: Each person in a network has, potentially, the ability to share, shape and change the content of the information being exchanged.

Crosbie uses the following example to illustrate this idea:

> Imagine visiting a newspaper website and seeing not just the bulletins and major stories you wouldn't have known about, but also the rest of that edition customized to your unique needs and interests. Rather than every reader seeing the same edition, each reader sees an edition simultaneously individualized to their interests and generalized to their needs.

Ownership and control

⚠ Preparing the ground

The distinction just drawn between old and new media forms is important when considering the relationship between media ownership and control, since the old and new media involve potentially different relationships between owners, controllers, producers and consumers. To understand this, we need, initially, to define what we mean by **owners** These, as you might expect, are the people who own whatever medium in being used to communicate information. We can identify two *basic* types of media ownership.

- **Private ownership**, where companies are owned by individuals, families, shareholders and so forth. Rupert Murdoch, for example, owns a controlling interest in News Corporation, a company that publishes books, films and magazines and broadcasts satellite TV programmes, among many other things.

- **State ownership**: The BBC, for example, is state owned – it is funded by the taxpayer and doesn't have private owners or shareholders. As an aside, however, we can note there are different *types* of state ownership around the world. In somewhere like China, for example, the government directly controls media content (the media is, in effect, state-run); the BBC, on the other hand, is overseen by a Board of Governors who, although directly appointed by the government, have a degree of independence from both the state and direct political control.

Ownership is significant here because owners have the potential to decide what sort of information an audience will be allowed to receive. For example, private owners may decide not to publish a book critical of their company, whereas state-owned companies may be subject to political control and censorship over what they can broadcast or publish.

Controllers are the people who actually run (or manage) a company on a day-to-day basis – the editor of a newspaper or the head of a film studio, for example. Usually – especially when talking about very large media companies – managers are not outright owners of the company for which they work (although they may own shares in that company).

Debates over the relative importance of ownership and control have traditionally been framed in terms of the significance of a *separation* between ownership of, and management roles within, media companies to prevent, in **Paul Mobbs'** ('Media Regulation and Convergence', 2002) phrase 'Undue influence over, or bias in, content'. In other words, in this section we are going to examine the extent to which there is a separation between the roles of owners and managers (controllers) within the mass media that, in turn, relates to debates about the control of information.

In basic terms, those writers who argue owners are the most significant players in the media industry suggest they use their control over information to show the world in a particular light (one favourable to their own particular viewpoint). On the other hand, those who argue managers are most

significant are suggesting this creates a diversity of media involving different forms and sources of information, such that audiences are able to pick and choose information to suit their own particular tastes and, indeed, prejudices.

Digging deeper

We can dig a little deeper into the background to this debate, prior to examining some sociological explanations of the relationship between ownership and control, by identifying and explaining a number of significant ideas.

Concentration of ownership refers to the idea that the ownership of various media (television, books and newspapers for example) is increasingly restricted to a relatively small number of companies. Table 3.1, for example, demonstrates this idea in terms of the ownership of national newspapers.

In the wider global context, **Nenova** et al's ('Who Owns the Media?', 2001) examination of media in 97 countries found that 'almost universally the largest media firms are owned by the government or by private families'.

The concentration of media ownership (on both a national and global scale) is important for a couple of reasons.

- **Product diversity**: If the number and range of information sources is restricted, audiences increasingly come to depend on a small number of media corporations for that information. However, since even in terms of the above table, British consumers have a choice of nine national daily newspapers, the concentration of ownership doesn't necessarily affect the range of products on offer (Table 3.1).

Daily Mail, Mail on Sunday	Daily Mail and General Trust
Daily and *Sunday Mirror, People*	Trinity Mirror
Daily Star, Daily and *Sunday Express*	Northern and Shell
Daily and *Sunday Telegraph*	Telegraph Group
Guardian, Observer	Guardian Media Group
Independent, Independent on Sunday	Independent Newspapers
News of the World, Sun, Times, Sunday Times	News International

Table 3.1 English newspaper ownership 2003
(Source: Department for Culture, Media and Sport)

The question here, therefore, is, does concentration affect information diversity?

- **Information diversity**: **Robert McChesney** (*Rich Media, Poor Democracy: Communication Politics in Dubious Times*, 2000), for example, argues we have the 'appearance of choice' in various media – lots of different products all selling much the same sort of (limited range) of ideas. As he argues about MTV: 'it's all a commercial. Sometimes it's an advert paid for by a company to sell a product. Sometimes a video for a music company to sell music … Sometimes a set filled with trendy clothes to sell a look that includes products on that set'.

- **Compaine** ('Mergers, Divestitures and the Internet', 2000), on the other hand, argues such an interpretation is mistaken – the global trend is not necessarily for an increased concentration of media companies. In addition, he argues media organisations are not static entities – they develop, grow, evolve – and disappear.

In 'The Myths of Encroaching Global Media Ownership', 2001, for example, he notes how the dominant global media companies in the 1980s were not necessarily the dominant media companies in the year 2000. For example, ten years ago Amazon.com didn't exist. In 2005 it's one of the world's largest media outlets – will it still exist in 2015?

Conglomeration is a second important aspect of media ownership and involves the idea the same company may, through a process of *diversification*, develop interests across different media. For example, Silvio Berlusconi (the current Italian Prime Minister), through his ownership of Fininvest, has a diverse range of media interests – television, book, newspaper and magazine publishing and so forth. One important – and useful if you are a large, transnational company (one that operates in a number of countries) – aspect of conglomeration is **diagonal integration**. *Cross-media ownership* can be used enhance the profile and profits of different businesses. Rupert Murdoch, for example, used ownership of *The Sun* newspaper to promote his satellite company Sky Broadcasting (later called BSkyB after it took over a competitor company) in its early years when it was losing money. The Sun ran competitions to win satellite dishes and subscriptions, gave

Sky and terrestrial (BBC and ITV) programme schedules equal space (even though Sky had a fraction of their audience) and publicised Sky through feature and entertainment stories.

Murdoch also wanted to attract subscribers by offering 'first-run' films before they were available to rent. However, to protect cinema and rental markets, Hollywood Studios refused to allow TV companies to show their films until at least two years after their initial release.

Murdoch solved this problem by buying a film studio (20th Century Fox) to supply Sky with films – which eventually forced other studios to follow suit.

In the next section (dealing with the relationship between the mass media and ideology) we will pick up and develop the above ideas in more detail, but to complete this section we can outline a number of different perspectives on the ownership and control debate, starting with those suggesting ownership is most significant and ending with those arguing the reverse – that control is most significant.

Traditional (Instrumental) Marxism

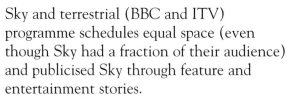 ## Preparing the ground

This variation of Marxism takes a distinct position on the relationship between ownership and control of the media, based on **social class**. An individual's economic position in society (their class) influences the way they see and experience the social world. For instrumental Marxists, society is seen in terms of a particular class structure involving a distinction between the bourgeoisie and proletariat (upper and lower classes). Those who own the means of production (the bourgeoisie) are the most powerful and influential grouping in any society and they try to keep their powerful position through their ownership and control of **ideological institutions**. Cultural institutions, such as the media, are used as a tool (or *instrument*) to spread ideas favourable to the bourgeoisie throughout society. Writers such as **Milliband** (*The State In Capitalist Society*, 1973), argue the ruling class has a common **economic status** (as owners and controllers – people who are generally drawn from the same social class) and **cultural background**, created and reinforced through education (public schools, Oxford and Cambridge Universities etc.), family networks, interlocking directorships (where the same person is a director of numerous different companies), media ownership and so forth. **Scott** (*National Patterns of Corporate Power*, 1991) for example, noted the significance of banks and insurance companies in the USA and Europe as centres of corporate networks through which businesses develop and are controlled.

Digging deeper

From this perspective the relationship between ownership and control of the media is straightforward.

- **Owners** have ultimate control over a company – they decide, for example, who to employ to run their businesses.
- **Managers** only 'control' a business (such

135

as a newspaper) in the sense they oversee its operation. The editor of a newspaper may control things like the stories appearing each day, the hiring and firing of employees and so forth. The owner, however, ultimately controls the political stance of the paper, the type of audience it aims to reach and the like.

Ownership and control, therefore, needs to be seen as part of the same process, which has two, interconnected, objectives.

• **Economic**: One objective, you probably

won't be too surprised to learn, is usually to make profits. However, a second (in some cases more important) objective is:

• **Ideological**, in the sense of trying to control how people see the social world. This aspect is significant because it is designed to create the conditions under which profit is not only created – and kept in private hands – but is seen as legitimate ('right and proper'). In other words one objective, common to both owners and controllers, is to protect and enhance the interests of a capitalist ruling

 Growing it yourself: editorial control?

Identify some of the ways owners try to ensure employees reflect their views (the following extracts may give you some ideas to get you thinking).

Investigating the Media (1991), Paul Trowler

The following was cut from Trowler's book (for HarperCollins – owned by News Corporation)

Source: http://www.lancs.ac.uk/staff/trowler/ressite/cut.htm#murdoch

> Murdoch is well known for intervening in editorial policy. He sacked Harold Evans, editor of The Times, after disagreements over policy. Frank Giles, former editor of the Sunday Times, said Murdoch would make a point of dropping into his office just to check on the first copies of the paper. Fred Emery, home editor of the Times in 1982 reported Murdoch as saying 'I give instructions to my editors all round the world, why shouldn't I in London?'.

'Patten and Murdoch Quarrel – David and Goliath Again?' (1998), Terry Boardman

> Worried that Patten's criticisms of China in his forthcoming book 'East and West – The last Governor of Hong Kong' would upset Beijing and thus spoil the strenuous efforts he had been making to reingratiate himself with the Chinese ... Murdoch, with his current audience of 36 million Chinese viewers and a potential further 240 million in mind, promptly ordered HarperCollins to drop the book.

'Newland Unleashed', *The Guardian***: 15/11/04**

> 'Black [the ex-owner of the Daily Telegraph] is not there anymore, the new owners do not interfere, it is basically down to us in a way it hasn't been for many years' ... The Barclays [the new owners of The Telegraph], he says, have not laid down a clear political line. 'There are still occasional conversations. I might call about something. Normal, friendly, conversations'.

Examples:

• Hiring people who reflect owner's views.

• Not hiring journalists who don't reflect the owner's views.

class and this is achieved, according to instrumental Marxists, through the media. Because the media is a major source of information about society it is used as a **tool** (or instrument) through which ideas, beliefs and behaviours are manipulated. Ownership and control, therefore, is used to create a picture of the social world beneficial to the interests of the most powerful people in society – and a key idea here is **false consciousness**. By their ability to control and limit the information people receive, a ruling class is able to control how people think – both directly and indirectly – about the things happening in society.

An example of false consciousness can be demonstrated with respect to the war in Iraq. From this perspective people were manipulated into supporting the war on the basis of Iraq having 'weapons of mass destruction' (which, we were repeatedly informed, could be used to launch an attack 'within 45 minutes'). We will return to this idea when, in the next section, we look at the relationship between the media and ideology in more detail.

Neo-(hegemonic) Marxism

⚠ Preparing the ground

Neo-Marxists such **E.O. Wright** (*Classes*, 1985) take a different approach to their traditional counterparts and, initially, the main points to note relating to this perspective are:

- **Social class** is *not* a static (unchanging) classification system; rather, it's seen (or conceptualised if you prefer) as a dynamic system of shifting and changing social relationships. This suggests:
- **Conflict**, divisions and contradictions occur *within* a dominant (or ruling) class.

Discussion questions: evaluating this perspective

To help you reflect critically about this perspective, think about and discuss the following questions.

- **Conspiracy theory**: Does this perspective develop a conspiratorial view of the media and the role of owners? Why do some parts of the media criticise the activities of powerful individuals, companies and governments?
- **Ruling class**: Do all members of the bourgeoisie have the same interests and, if so, what are they and how do media owners know what they are?
- **Choice**: In terms of old media there is a range of choices available, giving audiences access to different viewpoints; many people also have access to a wide range of new media. How easy is it for a ruling class to control the way people think when such choices are available?
- **Audience**: Are media consumers simply passive recipients of whatever owners want to publish, or are they more sophisticated and reflecting? Are some parts of the media audience (such as children) more open to influence than others?

A simple example here might be to note how some parts of the bourgeoisie in our society are pro-Europe while others are anti-Europe.

- **Class associations** can involve ethnic and gender dimensions (for example, individuals from some ethnic groups may be economically successful while seeing themselves, culturally, as not belonging to a middle or upper class).

- **Professionals** and **intellectuals** (the upper middle classes) have significant roles in the class structure. They occupy, according to **Poulantzas** (1975), 'contradictory class positions' – neither wholly bourgeois nor wholly proletarian. This, for neo-Marxists, is a significant idea in any explanation of the relationship between media owners and controllers.

 Digging deeper

In developing the above ideas we can note how neo-Marxists stress the distinction between:

- **social structures** – the web of social relationships surrounding us and

- **consciousness** – people's ability to interpret behaviour in many different ways.

They argue this is an important distinction because it is impossible for any individual (let alone a very large group such as a ruling class) to directly control how people think and behave (the 'conspiracy aspect' of traditional Marxism). Rather, they use the concept of *hegemony* to show how both owners and controllers are locked into a (structural) relationship that is, in one sense, mutually beneficial.

- **Owners** have to make profits – this is their guiding principle (since if businesses are unprofitable they may cease to exist).

- **Managers** also see profitability as important, since their jobs, salaries and lifestyles depend on it.

In other words, both owners and controllers have a basic *common interest* that binds them together, expressed in terms of **core values**. They are likely to share, for example, beliefs about the importance of profits, which in turn presupposes a (fundamental) belief in capitalist economic systems. Marginal disagreements may occur between these groups over such things as the most efficient way to make profits, but not over the basic principle of the need for profitability.

Although media owners and professionals share a common cause in promoting and preserving certain basic values this doesn't necessarily mean – as we have just noted – they will always agree on the best way to promote and preserve such values. From this perspective, managers enjoy **relative autonomy** (a certain amount of freedom to make decisions). Transnational media companies, for example, are too large and complex to be easily controlled by a single owner/board of owners on a day-to-day basis. They employ people (managers) who can be trusted to:

- **Reflect their views**: Editors who insist on ignoring the policies laid down by their employers are likely to find themselves unemployed, unless they:

- **Make profits**: As long as it is legal (and sometimes if it is not) the key principle is profitability – some modern media owners may not care too much about the behaviour and activities of their managers as long as the money continues to roll in.

Discussion questions: evaluating this perspective

To help you reflect critically about this perspective, think about and discuss the following questions.

- **Owners**: Is the significance of their role exaggerated? For example, many media companies are owned by large pension funds, making the role of managers more significant (the only interest a pension fund has in the running of a company is whether or not it produces a good return on investment).
- **New media**: How do things like the Internet fit into this equation? If people can effectively 'search the globe' for information, does this make questions of media ownership and control irrelevant?

Pluralism

⚠ Preparing the ground

An alternative way of looking at the relationship between ownership and control is a framework that stresses how social groups compete against each other in the economic market place. For example, two types of group we could note are:

- **interest groups**, an example of which might be a *business* (such as a publishing company) pursuing some economic or social objective
- **status groups**, for example, a *Trade Union* publishing information specific to the members of a particular occupation. One aspect of the Union's role might be to promote and enhance the reputation (status) of its membership.

From this perspective, societies involve groups pursuing their own (sectional) interests and, in so doing, they create:

- **explicit competition** involving, for example, different newspaper groups competing for readers
- **implicit competition** involving political groups promoting different economic, political or cultural views they want reflected in the media.

For pluralists, competition is based on the desire for *power*, which can, for example, be expressed in terms of:

- **economic** power – such as making profits or gaining market share
- **political** power – such as influencing decisions made by governments.

⚠ Digging deeper

Media owners are clearly powerful players in any society since they are in a position to have their views heard. However, Pluralists argue those who control the day-to-day running of the media are also powerful, for a couple of reasons. Modern ('joint-stock') media companies tend to be owned by groups of shareholders rather than by all-powerful individuals. **James Burnham** (*The Managerial Revolution*, 1943), for example, argued that, where no single shareholder had overall control of a business, this meant directors and managers were the main policy-makers. Thus, the day-to-day running of a business was in the hands of a **technocratic managerial elite** – people whose job it was to run a business in the best interests of the shareholders. This is a powerful group, according to pluralists, because their job depends on knowing what an audience wants and being able to provide it.

To survive, a business must compete successfully in a market place which means consumers (the people who buy the product being sold – or not as the case may be)

influence the behaviour of an organisation: if consumers don't like – or more importantly buy – what's on offer the seller either improves or changes their product or they go out of business.

For pluralists, the private ownership of the media is significant because it promotes

Discussion questions: evaluating this perspective

To help you reflect critically about this perspective, think about and discuss the following questions.

- **Murdock** and **Golding** ('Capitalism, Communication and Class Relations', 1977) argue Pluralists overstate the distinction between owners and managers – do you think the interests of these two groups really are as separate as Pluralists claim? Although owners may not *personally* oversee the content of the media they own, how likely is an owner to employ managers opposed to their social and economic interests?
- **Shareholding**: Are individual owners more powerful than pluralists suggest? Although modern companies may have many shareholders, it's still possible for individuals to control a business. Rupert Murdoch, for example, has a 35% share in News Corporation, giving him control over the company. As James Curren ('Global Media Concentration', 2000), notes:

   The power potentially at the disposal of media owners tends to be exerted in a one-sided way . . . this power is qualified and constrained in many ways – by . . . consumers and staff, the suppliers of news, regulators, rival producers, the wider cultural patterns of society. But it is simply naïve to imagine that it does not exist.

- **Old and new media**: Although the development of the Internet makes it more difficult now, than in the past, for owners to control what their audience see, read and hear, old media (such as newspapers and television) may have far larger audiences than most new media; they may also be *trusted* more by the general public as sources of information. How significant are new media, therefore, in ensuring a diversity of views and opinions in our society?
- **Diversity**: Does media diversity guarantee choice? For example, if I want to watch reality TV shows (like *Big Brother*), I have a wide range of programmes from which to choose on various channels. However, does this 'choice' alter the fact these programmes are basically offering slight variations on the same theme? This idea also leads to questions of:
- **Regulation**: To what extent should governments be involved in the oversight and regulation of media companies and the activities of their owners? **Richard Collins** ('Comments on the Consultation on Media Ownership Rules', 2002), for example, argues:

   Promoting effective competition will not necessarily achieve pluralism and diversity . . . the potential economies of scope and scale in the media sector may mean that supply can efficiently be provided by few, or very few, firms. Accordingly, regulatory action to ensure pluralism and diversity is likely to be required.

competition and *diversity*. As **Bernard** and **McDermott** ('Media Ownership Rules', 2002) put it: 'Current media ownership rules in the UK prevent any one entity acquiring excessive influence in the sector, thereby ensuring plurality of voice and diversity of content'.

Different perspectives on the nature of the relationship between ownership and control of the media are, as we have just seen, significant in terms of both how the media is controlled and the information created and distributed to audiences. In the next section, therefore, we need to explore the significance of this 'information distribution' in terms of the relationship between the mass media and ideology

Ideology
Introduction

In the previous section we touched upon a number of ideas relating to different explanations of the relationship between the mass media and ideology and in this section we can develop these ideas to provide a more in-depth analysis of the ideological role of the mass media.

⚠ Preparing the ground

The concept of *ideology* has a relatively short – but chequered – history. First coined in the early nineteenth century (by a Frenchman, Destutt de Tracy), its original meaning was the 'science of ideas' – a science to be used to evaluate the truth or falsity of different ideas. However, somewhat ironically, the term came to have a different meaning in the twentieth century; if something was 'ideological' it was held to be based on *untested ideas* and was, as **Blake** ('What is Systematic Ideology?', 2004) notes, not to be believed because it involved a *partial*, or *biased*, account – a meaning that, in some respects, we find attached to present day uses of the concept.

More recently, postmodernists have tended to reject its use (preferring instead to use concepts like *narrative* and *discourse* because of their more precise definition and usage – although the term is still implicitly used when postmodernists refer to the idea of *metanarratives*. Whatever you may think about postmodernism, a useful way to understand the concept of ideology is to think about the idea of a *narrative* (or story if you prefer).

From this exercise, we can identify a number of characteristics of ideologies.

- **Interrelated beliefs**: The important idea here is the beliefs we hold about something are related to each other. For example, you may believe the purpose of education is to achieve qualifications. This basic (or core) belief will influence other beliefs, such as how to achieve qualifications (through attending school, for example), your relationships with others in the education system and so forth.

- **Norms and values**: Ideologies involve ideas about norms (for example, your family ideology may see it as the norm for parents to raise their own children) and values (you may, for example, believe parents should provide for their children).

- **Truth or falsity**: The ideas that make up a particular ideology don't have to be true – you only have to believe them. It may or may not be true, for example, that the purpose of education is to achieve qualifications, but if you believe this is – or is not – the case it will influence how you behave in school.

- **Collective/personal**: Ideologies can be believed by large numbers of people (for example, many people in our society believe in conservative and socialist political ideologies) or they can be unique, personal, things (you may, for example, believe you were once abducted by aliens from the planet Zilog who, after conducting extensive experiments, then returned you to earth with superior powers of intelligence).

⚠ Digging deeper

We can develop these ideas by noting a couple of definitions that extend the concept in various ways. **Martin Joseph** (*Sociology For Everyone*, 1990), for example, argues ideologies involve:

- **A set of beliefs**.
- **Explanations** for something (for example, why some people are rich and some poor in our society). **Penny Henderson** (*A-Level Sociology*, 1981), for example, notes: 'An ideology is a pattern of ideas, both factual and evaluative [based on our values], which claims to explain and legitimise the social structure and culture of a particular group in society'.

- **Justifications** for people's behaviour (for example, why women, in the main, do the majority of housework in our society). Henderson again notes how ideologies are used 'to justify social actions which are in accordance with that pattern of ideas.'

- **Social groups**, in the sense ideologies are learnt and relate, in some way, to people's behaviour.

- **Mapping**: **Steve Chibnall** (*Law-and-Order News*, 1977) introduces a useful idea to help us understand the concept when he notes: 'Ideological structures permit events to be "mapped", i.e. located within wider contexts and related to similar events'.

In other words, if we think about ideologies as a form of *mental map* that can be used to tell us not only where we have been (our personal and social history) but also the right route to take to get us safely to where we want to go, we start to understand both a function of ideology and, by extension, its power and significance in relation to the mass media.

In relation to this last point, imagine, for example, society is like 'uncharted territory'; to travel around it we can:

- **Experience** it for ourselves. In other words, we map the territory as we go along, creating a *personal ideological map* of the society in which we live.

- **Buy** a map someone else has already created.

If you think about this for a moment, we actually combine these two things as we move through society. On the one hand, people (such as parents and friends) socialise us, using the mental maps they have developed and, on the other, we experience things 'for ourselves' (self-socialisation); in this respect, we combine the two to create our map of society.

At this point you could be forgiven for wondering what this has to do with the mass media. The answer is the media are a *socialising agency* (a potentially very powerful one) who, in essence, try to sell us **social maps** (or ideologies) that explain where we have been as a society and, potentially, where we should be going.

What we need to do next, therefore, is to look at how different sociological perspectives explain the significance of the mass media's role in creating and perpetuating ideological maps since, as **George Orwell** (*Nineteen Eighty-Four*, 1949) argued: 'Who controls the past controls the future. Who controls the present controls the past.'

Traditional (Instrumental) Marxism

⚠ Preparing the ground

Traditional Marxist perspectives emphasise an important role of the media as being one of *policing the values* of (capitalist) society. In this respect, we can note three initial points:

- **Owners and controllers** are powerful, both in terms of economic ownership ('those who own the physical means of production') and the ownership of ideas (control over the 'mental means of production' – how people think about their world and how they behave on the basis of the beliefs they are encouraged by the media to hold).

- **Ideology**: Media owners are able to control ideas because they control the information people are allowed to have. In other words, the media are not just biased (all forms of ideology, as I have suggested, involve bias because they select certain types of information as important and discard other, alternative sources and interpretations) but *consciously biased*; they propagate a *world view* (or ideology) that explicitly favours the rich and powerful.

- **Manipulation**: This perspective is sometimes portrayed as offering a *manipulative model* of media bias, in the sense those who own and control the media use it as a tool to manipulate public opinion in ways favourable to a ruling class.

From this perspective, therefore, the media is an (increasingly) important agency of *social control*. Media ownership affords the ability to manipulate information and ideas and, in basic terms, if you own a newspaper and want to put across a particular version of events there's no-one to stop you doing just that. Social control, therefore, involves things like:

- **Access**: People whose views reflect those of media owners are given access to the media, whereas those whose views do not are denied access to air their (alternative or contradictory) ideas.

- **Dominant ideology**: Related to questions of access, from this perspective ideas favourable to a ruling class are consistently highlighted and promoted in the media. For example, daily newspapers in our society consistently seek out and promote the views of business leaders, whereas the views of Trade Unionists are rarely featured unless they agree with the line taken by business or they are being subjected to a process of:

- **Marginalisation**: On occasions, alternative views are not simply ignored but explicitly attacked. In other words, alternative interpretations of events are *marginalised* (pushed to the edges of any debate) by being labelled as 'extremist', 'misguided', 'lunatic' and so forth.

The **Glasgow Media Group's** series of *Bad News* books contains a range of examples illustrating how television news, for example, manipulated the way business and trade unions were portrayed during strikes in the 1980s and **Mustafa Hussain** ('Mapping Minorities and their Media', 2002) outlines how ethnic minority groups have been targeted by the Danish media when he notes: 'The media . . . began to display openly an anti-immigrant and anti-Muslim rhetoric . . . ethnic minorities' exclusion and marginalisation in the . . . mainstream media . . . remains quite conspicuous'.

- **Entertainment and diversions** that stop people thinking about how they are exploited and oppressed.

- **Scapegoating**, which, for example, involves identifying particular social groups as the cause of social problems – in the examples here, asylum seekers are portrayed as the cause of 'racial problems'. For instrumental Marxists, scapegoating is designed to create divisions within and between social classes, ethnic groups, genders and the like.

War on minicab sex attackers: 27/11/03 From *The Evening Standard*.

[This report] used one case out of 167 – a rapist jailed last March who happened to have applied for asylum – to illustrate news that police can now take DNA samples from minicab drivers stopped for operating without a licence. The story warned that such sex attacks by 'illegal minicab drivers' are likely to increase over the Christmas period.

SWAN BAKE Asylum seekers steal the Queen's birds for barbecues: July 2003 From *The Sun*.

'Callous asylum seekers are barbecuing the Queen's swans, The Sun can reveal. East European poachers lure the protected Royal birds into baited traps, an official Metropolitan Police report says.'

Steve Knight of the Swan Sanctuary said he could not confirm the incident described ever happened.

Source: http://www.ramproject.org.uk/

Digging deeper

From this perspective, the role of the media is that of ensuring the views and interests of a ruling class are presented to the rest of the population in such a way as to ensure people accept things like social and economic inequality as 'normal and right'. The media, through their owners, are tightly integrated into both economic and political elites in ways that reflect the basic interests of such groups.

The roots of this media perspective can be traced to Germany in the 1930s and the work of the *Frankfurt School* – a group of writers who developed ideas about both the nature of the media in *totalitarian societies* (ones ruled by a dictatorship, such as in Nazi Germany) and, most importantly, concepts of **mass society: Kristina Ross** ('Mass Culture' 1995) notes a *mass society* is one where 'the masses' (as opposed to the small ruling elite) have the following characteristics.

- **Wide dispersal** across a geographic area. People are not in daily face-to-face contact with each other and this creates:
- **Social isolation**: People have little or no meaningful contact or social interaction. What interaction there is (work, for example) is largely *instrumental*. In other words, people lack strong social ties binding them together in communities.
- **Anonymity**: Where social interaction is limited, people rarely feel they are part of a functioning social group, community or society – which is where the media enters the picture; Ross suggests that if society is characterised by 'demographically heterogeneous [mixed] but behaviourally homogenous [similar] groups', the media can be used to create a sense of community and culture.

Hence, the importance of a related idea, namely **mass culture**. The 'culture of the masses', sometimes called – not entirely accurately – *popular* or *low* culture (to distinguish it from the *high culture* of the social elite) is the *social glue* that binds mass society. From this perspective, it provides the 'things in common' (such as values and beliefs) socially isolated individuals can share to create the *illusion* of a common culture – the characteristics of which are:

- **Manufacture**: This culture is artificial, in the sense of not being created by the people who consume it. People are, as **DeFleur** and **Ball-Rokeach** (*Theories of Mass Communication*, 1989) note merely '. . . acted upon by external forces'.
- **Mass Production**: As **Fiske** ('Popular Culture', 1995), *notes*: 'The cultural commodities of mass culture – films, TV shows, CDs, etc. are produced and distributed by an industrialized system whose aim is to maximize profit for the producers and distributors by appealing to as many consumers as possible' – an idea related to the concept of a:
- **Lowest Common Denominator** (LCD): To appeal to 'the masses', cultural products have to be safe, not intellectually demanding and predictable. In other words, to appeal to 'as many consumers as possible' they have to be bland, inoffensive and relatively simple to understand.

Growing it yourself: LCD culture

Using the following table as a guide, identify examples of the 'cultural artefacts' of mass culture (I've identified some to get you started). Briefly explain why each artefact you've identified can be considered part of 'LCD culture'.

Medium	Examples	Explanation
Print	Mass circulation newspapers (*The Sun*, *The Mirror*) *FHM, Nuts, Just 17* ...	Focus on 'celebrity' gossip and trivia.
Electronic	Reality TV shows (*Big Brother, Wife Swap* ...) Soap operas (*Coronation Street, EastEnders* ...) MTV	Subjecting people to intrusive surveillance, ritual humiliation and conflict for our 'entertainment'. Involvement in the lives of 'realistic communities'. Dealing with 'real life' issues (AIDS etc.).

Neo-(Hegemonic) Marxism

Preparing the ground

From this perspective, the role of the media is a complex one that reflects the complexity of class relationships and interests. In this respect, the ideological role of the media is considered in terms of how they act to create and sustain a broad political consensus in society around a set of core or 'fundamental' values. By their ability to do this, the media are able to reflect a variety of different opinions while, at the same time, absorbing critical views that may threaten the stability of the system.

Society as a supermarket

A simple way to understand how this works, is by using the analogy of the supermarket to represent society.

- **Core values**: To shop successfully in the supermarket, you have to accept a number of basic values. These include things like: paying for the food you want; not eating something before you pay for it; not going behind the counters or into the storerooms and so forth – it actually doesn't matter what these core values are, you simply have to recognise they exist (and that you'll be punished in some way if you deviate from them).

- **Conflict values**: Once inside the supermarket, you are faced with an array of choices to make: Premium or Value baked beans? Persil or Daz? Pay by cash or by credit card? These choices are real, but also limited – you can only buy what's on the shelf. If you value freerange eggs but they are not on sale you can't have them. You can, of course, go to the farm shop that's handily situated just next door, but the general process is the same – the eggs may be freerange but they are not free, so even though you're making a choice, core values are still preserved. Supermarket owners prefer you to buy certain things (and the advertising industry depends on convincing you one brand of toothpaste is better than another) and they use certain tricks and techniques to shape your choice – special offers, brighter packaging, eye-catching displays and so forth are all designed to make you choose one product over another.

Keeping the above ideas in mind, we can relate them to an understanding of the ideological role of the media which, from this perspective, is not one of providing a 'common culture for the masses'; the concept of mass society is seen as unrealistic and over-simplified – think of the range of (cultural) choices available within the supermarket, for example.

Rather, the role of the media is considered in terms of how it helps maintain the broad status quo in society (protecting those core values). Just as a major problem for a supermarket owner is how to win customer loyalty (and increase profits), the central problem for a bourgeois (ruling) class is how to win control of people's behaviour in a way that encourages them to contribute to their own (economic) exploitation. The key idea here, therefore, is the **manufacture of consensus**. The media, from this perspective, play a crucial role in both *socialising* audiences and, by extension, *manufacturing* a consensus around which people can be socialised (those core values again). In other words, people have to either accept fully the core values of the society in which they live or, if they try to reject them, be unable to change them. We need to look next, therefore, at how this ideological process of manufacture works.

⚠ Digging deeper

For hegemonic Marxists, the role of the media is an implicitly ideological one – the trick is to influence the way people think about their world while appearing to do no such thing. The manufacture of consensus is, therefore, achieved in a number of ways, using a number of devices.

- **Hierarchy of access**: Traditionally, access to the media (in terms of producing a newspaper, film or television programme and creating information that reaches a wide audience) has been restricted by both cost (producing and distributing a national newspaper is, as you might have guessed, very expensive) and the fact that in order to be 'heard' (as a reporter, for example) you have to work for a media owner.

The development of the **new mass media** has, of course, made this process easier and more accessible, although access restrictions still apply – you need a computer, Internet access, the ability to set up web pages, web logs (or 'blogs' – a type of online diary) and so forth. Having noted this, access to some forms of new media is significantly cheaper and, in a sense, poses a problem for instrumental Marxist perspectives because it holds out the prospect of a much wider spread of views being heard. For hegemonic Marxists, however, this isn't a particularly significant development, one reason for this being:

- **Hierarchies of trust**: Information (such as news) is not equal, in the sense that people place different levels of trust in information depending on how they perceive its source. **Hargreaves** and **Thomas** ('New News, Old News', 2002), for example, found most people (91%) used and respected television news (comparable figures were: 73% for newspapers, 59% for radio and 15% for the internet). In addition, young people were more likely to 'pay attention' to broadcast news 'when they know something interesting is going on'. Having said this, they also found a minority (43%) thought television news represented all sections of society and 'The internet is now the preferred news medium among some younger ethnic minority groups'.

- **Voices**: In general, the old mass media (and to some extent the new) give greater access and prominence to 'The Great and the Good'; in other words, the views of the rich and the powerful are more likely to be sought out and reported. They are also more likely to be given a platform (a newspaper article, a TV programme and the like) that lets them speak directly to an audience (rather than have their views reported by a journalist). Hegemonic Marxists argue this results, in part, from the way the media is organised (something we will investigate in more detail in a later section) rather than it being 'consciously biased reporting'. **Philo** and **Berry** (*Bad New from Israel*, 2004), for example, capture this idea when they report the following from a female journalist:

I think, 'Oh God the Palestinians say this and the Israelis say that' and I have to . . . make a judgement and I say this is what happened . . . I know it's a question of interpretation so I have to say what both sides think and I think sometimes that stops us from giving the background we should be giving, because I think well, bloody hell, I've only three minutes to do this piece and I'm going to spend a minute going through the arguments.

- **Audience**: Just as with different supermarket products, different types of media can be aimed at different audiences; readers of the *Daily Mail*, for example, don't usually read *The Guardian*. Although these two newspapers have different political values (the *Mail* is politically conservative and leans towards a New Right view on things like family life, national defence and sexuality, whereas *The Guardian* is politically liberal) they share many core economic and political assumptions about the society in which they operate.

- **Gatekeeping** describes the idea information presented to an audience is filtered through a (potentially) large number of people, each of whom have to make decisions about what to include and exclude. Gatekeepers include media controllers (such as editors and journalists) but also, on occasions, owners. Gatekeepers also have control over the way information is presented to an audience – which relates to some of the ideas we have just outlined.

- **Agenda setting**: The media conform to certain *taken for granted* beliefs about society and, by so doing, *set the agenda* for

debate. An obvious example here is sexual deviance – paedophilia, for example, is absolutely 'beyond the pale' and not up for discussion; any newspaper that advocated this form of sexuality would rapidly find itself in trouble with readers, politicians and the police.

- **Preferred readings**: Just as supermarkets have ways of convincing people to buy one product rather than another (even through they may be side by side on the same shelf), so too does the media. A *preferred reading*, as the name suggests, is the thing or things the producer of a newspaper article, for example, would like

Discussion point: sexual agendas

Now she's Flabby Titmuss
The Sun **02/09/04**

'BRAZEN Abi Titmuss flashes her boobs yesterday — as she also reveals her new **DOUBLE CHIN**.

The ex-nurse has been living it up since splitting from shamed John Leslie with TV work and partying.

But blonde Abi, 28 now appears to be piling **ON** the pounds as well as earning them. The satellite porn TV presenter revealed her look at a London bash. Perhaps she wants an even bigger profile'.

Double trouble... Abi bares her boobs... and her chins.

Svelte... Abi in her slimline days.

What sort of sexual (and other) agendas are being set in this report? You might want to think about the following:

Sexuality   How are the 'Before' and 'After' pictures used to suggest 'desirability'?

Celebrity   How is the reference to 'shamed' used to suggest approval/disapproval (John Leslie was cleared in court of a rape charge)?

Weight   What are we being told about body shape and size?

What other agendas can you identify in the report/pictures?

you to believe (without you particularly noticing your opinions and beliefs are being influenced – just like advertising, in some respects). One way to do this is through the use of headlines and sub-headings telling you what to expect before you've read the article; another way is to use captions to tell you what a picture is about or – more significantly perhaps – what it *means*.

If you look at the pictures of Abi Titmuss in the previous exercise, you can see how this process works.

- **The headline** tells you the purpose of the story, a reasonably famous woman has put on weight – and that is a bad thing. You know this because of the word 'flabby' – something not considered attractive.

- **The pictures**: One is clearly posed (the one you're encouraged to consider as the desirable version) whereas the other catches the model in a decidedly unflattering pose.

- **The captions** reinforce the headline's suggestion. 'Svelte', for example, tells you what one picture means, whereas as 'Double trouble' is a simple play on words to highlight both her breasts and her extra chin (and as you may know, for *The Sun*, while large female breasts are considered desirable, overweight women most certainly aren't).

This also illustrates a technique for studying the media called **semiology**, which can be used to interpret the 'hidden messages' embedded within a piece of text. For example, when you look the pictures, there are two levels of meaning.

- **Denotations** or what something *is* – in this instance, pictures of a young women. If you are not told who she is, or the significance of the pictures, this leaves any possible interpretation open to you, the audience. Therefore, as part of the *preferred reading*, you need to be told *why* these pictures are significant, which involves:

- **Connotations** or what something *means*. In this instance, the headlines and captions tell you very clearly how you are *supposed* to understand the story, but if you are interested (and even if you are not), there are other techniques being used to influence your interpretation. In the 'Svelte' picture, for example, the model has her head slightly bowed towards the camera – a submissive gesture in our culture. This is used to present two ideas (at least); firstly, it is a coy gesture used to suggest availability and desire. Secondly, it is a gesture frequently used by children, (they bow their head when being told off, for example) and it suggests youth (something the newspaper uses to symbolise attractiveness).

Pluralism

⚠ Preparing the ground

In this final section we can outline a range of different interpretations about the ideological role of the mass media to the ones we have just examined. These views can be loosely grouped under the banner of pluralist perspectives. The distinguishing characteristics of these perspectives (aside from offering a different interpretation to Marxist perspectives) are:

cookery enthusiasts to name but three). A diversity of media exist and people can choose from different sources of information. This applies, as we have seen, to both old and new media – access to the Internet, for example, means people can get information from both national and global sources.

- **Policing**: A variety of media, reflecting a range of different viewpoints, means the activities of the powerful can be scrutinised, exposed and criticised, which reflects a form of:

- **Social control**, whereby the diversity of old and new media means some sections will represent the interests of 'ordinary people'. The media can, for example, highlight for public scrutiny the activities of the powerful and, by so doing, call such people to account for their behaviour.

 # Digging deeper

The general pluralist perspective has, according to **Graham Thomas** ('Political Communication', 2004), a number of key features, which include:

- **Public debate**: A plurality of media facilitates freedom of speech and allows for public debates around issues. A vigorous public debate, for example, arose around the decision to go to war with Iraq in 2003.

- **State control** of the media, in democratic, pluralist, societies is *indirect*; government doesn't directly control or censor information. Its role is, by and large, a *regulatory* one – it sets certain parameters (or limits) for things like media ownership. The government may also, through associated agencies like the

Office for Communications (Ofcom), set standards for public decency and so forth for things like advertising and broadcasting.

- **Political opinions**: A wide range of opinion is covered within both old and, especially new media. Many of these views may be hostile to the government, media owners and so forth.

- **Attitude formation**: The key argument here is the media do not create people's attitudes; rather, **Thomas** argues, they 'reflect and reinforce them, corroborating attitudes rather than creating them . . . the rather conservative attitudes of the [British] press reflect the prevailing attitudes in society'.

New right perspectives, while echoing much of the above, take issue with the role of government in relation to:

- **Ownership**: The New Right see government media ownership (such as the BBC in Britain) as working against the interests of consumers by distorting economic markets. Since the BBC, for example, is guaranteed funding from the taxpayer (through a licence fee levied on television ownership) it doesn't have to compete against other channels for viewers and revenue. Thus, government media ownership can be used to limit or remove:

- **Competition**: In 2002, for example, the BBC was given a central role in the development of computer software for use in schools. The argument here (whether or not it's true) is that small software companies cannot compete against the BBC's power to distribute free software and this, it's argued, stifles innovation.

From this perspective, competition through diverse media ownership is seen as guaranteeing consumer choice.

- **Convergence**: This relates to the way different types of media can combine to create newer forms (for example, streaming television pictures over the Internet). Unlike Marxist perspectives, New Right perspectives see processes like convergence as something that should be encouraged, rather than discouraged through regulation. Rules governing (and to some extent preventing) cross-media ownership, it is argued, prevent companies developing these new technologies.

- **Regulation**: Anything that hinders the working of economic markets is, therefore, undesirable since only free markets can deliver innovation and economic development. As Tessa Jowell, Secretary of State for the Department of Culture, Media and Sport (2004) put it: 'For too long, the UK's media have been over-regulated and over-protected from competition'.

In terms of newspaper publishing, the chairman of the Press Complaints Commission, **Christopher Meyer** argued, in a speech to the Newspaper Society (2003): 'Any infringement of self-regulation would not just erode the freedoms of the press ... it would curtail the freedoms of the citizen, who, in a democratic society, will always depend on media uninhibited by both control by the state and deference to the establishment to protect their liberty'. **Compaine** ('The myths of encroaching global media ownership', 2001) also argues: 'even corporations must respect the discipline of the market. A diverse media

reflects the plurality of publics in modern society. This is democracy in action'.

Postmodern perspectives can be (very loosely) included within a general pluralist perspective for a couple of reasons relating to:

- **Ideology**: Although postmodernists prefer to talk about the media in terms of *narratives* and *metanarratives* rather than ideologies (the difference – for our purpose at least – is probably academic) they question Marxist arguments about the ideological role of the media.

- **Globalisation**: In a world that, to use **Marshall McCluhan**'s famous phrase (*The Global Village*, 1989), increasingly resembles a 'global village', the media can't be subject to the kinds of controls, checks and balances – characteristic of modern societies – that restricts the free flow of ideas and information.

Where postmodernism differs from Marxist, Pluralist and New Right perspectives is in the characterisation of **information structures**. Whereas the modernist perspectives we have examined view information *hierarchically* (the flow is from producers – at the top – to consumers at the bottom), postmodernists (as I suggested earlier) view information in terms of *networks*. **Castells** (*The Information Age*, 1996) suggests postmodernists characterise societies in terms of the way 'networks have become the dominant form of social organization'. For this reason **power** (in terms of control over the production and distribution of information), is no longer concentrated within institutions (media organisations, governments and so forth) but within *social networks* where information is both produced and consumed by the same

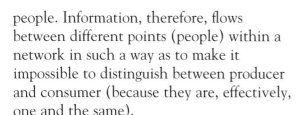

people. Information, therefore, flows between different points (people) within a network in such a way as to make it impossible to distinguish between producer and consumer (because they are, effectively, one and the same).

In this respect, **Tuomi** ('The Blog and the Public Sphere', 2002), identifies the characteristic features of postmodern media (and web logs in particular) in terms of:

- **User as producer** – they are, as I have just suggested, the same people.

- **Backstage is frontstage**: This reflects **Goffman's** idea (*The Presentation of Self in Everyday Life*, 1969) of social interaction as a performance; just like an actor in a play, we prepare and evaluate our public (or *frontstage*) performances 'backstage' – in private, as it were. Tuomi adapts this idea to argue that with something like a web log or chatroom there is no *backstage* – all interaction is played out within the confines of the medium – an idea developed by writers such as **Meyrowitz** ('Medium Theory', 1994).

- **Content reflects interpretation**: In other words, the way different people in the network interpret information contributes to the development of the media – a reversal and rebuttal of the Marxist idea of a *preferred reading*.

The main implication of the above – and postmodern thinking generally – is we have to discard (modernist) concepts such as truth or falsity when thinking about the ideological role of the media. All knowledge, from this perspective, is ideological – which makes it a fairly pointless exercise trying to argue some forms of information are more

(or indeed less) ideological than any other form of information.

To identify and explore postmodern concepts (not just those relating to the media) in more detail, see:
http://www.sociology.org.uk/kc1_home.htm

In this section we have outlined various perspectives on the ideological role of the media (which linked to debates about the relative significance of media ownership and control) and, in the next section we can examine some of the ways media ideologies influence (or not as the case may be) the selection and presentation of media content.

Selection and presentation

Introduction

This section focuses on what **David Barrat** (*Media Sociology*, 1992) has termed the 'social context of media production' or, in less technical terms, different explanations of the processes of selection and presentation of media content. In other words, having examined things like the significance of ownership and control and different interpretations of media bias, we now need to look more closely at some of the factors affecting the way media content is created and distributed.

To do this we can group such factors – for no better reason than our theoretical convenience – around the idea of economic, political and cultural influences on the general process of media production.

⚠ Preparing the ground

The world, as someone probably once said, is a big place. Whether we consider it at a global, national or local level, it is clear there is a lot of information swilling around, some of which finds its way into the media, the majority of which doesn't (for a variety of different reasons). We need, therefore, to think about the information, considered in its very widest sense, that does find its way into the media and, to do this, we need to initially think about two things in terms of media content:

- **Selection** refers to the processes involved in deciding what will appear in the media. As I have suggested, some form of selection process must take place on a daily basis since, on the one hand, the amount of potential content is vast and someone, somewhere, has to decide what – and what not – to select; on the other hand, the selection process is not arbitrary or random. Conscious decisions are made about content that reflect, as we will see, a variety of influences – economic, political and ideological.

- **Presentation** refers to the way this content, once selected, is transmitted to an audience. Media content isn't just placed into the public domain 'as is'; it is subject to a variety of processes and packaging before it reaches an audience and we need to understand how the presentation of content is also part of a social construction process.

The selection and presentation of content are not, of course, unrelated processes. A newspaper, for example, may decide to both select a particular story – from the many available each day – and to present it in a particular way (ideas we have previously met when we noted concepts such as *gatekeeping* and *agenda-setting*). The warm up exercise opposite should help to clarify these ideas.

If you deconstruct (take apart) this report carefully, you will notice how it uses a combination of *selection* and *presentation* to produce content reflecting a particular viewpoint – that 'Britain's youngsters' appear to be indulging in a veritable orgy of drink, drugs and violent, anti-social behaviour. This, I would argue, is not actually supported by the *facts* – as opposed to *opinions* – presented (did you, for example, note the way the headline and sub-heading refer to 'all youth', whereas the survey actually related to a tiny percentage of British youth?).

The type of analysis you have just done illustrates some – but by no means all – of the social processes involved in the selection and presentation of media content. What we need to do next, therefore, is to identify and outline some of these processes.

Economic factors

A range of economic factors come into play when considering media content. These include:

- **Costs**: *Production and distribution* costs, especially considered in terms of old media (although new media costs shouldn't be discounted – some forms, such as news web sites, may be just as, if not more, expensive to set up and run as their old media counterparts), influence the selection and presentation of content since they impact on things like:

WARM UP: SELECTING AND PRESENTING

Have a look at the following newspaper report and think about the following:

- What facts can you identify?
- What opinions can you identify?
- Do the facts presented support the opinions voiced?

Using the *factual* material in the story, re-write the article to show 'British youths' are actually law-abiding.

Shame of our kids
News of the World 19/05/02

BRITAIN'S youngsters are sinking into a pit of crime, drink and drugs, a shock poll reveals.
More than a quarter of **ALL** children aged up to 16 admit breaking the law. And the same proportion of kids excluded from school say they have taken heroin, crack or ecstasy. For the first time research lays bare the frightening extent to which Britain's teenagers are rejecting normal society.

The poll exposes a generation of kids who have minimal respect for the law, who embrace a culture of drink and drugs, and who often move on to commit serious crime.

The poll found **HALF** of all 15-year-olds had been offered cannabis. Around **ONE IN FIVE** had been offered a Class A drug such as heroin, crack or ecstasy. The survey discovered that more and more youngsters are losing respect for the police – by committing petty offences such as fare-dodging, graffiti and criminal damage. And serious offences such as car theft, violence and carrying weapons such as knives and guns are on the rise. The research among youngsters aged from 11 to 16 and excluded from school reveals the most frightening facts of all. Besides the quarter who have tried hard drugs, a shocking **78 PER CENT** admit to regularly drinking alcohol. More than **50 PER CENT** drink on street corners or in parks after illegally buying alcohol from an off-licence. **ONE IN FOUR** of expelled kids boasted about stealing mobile phones. Astonishingly, **64 PER CENT** of them each break the law 44 times a year. **ONE IN FIVE** carries a **KNIFE** and **ONE IN 12** boasts of carrying a **GUN**. More than 10,000 pupils are excluded from school **EVERY YEAR**.

- **News gathering**: A national newspaper or television company, for example, will have many more resources at its disposal (journalists, production and administration staff and so forth) than a local newspaper or television company. Having said this, news agencies (organisations, such as the Press Association or Reuters that collect and sell news material) are often used by media outlets to lower the cost of news reporting.

- **Production values** relate to the *quality* of the product presented to an audience. The BBC, for example, routinely spends more on its programmes than small satellite TV channels and, consequently, tends to produce material with higher production values. Within different forms of media programming, costs may also vary and this goes some way towards determining how content is selected and presented. For example, it is much cheaper to show a video produced by a record company to support one of its artists than it is to produce a one-hour episode of original TV drama (the average cost of which **Chung** (2004) notes is currently around £250,000).

- **Distribution**: The physical delivery of some media forms (such as newspapers, magazines and books) also determines, to some extent, the selection and presentation of content. Print media, for example, have restrictions on space (with associated additional costs related to the production of extra pages in a newspaper or magazine, for example) that don't apply to new media (such as web pages – the cost of whose distribution is relatively minimal).

- **Technology**: A further factor affecting both production and distribution costs is the level of technology available and used. For example, a global media company can select programming from a wide and diverse range of sources unavailable to individuals producing small web sites or documenting events in their local community through a web log. In addition, we can talk here about:

  - **Push** technologies: Content providers (such as a newspaper, book or television producer) send information regardless of whether or not it has been specifically requested; unrequested (or spam) email is a new media example of such technology.

  - **Pull technologies**: The audience can request specific forms of information from a content provider. When you type a URL into a web browser, for example, you are using a simple form of pull technology.

  - All media has some pull element (you choose to buy *Cosmopolitan* rather than *FHM*) but computer technology takes selection and presentation to a different level since, in theory, the audience can request information from a wide variety of sources tailored to their specific needs – news focused on stock-market information, sport or education delivered to your computer desktop, for example.

- **Competition** between media providers takes place on a number of levels and affects the selection and presentation of content in a variety of ways.

  - **Intra-medium** (within the same medium) competition may result in different organisations capturing or losing different kinds of content. For example, live Premiership football has been an important part of the satellite company BSkyB's audience strategy – it has successfully sold subscriptions to its channels on the back of this 'premium content' (content people are willing to pay extra to receive). However, since BSkyB has exclusive rights to this content, other broadcasters are unable to offer a similar service. The BBC, for example, can currently (2004) show recorded highlights and ITV are restricted to showing brief clips as part of its news service.

- **Inter-media** (between different media) competition, on the other hand, results in content being selected and presented in ways tailored to the particular strengths of the medium. Music, for example, is packaged differently on radio than it is on TV channels such as MTV or VH1 (where full use is made of the visual dimension to sell the music to an audience).

- **Profits**: For privately owned media, profitability is an important influence on selection and production processes since the creation of profits may be dependent on a precise knowledge of the audience for your content. In technical terms this is known as an *audience demographic* – understanding audience characteristics in terms of things like age, class, ethnicity and gender as well as less tangible things like lifestyles and tastes.

  The audience demographic for the Disney Cartoon Channel, for example, is likely to be very different to that of God TV (a Christian religious channel) and, consequently, media content has to be selected and presented with the audience in mind; if it is not, market share (and profits) may be lost as a potential audience turns to a different provider to give them the content they want.

- **Marketing** relates to the ability to select and present content in different – and appropriate – ways for different markets and audiences. The Hollywood film industry, for example, has developed a way of making films that sell in the widest possible markets and appeal to the largest number of people by the use of:

- Simple themes that translate easily into different cultures, for example, the juxtaposition of 'Good' against 'Bad'; the idea that although 'good' people will suffer trials (and 'bad' people might win small victories), the former will ultimately triumph.

- Standard plotlines: Think about how many films revolve around the 'boy meets girl, boy loses girl, boy gets girl in the end' plotline.

- Global stereotypes: The lone, rugged, individual; the straight cop in a corrupt society; the evil drug-trafficker . . .

Political factors

The selection and presentation of information is, to some extent, governed by political rules governing media content, in which respect we can note ideas like:

- **Censorship** (or media regulation): Western governments rarely operate a system of *direct* media censorship (although in times of 'national emergency' – such as war – this may change). During the second Gulf War ('Operation Iraqi Freedom', 2003) the British and American governments operated a system of 'embedding' reporters within fighting units. **Andrew Gray** (*Embedding Gave War Reporters Access – and Anxiety*, 2003) noted this had both advantages ('first-hand' experience of the conflict, the documentation of the horrors and personal dramas of war and so forth) and disadvantages (reporters identifying too closely with the people protecting them and self-censorship of criminal actions, for example). Having said this, the British government does operate forms of **direct media censorship**, which include:

- **The Official Secrets Act**: Information the government decides is a 'state secret' (or *classified information* to give it its technical name) cannot be published.

- **Defence Notices** (the 'D-Notice' system) are similar to Official Secrets but cover *non-classified information* about the armed forces. Although this is largely an informal, non-statutory, system, the 'D-Notice' Committee has the power to advise about and, in some instances, censor, the publication of information.

- **Positive vetting** of government employees (including those at the BBC) involves checks being made on the background of all prospective employees. Having first-hand knowledge of this process, I wasn't particularly convinced of its thoroughness (although I did remove my copy of Karl Marx's *Capital* from view prior to being interviewed, just in case . . .).

- **Legal rules and regulations** cover a

Discussion point: banned

1. 2DTV: George Bush

2. Benetton

3. Club 18-31 Holidays

4. Wonderbra

Three of these adverts received complaints in the UK on the basis of 'taste and decency'; the fourth was banned on grounds of 'offensiveness to the President.'.

Identify as many reasons as you can for censoring/not censoring media content.

Discuss your reasons.

range of things in relation to advertising and broadcasting. Some television companies, for example, operate a 'watershed' (starting at 9 pm) before which sex, violence and swearing is limited.

- **Indirect media censorship** can be noted in a couple of ways.

  - **Commissions** overseeing media content. These are *technically independent* of direct government control, although since they're usually government-funded their actual level of independence may, in practice, be limited. The Office for Communications (Ofcom), for example, recently (2003) took over the regulation of UK communications industries (replacing the Broadcasting Standards Commission, Independent Television Commission, Office for Telecommunications (Oftel), the Radio Authority and the Radio Communications Agency).

  - The Advertising Standards Authority regulates advertising content, while the Press Complaints Commission (funded by the newspaper industry), 'deals with complaints from members of the public about the editorial content of newspapers and magazines'. The Campaign for Press and Broadcasting Freedom (CPBF) however, argues ('Britain's Media', 1997) the Commission 'has no effective powers, because of its self-regulatory role, as either a press watchdog or a vehicle for redress'.

- **Distribution networks** – which may, at first sight, seem an obscure form of indirect censorship. However, we can see

their potential for censorship in two main ways:

- **Physically distributing** print media (two companies – W.H. Smith and John Menzies – for example, controlled over 50% of the UK wholesale and retail distribution markets for newspapers and magazines in 1996). Whereas in France, for example, retailers are prevented by law from refusing to stock a periodical on commercial grounds, no such restrictions apply in the UK. Small circulation periodicals may be effectively 'censored' because the public have difficulty buying them or even knowing of their existence.

- **Copyright restrictions** on the distribution of, for example, electronic content (such as the aforesaid monopoly of BSkyB on the broadcasting of live Premiership football).

- **Bettina Peters** (*Corporate Media Trends in Europe*, 2001) argues:

  Companies in control of distribution networks ... use their position as 'gatekeepers' to distribute mainly information and programme services of their own media group thus limiting free access.

- **Self-censorship** (or self-regulation) plays a part in the selection and presentation of media content, in terms of:

  - **News values** (discussed in more detail in the next section): This relates to the idea all media organisations have certain operating values. Such values may mean organisations don't publish certain things because their audience doesn't want it – The Times, for example, doesn't print pictures of topless women (because it is aimed at a high-culture audience) whereas its sister paper *The Sun* makes semi-naked women a selling point for its (popular culture) audience. Owners and controllers also apply values when deciding whether or not to select and present particular stories. **Lanson** and **Stephens** (*Writing and Reporting The News*, 2003), for example, argue factors such as the impact of an event (things that affect a lot of people personally, for example, are more likely to be reported) or its uniqueness (unusual situations are more likely to be featured than run-of-the-mill events) are important news values.

- **Omission** – or the failure to report something – is not uncommon in the media. The French, for example, knew nothing of President Mitterrand's sexual affairs until after his death; similarly, President Clinton's affair with Monica Lewinsky – although common knowledge to many journalists – was not reported until the story was broken on an Internet news site. During the 1990s, little or nothing appeared in the British media concerning the British bombing of Iraq following the 1991 war – and the effect of economic sanctions on the country was rarely – if at all – mentioned in the mainstream media.

- **Advertising**: Most forms of privately owned media rely on advertising income for their profitability and, consequently, are unlikely to behave in ways that upset their principal advertisers. **Noam Chomsky** (*Necessary Illusions: Thought Control in Democratic Societies*, 1989), for example, documented a number of occasions where pressure from advertisers resulted in articles and programmes being

withdrawn or 'amended'. Similarly, **Lee** and **Solomon** (*Unreliable Sources: A Guide to Detecting Bias in News Media*, 1990) point to examples of pressure by advertisers in the USA: 'In 1989, Domino's Pizza cancelled its advertising on *Saturday Night Live* [a satirical TV programme] because of the show's alleged anti-Christian message'.

Digging deeper

Debates about media content have tended to revolve around the manipulation/hegemony/pluralism axis we've previously outlined and, while you will be pleased to know I don't propose to go over this ground again, you should keep these ideas in mind since they provide a theoretical context for the interpretation of the material in this section. In this respect, although economic and political factors are important in relation to media content, we can dig a little deeper by examining a range of **cultural** (or ideological) **factors** surrounding a significant aspect of the mass media, namely the production of news. This particular area provides a wealth of material we can use to illustrate how media content is culturally selected and presented and we can begin by noting ideas about the **social construction** of 'news'. In basic terms, this involves the idea that 'what counts as news' is *socially determined*. Although everything that happens in a society is potentially news, the key factor that turns an event (or activity) into 'news' is that someone with the power to construct and enforce such labels decides it's *newsworthy*. In this respect, news is not a neutral, non-ideological, category; rather, it involves a set of *ideological prescriptions* (rules or agendas) that serve to classify events in particular ways.

This being the case, news is whatever people with the power to classify/report an event decides it will be (although, as you are aware, where definitions of news differ between, for example, a producer and their audience, something has to give – either people have to be persuaded they really are receiving news or the provider has to alter their definition to fit that of the audience). Be that as it may, we can think about the social construction of news by identifying some factors that influence the classification of information as news.

News values are, as I have suggested, the values used by organisations and individuals (such as editors, sub-editors and journalists) to guide their understanding of what is – and what isn't – newsworthy. **Steve Chibnall** (1977) in his analysis of British newspaper crime reporting defines this idea as: 'The criteria of relevance which guide reporters' choice and construction of newsworthy stories … learnt through a process of informal professional socialisation' and various writers have, over the years, isolated and classified journalistic news values.

Galtung and **Ruge** (1973), for example, identified news values and their meaning as shown in the table below.

News value	Meaning
Frequency	The duration of an event is an important consideration for different media (visual media like to feature fast-moving stories with plenty of action).
Size	How large and important is the event (in general, bigger equals more newsworthy)?
Unambiguous	The more clear-cut an event, in terms of the issues involved, the more likely it will be defined as news. If an event is complex it will be reduced to simple, clear, issues.
Meaningfulness	The closer the fit between the event and an audience's cultural background, the more newsworthy the event becomes. In our society, for example, 1000 people killed in a far off country is usually less newsworthy than 10 people killed in England.
Consonance	The ability to predict or want something to happen makes it news and relates to ideas such as *folk devils*, *moral panics*, *self-fulfilling prophecies* and *agenda setting*. If the predicted events don't happen, that too becomes news.
Continuity	The extent to which a news story can be given a context – a past and a future, for example.
Composition	News organisations like to feature a mixture of different stories (human interest, celebrity gossip, financial news, comment, etc.).

Steve Chibnall added the following ideas:

News Value	Meaning
Immediacy	'News' is, by definition, what's happening now.
Drama	The more dramatic an event, the more likely it is to become news.
Personalisation	'Important people' (defined in terms of the audience – celebrities are important to readers of The Sun and Mirror, politicians are important to readers of The Times and Telegraph) are given more attention and prominence. Stories also have more value if they can be *personalised*; that is, given a human interest angle.
Titillation	Sex is used to sell some newspapers, magazines and TV programmes.
Convention	Events are explained in ways familiar to an audience and their expectations.
Structured Access	Some people (*primary definers* such as reporters and experts) are given more opportunity than others to define the meaning of an event. This involves *hierarchies of credibility*, where more importance is given to some commentators than others.
Novelty	If an event is unusual or rare it is more newsworthy. New angles on an old event can also be newsworthy.

Lanson and Stephens (2003) noted a few more:

News Value	Meaning
Weight	An event's significance in relation to other, current, stories.
Controversy	Arguments and debates increase the value of news.
Usefulness	The extent to which the story helps people to understand the meaning of something.
Educational value	The extent to which people may be taught something of value.

 Growing it yourself: news values

You will need access to a range of popular tabloid and broadsheet newspapers for this exercise.

Divide into small groups, each taking responsibility for one type of newspaper.

Using the categories of 'news values' identified above, briefly examine each story to see if it conforms to one or more of these values (write down the values represented in the story). Once finished, construct a table like the following and identify the type of story that fits each news value.

News value	Title of newspaper: Story
Size	
Drama	
Etc.	

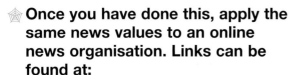

Once you have done this, apply the same news values to an online news organisation. Links can be found at:

http://www.sociology.org.uk/as4aqa.htm

If, as suggested in the previous exercise, news is not just 'something that happens' (plenty of things happen in the world without ever being classified as news), it follows that the news values of a media organisation are clearly important in terms of the initial selection of events.

However, in terms of the way news is *presented*, a further process – that of interpretation/explanation – comes into play. Hegemonic Marxists (among others), for example, argue the significance of an event is also interpreted *for* an audience – an idea that relates to the concept of preferred reading we've previously encountered or, if you prefer a (post) modern turn of phrase, the 'spin' put on the event. This involves, according to **Chibnall** (1977) the use of:

- **Legitimating values**, involving positive and negative ideas used in news reports to provide *cultural cues* that 'tell' an audience how to interpret something (without actually appearing to do so). For example, in the UK when discussing politics, the media tend to use the following ideas to symbolise positive and negative values:

Positive values	Negative values
Consensus	Conflict
Moderation	Extremism
Order	Disorder
Honesty	Corruption
Communication	Spin
Good	Evil
Democracy	Dictatorship

Thus, positive (legitimate) values and negative (illegitimate) values structure the way we 'read' information and they constitute part of what postmodernists call a:

- **Discourse** (one which, in this instance, refers to news media). **Fiske** (*Television Culture: popular pleasures and politics*, 1987), for example, sees a discourse as a *system of representation*, developed to circulate ideas, beliefs and values about something, that creates a framework for its interpretation by an audience. In other words, part of the function of a *news discourse* is, as we have seen, to define the concept of news itself (different discourses may define it differently). Once this occurs, further refinements take place, involving the ability to define the meaning of something (as 'good or evil', 'freedom fighter or terrorist' and so forth). This definition of meaning, of course, indicates to an audience how they are *supposed* to interpret something and, in some instances, determines their response to whatever is being presented as news. A good example of this is to use **Stan Cohen**'s (1972) concept of:

- **Folk devils**, that involves the periodic identification and selection of individuals or groups as being deserving of special attention, usually because they are believed (rightly or wrongly) to represent a challenge or threat (real or imaginary) to the existing moral order. Current folk devils, for example, might be 'asylum seekers' (portrayed in news discourses as 'foreigners' arriving in this country to seek a better life than that found in their country of origin) and, of course, 'terrorists' (people who seek to disrupt or destroy our way of life through illegitimate means).

165

Folk devils, in a sense, represent a way of creating a sense of *social solidarity* amongst a population by identifying people who are 'not like us' ('outsiders' or 'others' to use common sociological conceptualisations). Usually, the creation of folk devils in news media is accompanied by a process that presents them in terms of:

- **Moral panics**: These, as you might guess, involve the idea folk devils are sufficiently threatening to require some sort action to be taken to counteract or neutralise their influence. A classic example here might be the panic over the influence of so-called 'video nasties' in the early 1980s and the subsequent introduction of the *Video Recording Act* (1984); prior to this Act videos, unlike films, did not have to be classified by the British Board of Film Classification.

- **David Lusted** (*The Media Studies Book*. 1991), for example, points out how this particular moral panic centred around the development of a new form of technology (the video recorder) that offered a new freedom for audiences to control how they watched films and television. The suggestion here is that such freedom challenged traditional media conceptions of control and led to demands for limits to be placed on this new medium (through indirect means – by focusing on the 'danger to vulnerable children' a consensus could be generated around the desirability of censorship).

Synoptic link – Crime and deviance: The concepts of folk devils and moral panics can be applied to 'the social construction of, and societal reactions to, crime and deviance, including the role of the mass media'.

Moral panics have a number of features we can briefly note.

- **Scapegoating and stigma** involves individuals or groups being targeted for special treatment, usually by focusing on their perceived *deviance*.

- **Social control**: They represent one way of 'cracking down' on behaviour seen as undesirable by the media. This often occurs (as in the case of video nasties and asylum seekers) during periods of social crisis or change and, arguably, represents attempts to limit the impact and pace of such change. **Hall** et al (*Policing the Crisis*, 1978), from a Marxist perspective, attempted to link a moral panic over 'mugging' in the 1970s to an economic 'crisis in capitalism', arguing the media used such folk devils to distract people's attention from the real problems in society at that time (high levels of unemployment and social unrest, for example).

In terms of a more contemporary example, the US-led 'War on Terror' has seen the introduction, in the UK, of a wide range of government actions designed to 'limit the ability of terrorists to launch attacks on this country' that impact directly on individual (non-terrorist) freedoms; the possible introduction of identity cards, for example, is a case in point, as is the ability to detain non-British nationals 'indefinitely' in prison without charge or trial.

Alternative explanations of moral panics, however, focus on how they reflect news values relating to:

- **Audience share**: A dramatic,

sensational, story can be used to increase audience figures or ratings. This is particularly apparent during 'quiet periods' in terms of news when the lack of anything significant to report often results in 'folk devil' stories appearing in the media.

- **Moral entrepreneurs** (people or groups who take it upon themselves to 'protect public morality') who use news media to promote their individual or group agendas. **Mary Whitehouse**, for example, skilfully used newspapers to promote her National Viewers and Listeners Association (NVALA) campaigns against the 'lowering of public standards of decency' by the broadcast media. It is also not unknown for groups such as political parties to try to promote certain ideas and issues in the media for political gain.

Finally, in this respect, we can note a further concept related to the above, namely the:

- **Amplification of risk**: The concept of *media amplification* was originally floated by **Leslie Wilkins** (*Social Deviance*, 1963) when he developed the idea of a *deviancy amplification spiral* to suggest one result of the way the mass media select and present content related to crime and deviance was an increase (amplification) in the behaviour they were concerned to control. In other words, by publicising certain types of behaviour (such as drug-taking among young people) the media not only served to attract people to the behaviour but also led to deviance becoming criminalised.

> **Synoptic link – Crime and deviance**: The concept of deviancy amplification can be applied to 'the social construction of, and societal reactions to, crime and deviance, including the role of the mass media'.

- A further aspect of any amplification process is the idea of risk or, to put it another way, the public's perception of danger. **Frewer** et al ('The media and genetically modified foods', 2002), for example, showed how perceptions of risk relating to genetically modified food increased after extensive media reporting in the UK in 1999, whereas **Pidgeon** et al (*The Social Amplification of Risk*, 2003), highlight the way various issues have been increasingly used by media organisations to amplify the actual risks from a range of things (such as AIDS, nuclear power, and the Year 2000 computer bug).

Issues surrounding selection and presentation are many and varied and, in this section, we have identified a range of ways this overall process influences the (social) construction of media content. We can develop and apply many of the ideas we've discussed here in the next section when we look in more detail at the way different social groups (considered in terms of characteristics such as age, class and sexuality) are represented in the media.

Representations
Introduction

This section considers the role of the mass media in representations of age, social class, ethnicity, gender, sexuality and disability and it is important to note the emphasis on the word *role*; the focus is not so much on representations themselves but rather it is on the part played by the mass media in the representation of different groups. In other words, this section doesn't consist of a long list of examples of the way different social groups are represented (although some examples will, of course, be necessary). The main interest here is on how the media contributes to the creation of identities, based on the concepts we have just identified, by the way it represents different groups.

More specifically, this section focuses on the media's role in the creation, promotion and maintenance of *social identities* (its general role as a socialising agency); the final section – which looks at audiences and theories of media effects – focuses on the idea of *personal identities* and how they relate to social identities.

Gerry Connor ('Representation and Youth', 2001) expresses this distinction nicely when he notes: 'representation is not just about the way the world is presented to us but also about how we engage with media texts . . . This concept of representation is, therefore, just as much about audience interpretation as it is about the portrayals that are offered to us by the media.'

⚠ Preparing the ground

Before we start to examine the role of the media we need to clarify some basic ideas:

- **Identities**: The concept of social identities is outlined in the 'Family and social change' section of this textbook, so I don't propose to outline it further. If you are unsure about the meaning of this concept (and the related one of personal identify) it would be helpful to review it before continuing.

- **Representations**: **Daniel Chandler** ('Media Representation', 2001) argues representation refers to how the media socially constructs realities in terms of certain *key markers* of identity. As I have suggested, some key markers we are interested in are class, age, gender, ethnicity and disability – which gives us the mnemonic **caged** and, rather neatly I thought, encapsulates the idea of the way social identities constructed through the media are used to lock people into identities such as 'male' or 'female' (we are also interested in the key marker of sexuality, but that didn't fit so well).

In this respect, our interest in how social groups are represented focuses on the role of the media in terms of how representations of, for example, gender, contribute to the creation of social identities of masculinity and femininity. What we are interested in here, therefore, is how the media uses representations for a variety of intended and unintended purposes, to construct social identities.

Before we continue, a word of caution needs to be added. The key markers I have identified are *transgressive categories*. In plain English this means 'in the real world' these categories aren't self-contained; a woman, for example, may be represented differently in the media depending on her class, age and sexuality – we need, therefore, to keep this idea in mind throughout this section.

- **Stereotypes** involve a one-sided or partial representation of, for example, a social group (such as 'white people'); in other words, they involve oversimplified expressions of group characteristics and usually accentuate some feature in a negative way (although sometimes groups can be positively stereotyped). For example, blonde women are often stereotyped as 'bimbos' (and their male equivalent may be stereotyped as 'himbos').

Media stereotypes are not necessarily used in a simple ideological or biased way (to demonise a particular social group, for example). Often – as in television advertising where a message has to be transmitted and understood in about 30 seconds – they are used to ensure a wide audience quickly understands the background to something. In this respect, stereotypes are often used as *codes* to familiarise an audience with particular situations.

WARM UP: STEREOTYPICAL REPRESENTATIONS

Divide the class into six groups and, using the following table as the basis for the exercise, each group should choose one key indicator and identify as many contemporary examples of media stereotypes/ representations as they can.

Each group should then share its examples with the rest of the class to create an overview of stereotypical representations.

Key Indicator	Examples of media stereotypes/representations
Class	
Age	
Gender	
Ethnicity	
Disability	
Sexuality	

'Mr Muscle' drain cleaner uses a simple stereotype of a 'wimpy man' to show how easy it is to unblock a drain.

We can build on this exercise (which should have demonstrated your extensive knowledge of stereotypical media representations) by considering the media's role in the production and promotion of representations based on each of the key indicators we've identified.

Class representations

These can be examined in terms of a number of ideas.

- **The gaze:** This concept – originally developed by **Laura Mulvey** ('Visual Pleasure and Narrative Cinema', 1975) as a way of expressing the idea of male power and control over female representation in Hollywood films – can

News images of the working classes are often framed in term of conflict, whereas fictional images often reflect idealised images of 'community'. And conflict.

be applied to understand representations of social class across a range of media in a number of different ways.

For example, think about how the media presents information – through whose eyes do we see the world? Almost by definition, it's through those of middle class professionals or upper class owners (depending on where you stand in the ownership and control debate). News reporting, for example, involves a representation of reality that **Fiske** (1987) calls the *transparency fallacy* – a rebuttal of the idea that news reporting represents a neutral 'window on the world', reflecting events as they unfold.

- **Invisibility: Don Heider** (*Class and News*, 2004) suggests class visibility or invisibility is related to journalistic (and audience) news values when he argues that: 'people in [American] news rooms each day either choose to cover or not to cover stories depending on whether they think a particular audience will be interested. In many cases, if the victim of a crime is poor, the story won't be given

the attention it would if it were someone with wealth or influence.'

- **Ghettoisation** represents the idea that, where some groups (in this case the working classes) feature in the media, they are restricted to a fairly narrow range of appearances or situations. An obvious positive area is sport (especially male professional sport). On the negative side, there is the association with crime and industrial unrest. Middle-class representations tend to be broader, involving a wider range of representations across professional employment, taking in work, sport and cultural associations (music, fashion and so forth).

- **Stereotypes** relating to class abound in the media – from lovable working-class cheeky chappies (Alfie Moon in *EastEnders*) to sinister and shadowy upper-class cliques. Interestingly, portrayals of the upper classes in recent years in areas such as film and broadcasting have tended to display the same level of limited representation found among the working class. Films such as

Michael Moore's *Roger and Me* (1989) and *Fahrenheit 9/11* (2004), **John Sayles'** *Silver City* (2004) or television programmes such as C4's *The F***ing Fulfords* (2004) provide examples of how the upper classes (especially their rich and powerful members) are represented – with increasing frequency – in electronic media.

- **Marginalisation**: The Glasgow Media Group's study of television reporting of industrial disputes (*Bad News*, 1977) argued lower social classes had less direct access to the media and less control over how they were portrayed. This study has, however, attracted widespread criticism within the media – **Martin Harrison** (*Television News: Whose Bias?*, 1985), for example, argued that the study was unrepresentative of industrial relations and selective in its interpretation of evidence.

- **Codes** are things that tell us something about someone – such as their class or sexual orientation. In this instance, social class is represented through a number of subtle – and not very subtle – codes. **Jack Fawbert** (*Social class, replica football shirts and televisual communication*, 2003), for example, notes how the 'replica football shirt' is used throughout the media as shorthand for working class – in much the same way the business suit and the hand-made suit denote middle and upper class respectively. One of the interesting things to note here, of course, is the way changing codes reflect changes in society – 40 years ago, the bowler hat, trilby and flat cap were equivalent class codes. The question is, of course, as **Fawbert** notes: 'Are the media responsible for creating such representations or are they simply articulating (putting into practice) something already existing within society?'

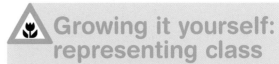

Growing it yourself: representing class

This simple piece of content analysis can be used to understand media representations of social class.

In small groups, each group needs a daily newspaper, the pages of which can be divided among group members. Skim through each story, noting the occupation of people in the story and the context in which they appear (the following table provides an example for you to follow).

Occupation	Context
School caretaker	Theft of a bike from school grounds (crime)
Further examples	

Once you've done this, rearrange your list into manual (working class) and non-manual (middle-class) occupations. Is each broad social class generally represented differently and, if so, how?

Age representations

These have a number of facets.

- **Categorisation**: Age – perhaps more than any other key marker – involves different categories focused on different interests, attitudes and needs:

  - **Children**, for example, as **Buckingham** et al ('Public Service Goes To Market', 2004) note, 'have always been seen as a "special" audience in debates about broadcasting – an audience whose particular characteristics and needs require specific codes of practice and regulation'. This group, as far as broadcasting is concerned, is subject to particularly strong forms of censorship (in terms of what they're allowed to watch, when it can be watched and so forth). This, in part, reflects the way children are viewed in our society – as a particularly vulnerable group, easily influenced by the media.

- **Youth**, on the other hand, are often represented in terms of being 'a problem'; for example, they are often portrayed as rebellious, disrespectful, ungrateful, sex-obsessed and uncaring. They are also, to take one example, frequently represented as being 'apathetic about politics', although **Lisa Harrison** ('Media Representations of Young People in the 2001 British General Election', 2002) suggests it is not so much a lack of political interest and more a question of how political parties communicate with young people that is in question here – young people tend to use traditional media far less than they use new media.

- **Elderly** people have also traditionally been represented as social problems (a burden on younger people, the National Health Service and so forth). They have also generally been portrayed unsympathetically – as senile, ill (both mentally and physically), unattractive and so forth. However, although such images still appear, the changing nature of representation is reflected, in television for example, in more sympathetic portrayals that mirror, in part, the changing nature of television audiences

– more elderly viewers, for example, who demand programming that reflects their interests and abilities.

- **The gaze**: Since the media, by-and-large, are controlled by adults (and mainly middle-aged, white, male adults), it is not surprising to find children, young people and the elderly are largely viewed through the eyes of this group.

On one level, for example, we see young people represented in terms of their 'innocent and uncorrupted nature', whereas on another we see them represented in terms of their unruliness and need for control **Geoffrey Pearson**'s *Hooligan: A History of Respectable Fears*, (1983) is a useful documentary source here, demonstrating how 'unruly youth' have been represented in the media over the past 150 years).

One form of gaze recently turned towards children and youth has been in relation to computer games and technology. The Internet, for example, is viewed as both a potentially positive (educational) medium and as a dark, dangerous place where all kinds of traps (and worse) await the innocent and unwary. The (old) mass media's attitude towards the Internet reflects a number of aspects of 'the adult gaze':

- **Social control**: Adults urged to control their children's use of the medium.

- **Technological control**: in situations where children probably know more about the medium than their parents, faith in technology (guardian software/censorship software etc.) replaces faith in adults.

- **Sexual agendas**: The vision of

uncorrupted youth falling prey to sexual predators via chatrooms and the like is almost Biblical (youth as the Garden of Eden and paedophiles as the snake). Once again, youth is an arena for folk devils and moral panics, although in this instance young people are not directly implicated in this particular panic.

- **Normality**: The category of youth – possibly because it is relatively difficult to precisely define in terms of specific ages – is represented through various media in ambivalent terms; that is, representations are constantly changing, reflecting the various ways youth can be a highly fragmented category – in terms of media stereotypes at least.

A dominant form of representation over the past 40 years, however, has been the distinction between 'normal' and 'abnormal' youth, with the former being largely defined by default in opposition to various spectacular forms of youth subcultures (spectacular in the sense of the way such subcultures have blazed a short but very bright trail across the media skyline). Categories such as Teddy Boys (ask your grandparents), Mods and Rockers, Skinheads, Hippies and Punks, for example, have all at one time or another featured heavily in the media as examples of abnormal youth (focusing once again on the idea of folk devils at the very centre of repeated moral panics surrounding 'the Nation's Youth').

- **Invisibility**: Although not as evident as it once was, the elderly have, at least in the recent past, been something of an invisible group as far as the media are

concerned. This, however, is changing for three reasons.

- **Ageing population**: There are more elderly people (currently 15 million over 55) as a percentage of the overall population than ever before, making them a significant viewing segment – the heaviest viewers of television, averaging 35 hours a week, according to **John Willis** ('Over 50 and overlooked', 1999).

- **Affluence**: The 'Grey Pound' (the amount of money the elderly have available to spend on consumer goods) is increasingly attractive to the advertisers who fund large areas of the British media. According to the Henley Centre, for example, around 80% of wealth in Britain is held by those aged 45+.

- **Media professionals**: The mass media is a relatively new phenomenon in our society (it is only in the past 40 years, for example, that television has become a mass medium) and, as the people who own, control and work in the media grow older it's possible their interests are reflected in new and different representations of the elderly.

- **Stereotypes**: The above notwithstanding, **Willis** (1999) notes that: 'older people were often crudely stereotyped in drama, with 46% of fictional portrayals showing them as grumpy, interfering, lonely, stubborn and not interested in sex. Older women are often seen as "silly", older men as "miserable gits"'.

In some situations, middle-aged or elderly men (in particular) are used to add a sense of seriousness/moral gravity to a situation; news readers (such as Trevor McDonald) and current affaires presenters (such as David Frost), for example, often fall into this category.

'Advertising concentrated on false teeth and stair lifts' (Willis, 1999) – although not necessarily at the same time.

- **Ghettoisation**: Different age groups are neatly compartmentalised into discrete (separate and self-contained) categories. The conflicts that supposedly arise at the point where adults meet youth, for example, is an unending source of inspiration for media writers (from 'The Simpson's' onwards).

Connor (2001) also points to the way ghettoes exist *within* age groups and media: 'In print … youth magazines are often split along gender lines and it is difficult to find any popular magazine that crosses the gender divide'. **Willis** (1999) notes, in terms of television: 'Everyone over the age of 55 tends to be lumped together as if they were a completely homogeneous group.'

Gender representations

These can be consider in the following terms:

- **The gaze**: At its most obvious, the male gaze refers to areas such as pornography or the use of female bodies in advertising; less obviously, it refers to how images of women are presented from both the male perspective and for the gratification of a male audience – the viewer becomes a *spectator* (or *voyeur* in some cases), who looks, through male eyes, at women reduced to *objects* (a series of body parts).

While this form of gaze is still evident, feminist writers such as **Nuria Enciso** ('Turning the Gaze Around', 1995) argue women have become more adept at developing a female gaze. **Eva-Maria Jacobsson** ('A Female Gaze?', 1999), for example, argues it is increasingly possible (in some areas of the media) for women to develop a female gaze that encourages

This (Jean Paul Gaultier) advert uses a naked woman to sell perfume

the viewer to see both men and women in non-sexist ways – although Enciso notes this 'reversal of the male gaze' may simply result in men being viewed as objects by women.

- **Stereotypes** take a number of forms, but the most obvious ones include:

  - **Body shape** – traditionally this focused on women but is increasingly relevant for men (although men are allowed a greater range of culturally acceptable body shapes). This does, of course, form part of a wider set of ideas surrounding cultural debates about beauty and how women, in particular, should look (especially in terms of the unstated assumptions that female beauty is both heterosexual and largely for the benefit of the male gaze).

  - **Masculinity** and **femininity** are also heavily stereotyped across a range of media (although factors such as age and class are significant components of the overall picture – young masculinity, for example, is represented in different ways to elderly masculinity).

    Helen Macdonald ('Magazine advertising and gender', 2003) also identifies differences in the way men and women are represented in magazine adverts. Alcohol adverts, for example, generally demonstrate traditional gender differences, in terms of the way men and women are sold different types of drink. Adverts aimed at men, for example, showed a restricted range of drinks 'allowed' to men (mainly beer and spirits) and also maintained a 'harder', more individualistic, image of masculinity associated with alcohol.

Adverts aimed at women, on the other hand, emphasised a 'softer', more social, aspect to drinking (bringing people together, easing tensions and so forth) as well as allowing women a greater range of alcoholic options (wine and liqueurs, for example).

However, a certain category of female (popularly labelled 'ladettes' to emphasise their similarity to 'lads') were seen to both challenge these stereotypes and break down the gender barriers between the sexes. This type of femininity seemed to emphasise the ability of women to behave in much the same kind of way as their male counterparts (drinking pints, 'behaving badly' …).

This change in representation indicates, for **Macdonald**, 'that gender is not static and woman are permitted to take on certain masculine behaviours in certain situations.'

- **Sexuality**: Female sexuality is frequently used to sell consumer goods and, in this respect, a particular form of (hetero) sexuality is often used, combining body shapes (thin, large-breasted and so forth) with patriarchal notions of 'availability'. Lynx deodorant, for example, in 2004 advertised using the suggestion young women are sexually attracted to the men who use it (although how this passes the Advertising Standards Authority's requirement an advert be 'honest and truthful' escapes me).

- **Normality**, in terms of gender concepts and relationships, is invariably represented in terms of heterosexuality and, while the wilder representations of gay males and females are largely a thing of the past, homosexual relationships are rarely portrayed as being part of a 'normal' gender discourse.

Dominant females, for example, are often represented as figures of fun or (deviant) sexuality, although there are significant exceptions – Sigourney Weaver's character (Ripley) in the film *Alien*, for example, was physically and mentally stronger than any of the characters around her. However, this type of representation seems to be just that – a significant exception from the norm.

- **Bodies**: Representations of male and female bodies are important, especially in terms of how they have both changed (think about the current emphasis on images of *sexualised male bodies* – the 'six-pack', for example, held up to be sexually desirable for women and culturally desirable for men) and, to some extent, not changed – the way female bodies, for example, are displayed in magazines and on television. We can see this in terms of:

  - **Advertising**: A significant recent development is the use of bodies as both 'walking advertising spaces' (for global brands such as Nike) and as a means of making gender statements. In this respect, **Ros Gill** ('From sexual objectification to sexual subjectification', 2003) uses the example of T-shirts with the slogan 'Fit chick unbelievable knockers' to demonstrate the idea of both 'sexualised self-presentation' (women having the freedom to advertise their sexuality) and as an example of how women collude in their own objectification (being seen as one-dimensional sexual objects rather than rounded individuals). As she argues:

Growing it yourself: representing gender

As a class, identify consumer products that could be advertised to men and women (I've listed some suggestions below to get you started).

Split the class into small groups and then pair each group with another group (for example, if the class has six groups of three people, this will become three paired groups). Each paired group then needs to choose a product to advertise. Once this is agreed, the task is to design a poster to advertise the product.

For one paired group, the task is to advertise the product to **men**.

For the other paired group the task is to advertise the same product to **women**.

Possible products to advertise: boxer shorts, beer, personal computer, shirt, briefcase, nail varnish, dishwasher, picture frame.

Once the paired groups have completed their advertising posters they should present and explain their poster to the whole class in turn.

A generation ago many women were ... fighting not to be portrayed in this ... manner, not to be reduced to the size of their breasts, or to be consumed only as sexual objects, and yet today young women are actually paying good money ... to present themselves in this way.

- **Objects of desire**: Female (and to a much lesser extent, male) nudity in the media has, in recent years, become a matter for debate. On the one hand, feminists, such as **Gill**, have argued women in general are exploited by displays of naked/semi-naked female flesh because it represents women as consumer objects (or commodities to be 'bought and sold'), whereas an alternative interpretation is that such displays *empower* women by not only allowing them to express their sexuality but to get paid for doing it – a view expressed in the following extract from *The Sun* (2004)

'[Big Brother 5's] Shell believes our topless shots are works of art, which could one day hang in the **TATE**.

She said: "Those who sneer at Page 3 lack intelligence. It's beautifully shot and tastefully pioneered the celebration of the female form".

"In many ways it emancipated women, letting them exploit their assets, earn cash and keep control. I see it as a modern art form."'

- **Identities**: In relation to the material we've examined so far, the general impression seems to be of a confused (and confusing) situation in which men and women are represented in terms of both traditional stereotypes and ways that challenge, confront and break down these stereotypical gender barriers. This shouldn't, however, be too surprising for reasons relating to the *heterogeneity* of:

  - **Gender**: 'Men' and 'women' are not (as I've suggested) *homogenous* (all the same) categories; age differences, for example, have a significant impact on both social identities and how gender is represented in the media.
  - **Media**: Similarly, 'the media' is not a simple homogeneous category; it covers a wide range of different types that aim at – and appeal to – a range

of different gender categories (considered in terms of class, age, ethnicity and so forth).

This 'confusion' is, of course, echoed in sociological interpretations of the nature and meaning of media representations of gender. On the one hand, there is a general recognition of:

- **Change** – young people today, for example, are different – in terms of attitudes and behaviours – to previous generations.
- **Fragmentation** reflects the idea that, with generational changes, it makes it harder – if not impossible – to talk about 'men' or 'women' as useful gender categories. Rather, we need to think in terms of the different ways it is possible to be 'a man' or 'a woman' in our society.
- **Fluidity**: Gender identities are not fixed and unchanging. Fragmented social identities are reflected in the way people start to see themselves (their *personal identities*) in new and different ways, some forms of which involve identities that have little or no apparent permanence but which change from day to day and situation to situation.

On the other hand, how this situation is interpreted differs:

Ros Gill (2003), for example, argues contemporary representations of women, while no longer depicting them as 'passive objects' of the male gaze, are not 'liberating' but rather they are another – more exploitative – form of what **Susan Bordo** (*Unbearable Weight: Feminism, Western Culture and the Body*, 1993) has termed a 'new disciplinary regime'. In other words, although media representations of women offer the 'promise of power' by suggesting they can choose whether or not to become 'sex objects', this promise is illusory since, whether they choose it or not, the objective is to please men.

David Gauntlett (*Media, Gender and Identity: An Introduction*, 2002) on the other hand, takes the view that '*within limits*, the mass media is a force for change'. He argues, for example, that traditional views of women (as a housewife or low-status worker) have been replaced by 'feisty, successful "girl power" icons'. Men have changed, from 'ideals of absolute toughness, stubborn self-reliance and emotional silence' to a greater emphasis on emotions, the need for help and advice and the 'problems of masculinity'.

In this respect, **Angela McRobbie** (*In the Culture Society: Art, Fashion and Popular Music*, 1999) argues the media have (partly in response to traditional feminism), adopted and adapted a form of 'popular feminism', whereby social and sexual inequalities are expressed (through the media and by women) in terms of 'a raunchy language of "shagging, snogging and having a good time".'

Ethnic representation

As with the other categories we have considered, a striking feature of ethnic representation is the change from the *crude* forms of stereotypical, negative and demeaning representations of 'black people' prevalent in even the recent past (see, for example, hugely popular television sitcoms

Discussion point: art or artifice?

This exercise relates to the work you've just done on 'objects of desire' and identities. You should be able to draw on material like *The Sun* article and the work of Gill, Gauntlett and McRobbie.

In small groups, make two lists (based on the following table). One list should focus on reasons why semi-naked pictures of women in the media are exploitative (of both men *and* women), the other should focus on how such pictures empower women.

As a class, compare your lists. What conclusions can you draw from this debate (it would be interesting to see if males and females in the class draw similar or different conclusions and, if so, why)?

Exploitative?	Empowering?
Demeans women by reducing them to objects	Well-paid work
Encourages women to participate in their own exploitation (Gill)	Women exploit men by making themselves objects of sexual desire.
Further examples?	

such as *Love Thy Neighbour* in the early 1970s in which blacks were described as '*sambos*' and '*nignogs*'), to forms of representation that are, at least in some respects, less stereotypical.

However, the main question to note here is the extent to which changes in media representation reflect real changes (towards less overtly biased and stereotypical images, for example) or what **Stuart Hall** ('The Whites of Their Eyes', 1995) has called **inferential racism**. While representations are less overtly and crudely racist, ethnic groups are still discussed and represented in ways that stress their difference (usually in cultural, rather than biological, terms) and problematic nature (for example, debates about ethnicity revolving around ethnic groups as the source of social problems).

- **Under-representation**: According to the Office for National Statistics (2004), in 2001, approximately 8% of the British population (5 million people) were classified as belonging to 'non-White' ethnic groups. However, when it comes to participation in areas of the media such as television, ethnic minorities are, according to **Annabelle Sreberny** (*Include Me In*, 1999) 'represented by two-dimensional characters, and . . . often negatively stereotyped'. Examples of **stereotyping** noted by Sreberny included *Coronation Street* introducing a black character (Marcus Wrigley) who promptly helped burgle a house and an Asian family (the Desai's) who took over – as if you couldn't guess – the corner shop. An Independent Television Commission survey (2001) also found 'The use of stereotypes in TV advertisements can reinforce racism and school bullying'.

  Rachel Morris ('Gypsies, Travellers and the Media', 2000) also points to another ethnic group (Roma) who have been increasingly stereotyped in the national print media in two ways. Firstly, for *not* fitting the 'stereotype that has been carved out for them: the "true" Gypsy' and secondly in terms of negative

characterisations such as being 'dirty, thieving, parasitic, living outside the law' and so forth.

- **Over-representation**, on the other hand, derives in part from some of the ideas we have just noted and relates to areas such as:

  - **Crime**: **Beata Klimkiewicz** ('Participation of ethnic minorities in the public sphere', 1999) points to the way ethnic minorities most frequently feature as agents of both domestic criminality and international terrorism.

  - **Victimisation**, where the reporting of 'natural disasters', such as floods and famines in places like Africa features heavily in international news reporting. **Klimkiewicz** also suggests ethnic minorities in Britain feature most heavily in news media as victims of racism and discrimination. This is somewhat ironic in light of an ICAR report ('Media image, community impact', 2004) that showed how negative newspaper coverage of asylum issues could be linked to violence and harassment of ethnic minorities.

- **The gaze**: With notable exceptions (which somewhat prove the rule) such as comedy programmes like *Goodness Gracious Me* (an all Asian cast – the title is an ironic reference to film and television stereotypes of Asian speech), ethnic minorities and their lives are generally viewed through a white (largely middle class) gaze.

  Ben Carrington (' "Race", Representation and the Sporting Body', 2002) notes how apparently 'positive' black identities are constructed around cultural spaces like sport, fashion and music (rap and hip-hop, for example). As he argues 'Consumers can now enjoy the spectacle of blackness 24-7, in a way which is no longer threatening by its mere presence, for those who now actively desire a taste for "a bit of the other"'. However, he also notes the 'spectacle of "hyperblackness"' highlights how such representations promote stereotypes of 'black bodies' that reflect white perceptions of race conceived in terms of 'athleticism and animalism' (the idea these features of black excellence are somehow 'natural').

The white gaze also, of course, extends into other areas (the lack of ethnic minority ownership and control within the media, for example) and is probably most evident in relation to concepts of:

- **The other**: One significant feature of non-white representation (in both the media and society generally) is the way ethnic minorities are frequently discussed in terms of their 'otherness' – how 'they' are different from 'Us'. In this respect, representations are produced against a social background that constructs ethnicity in terms of not just 'difference' (since we are all, in some way, different) but significantly in terms of *social problems*. This representational discourse emphasises two main strands; firstly, the idea of ethnic minorities as:
  - **Cultural problems**: Although it is no longer socially acceptable for the mainstream media to express openly racist ideas and attitudes (forms of *institutional racism*, evident in the recent past that saw it acceptable to

talk and write about 'blacks' in discriminatory terms), racism is still apparent, but framed in a different way. **Paul Gilroy** ('One Nation under a Groove', 1990) has termed this **cultural racism** (or the '**new racism**') because of the way it focuses on ideas like 'cultural differences' between white and non-white ethnic groups (in areas like language, family life and so forth). **Sreberny** (1999) noted the tendency for the media to think about Asian family life in terms of 'arranged marriages'; more recently, this focus has turned to the concept of 'forced marriages' and issues of violence surrounding this idea. (**Anthony Browne**: 'Age bar to curb forced marriages': *The Times*, 14 May 2003).

In turn, these ideas link into immigration and political asylum (the 'problem' of 'economic migrants'). The headline 'Forced marriages targeted' (BBC News, 14 May, 2003), for example, suggested changes to immigration law were 'a response to widespread concern about schoolgirls being forced into marriages with men from their parents' home countries, who go their own way once they have been granted residency in the UK'.

The second representational strand is that of:

- **Threat**, which represents ethnic minorities in terms of both a **cultural threat** (presenting challenges to a 'British' way of life – see 'arranged and forced marriages', for example) and a **physical threat** which occurs on both a *societal level*, considered in terms of the various representations of 'Muslims' and 'Terrorists' following the September 11th terror attacks, for example, and a *personal level*. Periodic moral panics about 'black criminality', for example, have been highlighted by writers such as **Stuart Hall** (*Policing the Crisis*, 1978) when he talked about 'black muggers' as folk devils in the 1970s. More recently, the identification of 'muggings in London' as being 'predominantly a black crime' by the Metropolitan Police (**Hugh Muir**, 'Sometimes a mugger's race does matter': *Evening Standard*, 6 February 2002) can also be seen as part of the representation process.

Rosalind Yarde ('Demons of the day', 2001), argues this 'discourse of threat' is not a recent phenomenon when she notes: 'Asylum crisis, hordes of refugees – after 40 years, papers are still telling the same old lies'. She also points out:

> Since September 11, the stereotypes have become interwoven and confused. The storylines have blurred. The demons have interchanged . . . the newspapers chant Asylum seekers, Muslims, Terrorists! . . . It used to be All muggers are black! . . . then like Chinese whispers, the message altered to All blacks are muggers!

> Now I watch as three become one. The asylum seeker, the Muslim, the terrorist are transmogrified into – the Muslim, terrorist, asylum seeker. All encapsulated in headlines such as: 'Asylum seeker who helped the hitmen' (*Daily Mail* 19/09/01)'.

Disability representations

These can be considered in the following way.

- **Labelling**: The first thing we can note about representations of 'the disabled' is the label itself since it involves, by definition, a concept of inequality – to be

disabled is somehow not as good as being 'abled'. **Lynne Roper** ('Disability in Media', 2003) argues we should distinguish between *impairment* – a real physical or mental state involving limitations in some situations – and *disability*, which she argues is a cultural construct. That is, a label implying notions of 'damage' and inability.

An alternative way to think about this area, therefore, is to use the label 'differently-abled' (or '**difabled**'); this suggests, I hope you'll agree, a sense of difference without the negative connotations.

- **Under-representation**: The Labour Force Survey (2001) estimated nearly seven million adults in the UK are disabled – a minority, to be sure, but at nearly 15% of the adult population, a significant minority. However, a striking feature of media representations of the difabled is their *omission*; **Paul Darke** ('Introductory Essay on Normality Theory', 2003), for example, notes: 'whereas there used to be (within the last five years) a number of... Disability... series on a number of UK television channels there is now none'. Part of this decrease, he argues, is caused by an *increased* number of television channels; greater competition and the need to maximise audience numbers to attract advertising has resulted in a decline in 'minority interest' programming.

This is not, of course, to say difability itself is always absent from mainstream media. Under certain circumstances (war, for example) images of disability (sic) are frequently used and these serve to highlight:

Discussion point: what's in a name?

Kelly Holmes won two gold medals at the 2004 Olympics – and you didn't. Compared to her, therefore, does this make you:

- Disabled?
- Differently abled?

Support your argument with clear reasons.

Kelly Holmes – double gold medal winner: Athens 2004

- **Normality** and abnormality, which clearly feature in portrayals of difability, given 'the disabled' can be easily represented in terms of their physical or mental differences. Aside from offering reassurance to the able-bodied ('they' are different to 'us') the focus, according to **Barnes** and **Mercer** ('Exploring the Divide', 1996) is on 'disability as deviance' – or, as **Ashwin Bulsara** ('Depictions of people with disabilities in the British media', 2001) argues

'Disabled people have been presented as socially flawed able-bodied people rather than as disabled people with their own identity'. This, of course, leads us to:

- **Stereotypes**: The argument here is that, for the media, difabled people are interesting *because of* their disability, not as people in themselves. The focus of attention therefore – the thing that defines 'disabled identity' – is their physical or mental difference (although, as with most stereotypical representations, there are exceptions – the physicist, Stephen Hawking (below), for example, is valued for his intellectual abilities).

Jenny Morris ('A Feminist Perspective', 1997) has also noticed a curious aspect of disability stereotyping: 'most disabled characters in film and television in recent years have been men'. She attributes this to the media using disability as a 'narrative device to express ideas of dependency, lack of autonomy, tragedy etc.' and 'Women do not have to be portrayed as disabled in order to present an image of vulnerability and dependency'.

Stephen Hawking

- **The gaze** has two aspects here. Firstly, the world, as expressed through the media, is almost exclusively seen through the eyes of the able-bodied. Where the difabled appear, they do so largely as 'objects of curiosity' – to be looked at and explained, rather than as 'normal people' living their lives in a world organised in terms of the needs of the able-bodied. Secondly, where the gaze of the latter falls on the disabled, it does so, according to **Colin Barnes** (*Disabling Imagery and the Media*, 1992) in ways that categorise 'the disabled' in highly stereotyped ways – as the following exercise demonstrates.

Sexuality representations

These refer mainly to differences within and between heterosexual and homosexual representations and we can discuss the role of the media here in the following terms.

- **Normal** and abnormal sexuality is a recurring feature of tabloid newspapers, whereby various aspects of sexuality (especially male homosexuality) are represented in ways that 'define the normal'. For example, homosexuality has been variously linked in the British tabloid press to both paedophilia and AIDS (*The Sun*, for example, describing it as a 'Gay Plague' even in the face of evidence to the contrary – the use of 'plague' is also interesting here since it, probably consciously, echoes the idea of biblical plagues – punishments visited on humanity by God).

Gareth McLean ('It's a Male Thing', 2002) however, argues the nature of tabloid press *homophobia* (fear of homosexuality) has changed in the face

 Growing it yourself: stereotype spotting

Barnes argues media portrayals of disability fall into 10 basic categories (see table below). Can you find examples in the media of each category?

Representation	Media Examples
Pitiable and pathetic	
Object of violence	
Sinister and evil	Nick Cotton (*EastEnders*)
Curiosity	Dustin Hoffman (*Rain Man*)
Super cripple (someone able to overcome their disability)	Christy Brown, writer (*My Left Foot*) Stephen Hawking.
Own worst enemy	
Burden/dependent	
Sexually abnormal	
Incapable	
Normal	

of changing public attitudes: *The Sun* 'that once printed "10 Ways to Spot a Gay Priest", allowed Garry Bushell to call gay people "poofters" and announced a "gay cult" was undermining public morals ... now recognises that much coveted younger readers will not tolerate the knee-jerk bigotry that previously passed for balanced coverage.'

- **Natural** and unnatural sexualities. A couple of interesting areas are covered here.

  - **Love**: The media continuously reinforces this concept (although, unlike in the recent past, no longer necessarily in the context of marriage) as a *natural* state of being for heterosexual – and, increasingly, homosexual – couples.

  - **Deviance**: Although the tabloid press in particular relishes the idea of 'deviant sexuality' – whether it's 'three-in-a-bed sex romps' or some form of sexuality deemed 'unnatural' – the media tends to see one-to-one sexuality as natural, normal and desirable.

    In the recent past, media concepts of deviant sexualities focused, as I have suggested, on homosexual behaviour (male homosexuality has only been legal in this country for about 40 years); however, with increasing public and media acceptance of such sexuality, the focus has turned towards areas such as paedophilia – recent moral panics over this practice have resulted not only in public demonstrations and violence against 'paedophiles', but also legal changes to prevent, for example, 'grooming' through internet chatrooms. A

significant development here has been the *sexualisation* of some forms of child/adult behaviour; in other words, many forms of adult involvement with children have been reconceptualised and reinterpreted as sexual behaviour.

- **Transgressive sexualities** (forms of sexuality that cut across gender categories) also tend to both lack expression in the media and invite scorn, derision or fear. A neat example here might be the relationship between sexuality and disability; the physically and mentally disabled are rarely represented in a sexual way, either as sexually active beings or as sexually attractive.

- **The gaze**: In general, although alternative forms of sexuality (such as male and female homosexuality) are increasingly represented in the media (in terms of press reporting, TV programming and advertising, for example) **Jayne Caudwell** ('Tipping the Velvet: Straight [forward] voyeurism?', 2003) argues numerous writers have suggested this increased representation represents a form of (male) heterosexual voyeurism – in effect, an example of the way straightforward pornographic images have effectively crossed-over into mainstream (or, indeed, *malestream*) culture.

  In addition, in programmes such as *Queer Eye for the Straight Guy* (Channel 4: 2004), we find a form of gaze that, while seemingly homosexual (a bunch of gay men putting a heterosexual man straight (pun intended) about clothes and culture), is mainly viewed through a heterosexual lens. In other words, such programmes are not about gay men, as such, but about selling a certain type of lifestyle – cool, hip, fashionable and ever-so-slightly dangerous – to a heterosexual audience.

In relation to advertising, there has certainly been an increase in homosexual representation (although whether this reflects the media leading changes in public attitudes or – more likely perhaps – finally latching on to more tolerant audience attitudes is an arguable point). However, where gay men feature they tend to be presented as 'stereotypical gays' – camp, suggestive but ultimately sexually unthreatening.

The male gaze is not, of course, restricted to homosexuality; the heterosexual youth magazine market, for example, has developed in recent years with (non-pornographic) magazines such as *Zoo*, *Nuts*, *FHM* and *Loaded* featuring a diet of 'Birds, Booze and Football' as a way of attracting readers and advertisers. Magazines aimed at women, however, tend to stress how to attract the male gaze – including advice on looking pretty, how to attract a man and so forth. Alternatively, writers such as **Gauntlett** (2002) argue women buy magazines like *More* and *Cosmopolitan* for reasons of self-esteem, reassurance and so forth.

- **Codes**: One interesting change in the way homosexuality is represented is that the language used to describe gay men and women no longer relies on the kind of semiological (symbolic) references to gay sexuality common in even the recent past (a classic example being the term 'confirmed bachelor' used by newspapers to suggest male homosexuality). This partly reflects changing audience attitudes (as noted above), but it also reflects the way gays have organised to promote their own sexuality (the adoption of the term 'Queer Theory', for example, to describe a growing body of social research into gay culture and lifestyles has consciously adopted a term of abuse directed at homosexuals and, by so doing, neutralised its negative impact).

McLean does, however, point to a changing media discourse of homosexuality; it may no longer (or increasingly rarely) be represented as an 'illness' or something secretive and shameful, but as he notes: 'sly homophobia is still rife ... the fact [Pop Idol winner, Will Young's] coming out was seen as a "confession" ... is indicative of the idea that homosexuality is something of a sin, a foible to be "admitted" (does anyone, for example, ever have to "confess" or "admit" to being heterosexual?)'.

Similarly, media representations of lesbianism have changed significantly over the past 25 years; depictions of 'butch, shaven-headed, women in dungarees and boots' are largely redundant images (although, on occasions some tabloid newspapers resurrect it, especially if they want to criticise radical feminism). However, as I've noted, writers such as **Caudwell** (2003) question the extent to which current media representations of lesbians simply reflect a changed male (political) gaze. In the recent past the media associated lesbianism with feminism – as something to be feared, ridiculed and marginalised; the decline in feminism's influence perhaps reflects the decoupling of lesbianism from feminism – returning it to its pre-feminist status as a male fantasy.

 Digging deeper

When we reflect on the role of the media in the creation and promotion of representations relating to the kind of indicators we have discussed in this section, we need to keep in mind the following ideas.

- **Mediation**: As we have seen earlier with Fiske's idea of a *transparency fallacy*, the world presented through the media is not 'real', in the sense of our witnessing or experiencing it first-hand; rather, what we get is a *reconstructed reality* – one that is filtered (or mediated) through a media lens. In other words, the media presents

us with an interpreted view of things like gender, class, sexuality and disability. In this respect, when we talk about mediation we are thinking about:

- **Stereotypes**: There is little doubt the media, in terms of representation, deals in stereotypical constructions; however, one question here, perhaps, is the extent to which media stereotypes constitute **misrepresentations**. When we argue, for example, that someone or something is *misrepresented* by the media (because it involves over-simplification, mediation or stereotype), we start to dig into a range of interesting ideas. On one level, for example, we could note **Andy Medhurst**'s ('Tracing Desires', 1998) observation in relation to sexuality that stereotypical representations of gay men or women are

 Growing it yourself: representations

One way of understanding media representations is to do your own research, using a variety of media and generating a range of different examples of the way different groups are represented. The following table illustrates how this can be done, using a range of categories we've already noted for you to apply across the key markers we've identified.

Concepts	Class	Age	Gender	Ethnicity	Disability	Sexuality
Invisibility						
Codes						
Annihilations						
Under-representation						
Ghettoisation						
Marginalisation						
Categorisation						
Normality						
The gaze						
Bodies						

In small groups in pairs, choose a category (class, for example) and find/suggest relevant examples for each of the concepts we've identified.

'the means through which ideologies about sexuality are circulated'. In other words, by representing gay men, for example, as 'effeminate' or 'camp', the media is articulating not just a simple representation of homosexuality but rather, as **Mitchell** (*Picture Theory*, 1994) suggests, 'representation constructs knowledge' – through the representation of something we may come to (mis)understand it.

Medhurst argues it is a mistake to see stereotypes simply in terms of misrepresentation since, as he argues, if we reject the kind of media stereotype about 'gay men' we have just noted, how can we replace it, except by 'creating another stereotype [which] would do away with "gay men are effeminate" and replace it with "all gay men are masculine"; a positive image is really only a stereotype that suits my ideology rather than yours'. These ideas, therefore, lead us to consider another level of misrepresentation when we think about the nature of any relationship between representations and **reality**. If we think about the idea of something being represented through the media it suggests, as **Stuart Hall** (*Cultural Representations and Signifying Practices*, 1997) argues, there must exist the thing that is being portrayed. The use of this idea suggests that somewhere, 'out there', is a reality – a 'set of unchanging meanings' as Hall puts it – to be represented. Thus, for the media to produce *representations* of reality (which aren't real precisely because they *represent* 'that which is real') it follows there must, ultimately, be something that is 'really real' – otherwise it couldn't have

a representation; there would, by definition, be nothing to represent.

To take this (slightly mind-boggling) idea further we can consider an alternative way of looking at media representations than the one that has been used throughout this section.

Postmodernist writers, such as **Jean Baudrillard** (*The Gulf War Did Not Take Place*, 1995), argue representations should not be considered in terms of things like distortions, misrepresentations or, indeed, simple reflections of 'reality'; this is because, for such writers, representations *are* reality. We can develop this idea in the following way: when we think uncritically about the word 'represent' it suggests the media re-presents something (like 'news') in a way that's somehow different to the original event; in other words, 'Something Happened' (to borrow **Joseph Heller**'s evocative phrase) and now it's being described (*re-presented*) to us. Conventionally, therefore, we contrast 'the real' (the 'something' that 'happened') with the representation and examine the media (and the various processes involved in things like 'news production') to see if we can disentangle the *real* from the *not real*. We can perhaps understand this quite complex idea more easily in the following way.

When Baudrillard argues that 'the [first] Gulf War didn't happen' he's not saying there was no war. Rather, he's saying 'the reality of the war' is different depending on who you were, where you were and what your source of information was. For example, soldiers fighting in battle had one experience of the war; civilians caught up in the fighting had another;

journalists reporting the war another still and people reading about and watching the war from the comfort of their living room had yet another.

In other words, the Gulf War (as, by extension, is everything presented by the media) was *experienced* as *multiple realities*, all of which are real and, of course, none of which are real, since they are simply representations of reality from different viewpoints. Thus, the 'reality of the war' can't be found in any one of the things I have just noted since they were all, in their different ways, 'real' experiences – they are all equally valid *narrative accounts* of the war. In this respect, Baudrillard uses the term **hyperreality** to express how different narrative accounts sit side by side, interweave and conflict in an ever-changing pattern of representation built upon representation until they form a 'reality' in themselves – something that is 'more real than reality' since, in the case of the Gulf War, for example (or any event you care to name – the Crusades, the Second World War, the death of Princess Diana . . .) our knowledge of 'what happened' simply derives from a range of different representations from which we pick-and-choose to suit our own particular prejudices or beliefs. Baudrillard calls this **simulacra** (or 'representations that refer to other representations') – in basic terms, *simulations* that are themselves the reality they depict. What this means, I would argue, is that to talk about media representations as distortions or misrepresentations of some hidden or obscured 'reality' (or 'deep structures' as post-modernists like to term them) is,

from a postmodern perspective, to miss the point entirely; The media don't simply 'mediate the message'; the media – to coin a phrase – *are* 'the message'.

In this and the previous sections we have examined a range of ideas surrounding the media, from the significance of the distinction between ownership and control, through ideas about media ideologies and the various ways social groups are represented. In the final section we can bring these ideas together by examining possible *media effects*; how audiences are influenced – or not as the case may be – by the media.

The media and their audiences

Introduction

In this final section we are going to look at different explanations of the relationship between the mass media and their audiences, largely in terms of what are called 'Media Effects'; that is, a selection of theories that seek to identify how – and in what ways – the media affect our behaviour.

Although there is a certain chronology to Effects theories – one that reflects changing academic developments and fashions (as a general rule, theories that argue the media *directly affects* audiences precede theories that take a more critical look at audience behaviour) – the approach here will be to consider various theories in terms of three categories of effect.

- **Direct**: These are sometimes called *mediacentric* or **transmission** theories

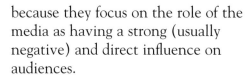

because they focus on the role of the media as having a strong (usually negative) and direct influence on audiences.

- **Limited**: These are sometimes called *audiocentric* or **diffusion** theories because they focus on the various ways audiences *use* the media to satisfy their own particular needs. For these theories, the mass media has few, if any, direct effects.
- **Indirect**: Theories in this category, while arguing for a range of media effects, sees these as slow and cumulative, rather than quick and direct.

There are two main reasons for using this type of categorisation.

- **Persistence**: Theories that have been challenged or disproved do not necessarily just 'fade away' – they may well reform, evolve and reappear at a later point in a different form. A simple 'theoretical timeline' may not capture these relationships and changes very convincingly.
- **Common sense**: Although academic sociologists may decide a particular theory is redundant, this doesn't mean media commentators or their audiences feel the same way. *Common sense* ideas about media effects often persist, regardless of the efforts of media sociologists to debunk them. In addition, we often find very simple – and simplistic – theories of media effects persist precisely because they represent a way of making the incomprehensible understandable to those not schooled in the darker arts of media theory.

WARM UP: FEELING THE FORCE?

This short exercise is designed to start you thinking about your own beliefs (positive and negative) about how the media affects audiences.

In small groups discuss/identify three or four examples of possible positive and negative effects – situations, for example, where you think the media influences people in some way. These can be from your own experience or from what you have seen, read or heard in the media.

Positive effects?	Negative effects?
Entertainment for the lonely	Does it frighten/panic some people?

Once you have done this, share your ideas with the rest of the class and, for each of the effects identified, discuss whether you think they:

- Affect everyone equally (and if not, why not?)
- Affect an audience directly or indirectly.

One of the things this exercise will have demonstrated is the significance of **Curren's** argument (*Media and Power*, 2002) that: 'The conviction ... the media are important agencies of influence is broadly correct. However, the ways in which the media exert influence are complex and contingent'. We can translate this idea into a relatively simple statement: We know the media affect people, but the crucial questions are how – and in what ways – are audiences influenced? We can begin to explore these questions by examining a range of 'Media Effects' theories.

189

Direct Media Effects

⚠ Preparing the ground

One of – if not the – oldest form of Effects theory is based on the idea of a relatively simple, direct and effective relationship between the media (as producers and transmitters of messages) and their audience (who both receive and act on such messages). This theory has two basic forms.

- **Hypodermic syringe** (or *magic bullet*) models: At its most basic, this theory suggests the media transmit 'messages' (ideas, information, beliefs and so forth) that are then picked-up and acted upon by the audience (receivers). Media messages, therefore, are a bit like a drug injected into the body that is the audience.

This theory, as you might expect, presupposes a number of things.

- **Effects** are direct and measurable – we can see the effect of messages on an audience in terms of a **cause and effect** relationship. The media (cause) does something and the audience reacts (effect) in some way.

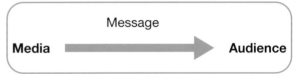

The Hypodermic Model

- **Immediacy**: For the media to be a cause of audience behaviour there has to be some sort of *immediate* audience reaction (otherwise we could not be sure the media was the cause of changes in people's behaviour).

- **Audience**: The consumers of media messages are *passive receivers* (as opposed to *active interpreters* – an idea we will develop in relation to other effects theories) of media messages. The reason for this is found in the idea of **mass society**. As we've seen in an earlier section, this argues people are *socially isolated*; in other words, they have few, if any, strong links to social networks (family, friends, communities and so forth) that provide alternative sources of information and interpretation. In this situation, therefore, audiences are receptive to whatever the media transmits because they depend on it for information.

A second form of this type of theory is a:

- **Transmission** model: Developed originally by **Shannon** and **Weaver** (*The mathematical theory of communication*, 1949) this suggests a slightly more sophisticated form of relationship between the media and their audience, in a couple of ways.

- **Senders**: It splits the transmission process into two parts; the *information source* (which can be anything – a government announcement, for example) and the *transmission source* (a television report of the announcement, for example).

- **Receivers**: Although media messages can be directly sent to a receiver (such as an audience watching a news broadcast), it's possible for people who are not watching the broadcast to also receive the message (or at least, a form of the message) through their interaction with people who did watch it (in other words, people may pass on messages to those who haven't personally experienced them).

This theory also introduces the concept of:

- **Noise** or **interference** – which can be anything that distracts an audience. For example, when watching a news broadcast, someone may leave the room to make a cup of tea, thereby missing some part of the message.

As we will see in a moment, this variation on the basic 'direct effects' theory paved the way for a more-critical understanding of how the media relates to its audience. However, before we look at such theories, we can identify some criticisms of this general transmission model (to give it a critical kicking, as we say in the trade).

Note: If you wanted to classify this type of theory in terms of sociological perspectives, the closest fit (at least for the earliest types of transmission theories) would be the New Right (later versions, focusing on ideas like globalisation and new types of mass society theory, can, however, be associated with New Left/Marxist perspectives).

⚠ Digging deeper

As **David Gauntlett** ('10 Things Wrong with the "Effects Model"', 1998) has argued, there are problems with transmission theories we can summarise in the following terms:

- **Audience**: As we have seen, original versions of this theory treated audiences as uncritical, gullible, individuals easily influenced and led by whatever they read, saw or heard in the media.

One particular piece of evidence often cited to support this idea (and the theory itself) is **Orson Welles'** infamous *War of the Worlds* broadcast (1938), a radio play cleverly designed to simulate a Martian attack using the news broadcasting techniques of the time. The received wisdom here is that many Americans believed they were hearing about a real invasion and panicked in a variety of ways; the evidence for this 'mass hysteria' is, however, actually quite thin.

From an audience of around 6 million people, *some* people clearly did feel unsettled by what they heard (a police station in the area of the supposed invasion answered around 50 calls from worried residents), but accounts of people 'fleeing to the hills' have been grossly exaggerated over the years. The remarkable thing about this story is not so much people believed what they were hearing, but that the behaviour of the vast majority of listeners was not influenced or changed in any appreciable way.

- **Artificial conditions**: Most research into transmission effects has taken place under conditions (in a laboratory for example) that inadequately represent the real situations in which people use the media. **Bandura, Ross** and **Ross**'s 'Bo-Bo doll' experiment ('Transmission of aggression through imitation of aggressive models', 1961), for example, is frequently cited as evidence that watching violent TV programmes produces violent behaviour in children (although I suspect that if anyone was selectively fed a diet of violence they might want to take out their frustration by bashing a large plastic 'Bo-Bo' doll over the head for a few minutes). One of the (many) weaknesses of the study was that the children in the study were 'rated for violence' by adult assessors, which beg questions about the objectivity of the research.

  Belson's study (*Television Violence and the Adolescent Boy*, 1978) is also cited as evidence that prolonged exposure to violence in the media produces violent behaviour (in young males). **Hagell** and **Newburn** ('Young Offenders and the Media', 1994), on the other hand, found a general lack of interest in television (violent or otherwise) among young offenders (they had, presumably, better things to do with their time – or perhaps watching televised violence has a pacifying effect on people's behaviour) – which raises questions about:

- **Immunity**: If the media have direct and immediate effects, why are some (most?) people immune to these effects? This applies equally to media researchers (**Frank Longford**, for example, was a celebrated anti-pornography campaigner

in the 1960s and 1970s who visited numerous strip clubs and viewed hardcore pornography without seemingly being affected by his experiences) and to audiences – the vast majority of listeners to the *War of the Worlds* broadcast, for example, were unaffected by it. In the same way, people seem able to view violent media content without necessarily imitating the violence they see depicted.

You might be forgiven, at this point, for thinking that transmission models would finally be laid to rest. However, they tend to resurface from time to time, usually in a slightly different or amended form:

Transmission theories are dead – they just refuse to accept this fact.

- **Cumulation theory**, for example, suggests media effects can be cumulative, rather than immediate. Thus, prolonged exposure to violent films or computer games, for example, can result in both changed behaviour and, in the case of violence, *desensitisation* (in other words, the more you are exposed to violent images, the less likely they are to stimulate you, so you seek out increasingly violent material – notice the drug/addiction theme still running here).

Eventually, you become so desensitised to violence you are less likely to be moved, shocked or appalled by real violence. The basic idea behind this version is closely related to a significant change in Transmission theories, namely:

- **Vulnerable audiences**: Rather than everyone being 'at risk', the focus sometimes moves to the idea 'some audiences' are more likely than others to be affected by the media – an obvious 'vulnerable' category being children. This follows from their lack of social experience and, of course, their tendency to copy behaviour around them. Actual evidence for effects tends to be *anecdotal* – the media claim, rather than prove, a relationship between, for example, violent behaviour and violent play.

Researchers such as **David Buckingham** (*Moving Images*, 1996) and **David Gauntlett** (*Moving Experiences*, 1995) have demonstrated how even very young children have a quite sophisticated level of media literacy – they understand more about the media and how it works than adults give them credit for (they are able to distinguish between fictional and factual representations of violence, for example).

Guy Cumberbatch ('Legislating Mythology', 1994) also warns against misleading, partial and slipshod 'effects research'. Responding in 1983 to newspaper headlines such as 'Half of children see film nasties' (*The Daily Mail*), his research showed 68% of the 11-year-olds he studied claimed to have seen what, at the time, were considered exceptionally violent films (so-called '*video nasties*' – a moral panic that arose

around the time Video Cassette Recorders (VCRs) were becoming common in the home). As **Cumberbatch** notes, moral panics about detrimental media effects often occur at times of technological change (as is currently the case with computer games). By the way, if 'two-thirds of 11 year-olds' seems a lot, the key point to remember here is these children were admitting to viewing films (*Blood on the teeth of the vampire!*) that didn't actually exist …

- **Academic arguments**: **Anderson** et al, in their review of 'effects research' ('The Influence of Media Violence on Youth', 2003) argue: 'Research on violent television and films, video games and music reveals unequivocal evidence media violence increases the likelihood of aggressive and violent behaviour in both immediate and long term contexts'. **Cumberbatch** (Office of Film and Literature Classification Conference, 2003), however, rejected this claim in less than flattering terms when he argued: 'If this analysis was a car, the door would fall off in your hand and the thing would collapse half way up the street.'

Limited Media Effects

⚠ Preparing the ground

Alternative ways of theorising media effects developed in the 1950s – partly as a reaction to the relatively crude *behaviourist* ('monkey see, monkey do') notions of direct effect theorists and partly as a development of such theories. We can examine a couple of these models by way of illustrating how they argued for a greater understanding of the role of audiences in the effects equation.

Diffusion theories focus on the way media messages spread throughout an audience and are based on the idea of a *trickle-down effect*. In other words, although messages may originate in the media, they are received by an audience in a couple of different ways.

- **Directly** – by personally viewing a news broadcast, for example.
- **Indirectly** – through social interaction with people who received the message directly, through other media sources reporting the original message or, indeed, a combination of the two.

In other words, diffusion theories reflect a form of 'Chinese Whispers', whereby an original message is continually relayed throughout an audience and, at each stage of the retelling, the message may be subtly changed or reinterpreted – think, for example, about how gossip is relayed through a population.

A classic version of this theory is **Katz** and **Lazarfield**'s (*Personal Influence*, 1955) **Two-Step Flow** theory, where they argued messages flowed from the media to *opinion formers* (people who directly received a message, were interested enough to want to relay it to others and influential enough for others to take the message on board).

In this respect, the majority of an audience received the original message in a form mediated through influential people in the *primary groups* to which they belonged (family or friends, for example). The key element in this type of theory, therefore, was

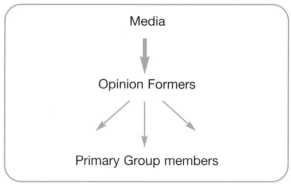

'Two-Step Flow' Model

an audience's involvement in primary groups where media messages were discussed – or, as **Katz and Lazarfield** put it, a recognition of the 'importance of informal, interpersonal relations'.

This version of diffusion theory, therefore, has three main elements.

- **Primary social groups** are a more significant influence than the media.
- **Interpersonal sources** of information are significant influences on how people receive and respond to media messages.
- **Limited direct effects**: Any changes in people's behaviour are likely to result from the way media messages are interpreted, discussed and reinterpreted within primary groups, rather than from any direct media influence. As **Joseph Klapper** (*The Effects of Mass Communication*, 1960) put it: 'Mass communication ordinarily does not serve as a necessary and sufficient cause of audience effects, but rather functions among and through a nexus [network] of mediating factors and influences' – such as, various types of **selective**:

  - **perception**: we notice some messages but not others

- **exposure**: we choose what to watch and read, consistent with our beliefs
- **expression**: we listen to what people important to us think
- **retention**: we remember the important things, consistent with our beliefs.

We can see these ideas in relation to how, for example, in recent years the UK media has transmitted messages about the possible dangers of mobile phone use ('New Mobile Phone Danger': *Daily Express*, 2000); despite the possible dangers, the use of such phones hasn't declined, let alone stopped. One reason for this might be a general audience consensus/belief such warnings are either untrue or exaggerated.

Another way of looking at this (and Klapper's ideas about audience selection) is through **Leon Festinger**'s concepts (*A Theory of Cognitive Dissonance*, 1957) of:

- **Cognitive assonance**: In basic terms, if a message fits with our personal and social (primary group) beliefs we are more likely to consider it favourably.
- **Cognitive dissonance** involves the reverse idea. If the message doesn't fit with what we want to hear then we respond by dismissing it, doubting it, ignoring it and so forth.

Both these ideas fit neatly with 'Two-Step Flow' theory since opinion formers within a group are likely to be seen in terms of the assonance of their message.

A second type of theory – related to the above – which takes the idea of a separation between the media and their audiences even further is **uses and gratifications**. This theory is interesting because it reverses the way we've been looking at the relationship between the mass media and their audiences for most of this chapter. It suggests audiences 'pick-and-choose' both media and messages – in other words, they *use* the media to satisfy their individual and group needs (gratifications). Thus, rather than asking what the media does *to* people, the theory looks at how different people, in different situations, use the media for their own ends. **Blumler** et al ('The Television Audience', 1972), for example, suggest there are four basic *primary uses* for the media:

- **Entertainment** – media used as a diversion from the problems of everyday life, for example. Alternatively, people may seek entertainment 'for its own sake' (or, indeed, for a 1001 different reasons).
- **Social solidarity**: In societies where the media is part of everyday life, it can be used as the basis for social interaction (talking about the latest events in a soap opera, discussing the news or arguing about who you think will be evicted from reality TV programmes like *Big Brother*). A shared knowledge of the media gives people common ground about which to talk (much like we often use the weather as a topic of conversation), which gives it an *integrating function* – we can feel part of a social group (solidarity) on the basis of our common interests and preoccupations. Even in the virtual world of Internet chatrooms and message boards (where people may not physically know each other), like-minded people can discuss things that are important to them.

Severin and **Tankard** ('Uses of Mass Media', 1997) found the most frequent users of the media were those who were lonely and/or socially isolated, which suggests for many people the media are an important source of companionship.

- **Identity**: We use the media in different ways to create or maintain a sense of 'who we are'. This may involve reading lifestyle magazines (such as *Hello* or *Homes and Gardens*), using the media as role and style models or, as is increasingly the case, seeking help from magazines and manuals about personal behaviour and problems (through self-help books such as **Milton Cudney's** ever-popular *Self-Defeating Behaviors* (sic), 1993).

- **Surveillance**: In a complex world, the media provides us with news and information about that world. We may use it to keep in touch with what is happening, for reassurance, personal education and the like.

In terms of this theory, the media are:

- **powerless**, considered in terms of their ability to directly influence or change behaviour

- **neutral**, in the sense of not really having any direct affect on attitudes

- **unimportant** as far as researchers are concerned, since the object of study is the *active audience* rather than the media itself.

We can also note a further theoretical variation on diffusion models, namely **Reinforcement Theory**, which focuses on the social context of media use. In other words, the way the media may affect us is dependent on the social groups – and interaction therein – to which we belong.

Klapper (1960), for example, argued people's beliefs were related to the social groups to which they were attached (primary groups being the most significant) and one

 Growing it yourself: uses and gratifications

Using the following table as a template, apply Blumler et al's ideas to your understanding of media use, on both a personal level and in terms of the way you think others may use the media to satisfy certain personal and social needs

Primary Uses	How I use the media	How others may use the media
Entertainment	MTV – Keeping up to date with my favourite music	Relaxation
Social solidarity		
Identity		Reading *The Guardian* reflects their view of society
Surveillance	I'm going to Florida – are there any hurricanes imminent?	

important role of a secondary group such as the media was to reinforce – either positively or negatively – the beliefs we have already formed. This, therefore, suggests a 'media effect' of sorts.

Finally, 'limited effects' approaches are neatly summed up by **Bernard Berelson**'s (*The People's Choice*, 1948) wonderfully imprecise argument that: 'Some kinds of communication on some kinds of issues, brought to the attention of some kinds of people under some kinds of conditions have some kinds of effects' – and you can't be more definite than that.

 # Digging deeper

Theories of limited media effects provided a welcome antidote to the kind of 'simple and direct' media effects that characterised (and still characterise, perhaps) Transmission models. We can, for example, see this very clearly if we consider the relationship between the media and **violent behaviour**. Transmission models have been implicitly criticised, methodologically, by *diffusion approaches* for assuming what they should be testing. For example, simply because we often find people who behave violently enjoy violent forms of media doesn't mean one (the media) causes the other – an idea called the **stepping-stone theory**, (one used extensively in discussions of deviance and illegal drug use, for example), which argues violent people consume violent media and then commit acts of violence as the 'thrill' they get from the former escalates into the latter.

An alternative interpretation here is, that for certain audiences, violent behaviour is something they enjoy (whether it be real or imaginary violence). If this is the case it's

hardly surprising to find a correlation between the two areas; if I like fighting with people in the street, for example, I probably also like to read violent material, watch violent films and listen to aggressive music – in other words, whereas the two may go together (people who like gardening probably read gardening magazines and watch gardening programmes), we can't easily (if at all) disentangle one from the other. In other words, which comes first? Do I watch violent films because I like violence – or does watching violence make me violent?

However, limited effects models do have some major problems we need to consider.

- **Tautology**: If a theory is *tautologous* it contains its own proof – in other words, it involves a *circular argument*; it cannot be disproven because it cannot be objectively tested. **Uses and gratifications**, for example, draws on functionalist ideas (the media performs certain functions for both society and the individual) and suffers from a similar problem. With Functionalism, the tautology comes from the idea 'everything in society exists for a purpose' – if it exists, it is functional because if it wasn't functional it wouldn't exist.

In the previous exercise, it should have been easy to identify a range of people's uses and gratifications; the problem, however, is that being able to do this doesn't test the theory. For this theory to be 'true', you merely have to identify some uses that some people at some time get from the media. Thus, if I use the media to gratify my needs, such needs explain why and how I use the media – but it doesn't explain where my 'needs' come from in the first place. In other words, we have no way of knowing if the media create – or simply reflect – my needs.

- **Choice**: For an audience to be *active* in terms of their media use, they have to be able to choose between different media options. For example, if I don't like the liberal politics of *The Guardian* I can choose the *Daily Telegraph* as a newspaper closer to my views. In some ways, the two are very different (one is anti-hunting, the other pro; one is anti-Europe, the other isn't and so forth).

While we shouldn't overlook the importance of these differences, in other ways the two newspapers are similar and, in this sense, my choices are limited by the range of media available. Both, for example, promote similar economic ideas about capitalism; both give more credence and space to the views of employer organisations and the ideas of the rich and powerful.

When I read each paper I am subjected to advertising and while the adverts may be different, their function is the same; to persuade me to part with some of the massive amount of money I'm being paid for writing this book (I wish). This idea of consumption ('I shop, therefore I am') can be related to issues of:

- **Identity**: Diffusion models, apart from seeing active audiences, suggest the media is, at best, a *neutral medium* (it has few, if any, effects) and, at worst, completely ineffective in its ability to influence. Such models, therefore, separate the audience from the medium, in the sense I may choose to watch television and may have the choice of many different channels. Within those channels a range of

different types of programming (such as film, drama and quiz shows) are available, within each type (or genre) I can choose, for example, romantic comedy as opposed to horror films and so on, almost ad infinitum. In other words, I chose the media that fit my sense of identity (because they satisfy my needs).

However, the obvious point to note here is the media cannot simply reflect the massive diversity of individual needs this situation implies – at some point my needs cannot be ideally satisfied and I may have to settle for whatever the media is offering. In other words, my behaviour is changed – subtly to be sure, but changed none the less. What this suggests, therefore, is the:

- **Relationship** between audience and medium is more complex than diffusion models suggest.

- **Cultural factors** always intervene in the relationship. At its most blatant, if a newspaper doesn't exactly meet my (political and ideological) needs, I have to settle for the 'closest fit' between my needs and what's on offer; at its most subtle, it suggests the media (consciously or unconsciously) introduces small behavioural changes to their audience. Thus, in relation to something like the Two-Step Flow theory we could note the importance of a cultural factor such as:

- **Authority**: In some situations, we look to the media to *lead* our behaviour – to tell us not only what is happening but, most importantly perhaps, how we should think about and interpret the significance of whatever is happening. A further cultural factor at work here is diffusion models assume audiences have an almost unlimited *range* of information available, so that all sides and all possible interpretations are covered – but this is not necessarily the case.

Leaving aside your personal feelings about 'violent youths', 'paedophiles' and 'illegal immigrants', they, for example, have no-one putting across their side of the story in the mainstream media. In such situations it's not beyond the bounds of reason to question how 'ineffective' the media actually are (which, spookily enough, is what we're going to do next).

Indirect Media Effects

⚠ Preparing the ground

It is tempting to see the next group of theories (gathered for convenience around the label '**cultural effects**') as some sort of middle ground between the 'direct effects' and 'limited effects' theories we have previously examined. This, however, would be a mistake because cultural effects theories view the media as a very powerful influence in society. Although we have already met the main ideas associated with such theories – when we examined hegemonic theories of media and ideology – we can apply them to an understanding of media effects by noting how these theories see the media as a **cultural** (or ideological) **institution**. In other words, its primary role is to promote – and police – cultural values, or, as **Newbold** ('Approaches to Cultural Hegemony within Cultural Studies', 1995) puts it: 'Cultural

effects theory suggests the media is embedded in the relations that constitute a particular society, working both to produce and reflect powerful interests and social structures'.

From this (neo-Marxist) perspective, therefore, we're looking at the media as an *agency of social control* and, in this particular respect, how the control of ideas – the way people think about the world – can be used to influence behaviour. However, as Newbold suggests, we are not thinking here about direct control, in the sense of forcing people (consciously or unconsciously) to behave in certain ways; rather, the media acts at the institutional (large group) level of culture, not at the level of individual beliefs. In other words, the media exercises social control through its actions as a **socialising agency**, advising and guiding audiences and, by so doing, exercising a *hegemonic role*. We can, for example, see this idea in terms of **George Gerbner**'s ideas ('Communications Technology and Social Policy', 1973) concerning **Cultivation Theory**, which argues television cultivates distinctive attitudes in its audience, rather than directly influencing their behaviour. As **Daniel Chandler** ('Cultivation Theory', 1995) puts it: 'Heavy watching of television is seen as "cultivating" attitudes which are more consistent with the world of television programmes than with the everyday world. Watching television may induce a general mindset about violence in the world, quite apart from any effects it might have in inducing violent behaviour'.

The key idea here, therefore, is 'induce a general mindset'; the hegemonic role of the media creates a situation in which some beliefs are subtly encouraged and others discouraged and, as it establishes this role, its effects are:

- **Slow**: Attitudes and behaviour don't change overnight. Rather, media effects have to be measured in terms of a slow 'drip' of change; in other words, small, gradual and long-term effects that are:

- **Cumulative**, in the sense the media establishes and builds on the general ideas being propagated. It uses a number of standard techniques to achieve a cumulative effect – the consistent promotion of some ideas and not others, the marginalisation of dissenting views and voices, the repetition of certain ideas until they assume a 'common sense' or *taken-for-granted* status.

- **Directional**, in the sense of being limited to particular influences. Only very rarely can the media directly change people's beliefs or behaviour; rather, it operates on the level of leading people in certain directions or ways of thinking.

Gerbner et al ('Living with Television', 1986) draw a parallel between television and religion in terms of its basic cultural functions: 'the continual repetition of patterns (myths, ideologies, 'facts', relationships, etc.) which serve to define the world and legitimize the social order'.

Perhaps the most influential cultural effects theory in recent years has been the **Encoding/Decoding** model developed by, among others, **Stuart Hall** ('Encoding/ Decoding', 1980). This involves what is sometimes called a *reception theory* and is based on the idea media messages always have a range of possible meanings and interpretations – some intended by the sender (a newspaper owner or the author, for example) and others read into the message by the audience. For example, even a very simple media text (such as an advert) will involve:

- **Encoding**: The originator of a message has a point they want to get across to the audience. The main point of an advert, for example, might be the simple message 'Buy this product' (it is more complicated than this in reality – not all adverts, for example, are designed just to sell products, but we can keep it simple for our illustrative purpose).

- **Decoding**: The audience viewing the advert will interpret (decode) its message in a variety of ways, depending on such factors as their social background, the context in which the advert is seen and so forth. Thus, how an audience receives and understands even a very simple message will depend on a potentially huge range of factors. For example, if I am not in the habit of buying cheap deodorant, I am unlikely to be very receptive to such an advert. On the other hand, if I see the advert when I'm thinking about a cheap Christmas present for a relation I don't particularly like, I may be receptive. The key idea here, therefore, is:

- **Relative autonomy**: In one sense, I am quite free (autonomous) to interpret a media text in whatever way I choose, depending to some extent on a range of factors (can I afford to buy what's being advertised? Do I really need the product?) On the other, I'm being bombarded with messages that may, in some circumstances, be difficult to resist.

For this model, therefore, media messages have a number of possible effects, depending to some extent on the message itself (how cleverly it's constructed, for example) and to other extents on things like my personal cultural background and situation (I may *want* to buy the Porsche 911 I've seen advertised but since I can't afford it, I won't). Hall suggests at least three main ways a media message can be read by an audience.

- **Hegemonic**: The audience shares the assumptions and interpretations of the author and reads the message in the way it was intended. Buying a Porsche 911, for example, is something I *need* to do because I can afford it and it will send a message to others about my social status (ironically, of course, I can't actually control what that message may be).

- **Negotiated**: For this type of reading the audience will broadly share the author's views, but may modify their interpretation in the light of their own particular feelings, beliefs or abilities. For example, although I know a Porsche is desirable – and would love to own one – I'll settle for a car that is better suited to my financial and family circumstances.

- **Oppositional**: As someone concerned about the environment, I believe cars are generally not to be encouraged. I would certainly not buy a Porsche because it uses too much petrol and pollutes the environment.

In terms of the above, therefore, we can look at three basic forms of cultural effect.

- **Agenda setting**: As we have noted in a previous section, the media, according to **McCombs** and **Shaw** ('The agenda-setting function of mass media', 1972) identify and select the ideas people are encouraged to think about. An obvious – and over-simplified – example here might be sports reporting. A casual glance

Discussion point: more than words can say

We can illustrate the above ideas by thinking about the following:

Imagine you owned a Porsche 911. List some of the things you want it to say to other people about you.

Reverse the gaze and imagine you see someone driving a Porsche 911. List some of the things you think it says about this person.

through most daily newspapers suggests football is the most important sport in this country – the column inches devoted to reports of matches, boardroom intrigues, managerial sackings and the like far outweighs the attention given to other sports throughout the year. In this respect, while newspapers are unlikely to make you change the team you support, they are *setting the agenda* for what people talk about. If this is true for sport, then it may also be true for areas such as politics and economics.

As **Severin** and **Tankard** (1997) argue, the media have the power to put certain issues in the public sphere – **Denis McQuail** (*Mass Communication Theory: An Introduction*, 1994), for example, noted a clear relationship between the order of importance attached to issues by the media and the significance given to those issues by politicians and the public.

However, as **McCombs** and **Estrada** ('The news media and the pictures in our heads', 1997) note, being told what to think about doesn't guarantee the media 'tell us how and what to think about it, or even what to do about it'. A further process, according to cultural effects theorists comes into play here, namely:

- **Framing**: In this respect, issues and stories are framed in ways that suggest to audiences how they *should* be interpreted. In other words, as we have seen earlier, issues are framed in terms of *preferred readings* and *dominant interpretations* – audiences are, therefore *primed* to understand issues (hence this idea is sometimes called *priming theory*) in terms of what **Simon** and **Xenos** ('Media Framing and Effective Public Deliberation', 2000) call 'elite discourses' – in other words, in terms of the way media owners and journalists want their audiences to understand an issue.

In *The Battle for Public Opinion*, 1983, **Lang** and **Lang** found framing worked by using language an audience could understand; in other words, by simplifying issues the media could effectively frame events and set the agenda for their discussion. A more recent example might be the way something like terrorism is reduced to simple ideas, language and solutions. The phrase 'Muslim Fundamentalist' – used repeatedly in the context of terrorism – is a *priming phrase* used by some media to lead their audience to the conclusion the two are inextricably connected. This, in turn, leads us to consider a further cultural effect.

- **Myth making: George Gerbner** ('Reclaiming Our Cultural Mythology', 1994) argues the media have grown so powerful and pervasive in modern (global) societies they create *mythical realities* for those audiences who immerse themselves in media content. In other words, the heavier your media consumption (whether it be watching television, reading newspapers or surfing the Internet) the more likely you are to be drawn into a 'fantasy world' of the media's creation.

For example, we are aware media reporting of crime and violence is far more exaggerated than its actual occurrence in our society. Gerbner (1994) argues, 'heavy television viewers' (watching more than three hours per day) are drawn into 'a distorted concept of reality'. As he notes: 'Most of the violence we have on television is what I call happy violence. It's swift, it's thrilling, it's cool, it's effective, it's painless, and it always leads to a happy ending because you have to deliver the audience to the next commercial in a receptive mood.'

Such exposure, he argues, leads to the development of *mean world syndrome* – the belief, in short, the world is a harsher and meaner place than it is in reality because 'programming reinforces the worst fears, apprehensions and paranoia of people.'

Digging deeper

On the face of things, cultural effects theories seem to represent a significant step forward in understanding media effects. However, they do have both methodological and conceptual problems. **Methodological** problems relate to the idea of proving or disproving cultural effects arguments and we can note a couple of such problems.

- **Measurement**: Although these theories suggest the media does have some form of socialising/social control effect, the main problem is how to measure such effects. If they are, by definition, slow, cumulative, indirect and long term, it means that, at best, they will be extremely difficult to identify and track and, at worst, it will be all but impossible to disentangle specific 'media effects' from a wide range of other possible causes. In other words, how is it possible to say with any degree of certainty that attitude or behavioural changes are the result of media – as opposed to some other – effects?

  Cultivation theories also involve some clear problems of measurement and interpretation. For example, the idea 'heavy television viewers' are more open to media influence begs a number of questions: How many hours do you need to watch to be a 'heavy viewer'? How does a researcher decide this figure and, perhaps more significantly, how does the social context of viewing (alone, with family etc.) impact on such ideas?

  In addition, problems of proof relate to:

- **Tautology**: Just as *diffusion models* have problems with proof, so to do cultural effects models. The basic problem here relates to the identification and tracking of effects we have just noted; what exactly is a 'media effect'? Just about anything can be advanced as evidence of the basic theory. If, for example, we are somehow able to identify an effect, this proves the theory (it demonstrates, for example, the media's hegemonic role); on the other hand, an inability to identify effects doesn't disprove the validity of the theory since we could argue 'oppositional readings' of media messages explain why there are no effects.

Conceptual problems, on the other hand, relate to the ideas used within cultural effects theories. For example:

- **Preferred readings**: This idea, although apparently straightforward, is fraught with problems. **John Corner** ('Textuality, Communication and Power', 1983) for example, argues it is difficult to discover which – if any – reading is a dominant one in a situation where, as cultural theorists admit, there are many possible readings. In addition, **Kathy Myers** ('Understanding Advertisers', 1983) argues it would be in the interests of advertisers to create a range of preferred readings for their product to appeal to as wide an audience as possible on a range of different levels. In such situations it doesn't make much sense to somehow restrict the advert to a single, preferred, reading that can be rejected (or opposed) by the people you are trying to influence.

  A further problem is that in order to identify a preferred reading we presumably either have to research an audience to discover their understanding of a media text or trust to our own media literacy as researchers. In the first instance, as **Justin Wren-Lewis** ('The Encoding/Decoding Model', 1983) argues, does the possibility an audience will interpret a certain message as the 'one intended by the author' necessarily mean this is the preferred reading? Apart from the problem of *author intention* that is discussed in more detail below, we can't simply assume, as I have noted, there is a single dominant reading, nor can we assume the reading identified and understood by the majority of an audience is actually the preferred reading – they may, for example, simply have latched on to a reading they prefer.

In the second instance we arrive at a general problem of:

- **Semiological analysis**: Cultural effects theories depend on this type of analysis (the basics of which we have covered in the *Research Methods* chapter) because they argue a media text has a number of possible interpretations. However, as **Shaun Moores** (*Interpreting Audiences: The Ethnography of Media Consumption*, 1993) notes, one problem for a researcher is a form of 'imposition effect'; that is, if we are sure a preferred reading exists there is the possibility that, by trying to identify it, we simply impose *our* reading of the text on both the author and the audience.

- **Essentialising the reader**: A final problem, related to the above ideas, is one noted by **Rob Stam** (*Film Theory*, 2000) when he argues cultural effects theorists tend to resolve the problem of semiological analysis by giving primary importance to

the audience in any interpretation/decoding. However, the logic of such an argument, Stam suggests, is we assume audiences have essential characteristics (they can be relatively easily grouped – as 'oppositional readers' – for example) when the reality is they may hold contradictory, illogical and fragmented levels of understanding. In other words, 'asking the audience' may not be a very fruitful way of establishing effects – not least because it begs the question about media effects in the first place: does an audience interpret a message because of its unique cultural characteristics or, conversely, because it has been shown how to interpret the message by the media?

The last word(s)

To complete this section we can note a couple of further dimensions to the general debate surrounding media effects. The first of these we can call **ethnographic** analyses of audiences: In terms of this general model, the debate has moved on in a couple of ways: firstly, away from an analysis of 'the media' to a cultural analysis of audiences and the various ways they interact with different media. Secondly, analysis has moved away from the idea of *mass audiences* – their actions and reactions – to an interest in audiences *differentiated* by general categories like age, gender and ethnicity as well as by more individualised categories such as cultural and technological competence. In some ways this *epistemological shift* (a change in the way sociologists think about how to generate reliable and valid knowledge about the way audiences use the media) reflects a postmodern-tinged concern with the nature of personal and social identities, an important component of which in the twenty-first

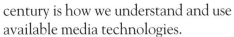

century is how we understand and use available media technologies.

To get a flavour for these approaches (which, as the term *ethnography* suggests, involves the researcher immersing themselves in the cultural behaviour of the people they are studying – observing, questioning and participating in that behaviour, for example), we can note three basic strands to this general approach.

- **Social space**: This particular strand focuses on the way the media is integrated into different *spaces* – especially, but not exclusively, the *private space* of the home. In this respect, understanding how audiences use the media involves examining how domestic spaces are structured – from relatively simple issues such as 'who uses what media in what contexts for what purposes', to more complex issues about control and ownership of technology (who controls the TV remote in your family?) and how media use fits into the general flow of domestic behaviour.

- **Cultural competence**: This strand focuses on understanding how audiences bring different levels of media literacy and competence to their use of the media at their disposal. An obvious example here is the Internet and debates over the extent to which children should or should not be supervised (through both parental and software controls). How people use the media – and what they take from it – will depend to varying extents on their familiarity with that media; this extends from things like understanding the conventions of films, through the expectations we have for different media, to the ability to master different technologies. To use a simple example, although I

consider myself media literate (I can spot a conventional code at 20 paces . . .), the 'joy of text' remains a mystery to me – I have no idea how to send or receive text messages. This, in a sense, make me media illiterate and leads to a further focus:

- **Technology**: This model focuses on how we engage with technology – the media hardware and the software that increasingly surrounds us. Forty years ago British audiences had to cope with television (black and white with two channels, both of which shut down around midnight and daytime TV was but a glint in some advertising executive's eye) and radio – four stations, all government controlled.

Now, I am surrounded by technology – 200 television channels (the majority of which I watch for about 10 seconds as I continue my fruitless search for something interesting), a digital radio I've no idea how to tune, a computer that can stream films to my desktop, access to hundreds of radio stations around the world, email, message boards, chatrooms, web blogs and a mobile phone I don't know how to answer.

Interesting as these ideas (and my inability to keep pace with technological change) are, a second dimension to the debate revolves around a **theoretical approach** to understanding media and audiences. This type of approach suggests the type of theories we have examined here (from transmission though diffusion to cultural effects and ethnographies) have been looking for the wrong things in the wrong places in the wrong ways (and you can't get more wrong than that). Conventional effects theories, for example, assume a separation between 'the media' and 'the audience', albeit in different ways; transmission theories assume the media is dominant, diffusion theories the audience dominates and cultural theories suggest the media dominates in some areas, audiences in others.

Postmodern approaches, however, focus on the concept of **meaning**. The majority of conventional media effects theories assume, to varying degrees, a separation between 'the media' and 'the audience', such that one sends out some sort of information that may or may not be received by audiences in different ways. However, if we consider the work of someone like **Janet Staiger** (*Perverse Spectators: The Practices of Film Reception*, 2000), she reworks *reception theory* to argue, for example, **immanent meaning** (the idea the meaning of something like a film or a news broadcast is fixed and unchanging) is not a useful concept. Audiences, in effect, are *perverse spectators* in that they use media in their own way and for whatever purpose.

Activated meanings are created through the various ways an audience interacts with the media. In other words, the meaning of something like a soap opera is effectively created and expressed in numerous ways by whatever a viewer brings to their consumption and enjoyment – or otherwise – of the programme. The significance of this idea, of course, is that the *meaning* of *EastEnders* changes each and every time it is viewed, making it impossible to quantify any form of 'media effect' in any meaningful way. Any 'effect' is changed each time it is identified.

This idea holds true for both the present – the meaning of a media text is changed immediately it is consumed – and, most obviously, the past (films, for example, that were once considered shocking are now more likely to elicit laughter than fear).

Audience as media

Perhaps the most radical way of understanding audience and media is to think about the changing face of media technology and use. If we think, for example, about new mass media (such as weblogs), the circle is completed by the idea the audience becomes, at one and the same time, both the *producer* and *consumer* of media texts. In other words, the audience *is* the media and the media *is* the audience – the two are interchangeable and indistinguishable since the one is a reflection of the other.

This idea (still in its earliest days since access to and understanding of new media technologies is still in its infancy and is shot through with debates about media literacies, competencies and the uneven spread of technological development) is noteworthy because it suggests a different direction for media research and effects theories. It takes the idea of the 'death of the author' (although an author may have some idea about how they would *like* an audience to receive and understand their text, each reader effectively interprets the text in terms of their own ideas, beliefs and so forth) to new extremes of interpretation since it becomes technologically possible to be both author and audience at one and the same time.

Growing it yourself: author and audience

The message board you can find at www.sixthform.info/forum can be used to explore the above ideas – either individually or as a class.

As you use it, think about how you are performing the dual roles of both audience and mass medium.

Whatever your personal view of school (the happiest days of your life or, in my case, a miserable battle against boredom, petty rivalries and having to get up way too early on cold winter days), there is little doubt education, as a social institution, has an important role to play in our society. Whether you view that role positively or negatively, we need to examine a range of perspectives (structuralist, interactionist, postmodern and New Right) that offer 'different explanations of the role of the education system'.

WARM UP: WHAT'S THE POINT OF EDUCATION?

Most of us spend at least 11 years in some sort of educational institution, so we should know something about what happens in schools. To get you thinking about the role of education therefore, identify as many things as you can relating to two types of learning:

- formal learning (the things schools are supposed to teach us) and
- informal learning (the things we learn that are not always openly taught).

I have identified one of each to get you started.

Formal Learning	Informal Learning
Curriculum subjects (English, Maths, etc.)	How to deal with people who are 'not family'

Structuralist perspectives

Preparing the ground

In this section we are going to examine three main structuralist perspectives on the role of education – functionalism, Marxism and feminism – and we can begin by identifying the major ideas that characterise each perspective.

Functionalism

Although this perspective has generally declined in sociological importance in the UK over the past 20 or so years, its influence in shaping educational policy shouldn't be underestimated. This is partly because the basic ideas that sit at the heart of this perspective – ideas about *consensus*, *competition* and *achievement through merit*, for example – sit relatively comfortably with modern Conservative, Liberal and Labour political ideas. For functionalists, arguments about the role of education focus on: **institutional relationships** and *functional linkages* with wider society. In particular, the focus here is on how education links to other social institutions, such as the family and the workplace. The complexity of modern social systems means the education system becomes, in effect, a bridge between these institutions in a couple of ways. Firstly, on an institutional level, social systems with a variety of different types of employment must develop ways of managing their human resources. While a society may need doctors, police officers and manual labourers, there's little point producing so many trained doctors they cannot get employment because there is no demand for their services. Secondly, on an individual level, the education system functions as an agency of **secondary socialisation**. In this respect, education is an institution that 'broadens the individual's experience' of the social world and, in so doing, prepares children for adult role relationships in the workplace and wider society.

For the education system to function properly on both the institutional and individual level it must, according to Functionalists, be **meritocratic** – a concept that reflects the idea that rewards (such as high pay, high status, jobs) are *earned* on the basis of our merits (things like skills, knowledge and effort) rather than simply *allocated* on the basis of who you know or how rich or poor your family is.

Education systems, in this respect, have to be competitive because children have to prove themselves willing to 'work to achieve'. For a merit-based system to function correctly, there must be equality of opportunity since if some are disadvantaged

(discriminated against or denied the opportunity to show their worth) society cannot be sure the best people occupy the most important adult roles.

As **Parsons** ('The School Class as a Social System', 1959) put it:

> ... it is fair to give differential rewards for different levels of achievement, so long as there has been fair access to opportunity and fair that these rewards lead on to higher-order opportunities for the successful.

Marxism

Marxist perspectives haven't been particularly influential in terms of government policies (hardly surprising since they are highly critical of capitalist societies). However, ideas about the role of education have, arguably, filtered down into the teaching and learning process and some key ideas for Marxists include:

- **Cultural reproduction**: This concept involves the idea of *secondary socialisation*, but with a twist. **Louis Althusser** ('Ideology and Ideological State Apparatuses', 1971) argues that the economic system (capitalism) has to be reproduced from one generation to the next. In other words, each new generation has to be taught the skills, knowledge and ideas required for them to take up positions in the workplace.

The twist, however, is schools don't just select, allocate and differentiate children (through testing and public examinations) in the interests of society as a whole – education is not meritocratic. Rather, the role of education is to ensure the sons – and increasingly daughters – of the powerful achieve the levels of education required for them to follow in their fathers' – and mothers' – footsteps into professional employment. The trick, in other words, is to educate most people 'just enough' for them to be useful employees and a small number 'more than enough' to take up high-powered work roles.

- **Hidden curriculum**: This reflects the way ideas about the social world – and the individual's place in that world – are transmitted through the education system. Schools, as part of the daily teaching process, don't just teach formal subjects – they also teach 'hidden' values such as competition, individual learning and achievement, and qualifications as a way of measuring people's worth.

- **Education and society**: The link between the two is one where the education system responds to the demands of employers – there is a correspondence between what employers want (socialised workers differentiated through qualifications etc.) and what schools provide.

Feminism

Although the main focus of feminist educational research (gender inequality) has remained largely unchanged over the past 25 years, the emphasis of this research has moved from explaining why girls achieve less than boys (because, in the main, they don't anymore) to explaining how girls learn to cope with a range of school and workplace disadvantages.

Feminist research in the past shouldn't necessarily be dismissed as being outdated and irrelevant to our (present-day) understanding of the role of education. Although these studies originally focused on explanations for female underachievement they are, arguably, still relevant as explanations for differences in career choice and progress. In addition, these explanations assume a new relevance as political concerns about boys' underachievement have led to an educational focus on ways to help them 'overcome the gender gap' (usually involving a resurrection of ideas and practices criticised in feminist research over the past 25 years …). Broadly speaking, feminist explanations of female disadvantage, centre around the following ideas:

- **Socialisation** research. **Eichler** (*The Double Standard*, 1980) highlighted how differential socialisation experiences – and different social expectations – of males and females help to construct different gender identities and adult role expectations. In the past, for example, the education system contributed to the way women saw their primary adult role in terms of the private sphere of the family (as mother and housewife, for example) and, although female horizons have widened somewhat over the past 25 years, feminists have argued traditional assumptions about masculinity and femininity continue to influence both family and work relationships.

Norman (*Just a Bunch of Girls*, 1988), for example, argued *teacher* expectations, especially in early-years schooling, emphasised female roles related to the mother/carer axis and, while this may no longer *automatically* translate into women seeing their primary role in terms of caring for their family, it is clear – as we will see when we dig a little deeper in a moment – female work roles continue to be framed around the basic idea of different male and female capabilities.

Thus, although nearly 25 years ago, **Stanworth** (*Gender and Schooling*, 1981) found A-level pupils underestimated girls' academic performance and teachers saw female futures in terms of marriage, child rearing and domestic work (while future careers were stereotyped into 'caring' work such as secretarial, nursing and so forth) the question we have to consider is the extent to which, for all the evident changes in male and female educational performance, the general picture is still broadly similar in terms of the adult roles performed by women in our society.

- **Identity**: Following from the above, feminist research in the recent past focused on ideas like the gendering of the school curriculum, in terms of how pupils saw different subjects as 'masculine' or 'feminine'. Such gendered perception, it was argued by writers such as **Woods**

('The myth of subject choice', 1976), helped to explain things like lower levels of female participation and general achievement in science subjects. Similarly, policy initiatives, such as Girls Into Science and Technology (GIST), explored why girls were underrepresented in science subjects (the basic reasons were science was seen as both difficult and demanding and, interestingly, the image of scientists was unflattering and unfeminine).

Despite the introduction, in 1988, of a National Curriculum that ensured all pupils studied subjects such as science and maths (traditionally perceived as masculine subjects) up to GCSE, the evidence from post-16 education suggests the type of gendered curriculum identified by Woods still exists, as table 4.1 demonstrates.

Thus, although the focus of feminist research in this particular area may have changed, over the years – from concerns about female underachievement to concerns about gendered participation – the post-16

Subject	% Males	% Females
Physics	78	12
Computer Studies	76	14
Economics	74	16
Mathematics	60	40
Biology	38	62
English Literature	25	75
Social Science	24	76
Home Economics	3	97

Table 4.1 United Kingdom GCE A level or equivalent entries for young people: by selected subject, 2001/02
[Source: Social Trends 34 (2004)]

evidence (where students are given a free choice of subjects to study) suggests participation levels are related to concepts of male and female identity. If this is the case, it seems unlikely the causes of this gendered participation only begin after the official school leaving age. Thus, past feminist research into the school curriculum still has both currency and usefulness. **Spender** ('Invisible Women', 1983), for example, argued that the curriculum was geared towards the needs and interests of boys, so as to render girls 'invisible' within the classroom. Similarly, **Deem** (*Schooling for Women's Work*, 1980) argued the school curriculum and subject choices were highly gendered and **Mahony** ('Schools for the Boys?' 1985) demonstrated how girls were frequently *marginalised* in the classroom by both boys and teachers. In addition, he pointed out how staffing structures reflected male importance in the workplace (the highest status teaching jobs were – and remain – occupied by men).

 Digging deeper

Functionalism

We can expand the ideas we have just noted in the following way.

- **Secondary socialisation:** Talcott Parsons (1959) called this process the 'emancipation of the child from primary attachment to the family' and it involves:

  - **Instrumental relationships** – or relationships based on what people can do for us in return for the things that we can do for them. Most of our adult relationships take this form (as opposed to the *affective* relationships experienced between people who share a close, personal, friendship). In school, instrumental relationships with teachers are different to affective relationships with friends.

- **Social control**: Two types are significant here: firstly, learning things like acceptable and unacceptable behaviour and, secondly, learning self-control – the child has to learn how to deal with things in an even-handed way. For example, by learning:

- **Deferred gratification** – we can't always have what we want when we want it (immediate gratification). In educational terms, successful students put up with things they may dislike (boring lessons, the lack of money . . .) in the expectation of passing exams and gaining access to high pay and high status occupations. This relates to a further function of education, the:

- **Transmission of cultural values** – or as **Parsons** (1959) puts it, the '*internalisation* of a level of society's values and norms that is a step higher than those learnt within the family group'. Through interacting with others, children learn and internalise (adopt as part of their personality) wider cultural values. For example, they start to understand something of their history and geography as well as general cultural values (such as equality of opportunity, individual competition and so forth). This, in turn, is related to:

- **Social solidarity** – the idea that, as unique individuals, we have to establish things 'in common' with others if we are to live and work together; we have, in short, to feel we *belong* to larger social groups (such as a school or a society). The promotion of social solidarity involves *social integration* – any institution, such as a school, has to develop *mechanisms* for helping people feel they belong.

Growing it yourself: social integration

Draw a similar table to the one below and identify some of the ways schools try to promote social solidarity (school uniform is an example of a mechanism)

Integrating mechanism	How does it promote solidarity?
School uniform	Everyone looks the same . . .
Further examples?	

- **The co-ordination of human resources** relates to the school's links with wider society and it involves things like:
  - **Role allocation** – preparing children for their future adult roles, which is achieved by:
  - **Social differentiation**: Since work roles are clearly different (some require higher levels of skill and knowledge, others do not), pupils have to be 'made different'. One way the school does this, of course, is through *testing* and *examinations* – which have to be objective demonstrations of ability (everyone should have the same opportunity to take and pass such tests). This is because adult roles have to be *achieved* (on merit) rather than *ascribed*.

- **Social stratification** (groups occupying different levels in society) is the inevitable outcome of the process just described and the classic functionalist statement of the necessity for – and inevitability of – stratification is **Davis** and **Moore**'s ('Some Principles of

Discussion questions: functionalism

To help you evaluate some of the ideas we have just examined, think about – and discuss – some or all of the following questions.

- **Merit**: Is educational achievement based on individual merit and do schools provide equality of opportunity? Or do factors such as parental income (buying private education, for example) give some children distinct advantages over others?
- **Role allocation**: If adult roles are allocated on merit – those who achieve the most in education receive the most in the workplace in terms of pay, conditions and status for example, why is it that women – who now generally out-perform men in the education system – rarely occupy the highest paid jobs in our society?
- **Intelligence, attainment** and **employment** are assumed to be closely related (the brightest achieve the most and get the best jobs). As with role allocation, however, why aren't women better represented in higher income professional work?
- **Functional importance**: Who is more functionally important to society – a road sweeper (£4–£6 per hour) or a financial accountant (£25–£35 per hour)?

Stratification', 1945) argument that stratification represents a mechanism through which those who are most able and talented intellectually are allocated work roles that offer the highest rewards in terms of income, power and status. As Davis argues: 'Education is the proving ground for ability and hence the selective agency for placing people in different statuses according to their abilities'.

Marxism

In developing these ideas further, we can note the following:

Cultural reproduction: For **Althusser** (1971), this involved:

- **Formal education**: Children have to learn the skills and knowledge (literacy and numeracy, for example) they will need in the workplace.

- **Access to knowledge**, is restricted through control of subjects appearing on the curriculum. The higher you go in the education system, the greater your access to knowledge. Restricting access is also useful as a way of limiting children's ambitions and expectations by:

- **Structuring knowledge**: Preparing people for the differing levels of knowledge required in the workplace involves creating different levels of knowledge in the school. For example, academic (theoretical) knowledge (such as AS-levels) is valued more than practical (vocational) knowledge because the former is the type most useful for professional workers. Similarly, some forms of knowledge are

more *valid* than others (the ability to do algebra, for example, is considered more valid than the ability to remember who played in goal for Chelsea in the 1970 Cup Final – Peter 'The Cat' Bonetti, in case you're wondering).

- **Social control**: Children have to learn to accept and respect 'authority', since this will be important in the workplace. As you will know from your own education, the higher you go, the looser the controls on your behaviour (by the time you reach A-level you can be largely trusted to 'do the right things').

- **Commodification of knowledge**: testing and exams are part of a process where knowledge is given an *economic value*; in other words, it can be bought and sold. This is important because knowledge, unlike skills (such as the ability to mend a car), can't be easily valued unless you certificate it. Your knowledge of sociology, for example, will be economically worthless unless you pass your AS-level.

- **Ideological State Apparatuses** (ISAs): The content of education is controlled by the State and, for Marxists, this is the means by which the way people think about the world is conditioned by what they learn in school (both in the formal and hidden curriculum). This, in turn, is related to:

- **Social learning**, which refers to the role played by teachers in 'transforming pupil consciousness'; that is, ensuring they accept 'the realities of life' and, by extension, their likely future social positions.

213

- **Hegemony**: Antonio Gramsci (*Selections from the Prison Notebooks*, 1971) used this term to describe the idea of legitimate leadership. In other words, people obey authority because they believe it right to do so. For example, most people would accept Tony Blair has a right to exercise political leadership because he was democratically elected. As **Dominic Strinati** ('An Introduction to Theories of Popular Culture', 1995) put it, 'Dominant groups in society ... maintain their dominance by securing the "spontaneous consent" of subordinate groups'. This idea is important, when thinking about the role of education because if people believe education is meritocratic they will believe failure is their fault, not that of a system designed to ensure their failure.

- **Correspondence Theory**: **Bowles** and **Gintis** ('Schooling in Capitalist America', 1976) argued education is a proving ground in which the organisation of the workplace is reflected in the organisation of schools. Education, therefore, becomes a test of control and conformity – those who conform are allowed into the higher areas of education (and, by extension, work) whereas those who do not are excluded. The unstated role of education, therefore, is *cultural reproduction*: workplace inequality is reflected and reproduced in the organisation of schooling.

- **Social Reproduction**: Pierre Bourdieu ('The Forms of Capital', 1986) attacks the idea that education systems are meritocratic (see below); for Bourdieu, their real role is to reproduce the power and domination of powerful social classes, something achieved through **habitus**. An easy way to grasp this idea is to think

 Growing it yourself: school and work

The following table explores the relationship between work and school by identifying/explaining possible areas of correspondence. Some parts have been left blank for you to complete.

Once you've done this, expand the table by identifying and explaining further possible areas of correspondence (e.g. tests and grades).

School	Work
Schools arranged hierarchically (top to bottom)	Workplace has different levels (e.g. managers, senior managers, etc.)
	Employers have authority over employees
Students have no say in curriculum	
School uniform	
	Tea breaks
Further Examples	

about the idea of a habitat – the environment in which a group lives and flourishes. The natural habitat of fish, for example (the environment it needs) would not be suitable for humans (and vice versa). For Bourdieu, schools are the 'natural habitat' of the middle and upper classes – they reflect their interests, values and beliefs. The working-class child is like 'a fish out of water' – their values and beliefs are different because of **cultural capital** – the idea, in basic terms, that our social backgrounds give us certain advantages and disadvantages. Thus, working-class and middle-class children enter the education system with skills and abilities (such as how we speak and express ourselves) that advantage the middle-class child (because their cultural background is similar to that of the school). Thus, working-class children have to 'learn how to learn' before they can actually learn the things on the school curriculum – which gives them a decided disadvantage in the educational game.

- **Farkas** ('Family Linguistic Culture and Social Reproduction', 2001), for example, found significant linguistic and vocabulary differences between different social classes of white and black children in the USA which, he argued, disadvantaged working-class children in both pre-school and school environments.

- **Meritocracy**: Bourdieu is critical of this idea because differences in *cultural capital* influence the relative starting points of students (middle and upper class children have a hidden advantage). However, as he notes, the objective of schooling is cultural reproduction by progressively eliminating lower class children from the school system in ways that make their failure appear their own fault – by examination failure and self-elimination (they give up and leave school at the earliest opportunity).

Discussion point: equal opportunities?

This is a simple demonstration of how equality of opportunity (giving people the same chance to demonstrate their abilities) can actually be unfairly biased by 'cultural background'.

Select two students, one tall, one short. Stand them next to each other and explain their educational future rests on a single target – whoever can jump and reach highest wins.

A discussion about how the competition could have been made fairer (should the shorter student have been allowed to stand on a chair or given a helping hand?) can set the scene for a consideration of **compensatory education** (the idea some children, because of their 'deprived' social background, should be given additional help within the educational system to compensate for their deprivation).

Growing it yourself: cultural capital

Imagine three people (one French, one German and one English) go into a shop in France (the 'dominant culture', in this respect, would be French).

- The French person speaks the language.

- The German person knows some French.

- The English person knows no French.

The objective is to buy 7 oranges, 1 kilo of flour and 1 litre of cooking oil.

Write a brief explanation (100–200 words) explaining how cultural capital advantages or disadvantages each person in this situation.

When you've done this, imagine the French person is like an upper-class child, the German a middle-class child and the English a working-class child. Write a further brief explanation (200+ words) explaining how their cultural capital advantages or disadvantages them within the school.

Discussion questions: Marxism

To help you evaluate some of the ideas we've just examined, think about – and discuss – some or all of the following questions.

- **Correspondence**: Is the 'correspondence between school and work' a sleight-of-hand? For example, is it possible to find a connection between *anything* that happens in schools and the workplace (try it and see)? If you can, what does it tell us about the usefulness of this theory?

- **Perspectives**: The similarities between Marxism and Functionalism can, at times, be striking – are some Marxist perspectives just, to use **Jock Young**'s phrase (*The New Criminology*, 1973), 'Left-wing Functionalism'? To explore this idea, identify some of the similarities and differences between Functionalist and Marxist explanations of the role of education.

- **Social Control**: Are teachers really 'unwitting agents' of social control for a ruling class? Identify and explore some of the ways teachers, through their behaviour, both enforce and undermine the relationship between education and the workplace.

If you are feeling confident, you might like to explore the following questions.

- **Arguments**: How significant are arguments within Marxism? **Poulantzas** (*Classes in Contemporary Capitalism*, 1975) for example, argues schools are '*relatively autonomous*' institutions (that is, governments actually give schools and teachers quite a bit of freedom to act and interpret the curriculum – albeit within certain limits). How different is this from **Althusser's** argument?

- **Dominant ideologies**? Similarly, **Urry, Abercrombie** and **Turner** (*The Dominant Ideology Thesis*, 1975), prefer Gramsci's concept of hegemony, rather than the idea of there being a 'dominant ideology' in our society. Is there really a clear set of 'ideas about the role of education' in our society and, if not, can you identify what these competing ideas might involve?

Feminism

As I have suggested, the focus of feminist research has changed somewhat in the light of increasing female achievement, something that is reflected in two main ways:

- **Work**: Despite their educational achievements, women consistently lose out in the workplace. As **Treneman** ('Will the boys who can't read still end up as the men on top?', 1998) notes: 'The statistical under-achievement of boys in schools is nothing compared with the statistical over-achievement of men in life' (the pay gap between men and women still, for example, reveals an average 20% difference over an individual's lifetime).

- **Warrington** and **Younger** ('The Other Side of the Gender Gap', 2000) noted that male and female career aspirations still reflected traditional gender stereotypes (childcare, nursing, hairdressing and secretarial for girls, computing, accountancy and plumbing for boys) and **Gordon** ('Citizenship, difference and marginality in schools', 1996) found that, although teachers frequently praised girls' efforts, they reported finding boys more interesting to teach and gave more time and effort to motivate and retain their attention – once again suggesting the different levels of importance teachers give to male and female work.

- **Roger** and **Duffield** ('Factors Underlying Persistent Gendered Option Choices', 2000) suggest a number of reasons why girls tend to avoid science subjects that are equally applicable to a range of gendered curriculum choices.

  - **Primary socialisation** entrenches concepts of gender identity in males and females, conditioning the choices they make in school.

  - **Role models**: In primary teaching, for example, nearly 90% of classroom teachers are female, leading to an early connection between gender and work.

  - **Careers** advice tends to reinforce traditional male–female work roles.

  - **Work experience** places boys and girls into traditionally stereotyped jobs. **Jeannie Mackenzie**'s study of 'school-based work experience' placements ('It's a Man's Job ...', 1997) found, for example:

45% of girls [in the study] were allocated to caring placements but these did not always reflect their choices. Boys who did not get their preferred placement tended to be allocated to occupations which were regarded by them as either neutral or as traditionally male while girls who were unsuccessful were allocated to traditionally female occupations.

- **Identity**: The emphasis here is on understanding different levels of achievement amongst females by examining different forms of identity (how class and ethnicity, for example, impact on gender). **Warrington** and **Younger** (2000) for example, found very little difference between the percentage of boys and girls who leave school with no qualifications.

Diane Reay ('"Spice Girls", "Nice Girls", "Girlies", and "Tomboys"', 2001) found a variety of female identities developing in the primary classroom, including, most interestingly, as the following exchange suggests, girls who wanted to be like boys:

Jodie: Girls are crap, all the girls in this class act all stupid and girlie.
Diane: So does that include you?
Jodie: No, cos I'm not a girl, I'm a tomboy.

Discussion questions: feminism

To help you evaluate some of the ideas we have just examined, think about – and discuss – some or all of the following questions.

- **Achievement**: If girls out-perform boys at GCSE and A-level should we, as a society, be more concerned about explaining the relative underachievement of boys in our education system? You might, for example, want to consider possible reasons for female achievement and male relative underachievement (what changes in school and society, for example, might have caused this change in achievement?).
- **Gendered curriculum**: Why does it matter that males and females tend to study different subjects in post-16 education?
- **Work and adult roles**: Why does it matter that males and females tend to do different types of work?
- **Social change**: Is the future of work female? Although men still dominate higher levels of paid employment, is the position of women slowly changing? Have the changes in educational performance and achievement of girls had enough time to filter into the workplace?

If you are feeling confident, you might like to explore the following questions.

- **Research**: Is the large body of feminist evidence built up in the 1970s and 1980s to explain female underachievement now largely irrelevant?
- **Identity**: Does the change in focus of some contemporary feminist research (to look at class and ethnic identities as well as gender) call into question the need for feminist theories of education?

Interactionist perspectives

Preparing the ground

Interactionist perspectives focus on the role of education as a *process* rather than a *system*. In other words, they're interested in examining the idea that education is a social construction whose role isn't fixed and unchanging but, on the contrary, fluid and open to a wide range of interpretations. A classic example of this is the question of whether the role of the education system is one of two things.

- **Education**: **John Dewey** (*Democracy and Education*, 1916) argued education should be 'transformative'; focusing on individuals and their social, psychological and moral development as people. Education, in this respect, involves providing the means for individuals to achieve their 'full potential' (whatever that may, in reality, turn out to be).
- **Training**: The role of education is to give people the knowledge and skills they need to perform specific work-related roles (doctor, mechanic, etc.).

This general debate in our society over the role and purpose of schooling is played out in a number of areas, two of the most significant being:

- **Outside the school**: The role of education is never clear-cut and uncontested; various interest groups (parents, teachers, governments, businesses) have an input into the system, trying to shape it to reflect their interests, prejudices and concerns. Some groups, of course, are more successful in having their views heard (government and business organisations over the past 20 years, for example, have been powerful shaping forces in education). The dominance of these groups has resulted in the role of education being 'officially' defined in terms of its *training role* – the objective (through policies such as the National Curriculum, Key Stage testing, literacy hours in primary schools and so forth) is to produce 'a highly skilled and trained workforce'.

- **Inside the school**: While official declarations and definitions of the role of education are important influences on behaviour within schools, the relationship between the various *actors* involved in 'doing education' (teachers and their students, for example) is important and worthy of study. This is because interactionists want to consider

how these social actors *interpret* their roles within the context of the education system itself.

To illustrate this with a simple example, the sociology course you're following (for whatever reason – you like the subject, your friends took it so you did too, you ticked the wrong box when deciding your options and now you're stuck with it ...) has, in terms of its *structure and content*, been decided by the exam board (or awarding body as it's now known). Thus, if you want the qualification you have to study what is laid down in the specification. However, teachers don't all teach sociology in the same way – for some the objective may be to get you through the exam, for others it may be to provide an 'interesting learning experience' on a wet Friday afternoon.

The main point here is that what happens 'inside schools' is a process that can be shaped – but not determined – by official definitions of the role of education.

Discussion point: education or training?

One way of demonstrating this idea is to decide the purpose of education. Does it involve 'educating people' (and if so, how? Should you be allowed to study what you want, when you want?) or does it involve 'training people' (giving them specific work skills?) – or maybe it's a combination of both?

To help you organise your discussion, draw the following table and identify relevant points you can use to argue your case about the purpose of education.

Education?		Training?	
Advantages	Disadvantages	Advantages	Disadvantages
Pupils and teachers can focus on material they enjoy learning	Are there things we must learn to take our place in adult society?	You get the skills you need to get a job	What if the skills you've learnt are no longer needed?

Add your own ideas to these lists.

⚠ Digging deeper

Interactionist perspectives focus explanations about the role of education on what happens *inside schools*, mainly in terms of **school processes**. These involve ideas about how educational roles are interpreted and negotiated 'at the chalk face'. In this respect, Interactionists employ a range of ideas to understand the ways teachers and pupils *construct* 'education'.

- **Labelling theory** has traditionally been used to describe how teachers, as powerful actors in the education game, classify (or stereotype) students and, by so doing, influence the way they understand their role and status within the school. **Pauline Padfield** (' "Skivers", "saddos" and "swots" ', 1997), for example, has explored the way 'informal reputations' gained within the school influenced official definitions of pupils.

Labelling theory has been used to show how school processes such as *streaming* (grouping by ability on a yearly basis), *banding* (students taught at different levels, for example, Intermediate and Higher Maths) and *setting* (grouping by ability on a subject-by-subject basis) are *divisive* (they encourage students to think of themselves – and each other – in terms of fixed educational abilities).

Ruth Lupton's study (*Do Poor Neighbourhoods Mean Poor Schools?*, 2004) notes the decision made by the head teacher of one school to abandon banding: 'principally to counter problems of low self-esteem among pupils in the lower band. Within the context of the selective system and the school's poor performance and reputation, mixed

ability teaching was seen as an important way to give all pupils the message they were equally valued'.

Additionally, we increasingly have an educational system, as **Hattersley** and **French** ('Wrong Division', 2004) point out, that labels whole schools as either 'good' (academically successful) or 'bad' (academically failing) – and the consequences of the latter label frequently means closure.

Discussion point: school labels

You have probably got some knowledge about schools and colleges in your area (by reputation at least). As a class, identify the things you know about these institutions. What sort of reputation do these schools and colleges have and how do you think it affects people's general perception of them?

Can you identify any ways schools/colleges with poor reputations have tried to 're-label' themselves to try to change people's perceptions (for example, where I live Secondary Modern schools that had a poor reputation have re-named themselves 'Community Schools').

- **Self-concepts**: The concept of labelling relates to this idea in terms of questions like: How do you know if you are a good or bad student? How does your teacher know if they're good or bad at their job? How good is the reputation of your school?

These questions relate to how we see ourselves and, for Interactionists, self perception is fluid and intangible, mainly because we look to others to tell us how we are doing (you may, for example, look to your teacher to tell you how 'good' or 'bad' a student you are. Equally, your teacher may look to you to tell them something about their abilities as a teacher). Labelling is an important aspect of this process of *self-construction* (if your teacher continually gives you poor grades or students continually misbehave in a class we soon start to get the picture), based on the idea of:

- **Reference groups** – the people we use to check 'how we're doing' in whatever role we are playing. Not everyone in our reference group is equally important; *significant others* are people whose opinion we value while *insignificant others* are people we don't really care about (if your teacher isn't a significant other, you won't particularly care how they label you – although the labels that stick will always have consequences). This idea can of course, be applied to whole schools as well as groups and individuals within them. One outcome of all the processes just described may be a:

- **Self-fulfilling prophecy** – a prediction we make that, by making, we bring about. On an individual level, if we're labelled by teachers as 'dim' because, despite our best efforts, we get poor grades then perhaps we start to see our self in terms of this label and stop trying to get decent grades (what's the point – we're dim) and, in effect, confirm the teacher's label.

Robin Nash (*Keeping In With Teacher*, 1972) demonstrated how the values held by teachers about 'good' and 'bad' pupils were rapidly transmitted to pupils through attitudes and behaviours. Nash concluded: 'Certainly children of low

Discussion questions: interactionist perspectives

To help you evaluate some of the ideas we have just examined, think about – and discuss – some or all of the following questions.

- **Labelling**: Is this idea applied in a deterministic way (that is, does it suggest labelling always has a specific outcome?). In your experience, for example, is it possible to overturn negative labels and – if so – how?

- **Outside school factors**: How important are things like government policies, cultural capital and so forth in shaping school and pupil performance and achievement?

- **Self-concept**: To what extent do you agree/disagree that 'a weakness of Interactionist theory is that individuals are seen in isolation from wider social influences and stresses'? In other words, are schools the most important influence on how we see our self in educational terms? For example, identify and consider some ways teachers are important for pupil self-concepts and then think about how other social groups may influence our educational performance.

- **Setting and banding**: What positive features of these practices can you identify?

- **Inside school factors**: Do Interactionist theorists overstate the importance of these in explaining the role and purpose of education?

social origin do poorly at school because they lack encouragement at home, because they use language in a different way from their teachers, because they have their own attitudes to learning and so on. But also because of the expectations their teachers have of them'.

This concept also applies to whole classes of students who may be labelled in this way. Studies abound (**Stephen Ball**'s *Beachside Comprehensive*, 1981, **Paul Willis**'s *Learning to Labour: How working-class kids get working-class jobs*, 1977, **Cecile Wright**'s *Race Relations in the Primary School*, 1992 and **Troyna** and **Hatcher**'s *Racism in children's lives*, 1992) to demonstrate how this occurs through practices such as streaming, setting and banding, ethnic stereotyping and so forth.

Finally, whole schools may be enveloped by a self-fulfilling prophecy. If schools do badly in league tables of GCSE results, middle class parents stop sending their children to the 'bad school', whose results may continue to fall.

Postmodern perspectives

⚠ Preparing the ground

Postmodernist views on the 'role of education' are difficult to categorise for the deceptively simple reason that, as **Clinton Collins** ('Truth as a communicative virtue in a post-modern age', 1993) suggests: 'The term describes cultural changes happening to people throughout the post-industrial world, willy-nilly'.

Postmodern writers are like football commentators, describing the action for us as it unfolds (sheepskin coat optional)

The 'willy-nilly' tag is important because it suggests postmodernism is concerned with describing cultural tendencies and processes, in all their (glorious) confusion, for both our amusement and, probably, bemusement. In other words, postmodernists don't have a view, as such, on the role of education since this would suggest there is some essential 'right' or 'wrong' position on the subject. What they do have – which I propose to outline – is ideas about the relationship – and tension – between two competing, increasingly opposed, processes.

Modern institutions, such as schools, were born out of the Industrial Revolution and the development of modern society. As such, they exist to serve a number of purposes all of which, according to writers such as **Foucault** (*Discipline and Punish*, 1977), are to do with power ('Everything reduces to power', as he helpfully puts it). The power principle, in this context, relates to how the modern state tries to exert social control through institutions such as education.

The other side of this spectacle are **postmodern people** – the increasing *resistance* and *decentralising attitudes* of students (and indeed teachers) to the *centralising tendencies* of modernist education systems.

In other words, we have a situation where, on the one hand, the education system has, over the past few years, been subjected to increasingly centralised control by, for example, the government. This idea of 'control from the centre' has been evidenced by things like the introduction of a:

- **National curriculum** that sets out the subjects to be taught in all state schools.
- **Key Stage testing**, at ages 7, 11 and 14, that sets attainment targets in English and maths for all pupils.
- **Literacy** and **numeracy hours** introduced into primary schools in 1998. Commenting on the introduction of the literacy hour, the National Literacy Trust (2004) noted:

The National Literacy Strategy is an unprecedented intervention in classroom teaching methods. [It] describes term by term how reading and writing should be taught ... The policy requires primary teachers to teach a daily English lesson in which pupils are taught for the first half of the lesson as a whole class, reading together, extending their vocabulary ... and being taught grammar, punctuation and spelling.

On the other hand, however, we have a situation that **David Elkind** ('Schooling the Post-Modern Child', 1998), characterises in terms of the idea that: 'Whereas modern childhood was defined in terms of differences *between* age groups, postmodern childhood is identified with differences *within* age groups'. In other words, there is a sense of what **Phil Willis** ('Social class "defines school achievement"': *The Guardian*, 23/04/03) describes as 'Decentralising education from government and reducing the number of tests and targets' in order to '... free schools up to deal with the needs of individual children'.

Digging deeper

We can develop the distinction between *modern institutions* and *postmodern people* in the following way.

Modern institutions

The idea of control, for postmodernists, works on two levels.

- **Intellectual** control involves how people think and act in a number of ways.
  - The **curriculum**, for example, specifies the things (subjects) considered worthy of being known and its content is controlled down to the finest detail (think about the sociology specification or government initiatives involving things like literacy hours and detailed lesson plans for primary school teachers).
  - **Knowledge** is also controlled in terms of what you learn. English literature, for example, involves learning 'classic texts' (Shakespeare, Dickens and so forth – sometimes called 'high culture' – what governments and educationalists view as the best possible examples of our culture) and largely excludes 'popular culture' (the books and magazines most people

actually read, the computer games they play, the films they watch …) that is considered, within the National Curriculum for example, as being largely unworthy of serious, detailed, study.

- **Sites of control**: In an overall sense, schools are sites which attempt (through their captive audiences) to distribute (and legitimise) certain forms of what **Provenzo** (*Teaching, Learning, and Schooling*, 2002) identifies as: language, practices, values, ways of talking and acting, moving, dressing and socialising (to name but a few). Schools, from this viewpoint, are not simply organised for 'education', but also for institutionalising the culture of powerful groups.

- **Physical control** involves both:

  - **Body**: Think about what you can and can't do in school. You must attend (or your parents may be prosecuted) and you must be in certain lessons (and places) at certain times. Once in those lessons there may be restrictions on when you can speak, who you can speak to, how you speak to them, as well as movement restrictions (such as asking permission to go to the toilet and not being in corridors when you should be in a lesson).

  - **Space**: Schools are increasingly introducing closed-circuit television (both inside and outside the classroom) for the purpose of patrolling and controlling space – who is allowed to be in certain spaces (classrooms, corridors, staffrooms) and when they are allowed to be there.

Postmodern people

For postmodernists, what we are seeing are changes in people's behaviour (under the influence of *globalisation* and cross-cultural contacts and exchanges) which include:

Active consumption: Mark Taylor (*Generation NeXt Comes to College*, 2004) argues students are changing: 'They are the most academically disengaged, or even compliant college students with all time low measures for time spent studying

 Growing it yourself: the school prison

Foucault (1977) likened schools to prisons in terms of their use of surveillance techniques. Are schools really like this and, if so, how?

Using the following table as a guide, identify some of the ways schools are like prisons in terms of how they attempt to control body and space.

Body		Space	
Prison	School	Prison	School
Electronic tags	Electronic registers	Cells	Classrooms
	Teachers	Warders	

and all time high measures for boredom and tardiness . . . bringing educational and social characteristics to campus that are challenging educators'. Taylor characterises these students in a number of ways (not all of them particularly flattering): Consumer oriented, wanting instant gratification, adaptable to new situations, sceptical and cynical to name but a few.

- **Differentiation**: **Elkind** (1998) suggests a key characteristic here is the idea of difference and, in a sense, the *fragmentation of identities*. In other words, students want to be recognised and treated as unique individuals rather than as groups (genders, classes. ethnicities and so forth). To use **Giroux**'s phrase (*Slacking Off*, 1994) students are increasingly 'border youths' whose identities cut across class, ethnicity and gender categories.

- **Sousveillance** (the opposite of surveillance – to watch from above) means 'to watch from below' and expresses the idea students (and teachers) are increasingly critical and dissatisfied with their treatment in the education system.

As **Hanafin** et al ('Responding to Student Diversity', 2002) argue:

Mainstream education is constructed on a flawed notion of intelligence and consequently disables many learners, perhaps even the majority . . . Through over reliance on a narrow range of teaching methods, students are denied access to curriculum content. Narrow assessment approaches further compound disablement. At its most extreme, mainstream education supports and structures unnecessary failure and exclusion.

In addition, we could also note here the development of new:

- **subjects**, such as media, film and cultural studies
- **ideas** about learning – **Howard Gardner**'s ideas about *multiple intelligences* (*Frames of Mind*, 1993), for example, express the idea that

. . . it was generally believed intelligence was a single entity that was inherited; and that human beings – initially a blank slate – could be trained to learn anything, provided it was presented in an appropriate way. Nowadays an increasing number of researchers believe precisely the opposite; that there exists a multitude of intelligences, quite independent of each other.

- **relationships** – the teacher as 'facilitator', helping students to learn.

Finally, postmodernists note, as I have suggested, some contributing processes to the above involve:

- **Globalisation** (of course), because it opens up new ways of thinking and doing and, as **Shen-Keng Yang** ('Educational research', 2002) notes, it also promotes a new interest in *local cultures* (your immediate and personal environment, for example).

- **Uncertainty** (both for students and teachers) about the teaching and learning process – what, for example, is expected of people? Have they made the right choices about what to study?

One upshot of uncertainty is a contradictory outcome to that noted by **Taylor** (2004). **Howe** and **Strauss** (*Millennials Rising*, 2000), for example, characterise the 'postmodern generation' as being well focused on grades and performance, interested in extra curricular and community activities, demanding of secure environments and more interested in maths and science than in humanities.

On the other hand, as we will see when we look at New Right perspectives, governments have responded to uncertainty by increased efforts at centralisation and control. The National Curriculum, Key Stage tests and so forth are all attempts, it could be argued, to maintain an outdated perception of the role and purpose of education.

New Right perspectives

⚠ Preparing the ground

New Right perspectives are difficult to classify because they tend to straddle an uneasy divide between, on the one hand, Functionalist theories (involving, for example, structural concepts like role allocation and social differentiation) and, on the other, individualistic views about people as consumers who exercise choices about the education their sons and daughters receive. Problems of classification notwithstanding, we can note how New Right perspectives generally focus on two basic areas.

- **Society**: Although Margaret Thatcher's (in)famous observation, 'There is no such

Discussion questions: postmodernism

To help you evaluate some of the ideas we've just examined, think about – and discuss – some or all of the following questions.

- **Surveillance**: Can things like CCTV in schools have positive aspects (such as creating a secure and safe environment)?
- **Postmodern people**: How aware are students and parents of their role as 'consumers' of education? Do you see yourself as a 'postmodern person' and if not, why not?
- **Identities**: How important (or unimportant) are things like class, gender and ethnic identities? Do people see themselves as 'individuals', part of large groups or, perhaps 'individuals within large groups'?
- **Patterns**: Is it possible to identify patterns of behaviour within school (for example, groups of boys and girls acting in specific, different, ways)? If so, what does this tell us about postmodern ideas?
- **Postmodern people**: Look again at how both Taylor (2004) and Howe and Strauss (2000) characterise 'postmodern students'; which, in your experience, is the more realistic characterisation (and why)?

thing as society, only individuals and families', suggests these perspectives take a rather dim view of sociological arguments about society and culture (they also take a dim view of sociologists, come to that), this is not to say they don't have strong views about the role of the state which, in basic terms, involves the idea the role of government is to guarantee the freedom of:

- **Individuals**: From this perspective, people are seen as consumers, able and willing to make informed choices about their lives and families (which, incidentally, is seen as the basic social unit in any society). However, they argue consumer choice is limited, in societies such as our own, by the way governments have allowed teachers to set the education agenda – an idea we will develop in more detail in a moment.

Rather than concern ourselves with trying to specify, from this perspective, the exact relationship between the individual and society, it's perhaps easier to think in terms of the relationship between individuals and the state (which includes things like political government, the Civil Service and social control agencies such as the police and armed forces). In this respect, New Right perspectives argue for a **minimal state**. In other words, the ideal role of government in any society is that of creating the conditions under which private enterprise can flourish and in which individuals can go about their daily lives with the minimum of political interference. The role of the state, therefore, is largely reduced to one that guarantees the safety of its citizens – both internally, through agencies such as the police, and externally through agencies such as the armed forces.

Although this characterisation oversimplifies New Right arguments somewhat, it does give a general flavour for the perspective and its emphasis on the rights and responsibilities of individuals (to provide, for example, for both themselves and their families) and the general belief that capitalism (and private enterprise) is the best possible way of ensuring the largest number of people have the highest possible standard of living.

These ideas, as I am sure you appreciate, mean that when we consider the role of education from this perspective the general argument is that government should not be involved in its provision.

⚠ Digging deeper

New Right perspectives on the role of education have been influential in both Britain and the USA in recent years and we can develop the ideas we've just noted in the following way.

Society

- **Business organisations** are seen as *wealth creators* and, as such, should be allowed to get on with the thing they do best (creating wealth if you have to ask), free from state 'interference'. In this respect:

- **Governments** are seen as bureaucratic organisations, unable to adjust quickly and easily to change. They should not involve themselves in areas (such as industry and commerce) where businesses can, it is argued, do a better job. The role of governments, therefore, is not to 'do things' (like manage schools or … err … railways) but rather to create the conditions under which businesses can successfully operate. One reason for this is:

- **Competition**: Businesses, unlike governments, are competitive organisations, forced to innovate (find new and better ways of doing things) if they are to capture and retain customers.

Individuals

As **Pateman** ('Education and Social Theory', 1991) notes, the New Right sees consumer choice as being limited by *producer capture*: 'Teachers (the "producers") have set their own agendas for schools when it should be parents (the "consumers") who set agendas for teachers. The New Right then argues for breaking up schooling monopolies and for enfranchizing the consumer'. The role of government, in this respect, is to guarantee:

- **Choice**: This is achieved in a variety of ways: by encouraging different types of school; allowing businesses a say in the building, ownership and running of state schools; encouraging fee-paying, private schools (thereby contributing to the diversity of educational provision and the enhancing of parental choice).

- **Standards**, in the sense of ensuring teachers teach the same curriculum, testing (at various Key Stages) to ensure schools are performing their role properly and to identify schools 'failing their customers'. League tables which show the 'best' and 'worst' performing schools are also designed to give consumers choice over where they send their children.

- **Training**, rather than education. The objective is to ensure schools produce students with the skills businesses need ('Key Skills', for example, such as maths and ICT). The New Right is keen on 'traditional subjects' (English, maths and science) and antagonistic to subjects like

media and film studies – and, of course, sociology.

- **Socialisation**: Schools have an important role here, not just in producing new consumers and workers, but also ensuring children have the 'right attitudes' for these roles. Part of this process involves (in a similar sort of argument to that used by functionalists) instilling respect for legitimate authority and the development of future business leaders.

Discussion questions: New Right

To help you evaluate some of the ideas we've just examined, think about – and discuss – some or all of the following questions.

- **Training**: Should schools be about more than simply training people for the workplace? If so, what sort of things should schools be doing to enhance individual experience of education?
- **Private schools**: Do they 'enhance consumer choice' or simply divide people on the basis of income? What arguments – for and against – can you identify?
- **Development**: What are the possible advantages and disadvantages of government control over the education system?
- **Curriculum**: Is the kind of school curriculum (in terms of subjects and content) you've experienced appropriate for the twenty-first century? What subjects, for example, should/shouldn't be on the curriculum?
- **Marketisation**: What are the possible advantages and disadvantages of private business control over the education system?

In this section we have looked, in general terms, at the role played by education in society from a variety of different perspectives. One of the roles we have touched on at various points is the idea of schools as areas of formal teaching and learning and how learning, in particular, is validated and certificated. In the next section we can develop this idea a little more by focusing on the concept of differential achievement – why some social groups do better or worse than others in our education system.

Differential achievement

Introduction

The focus of this section, (if you hadn't already guessed) is an examination of 'explanations of the different educational achievement of social groups by social class, gender and ethnicity'.

WARM UP: SOCIAL CLASS AND ACHIEVEMENT

This exercise is in two parts.

1. In small groups, create a table like the one shown. Each group should choose one of the areas indicated (family, work or school). For your chosen area, identify as many factors as you can that might give a child an educational advantage or disadvantage (I have noted a few to get you started).

Area	Possible advantages?	Possible disadvantages?
Family and home life	Positive parental attitudes to value of education	Poverty
Work	High income	Unemployment
School	Private schooling	Exclusion from school

2. For each factor you've identified within your chosen area, write a short explanation about how you think it might advantage or disadvantage a child's education. For example: 'Parental unemployment may mean a child has to leave school at 16 to get a job to help support their family'.

Once you have completed this, present your ideas and explanations to the rest of the class.

Social class

⚠ Preparing the ground

We can begin this section by identifying some of the ways social class impacts on educational performance at various levels of our education system, from achievement at Key Stage 1 (7 year olds) to participation at degree level. Once we have outlined the basic relationship between class and educational performance we can then move on to examine some explanations for this relationship.

Key Stages 1–3

Table 4.2 illustrates achievement differences between social classes using eligibility for Free School Meals (FSM) as a measure of attainment. This does, of course, assume (probably quite reasonably) pupils with FSM status come from the lower social classes.

The most notable feature of these figures is the comparatively lower performance of FSM pupils at all stages of compulsory schooling, (from Key Stage 1 to Key Stage 4 (GCSE)).

Key Stage 4

If we look in a bit more detail at Key Stage 4, by breaking the figures down into specific social classes, we can see more clearly the general relationship between class membership and achievement. Firstly, middle-class (professional) children perform comparatively better than working-class (skilled and unskilled manual) children – but there are also clear achievement divisions *within* the working class. Secondly, educational performance for all social classes has improved in recent years, although, as I have just noted, the performance gap between the higher and lower social classes is still apparent.

	1989	2000	2002
Professional	52	74	77
Skilled manual	21	45	52
Unskilled manual	12	26	32

Table 4.3 % of selected social classes gaining 5 or more GCSE grades A*–C
Source: Department for Education and Skills, 2004

	KS1	KS2	KS3	KS1	KS2	KS3	KS1	KS2	KS3	KS4 (GCSE)	
	Reading	English		Writing	Science		Maths			5 or more A*–C	No Passes
Non FSM	88	79	74	85	79	74	93	76	75	55.2	4.1
FSM	69	54	44	64	52	42	80	53	46	24.4	12.2

Table 4.2 % Achievement: Key Stages 1–3 (ages 7, 11 and 14) to Key Stage 4 (GCSE)
Source: Department for Education and Skills, 2004

Further and higher education

If we look at participation (or 'staying-on') figures for those in full-time further (post-16) education by social class, an interesting picture begins to emerge. Working-class participation, although still generally lower than middle-class participation, has increased significantly in recent times (unskilled manual participation, for example, has more than doubled since 1989). This suggests a couple of things.

• **Vocational qualifications**: Many working-class children stay on in education, post-16, to study for *vocational qualifications* that are directly related to specific occupations (bricklaying, for example) or types of occupation (tourism, for example) not offered during their period of compulsory schooling.

• **Educational value**: Many working-class children (and presumably their parents who may have to support them financially during their period of study) place a value on educational qualifications. The interesting thing to note here, perhaps, is the possibility such children have problems with their school (in terms of achievement, what they are required to study and so forth), not with the idea of education itself.

Finally, if we look at participation in higher (degree-level) education, a similar trend – in terms of middle-class (non-manual) children having a higher level of participation than working-class (manual) children – is again evident. However, we need to keep in mind that if relatively large numbers of working-class children are participating, post-16, in vocational education courses it makes it less likely they will be subsequently involved, unlike their middle-class peers, in higher education. It is, therefore, important to consider the idea that different social classes may develop different routes through the education system.

	1991	1998	2002
Non-Manual	36	48	51
Manual	11	18	19

Table 4.5 % Participation in HE by social classes
Source: Social Trends 34 (2004)

In terms of the figures we have just examined, the general patterns of achievement we have noted suggest the higher your social class, the greater your level of educational attainment. Sociologists have, of course, developed a number of possible explanations for this situation which, for convenience, we can examine in terms of two general categories: outside school factors and inside school factors.

	1989	2000	2002
Professional	68	82	87
Skilled manual	39	66	69
Unskilled manual	27	59	60

Table 4.4 % in full-time education at age 16 by selected social classes
Source: Department for Education and Skills, 2004

Outside school factors involve explanations focusing on the home background (both *material* and *cultural*) of pupils. These include, for example:

- **Material deprivation**, which refers to things like poor diet/nutrition, lack of private study facilities and resources, the need to work to supplement family income and so forth. These combine to give affluent (well-off) pupils a relative advantage in school (the ability to use computers and the Internet for homework/coursework, for example).

- **Attitudes** to education focuses on the idea that middle-class parents take an active interest in their children's education. **Diane Reay** ('Emotional capital', 2000) suggests middle-class mothers, for example, invest time and effort (or emotional labour) in their children's education. Working-class parents, on the other hand, either don't particularly care about their children's education (the classic argument being they prefer their children to leave school and start work at the earliest possible opportunity) or they fail to control their children's behaviour, which results in things like truancy, exclusion and underachievement. This links easily into:

- **Cultural deprivation** theory and the idea that working-class culture is somehow 'lacking' in the *attributes* (such as positive parental attitudes about the value of education) and *practices* (reading to children, helping with homework and so forth) that make the middle classes educationally successful. Solutions to cultural deprivation focus around 'compensating' working-class children for their cultural deprivation by providing extra educational resources to give them an equal opportunity to compete with their culturally advantaged middle-class peers. By and large, this type of theory has been submerged into:

- **Underclass** theory, which suggests a combination of material and cultural factors are the cause of educational failure among a class of people who are increasingly disconnected from mainstream society. According to New Right theorists like **Charles Murray** and **Melanie Phillips** ('The British Underclass 1990–2000', 2001), the underclass involves 'people at the margins of society, unsocialised and often violent ... parents who mean well but who cannot provide for themselves, who give nothing back to the neighbourhood, and whose children are the despair of the teachers who have to deal with them'.

Underachievement is explained by arguing that material factors (economic deprivation) and cultural factors (a *moral relativism* that fails to condemn unacceptable behaviour, for example) combine to produce, in **Phillips'** (2001) words, 'the *socially excluded* who are no longer just poor but the victims of anti-education, anti-marriage policies which have undermined personal responsibility'. This theory, therefore, identifies the underclass as a group mainly responsible for underachievement – through things like truancy, misbehaviour and general beliefs (state handouts and petty crime as preferable to qualifications and hard work, for example). In other words, this version of underclass theory blames governments (for creating a class of people dependent on state handouts) and parents (for failing to take moral responsibility for child care and socialisation). A different, more left-wing, take on this involves:

- **Class culture** theory, which argues different classes develop different values and norms based around their different experiences and needs. For the middle classes, educational qualifications are an important way of reproducing individual class positions, whereas for the working classes the work-based route to money and status has always been more important. Class differences are demonstrated in a variety of ways: deferred/immediate gratification, parental experiences of higher education – or not as the case may be – and so forth.

- **Class subculture** theory takes this a little further by arguing state schools are institutions dominated by 'middle-class norms, values, beliefs and ideologies' and some working-class subcultural groups succeed by adapting successfully to this school environment – whereas others, of course, do not. A modern version of this general theory relates to:

- **Identities**, which pinpoints changing male (and female) identities as causes of differential achievement; the idea, for example, some working-class boys develop a 'laddish, anti-school, anti-learning' culture. **Becky Francis**'s secondary school study (*Boys, Girls and Achievement*, 2000) argues that teenage boys used 'laddish' behaviour in the classroom as a way of offsetting the generally low levels of esteem they received from both teachers and (female) pupils (findings that link back to earlier subcultural studies – such as **Albert**

Cohen's *Delinquent Boys* (1955) – which focused on the idea of status deprivation as a cause of boys' educational disaffection).

- **Cultural capital** is an idea we have examined earlier and its application to educational achievement lies in areas such as those identified by **Reay** (2000) when she argued the importance of 'mothers' emotional engagement with their children's education' – in areas such as help and encouragement with school work and pressurising teachers to improve their children's performance. Middle-class women, according to Reay's research, were particularly successful in investing their emotional capital in their child's education.

Inside school factors (sometimes called the *hidden curriculum*) involve explanations for differential achievement that focus on:

- **Type of school**: Different types of school (private, grammar, comprehensive . . .) involve different levels of teacher, parent and pupil expectations – in other words, top performing schools, whether in the private or state sector, create a climate of expectation that pushes pupils into higher levels of achievement. In addition, status differences between schools also tell pupils something about their relative educational (and social) worth.

Gewirtz ('Can All Schools Be Successful?', 1998) demonstrated that, even within schools of similar status, there is a huge difference between a top state school and an inner city school labelled as 'failing'. In the latter, for example, she found, 'difficulties in staff recruitment and parental involvement, and strained relationships between management and staff as improvement agendas became hijacked by day-to-day fire-fighting'.

- **Class sizes**: Private (fee-paying) schools dominate school league tables, one explanation for this being teachers give more time to individual students because of smaller class sizes. According to the Department for Education and Skills (DfES), in 1999 average class size in state secondary schools was 20 pupils, whereas in private schools it was 10.

- **Teacher attitudes** involves the ideas of labelling and self-fulfilling prophecies (which we have explained previously).

The basic idea here is teachers communicate, (consciously and subconsciously), positive or negative beliefs about the value of their pupils. Pupils pick up on these ideas and, in the process, see themselves in terms of the labels given to them by their teachers (as intelligent or unintelligent, for example).

- **Social inclusion/exclusion** has one fairly obvious form (physical exclusion), which includes *self-exclusion* (truancy) as well as actually being barred from school (DfES figures for 2001 show 10,000 permanent school exclusions, for example).

Malcolm et al ('Absence from School', 2003) found broad agreement amongst Local Education Authorities (LEAs) and

Discussion point: schools

One of the schools pictured below is a public (fee-paying) school the other isn't.

Can you guess which is which?

What factors led to your decision? What educational and social advantages/disadvantages do you think there might be for pupils who attend either the fee-paying school (pictured left) or the state school (pictured right)?

teachers that absence correlated with lower attainment (which is not too surprising, all things considered).

Another, less obvious form of inclusion/exclusion is ability grouping (a general label for practices such as streaming, setting and banding). **Harlen** and **Malcolm**'s wide-ranging 'Setting and Streaming' (1999), for example, concluded educational performance was affected by many school processes – 'class size, pupil ability range, teaching methods and materials … and teachers' attitudes towards mixed-ability teaching'.

Hallam, Ireson and **Hurley** ('Ability Grouping in the Secondary School', 2001) noted how setting, for example, had both benefits for pupils (minimising disruptive behaviour) and disadvantages (stigmatising lower set pupils, the association between lower sets and unemployment, higher sets and good exam grades). They also noted a familiar trend in this type of research (from **Nell Keddie** 'Classroom Knowledge', 1971, onwards) – teachers giving 'more creative

work and privileges to higher set students while restricting lower sets to tedious, routine tasks'.

Hallam et al's research highlighting how high and low set pupils attracted different stigmatising labels ('thick', 'dumb', 'boffin', 'clever clogs') relates to ideas about:

- **Pupil subcultures**. As an explanation for differential achievement, this idea has a long and respectable history (see, for example, **David Hargreaves**' 'Social Relations In A Secondary School' (1967) and **Pete Woods**' 'The Divided School' (1979) – the latter noting the existence of *pro* and *anti* school subcultures, from ingratiating, compliant pupils, through ritualists 'going through the motions' to outright rebels).

More recently, **Martin Johnson** (*Failing School, Failing City*, 1999) has described schools in Northern Ireland where some pupil subcultures were marked by 'hostility and indifference' to learning, which correlated with high levels of absence and lower levels of educational achievement.

Finally, **Colin Lacey** ('Hightown Grammar', 1970) noted streaming and setting created the belief, even among relatively successful grammar school students, they were failures when compared to their peers. Thirty years later, **Power** et al ('Education and the Middle Class', 2003) found much the same sort of subcultural labelling process at work when they noted how successful middle-class students labelled themselves as failures for their inability to match the achievements of some of their high-flying peers.

Growing it yourself: pupil subcultures

In small groups (or as a whole class) use your experience of school/college life to identify as many pupil subcultures as you can.

Once you've done this, make a list of the general social characteristics of each group: are they, for example, single or mixed gender, middle or lower class? are these groups associated with setting/banding (and, if so, how)? The general social behaviours of these groups: are they, for example, pro or anti school?.

Digging deeper

Although we have identified a range of possible explanations for class-based differential achievement, we need to remember two things.

Firstly, as **Mairtin Mac an Ghaill** ('What about the Boys?', 1996) argues, social class origins remain the single best predictor of educational success or failure. **Demack, Drew** and **Grimsley** ('Myths about underachievement', 1998) also note, 'While school effectiveness research has focused on school differences, social class differences are still the largest differences of all and the children of professional parents have the largest advantage of all'.

Secondly, we should avoid the assumption that 'the majority' of working-class children are necessarily academic underachievers. Significant numbers do succeed educationally and they have been increasingly successful (albeit from a low starting point) over the past 15 years at GCSE. Working-class children are also increasingly present in post-16 education. The fact they remain, despite increases in recent years, under-represented in higher education also tells us something about the activities and preoccupations of this group.

Outside school factors

- **Material deprivation**: Although studies over the past 40 years have shown there is no clear and simple relationship between poverty/deprivation and educational performance, there is, nevertheless, a link.

  Douglas's classic study ('The Home and the School', 1964) concluded material deprivation was too broad an explanation for relative working class failure because some materially-deprived children managed to succeed. Working class attainment also tended to fall *throughout* a child's education, suggesting other processes, within the school itself, contributed to differential achievement levels.

  Mortimore (*The Road to Improvement: Reflections on School Effectiveness*, 1998), however, argues that 'In any country in the world … there is a strong relationship between deprivation in the early years and later educational outcomes' and **Robinson** (*Literacy, Numeracy and Economic Performance*, 1998) concludes: 'A serious policy to alleviate child poverty might do far more for boosting attainment in literacy and numeracy than any modest interventions in schooling'.

- **Parental attitudes**: We need to be careful when suggesting attitudes and a lack of involvement by working class parents in their children's education are a cause of differential achievement. As **Hanafin** and

Lynch ('Peripheral Voices', 2002) argue, working-class parents are interested in their children's education and progress, but they 'felt excluded from participation in decision-making', which suggests the 'problem' lies not so much with parents but with schools – something addressed by New Labour educational policies that have attempted to involve parents in the running of their child's school. **Desforges**' literature review ('The impact of parental involvement', 2003), on the other hand, also suggests 'at-home good parenting' has a positive effect on achievement.

- **Cultural deprivation/underclass** explanations have a superficial attractiveness, but **MacDonald** and **Marsh** ('Disconnected Youth?', 2003) found 'no evidence of a distinct, deviant, underclass culture' in their research on Teesside, Middlesbrough. What they found was a complicated picture of 'marginalised youth' struggling to come to terms with their low status and social exclusion. As **Mac an Ghaill** (1996) notes, the problem is not the culture of working-class boys; rather, changes in the labour market (the decline in manufacturing jobs) have effectively excluded such boys from their traditional work in industry. This gives a useful comparison to the situation found by **Paul Willis** ('Learning to Labour', 1977) when he argued many working class boys were unconcerned with educational achievement because their objective was to leave school and start earning money – something that may no longer be as easy to achieve as it was at the time of Willis' study.

Inside school factors

Nell Keddie ('Tlnker, Tailor: The Myth of Cultural Deprivation', 1973), observed that if we, as sociologists, focus our attention on the supposed deficiencies of children (in terms of cultural deprivation, for example), we may not notice the shortcomings of schools – something particularly evident over the past 30 years in terms of strategies designed to improve the performance of underachieving students.

- **School effects**: Taking a range of general factors into account, **Ruth Lupton** (*Do poor neighbourhoods mean poor schools?*, 2003) concluded that 'neighbourhood poverty' and 'poor schooling' go hand-in-hand – the main question being, of course, which comes first; are schools 'poor' because of their ability intake or do schools – through processes such as labelling and self-fulfilling prophecies – fail to inspire and educate their pupils?

- **Value-added**: **Thomas** and **Mortimore** ('Comparisons of value added models', 1996) argue that, by controlling for social class and applying value-added analyses to educational attainment (measuring the relative improvement – or lack of same – of children within a school between, for example, one Key Stage and the next), schools can substantially raise pupil achievement.

- **League tables**: **Robinson** (1998) has additionally noted the impact of school league tables on achievement; while overall levels of achievement have risen in recent years, he argues this is at the expense of the lowest achieving children because teachers have concentrated their efforts on 'marginal pupils' (those just below the magic C grade at GCSE). Slight improvements in their attainment, Robinson argues, results in hugely improved pass rates at GCSE.

- **Study support**: A number of writers have noted how changing ways of supporting students can affect achievement. In 'The Impact of Study Support', (2001), **MacBeth** et al, for example, noted areas such as attendance, attitudes to school and attainment increased for students who participated in out-of-school-hours learning – something incorporated into New Labour educational policy in the shape of Extended Schools (discussed in more detail below).

To put the above into an overall context, **Lucy Ward** ('Pupils at good schools "gain 18 months"', 2004) notes that, according to DfES research, of differences in performance *between* schools:

- 73% is due to a child's level of achievement on starting secondary school
- 19% on the proportion of pupils qualifying for free school meals
- 8% on the effectiveness of teaching.

Gender
Preparing the ground

We can begin this section in a similar way to the section we have just completed on social class – by identifying some of the ways gender impacts on educational performance at various levels of our education system, from achievement at Key Stage 1 (7 year olds) to participation at

degree level. Once we have outlined the basic relationship between gender and educational performance we can then examine some possible explanations for this relationship.

Key Stages 1–3

According to DfES figures (2004), girls outperformed boys at every Key Stage in 2003, with the exception of Key Stage 2 Maths and Key Stage 3 science (where their levels of achievement were the same). If we include class-based factors in the analysis, a couple of points can be noted.

- **FSM children**: Both boys and girls in this category achieved less than their non-FSM peers. Among this group, girls outperformed boys at every Key Stage level with the exception of Key Stage 3 science and Key Stage 2 maths (where small percentage differences in achievement in favour of boys were apparent).

- **Non-FSM children**: The general pattern of achievement for this group was similar to the FSM group – girls outperformed boys with the exception of Key Stage 2 maths.

We can add a couple of points to the above.

- **Marginal differences**: With the exception of English at Key Stage 2 and 3, the percentage difference in performance between boys and girls (both FSM and non-FSM children) is marginal – 2 percentage points at most.

- **Social class**: the significance of social class should be noted here; FSM girls achieved less than non-FSM boys. This suggests, at the very least, social class is a significant factor in explaining male and female educational achievement.

Key Stage 4

The pattern of gender achievement at GCSE is, as you might expect, similar to that at Key Stage 1–3; girls, over the past few years have outperformed boys at this level. It is also significant to note that, over the past 15 years, the gender gap at this level has increased (as Table 4.6 demonstrates).

	1989	2000	2002
Male	28	44	46
Female	31	54	56

Table 4.6 % gaining 5 or more GCSE grades A*–C by gender
Source: Department for Education and Skills, 2004

Further and higher education

When we look at participation rates post-16 we find more girls than boys in further education. According to DfES figures (2004), for example, in 2002 75% of 16-year-old girls and 66% of 16-year-old boys were in full-time education. In terms of achievement, as Table 4.7 shows, girls achieve more than boys in terms of exam passes at A-level and its equivalent than boys.

	1996	2000	2001
Males	34	37	37
Females	42	46	47

Table 4.7 % achieving 1 or more A-level passes or equivalent by gender
Source: Department for Education and Skills, 2004

In terms of participation in higher education, according to Social Trends 34 (2004), more

women than men were studying full time for a first degree in 2002 (630,000 as against 519,000). The equivalent figures for 1971 were 173,000 women and 241,000 men).

Growing it yourself: gender and achievement

30 years ago explanations for differential achievement focused on why boys achieved more than girls in the education system. Today, the reverse is true.

Using the table below as a starting point, identify changes in both society and schools that might be responsible for changing patterns of gender achievement.

Outside school factors	Inside school factors
Increasing female employment	Teaching strategies
Changing nature of work	Curriculum changes
Further factors?	

As with the work we did on social class we can organise this section in terms of inside and outside school factors.

Outside school factors

- **Social changes**: From a post-feminist perspective, **Helen Wilkinson** (*No Turning Back*, 1994), identifed a range of changes that, she argued, represented a 'historic shift in the relationship between men and women'. These included:
  - **Cultural** changes, such as contraception, the availability of

abortion and the outlawing of sexual discrimination.

- **Labour market** changes that increasingly drew women into the workforce. The gradual change from manufacturing to service industries has seen the development of a 'knowledge-based' economy that 'values brains more than it does brawn' and demands flexibility and dexterity. **Wilkinson** identifies skills women have traditionally demonstrated in the home (or private sphere) – conflict resolution and interpersonal communiucation skills, for example – as increasingly valued in the (post) modern workplace (or public sphere). These changes mean an increased importance being placed by women on:

- **Educational qualifications** – the route into areas of the labour market traditionally dominated by men. In other words, by acquiring measurable credentials (qualifications), women are increasingly able to enter the workforce and compete for jobs with men. This change is reflected in:

- **Workforce participation**: According to the Office for National Statistics (Social Trends 34, 2004 in 1997), women in paid employment outnumbered men for the first time (11.248m to 11.236m). Against this, men still outnumber women in terms of *full-time employment* (in 2003, 11.5 million men and 6.7 million women were in full-time work) and, as of 2003, male employment has also overtaken female employment again (15 million to 13 million respectively).

- **Globalisation**: **Ros Coward** (*Sacred Cows: Is Feminism Relevant to the New Millennium?* 1999) identifies economic globalisation, which encourages greater workplace flexibility and opportunities for home working using computer technology, as further evidence of a seismic shift (or 'Genderquake' as **Wilkinson** terms it) in male–female relationships.

- **Socialisation**: Although such things are difficult to precisely track, there is evidence to suggest changes in female primary socialisation. **Carter** and **Wojtkiewicz** ('Parental involvement with adolescents' education', 2000), for example, found greater parental involvement, help and attention in the education of their daughters. In terms of how socialisation impacts on gender identities (especially conceptions of masculinity and femininity) **Isabella Crespi** ('Gender socialization within the family', 2003) argued that adolescents now have a range of possible gender identities available to them, rather than the restricted range (paid worker/domestic worker) of even the recent past. In this respect, two things may be happening to help explain changes in female achievement.

- **Opportunities**: Females have more opportunities to express a range of different 'femininities' – including ones that involve a career, rather than just part-time work.

- **Social change**: As changes occur in the workplace, these reflect back onto family socialisation processes. Parents, for example, change their perception of their children's future adult roles and, consequently, the relative importance they place on male and female educational achievement.

- **Identities**: The idea of changing male identities – what **Jones** and **Myhill** ('Seeing things differently', 2003) term 'hyper masculinity' (or laddishness to you and me) may also contribute to differential educational achievement as boys redefine their future adult roles. Both **Epstein** et al (*Failing Boys?: Issues in gender achievement*, 1998) and **Lydon** ('Man Trouble', 1996) pinpoint the idea of males losing control of both their unique identities and their lives as a result of changes in both female behaviour and the workplace. In this respect, the argument is that, as a result of changing identities, some boys see education as irrelevant to their future.

  Platten ('Raising boys' achievement', 1999) takes issues of identity further by arguing boys are increasingly victims of *negative gender stereotyping* when compared to girls (boys 'command' but girls 'request', for example). In other words, traditional male behaviour is reinterpreted (largely negatively) by teachers, which leads us to consider inside school factors.

Inside school factors

- **Labelling and stereotyping** explanations suggest a reversal of traditional forms of gender labelling, with girls increasingly being *positively labeled* (as high achievers who work hard and have least behavioral problems). Boys, on the other hand, are increasingly *negatively labeled* in terms of underachievement, laziness and behavioral problems (although class perceptions are also significant here, with working-class boys, in particular, attracting negative labels).

- **National curriculum**: Introduced in 1990, this made subjects such as maths and science compulsory to GCSE level and encouraged the breakdown of gendered subject choices (the idea that males and females, when given the choice, opt for different subjects). This resulted in increased female achievement in these subjects.

- **Coursework**: The expansion of this option, mainly through the introduction of GCSE, benefits girls because it demands steady, consistent, work over time (something which is, supposedly, more suited to the way girls work).

- **Curriculum initiatives** such as 'Girls into Science and Technology' (GIST) encouraged the breakdown of barriers around traditionally male subjects, whereas work experience initiatives introduced girls to the possibility of full-time work at an early age (although, as Mackenzie (1997) has demonstrated, there are arguments about whether or not girls and boys are still encouraged to follow 'traditional' employment options).

- **Identities**: **Francis** (2000) argues that changes within the school and wider society have altered the way girls construct femininity (they no longer see it mainly in terms of the home) whereas concepts of masculinity have remained largely unchanged. This fits neatly with the fact higher levels of female achievement over the past 25 years have *not* been at the expense of male achievement – the 'underachievement of boys' is relative to improvements in girls' achievement – it hasn't necessarily declined.

  Barbara Walker ('Understanding boys' sexual health education and its implications for attitude change', 1996) similarly identifies changing conceptions of masculinity, in terms of 'finding a role in a fast-changing world' as a challenge many young men are unable to resolve in the education system, an idea that leads into:

- **School subcultures**: These have traditionally been cited in explanations for male underachievement. **Barber** ('Young People and Their Attitudes to School', 1994), for example, identified three main types of underachieving male subculture.

  - **Disappointed** boys were not inclined to do much at school outside the maintenance of their peer group relationships.

  - **Disaffected** boys disliked school but used it as an arena for their general disaffection (bad behaviour, in other words).

  - **Disappeared** boys attended school as little as possible.

Similarly, the **Northern Ireland Department of Education's** 'Review of research evidence on the apparent underachievement of boys' (1997) linked male underachievement to 'anti-school subcultures and peer-group pressures'.

 # Digging deeper

It is, perhaps, ironic that current concerns over differential achievement have been framed in terms of boys' underachievement. As **David Spendlove** ('Sometimes it's hard to be a boy', 2001) has noted: 'With the examination period now upon us again, we await the inevitable results showing that girls have out-performed boys in all subjects

and at all levels. There then follows the usual media frenzy with headlines about boys' underachievement . . .'.

The irony here is that substantial numbers of boys have *always* 'underachieved' in our education system – a 'problem' that has only merited attention in the context of a *rise* in female achievement. In this respect, it is tempting, perhaps, to note **Cohen**'s observation ('A habit of healthy idleness', 1998): 'The question to ask is not "why are boys underachieving?" but "why are we concerned about it now?"'.

Be that as it may, it is useful to note two different ways the question of male underachievement has been framed. The first reflects a postmodern influenced concern with identities and **gender discourses**. Following the lead suggested by the **Queensland Department of Education** ('Boys Gender and Schooling', 2002), we can note how debates about gendered differential achievement have focused around four main ideas (or discourses if you're feeling a bit postmodern):

- **Boys as victims** suggests underachievement results from the 'feminisation of school and work', whereby male role models, ways of teaching and learning that have traditionally favoured boys and so forth have been replaced by ideas and practices favouring girls.

- **Failing Schools** locates the problem within the school, in terms of narrow measures of intelligence and achievement and teaching/testing regimes that favour female ways of thinking and working. In addition, schools fail to address or resolve problems associated with material deprivation.

- **Boys will be boys** focuses on the idea certain aspects of masculinity (aggression, later maturity and so forth) are biologically determined and, therefore, fixed at birth. Solutions to underachievement here focus on schools developing ways to 'engage boys effectively and actively'.

- **Gender relationships** focuses on how different notions of masculinity and femininity affect student beliefs and practices – for example, how students choose different subjects to study and why male classroom behaviour is more disruptive than female behaviour. The concern here, therefore, is the various ways gender identities are constructed and how they might be changed.

We can also note how, according to **Jones** and **Myhill** (2003), the concept of '**underachievement**' is constructed in a number of ways by teachers who are, they argue, increasingly likely to identify boys as 'potential underachievers'.

Ideas about what counts as 'underachievement' also vary in terms of gender. Female underachievement, for example, becomes invisible in the rush to identify and explain male underachievement. In addition, teachers rationalise achievement differences in terms of their perceptions of the nature of male and female abilities; female achievements, for example, are characterised in terms of 'performance' – understanding what an examiner wants and delivering it – whereas males are characterised in terms of 'ability'. Teachers, in other words, according to **Jones** and **Myhill**, define and re-evaluate their role in terms of how to stimulate boys' natural abilities.

The second (modernist) way reflects a concern with **social class**, rather than gender. In this respect, the question is framed in terms of the extent to which gendered educational achievement is *primarily* an issue of class rather than gender. **Murphy** and **Elwood** ('Gendered

Growing it yourself: solutions to underachievement?

Thinking about each of these discourses, use the following table as the basis for identifying how each might suggest solutions to male underachievement. Once you have done this, identify possible criticisms of these potential solutions.

	Boys as victims	Failing Schools	Boys will be boys	Gender relations
Solutions?		Different forms of testing		
Criticisms?			Assumes 'boys' are all the same ('homogeneous') and will respond to the same teaching styles.	

experiences', 1998), for example, note how recent improvements in female educational achievement is 'not shared by girls from low socio-economic backgrounds'.

Epstein et al (1998) have also questioned the idea of 'male underachievement' as a general category when they ask which boys underachieve, at what stages in the education system is underachievement apparent and, perhaps most importantly, what are the criteria used to measure underachievement? In addition, as I have suggested at the start of this section, DfES figures (2004) relating to class, gender and achievement at Key Stages 1–4 suggest social class is a significant factor here, given that the educational achievement of lower class girls is generally worse than that of higher class boys.

Gorard, **Rees** and **Salisbury** ('Investigating the patterns of differential attainment of boys and girls at school', 2001) also note that there is little difference in male/female attainment in maths and science and no significant gender difference at the *lowest attainment levels* for all other curriculum subjects. The 'problem', they argue, is one that exists among 'mid-to-high-achievers', where girls achieve higher grades than boys. Supporting this argument, a study by Birmingham's education authority (*Times Educational Supplement*, September 2000), demonstrated, 'the most disadvantaged pupils are boys from a poor, ethnic minority, background who were born in the summer, never went to nursery and spent their primary school years moving from school to school'.

Ethnicity

⚠ Preparing the ground

As with the previous sections on class and gender, we can begin this section by identifying some of the ways ethnicity relates to educational performance at various levels of our education system. Once we have examined the basic relationship between ethnicity and educational performance we can identify some possible explanations for this relationship.

Please note in the following, the identification of different ethnic groups (*Indian*, *White* and so forth) uses the UK Government's classification system for ethnicity.

Key Stages 2 and 3

For 2003, Department for Education and Skills figures (2004), show children from different ethnic backgrounds had different levels of achievement in English and Science. These were, in descending order of attainment

- Indian
- White
- Bangladeshi
- Black Caribbean
- Black African
- Pakistani.

We can add two things to the above.

- **Mixed ethnicity**: Noting how children from mixed ethnic backgrounds performed may tell us something about the influence of cultural factors on achievement levels. Thus, the top achieving ethnic group at this level in 2003 was White and Asian; interestingly, White and Black Caribbean children showed significantly higher levels of achievement than Black Caribbean children.

- **Gender**: Girls perform marginally better than boys for all ethnic groups in English and Science at this level.

Key Stage 4

At GCSE level, the pattern identified in the previous Key Stages is largely reproduced – the main exception being the relative underachievement of Black Caribbean ethnic groups. Although their performance has improved markedly over the past 15 years, they still appear, as a group, to achieve least at this educational level.

	1989	1998	2002
Indian	n/a	54	60
White	30	47	52
Bangladeshi	n/a	33	41
Pakistani	n/a	29	40
Black	18	29	36

Table 4.8 % with 5 or more GCSE grades A*-C by ethnicity
Source: Department for Education and Skills, 2004

When we include gender in the equation, we once more find girls outperforming boys in all ethnic groups (including mixed groups) at this level. Similarly, for all ethnic groups boys are more likely to leave school with no A*–C passes at GCSE.

Further education

One interesting thing to note about participation in post-16 education, as

Table 4.9 demonstrates, is the relatively low level of White – and the relatively high level of Black – participation.

	1989	2000	2002
Indian	n/a	92	91
Black	68	84	82
Bangladeshi	n/a	81	79
Pakistani	n/a	81	77
White	47	70	69

Table 4.9 % whose main activity is full-time education at age 16 by ethnicity
Source: Department for Education and Skills, 2004

Heidi Mirza (*Young, Female and Black*, 1992) has noted one reason for higher Black participation is the number of black women staying in education post-16. More recently, **Kamala Nehaul** ('Parenting, Schooling and Caribbean Heritage Pupils', 1999) has noted how black parents

> . . . valued education for the enhanced life chances it offered . . . The importance attached to education was reflected in the myriad of ways in which all parents supported children's schooling . . . the encouragement given to reading, the priority placed on talking regularly with children about the school day, the provision of materials and books for school, and the commitment to supporting homework.

These ideas are interesting – in relation to participation and achievement levels of black children – because, as with social class, they point us towards the idea that, in the case of some ethnic minorities (as with some social classes), problems related to differential achievement and participation appear to be more marked pre-16 than post-16.

When we consider patterns of ethnic educational achievement, the picture is complicated not only by class and gender but also, as I have suggested, by mixed ethnicities (or, if you want to be technical about it, 'hybrid ethnicities' – such as *'White and Black Caribbean'*). Keeping these ideas in mind, there are a range of explanations for differential achievement to consider.

Outside school factors

- **Social class**, as we have seen, (**Demack, Drew** and **Grimsley** (1998), for example) is a good general predictor of educational attainment and there is little reason to suppose this doesn't apply to ethnic minorities in the same way it applies to the (white) ethnic majority. Given Black and Asian minorities are relatively over-represented in the lower social classes it should not, according to this analysis, be too surprising to find lower educational attainment amongst these groups. However, one exception to this is the educational performance of Indian children who, in the main, are one of the most educationally successful groups in our society. We can explore this idea further, therefore, by looking at:

  - **Poverty**: The Cabinet Office Performance and Innovation Unit (2002) noted a couple of interesting points. Firstly, that employment rates are lower – and unemployment rates higher – for ethnic minorities. Within South Asian minorities, Pakistani and Bangladeshi families are four times more likely to be poor than a White family. Indian families, on the other hand, generally had incomes comparable to White families. The 2001 Census (2003) confirms these trends. In addition, even working

Pakistani and Bangladeshi households are likely to experience poverty.

- **Family structures** correlate with differential educational achievement in the sense children from single-parent families, for example, do relatively badly across all ethnic groups. Black Caribbean families have the highest rates of single-parenthood and the lowest rates of educational achievement. **Summerfield** and **Babb** (Social Trends 34, 2004) note 22% of White families were headed by a single parent in 2001, compared with 11% for all Asian British and 48% for Black Caribbean families.

  Asian family life, on the other hand, is often (stereotypically) characterised as tight-knit and supportive (highly-pressurising even) which leads to greater achievement. While **Goodwin** ('Social Support and Marital Well-being in an Asian Community', 1997) found 'a strong sense of inter-family cohesion and regular contact with immediate family is actively encouraged and maintained' amongst Hindu-Gujarati (Indian) families, **Berridge** et al ('Where to turn?', 2000), found that 'close-knit communities could generate social isolation, and that families undergoing acute stress could feel a sense of shame about their difficulties'.

- **Parental involvement/attitudes**: One significant idea here is the development of 'Saturday schools' amongst Black Caribbean communities (**Heidi Mirza**: 'Black supplementary schools', 2001). Their existence and increasing popularity is, according to **Mac an Ghaill** ('Black voluntary schools', 1991), indicative of a general dissatisfaction, among black parents and children, with 'White institutions' that seem to regularly fail them – an idea we'll explore in more detail in a moment. When considering this idea as a possible explanation for differential achievement (in basic terms, White and Indian parents, for example, have different attitudes to – and involvement with – their children's education, **Nehaul**'s work (1999) offers evidence to contradict this type of explanation).

- **Identity**: The underachievement of Black Caribbean boys is a striking feature of our education system. In addition, as they move through school, achievement seems to fall (until, at GCSE, they have the worst academic performance of all children). Black Caribbean girls perform significantly better at GCSE (although achievement levels are lower than for any other group of girls). White and Black Caribbean boys also achieve more, which suggests identity (and possibly concepts of masculinity that lead to rebellion against 'White' schooling) may be significant factors in the explanation for the decline in performance of Black Caribbean boys.

Inside school factors

- **School cultures** covers a general range of possible explanations.
  - **The school curriculum**, for example, may involve, according to **Blair** et al ('Minority Ethnic Attainment and Participation', 2003) teaching practices and expectations based on cultural norms, histories and general cultural references unfamiliar to many ethnic minority pupils.
  - **Role models**: **Blair** et al (2003) also

point to a lack of role models within the school for ethnic minority pupils. Statistics for school teachers are not currently (2004) available, but in FE colleges 7% of staff were drawn from ethnic minority groups (which is roughly in line with their representation in the general population). In Scotland (not, admittedly, the most ethnically diverse or representative part of the UK), 1% of secondary and 0.4% of primary teachers were from ethnic minorities (Scottish Executive National Statistics, 2004).

- **Racism**: **Aymer** and **Okitikpi** ('Young Black men and the Connexions Service', 2001) argue that Black Caribbean boys are more likely to report negative experiences of schooling, some of which include racial abuse and harassment from their peers. It is perhaps instructive to note, therefore, **Kerr** et al ('England's results from the IEA International Citizenship Education Study', 2002) found British students had *less positive* attitudes towards 'immigrants' than in many other countries. This, they argued, was likely to shape peer group interaction.

Although school cultural factors can be significant, they may be too generalised to adequately explain the intricacies of ethnic group attainment differences (why, for example, should high achieving Indian pupils experience less racism than lower achieving Black Caribbean pupils?). We can, therefore, look at a range of more targeted explanations.

- **Teacher–pupil interactions** focus on the specific relationships found within different schools. The Runnymede Trust ('Black and Ethnic Minority Young People and Educational Disadvantage', 1997) argued a range of hidden processes occur within schools that 'deny equal opportunities'. Ethnic minority students, for example, reported:

- high levels of control and criticism from teachers

- stereotypes of cultural differences, communities and speech that betrayed negative and patronising attitudes.

Diane Abbott (a black Labour MP) has argued (see: **Gaby Hinsliff** ' "Scared" white teachers fail black students', 2002) that 'white women teachers' fail to relate to black boys because they are frightened and intimidated by them. A failure to challenge disruptive behaviour, she argues, leads to an escalating situation which results in black boys being excluded from school (Black Caribbean boys are more frequently excluded than any other ethnic group).

Foster, **Gomm** and **Hammersley** (*Constructing Educational Inequality*, 1996), on the other hand, suggest the over-representation of Black Caribbean boys in low status sets and bands within the school is simply a result of 'unacceptable behaviour' on their part. **MacBeth** et al ('The Impact of Study Support', 2001) also noted schools are increasingly concerned about low ethnic minority achievement and take steps to address the problem – the use of out-of-school-hours learning support for example, served to raise achievement levels amongst Asian students in particular.

Labelling: Although we may – or indeed may not – reject the idea schools are 'institutionally racist' (the idea racist attitudes and practices go unchallenged – or are secretly encouraged – within schools), various forms of subtle labelling and stereotyping (intentional or otherwise) do seem to impact on ethnic achievement. Generally positive teacher attitudes to Indian pupils (based on the knowledge of their high levels of attainment) may be offset by negative beliefs about Black Caribbean pupils.

David Gillborn ('Education and Institutional Racism', 2002) thinks schools *are* institutionally racist, especially in the light of curriculum developments that, he argues, are 'based on approaches known to disadvantage black pupils'. These include: selection in schools by setting, schemes for 'gifted and talented' pupils and vocational schemes for 'non-academic' pupils. Teachers, Gillborn argues, 'generally underrate the abilities of black youngsters' which results in their assignment to low-ability groups, a restricted curriculum and entry for lower-level exams.

The Pupil Level Annual School Census (2002), for example, shows black pupils are more likely to be classified in terms of Special Educational Needs (SEN) – 28% of Black Caribbean secondary pupils as against 18% of White pupils. **Sammons** et al ('Special educational needs across the pre-school period', 2002) also suggest pre-school minority group children are more likely to be 'at risk' of SEN than White children. Again, whether this reflects beliefs about ethnic groups or is the result of socio-economic factors is a point for debate.

Stereotyping: **Figueroa** (*Education and the Social Construction of Race*, 1991) suggested teachers frequently limit ethnic minority opportunities through the use of culturally-biased forms of assessment (the way students are expected to speak and write, for example) and by consigning pupils to lower bands and sets on the basis of teacher-assessment. Teachers generally have lower opinions of the abilities of some ethnic minority groups, which results in a self-fulfilling prophecy of underachievement – something the Runnymede Trust report (1997) also suggests.

 Digging deeper

When examining explanations for the educational underachievement of some ethnic groups relative to other ethnic groups, it is easy to overlook the fact one of the largest groups of underachieving pupils is White working class boys. Thus, while explanations focusing on factors such as racism, school processes and teacher–pupil relationships are significant in explaining *some* forms of ethnic underachievement, they don't necessarily apply to this group. When studying *all* forms of differential achievement, therefore, we need to keep in mind how class, gender and ethnic factors intersect and, in this respect, we can note a number of ideas, beginning with the observation that **achievement** is a relative concept. In other words, it depends on:

- **What** we measure – is it, for example,

measured in terms of simple exam passes (and, if so, at what level and grade?) or can it be measured in terms of participation rates in, for example, post-16 education and training?

- **When** we measure it – again, the point at which we measure achievement will be significant. In addition, ethnicity is a changing status, in the sense changes occur over time. Bangladeshi children, for example, are one of the most recent immigrant groups to the UK. Their achievement levels (initially amongst the lowest for all ethnic groups) have increased significantly over the past few years.

- **How** we measure it – are we, for example, interested in exam passes or in progress made from different starting points (a *value-added* assessment)?

This idea suggests the concept of achievement involves at least two related ideas.

- **Meanings**: The concept of achievement can mean different things, depending on how you specify its possible measurement.

- **Measurement**: For example, is it measured in terms of a *product* (such as an exam grade) or in terms of a *process* (such as a value-added assessment that measures the progress made by a pupil between a measurable start and an end point – such as, for example, the distance travelled, in terms of achievement, between GCSE grades and A-level grades)?

If we measure achievement in terms of *product*, no account is taken of the social and cultural backgrounds of different pupils (their cultural capital, to use

Bourdieu's (1986) concept). If, on the other hand, we measure achievement in terms of **process**, recognition and understanding of different levels of cultural capital can be built into the measurement process.

Discussion point: the education race

To understand the difference between the measurement of achievement in terms of *product* or *process*, think about education and achievement in terms of a race.

Everyone starts at the same point. The aim of each pupil is to compete and cross the finishing line first (to gain the highest level of educational achievement). Although the race involves a certain *equality of opportunity* (everyone is allowed to enter), some pupils have their legs tied together, while others have large, heavy, weights strapped to their bodies Other pupils are able to cycle to the finish line. These ideas symbolise the advantages and disadvantages some children may have because of the social and cultural background.

Consider these questions:

• Is this race fair?

• Is it fairer to measure achievement in terms of product or process (keeping in mind that the children with their legs tied together may make substantial progress in the race, but they lag far behind the cycling pupils)?

• Which social groups benefit the most from measuring achievement in terms of product?

Underachievement is, similarly, a *relative* concept. If we look, for example, at Black

Caribbean achievement in terms of GCSE passes, then evidence of underachievement (within and between ethic groups) is not difficult to find. Alternatively, if we look at *post-16 participation* in full-time education, White children, as we have seen, seem to participate least.

• **Participation**: In addition, evidence of underachievement in compulsory education should not automatically be considered evidence of wider underachievement. As noted earlier, Black Caribbean Saturday schools don't appear to have significantly impacted on performance at GCSE level. However, since post-16 participation rates for black children (especially in FE colleges), ranks second only to Indian children, this suggests black parents – and children – value education but have problems with the kind of education offered in schools.

Further education seems to meet the needs of this ethnic group in ways that schools don't, an explanation supported by **Aymer** and **Okitikpi** (2001), among others – such as **Blair** et al (2003), who suggest colleges 'Can provide a space where young Black men are supported by a community of Black students, an opportunity to study a curriculum that celebrates Black cultures and histories and to develop positive relationships with tutors'.

• **Social class**: Just as we shouldn't underestimate the importance of ethnicity and gender, social class is also significant. As **Blair** et al (2003) note, children who receive Free School Meals are less likely to achieve than children of the same ethnic group who do not qualify for FSM.

A final word, in this respect, might be to note **Gillborn** and **Gipps**'s observation ('Recent Research on the Achievements of Ethnic Minority Pupils', 1996) that, whatever a student's gender or ethnic background, those from the higher social classes, on average, achieve more in terms of exam passes and grades.

The question of differences in achievement between social groups is an important one in our society and, for this reason, we have spent some time looking at what sociologists have to say on the matter. In the next section, however, we can look at how government, through the development of various social policies, have been – and continue to be – concerned about the best way to resolve the social problem of different levels of achievement between social classes, genders and ethnic groups.

State policies

Introduction

During the 1997 election campaign, when asked to name his government's 'top three priorities', should a New Labour government be elected, Tony Blair replied 'Education, education, education', something I mention not because it's particularly profound but rather because it symbolises an increasing state (government) interest in education over the past 25 years. The identification and examination of state policies in this period will be the main focus of this section – although we will also need to understand something of the relatively brief (and sometimes not very glorious) history of government-sponsored educational provision in our society.

WARM UP: EDUCATIONAL POLICIES

Having experienced 'education' for some considerable time, you'll be aware of state polices that have affected education over the years. Initially in small groups, use the following table (I have included a couple of policies to get you started) as a basis for identifying recent educational policies.

Once you have done this, come together as a class to share your knowledge of policy and discuss whether you believe these policies have had positive or negative effects on your experience of schooling.

Policy	Positive effect?	Negative effect?
Comprehensive schools	All pupils receive a similar education	Very large schools that mean individual pupils can feel lost and unimportant within the school.
National Curriculum	Everyone is taught the same subjects	Everyone has to study the same things – lack of individual choice.
Key Stage testing	Progress is monitored to identify educational weaknesses that need improving	Pupils feel pressurised and stressed by constant testing.
Additional policies?		

Nineteenth-century education

⚠ Preparing the ground

It may be surprising to learn (but, then again, it might not) the history of government involvement in the provision and regulation of education in Britain is not a very long one. It is only over the past 100 years or so – dating from the *Forster Education Act* (1870) – that governments have sought to provide education for the mass of the population. These early attempts were not particularly successful, although the fact the elementary schools established in 1870 were neither free nor compulsory probably explains the general lack of participation in them by the majority of the working classes. Various attempts were made, over the following 60 years, to 'educate the working class' with varying degrees of success.

⚠ Digging deeper

If the impact of these attempts to provide schooling was not particularly great (in terms of the numbers of children experiencing state education), the role of education, if not explicitly defined, was laid-out in terms of meeting two needs:

- **economic** – the increasing need, as modern, industrial society developed, for a literate and numerate population to work machines in factories

- **political** – the need for a population

socialised into the demands of an increasingly complex division of labour (in particular, one that was well-schooled in the disciplines required by factory forms of production).

As we will see, despite the many recent changes to our education system, it is arguable the role of education – at least in terms of how it is generally seen by the state – probably hasn't changed a great deal. However, in terms of impact and experience, the following was arguably the most influential education act of the twentieth century.

1944 Education Act

⚠ Preparing the ground

This educational reform introduced two main elements into the role and experience of education.

- **Universal education**: Free, compulsory education for all between the ages of 5 and 15 (until this point secondary schooling wasn't free, although elementary schools had a *nominal* leaving age of 14 for most children who bothered to attend).

- **Tripartite system**: Although, as **David Bell** ('Change and continuity: reflections on the Butler Act', 2004) notes, the 1944 Act didn't specify a tripartite *system* (there was simply 'heavy guidance' from the Ministry of Education in this direction), the school system was reformed with the introduction of compulsory secondary schooling after the age of 11, based on three types of school (for, in effect, three types of pupil):

- **grammar** – providing an exclusively academic education

- **secondary modern** – providing a mix of practical (or vocational – providing skills required for the workplace) and academic education, with the emphasis on the former

- **secondary technical** – providing a largely work-related technical/vocational education.

The tripartite system had the following features.

- **Selection** for each type of school was based on an intelligence (IQ) test that claimed to identify different types of learner – in basic terms, those suited to an academic-type (theory-based) education and those suited to a vocational (practice-based) education. Students were tested at 10 (the so-called '11+' exam) and assigned a school on the basis of their test performance (with roughly the top 15–20% of pupils awarded grammar school places).

- **Parity of esteem** or, if you prefer, the idea each type of school was 'separate but equal'. Children were literally separated by attending different schools, but the idea of 'equality' was rather more questionable, for a couple of reasons.

  - **Bipartite education**: Few technical schools were built or established (partly because it proved difficult to quantify 'technical ability' in an IQ test and partly because of the expense) which effectively meant a two-school (bipartite) state system developed –

those who passed the 11+ went to grammar schools, those who failed went to secondary modern schools.

- **Status**: It quickly became clear grammar schools, attracting mainly middle-class pupils who were more likely to stay in school to take the General Certificate of Education (GCE) exams at 16, were held in higher regard (by universities, employers and, indeed the general public). They had greater status than secondary moderns, which attracted predominantly working class pupils who were supposed to work towards a (non-examined) School Leaving Certificate at 15.

A couple of exceptions to this general situation were:

- **Private schools**: Fee-charging schools were not covered by the Act and could operate outside its general scope. These, by and large, remained the preserve of upper-class pupils.

- **Comprehensive schools**: Local Education Authorities (LEAs) were given responsibility for introducing the educational reforms in their area and some chose to interpret the injunction to provide 'free and equal' education differently. In London, for example, eight comprehensive schools were built between 1946 and 1949.

 Digging deeper

The tripartite system, whatever its actual weaknesses in terms of scope and implementation, represented a clear statement of the role of education in modern society, in terms of the relationship between schools and the economy. It resembled a broadly functionalist perspective by defining the education system in terms of *differentiation* and *role allocation*. The relationship between academic schooling and professional careers, vocational schooling and non-professional/manual work is evident here (as indeed it was in the practice of each type of school – secondary moderns, for example, emphasised the learning of manual skills (woodwork, bricklaying and so forth) for boys and domestic skills – needlework, cookery and the like – for girls). In this respect, the system was underpinned by two main ideas.

- **Ability**: Children were defined, as I have suggested, in terms of differing abilities and aptitudes which, coincidentally or not, reflected both the economic structure of the time (a plentiful supply of manufacturing jobs, for example) and ideas about the respective roles of males and females. The latter's experience of secondary modern schooling, for example, focused primarily on the knowledge and skills women would need for their 'traditional' roles of wife and mother.

The concept of 'separate abilities' was, however, underpinned, as **McCulloch** ('The Norwood Report and the secondary school curriculum', 1988) has noted, by *psychological* ideas about the nature of intelligence. In particular, the academic/vocational division for different types of schooling reflected the idea, popularised by psychologists such as **Cyril Burt**, on whose research the tripartite system was largely based (although, in recent years, an unresolved controversy has raged over whether Burt falsified his original research data), that intelligence

was both *innate* and relatively *fixed* at around the age of 10 or 11.

- **Academic/vocational** aptitudes were reflected in the basic premise of the tripartite system, with secondary modern schools being organised – at least initially – around a vocational type of education designed to prepare boys for various forms of skilled manual work (agricultural as well as industrial) and girls for lower level non-manual occupations (secretarial, office and nursing, for example) that reflected both their general economic position and family role – working class women were generally expected to work until they married and then replace full-time work with domestic responsibilities.

This system had a number of significant effects.

- **Compulsory education** became fully established for the mass of the population.
- **Social inequality** was not only embedded in the system, it was also routinised (made to seem to normal and inevitable) and ideologically justified (on the basis of the 'objective testing' of innate genetic characteristics).
- **Social segregation** was also established as a routine educational practice with the classes 'unofficially' separated in different schools.

The impact of the tripartite system on the experience of schooling for many pupils differed in terms of:

- **Labelling**: Grammar schools were seen as 'superior' in terms of both the education offered and the status of the children who attended. Grammar school teachers were

254

also more highly qualified – and paid more – than their secondary modern counterparts.

- **Stereotyping**: Secondary modern children faced two related forms here. Firstly, the fact of failing the 11+ and, secondly, in terms of the idea they had lower natural levels of intelligence.

- **Gender**: Apart from the differences in what girls and boys were taught, there were more grammar school places available for boys than girls (a legacy of the pre-1944 situation of single-sex secondary schools). This meant girls with higher measured levels of IQ were often denied places at grammar schools in favour of boys with lower measured IQs.

Comprehensive schooling

⚠ Preparing the ground

The gradual domination of secondary education by comprehensive schools was:

- **Protracted**: A lengthy process, mainly started in 1950s, encouraged by Wilson's Labour Government in the 1960s (*Circular 10/65* tends to be seen as the start of a 10-year effort to reform the tripartite system) and finally (almost) completed by Shirley Williams (the then Labour Education Minister) in 1976 when an Education Act instructed all councils to 'prepare plans for Comprehensive schooling' in their area.

- **Challenged**, not least by influential advocates of grammar schooling but also

by some LEAs who fought to retain grammar schooling through the Courts. Hence:

- **Partial**, given that some LEAs (having 'produced plans' for comprehensive schooling never implemented them) still operate grammar schools – around 160 such schools still exist within the education system in various parts of the country – mainly those with a history of Conservative council control. Some grammar schools also avoided becoming comprehensive by becoming public, fee-charging schools.

The introduction of comprehensive schooling reflected three basic ideas.

- **Selection** (by IQ test) was abolished because it was educationally (and socially) divisive. All children, regardless of prior academic achievement, would receive the same secondary education in the same school. *Mixed ability teaching* (where children of differing levels of attainment are taught in the same class, by the same teacher, the same curriculum to the same level) was seen as the way forward.

  25 years later, the jury is still out on this one – **Hallam**, **Ireson** and **Hurley** (2001) suggest some subjects (English and humanities) were considered by teachers as more appropriate for mixed ability classes than others like maths and modern languages. A new exam (GCSE) was phased in to replace the Ordinary Level ('O-level') and Certificate of Secondary Education (CSE) divide (the latter was aimed at a lower level than 'O-level').

- **Social integration**: One of the guiding principles of comprehensive schooling was the desire to remove the socially divisive tripartite system. Education, therefore, was used to promote social mixing. Initially, this meant ensuring each school had a mix of different social classes, although this ideal has effectively been replaced by a form of 'self-selection' by catchment area (you become eligible to attend the school if you live within a certain radius of it).

- **Economic changes**, in tandem with a desire for a more *meritocratic* education system, were also an important motor of change, for three reasons.

  - **Work**: The decline in manufacturing industry meant fewer manual jobs available as a 'vocation'.

  - **Technological** changes produced an increasing demand for a better educated general workforce.

  - **Gender**: Increasing numbers of women were involved in the workforce, creating a general resistance to the type of 'traditional' education they received in secondary modern schools.

⚠ Digging deeper

Comprehensive education attempted to change the general role of the education system in a couple of ways.

- **Ideologically**: Comprehensive schools represented the idea social class divisions could be abolished through a system of education that encouraged 'social class mixing', *equality of opportunity* and achievement through talent and hard work. In other words, it represented ideas about *social integration*, *meritocracy* and *egalitarianism* (equality). In this respect, we can see these ideas reflect a general

Functionalist view of society, with its stress on consensus, shared values and the allocation of adult roles through proven merit.

- **Economically**: A central theme of comprehensive education was that the population contained a larger *pool of talent* than was generally recognised by any previous system. The changing nature of economic production – and the increasing importance of service industry – led to a reappraisal of both the purpose of education and the general skills/qualification base. The role of education, in this respect, was to respond to the changing economic needs of society by producing a highly educated, skilled and trained workforce.

The impact of comprehensive education was felt in a number of ways.

- **Provision**: New purpose-built co-educational schools, for example, developed in many areas to replace closed/amalgamated schools. A comprehensive school, for example, might typically replace a couple of grammar schools (boys' and girls') and a secondary modern school – creating a large institution with better facilities and more curriculum choice.

- **Exams**: The school leaving age had been raised to 16 in 1972 and this was accompanied by the gradual introduction of a new GCSE exam taken at 16 by all students. Differentiation *between* exam systems (pupils of different abilities taking different exam levels) was replaced by differentiation *within* a single exam system.

- **Grammar** and **public schools**: The continued existence of these schools within a nominally 'Comprehensive' system created problems in that parents who had the money and/or desire could continue to buy a different (higher status) type of education, perpetuating the class divisions comprehensive education was (theoretically) designed to remove.

In some respects, Comprehensive schools did provide a different set of experiences for both teachers and pupils.

- **Size** of schools, for example, was generally larger and more impersonal.
- **Labelling**: Children were no longer stigmatised by the label of failure at 11.
- **Gender**: New opportunities for girls (especially working class girls) developed as they followed a similar curriculum to boys (although some differences remained in terms of a gendered curriculum choice – girls were still expected to take subjects such as Home Economics, for example).

On the other hand, some school practices simply transferred from the tripartite system to the comprehensive school (as part of a *hidden curriculum* discussed in more detail in the final section).

- **Streaming**, **setting** and **banding**, for example, developed to differentiate pupils *within* the school. The general outcome was to find middle-class children in the higher streams, sets or bands and working-class children in the lower streams, sets or bands, which, of course, raised the question of:
- **Labelling**: These practices effectively created a system of positive and negative

labelling within the school – with some pupils being almost entirely separated from others. Another form of selection and separation involved:

- **Catchment areas**: Originally, schools were supposed to have a social mix of pupils (which invariably meant some children faced long journeys to school) but fairly rapidly this devolved into 'selection by area' – inner city schools attracted high levels of working class kids and suburban schools attracted middle class kids.
- **Regional differences**: As **Linda Croxford** ('Inequality in Attainment at Age 16', 2000) notes, different parts of the UK operated different systems – in Scotland and Wales all state-funded secondary schooling was comprehensive, in Northern Ireland it was selective, and England had, as we have seen, a number of regional variations. Croxford's research also noted:
  - **social segregation** was lower in Scotland and Wales
  - **attainment** was, on average, the same in Wales, England and Northern Ireland, although girls outperformed boys in all four systems
  - **social class** was a major determinant of attainment, although it made less difference in Scotland than in England.

Discussion point: different pupils/different schools?

Should pupils be taught in different types of school?

Use the following table as the basis for exploring arguments for and against this idea.

Different Schools	
Arguments for	Arguments against
Some pupils want to develop academic skills, others want to develop vocational skills.	Socially divisive.
Further arguments?	

1979–1997: The Conservative years

Preparing the ground

In 1976, the then Labour Prime Minister James (later Lord) Callaghan gave a speech at Ruskin College in Oxford to initiate a so-called *Great Debate* about education (which, true to form, was neither 'Great' nor a 'debate'). Although no major educational reforms came from this speech, it paved the way for major reforms under the Thatcher (Conservative) government elected in 1979, in two ways.

- **Basic skills**: It suggested schools were failing to instil 'basic skills' in their pupils. As Callaghan stated: 'I am concerned . . . to find complaints from industry that new recruits from schools sometimes do not have the basic tools to do the job'. In 1978, the Youth Opportunities Programme (YOP) was introduced, aimed at 16–18 year old school leavers, paying a small allowance as part of its training programme. Interestingly, it was described at the time, by Albert Booth the Employment Secretary, as a 'New Deal' for the young unemployed – an evocative echo of the American 'New Deal' programmes of the 1930s credited with dragging America out of the deep economic recession of the period.

- **Core curriculum**: It floated the idea of a 'core curriculum of basic knowledge' (about which, more in a moment).

These ideas, it could be argued, set the agenda for two major developments during the 1980s.

New Vocationalism

High levels of youth (especially school-leaver) unemployment in the early 1980s led to the development of the *New*

Vocationalism (presumably to differentiate it from the 'Old Vocationalism' of the tripartite system). New emphasis was placed on the idea of *training*, as opposed to *education* (remember the distinction we made in an earlier section?); initially, the focus was on post-16 training, with some forms of vocationalism gradually introduced into the pre-16 curriculum. During the 1980s, a range of New Vocational schemes were initiated, developed . . . and discarded.

- **Youth training schemes**: Introduced in 1980 (as a development of YOPs) and aimed at unemployed school leavers, these offered job training with trainees receiving a small payment over-and-above any state benefits they received. This expansion of YOPs was described by James Prior, the then Employment Secretary, as a 'New Deal' for young people (are you beginning to see a theme developing here?)

- **Technical and Vocational Education Initiative** (TVEI): This initiative – piloted in 1982 and fully introduced in 1987 – marked an important development because it aimed to introduce technical/vocational education to 14-18-year olds *within* schools. As **Bell** et al ('TVEI and the Education–Industry Relationship', 1988) noted at the time 'TVEI remains unambiguously education-led'.

  TVEI was a series of *initiatives*, rather than a vocational curriculum, some of which came from government (Records of Achievement and 'work experience', for example) and some from schools (such as developing the use of Information Technology and equal opportunity schemes for expanding the number of women going into traditionally male forms of employment).

- **Youth Training Scheme** (YTS): Introduced in 1983 as a one year, post-16, course. The original intention was for YTS to be a logical vocational extension of TVEI courses developed in schools. In 1988, the 'Youth Training Guarantee' required all unemployed 16 and 17 year olds to register with YTS – which was renamed 'Youth Training' (YT) – for education or training.

- **Vocational qualifications**: Two forms of qualification were introduced in 1986; the **Certificate of Pre-Vocational Education** (CPVE) – a one-year, post-16 course designed as a preparation for work or further vocational study.

  - **National Vocational Qualifications** (NVQs) introduced the idea of *workplace competencies* – every job had a set of identifiable, measurable, skills. Every job could, in theory, be vocationally certified – the main drawback, however, was you initially had to be doing a job before you could achieve the qualification (so it is debateable how much NVQ contributed to 'training'). However, for various reasons aspects of NVQs were introduced into schools and led, directly, to the introduction, in 1993, of GNVQs.

  - **General National Vocational Qualifications** GNVQs were offered at three levels – Foundation, Intermediate (equivalent to GCSE) and Advanced (equivalent to A-level). The latter was subsequently renamed the Advanced Certification of Vocational Education (AVCE) and are know to be known as Vocational A-levels. We can also note that, indirectly, the development of GNVQs led to the introduction of Key Skills with Curriculum 2000.

- **Modern Apprenticeships** were introduced in 1995 for 18–19 year olds and linked to NVQs. Designed to be a 'quality training' scheme, an ironic note here is the reintroduction of apprenticeship training after it was effectively abolished by the Conservative Government because it led to 'restrictive labour market practices' (New Right-speak for Trade Union involvement).

David Yeomans ('Constructing vocational education: from TVEI to GNVQ', 2002) neatly summarises the focus of the New Vocationalism when he notes it reflected a belief that: 'Better vocational education and training = Greater individual productivity = Economic growth'.

Education Reform Act (1998)

This was a major development for a number of reasons.

- **National curriculum**: Strange as it may seem, the subjects taught in schools were never specified by governments until 1988 (until this point, Religious Education was the only compulsory subject). The following table explains how the National Curriculum was originally constructed.

National Curriculum: 1988	
English	'Core subjects'
Maths	30 –40% of the timetable
Science	
Technology	
Music	
Art	Non-core subjects
History	50% of the timetable
Modern foreign language	
Geography	
Physical education	
Optional subjects:	
Religious education etc.	10%–20% of timetable if required.
Other requirements:	
• 'A daily act of worship' of a 'broadly Christian nature' (parents had the right to withdraw children from this).	
• Sex education	
• Citizenship Lessons added to curriculum in 2003	

- **Key Stage** testing was introduced at 7, 11 and 14 (Stages 1, 2 and 3). Key Stage 4 was GCSE. At the end of each Stage, children were assessed – using Standard Attainment Tests (SATs) – against national 'Assessment Targets' (the aim being to eventually ensure all children achieved a certain level of competence relative to their age). The original testing regime has been severely curtailed over the years – testing and teacher assessments of the core subjects at Stages 1–3 are now the norm.

- **Institutional freedom** involved the idea of 'freeing' schools from the 'bureaucracy' of local government control in a number of ways.

- **Grant-maintained** schools were directly funded by government, rather than through LEAs (and local taxation). To encourage schools to 'opt-out' of LEA control, generous funding packages were offered. For schools that didn't opt out (relatively few actually did) the:

- **Local management of schools** initiative gave head teachers and governing bodies direct control over how they spent the school budget.

- **City Technology Colleges** – new schools specialising in the application of Information Technology to all aspects of the curriculum were introduced, partly funded by private companies (at least in theory – some funding was forthcoming from a few wealthy individuals who supported the government's New Right agenda, but the bulk of the expenditure came from government; around 20 such colleges were actually completed). Finally, an

- **Open enrolment** policy was developed whereby popular and 'successful' schools were allowed to expand at the expense of 'unsuccessful' schools. Parents were, in theory, given more choice about where to send their children and LEAs couldn't set limits on school size to reduce parental choice.

Between the 1988 Act and the 1996 Education Act (whose main purpose was to consolidate all education reforms since 1944), a number of significant changes were made, which we can note as follows.

- **Higher education**: The following were gradually introduced:

- **student loans** (1988) replaced grants
- **student numbers** increased
- **polytechnics** (once considered a vocational form of HE) were given university status (1993).

- **Parents' Charter** gave parents the right to information from a school about its performance.

⚠ Digging deeper

With the development of vocational education and the 1988 Reform Act we can see the influence of New Right thinking on education during this period.

Role: The education system became more closely aligned with the needs of industry over this period, in terms of both the development of explicitly vocational elements and the range of subjects that schools could teach. The 'core curriculum' of English, maths and science, in particular, was designed to satisfy employer-led demands for workers with 'basic skills' of literacy and numeracy. At the time, some writers (for example **Lacey**: 'Professionalism or Bureaucracy?', 1985) argued such *prescription* (that is, setting out the subjects that had to be taught in all state schools) would not improve the quality of education but, rather, result in greater bureaucracy.

Opinions about the New Vocationalism are generally divided.

For some, such as **Dan Finn** ('Education for Jobs', 1988), youth training schemes involved:

- **cheap labour** for employers
- **bonded labour** – 'trainees' who left a job risked losing state benefits

- **pretend jobs** – many trainees were either on 'work creation schemes' devised and funded by government or in work offering no prospect of further employment once the 'training period' was over (and the government subsidy ended)

- **little training** – and certainly not in the skills required for work in a high technology, service-based, economy

- **hidden subsidies** that shifted the burden of training costs from employers to the taxpayer.

In addition, for Marxist writers such as **Bates** et al (*Schooling for the Dole*, 1984) and **Bates** and **Riseborough** (*Youth and Inequality*, 1993), the New Vocationalism had a number of features.

- **Class division**: Most (white) middle-class pupils followed the academic education route to high pay, skill and status employment whereas (white and black) working class pupils were encouraged along the vocational route to lower paid/lower status work.

- **Social control**: Taking potentially troublesome, unemployed youth 'off-the-streets' and subjecting them to workplace discipline.

- **Lowering wages** for all young people by subsidising some employers.

- **Lowering unemployment** figures.

Feminist writers also criticised vocationalism for channelling girls into 'traditional' female areas of the workforce – hairdressing, secretarial and 'caring professional' work such as nursing.

On the other hand, the new vocationalism had a couple of positive features.

Yeomans (2002) notes the general political belief that 'education in general, and vocational education in particular, will have an economic pay off remains strong and continues to have a powerful influence on the education policy of the major political parties'.

Sue Heath (*Preparation for Life? Vocationalism and the Equal Opportunities Challenge*, 1997) suggested TVEI, for example, helped involve women in areas of schooling (and eventually work) that were traditionally male preserves by insisting on equal opportunities.

Impact: Lee Murray ('How far did the 1998 Education Act usher a radically new direction in British Education?', 2002) argues most of the Act's reforms (such as CTC's and 'opting-out') had very little impact on the education scene; the actual curriculum didn't change that much and Key Stage testing has been generally watered down over the years. However, one way Conservative Government changes impacted was by setting the agenda for subsequent educational reform under New Labour in the 1990s (as we will see in a moment).

Experience: One interesting thing to note, in this context, is how the changes just outlined reflect some of the contradictions in New Right thinking (contradictions which, it could be argued, have been carried through to New Labour's education policy in the twenty-first century). In this respect we can note two tendencies.

- **Economic liberalism**, relating to control of school budgets and decision-making about teaching resources etc. One objective here seems to have been to remove schools from local government control and influence.

- **Centralised control** of the 16–18 curriculum. Post-16 vocational training had, for example, a strong compulsory element (school-leavers who refused training could have state benefits removed) whereas, as we have noted, the secondary school curriculum (and eventually that of primary schools too) became increasingly prescriptive; what could be taught – and even how it was to be taught – was effectively decided by the government.

In this respect, New Right perspectives (like their postmodern counterparts) recognise the significance of economic change but, unlike the latter, want to retain highly centralised control over some areas of society (schools and family life for example).

Finally, we can note a couple more points relating to the experience of education.

- **Curriculum of the Dead: Stephen Ball** ('Education, Majorism and the "Curriculum of the Dead"', 1995) argues that Conservative reforms tried to 'deconstruct the comprehensive, modernist curriculum and replace it with an ... authoritative curriculum of tradition' – in other words, an attempt to specify a school curriculum that focused on learning 'facts' and which gave central importance (by enshrining them in law) to traditional curriculum subjects such as maths and science. It was, almost literally a 'curriculum of the dead' because this is where its focus, according to **Ball**, lay – the distant past.

- **Education *or* training**: For all the recent changes in the education system (including ones we will examine in a moment), the central problem of, to paraphrase **John Lea** ('Post-compulsory education in context', 2001), 'What are schools for?' remains unresolved. **Pete Abbs** (*The Educational Imperative*, 1994), for example, argues against the idea that 'the first task of teachers is to serve the economy, to turn out skilled robots and uncritical consumers for the hi-tech age'.

 Growing it yourself: what are schools for?

Use the following table as the basis for thinking about these two ideas about the purpose of schooling.

The main purpose of schools is to:	Arguments for	Arguments against
Educate young people for adult life		
Train young people for work		

1997–2004: New Labour

Preparing the ground

The scope and diversity of educational changes seems to have accelerated over the past seven years and covers all aspects of education, from primary, through secondary to tertiary (higher education). For our convenience, we can categorise these changes under the following headings.

Primary education

- **Literacy and numeracy** hours were introduced as part of the curriculum and all primary pupils to have one hour each day devoted to reading and writing. The prescriptive nature of the strategy (telling teachers *how* to teach as well as *what* to teach) was unique, at the time, for primary education.
- **Nursery education** encouraged through the use of tax credits for parents.
- **Class sizes** of more than 30 children at Key Stage 1 were made illegal in 1997 (although it is debatable how strictly the law is enforced).

Secondary education

- **Curriculum 2000**: A-levels split into two qualifications (AS and A2) and Key Skills introduced (Main skills: Communication, Application of Number and IT. Wider skills: Improving Own Learning, Working with Others and Problem Solving) as part of 'basic skills' strategy.
- **Types of school**: Within the comprehensive system, school diversity has developed along the following lines.
  - **Specialist schools** – specialising in a particular curriculum area (such as modern languages), these schools can select up to 10% of their intake by 'aptitude'.
  - **Beacon schools** are given increased funds to spread 'high quality teaching practice' amongst lower-performing schools.

- **Foundation schools** (as part of the 'Five Year Strategy' – see below) will be allowed to set their own curriculum.
- **Academies** (the latest addition) will be established in partnership with private sponsors, located in disadvantaged areas and encouraged to specialise in certain curriculum areas. These schools may also select up to 10% of their intake by aptitude.

- **Tomlinson Report** (2004): This review of the 14–19 curriculum recommended, among other things, the reform of examinations such as GCSE and A-level into a School Diploma modelled on the International Baccalaureate.

Mike Tomlinson, author of the Tomlinson Report (2004)

A more-detailed examination of the Report can be found at the end of this section.

- **Home–school agreements** (where parents promise to ensure children attend school etc.) made legally binding, although never enforced.
- **Targets**: Literacy strategy and learning targets introduced (Moser Report, 1999).
- **Education Maintenance Allowance** (EMA) introduced for 16 year olds in full-time education, 2004. Payment depends on attendance targets being met by individual students.
- **Performance Indicators** (commonly known as league tables) were expanded to include all primary and secondary and

schools in England (Scotland and Wales abolished such tables). Based initially on GCSE/A-level results and, increasingly, Key Stage SAT results, these tables have been extensively criticised for their bias in favour of schools with selective intakes (Public and Grammar schools) and bias against schools with high levels of SEN ('Special Educational Needs') and Free School Meals (FSM) children.

To counteract this in-built disadvantage, the government now publishes 'Value-Added' League Tables measuring progress (rather than actual level of achievement) made by a pupil between, for example Key Stage 3 and 4.

- **Social inclusion**:

  - **New Start** scheme aimed to target 'disaffected or underachieving' 14–17 year olds by encouraging schools to develop new ways of motivating such pupils.

  - **Vocational Training**: 'Disaffected' 14–16 year olds allowed to spend part of the school week at FE College or work experience.

  - **Excellence in Cities** (2000) introduced a range of ideas, including: Learning Mentors and Support Units, City Learning Centres, more Beacon and Specialist schools, support for Gifted and Talented pupils and small Education Action Zones (that involve clusters of Primary and Secondary schools joining forces with parents, LEAs and local business to improve educational services).

  - **Sure Start** (2000) programmes designed to improve services to poorest pre-school children and families to prevent truancy and increase achievement. Additional schemes aimed at pregnant teenagers to help them back to education/employment.

  - **Extended Schools**: Following an American model, schools offer a range of services/facilities (crèches, support for parents, curriculum and leisure opportunities for pupils outside the traditional school timetable) to engage pupils and parents in their child's education. **Wilkin** et al ('Towards the development of extended schools', 2002) found a positive impact on 'attainment, attendance and behaviour' by offering activities that increased 'engagement and motivation'.

- **Vocational**: Whether we consider these changes in terms of the new 'new vocationalism' (as it were) or simply an extension of existing vocational initiatives, a number of developments are worthy of mention:

  - **Integrating provision** has involved attempts to link post-16 training more-closely with school and work. National Traineeships, for example, were an early introduction, designed to provide a link between school leaving and Modern Apprenticeships.

  - **New Deal**: Showing either a distinct lack of imagination or a touching faith in the past, this required all unemployed under 25s to take either a subsidised job, voluntary work or full time education/training.

  - **Careers**: All schools must provide careers education for 13–18 year old pupils. '*ConneXions*' (the renamed 'Investors in Young People' careers' service) was introduced – with a 'cool' name, presumably to appeal to 'The Kids'.

- **Providers**: Training and Enterprise Councils (TECs) replaced by Learning and Skills Council (LSC).
- **Work experience** expanded to a two-week placement for all state maintained school pupils. As part of increased vocational awareness, pupils were also to be taught 'job skills' such as interview techniques.
- **Vocational GCSEs** introduced to replace Intermediate GNVQs.

Post-16 education

- **Dearing Report** (1997) – a major review of Conservative education policy that led to changes in Key Stage testing as well as laying the ground for the subsequent reform of the 14–19 curriculum (the Tomlinson Report, 2004 – discussed in more detail below). Also recommended students should be charged for their tuition fees (so you know who to blame).
- **Teaching** and **Higher Education Act** (1998) created a new system of student loans and fees. Grants largely abolished but 'poorer families' exempted from fees after political criticism that working class students would be unfairly penalised.

  Participation: Target of 50% of under-30s to 'experience Higher Education' by 2010.

Five Year Strategy

Having looked at policy in the recent past, we can finish by outlining New Labour's plans for the future (assuming, of course, they are re-elected), unveiled in July 2004 as part of a five year strategy.

- **Providers**: Greater private industry involvement in the funding, owning and running of schools. New providers (parent groups, religious organisation and businesses) can set up new schools.
- **Personalised learning** will expand, with the objective being to 'tailor the curriculum' to the needs of each individual pupil. This, however, is likely to raise serious labelling issues.
- **Schools**: The aim is to expand 'good schools' and close 'failing schools' (replacing them with Academies). Greater control over attendance and behaviour will be introduced, part of which involves the expectation every school will have a uniform and code of conduct. The 'extended schools' experiment will itself be extended and specialist schools will be allowed to develop a second 'specialism'.

Ten Year Strategy

Looking even further into the future, the Tomlinson Report (2004) is intended to form the basis for wide-ranging reform of the 14–19 curriculum and, as such, it is worth outlining the Report's main recommendations (even though, at the time of writing, it's not clear whether the government intends to implement them all). The basic recommendations are '. . . to replace existing 14–19 qualifications including A levels, AS levels, AVCEs, BTECs and GCSEs' with a diploma framework. There will be four levels of attainment:

- Entry
- Foundation
- Intermediate
- Advanced.

Achievement at each level is recorded as a *pass, merit* or *distinction* and 'Detailed performance records' would be available to teachers, employers, universities and colleges, recording the grades achieved in particular components of the diploma.

As the following table shows, the diploma is built around three areas.

- **Main learning**: Most time would be spent on these subjects.
- **Core learning**: The focus here is on students gaining 'a minimum standard in functional communication, mathematics and ICT for each diploma'. An extended project (to replace 'most externally assessed coursework' would be part of all core learning, as would participation in 'sports, arts, work experience and community service. Their participation would be recorded on their diploma, but would not be compulsory'. Personal reviews and evaluations of learning would also feature here.

- **CKSA**: The focus here is the development of skills (problem solving, teamwork and study skills, for example), rights and responsibilities, active citizenship, ethics and diversity.

National Curriculum (14–16) subjects would be retained as options within the diploma. However, the report proposed 'up to 20 subject mixes. Young people could choose an "open" diploma with a subject mix similar to GCSEs and A-level combinations. Alternatively they could choose a diploma specialising in an employment sector or academic discipline'.

Vocational education and training can be either integrated into 'open diplomas' (mixed with academic subjects, for example) or followed as distinct 'vocational pathways' (routes through the various options and qualifications). In theory, 'schools and colleges, working with training providers, could tailor programmes to each young person's needs and abilities' which, in turn,

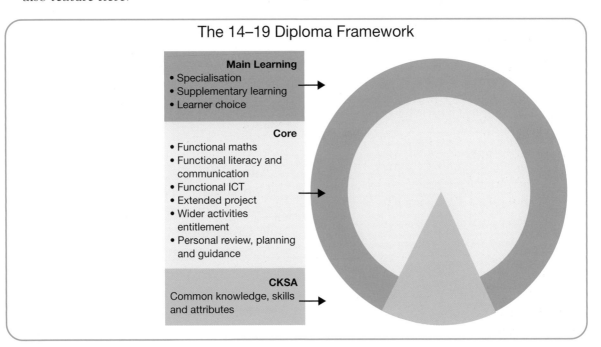

The 14–19 Diploma Framework

is seen by Tomlinson as a way of tackling social exclusion (in the form of 'disengagement and poor behaviour')

Assessment: An interesting notion here is that 'students sit too many external exams'. The proposal, therefore, is for fewer external tests and more teacher assessment, although formal exams would be retained and 'External exams would also remain in the advanced diploma as well as for communication, mathematics and ICT in each diploma'.

Potential problems of *teacher labelling* and *stereotyping* impacting on their assessments of pupils would be resolved using a system of external moderators who would sample teacher assessments.

⚠ Digging deeper

Role: New Labour policies shaping the role of education in the twenty-first century reflect a range of functionalist and New Right perspectives and ideas. Functionalist ideas, for example, are reflected in areas such as:

- **Social solidarity**: One of New Labour's major concerns has been with *social exclusion* (a form of underclass theory linking educational underachievement, crime, delinquency and poverty). Education policy, therefore, has focused on measures to combat truancy, the introduction of Extended schools as a way of involving all sections of the community in the educational process and the development of different types of schools (Specialist, Foundation, Academies and so forth) as a way to raise achievement among the worst performing (academically) sections of society. Vocational forms of education have also

been developed as a means of raising achievement through social inclusion.

- **Social integration**: Measures such as school uniforms, codes of conduct and home–school agreements are classic *integrating mechanisms*, designed to promote social solidarity. The development of Extended schools also reflects the idea involving parents in the education of their children helps to control behaviour and increase achievement.

New Right perspectives, on the other hand, are increasingly reflected in ideas like:

- **Marketisation strategies** – the way to improve educational performance is to 'open schools up' to commercial influences. This involves a range of initiatives, from commercial funding of school building (the *Building Schools for the Future* programme – due to begin in 2005 – for example, involves capital spending by both the government and private industry, whereas the *Seed Challenge* initiative involves capital spending by government on a school if the school can attract 'matching funds' from non-government sources) to commercial firms actually owning and running schools. Critics of such involvement – such as **Davies** and **Adnett** ('Market Forces and School Curriculum', 1999) – point to a couple of potential problems.
  - **Curriculum innovation** decreases because of uncertainty about its success or failure (and, in particular, the consequences of getting it wrong).
  - **Burden of change** falls disproportionately on those schools

with the least resources to innovate successfully.

In addition, we can also note:

- **long-term planning** is inhibited by the need to produce 'instant improvements'
- **competition** between schools for pupils may actually decrease innovation and improvement because schools simply develop ways of attracting a limited pool of 'high ability, high motivation' pupils.

- **Informed consumers**: One problem with the idea of *consumers* (parents to you and me) being able to pick and choose schools is that equality of opportunity is more apparent than real. For example, what happens if a school is over-subscribed with applications (more parents want their children to go to that school than it has places available)? If a school cannot expand, the provider (a school), rather than the consumer, may end up choosing which pupils it accepts.

The experience of school performance (league) tables is a good example of how consumer choice may be limited. The rationale for the hierarchical ranking of schools (one on top of the other) is to allow consumers to judge the effectiveness of their local schools. However, such tables may lack validity for a number of reasons.

- **Special needs**: Schools with few SEN pupils have higher average academic performance.
- **Resources** are not distributed equally across all schools (inner city comprehensives, for example, fare worse in this respect than suburban public or grammar schools).

- **Social class** factors, rather than what happens within a school, may have more influence on exam results. Schools with large numbers of working-class children, for example, achieve less on average than schools with a largely middle-class intake.
- **Exam values**: Schools develop ways of 'improving their performance' by manipulating exam entrance. For example, they may be reluctant to accept lower class pupils (those who, historically, perform least well educationally); greater time, effort and teaching resources may be given to 'marginal students' (those who, with extra help can achieve five A–C GCSE grades) at the expense of pupils considered unlikely to reach this target.
- **Self-fulfilling prophecies**: High ranking schools attract more middle-class pupils who, historically, achieve most educationally.

- **Impact**: Changes to educational provision have impacted on both providers and consumers in a number of ways:
  - **commercial input** into school building and ownership
  - **centralised direction** of the school curriculum, teaching methods, what pupils should wear to school and so forth
  - **failing schools** and the consequences of not meeting (centralised) government performance targets
  - **competition** between schools for pupils (especially those pupils with the 'right' attitudes and motivations).
- **Experience**: While it is always difficult to

evaluate the experience of schooling, we can note a number of general developments.

- **Social inclusion** has involved attempts to both increase levels of achievement and to ensure pupils from social groups who have, historically, been largely excluded from schooling are reintegrated into the system.

- **Training**: Greater emphasis, in recent years, has been placed on the relationship between education and work. While this has positive aspects (allowing students to follow vocational courses closely integrated to their needs and preferences) it also has rather less positive consequences in terms of:

  - **selecting** students for 'vocational training'

  - **specialisation** at a too early age

  - **training** that doesn't particularly match the changed economic situation (for example, vocational training that doesn't include high levels of ICT)

  - **academic/vocational** class divides in our educational system are perpetuated (in crude terms, middle-class pupils receive a high status academic education and the rest don't).

As **Rutherford** ('Education as a Frontier Market', 2003) argues: 'Education and training is changed from the social provision of a public good, into a services market involving private transactions between customers and providers'.

- **Curriculum changes**: Some changes can, once again, be viewed in a generally positive light. **Michael Fielding** ('Students as Radical Agents of Change', 2001), for example, has noted

opportunities for student involvement in the teaching and learning process through curriculum initiatives (which, presumably, would involve the new requirement on schools to teach Citizenship).

Attempts to simplify the school curriculum by offering different routes through the school (in terms of academic/vocational subjects, Foundation, Intermediate and Higher levels and so forth) may help to clarify pupil choices and the possible introduction of a School Diploma may also broaden pupil experience by widening their choice of subjects.

Conversely, however, **Fielding** also notes a conflicting tendency within schools; the over-emphasis on exam performance and education as a series of 'measurable outcomes', serves to limit both choice and channel pupils into an increasingly narrow set of educational experiences.

This section has covered the development and application of educational policy over the past 50 years, from the introduction of universal, free, education to the recently published Tomlinson Report that charts the proposed way forward for the next 10 years. As such, it represents a logical development of the ideas about education as a social institution discussed earlier in the chapter. In the final section, however, we are going to focus on another side to the educational debate, namely understanding what goes on 'inside schools' in terms of the relationship between adults and children.

School relationships and processes

Introduction

In this final section we are going to examine debates about schooling as a social process; in other words, we need to look more closely at what goes on 'inside schools', in terms of the organisation of teaching and learning, teacher/pupil relationships, the influence of the hidden curriculum and the development of pupil subcultures.

As you will note, we have touched on some of these ideas in earlier sections but we need to develop them in more detail to arrive at a rounded picture of education in our society.

⚠ Preparing the ground

The organisation of teaching and learning

We can categorise these processes in terms of two main ideas.

- **Social organisation** refers to how education is organised in terms of things like the educational policies we examined in the previous section. The social organisation of education, therefore, sets the basic context for the:

- **Sociological organisation** of teaching and learning, which involves examining areas like:

  - **School and classroom organisation**: How is teaching and learning physically organised?

  - **Curriculum organisation**: for example, what must be taught in schools.

  - **Socialisation** and **social control**: How is it established and exercised?

  - **Teaching styles**: Are there different theories of teaching?

  - **Learning styles**: Are there different theories of learning?

WARM UP: TIME TRAVEL

Imagine you have been transported back in time to 1904 – what differences and similarities do you think there might be between the early twentieth and early twenty-first century school/classroom?

Edwardian classroom – early twentieth century

Modern classroom – early twenty-first century

Similarities	Differences
Going to school	No physical punishment

You will, no doubt, have established, some fairly obvious similarities between Edwardian and contemporary schooling. For example:

- school as a place you go to learn
- you are taught by teachers (adults)
- you may wear uniforms (although this depends on the school).

There are, of course, some obvious differences: relationships with teachers may be friendlier and their style of teaching different; discipline is very different (corporal punishment (physical beating) is no longer allowed) and, of course, the technology of the Edwardian classroom was very different – writing with chalk on a piece of slate probably doesn't quite match today's computers, data projectors and electronic whiteboards – although most students probably still record their work in ink, on paper).

In the following we can look at some significant aspects of the organisation of teaching and learning (a few of which, I suspect wouldn't have seemed too different to pupils 100 years ago).

- **Social structures**: By and large, schools are *hierarchical structures*, not only in terms of the power/authority relationship between adults (teachers, administrative and support staff) and pupils (who, by-and-large, have very little power within schools and are consequently unable to officially influence the teaching and learning process), but also in terms of the general authority structure within the school.

Growing it yourself: school hierarchies

This exercise can be completed in small groups or as a whole class, depending on your knowledge of different types of educational institution.

Draw an organisational chart, based on your knowledge of primary/secondary school/college, to include everyone – from the head teacher/principal down to the youngest year group pupils (if you're lucky, your teacher may have a chart available for the teaching staff which you can adapt for this purpose).

Indicate, where known, the gender and ethnicity of the staff occupying the positions of authority you've identified.

Discussion points

You might like to consider: What are the social characteristics (age, gender, etc.) of the most/least powerful people in the organisation?

What levels of respect/obedience are people in the organisation expected to show towards each other? (For example, how are pupils expected to act towards staff and vice versa?)

- **Bureaucratic organisation**: Schools are, in some ways, bureaucracies organised, for teaching and learning purposes, around basic principles designed to maximise their efficiency as *people processors*. In other words, schools are modern institutions, an idea expressed by the American educationalist **Ted Sizer** (*Horace's Compromise The Dilemma of the American High School*, 1984) when he

argued schools tend to be organised around principles of:

- **Uniformity**: They operate, in other words, with little concern for the needs of individuals (teachers or learners) and emphasise a narrow definition of achievement (how many tests are successfully passed) rather than the quality of student understanding.

- **Quantification** is the main way the value of a school, its teachers and students is expressed. 'Success' is measured in exam passes and league table position.

- **Expectancies**: Schools (and by extension teachers and students) are set targets, determined at a national, government, level, for student learning (all 7 year olds, for example, should achieve Key Stage 1 in reading, writing and maths).

- **Division of labour**: This is highly fragmented (split into small parts) and tightly controlled. The school day, for example, is divided into rigid lessons and what is taught is not open to negotiation.

- **Individual responsibility** is limited; learning is controlled (by the needs of testing regimes, for example) and there's little scope for individual development or expression. Students are generally expected to learn similar things, at similar times, in similar ways.

Whether or not your experience of schooling fits exactly (or even inexactly) with the ideas we've just noted, have a look at the following examples of two different kinds of educational philosophy

Summerhill School (founded by A.S. Neill in 1921)	
Schooling norms	**Schooling values**
Children can follow their own interests	Provide an environment so children can define who they are and what they want to be.
No compulsory assessments or lessons	No pressure to conform to artificial standards of success based on predominant theories of child learning and achievement.
Children are free to play when and how they like	Spontaneous, natural play not undermined or redirected by adults into a learning experience for children.
All school rules and decisions made democratically by children and adults	Create values based on the community. Problems are discussed and resolved openly and democratically.
Boarding fees range from £5300 to £6550 depending on the age of the student. http://www.summerhillschool.co.uk	

Steiner Schools
'The school curriculum is designed to meet the needs of the child at each stage of their development. Children enter classes according to their age rather than academic ability and the teacher is free to present subject material in an individual way that aims to awaken and enthuse the children, encouraging them to discover and learn for themselves. In this way the child is not educated solely in the '3 Rs' but also in the '3 Hs' – Hand, Heart, Head – the practical, feeling and thinking capacities'.
Rudolf Steiner School: Kings Langley: http://www.rudolfsteiner.herts.sch.uk/

 Growing it yourself: alternative schools

What are your views on institutions like Summerhill and Steiner Schools?

Split into two groups:

- group one should identify possible advantages of this type of schooling
- group two should identify possible disadvantages.

Combine your observations into a table similar to the following:

Advantages	Disadvantages
Pupils learn at their own pace.	What if people don't learn anything?
Variety of learning techniques	What if people don't behave?

Once you've done this, you might like, as a class, to consider the strengths and weaknesses of these types of school compared to your school/college.

about how teaching and learning should be organised:

- **Curriculum**: The teaching and learning process in schools is constrained by the nature of the school curriculum, in terms of what can or can't be taught. Two things are useful to note here. Firstly, how little the school curriculum actually changed over 100 years. Compare, for example, the National Curriculum subjects noted in the previous section with:

The Board of Education Curriculum: 1904	
English	Manual Work (boys)
Maths	Domestic subjects (girls)
Science	Physical Exercise
History	Foreign Language
Drawing	Geography
Music added shortly afterwards	

Secondly, the relevance of the curriculum – in terms of the usefulness or otherwise of what is taught – is rarely questioned, although, having said that, **John White** (*Rethinking the School Curriculum*, 2003) has argued: 'Many subjects are bogged down in values held over 100 years ago. They need to be freed from the dead weight of custom and from the shackle of the assessment system before they can focus on what is really important'. He argues, for example:

- **History** contains little of relevance to the twenty-first century.
- **Science** is laboratory-based, employing techniques no scientist currently uses (the Bunsen burner!)
- **Music** – one of the most important aspects of pupil culture – is reduced to the study of dead, white, European classical composers.

The Royal Society for the Arts has argued a curriculum for the twenty-first century ('Opening Minds', 1998) should be based around five 'competencies':

- **learning**: being taught how to learn, think and critically reflect
- **citizenship**: focusing on behaviour, rights and responsibilities
- **relationships**: understanding how to relate to others
- **managing situations**: dealing with change and so forth
- **managing information**: how to access and judge the value of different sources.

- **Teaching** and **learning styles**: Having suggested schools are bureaucratic institutions that don't seem to have changed much over the past century in terms of how they organise knowledge and information, in recent years a great deal of work has gone into thinking about how teachers teach and students learn. The impact of new technologies (the Internet, interactive white boards, CD-ROMs and so forth) on teaching styles should not be underestimated since, although it may be much the same old curriculum, technology opens up new ways to teach and learn (although we are, of course, only at the beginning of any exploration of how such technology impacts on the organisation of teaching and learning).

Similarly, developments in teacher and student understanding of learning styles (differences, for example, in the way different students process information – visually, verbally and the like) are starting to have an impact, as is the idea of things like **Howard Gardner**'s concept of multiple intelligences (*Multiple Intelligences after Twenty Years*, 2003) which argues students possess a range of 'intelligences' (interpersonal, emotional, musical and so forth) as well as the ones (language, mathematical and spatial) traditionally recognised and tested (in exams and IQ tests) in schools.

The hidden curriculum

Philip Jackson (*Life In Classrooms*, 1968) argued the hidden curriculum involves the things we learn from the experience of attending school. It is, therefore, a form of socialisation process, involving a mix of formal and informal techniques.

Meighan ('A Sociology of Education', 1981) suggests: 'The hidden curriculum is taught by the school, not by any teacher ... [it involves] an approach to living and an attitude to learning'.

Skelton ('Studying hidden curricula', 1997) suggests it involves: 'That set of implicit messages relating to knowledge, values, norms of behaviour and attitudes that learners experience in and through educational processes. These messages may be contradictory ... and each learner mediates the message in her/his own way'.

In this respect, **Carrie Paechter** ('Issues in the study of curriculum', 1999) suggests the hidden curriculum has two basic dimensions:

- **Intended** aspects are the things teachers 'actively and consciously pursue as learning goals'. These include, fostering certain values (politeness, the importance of order, deference to authority and so forth) and discouraging others (bullying and sexism, for example). It is 'hidden' in the sense these things are not part of the formal curriculum, but teachers and students are probably aware of many of the processes going on in the school (some of which may actually be explicit, in terms of things like anti-racism or anti-sexism policies).

- **Unintended** aspects might include the messages teachers give to students in the course of their teaching – things like status messages (whether boys appear to be more valued than girls – or vice versa), messages relating to beliefs about ability (whether teachers believe it is 'natural' or the product of 'hard work') and so forth.

Have a look at the 'Discussion point' opposite. Having established what we mean by this concept (and, I trust, how the interpretation of its meaning reflects Skelton's argument), we can identify some aspects of its content in the following terms:

- **Status messages** covers a number of areas related to ideas we develop about our 'worth' in the eyes of others. This includes, for example:

  - **Type of school**: State or private, grammar or non-grammar, for example.

  - **Streaming/banding/setting** and how membership of 'high' or 'low' academic groups impacts on pupil perceptions of themselves and others.

Discussion point: images of the hidden curriculum

How would you interpret the meaning of the following?

Primary science

Primary cookery

Secondary science

What do these examples tell us about the hidden curriculum?

- **Academic** and **vocational** courses and subjects have different statuses in our educational system. The introduction of 'Vocational GCSEs' for example, reflects the implicit assumption academic GCSEs are not suited to the abilities of some students (and it probably doesn't take too much imagination to guess the social class of students who will be encouraged to take these new qualifications).

- **Class position** – how ranking in terms of academic success or failure affects children's self-perception and value.

- **Classroom organisation** – in terms, for example, of authority within the classroom (teacher at the front, directing operations or a situation in which there is no clear authority ranking).

- **Socialisation/social control** messages relate to ideas about what is required from

pupils if they are to succeed educationally. Some of these ideas refer explicitly to the way pupils are encouraged to behave within schools (for example, the various classroom processes that involve order and regularity – attendance, punctuality and so forth) whereas others are less explicit and relate to the things pupils must demonstrate in order to 'learn how to learn'. That is, learning to conform not just to the formal rules of the school but also to the informal rules, beliefs and attitudes perpetuated through the socialisation process. These include things like recognising:

- **Authority**, in terms of the powerful role played by the teacher within the classroom – not simply in terms of organisational rules (when to speak, where to sit and so forth) – but also in relation to:

- **Learning**, which may involve ideas like individualism (learning is a process that should not, ultimately, be shared) and competition (the objective is to demonstrate you are better than your peers). Learning also involves ideas about what is to be learnt in terms of:

- **Knowledge**: Teachers, for example, select and present certain ideas as valid. To pass exams (and thereby succeed in educational terms), the pupil has to learn to conform to what the teacher presents as valid knowledge.

- **Assessment** is an integral part of the hidden curriculum because it involves the idea learning can be *quantified* (through tests and exams) and that, consequently, only quantifiable knowledge is valid knowledge. Assessment is, of course, crucial to various forms of teacher labelling and stereotyping that go on within schools and classrooms and contributes to pupil (and indeed teacher) identities.

- **Identities**: These are a significant aspect of the hidden curriculum, not just in terms of the things we've already noted (different senses of identity related to types of school, how pupils are perceived, categorised and treated and the like), but also in terms of ideas like class, gender and ethnicity. **Hill** and **Cole** (*Schooling and Equality: Fact, Concept and Policy*, 2001), for example, argue the hidden curriculum functions to exclude particular groups (especially working class children, but also such groups as the mentally and physically disabled).

- **Elizabeth Burn** ('Do Boys need Male Primary Teachers as Positive Role Models?', 2001) argues current government preoccupations with initiatives relating to boys' achievement (male role models, after-school learning clubs, boy-friendly curricula, single-sex classroom groups . . .) sends messages about achievement to both males and females – that boys have 'a problem', for example and the achievement of girls is both devalued and (perhaps) part of the problem. Similarly, **Emma Smith** ('Failing Boys and Moral Panics', 2003) questions the idea of framing debates about underachievement in terms of 'failing boys'.

Questions of identity are also related to **subject choice** in terms of what students choose to study (mainly post-16 under the conditions originally set by the National Curriculum, but some forms of choice at Key Stage 3 – decisions about vocational or academic GCSEs for example – are gradually being introduced) and why they make these choices.

A wide range of evidence suggests males and females make different subject choices when given the opportunity. These choices are not just influenced by the people around us (**Cooper** and **McDonald** ('Why Science?, 2001), for example, found both parents and teachers influential in a student's choice of degree courses) but also by perceptions relating to masculine and feminine identities. **Caroline Bamford** ('Gender and Education in Scotland', 1989) noted the research evidence suggested more boys take subjects like science, geography, technical drawing and computing, whereas more girls take secretarial studies, biology, French, home economics and history.

Abbot and **Wallace** (*Feminist Perspectives*, 1996) also point out feminist research has shown how concepts of masculinity and femininity are influenced by factors such as:

- **Academic hierarchies** – how the school is vertically stratified in occupation terms (men at the top being the norm).

- **Textbooks** and **gender stereotyping**: Males appear more frequently and are more likely to be shown in active ('doing and demonstrating'), rather than passive, roles. **Lesley Best** ('Analysis of sex-roles in pre-school books', 1992), for example, used Content Analysis to demonstrate how pre-school texts designed to develop reading skills remain populated by sexist assumptions and stereotypes.

David Gillborn ('Citizenship, "Race" and the Hidden Curriculum', 1992) also notes how the hidden curriculum impacts on ethnic (as well as gender and class) identities through citizenship teaching, where the content of the subject teaching (democracy, racial equality, etc.) frequently clashes with the 'learned experiences' of black pupils.

- **Formal curriculum**: Decisions about what subjects should be studied, how they should be studied and the particular content of each subject are also significant aspects of the hidden curriculum. **Paechter** (1999), for example, argues:

  - **Subject learning** – as opposed to process learning – is generally considered more important in our education system. For example *critical thinking* is a *process* where we learn how

to assess and evaluate knowledge. However, somewhat ironically, its value is only realised when it is turned into a subject to be studied.

- **Specialisms**: Each subject has its own special skills and knowledge and the curriculum becomes increasingly specialised as students progress through the system.

- **Hierarchy**: Some subjects are more important than others (English, maths, science and ICT have special places in the school curriculum; social science, media studies etc., barely get a look-in).

  White and **Bramall** ('Why Learn Maths?', 2000) question this hierarchy when they argue against forcing children to learn high levels of maths: 'The maths we need for everyday life and work is mostly learnt by the end of primary school'.

  Michael Reiss ('Representing Science', 2001) similarly questions the value of science as a National Curriculum subject when its teaching is '...putting pupils off further study of science by limiting the subject to tedious experiments that have little connection to everyday life'.

- **Teaching** within schools assumes teachers, as the 'organisers of learning for others', are a necessary aspect of schooling. This raises a number of interesting questions (for example, are teachers actually needed?) about the nature of knowledge and learning. Even the development of electronic learning (delivered via the Internet, for example), assumes the presence of teachers to organise and direct learning.

Teacher/pupil relationships

We have considered aspects of this relationship at various points (in terms of labelling, stereotyping, self-fulfilling prophecies and differential achievement, for example) and so, you'll be relieved to know, I don't propose to go over this ground again. However, there are further aspects of this relationship that can be usefully explored here.

- **Switching-on: Cano-Garcia** and **Hughes** ('Learning and thinking styles', 2000) argue this relationship is significant in terms of how successful (or unsuccessful) pupils are in switching-on/conforming to teaching styles. They argue, for example, the most academically successful students are those who can work independently of the teacher within a fairly rigid set of teacher-controlled guidelines and procedures. In other words, successful pupils understand what the teacher wants and develop 'teacher-pleasing behaviours' designed to provide it.

- **Switching-off**: The other side of this idea, of course, is what **Barrett** ('Middle schooling', 1999) has termed 'switching-off' – the idea that where pupils fail to see what they're supposed to be learning as 'useful now, as well as in the future' turns a large number off, in terms of learning. In addition, switching-off also seems to occur when pupils feel they lack power to influence the scope, extent and purpose of their studies.

  Seaton ('Reforming the hidden curriculum', 2002) expresses these two basic pupil orientations more academically as 'learned dependence' on the one hand and 'experienced alienation' on the other.

- **Tacit agreements**: These two ideas (switching-on and switching-off) capture, in a small way, one of the problems teachers face in the teaching and learning process – *contradictory demands* made by a fragmented student body (which is a posh way of saying some students like some things and others don't).

  This is not particularly a problem, however, when teacher and pupils are acting in tacit agreement about the purpose of education. It is probable middle-class children gain no more and no less satisfaction from their schooling than working-class children; **Barrett**, however, suggests the former are more likely to *tacitly agree* with teachers about the purpose of education – the accumulation of credentials (qualifications) – and be more inclined, therefore, to participate in teacher-pleasing behaviour.

  One important aspect of the *breakdown* of teacher – pupil relationships we need to note, in this context, is of course *pupil violence* towards teachers and other pupils. DfES figures for 2004 show nearly 300 pupils were expelled for assaults on adults, in addition to nearly 4000 fixed period suspensions. There were also 300-plus expulsions and 12,800 suspensions for attacks on fellow pupils.

- **Teaching styles**: In terms of the different ways teachers interpret their role, we could note four basic categories of teaching styles:

  - **teacher-centred**, where the teacher directs and informs the class
  - **demonstrator**, where although the class is teacher-centred and controlled, the emphasis is on demonstrating ideas

and encouraging students to experiment

- **student-centred**, where the role of the teacher is defined as helping (or facilitating) the student to learn by giving them responsibility for their own learning
- **delegation** styles involve requiring students to work independently on tasks, at their own pace.

Discussion point: teaching styles

As a class, you might like to discuss which type of teaching style (or mix of styles) you prefer – and why.

What, for example, are the strengths and weaknesses (from both the teacher and student viewpoint) of each style?

✸ **In terms of the ideas at which we have just looked, you might find John Gatto's arguments ('The Six-Lesson Schoolteacher', 1991), interesting. You can find the article at:**
www.sociology.org.uk/as4aqa.htm

Pupil subcultures

This final section brings together, in a variety of ways, the general ideas we have just examined in terms of how teaching and learning is organised, the formal and hidden curricula and how teacher–pupil relationships develop and impact on pupil orientations towards school and education (not necessarily the same things – you can hate school but value education and, of course, vice versa).

Traditionally, the sociology of pupil subcultures has focused on the identification of two basic subcultural types.

- **Reactive** subcultures develop, as the term implies, as a reaction to what someone is doing – in this instance, the school or teachers. In other words, this body of theory argues school subcultures develop out of the dissatisfaction of some groups of pupils with their treatment within the school.
- **Independent** subcultures are similar but involve the idea particular subcultural groups already exist within the school (they have developed *independently* of any adult input) and are subsequently *labelled*, in some way (positively or negatively) by those in authority.

In addition, these – again traditionally – have been subdivided into:

- **pro-school subcultures** – groups of pupils who, for whatever reasons, see schooling in a positive light
- **anti-school subcultures** – pupils who, as you might expect, aren't too keen on school or what it has to offer.

The literature is heavy with studies identifying these types – **Hargreaves** ('Social Relations In A Secondary School', 1967) and **Woods** ('The Divided School', 1979) for example and **Johnson** ('Failing School, Failing City', 1999) more recently in relation to Northern Ireland schools. Much of the research (including **Willis**'s *Learning to Labour*, 1977) focused on the idea of:

- **Counter-school subcultures** – how pupils – usually young, white, working-class boys – developed subcultural groups as an alternative to the mainstream culture of schools. **Woods**, for example, adapted

Merton's *Strain Theory* of deviance (*Social Structure and Anomie*, 1938) to argue for a range of different subcultural responses (adaptations) to school culture – from *ingratiators* (pupils who try to earn the favour of teachers – the most positive adaptation) at one extreme to *rebels* (who explicitly rejected the culture of the school) at the other.

While much subcultural theory focused on 'lads' (and, by and large, 'bad lads') and their behaviour, to explain how and why this group is complicit in its own educational failure, some research also included girl's behaviour. **Sue Lees** (*Sugar And Spice: Sexuality and Adolescent Girls*, 1993), for example, noted how female subcultures developed around:

- **Pro-school girls**, which included those who intrinsically valued education (seeing school as enjoyable and worthwhile) and those who took a more extrinsic or instrumental approach to their studies (they saw qualifications, for example, as a necessary means towards a desired end and didn't particularly value school 'for its own sake'). In addition, some girls saw school as an enjoyable place for socialising with friends, without necessarily seeing qualifications as being particularly important.

- **Anti-school girls** included some subcultural groups who saw school as a pointless waste of time, an unenjoyable and uncomfortable period in their life they have to get through before being able to escape into the adult world of work and family.

In addition, writers such as **McRobbie** and **Garber** ('Girls and Subcultures', 1975) and **Christine Griffin** ('It's Different For Girls', 1986) have used subcultural theory to explain how and why girls develop different kinds of response to their treatment and experiences within school and society.

In general, the majority of 'traditional' subcultural analysis focuses on the idea of pupils and teachers reacting, in some way, to each other's behaviour (in terms of *status-giving* or *status denial*, the acceptance or rejection of authority, labelling processes and so forth). However, more recently, writers such as **Mac an Ghaill** (*The Making of Men*, 1994) have changed the focus to that of masculinity and femininity, as well as developing a class and ethnic approach to understanding pupil subcultures. **Mac an Ghaill**, for example, identifies working-class subcultural groups such as *New Enterprisers* – boys who want to be self-employed – and *Real Englishmen* – middle-class boys disaffected with their school experience. In addition, recent developments have led in two main directions.

- **Subcultural theory** has been questioned, not so much in terms of the behaviour it seeks to explain, but more in terms of the idea of subculture itself. For example, we need to ask if pupil subcultures really exist, since there seems little evidence these groups develop any real forms of *cultural production and reproduction* within the school setting (that is, there is not much evidence of cultural identities nor any coherent and consistent way of recruiting and socialising new members). In addition, the concept of subculture suggests some sort of permanence and rigidity within groups, whereas recent types of research suggest this is not the case.

- **Identity** has become the new focus for explaining pupil behaviour. **Rob Shields** (*Lifestyle Shopping*, 1992), for example, argues 'post-subcultural theorising' thinks about identity in terms of its fragmentation (lots of different identities co-existing within schools, for example), rooted in 'fleeting gatherings' rather than rigid groups and focused on consumption (the things you buy and use – which can be real, in the sense of actually buying stuff, or metaphorical, in the sense of buying into a particular lifestyle).

  - **Lifestyle shopping: Sara Delamont** ('Gender and the Discourse of Derision', 1999), for example, has linked achievement and underachievement in the observation of female *lifestyle shopping* – the general rejection of 'failing working boys' who were not seen as having either the educational/work prospects or attitudes that make them particularly attractive future partners.

  - **Neo-tribes: Andy Bennett** ('Subcultures or Neo-tribes?', 1999) also points to a different way of conceptualising *pupil subcultures* with the concept of neo-tribes; dynamic, loosely bound groups involving a range of different – and fleeting – identities and relationships centering around lifestyles rather than a 'way of life'. In other words, this concept questions the idea of subcultural groups (something relatively permanent and tangible) and replaces it with the idea of loose-knit associations and interactions that chop and change over time (in a postmodernist sort of way).

⚠ Digging deeper

As we have seen, school relationships and processes are both complex and inter-connected (for example, the hidden curriculum links into teacher–pupil relationships which, in turn, influences the development of pupil subcultures/styles). In this final section, therefore, we need to establish a general framework within which we can interpret these ideas. This framework can be developed around two school processes identified earlier, namely the *formal and informal* (or hidden) curricula. In this respect, we are interested in examining the formal curriculum in a little more depth since this aspect of school organisation arguably sets the tone for the informal curriculum.

One of the first sociologists to question the ideological nature of the formal curriculum was **M.F.D. Young** (*Knowledge and Control*, 1971) when he argued the way knowledge is categorised, presented and studied is significant for any understanding of school organisation and processes. If people believe it is possible to identify the 'most important' areas of knowledge in society, then some form of consensus is manufactured – and on this consensus can be built a system of testing and evaluation and individuals can be evaluated against their knowledge and understanding in a way that appears:

- **objective**: since there is agreement about what constitutes knowledge, testing can be measured against known standards of competence

- **fair**: pupils can be evaluated in terms of the extent to which they reach certain standards

- **meritocratic**: success or failure in reaching agreed standards can be expressed in terms of individual characteristics. If standards exist and children have an equal opportunity to achieve them then success or failure is down to individual levels of effort, motivation and so forth.

Young (from a Marxist perspective) argued the formal curriculum reflected the interests of powerful social groups in terms of the way knowledge was:

- **selected** – involving decisions about which subjects appear on the curriculum, the content of each subject and so forth

- **organised** – involving decisions about how teachers teach (alone or in groups, for example), how pupils should work (competitively or cooperatively, etc.), classroom organisation (who is in control) and the like.

- **stratified** within the classroom, the school and society. This involves thinking about why theoretical knowledge is considered superior to practical knowledge, the division between vocational and academic subjects, how subjects are *compartmentalised* (taught separately) rather than *integrated* (related to each other), teaching children different levels of knowledge, based upon assessments of their ability and so forth.

In a similar way, **Michael Young** ('Knowledge, learning and the curriculum of the future', 1999) argues that the formal curriculum is changing, in various ways, as our society changes (under the influence of global economic and cultural factors, for example).

Curriculum of the past	Curriculum of the future
Knowledge and learning 'for its own sake'	Knowledge and learning 'for a purpose'
Concerned with transmitting existing knowledge	Focus on creation of new knowledge
Little value on relationships between subjects	The interdependence of knowledge areas
Boundary between school and everyday knowledge	Link between school and everyday knowledge

Finally, we can finish by developing these basic ideas a little further, using **Bernstein**'s argument ('On the Classification and Framing of Educational Knowledge', 1971) that the way knowledge is organised (in his terms 'classified and framed') has consequences for the kinds of messages children receive about the nature and purpose of education.

Discussion point: classification and framing

Have a look at the following table that outlines Bernstein's ideas.

Characteristics of strongly classified and strongly framed knowledge	Characteristics of weakly classified and weakly framed knowledge
There are right answers and these are already known.	There are no right answers. Education is a process of explanation and argument.
Pupil's personal experience is largely irrelevant (unless specifically requested as an example and then it will be right or wrong).	The personal experiences of pupils are always important.
Knowledge is divided into subjects. When one is being studied, other subjects are irrelevant.	Subject boundaries are artificial. Pupils should link various forms of knowledge.
'Education' is what goes on within the school.	'Education' never stops. It occurs everywhere.
Teachers determine the time and pace of lessons.	The pace of learning is determined by the pupil and their interests.
Education involves matching the individual performance of pupils against fixed standards.	Education is seen as a process of personal development.

Now, in small groups or as a class, consider the following questions.

• In your experience, which type of framing (weak or strong) most closely matches your experience of schooling and why?
• Which of the two types of classification and framing most closely matches government educational policies over the past 20 years?
• Which type of framing most closely matches the Summerhill school curriculum?
• Is sociology 'weakly' or 'strongly' framed (and why)?
• If you have experience of e-learning (via the Internet for example) in your school/college, is this knowledge strongly or weakly framed and classified?

INTRODUCTION

The general theme of this chapter is wealth, poverty and welfare and its relationship to *social inequality*, with the main focus being on understanding how things like wealth, income and poverty are unequally distributed in our society.

We can start to explore this theme, therefore, by thinking about 'different definitions of poverty, wealth and income' since, as **Ruth Levitas** ('Defining and Measuring Social Exclusion', 1999) notes: 'definition precedes decisions about measurement'. Given we will be measuring these ideas at various points, it will be helpful to establish what it is we are trying to measure.

Wealth, poverty and welfare

WARM UP: THINKING DEFINITIONS

To get you started, in small groups, use the following table as the basis for identifying and discussing what you already know about:

Income	Wealth	Poverty
Money you earn	Things you own	Not enough to eat
Further examples		

Defining income

⚠ Preparing the ground

Income, on the face of things, is not particularly hard to define; it refers to the monies received by an individual over a specified time period (usually, but not necessarily, a year). In this respect, it is a simple *economic indicator* of value that, consequently, can be objectively quantified (or measured). It can also be one of two types:

- **earned** (or **active**) income is money received for doing something (like paid employment)

- **unearned** (or **passive**) income, on the other hand, comes from things like investments (such as dividends from stocks and shares), rents and so forth.

As **Ian Townsend** ('Income, Wealth & Inequality', 2004) notes, it is important not to confuse *earnings* (money from paid work) with *income*; the two ideas, although related, are not the same – income, for example, may include 'savings and investments, benefits and occupational pensions, in addition to wages'.

A few related ideas we can note are:

- **gross** income involves the total amount of an individual's income – earned and unearned – before any direct taxation (such as income tax)

- **net** (or disposable) income is the amount left after various forms of direct taxation have been deducted

- **discretionary** income refers to the amount of money someone has available to spend once essential items (food, clothing, transport to work and shelter for example) have been deducted.

Although the basic definition of income is fairly straightforward, a couple of complicating factors enter the equation (you just knew they would, didn't you?) when we think about the possibility of using it as an indicator (or measure) of something like social inequality or poverty.

- **Individual** or **household**: Although incomes are earned individually, within family groups or households they are likely to be pooled (or aggregated), a situation further complicated by the number of incomes being pooled (a single adult contributing to the economic upkeep of the family or a number of adults contributing their income, for example). When income is defined at the level of a family or household, the term:

- **Equivalised income** is frequently used, especially if we want to compare families and households on the basis of their needs; a single adult household, for example, needs a lower income than a two adult with children household to maintain a similar standard of living. Most official statistics in this area use an 'equivalence scale', such as that devised by **McClements** ('Equivalence Scales for Children', 1977), to compare incomes between different households.

Module link – Family Life: The idea of different types of family or household group is significant in terms of family diversity.

- **National**, **international** or **global**: When making comparisons between different countries, national income figures are a useful starting point. Global comparisons, for example, can be used to locate a country's total income within a world context, whereas international comparisons can be used to compare the total income of a country like Britain with its equivalent economic competitors (such as France or Germany). However, a simple comparative focus on national income levels – while undoubtedly interesting and useful – may mean we overlook wide disparities of income *within* a society.

⚠ Digging deeper

Although defining income, as we have seen, is not too difficult, such a definition – although necessary – is not particularly useful or meaningful. What would be useful and meaningful is the ability to think about income in terms of its **relative distribution** in our society. That is, how different levels of income are distributed within and between different social groups. If we can discover this it will go some way towards helping us understand concepts such as poverty and, of course, why some individuals and groups are more unequal than others.

To make income meaningful, therefore, we need to measure it – and this, as we are about to discover, is not as simple and straightforward as you might expect, for a couple of reasons.

- **Masking**: Some groups in society have the ability to hide their real income from the prying eyes of tax officers (and sociologists of course – although they are probably slightly more concerned about the activities of the former).

The wealthy, for example, may employ accountants to find (legal) ways of minimising their income for tax purposes. **Prem Sikka** ('Socialism in reverse', 2003), for example, estimates UK tax avoidance schemes (legal ways of avoiding taxation) cost the government £25 billion each year.

On the other hand, some groups may minimise their declared income by working in the:

- **Hidden economy**, where income is either from illegal sources (such as theft or drug-dealing) or paid 'cash-in-hand' (that is, paid directly to an employee without the money being declared for tax purposes by either the employer or employee). **Dilip Bhattacharyya** ('On the Economic Rationale of Estimating the Hidden Economy', 1999) for example, argues the existence of 'unrecorded economic activities' casts doubt on national income estimates and, by so doing, has implications for social and welfare

American property developer Leona Helmsley (pictured) once famously said 'Only little people pay taxes'

This was, of course, before she was imprisoned for four years (in addition to a $7 million fine) for failing to declare her true earnings to the US tax authorities.

policies (which we will discuss in more detail later).

Leaving these complicating factors aside, measuring 'net disposable household income' involves, according to **Simon Lunn** ('Low-Income Dynamics 1991–2001', 2003), counting, where applicable, all of the following:

- net employment earnings
- profit or loss from self-employment
- social Security benefits and tax credits
- occupational and private pensions
- investments and savings
- maintenance payments (if received directly)
- educational grants and scholarships (including loans)
- payments in kind (such as luncheon vouchers or free school meals).

Although defining and measuring income can, as I have suggested, be difficult, once we have done these things it becomes fascinating to think about how income is distributed unequally in our society across a range of social categories, beginning with social class.

Social class

Although there is no great surprise in the observation class differences in income exist (in general, the higher your social class, the higher your overall income), a couple of points can be noted.

- **Proportion**: According to **Andrew Shephard** ('Poverty and Inequality in Great Britain', 2004), income in our society is disproportionately skewed towards the higher social classes, as the following table illustrates:

Population %	Share of total UK Income
Richest 1%	8%
Richest 10%	28%
Poorest 10%	2.8%

Table 5.1 UK Income Share: 2002–2003

- **Increasing income inequality**: Over the past 40 years, higher income groups have increasingly taken a higher share of

1961 – 1979	Income rises were fastest for the lowest groups.
1979 – 1992	Income for the poorest 30% was largely static: incomes in general rose by 36%.
1992 – 1995	Income of poorest rose slightly faster than for other groups.

Source: J. Hills, 'Income and Wealth', 1998

national income. The rise in income inequality is not, however, an even upward movement. As **John Hills** ('Income and Wealth', 1998), for example, notes:

The Institute of Fiscal Studies ('Inequality, income distribution and living standards', 2000) suggests that, although 'the widely charted rise in income inequality in the 1980s was checked during the recession of the early 1990s ... inequality has since begun increasing again' and **Shephard** characterises the current situation as one of 'Increasing inequality, yet increasing redistribution' – which suggests although over the past few years there has been some redistribution of income among social classes, it has largely been from the higher classes to the middle classes.

Thinking about these ideas, we can identify a number of reasons for income inequality in the recent past.

- **Technological changes**: The development and application of computer technology over the past 25 years has had a number of consequences for income inequality in our society, related to the changing nature of employment. In the 1980s, for example, the decline in manufacturing (such as car production) and extraction industries (such as coal mining) led to an increase in (mainly working class) unemployment.

The rise in service industries (such as banking and finance services, data processing and so forth), has, on the other hand, had a couple of consequences we can note here. Firstly, the growth of relatively low-paid work in areas such as call centres and, secondly, an increase in the income of some parts of the middle class as employers pay an income premium for skills, knowledge and qualifications.

- **Trade Unions**: The decline in the number of people joining unions has lessoned their ability to raise wage levels for the poorest sections of our society.

- **Unemployment**: Although at around 1.5 million people this is far lower than in the early 1980s (where an estimated 3–4 million people were unemployed), substantial numbers of individuals and, more importantly, households, who rely for their income on state benefits are among the poorest in our society.

- **Benefit changes**: Payments were once linked to rises in income, but are now linked to price rises. In a low price-inflation economy (where prices rise slowly, if at all), the value of welfare benefits has declined in relation to work-related incomes.

- **Tax changes**: The highest rate of income tax is now 40% (for those earning over £40,000), which contrasts with rates reaching 80% – 90% in the recent past. Those on higher incomes, therefore, now get to keep more of that income.

  In addition, there are a couple of useful concepts we can apply in this context (and, as we will see, in relation to areas such as gender, age and ethnicity).

- **Vertical segregation** refers to the way the workplace is *hierarchically structured* ('top to bottom'); within occupations, for example, there is normally a grading structure whereby those at the top earn significantly more than those at the bottom (a head teacher for example, earns more than a classroom teacher).

- **Horizontal segregation**, in this context, refers to the idea different occupations have significantly different rates of pay. Middle-class occupations (such as a doctor or lawyer) are segregated from working-class occupations (such as bricklayer or road sweeper) on the basis of skills, knowledge and qualifications.

Age

Income differences, for a variety of reasons, are linked to age in two main ways.

- **Individually**: In general, the incomes of the young are lower than those of other age groups (with the possible exception of those aged 65+). One explanation here is that of *career seniority* linked to levels of skills, knowledge and qualifications. Vertical workplace segregation, for example, may be a factor in age-related income inequalities in some occupations (such as further education lecturing, where individuals move up the pay scale for each year of experience they gain).

- **Life cycle**: **Rownlinson** et al ('Wealth in Britain', 1999) argue significant income inequalities are related to life cycle differences. Thus, 'young, childless, couples' for example, generally have higher (household) incomes than young single people or young couples with children. For couples with children, **Rownlinson** et al noted three significant factors in relation to income.

  - **Single parents** had significantly lower incomes than dual parent households.

  - **Age of children**: Lower income families were more likely to have children of pre-school age.

- **Age of mother**: Where women delayed childbearing (until their early 30s, for example), this had less impact on family income levels. This is probably due to middle-class women, in particular, delaying childbearing until they have established a career to which they can return after child birth.

Rigg and **Sefton** ('Income Dynamics and the Life Cycle', 2004) also point to the way life cycle factors affect income when they note: 'Mothers typically reduce their employment activity when they have children and retirement is usually, though not always, associated with a reduction in employment activity'.

One interesting feature of the elderly and retirement is the observation that, although this group tend to have significantly lower incomes (especially single elderly people) they are often one of the *wealthiest* social groups (mainly because of outright house ownership and the value of private pensions).

Gender

Average female incomes have, historically, been lower than average male incomes. The Office for National Statistics (2004) noted, for example, the 'gender gap in average hourly pay of full-time employees' was 18% (women earn 82% of average male earnings) – a decline, it should be noted, from 26% in 1986. Although this figure hides significant differences in income across different social classes and occupations, we can note a number of reasons for the continuing difference.

- **Discrimination**: Despite progress we shouldn't discount the continued significance of overt (and covert) forms of sex discrimination within the workplace

as an explanation for gendered income inequality.

- **Vertical segregation**: Within many occupations, the top (highest-paid) positions are still predominantly filled by men. The concept of a *glass ceiling* is sometimes used to suggest the idea that, although women may not suffer overt forms of sex discrimination, they are still, by and large, unable to reach the top positions in companies in any great number.

- **Horizontal segregation** refers here to the idea many occupations are *sex segregated*, in the sense of being predominantly performed by either males or females. Female dominated occupations, for example, include areas such as teaching, nursing, shop and secretarial work and, in general, these types of work are lower paid than male-dominated occupations.

- **Dual labour markets**: Sociologists often distinguish between:

  - **primary** labour markets, involving, for example, large, technologically advanced, companies with high levels of profitability, job security, promotion, career prospects and wages and

  - **secondary** labour markets where the reverse is true – working conditions, job security and wage levels, for example, are normally considerably worse than in the primary market.

The fact that women generally tend to work in the secondary labour market, therefore, goes some way to explaining lower levels of female income. **Sommerlad** and **Sanderson** ('The Legal Labour Market and the Training Needs of

Women Returners in the United Kingdom', 1997) , for example, note: 'The primary market is conceptualised as male and characterised by male ways of working and career norms'.

Even where women are present in a primary market (as in the case of solicitors studied by **Sommerlad and Sanderson**), they occupy a *secondary position*, based on the idea of vertical workplace segregation. In other words, women in such professions generally have lower incomes than their male counterparts. Furthermore, **Sommerlad and Sanderson** argue the position of women within an organisation may be both fragmented and complicated, thus:

The secondary market is characterised by its own hierarchy: full-time women who have not taken a career break and who are childless, but who have not been accepted as 'honorary men', full-time women who have not taken a break, but who have dependent children, returners with children who are full-time and, at the bottom, returners with children, who work part-time.

Ethnicity

In relation to non-white ethnic groups we find a diversity of income levels related to specific cultural (such as family composition, size and type) and economic factors (such as type and level of employment). In an overall sense, factors such as those identified for

Discussion point: women on top? More women make the boardroom

BBC : 21/02/03

The number of women heading UK businesses has seen a sharp increase, according to the latest research from Cranfield School of Management. There are now more female directors than ever before leading UK companies listed in the FTSE 100 index.

The biggest increase was seen in executive director posts, where the number of women jumped from just 10 in 2001 to 15 in 2002.

- Women continue to hold only 7 per cent of all directorships.
- 39 of the UK's top companies still had no women directors.
- In Britain, Dame Marjorie Scardino of Pearson is still the only female chief executive of a FTSE 100 company, while 3i's Baroness Hogg is the only female chairman (sic).
- Most female boardroom staff: Marks & Spencer (27%)

Marjorie Scardino

As a class, think about and discuss the following:

- Why are more women not at 'senior management level'?
- Is it important for women to be represented at senior levels of a company (why/why not?)?
- What personal and social factors might contribute to the idea of a 'glass ceiling' in some occupations?

other social groups also apply to ethnic minorities. For example:

- **Racial discrimination** is a factor in the relatively lower levels of income experienced by minority groups compared to their majority (white) counterparts.

- **Vertical segregation** involves the fact ethnic minority group members (with notable exceptions – especially among those who have successfully established their own businesses) tend to be employed at lower organisational levels.

- **Horizontal segregation** operates by locating minority group workers in lower-paid occupations (such as nursing, for example).

- **Dual labour markets**: Ethnic minority groups are disproportionately found in secondary markets, where they experience lower job security and wages.

Against this general background of lower ethnic group incomes, **Richard Berthoud** ('Incomes of Ethnic Minorities', 1998) notes a wide diversity of income levels between different non-white groups. He identifies Pakistanis and Bangladeshis as being among the very poorest in our society for a number of reasons:

- **family size** tends to be larger than average
- **unemployment** is high among males
- **economic activity** is low amongst females
- **lower levels** of pay.

(Note how you can use the mnemonic **FUEL** to help you remember these reasons).

Indian and Chinese groups have higher levels of employment and, in general, their rates of pay – if not always household income levels – match white workers. Afro-Caribbean minority groups generally have higher levels of (male) unemployment, coupled with higher than average rates of single-parenthood. **Berthoud** notes that, although wage levels for men tend to be below those of their white counterparts, the same is *not* true for female pay rates.

Platt and **Noble's** study of ethnic diversity in Birmingham ('Race, place and poverty', 1999) confirms Berthoud's general argument; they found 'Bangladeshi, Black Caribbean, and Pakistani ethnic groups are over-represented in the low-income population'.

Defining wealth

⚠ Preparing the ground

Defining income is, you will no doubt be pleased to know, relatively straightforward compared to defining wealth. Although the Office for National Statistics (Social Trends 31: 2001) makes a relatively simple distinction:

- **income** represents a flow of resources over a period, received either in cash or in kind
- **wealth** describes the ownership of assets valued at a particular point in time.

The main (sociological) problem we have with defining wealth is deciding the relative importance of different types of **asset**, defined as the ownership of things (such as cars, houses and computers) that have an economic value – they can be sold for money, in other words. However, within this basic category there are two sub-divisions we can note:

- **Use**: If we think about economic assets in terms of *property*, this category involves the things we own for *personal use*; the home in which we live, the car we drive, the sociology books we read. The significance of ownership here is that, because it involves personal need or use, if we sell something we need, we may have to buy something similar to replace it.

  This dimension of wealth is clearly important when we are comparing cross-cultural wealth (and poverty), but less useful when we are comparing levels of wealth within a society. Part of the reason for this is a debate about whether or not the things we own for their *use value* (I need a house in which to live, a car to get me to work and sociology books to teach from) can be counted as wealth in the same way as things kept for their:

- **Value**: Property in this category refers to the things we own as *investments* – the things we accumulate for their worth and the value they will realise once sold. Stocks and shares are obvious examples here, but ownership of a second home also counts as wealth in this category. This is often called *marketable wealth*. However, just to complicate matters, a further dimension here is:

- **Non-marketable wealth** – this has neither a particular use, nor can it be sold. A *personal pension* is a classic example of this type of wealth.

In terms of the above, therefore, we can distinguish between two types of wealth.

- **Productive property** is a form of wealth that can create income (by selling something like a second home, ownership of a business, investments in things like shares and so forth).

- **Consumption property**, on the other hand, involves things owned for their use (such as a TV set). They don't create income, but they could be sold. However, they would have to be replaced if you wanted to maintain a certain standard of living.

Debates about how to define wealth are important since, as **Stephen Jenkins** ('The Distribution of Wealth', 1990) argues, if we can't easily decide how wealth should be defined and measured, this creates problems for our understanding of its distribution in society (understanding, in effect, who owns what and the social consequences of different levels of wealth ownership).

Such debates are important, however, because they shape our understanding of ideas like social inequality and poverty; if we include in our definition of wealth everything people own, the picture we get is one in which disparities of wealth (the difference between the wealthiest and poorest in our society) may not be as great as if we exclude those things owned for their use rather than their actual value.

⚠ Digging deeper

When we think about how wealth is distributed between social groups in our society we need to keep three things in mind.

- **Definitions**: As we have just seen, how you define wealth has implications for how we understand its distribution in our

Discussion point: what counts as wealth?

In small groups, use a table like the one below to identify those things we own (such as houses and cars) for their use and those things we own for their investment (income) value.

As a class, consider how debates over what constitutes wealth influence our understanding of wealth distribution in our society (for example, who are the wealthy in society?).

Wealth?	
Things owned for their use	**Things owned for their value**
Television	Paintings
Personal computer	Stocks and shares
House	Second home
Further examples	

society (if we exclude, for example, home ownership from our definition the picture we get will be of a more unequal society in terms of wealth than if we include it).

- **Measurement**: In this instance we are less concerned with what counts as wealth and more with how to reliably and validly count people's actual wealth. This is not always easy, for similar reasons to the measurement of income.

  - **Masking**: The wealthy, for personal and tax reasons, can restrict our ability to estimate their wealth accurately. This may involve moving wealth 'off-shore' (to countries with relatively lax

tax and disclosure laws) or *gifting* money and property to relatives to avoid inheritance taxes – and since much of our knowledge about the wealth of the very rich is only revealed when they die (from their wills), we need to be aware this type of source may understate the extent of individual wealth.

  - **Hidden economy**: This may involve both wealth accumulated by criminal means or, as in the above, exploiting various legal loopholes to hide actual levels of real wealth from tax authorities.

- **Process**: **Rownlinson** et al (1999) identified four major factors in the ability to accumulate wealth (not including, of course, the ability to inherit it from your parents).

  - **High income**: The highest income groups are more likely to use part of their income for investment (savings, stocks and shares, etc.). **Townsend** (2004), for example, noted that 'almost 70% of investment income is received by those with incomes above £20,000 a year'.

  - **Lifestyle** – which included attitudes towards saving (and, most importantly, the ability to save).

  - **Knowledge** relating to investment schemes and opportunities was a significant factor in wealth accumulation.

  - **Availability** of suitable savings and investment schemes.

Keeping these ideas in mind, we can make some general statements about the distribution of wealth in our society.

Social class

There is a strong relationship between social class and wealth. In terms of its general distribution, for example, the Office for National Statistics (2003) provides the following breakdown:

Total market-able wealth of:	Percentage		
	1976	1999	2001
Top 1%	21	23	23
Top 10%	50	55	56
Top 25%	71	74	75
Bottom 50%	8	6	5

Table 5.2

When we look at total marketable wealth (which includes the value of houses), the picture we get is one of:

- **inequality**: the wealthiest half of the population, for example, currently holds 95% of the nation's total wealth
- **increasing inequality**: over the past 25 years, the wealthy have taken a greater share of the nation's wealth.

If we exclude the value of dwellings, the picture is, as might be expected, one of even greater inequality. According to the Office for National Statistics (2003), the top 50% of the population control 97% of the nation's wealth and one-third of all wealth is owned – as table 5.3 illustrates – by just 1% (approximately 60,000 people if we include children) of the population.

This situation has led **Townsend** (2004) to argue for the significance of **wealth**

Market-able wealth, less value of dwellings, of:	Percentage		
	1976	1999	2001
Top 1%	29	34	33
Top 10%	57	72	72
Top 25%	73	86	86
Bottom 50%	12	2	3

Table 5.3

exclusion. The number of people with the least wealth (those with no savings or investments) increased in the twentieth century. Ten per cent of the UK population had no discernable material wealth at the end of the century (a figure that rises to 20% in the 20–34 age group).

A significant factor in the relationship between social class and wealth is:

- **Inheritance**: Not only can wealthy individuals' marketable wealth be passed, on death, to their offspring, the value of any non-marketable wealth may also be realised at this point. One consequence of this system is:
- **Elite self-recruitment**: The wealthy – by their ability to pass their wealth down the family line to their offspring – perpetuate wealth inequalities, effectively ensuring the recruitment of their sons – and, increasingly, daughters – to the ranks of the wealthy.

The existence of 'death duty' taxation also helps explain what little wealth redistribution there has been over the past 50 years in the UK; the very wealthy seek to minimise their tax liabilities by passing wealth down the family line *before* they die. Although, historically, inheritance has been through the male line (*patrilineal descent*), the increasing likelihood of all children being included may slightly dilute the overall wealth of the very wealthiest in the population by spreading wealth across a number of different children.

Age

If we think about age-related wealth in terms of an individual's *life cycle*, over their lifetime people are more likely to build up marketable wealth, which suggests wealth inequality is built into our economic system. **Rownlinson** et al (1999) noted how wealth increased with age, peaking in the 60–69 age group. The least wealthy life cycle groups were 'young single people (under the age of 35) and lone parents'.

Gender

Although, as I have noted, in the past wealth was generally passed down the male line, this practice is not as prevalent as it once was. However, in terms of *wealth creation*, men are much more likely to feature among the self-made wealthy than women (something related to economic practices and opportunities – we could think about how vertical and horizontal workplace segregation apply here).

Ethnicity

Among non-white ethnic groups, those of Asian origin (especially Pakistani origins) are most likely to feature in the least wealthy 10% of the UK population. Those of Chinese origin, on the other hand, are most likely – among all ethnic minority groups – to appear in the wealthiest 10% of the population.

Region

Anne Green ('The Geography of Poverty and Wealth', 1994) noted changes in the traditional distribution of wealth in the UK during the 1980s – areas formerly dependent on large-scale extraction industries (such as coal mining) and manufacturing saw a general decline in their share of the nation's wealth; the South East and London (where the commercial focus is on *service industries*) saw their proportionate share of wealth increase. This process has continued into the twenty-first century.

Defining poverty

⚠ Preparing the ground

Although you won't thank me for this, it is probably fair to warn you our ability to define poverty presents us with some subtly different problems compared to our ability to define concepts such as wealth and income. The good news is there are two basic types of definition we can use (I will leave the bad news about them until you've understood what's involved).

Absolute poverty

This definition is based on the idea we can identify the minimum conditions for the maintenance of human life. **Seebohm Rowntree** (*Poverty, A Study of Town Life*, 1901), for example, was one of the first to identify a minimum subsistence level, below which people were to be considered poor.

He also distinguished between what he called:

- **primary poverty** – a situation in which individuals or families lacked the means to provide the basic necessities of life (food, clothing and shelter, for example) and

- **secondary poverty** – a situation in which, although people have sufficient means to sustain life, they fail to do so adequately because they spend at least part of their income on things that aren't essential (a classic example here might be spending on things like alcohol and tobacco).

In this respect, we can think of this type of definition as being based on human *biological* needs. A more modern version of absolute poverty, however, might be evidenced by **Gordon** and **Townsend** et al's study (*Child Poverty in the Developing World*, 2003), which defined poverty on the basis of seven basic needs, as shown in the table below.

However we specifically define absolute forms of poverty, this type of general definition rests on the ability to draw a poverty line by which to identify basic human requirements (in the manner of **Gordon** and **Townsend** et al's study). In basic terms, if you do not have these things, you are poor.

As we will see in a moment, there are advantages and disadvantages to defining and measuring poverty in absolute terms. However, we need to note a significant problem (one that led to the idea of defining poverty in **relative** terms – something that is discussed further below) with absolute definitions, namely the concept of **minimum needs**. Although human life has certain minimum needs (a given amount of food and water each day, for example), this type of 'absolute definition' is not particularly useful when it's applied to societies (such as Britain in the twenty-first century) where very few – if any – people are unable to meet these 'minimum needs'.

Gordon and **Townsend** et al's study, for example, found 35% of children in the Middle East & North Africa were in absolute poverty – applying the same measures in their study to children in Britain would probably conclude no – or very little – poverty existed in our society. Although in absolute terms this may be true, it is not a very useful way to think about poverty, mainly because there are considerable differences in general living standards in our society – some people, in basic terms, have more of the 'good things in life' than others – and we need to understand the significance of this type of difference. For this reason, an alternative way of measuring poverty focuses on the following.

Basic Needs	'Child Poverty in the Developing World', 2003
1. Clean water 2. Sanitation 3. Shelter 4. Education 5. Information 6. Food 7. Health	'If the household or individual does not have access to a particular basic need, they are defined as "deprived". Those who are deprived of two or more of the seven basic need indicators are defined as being in "absolute poverty"'. Townsend Centre for International Poverty Research [http://www.bris.ac.uk/poverty/child%20poverty.html]

Relative poverty

If, at least in its original formulation, the concept of absolute poverty focused on the idea of *biological* needs, the concept of relative poverty – articulated through the work of **Peter Townsend** ('Measuring Poverty', 1954) and **Townsend** and **Abel-Smith** ('The Poor and the Poorest', 1965) – added the idea of **cultural needs** to the definition. In other words, **Townsend** (among others) argued poverty in affluent (wealthy) societies wasn't simply a matter of biology – someone should be considered poor if they lacked the resources to participate fully in the social and cultural life of the society in which they lived.

This type of definition introduced the idea poverty was related in some way to the 'normal and acceptable' standard of living in any society (whatever this may be). **Mack** and **Lansley** (*Poor Britain*, 1984) express this idea quite neatly when they note: 'Poverty can be seen in terms of an enforced lack of socially perceived necessities'. The key idea here is 'socially perceived'; what one society at one particular time sees as being 'unnecessary' may, in another society or at another time, be seen as essential.

By considering poverty in terms of cultural needs, therefore, we can accommodate ideas of:

- **Cross-cultural differences**: Different societies, for example, have different living standards – life in East Africa, for example, is not the same as life in East Anglia.

- **Historical differences**: In our society, life is very different for the majority of the population today to what it was 200 years ago. What may have been considered an acceptable living standard at the start of the nineteenth century would probably not be considered acceptable today.

- **Demographic differences** takes the idea of *cultural relativity* further by noting that, even within the same society, there are differences between social groups (such as young people and the elderly). A 'normal and acceptable' living standard for a teenager may not necessarily be viewed in the same way by an old age pensioner.

Growing it yourself: getting by?

In small groups, use the following table as a template for deciding what the biological and, more significantly, cultural needs are for people in our society.

As a class, compare your different lists and, after a full and frank discussion (otherwise known as an argument), decide what you believe the minimum biological and cultural needs are for our society.

When thinking about cultural needs, think about the things you feel people really *must* have to participate fully in the cultural life of our society.

Our Biological Needs	Our Cultural Needs
Enough food to prevent starvation	Telephone Shoes

Digging deeper

In the following sections we are going to look at the concept of poverty in more detail, so we're not going to think about things like the extent of poverty in our society just yet. Instead, we can look a little more closely at how poverty is defined and measured and the respective advantages and disadvantages of such definitions and measurements.

We can begin by noting poverty (unlike concepts such as income and wealth) is not something we can directly measure, since it is not immediately quantifiable. To *operationalise* (define and measure) the concept we need to identify certain *indicators* of poverty (in the way you've just done in the previous activity, for example).

In this respect, all definitions of poverty (either absolute or relative) are essentially based on the same idea, namely we can – somewhere and somehow – draw a *poverty line*, below which people are to be considered poor and above which they are to be considered not poor. The argument, therefore, is not particularly over whether absolute or relative definitions are superior or inferior (since both types, ultimately contain an absolute definition somewhere along the line). Rather, the argument over definitions falls in two main categories.

- **Indicators**: The main question here is whether we use *biological* or *cultural* indicators (or perhaps both) as the basis for any definition: *Absolute definitions* are more likely to use the former (because they provide a basic yardstick against which to measure human needs in general), whereas *relative definitions* are more likely to use the latter (because they provide a flexible set of indicators that can be applied to specific societies at different times).

- **Measurement**: Related to the above, we have to decide what features of social life are to be used as indicators of poverty.

Relative definitions, for example, use a range of different indicators depending on the preferences of their creators – an idea we can briefly outline in the following way.

Measuring relative forms of poverty involves varying levels of complexity and depends, to some extent, on what the researcher is trying to achieve and the resources they have available. We can get a flavour for the various ways of defining and measuring poverty by identifying a variety of different models using a basic classification suggested by **Stewart** et al ('Everyone agrees we need poverty reduction, but not what this means: does this matter?', 2003).

- **Monetary** models involve using income (either directly or in terms of the ability to buy certain goods and services defined as 'necessities') as the basic definition and measure of poverty. For example:

  - **Households below average income**: In the UK, this measure sets a relative household poverty line at 60% of *median net income* (the median is found by arranging income values in order and then identifying the one in the middle – if the median income was £100 per week, for example, the poverty line would be drawn at £60 per week).

  In the European Community, however, a figure of 50% of median net income is used as a poverty line – which demonstrates how problems of definition may occur even when we use a relatively simple monetary indicator of poverty.

- **The World Bank** uses the formula of '1$ a day' (approximately 60p) as the economic measure of world poverty – if your income is above this level you are not classified as poor.

- **Budget standards: Tom Startup** ('Poor Measures', 2002) advocates a measure of poverty based on the idea of the cost of a 'basket of goods and services'. This involves identifying basic biological and social necessities, estimating their cost and setting a poverty line at this level. A variation on this idea involves:

- **Basic necessities surveys: Rick Davies** ('Beyond Wealth Ranking', 1998) argues poverty can be defined as 'the lack of basic necessities'. However, what these necessities may be is not pre-defined by the researcher; rather, they are identified during the research process.

  The researcher may, for example, start with a list of items (such as a television) and events (the right to an education, for example) and these are accepted, rejected or modified by respondents as they see fit. These approaches are similar to the **participatory models approach** (see below) but are usually classified as *consensual approaches* to defining poverty because they're based on a *popular consensus* about what constitutes 'basic necessities'.

- **Capability** approaches focus on what **Sen** (*Development as Freedom*, 1999) has termed 'indicators of the freedom to live a valued life'. In other words, they focus on understanding poverty as a set of *lived experiences* (things people can or cannot

do) rather than a simple monetary approach. What these capabilities may be differs both historically and cross-culturally and involves identifying a range of indicators of deprivation (the ways some people are deprived of the things a society takes for granted as being part of a normal and acceptable standard of living). We can, for example, note a couple of capability-based concepts.

- **Relative deprivation**: Writers such as **Peter Townsend** (*Poverty in the UK*, 1979) and **Mack** and **Lansley** (1985) used a range of different indicators of deprivation to measure people's quality of life. Townsend, for example, included things like household amenities (a refrigerator and fixed bath, for example), how often people went out to visit friends or for a meal, as well as the type of food people bought and ate.

  Townsend's 'Material Deprivation Score' analyses (1991 and 2001) for the National Public Health Service for Wales are more recent examples of this approach, using a simplified index of deprivation based on four census-based variables, namely the percentages of households with no car, not owner occupied, unemployed, and overcrowded.

- **Indices of deprivation**, although measuring a range of deprivation indicators in a similar way to the ones noted above, involve broader estimates of people's overall quality of life. The **Social Disadvantage Research Centre** ('English Indices of Deprivation', 2004), for example, used indicators such as levels of income, employment and experienced crime (among other factors) to create an *index of material deprivation*.

The main difference between the two (similar) approaches is their focus: *relative deprivation* approaches tend to focus on individuals and households, whereas *indices of deprivation* approaches broaden the scope to include wider community factors (such as levels of crime in an area).

- **Social exclusion** approaches represent a more recent way of thinking about how poverty and deprivation affect people and the society in which they live. They focus, as you might expect, on trying to measure the various ways people are excluded from participation in the activities and experiences we take for granted as part of our general lifestyle.

A range of indicators can be used to measure social exclusion. For example, 'Opportunity for All: Tackling Poverty and Social Exclusion', 2003 (Department of Works and Pensions) identified a variety of ideas (levels of rural poverty, unemployment, urban deprivation, child poverty, health care and so forth) that, taken together, represent some of the ways people are socially excluded.

Palmer et al ('Monitoring poverty and social exclusion', 2003), on the other hand, used indicators related specifically to different age groups (children, youth, adults and the elderly) as a way of measuring exclusion. Within each group they looked at different factors (such as birth weight and exclusion from school for children, winter death rates, levels of anxiety and access to services for the elderly) to arrive at a comprehensive 'index of exclusion'.

- **Participatory** approaches are similar to *consensual approaches* in that they are based on the idea of asking people to define what they mean by poverty. However, as **Bennett** and **Roberts** ('From input to influence', 2004) argue, a major difference here is that the *meaning* of poverty is constructed through 'discussions with people with past or present experience of poverty'. This approach, they argue, takes control over definitions away from governments and researchers and returns it to the people with direct, first-hand experience of the matter.

A similar *ethnographic approach* (allowing the poor to 'speak for themselves') was advocated by **Beresford** et al ('Poverty First Hand', 1999) as a means of *understanding*, as opposed to simply *representing*, poverty. The main objective of such approaches, therefore, is to discover ways of eliminating poverty and social exclusion based on how the people involved actually experience such things.

Although this type of approach can be criticised (it's not just the poor, for example, who have an interest in both defining and eliminating poverty), **Robert Chambers** ('Poverty and Livelihoods', 1995), defends participatory approaches by asking: 'Whose reality counts? The reality of the few in centres of power? Or the reality of the many poor at the periphery?' He justifies such approaches by arguing they have the potential to bring 'poor people's problems and priorities' to the attention of national policy makers.

To complete this section we will look briefly at a number of advantages and disadvantages to absolute and relative definitions of poverty.

Growing it yourself: constructing exclusion

This exercise builds on the one you've just done, using a participatory approach to understanding poverty. In the previous exercise you looked generally at minimum biological and cultural needs for our society. In this exercise you are required to identify the kinds of things (such as personal use of a television) and behaviours (going out once a week, perhaps?) you consider essential for full and active participation in the 'normal lifestyle' for *your age group*.

In small groups, copy the following table and use it to identify 'essential objects and behaviours'. Once you've done this, discuss your ideas with the rest of the class to arrive at a 'participatory picture' of inclusion/exclusion for your age group.

Age Group Essentials	
Objects	Behaviours
Personal stereo	Going to cinema one a month
Further examples	

As a further piece of research, ask people of a *different* age group for their views on the essentials of a 'normal lifestyle' for their group; if you compare the different views, you will arrive at a picture of how different groups in our society may see themselves as having different lifestyle needs.

If, for the sake of argument, we consider **absolute** forms of poverty in terms of indicators related to human biological needs

we can note a number of advantages to this form of measurement.

- **Standardisation**: The basic definition of poverty never changes, since human beings, wherever they live in the world, all have the same basic needs in terms of the things required to sustain life. Thus, when we measure poverty we are always applying the same set of rules. This makes measurement:

- **Objective**: Once we have decided what constitutes minimum or essential human needs, our definition – and hence measurement – doesn't change. **Jane Falkingham** ('A Profile of Poverty in Tajikistan', 2000), for example, notes absolute definitions are based on objective norms; we are always, in other words, applying the same definition of poverty wherever and whenever we try to measure it. This, of course, makes the concept:

- **Transferable**: Once we have identified norms that define poverty, they can be consistently applied across all societies, which allows us to compare levels of poverty on a global scale, regardless of different levels of social and technological development within different societies.

- **Social change**: Because biological needs don't change over time, absolute measures allow us to track historical changes to the levels of poverty in the same society.

- **Poverty**: This type of definition does exactly what it says on the tin – it measures poverty. It doesn't try to measure concepts like *deprivation*, *relative deprivation* or *social inclusion* and *exclusion*. It has the advantage, therefore, of being simple, clear, consistent and easily understandable as a way of measuring poverty.

Having said this, *absolute approaches* do have several *disadvantages*, which we can note in the following terms.

- **Basic needs**: Historical and cross-cultural differences in terms of living standards make it difficult to apply a standard 'biological needs' test of poverty in any meaningful way. Using a 'minimum subsistence level' test in modern Britain, for example, would, as I have previously suggested, result in very little (if any) poverty being found.

- **Social change**: Related to the above idea, it's clear, in our society, ideas about what is and what isn't an 'acceptable standard of living' have changed – even over the course of the past 50 years. As a society changes, therefore, concepts of poverty also need to develop to reflect these changes. Thus, we need to think about:

- **Poverty** itself, in the sense of what it means to us as a society. Some critics of relative measures argue, as we will see, relative definitions measure things like social inequality, deprivation and exclusion rather than poverty. In historical terms, however, it is clear that as living standards rise people's expectations about acceptable lifestyles change – and concepts of poverty (however defined) also need to change to reflect the fact we now live in a very different type of society to the one that existed 50 or 100 years ago. If societies and individuals change, should we keep to definitions of poverty that belong to a world that has disappeared?

- **Objectivity**: There are two points we can usefully make here. Firstly, any attempt to draw a poverty line – even one as basic as 'minimum nutritional needs' – cannot be truly objective. This follows because the concept of poverty itself is a subjective condition; if you think about it, my definition of 'minimum needs' may be different to your definition – and we have no objective way of choosing between them.

Related to this idea is the fact there is no such thing as a minimum level of human need. A child, for example, will have different minimum needs to an adult and an adult male manual worker will have different minimum needs to an adult male office worker. As these examples demonstrate, even apparently objective definitions of poverty may have a cultural (subjective) basis.

Secondly, simply because we may prefer *quantifiable* – as opposed to *qualitative* – ways of defining and measuring poverty, doesn't make the former any better – or indeed worse – than the latter. Ultimately, concepts of poverty reflect whatever a society and its members believe is an acceptable standard of living – which leads to the idea of **relative differentiation**.

Although, on the face of things, identifying needs doesn't appear to be a problem, a couple of questions arise. Firstly, as **Falkingham** (2000) notes, what exactly are people's 'needs' (are they merely biological or do they extend into cultural areas such as education)?; secondly, on what level do we measure need? For example, do we measure it in terms of individuals, families or households, or do we extend this to include communities? Alternatively, as I have just suggested, an elderly adult has different needs to a child or a pregnant woman. In this respect, it's not simply a matter of defining a set of 'human needs' and applying them uncritically to a population that is *relatively differentiated* (that is, a population with different biological and cultural needs).

Relative definitions of poverty, on the other hand, have a number of advantages, leading from – and reflecting to some extent – the criticisms we have made of absolute definitions.

- **Realism**: Relative definitions – even the simplest ones that focus on income or budgetary requirements – more realistically reflect the nature of modern lifestyles; life in our society is, arguably, more than just the pursuit of a minimum standard of living. This follows because of:

- **Social differentiation**: As I have suggested, although we are all human this doesn't make us the same; on the contrary, people are different in a number of (socially constructed) ways. If such differences – even if we minimally consider them in terms of class, age, gender, ethnicity and region – are real, it follows any definition of poverty must attempt to reflect and capture the richness of people's social behaviour – an idea that leads us to:

- **Complexity**: If our society is a complex place, considered in terms of culture and lifestyle for example, any concept of poverty – expressed perhaps in terms of relative forms of deprivation and social exclusion – must, of necessity, be complex. Relative definitions, because

they attempt to measure a variety of different dimensions of life and lifestyle, are more likely than absolute definitions to accurately represent people's behaviour, attitudes and expectations.

In addition, therefore, we need to be aware poverty is not simply about being *economically poor* – it must also be considered in terms of things like access to education and health, general life chances, risk of illness and so forth.

Although relative definitions have significant advantages, in terms of how they conceive, theorise and attempt to measure poverty, the range of different measures and perspectives involved make for some significant *disadvantages* we can outline as follows.

- **Meaning**: **Simon Maxwell** ('The Meaning and Measurement of Poverty', 1999) notes how, over the years, the meaning of 'poverty' has evolved – not just in terms of ideas like deprivation and exclusion, but also in terms of more specific ideas about what is actually being measured. He notes, for example, seven different basic meanings in current use:
  - income or consumption poverty
  - human (under)development
  - ill-being
  - (lack of) capability and functioning
  - vulnerability
  - livelihood unsustainability
  - lack of basic needs.

Such diversity of meaning makes it difficult to know what, if anything, is being measured using different types of relative definition. In addition, the question arises here of who decides the meaning of poverty? What happens, for example, in a situation where someone can be objectively defined as 'poor' but they refuse to consider themselves poor? This raises the problem of:

- **Subjectivity**: Although, to some extent, true of all ways of defining and measuring poverty, relative definitions and measurements raise a number of significant problems. For example:

  - **Objective measurements** used as indicators of relative poverty (such as in income or budget approaches), raise the question of who decides where a poverty line is drawn (as we have seen in relation to the difference between UK and European Community income-based definitions).

  - **Consensual definitions** have similar problems – people may lack knowledge and experience of poverty when they're asked to decide what features of social life represent 'normal' and 'acceptable' aspects of our general standard of living.

  - **Ethnographic (participatory) definitions** involve the basic problem that, in order to involve 'the poor' in the creation of definitions of poverty you have to categorise people as poor in the first place (which sort of limits the effectiveness of such studies).

- **Differentiation**: In the same way that a differentiated population creates problems for absolute definitions, the same is also true for relative definitions unless they are sufficiently clearly defined to reflect possible differences in population expectations and standards. This means that:

- **Indicators of poverty** cannot be easily standardised. Cross-culturally and historically there will be different living standards that need to be reflected in the indicators used.

- **Poverty**: A pertinent criticism of relative definitions is they lose sight of poverty, as such, and instead become measures of *social inequality*. In other words, in an affluent society people can enjoy a relatively comfortable standard of living – yet still be classed as 'relatively poor'. The problem, in this respect, is that poverty becomes a function of *definition* rather than *fact*; that is, in every society where social inequality exists – no matter what the general standard of living in that society – relative poverty will always, by definition, exist.

The fact different definitions of poverty exist should alert you to the idea that different explanations for the existence and distribution of poverty (and income and wealth for that matter) have been put forward by a variety of writers working within different social and economic perspectives. The next thing we have to do, therefore, is examine a range of such explanations.

Explaining Inequality

Introduction

This section focuses on the concept of social inequality – considered in terms of the ideas introduced in the first section of this chapter – and it involves outlining and examining a range of different explanations for the distribution of poverty, wealth and income between different social groups. In this respect we can consider a number of different perspectives on equality, firstly by outlining their key theoretical points and, subsequently, by applying these ideas to a specific understanding of inequality.

Functionalist perspectives

 Preparing the ground

Thinking about social inequality from a Functionalist viewpoint, we can identify a number of key ideas that inform this general perspective, the first of which, unsurprisingly, is that of **function**. We know, from previous work we have done on this perspective, that if something exists in society it does so because it performs some important task or function. The question here, therefore, is what are the functions of inequality?

WARM UP: THE FUNCTIONS OF INEQUALITY

Using the following table as a template, suggest ways social inequality (considered in terms of three key indicators – income, wealth and poverty) might be functional for society (I've given you a couple of ideas to get you thinking).

Type of Inequality	
Income and Wealth	Poverty
Motivates people to perform necessary work	The poor do society's 'dirty work'

To understand why inequality is functional, we need to understand the basis of inequality from a functionalist perspective. In this respect, we can note modern societies are:

- **Complex systems**: That is, they involve a huge range of political, economic and social roles that have to be successfully filled and performed if society is to both function (or exist) and develop. For example, focusing on economic roles, you'll be aware of a vast number of roles (or jobs) that need to be done; to take a few at random, we need doctors, police officers, traffic wardens, dentists, people to empty our dustbins, shelf-stackers, lifeguards and, last but by no means least, burger-flippers in McDonald's. In this respect, the working world is:

- **Differentiated** in terms of roles requiring different levels of skill, training, expertise and knowledge. If this is the case, societies have to find ways of allowing people to demonstrate they have the skills necessary to perform certain jobs – if work roles were simply allocated randomly, or on the basis of who you know we'd have a situation in which anyone who fancied being a dentist could set themselves up as such. I don't know about you, but personally if someone's going to put a drill in my mouth I'd prefer it to be someone trained in dentistry, rather than a bloke who used to be a garage mechanic. For Functionalists, the best way to allocate work roles is through the 'proven merits' of each individual – hence it's important society is:

- **Meritocratic**: That is, people are required to demonstrate their abilities (by working hard in school, for example) in order to qualify themselves for certain roles. Although **Davis** and **Moore** ('Some Principles of Stratification', 1945) have argued some roles are more 'functionally-necessary' than others – therefore, we have to ensure the best people fill them by giving them incentives and rewards (such as higher pay) – this isn't necessarily the case. Even if we leave aside the idea all roles are functionally necessary in some way – if they weren't they wouldn't exist – on what basis can we say the woman who sweeps my street is less functionally important than a bank manager?

If society is *meritocratic* (and it's not necessarily true that it is – but bear with me for the moment), it must therefore be based on:

- **Competition**, which develops in society for the performance of particular roles; some roles are more desirable, fulfilling and, of course well paid than others (which is a bit of a chicken-and-egg situation – do people compete for high paid jobs *because* they are well paid, or do they pay well because there's a lot of competition for them?). Stacking shelves in Sainsbury's is something most people could do after about five minutes training; learning how to carry out a heart transplant probably takes a little longer. Economic inequality, therefore, develops 'naturally' out of the:

- **Social division of labour**: As work is differentiated in terms of, for example, skills, qualifications and income levels, societies develop hierarchically (in the sense some jobs come to be seen as better than others).

Thus, for traditional functionalism, economic inequality is both functional and necessary for society – and to understand how inequalities of income, wealth and poverty are functional, we need to dig a little deeper.

⚠ Digging deeper

Perhaps the classic modern Functionalist statement concerning the functions of social inequality is that of **Herbert Gans** ('The Uses of Poverty', 1971), when he argued inequalities of income, wealth and poverty had '13 main functions' which we can group, for our convenience, into four main categories.

- **Economic functions** relate to ideas such as the poor being available to do 'society's dirty work' – the various menial tasks (emptying bins, flipping burgers and so forth) someone has to be prepared to do. The presence of a group of low-waged poor people also creates employment for middle class professionals (such as social workers, for example).

- **Social functions** cover areas such as *norm maintenance* – the poor 'can be identified and punished as alleged or real deviants in order to uphold the legitimacy of conventional norms'. The fact the poor are criminalised more than other social classes also, according to Gans, serves a *boundary-setting* function – it shows people where the limits of acceptable and unacceptable behaviour lie.

- **Cultural functions** include things like 'guaranteeing the status' of those who are not poor ('In every hierarchical society, someone has to be at the bottom') and as a guarantor of upward social mobility for those 'just above them in the class hierarchy'.

- **Political functions**: The poor, being relatively powerless (and less likely to vote than other social groups) can be scapegoated in various ways (for their laziness, lack of sexual morality, criminality and so forth.) Their existence also guarantees the existence of political parties to 'represent their interests', thereby providing a democratic counterweight to political parties representing the middle and upper classes.

While it is sometimes difficult to know when **Gans** is being serious and when he's taking the opportunity to poke fun at such arguments ('the poor help to keep the aristocracy busy, thus justifying its continued existence', for example), his ideas do give us a general flavour of the way Functionalists address the (sociological) problem of social inequality.

However, they are also indicative of what **Bolender** ('Robert King Merton', 2004) terms *neofunctionalism*; that is, developments in Functionalist thinking in the latter part of the twentieth century. **Gans**, for example, doesn't necessarily see poverty as beneficial to 'society as a whole' (although it may serve this purpose – poverty's political functions may encourage the democratic political process, for example); rather, he explains it in terms of how it is:

- **functional** for some groups in society (notably the middle and upper classes) and

- **dysfunctional** to other groups (the poor being the most obvious example here).

New Right perspectives

 ## Preparing the ground

In many ways the basic ideas underpinning New Right perspectives on social inequalities reflect those of the more basic forms of Functionalist argument, in that inequalities of wealth and income are generally seen as both beneficial to, and necessary for, the health of any given society. However, New Right theory has a number of distinctive strands relating to both the way they see the relationship between society and the individual and how they view inequality. On this basis, we can start to understand New Right perspectives in terms of:

- **Individualism**: This idea sits at the very heart of New Right thinking about the nature of both people and society; ideas about individual liberty and the freedom to pursue economic goals (such as becoming wealthy) are fundamental to this perspective. From these basic concepts spring a range of ideas about 'human nature' and social organisation – the former being based on ideas about:

- **Rationality**: People are viewed as rational beings who make *informed* choices about their behaviour. In this respect, individuals, not governments, are best placed to make these choices based on a:

- **Cost/benefit analysis**: That is, before they do something, rational, calculating, individuals weigh up the possible *costs* of their behaviour against any likely *benefits*; if the benefits outweigh the costs they will do something, but if the reverse is true, they won't (think about this in relation to crime; if the likelihood of being caught is high (the cost) this may outweigh any possible benefits and so the individual remains law-abiding). For this aspect of 'human nature' to operate effectively, social organisation has to be based, as with Functionalism, on:

- **Competition**: This is a vital aspect of economic organisation because it creates innovation, progress and wealth. Without economic competition, it is argued, society would simply stagnate – and such competition is guaranteed by the existence of:

- **Free markets**: Ideally, companies and individuals must be allowed to compete against each other, free from 'outside interference' – meaning organisations like Trade Unions and the state (the government and Civil Service bureaucracies, for example). Any interference in the workings of the market distorts competition and makes them less efficient, which is why New Right perspectives tend to be against:

- **Welfare systems** (such as the Welfare State in Britain). Any form of government-based welfare (such as unemployment or housing benefits) places limits on competition because it protects people from the consequences of their behaviour. For example, if I choose not to have children, why should I have to pay, through higher taxation, to educate other people's children? In other words, if you choose to have children you should, the New Right argue, take responsibility for ensuring they are educated.

We can apply this idea to economic behaviour generally. For example, faced with a decision about whether to accept a low paid job or receive a similar (or greater) level of government welfare benefit, any *rational person* would choose the latter. The consequence of this may be companies competing in global markets simply relocate to countries (such as India) where wages are lower. Not only does this contribute to higher levels of unemployment, it effectively creates a group of people who become 'unemployable'. If low skill, low paid work is exported to other countries, the existence of state-financed welfare systems simply means we create a group of people who have little or no incentive to work; it creates, in other words, a:

- **Dependency culture** – a situation where an increasing number of individuals and their families literally *depend* on government welfare for their existence. This, in turn, creates what New Right theorists such as **Charles Murray** (*Losing ground: American social policy, 1950–1980*, 2001) have termed an:

- **Underclass** – people who exist 'outside' the normal limits of society. They represent a group who effectively fail to participate in the day-to-day activity of the society in which they live. Such people, according to writers such as **Murray**, are dependent on state benefits, have little or no economic incentive to work, fail to take responsibility for their families or children and are over-represented in criminal activity.

This idea, in some respects, reflects Functionalist notions of *social solidarity* – the idea people need to feel connected to and responsible for others. The underclass, because it is not integrated into mainstream society through mechanisms such as work, is effectively excluded from the normal workings of mainstream society – except, of course, in terms of how their behaviour (high levels of illegitimacy, child and family neglect and criminality) impact on the quality of life in mainstream society.

⚠ Digging deeper

In terms of the above type of analysis, it is not difficult to understand how New Right perspectives generally view inequalities in income, wealth and poverty. We can outline these ideas in terms of four general categories.

- **Economic reasons**: Because, as I have suggested, people are seen as rational beings, they need incentives to behave in particular ways; if, as a society, people want a certain standard of living (one that involves comfortable housing, personal transport, the latest technology and so forth) they have to be *motivated* to work – and this is achieved, for the New Right, through individual responsibility, competition and the potential rewards of economic success.

A high income, for example, is a reward for working hard at school and university to get the qualifications required to become a doctor or a lawyer; in a meritocratic society, everyone has the chance to achieve these things – some choose to pursue such goals while others choose not to. The important point here, of course, is the incentive is present – people, in other words, have to be allowed to reap the rewards of their success (and, consequently, suffer the pains of their lack of ability, application or effort).

- **Social reasons**: For the New Right, societies are *moral systems* in the sense they hang together on the basis of how people view their relationship to others. Inequality, for example, is considered 'fair' if people are allowed the opportunity to be successful and, in so doing, keep the fruits of their efforts. Someone who, for example, 'creates wealth' by employing others should, in this respect, be allowed to benefit from their hard work, dedication and sacrifice. Welfare systems provided by governments, on the other hand, are *morally wrong* because they encourage people to live off the work of others.

Inequality, therefore, has social benefits because it encourages people to work to support themselves and their dependents (the family system is a crucial component of New Right thinking – it represents the 'social glue' that binds people together in productive work). Poverty, in this respect, is generally viewed in absolute *terms* (although, somewhat confusingly perhaps, it also has a *relative* dimension) in the sense that in modern, Western, societies (such as Europe and the USA) few – if any – people experience the absolute forms of poverty characteristic of some areas of Africa and South America. Poverty is, in this respect, relative for Western societies – it is simply part of the price that has to be paid for a dynamic, wealth-creating system.

- **Cultural reasons** for poverty (in particular), are bound up in the actions of governments (see below) in terms of the way their behaviour both enhances and restricts the expression of individual choices. In some ways the concept of choice (about whether to pursue educational qualifications, for example) is bound up in values, in the sense of people making rational decisions about how to behave (to marry and start a family, for example – or not as the case may be). The choices people make about their lives, therefore, affect their behaviour and help to explain the social distribution of income, wealth and poverty.

Bane and **Ellwood** (*Welfare Realities: From Rhetoric to Reform*, 1994) identify three main ways the choices people make relate to poverty and, by extension, inequality.

- **Rational choices**, as I have already suggested, involve the idea people decide how to behave. They 'survey the options available to them and make a rational choice of the option that will bring them the greatest satisfaction'.

- **Expectancy choices** involve the idea 'that people make choices based on whether they expect the decision to have the desired outcome'. If a society, for example, encourages people to study and work (because they see the future benefits for both themselves and their family) this is the route most people will choose.

- **Cultural choices** relate to the culture within which people live. Middle-class cultures, for example, tend to stress values such as deferred gratification, the importance of education as a means of social mobility and the like. Lower-class cultures, according to the New Right, tend to develop a *fatalistic* acceptance of poverty – they develop into a dependency culture or a culture of poverty; a cultural situation which

locks people into poverty. As Bane and Ellwood put it: 'If sanctions against a behaviour like unwed pregnancy are missing, it will occur'.

- **Political reasons**: For the New Right, the role of government is mainly one of creating the conditions under which people can successfully – and fairly – compete against each other for economic rewards. In this respect, government should support strong (dual-parent) families (and, by extension, *discourage* the development of single-parent families) and maintain the safety of citizens through law and order policies that allow people to go about their lives in relative comfort and safety. Governments should not involve themselves in welfare since this, it is argued, actually contributes to increased social and economic inequality in a number of ways – such as:

  - **Discouraging individual enterprise and responsibility**: Welfare, for example, has to be paid for by taxing those in work, leaving them with less of their own money and restricting their ability to provide for both themselves and their dependents. State welfare systems increase *social fragmentation* by creating resentment of the poor.

  - **Encouraging dependency** amongst the poor by locking them into a welfare system they either don't want to escape from (for reasons already noted) or cannot escape from because they would earn less money by working than if they remained on welfare benefits.

A crucial idea here, according to **Murray** (1984), is 'the destruction of status *rewards*'; as he puts it, although 'not everyone can be rich, a person can enjoy "status" by being a hard worker or a secure provider for his or her children'. If government policies have the effect of removing status differences and rewards, therefore, social problems develop.

Social democratic perspectives

Preparing the ground

These perspectives (think in terms of New Labour in Britain since 1997) share a number of ideas with both Functionalist and New Right explanations about the distribution of wealth, income and poverty (for example, the view some form of economic inequality is both necessary and desirable); where these perspectives diverge, however, is in relation to poverty, the social characteristics of the poor and – in a significant departure from New Right thinking – the role of the state in welfare provision.

In Britain, some social democratic approaches have attracted the label of a 'Third Way' (see, for example, *The Third Way: The Renewal of Social Democracy*, 1998 and *The Third Way and its Critics*, 2000, both by **Anthony Giddens**); in other words, they seek to develop policies and explanations that sit between, on the one hand, the New Right belief that social inequality is desirable and 'Old Left' (or Marxist) belief that it is undesirable.

In this respect, social democratic perspectives tread the line between, on the one hand, seeing income and wealth inequalities as positive features of any society (for reasons we will explore in a

The Third Way?

moment) and, on the other, seeing too great a level of inequality as being damaging for both society (in terms of social exclusion, the waste of human resources and the like) and the individual, considered in terms of the problems and suffering caused by poverty. In general, therefore, we can identify the key components of this perspective in terms of five main ideas:

- **Meritocracy**: Inequality, from this perspective, is desirable as long as it is based on merit. Those who work hard, use their abilities constructively and so forth should be allowed to accumulate private wealth and achieve higher incomes. Differences between individuals and groups in terms of income, therefore, stem from this idea of merit; people have different skills and levels of qualifications, for example, and differential rewards serve to motivate people to acquire the skills and knowledge needed by different economic sectors (the dedicated and talented are thus rewarded for their efforts by higher incomes). The ability to accumulate wealth also, of course, produces income differences, since the rich are allowed to live off the (unearned) income of their wealth.

Tony Blair, in a speech to the Institute for Public Policy Research (1999), expressed these ideas quite nicely when he argued there needed to be 'Ladders of opportunity for those from all backgrounds, no more ceilings that prevent people from achieving the success they merit'. These views are, in turn, related to the idea of:

- **Competition** based on people having different talents, aptitudes and abilities that, by and large, they are free to use in whatever way society deems legal. However, where social democratic perspectives take leave of New Right perspectives is over the idea of a:

- **Mixed Market Economy**: That is, an economy characterised by both *private* and *public* (state owned) economic activity. Economic ownership, in this type of economy, is mainly in private hands (either individuals or, more usually, shareholders), although in some circumstances the government may own an industry (such as the railways and coal mines in the UK from the middle to the latter part of the twentieth century – known as *nationalisation*). Even where governments don't directly own industries, however, they play an important role in the:

- **Regulation** of economic activity, through the legal and taxation systems, for example. Thus, the role of the state here might extend to things like equal opportunity laws (as happened Britain in the 1970s with the introduction of both the *Sex Discrimination Act* – making it illegal to discriminate on the grounds of sex – and the *Equal Pay Act* – making it illegal to pay men and women different rates for doing the same job). Governments may also legislate for things

like standards of workplace *safety*, a minimum wage and so forth. In addition, taxation policies may be designed to place limits on personal income and wealth and, in some instances, redistribute wealth via a:

- **Welfare state**: This involves a number of ideas; in Britain, for example, the state has provided 'free-on-demand' medical and educational provision, paid for by taxes on income (*production taxation*) and spending (*consumption taxation*). However, the main idea of interest in this context is that of the state, according to **Veenhoven** ('Social Equality and State-Welfare-Effort', 1992), 'Guaranteeing their citizens a minimum level of living, by providing income supplements and/or services'.

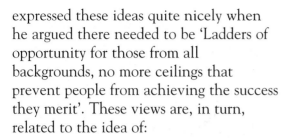 # Digging deeper

As I have suggested, social democratic perspectives explain the distribution of income, wealth and poverty in terms of the relationship between (capitalist) economic markets and the state. On the one hand, the logic of free markets dictates economic inequality is *necessary* while, on the other, the **role of the state** is one that limits the worst excesses of capitalism (in terms of the exploitation of workers, for example) and seeks to provide a safety net for those unable to compete effectively in the market place (the old, sick, disadvantaged and poor, for example).

David Marquand (*The Blair Paradox*, 1998) expresses this in the following terms: 'A meritocratic society is one in which the state takes action to raise the level of the talents – particularly the talents of the disadvantaged – which the market proceeds

Discussion point: regulating pay

Should the government act to prevent the wealthy receiving greater than average pay awards?

As preparation for discussing this question, make two lists based on the following:

1. Reasons why the wealthy should be allowed to earn as much as possible:
- they produce the nation's wealth
- in a free society people should be allowed to earn as much as they are worth.

2. Reasons why the 'pay gap' between rich and poor should be narrowed:
- decreases the sense of social exclusion felt by the poor
- the wealthy already earn more than their fair share of the nation's income.

Directors' pay increases by 16%

'Company directors' pay increased by more than 16 per cent over the past year.

Top executives in the UK's leading companies now earn over £1 million annually while other directors are being paid £650,100. The basic pay of directors in the country's top 350 companies went up by an average of 9%, but with bonuses this rose to 16.1%. Around one in 10 executives enjoyed wage hikes of 20% or more in the past year, although one in eight had no salary rise at all'.

The average pay increase for non-directors was 3–4% in 2003.

Source: ITN: 08/10/04

to reward. First, the state levels the playing field. Only then does the game commence'. In this respect, therefore, the state plays a number of roles.

- An **enabling role**, in the sense of regulating economic markets (where it can), providing services (such as education) and generally promoting equality of opportunity through, for example, the legal system.

- A **protection role**, whereby the socially vulnerable are given help (through such things as unemployment, housing and disability benefits) to provide a basic standard of care and sustenance.

- A **redistribution role**, whereby the tax system, for example, is used to fund the previous two roles.

Ruth Lister ('To Rio via the Third Way', 2000) characterises this aspect of the social democratic perspective as 'Reforming welfare around the work ethic', As she argues, 'It is work, or to be more precise paid work, which is the main focus of social security reforms designed to modify behaviour and to promote responsibility, as well as opportunity and inclusion'. The emphasis, she argues, within social democratic perspectives has moved from the concept of *social equality* to that of *equality of opportunity*, which involves:

- **Responsibilities**: The idea that the role of government is to encourage people to participate in the workplace wherever possible. Thus, various government schemes (aimed at getting, for example, lone parents into work by helping to provide childcare) are based on the idea the best way to help people escape from poverty is to turn them into working, productive, members of society.

- **Inclusion**: This involves the belief paid work – and the ability to support oneself and one's family – is the best way to tackle social exclusion. **Giddens** (1998), for example, suggests a redefinition of 'social equality' to mean '*social inclusion*' – the idea everyone should be encouraged, through state help if necessary, to play a part in the society in which they live.

- **Opportunity** reflects the central problem faced by government in a mixed market economy, namely that of how to promote social integration (or inclusion in New Labour terms) within the parameters of a fundamentally unequal society. The solution, in social democratic terms, is for governments to provide opportunities – through education, welfare training schemes and the like – for people to work.

Marxist perspectives

⚠ Preparing the ground

As a general perspective (focusing for the sake of convenience on the basic ideas shared by different types of Marxists), Marxism focuses on the idea of:

- **Conflict**: While this idea covers all types of social conflict, the main focus is on economic conflict and the relationship between:

- **Social classes**: At its most basic level, class conflict is based around the relationship between the:

  - **bourgeoisie** (or **ruling class**) – those who own and control the means of economic production (land, factories, machinery and so forth) and the

  - **proletariat** (or **subject class**) – those who sell their labour power (their ability to work) to the highest bidder.

In this respect, economic inequality – in terms of vast differences in income and wealth, for example – leads to social inequality (differences in social status, lifestyles and so forth) and is based on the concept of:

- **Profit** (or surplus value, as Marxists like to call it). In basic terms, surplus value is the difference between what an employer pays to produce commodities (goods and services that can be sold) – labour costs, general production costs, the price of raw materials and so forth – and the price for which they are able to sell these commodities.

For example, for the publisher of this book the difference between what it costs to produce (the writing, editing, publishing and distribution costs, for example) and the price for which they sell it to you, is their profit – the 'surplus value' added over and above the costs of production. The main reasons for the existence of profits are, according to Marxists:

- **Exploitation**: The relationship between those who own the means of production and those who do not is, fundamentally, one in which the former exploit the latter. This is because, in a capitalist economy, ownership involves the private retention of profit. In simple terms, owners pay their workers less than the cost of whatever it is they produce and, consequently, are able to keep (or appropriate) the difference between production cost and selling price for themselves. In this situation:

- **Inequality** is an inevitable feature of life in capitalist societies. The distribution of both income and wealth, for example, will always be unequal – there will always be those who are rich and those who, relatively speaking, are poor. This follows because of the economic structure of this type of society – inequalities of wealth and income are, by definition, built into the fabric of capitalist society; they are, in short, the very bedrock (or economic base) on which this type of society is built.

Digging deeper

Unlike functionalist, New Right and social democratic perspectives that, with varying degrees of enthusiasm, see economic inequality as necessary and/or desirable, it should come as no great surprise to learn Marxists see it as neither. Where social

democratic perspectives, for example, see the reform of capitalism as a major goal – through systems of progressive taxation (the wealthy paying increasingly higher rates of tax on their income and wealth, for example, to pay for social reforms) and the like, Marxists argue social and economic inequality can only be eliminated by the revolutionary overthrow of capitalism and the subsequent development of a communist society.

However, until such a society comes into being, Marxists focus on the key question of how social inequality – based on the unequal distribution of income and wealth – is maintained in capitalist societies. They answer this question in a number of ways:

- **Ideology**: As we have previously seen, writers such as **Louis Althusser** (1972) highlight the concept of 'Ideological State Apparatuses' (such as the education system) and their role in convincing people they live, for example, in the best possible type of society, that social inequality is inevitable and necessary and so forth. The role of cultural institutions such as religion and the mass media are also highlighted here in terms of their ideological (or socialising) role. From this perspective, religions such as Christianity have, for example, historically stressed the importance of accepting the social order as 'God given' and the media project a general world view favourable to the interests of the ruling class.

- **Force: Althusser** (1972) points to the idea of 'Repressive State Apparatuses' (such as the police and armed forces) as a factor in both maintaining social order and, by extension, protecting the status quo in society. In basic terms, if a society is fundamentally unequal and the role of the police is to uphold the law, their behaviour simply serves to 'maintain the existing unequal social order' (or, in other words, to keep things as they are).

- **Hegemony**: Part of this idea suggests people come to accept (enthusiastically or grudgingly) the existing social order. They may, for example, see it as 'right and proper' that inequality exists or they may, the other hand, want to change things but feel powerless to achieve such an aim.

Marxists point to a number of distinctive ways capitalist societies promote social inequality.

- **Economic means**: An example here might be the concept of a **reserve army of labour**. This involves the idea of people being brought into the workforce at times of full production and labour shortages and then sacked or made redundant in periods of economic downturn. Traditionally, women have, according to Feminist writers such as **Irene Bruegal** ('Women as a Reserve Army of Labour', 1979), been treated in this way – partly because of the housewife role many women are still expected to play. In this respect, the argument here is women can, more easily than men, be forced out of the public sphere (workforce) and into the private sphere (the home) because of their traditional role as domestic labourers.

In addition, groups such as the unemployed also constitute a reserve pool of labour that can be dipped into by employers when they need additional labour.

Terry Evans ('Part-time Research Students', 2002) has given this idea a somewhat novel twist by noting how, in Australia (as in many European countries) poorly paid and relatively low-status research students are employed on a part-time, casual basis to carry out university-based research. Once they are no longer required, they simply return to the pool of labour seeking further (short-term) work.

For Marxists, this idea of a labour reserve is important because it can be used to lower the wages of other employees. If a reserve army of labour exists in society – willing to be brought into and excluded from the workforce at various times – it lowers the job security of employees and makes them less likely to push for things like wage increases for fear of being replaced by people willing to work for less money.

- **Political means**: The role of the state is an important one in maintaining social inequality through the provision of welfare services. Strange as it may seem, Marxists tend to view the role of welfare provision as being crucial in maintaining inequality because it protects 'the poor' from the worst excesses of inequality. By providing a safety net, governments help to diffuse potential conflicts, lower rates of illegal activity and generally help to maintain the *status quo* from which the ruling class, quite literally, profit the most. Welfare, from this perspective, perpetuates inequality in a number of ways.

  - **Poverty** is marginalised in the sense few people, if any, are allowed to fall into the kind of abject poverty that might lead to a questioning of an economic system that allows some to enjoy vast personal income and wealth while others starve.

- **Policing**: Where governments provide for the poorest in society, one upshot of this is an increased surveillance of those who receive welfare benefits. Social workers, for example, become a form of '*soft policing*' because of their day-to-day involvement with their clients (checking on their current situation, offering advice on behaviour changes and so forth).

Feminist perspectives

⚠ Preparing the ground

You know, from the work you did on feminism in the opening chapter, there are a variety of different feminist perspectives. However, for the purposes of this section we will consider 'feminism in general', in terms of the way feminists have considered and explained social inequalities.

Unsurprisingly, the traditional focus of feminist perspectives on economic inequality has been on the fact women, historically, have lower incomes (as the box opposite demonstrates), own less wealth and are more likely to experience poverty, than their male counterparts.

We can explore Feminist explanations for the relative levels of male–female inequality in terms of a range of ideas.

- **Social Segregation**: Traditionally, men and women in our society have had differential access to – and participation in – different *social spheres*. For example, men have tended to be more heavily involved in the:

- **Public sphere** of the workplace, which gave access to a range of factors contributing to social inequality (income, social networks and wider relationships, for example). Women, on the other hand, were more likely to be involved in the:

- **Private sphere** centred on the home, domestic and family roles and responsibilities.

In such a situation, female dependency on men was fairly easy to demonstrate since it involved inequalities of power based on who earned and controlled family income and who didn't. As **Maureen Ramsay** ('Political Theory and Feminist Research', 1994) notes, Feminists have traditionally argued the separation of the spheres

> . . . affect [female] access to jobs and to participation in public life generally . . . inequalities at work reflect and reinforce [a] subordinate position in the private domestic sphere in that typical 'women's work' is an extension of their domestic roles, and the low pay and low status attached to this work mirrors the devaluing of their domestic tasks.

However, as Ramsay suggests, a distinct separation between the two spheres can't be easily maintained in the light of women's increasing participation in the workplace (and the suggestion men are far more involved in family life than in the past). Office for National Statistics figures (2004), for example, show female workforce participation is only marginally (13 million as against 15 million) less than male participation.

Although a clear 'public–private' sphere distinction can't be easily maintained in

Male/female income differences

Women way behind on pay
BBC News: 21/02/00

Women who choose career over family earn less during their working lives than male colleagues in the same job … many women were being paid less than men simply because of their sex.

This backs up figures from the Equal Opportunities Commission, which says that women get paid only 80% of the average hourly male earnings. The Equal Pay Act of 1970 was introduced to prevent exactly this inequality.

Universities 'break equal pay laws'
BBC News: 04/04/00

The pay *difference* between men and women of the same grade:

- Anatomy/physiology professors: £8,000
- Veterinary science professors: £7,000
- Agriculture/forestry lecturers: £4,950
- Nursing lecturers: £1,558

UK working mothers earn less
BBC News: 06/03/02

Career women's lifetime wage losses, compared to men:

- No qualifications: £197,000
- GCSE qualifications: £241,000
- Graduate qualifications: £143,000

Lifetime wage gap between mother and father of two

- Low skills: £482,000
- GCSE skills: £381,000
- Graduate skills: £162,000

Working mothers' pay compared to men. (Centre for Analysis for Social Exclusion, 1999)

- Women with one child paid 8% less.
- Women with three or more children paid up to 31% less.

relation to British society as a whole in the twenty-first century, we can make a passing reference here to **cultural** and **subcultural differences** in male–female participation in the different spheres. Some ethnic, age and social class groups, for example, maintain a stronger sense of gender separation than others (an idea that reflects what feminists term 'areas in which gender, class and ethnicity intersect').

However, even though it may no longer be the case there is a clear and rigid gender separation between the two spheres, we need to be aware the 'public–private' distinction may not have disappeared, as such, but merely changed in form. Feminists, for example, point to the way it seems to operate in terms of:

- **Economic segregation**: In its most general form, gender segregation operates, according to this perspective, in terms of a dual labour market.

  - **Primary labour markets** involve, according to **Marshall** ('Flexibility and Part-Time Work', 1999), jobs that provide 'security, career development, firm-specific training and an extensive benefits package'. They are also more likely to involve full-time, well-paid, work.

- **Secondary labour markets** on the other hand – as Marshall notes – 'provide little in the way of training, job security or internal promotion prospects'. They are also more likely to consist of low-paid, low-skill, part-time work whose 'most obvious and important characteristic . . . in the UK is that it is undertaken by women'.

  Walters ('Female Part-time Workers' Attitudes to Trade Unions in Britain', 2002) further suggests secondary labour markets are characterised by a 'plentiful supply of women seeking part-time work . . . and, until recently, poor legal and social protection as employees'.

This basic distinction goes some way to explaining gendered income inequality since women are more likely than men to be involved in part-time work (as Table 5.4 demonstrates):

Employee Status	Male	Female
Full-time	11.5	6.7
Part-time	1.2	5.1

Table 5.4 Office For National Statistics (2004): Employment Activity by Sex (millions)

Although **Edwards** and **Robinson** ('A "New" Business Case For Flexible Working?', 2003) characterise part-time work as a 'marginalised form of cheap labour and precarious employment largely found in low skill jobs that can be organised efficiently on a part-time basis',

writers such as **Atkinson** ('Flexibility or fragmentation?', 1987) and **Hunter** et al ('The "flexible firm"', 1993) have argued income inequality can't be exactly explained by different forms of labour market participation.

As **Marshall**, for example, notes:

It would seem females whose labour market participation is constrained by domestic responsibilities often end up working part-time for employers who offer less attractive terms for all their employees, rather than occupying peripheral jobs with firms who offer much better terms and conditions of employment to core workers.

This idea, therefore, leads to a consideration of:

- **Workplace segregation** as an explanation for economic inequality. As **Dolado** et al ('Where Do Women Work?', 2003) point out, this idea works in two ways.

  - **Vertical segregation** involves the idea particular occupations (and workplaces) are vertically stratified by gender; they involve clear gender divisions between those at the top and those beneath them. **Catherine Hakim** ('Job segregation: trends in the 1970s', 1981) expresses this idea in terms of: 'Vertical occupational segregation exists when men and women both work in the same job categories, but men commonly do the more skilled, responsible or better paid work'.

  In general – even in occupations where there is a gender mix – men occupy the higher positions (and receive higher levels of income) than women. **Sarah Wise** ('Multiple Segregation in Nursing Careers', 2004), for example, points out 'Men

[are] over-represented in higher nursing grades and spend less time getting there'.

One consequence of this, as the Equal Opportunities Commission ('Response to the Low Pay Commission's Consultation on Extending the National Minimum Wage to 16 and 17 year olds', 2004) notes is that 'Vertical segregation limits career development that would enable women to earn more'.

- **Horizontal segregation**, in this context, involves the idea men and women do different types of work. The Equal Opportunities Commission (2004), for example, notes: '75% of working women are still found in just five occupational groups':
  - associate professional and technical (e.g. nursing)
  - admin and secretarial work
  - personal services (such as caring for children or the elderly)
  - sales and customer service
  - non-skilled manual work.

The Commission argues: 'Jobs which are classified as women's work command lower wages than men's work even when they require similar qualification levels, leading to inequalities in pay and income'.

Although we have focused on explanations for income equalities related to gender, we can note how both wealth inequalities and poverty are also related to gender (we will examine the latter in more depth on the next section).

Wealth inequality, for example has both current and historical dimensions.

- **Current dimension**: In terms of the areas at which we've looked, women have fewer opportunities than men to accumulate wealth through working. It may, therefore, seem somewhat surprising to note that, according to Datamonitor (2004), there are more wealthy women in the UK than men ('Nearly 393,000 women holding more than £200,000 in cash, shares and bonds, compared with 355,000 men'). This situation is explained partly by the relatively low definition of wealth and partly in terms of **Rownlinson** et al's (1999) observation that the highest levels of wealth are found amongst the elderly; since women live longer in our society than men they are more likely to inherit their partner's wealth.

The *Sunday Times Rich List* (2004) paints a somewhat different picture of wealth amongst the very rich in our society. Of the richest 1100 people in Britain, 93% (1,022) were men.

- **Historical dimension**: Traditional forms of wealth distribution amongst families, for example, have followed the idea of *patrilineal descent* (inheritance down the male line). Until the nineteenth century, for example, women were effectively barred from wealth ownership and, as you might expect, change in this respect has been slow. Men, in general, have had far greater opportunities than women, historically, to accumulate wealth through inheritance.

 Digging deeper

In terms of the ideas at which we've just looked, for 'Second wave' feminist perspectives at least (see Chapter 1 for a discussion of this idea and its relationship to post-feminist or 'Third wave' perspectives) they are all, in their various different ways, underpinned by the concept of **patriarchy**. In basic terms, this involves the idea of *male domination* – something that, for feminists, is at the root of gender inequalities across all areas of society. Various forms of male domination (in the private as well as the public spheres) are supported, according to this perspective by **patriarchal ideologies** that seek to explain and justify men's continued domination and exploitation of women. In this respect, income inequalities, for example, are justified in various ways.

- **Male family wage**: That is, the idea men need to be paid more because, as *primary providers* their income is spread through the family group – an idea that ignores both the primary family role played by many women and the fact income levels between men don't reflect differences in family status; a single man doing the same job as a man with a family to support is paid the same wage.

- **Biological programming**: Some (non-sociological) perspectives (such as *sociobiology* – or *evolutionary psychology* as it now prefers to be known) argue males and females have different biology-based abilities and capabilities. **Men**, for example, are biologically programmed for aggression which makes them more suited to hunting and, its modern-day equivalent, the workplace. **Women**, on the other hand, are programmed for nurture, which makes them better suited to the home-making role. Sociological versions of this idea appear in the idea of a female:

- **Affective role** – the idea, common among traditional Functionalist writers such as

William Goode (*The Family*, 1964), women have a nurturing role to play as a counterpoint to male breadwinning roles.

As the information in the box opposite suggests, however we view the notion of patriarchy and patriarchal ideologies, in any society where economic inequality is encouraged, competition between men and women for control of resources (such as income and wealth) is likely to have a patriarchal element, given men have, historically, been better placed – both culturally and economically – to discriminate against women on the basis of sex.

Growing it yourself: economic inequality

In this exercise you are going to address the following:

'Assess explanations for the unequal distribution of wealth and income in contemporary Britain.'

As an extended piece of work you should aim to write between 500 and 750 words (more if you really want to).

To organise your answer, write 100–150 words on each of the perspectives we've examined in this section:

- functionalist
- New Right
- social democratic
- Marxist
- feminist.

Focus your writing on each explanation by re-reading the information provided and thinking about how it can be used to explain economic inequality from the particular viewpoint of each perspective.

Social Focus on Men (Office for National Statistics, 2001)
[Source: BBC News: 12/07/01]

UK is 'still a man's world'

Men are still getting a better deal at work and at home despite years of campaigning to promote sexual equality. Men do much less cooking and housework than women and are still rewarded better in their careers. The gender pay gap is still very much in evidence and men hold more high-powered jobs than women, even though more women are working.

Women outperform men at most levels of education but still earn less.

Family life is changing, with men no longer always being seen as the primary providers, but men are still not pulling their weight in the home: 'Traditional roles in the home may still exist with women undertaking the bulk of domestic chores.'

Work life: Men also still have higher wages despite equal pay legislation, and 'outnumber women in management and in many professional occupations'. This is despite evidence men are now 'outperformed by women at many levels of education'.

The average gross wage for men is £247 a week, compared with £119 for women.

The average gross earnings for women peak in their mid-20s at about £180 a week. Men, on the other hand, steadily rise in earning potential to an average £350 a week for the ages 35–50.

This section has looked at a variety of explanations for the distribution of income, wealth and, to a limited extent, poverty. In the next section, however, we are going to focus directly on poverty as a form of social and economic inequality by looking at theories that seek to explain both its existence and persistence.

The existence and persistence of poverty

Introduction

Discussion of different explanations of the existence and persistence of poverty in this section is organised around two main themes, based on an outline and examination of theories relating to:

- **individualistic** (or **cultural**) explanations of poverty
- **structural** explanations of poverty.

WARM UP: PERSONAL PERSPECTIVES ON POVERTY

Individually or in small groups (using the following table as a guide) identify:

1. As many **individual** reasons as possible for poverty (focusing on the idea it results from deficiencies in the behaviour of the **poor**).
2. As many **social** reasons as possible (focusing on the idea it results from the behaviour of the **non-poor**).

When you've exhausted all possibilities, as a group decide on a point score for each reason, based on the following:

- 5 points if you think it's a **very important** consideration
- 3 points if you think it's an **important** consideration
- 1 point if you think it's a **not very important** consideration

Total the points you've awarded in each column to arrive at an assessment of your personal perspective on poverty.

Individual Reasons	Social Reasons
The poor are idle and lazy	The rich take more than their fair share of economic resources
Further reasons ...	**Further reasons ...**
Total points	Total points

Individual (cultural) explanations

⚠ Preparing the ground

Explanations for poverty grouped under this general heading focus on the qualities possessed (or not as the case may be) by individuals and the groups to which they belong. This being the case, if poverty is a 'quality of the poor' it follows any explanation for its existence and persistence is based on some form of **absolute definition** of poverty (either biological or, more usually, cultural – a minimum level of earnings, for example). This follows because, if the behaviour of the poor is a cause of their poverty, any solution to poverty (something we will discuss in more detail in the next section) will focus on how the poor need to change their behaviour – which means there must be some form of poverty line against which to measure who is – and who is not – in poverty.

In terms of this general type of explanation, we can identify and discuss a range of different theories, beginning with the idea of a **culture of poverty**, originally developed by the anthropologist **Oscar Lewis** (*Five Families*, 1959; *The Children of Sanchez*, 1961). In his study of Mexican and Puerto Rican societies, Lewis wanted to understand poverty in a *cultural context*; that is, he wanted to understand how the poor adapted to and coped with the fact of their poverty; in this respect, he argued poverty, like any other form of cultural activity, was

socially organised. Rather than seeing poverty as simply being caused by random events (such as illness or disease) or natural forces that struck different people at different times, Lewis argued the persistence of poverty across generations meant it needed to be understood in terms of a **socialisation process**. In other words, adults who experience poverty as a set of objective conditions (such as the effects of long-term unemployment, low rates of pay for those in work, illness, disability and so forth) learn to cope with the fact of living in poverty and, in the process, pass this knowledge on to their children (in the same way those who live outside poverty pass their accumulated knowledge on to their children). The persistence of poverty, therefore, is explained by the way each generation socialises the next generation with the knowledge and skills required to live in poverty.

As should be apparent, if a culture of poverty develops it does so because it performs certain functions for the poor (hence we can associate writers like Lewis with a broadly functionalist perspective). These include:

- **Informal economies**: For example, the use of pawnbrokers as a way of budgeting on limited resources or informal borrowing and lending arrangements with friends and neighbours.

- **Present orientations**: The idea of 'living for today' and worrying about what will happen tomorrow or the next day when (or even if) it arrives.

- **Informal living arrangements**: For example, a lack of commitment to institutions such as marriage which would involve trying to provide for others as well as oneself.

On the other hand, a culture of poverty is, ultimately *dysfunctional* (damaging to both individuals and societies) because it represents a **self-defeating strategy**. By adapting and coping, the poor do not address the problems that create poverty in the first place (things like lack of employment and low wages). The development of *informal economies*, for example, may lead to the introduction of moneylenders into the *economy of poverty*. Borrowing money in this way may resolve a short-term problem (paying the rent, for example) but it creates a much more serious long-term problem since the money not only has to be paid back, but paid back with punitive rates of interest.

A further dysfunctional aspect of a culture of poverty is the 'absence of childhood'. **Lewis**, for example, noted children, at an early age, were expected to be economically *active* – to 'earn their keep' and contribute, if they could, to a family income; the problem here, of course, was the absence of schooling – low rates of literacy were common among the poor Lewis studied – and since education is one of the main (long-term) routes out of poverty the poor were, effectively (and unknowingly) perpetuating their own poverty.

Cultural theories have been influential as a way of studying and explaining the existence and persistence of poverty and, as you might expect, they have been revised and updated over the years. The following, for example, takes one particular aspect of the culture of poverty thesis – the idea the adaptive behaviour of the poor contributes to their continued poverty – and develops it into a theory of **the underclass**. This theory, associated with New Right perspectives in the USA – through political scientists like

Discussion point: self-defeating strategies?

In small groups, construct a table along the following lines, identify some of the 'strategies for coping' developed by the poor and indicate why they might be 'self-defeating' in terms of raising them out of poverty.

Coping strategy	Self-defeating?
Leave school as soon as legally allowed	Lack educational qualifications
Further Examples	

Once you've done this, combine your ideas with those of the rest of the class and discuss the extent to which such coping strategies contribute to a culture of poverty.

Charles Murray (*The Underclass Revisited* 1999) – and Britain, through the work of politicians such as **Frank Field** (*Losing Out: The Emergence of Britain's Underclass*, 1989 and *Making Welfare Work*, 1995), argues the very poor in the USA and – to a more limited extent – Britain, constitute a 'class apart' from mainstream society. They are, according to this argument, a class who not only exist at the very bottom of the society but who are also socially excluded in terms of income, life chances and political aspirations.

Mike O'Brian ('Beyond Poverty', 1997) notes New Right theorists frequently make an important (ideological) distinction between two groups.

- The **deserving poor** – those who, through little fault of their own, find themselves in poverty (and who, to some extent, try to lift themselves out of this situation – hence the idea they are deserving of help). This group, for example, might include the 'working poor' who struggle to exist on low wages.
- The **undeserving poor** – those who are (supposedly) happy to exist on the margins of society, living off state benefits, indulging in various forms of petty criminality and who, for whatever reason, make little or no effort to involve themselves in the day-to-day life of mainstream society.

Chris Jencks ('What is the Underclass – and is it Growing?', 1989) argues that, on the basis of this type of distinction, New Right perspectives generally talk about the undeserving poor in terms of three types of failure:

- **moral**: they routinely indulge in deviant/criminal behaviour
- **economic**: they are unable (or unwilling) to get paid work
- **educational**: they lack cultural and educational skills and qualifications.

The underclass, therefore, are seen to contribute to their own social exclusion by their rejection of the values and norms of wider society. In other words, membership of the underclass is defined in terms of the choices made by its members; for example, the failure to pursue educational qualifications leads to economic marginalisation and the development of a morality based around criminality and a dependence on the rest of society to support their deviant lifestyles through state benefits. In terms of who the undeserving poor actually are, their **membership** varies according to different writers. **Peter Saunders** (*Social Class and Stratification*, 1990), for example, identifies the underclass in terms of the poor, educationally unqualified and those irregularly or never employed.

Ruth Lister ('In Search of the "Underclass"', 1996), on the other hand, argues the New Right generally characterise membership in terms of 'those distinguished by their undesirable behaviour', examples of which include:

- illegal drug-taking
- criminality and casual violence
- illegitimacy
- failure to find and hold down a job
- truancy from school.

In addition, disproportionately represented amongst this class are:

- ethnic minorities (especially, but not exclusively, Afro-Caribbean)
- people trapped in run-down council estates or decaying inner cities
- young single people
- single-parent families.

For the New Right (especially in the USA), the development of an underclass is, somewhat perversely, also a consequence of the behaviour of mainstream society, in two main ways.

- **Welfare systems** providing various forms of economic support shield the poor from the consequences of their behavioural choices. By supporting poverty, welfare systems also support:

- **Deviant lifestyles** and **moralities**: The poor are shielded from the effects of the moral choices that contribute to their poverty. For example, single parents who choose to have children they cannot support (because they can't work and look after children at the same time) are actively encouraged by a welfare system that effectively pays (through benefits funded through taxation) for their (deviant) moral choices.

These ideas lead to a further theory of poverty, closely related to that of the underclass, namely a **dependency culture**: The basic idea here is the existence of state welfare systems and payments both *supports* and *traps* the poor in poverty, depending on the particular view of the underclass adopted. In this respect, we can note three basic views about the relationship between a dependency culture and the underclass.

- **Generosity**: Benefits are so high they provide the underclass with a comfortable existence for little or no effort.

- **Baseline**: Although benefits may not provide a comfortable lifestyle, the fact the poor can live without (officially) working means they are free to involve themselves in the *hidden economy* (the world of cash-in-hand, tax-free work as well as various forms of economic criminality).

- **Low-wage work**: Members of the underclass, almost by definition, lack the educational skills and qualifications to find highly paid work. Their working options, therefore, are largely limited to low-skill, poorly paid work. Where welfare benefits are pitched at even a reasonably generous level, therefore, it is not in the economic interests of the underclass to take low-paid employment. It is interesting to note, in this particular context, the New Right 'solution' to this problem is not to force employers to pay higher wages (since that would interfere with the workings of free markets) but rather to cut the level of state benefits.

In any of these situations, those who become dependent on the state for their existence become detached from wider society and are effectively excluded from participation in that society. **Mike O'Brian** (1997) characterises this New Right view of dependency in the following terms:

> Beneficiaries, it is argued, constitute a separate culture . . . with a different set of values and beliefs from the values and beliefs that exist in the society at large. 'Dependence' is a state enjoyed and relished. It is an argument . . . reflected, for example, in the . . . claim five-year-olds were entering school looking forward to life on social security benefit as their occupational aspiration.

In Britain, the idea of an underclass has tended, politically, to be expressed in a slightly different form. Although US New Right theorists (such as **Murray**) generally focus on the qualities of the poor as the cause of their poverty, British writers like **Field** have, in some senses, characterised the 'underclass poor' as victims of **forces of expulsion** from society, which include:

- unemployment
- widening class differences
- exclusion from rapidly rising living standards
- hardening of public attitudes to poverty.

In this respect, a softer version of underclass theory, largely associated with social

democratic perspectives on poverty, has developed around the concept of **social exclusion**. **Katherine Duffy** ('Social Exclusion and Human Dignity in Europe', 1995) defines social exclusion as the 'Inability to participate in the economic, political, social and cultural life of a society' (which, if you think about it, sounds very much like a definition of relative poverty). The notion of exclusion reflects, according to **Howarth** et al ('Monitoring poverty and social exclusion', 1998) 'Renewed concern about not just poverty, but the degree to which groups of people are being excluded from participation in work, lack full access to services and in other ways find themselves outside the mainstream of society'.

From this perspective, therefore, while poverty may have many causes, some relating to wider structural influences (such as economic changes within labour markets – discussed in more detail below – that create widespread unemployment) and some relating to the lifestyles and culture of the poor, the 'problem' for mainstream society is considered to be one of **social integration**. In other words, the political problem of how to ensure the poor do not become culturally (as well as economically) detached from mainstream society. The government funded Social Exclusion Unit, for example, has identified three general areas of potential social exclusion and suggested ways of reintegrating the excluded in terms of their:

- **Physical environment**: This involves integrating people by improving local and national transport systems, housing and neighbourhood renewal, community regeneration and so forth.

- **Cultural environment** measures involve cutting crime and teenage pregnancy, reducing the fear of crime, improving access to educational training and skills and ensuring health services are accessible to those who need them most.

- **Economic environment**: This involves understanding the causes of unemployment (and its relationship to areas such as health and crime). Social integration initiatives have also focused on paid work as an inclusive force. Schemes to involve the unemployed in training and employment (so-called 'welfare-to-work' schemes) have also proved a popular political solution to social exclusion.

Discussion point: inclusion and exclusion

In small groups, use the following table as the basis for identifying some of the ways the poor may be socially excluded from mainstream society.

For each way you've identified, what policies could be developed by governments to ensure social exclusion doesn't occur?

Forms of exclusion	Policies?
Living in run-down housing estates	
Truancy from school	Prosecute parents who don't send their children to school
Further examples	

In Britain, the social democratic concept of exclusion is subtly different from the New Right version of underclass theory; where the latter locates poverty in the behaviour and practices of the poor – **Horowitz** ('On the Dole in United Kingdom', 1995), for example, sees poverty as being explained 'more by self-destructive behaviour (sic) – crime, drug abuse, bearing children out of wedlock and a lack of commitment to education – than mere material want' – the former sees poverty in terms of a mix of *material* and *cultural* factors.

As **Welshman** ('The cycle of deprivation and the concept of the underclass', 2002) argues: 'In drawing on the concept of social exclusion, New Labour has been keen to distance itself from the longer-term "underclass" discourse'. Keeping this in mind, therefore, we can note how the idea of social exclusion has been based on the idea of a **cycle of deprivation** (pictured overleaf). For this type of theory, deprivation is usually considered in terms of *material* factors (such as a low family income) having cumulative, cultural, effects. A simple example might be parents living on a low income (material deprivation) means their children have a poor diet, which causes health problems and missed schooling and leads to educational failure (cultural deprivation) which, in turn, leads to low-paid, low-skill work.

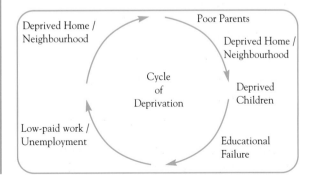

> **'Link between Poverty and Truancy'**
>
> Children are more likely to skip school if they come from poor families. Research carried out by Ming Zhang found a close link between poverty and truancy among primary school children. The study, examined statistics from London boroughs between 1997 and 2000.
>
> [BBC News: 07/07/02]

When these people start families of their own, the cycle begins anew.

An example of this type of theory might be expressed in the following report of research suggesting a link between poverty and school truancy.

This theory, as I have represented it, doesn't involve the poor being 'committed to poverty', nor are they (directly) to blame for their poverty (a process sometimes called *'blaming the victim'*). Rather, a range of social and economic factors, whose effect is *cumulative* (hence the idea of a cycle or chain of events), lead to the persistence of poverty down the generations.

 # Digging deeper

Although we will look more closely at cultural explanations in the next section (which discusses possible solutions to poverty), we can note a number of general ideas about the basic concept of **cultures of poverty**. When we think about this idea (as originally theorised and presented by Lewis) we need to ask three basic questions:

- **Do they exist**? Although the concept itself is a plausible one, it depends for its currency on the existence of a reasonably stable group of people, co-existing in poverty over time (and by time we're talking generations). The evidence we have suggests poverty – at least in Western societies such as Britain – doesn't necessarily have this basic characteristic.

Drever et al ('Social Inequalities', 2000), for example, note that, measured in terms of income, in the six years between 1991 and 1997, 50% of the bottom fifth of the UK population (in other words, the very poorest in our society) moved out of this category. This suggests, at the very least, a large population *churn*, something also suggested by **Jarvis** and **Jenkins** ('Changing places', 1997) when they note:

Although only a minority of the population have a low income in any given year, many more people experience low income at least once over a four-year period . . .
Fluctuations in income are experienced by people at all income levels. There is some evidence that mobility is greater in the very poorest and the very richest income groups.

On the other hand, **Jarvis** and **Jenkins** also note that, as ever, concepts of poverty largely depend on where a poverty line is drawn: '90% of those in the poorest tenth of the population remain in the bottom three-tenths a year later'. The situation is further confused if we focus on a particular group of poor.

Howard et al ('Poverty: the Facts', 2001), for example, argue poverty is likely to last longer for children, in the sense that where children are born into poverty (as opposed to becoming poor, for whatever reason, in later life) they find it very difficult to escape from that poverty – it is, they argue, something they carry with them into adult life. The Department for Work and Pensions ('Low Income Dynamics', 2002), confirm this idea when they note how movement out of extreme poverty in the UK tends to be not very far.

What these types of study suggest, perhaps, is that people experience different *types of* poverty throughout their lifetime – from extreme forms to less extreme forms (whatever, in practice, each form might involve). In other words, just because we may be able to classify people as 'poor' it doesn't simply follow they all have the same, shared, experience of poverty. If the evidence for the existence of a relatively stable group is, at best, inconclusive, a further question to ask is:

- **Are the poor homogeneous?**: In other words, if we assume, for the sake of argument, a 'hard core' poverty-stricken group does exist in our society, do they have the same basic social and cultural characteristics? When we look at 'the poor' in our society, although it's possible to identify broad groups with similar characteristics, the evidence for homogeneity – and hence the development of cultures of poverty – is patchy. We can, for example, note:
  - **Ethnic minority groups**, particularly Pakistani and Bangladeshi minorities, feature more heavily in poverty statistics, according to Oxfam ('The facts about poverty in the UK', 2003).
  - **Regional variations** in our society exist in the extent, experience and

distribution of poverty. **Department for Work and Pensions** ('Households Below Average Income', 2002) statistics, for example, show the North-East and South-West of England experience higher levels of poverty than the South-East of England.

- **Age variations**: Different age groups have different experiences of poverty – to be young and poor is different to being elderly and poor, for example.
- **Women** are more likely than men to be at risk of poverty (Department of Social Security: 'Households Below Average Income', 2001) and reasons for this include the greater likelihood of their being single-parents and, because of longer life expectancy, widows. This observation, however, leads us to our final question, namely:

- **Is poverty communal?** A significant aspect of cultures of poverty is their communal character; such cultures develop in a situation where the values and norms of the poor are continually reinforced by people in similar social situations. However, it's interesting to note how, when those in poverty speak for themselves, they repeatedly stress its isolating effects (as the following examples demonstrate).

> Poverty is isolating. You do not want anyone to know what you are feeling . . . you put on a brave face and do not let anyone into your private life.
>
> In part it is about having no money. It is also about being isolated, unsupported, uneducated, unwanted.

Source: UK Coalition Against Poverty Workshop 2000

In light of the above, **Karen Moore** ('Frameworks for understanding the intergenerational transmission of poverty', 2001) argues:

> 'Controversial 'culture of poverty' theories suggest people become and remain poor due to their beliefs and behaviours ... it may be more relevant to consider 'cultures of coping' among the poor, and 'cultures of wealth? among the rich and middle class as significant factors in keeping the poor in poverty'.

Rather than thinking in terms of a *culture* of poverty, **Moore** suggests we should view poverty in terms of **Inter-Generational Transmission (IGT)**. This represents a sophisticated attempt to understand the persistence of poverty in terms of the interplay between a range of cultural and structural factors. In addition, it provides a bridge between the overtly cultural theories we have just examined and the 'structural poverty' theories we'll consider in more detail in a moment. **Moore** outlines the key elements of **IGT** as being the 'Intergenerational transfer ... and absence of transfer of different forms of capital: human, social-cultural, social-political, financial/material and environmental/natural'. In other words **cultural transmission** is a complex process involving a wide range of possible *capitals* we can group, for convenience, under two main headings.

- **Material capital** involves things like parental ability to provide financially for children. **Gregg** et al ('Child development and family income', 1999), for example, used a *longitudinal study* of children born in 1958 to show how 'Social disadvantage during childhood is linked to an increased risk of low earnings, unemployment and other adversity by the age of 33'.

- **Non-material capital**, which includes things like cultural traditions, values and experiences. **Shropshire** and **Middleton** ('Small expectations: Learning to be poor?', 1999), for example, noted how non-material values were transmitted between generations. Children of single-parent families, for example, had 'lower expectations about their future than their peers' – they were, for example, less likely to consider professional qualifications and occupations.

Structural explanations

⚠ Preparing the ground

This type of explanation for the existence and persistence of poverty examines the way behavioural choices are limited (or extended) by structural factors in society. Whereas the kind of theories we've just considered (individual or cultural) share a couple of common themes (the behaviour of the poor is a social problem and the causes of poverty are found in the attitudes and lifestyles of the poor themselves), for this second set of theories the causes of poverty are located in areas such as the behaviour of governments and/or the wealthy and economic changes in society. We can identify a range of structural theories of poverty, beginning with the idea of **labour market changes**. Since the Second World War at least, our society – in common with

Growing it yourself: IGT

The following table provides general examples of each type of capital identified by Moore (p. 33).

Intergenerational forms of capital	
Type of capital	Example
Human	Labour contributions (from children/older people to working generation). Investment of time and capital in education/training. Knowledge/skills useful as part of coping and survival strategies.
Financial/material	Money and assets. Insurance. Inheritance, bequests. Debt.
Natural/environmental	Pollution and ill-health Lack of work in urban/rural areas Lack of affordable transport
Socio-cultural	Educational opportunities. Parental investment in child's education. Parents' experience of education. Traditions and value systems.
Socio-political	Ethnicity; gender; class; family background; religion; disability; access to key decision-makers.

For each type of capital in turn, write a paragraph (120-150 words) in the following format:

- **Identify** the type of capital you are discussing.

- **Define** what it involves.

- **Explain**, using an example, how its transmission between generations can advantage/disadvantage the poor and/or the non-poor.

many societies around the globe – has witnessed a relative decline in manufacturing industry, in terms of the number and type of products built and the number of people employed. One reason for this, as the following extract (**Roland Gribben**: 'Dyson production moves to Malaysia') illustrates, is the relocation of some manufacturing industries from the UK to other countries (where production costs are much cheaper).

Alongside this long-time decline, however, has been a general rise in the numbers employed in service industries (such as banking, information technology and communications at the well paid end and call centres and sales at the low paid end).

Dyson production moves to Malaysia
Roland Gribben: **21/08/03**

'Entrepreneur James Dyson was involved
in a fresh row over exporting jobs
yesterday after announcing he planned to
switch production of washing machines to
Malaysia with the loss of 65 jobs. The
decision means the end of manufacturing
for Dyson in Britain after last year's
decision to move vacuum cleaner
production to Malaysia, where production
costs are 30% lower. The transfer resulted
in the loss of 800 jobs'.

We can note how such changes have
impacted on poverty in a number of ways.

- **Unemployment**: Although this concept,
  for a variety of reasons, is difficult to
  reliably measure (different governments,
  for example, use different indicators of
  unemployment), it is clear one
  consequence of changing labour markets
  over the past 25 years in Britain has been
  fluctuating levels of unemployment –
  something that's especially true among
  manual workers (one consequence of the
  loss of manufacturing jobs). We need to
  note, however, unemployment and
  poverty – where they are related to the
  loss of such jobs – are:

- **Regional**: In this respect, experience of
  poverty in the UK can be characterised as
  fragmented. Areas, such as the North of
  England and Scotland, with high levels of
  manufacturing (such as car assembly and
  ship building) and extraction industries
  (such as coal mining) have experienced
  higher levels of unemployment than areas
  with lower levels of manufacturing and

higher levels of service industry, such as
the South East of England.

Bennett et al (*Dealing with the
Consequences of Industrial Decline*, 2000),
for example, note how 'Coalfield
communities remain blighted by
widespread unemployment, long-term
sickness and poverty a decade after the
collapse of the mining industry' and
Evans et al ('Geographic patterns of
change', 2002) have noted that although
'Every neighbourhood in England has
benefited from strong economic growth
and falling unemployment since the mid-
1990s', the rate of change has varied. This
has led, they argue, to greater polarisation
between the richest and poorest regions.

- **Income**: Although levels of measured
  unemployment have fallen in recent
  years, a further consequence of labour
  market changes has been the replacement
  of relatively high paid manufacturing
  work (especially semi and skilled manual
  jobs) with lower paid, insecure, service
  sector work. As **Bennett** et al (2000)
  note:

  Companies have been able to hire people
  willing to work flexibly for low wages, often
  in non-unionised workplaces. The new jobs
  have often been part-time . . . Much of the
  work created has gone to women – creating
  tensions in communities where men have
  traditionally seen themselves as
  breadwinners.

- **Globalisation**: A further structural
  development we can note is the
  insecurity of some service sector jobs (call
  centres being an obvious current example
  – as the following extract illustrates). The
  globalisation of telecommunications and
  computer technology, for example, has
  opened up opportunities for companies to

employ cheaper labour, in countries such as India, to service customers in the UK.

Profits of loss

Charlotte Denny: *The Guardian*, 25/11/03)

South Africa and India are the new destinations of choice for British companies looking to cut costs. Call centres and IT processing, and even such high-skilled work as pharmaceutical research, are being 'offshored'. White-collar workers are discovering they are as vulnerable to competition from cheaper workers abroad as steelworkers and shipbuilders a generation ago. Unions fear the service sector is about to repeat the experience of manufacturing, which has lost 3.3m jobs since 1980.

A second form of structural argument, related to the idea of labour market changes and the impact of economic globalisation, is the idea – largely associated with Marxist perspectives – that some form of poverty is **inevitable** in capitalist society. This follows because such societies are, by definition, unequal in terms of the distribution of wealth and income. In any economic system where competition is the norm, relative differences will always exist. The main question here, however, is how you define poverty. In **absolute terms**, for example, few people in our society could be considered poor; in **relative terms**, however, it is clear there are wide disparities between the richest and poorest sections of society. More controversially perhaps, we could note the idea of poverty as a **necessary** condition of capitalism – the idea that the existence of

the poor (or relatively deprived if you prefer) is useful for a ruling class since they can be used as a *reserve* army of labour whose existence can be used to control wage levels and hence profitability.

One aspect of this 'necessary and inevitable' relationship between poverty and capitalism is the concept of **social segregation**. Structural theories of poverty have suggested the existence of economically segregated groups leads to social segregation and, in some instances, physical segregation – the existence, for example, of private *gated communities* that are a feature of some US cities and which are increasingly common in the UK.

Atkinson and **Flint** 'The Fortress UK?', 2004), for example, found 'around 1000 such developments' which, they argue, relate to 'patterns of interaction and separation which suggest an attempt to reduce fears of victimisation and promote privacy'.

One downside of poverty (for a ruling class) is the fact the poor – as with other members of society – are *consumers*; if they can't afford to buy goods and services, profitability suffers. For many Marxists, therefore, the idea of a welfare system is significant, mainly because it provides some form of safety net for those at the bottom of society. This leads us to note a further aspect of structural approaches to poverty, namely the **structural limits of welfare**. Although this idea has numerous dimensions, we can understand it by noting an example of the limitations of welfare systems in relation to poverty – namely, the idea of a **poverty trap**. In any *means-tested* welfare system (that is, one in which people receive different levels of benefits based on things like their income and savings), the problem of a poverty trap is always likely to exist. This is because, as someone's income rises (they move, for example, from unemployment into work or from part-time to full-time work) their welfare benefits are accordingly reduced.

For example, if for every extra £1 earned through employment, state benefits are similarly reduced, this creates a disincentive to work (if you're unemployed) or to take full-time work (if you're employed part-time). This is because, effectively, you're not being paid any extra money for the extra work you do. In an attempt to reduce this 'disincentive to work', benefit reductions are increasingly staggered as earnings increase. However, according to Department for Work and Pensions figures ('Opportunity for All', 2004) over two million Britons are currently caught in a poverty trap.

One reason for this involves considering a slightly different example – a situation where an unemployed person with a family to support loses a range of benefit payments if they find employment. If the level of income they lose from the state isn't matched or exceeded by the income they can get from paid work, this individual (and their family) will, effectively, be worse off if they take paid employment.

A final aspect of structural approaches to poverty we can note is the idea of the **feminisation of poverty**. According to the **Institute of Development Studies** ('Briefing paper on the "feminisation of Poverty"', 2001), 'there is little clarity about what the feminisation of poverty means'. Notwithstanding this unpromising start, the concept generally relates to the idea the existence and persistence of poverty can be linked to female lives (as head of households) and experiences (of low-paid, part-time, work, for example). In this

respect, the argument is that women experience:

- more poverty than men
- worse poverty than men
- an increasing trend to greater poverty.

Elisabetta Ruspini ('Engendering poverty research', 2000), for example, argues any structural analysis of poverty needs to take account of its **gendered nature**. That is, the idea men and women – even of the same social class or ethnic grouping – experience poverty in different ways. For example, welfare and insurance systems reflect, according to **Glendinning** and **Millar** ('Poverty: the forgotten Englishwoman', 1999), 'their different access to, and levels of, income replacement benefits'.

 # Digging deeper

Structural approaches, as I have indicated, focus on the way economic organisation and relationships create and sustain both wealth and poverty. In this respect, although such relationships have clear *cultural* effects (in terms of who is – and who isn't – likely to experience poverty), structural poverty theorists argue that to understand the existence and persistence of poverty it is necessary to understand its wider theoretical context; people fall into – or fail to get out of – poverty *not* because of their individual and social character deficiencies but because of way society is structured against them.

Poverty, from this perspective, forces people to behave in certain ways. Thus, although **Lewis** originally argued cultures adapt to social and economic conditions and, in the process, develop and perpetuate self-defeating strategies, structural theorists argue these strategies are not necessarily chosen from a wide range of possibilities; rather, they are 'chosen' because they the only ones available to the poor. Rather than blaming the victims of poverty for their poverty, therefore, structural approaches seek to understand how and why there are victims in the first place. Given this observation, we can dig a little deeper into structural approaches by thinking, in the first instance, about poverty as **risk**. This approach starts by taking note of the structural factors in any society relating to poverty. For example, we have already noted a selection of these in terms of things like: the nature of the economic system; regional differences relating to different types of labour market (and how changes in labour markets result in differences in employment and unemployment) and the impact of globalisation on national and international markets. In addition, we have noted how the risk of poverty may be associated with cultural factors such as gender and ethnicity.

Once these structural factors have been theorised, poverty can then be generally mapped in terms of our ability to identify different social groups who are at greater risk of poverty than others. This concept of *risk-mapping* moves us away from the simple cultural identification of 'at risk' groups – characteristic of individual approaches to explaining poverty – for a couple of reasons.

- **Structural conditions**: Different structural conditions create greater or lesser risks of poverty (which, as ever, will always depend on how poverty is defined).
- **Poverty conditions**: We have noted a central problem with individualistic/cultural theories of poverty is the fact those considered to be 'in poverty' at any

given moment do not necessarily remain in poverty all their lives. On the contrary, the *cyclic nature of poverty* frequently means people (or whole groups) move into and out of poverty at different points in their *life cycle*. This suggests, therefore, that although the identity of 'the poor' may change – in terms of specific individuals – the condition of poverty itself remains; it simply involves different people at different times.

We can understand this idea by thinking about **Richard Berthoud**'s observation ('Incomes of Ethnic Minorities', 1998) that 'Pakistani and Bangladeshi families in Britain are almost four times as likely to be living on low incomes as white households'. Berthoud identifies four major 'risk factors' for these groups:

- high male unemployment
- low levels of female economic activity
- low pay
- large family size.

The point to note, here, is not that poverty is explained in terms of the specific cultural characteristics of these minorities; rather, it is that any group sharing these characteristics is likely to risk falling into poverty.

Similarly, **Bardasi** and **Jenkins** (*Income in later life*, 2002) found the 'risks of old-age poverty for those retiring early are strongly linked to occupation'. Managerial and professional workers, as you might expect, have a reduced risk of poverty – but so do manual workers. Clerical or sales occupations, craft and service workers (police officers and waiters, for example) on the other hand 'may be especially vulnerable if they stop work early'.

Although the general concept of *risk* can contribute to our understanding of poverty, attempts have been made to refine this idea in order to relate it specifically to structural factors. We can look at an example of this in terms of **memberships theory**. **Steven Durlauf** ('Groups, Social Influences and Inequality', 2002), argues this type of theory can be used to examine how poverty is related to the way 'various socioeconomic groupings affect individuals' and their behavioural choices, in terms of two different types of group.

- **Exogenous** group membership would include things like gender and ethnicity. In a sense, we can think of membership of these groups largely in terms of *ascribed* characteristics; for example, as we have seen with ideas like the feminisation of poverty or the relationship between ethnicity and poverty risk, individual life chances can be generally related to membership of such groups.

- **Endogenous** group membership, on the other hand, relates to the specific social and economic circumstances of the individual – **Durlauf**, for example, points to areas such as residential neighbourhoods, school and work relationships as being significant factors in the poverty/non-poverty equation.

In this respect, *memberships theory* examines the interplay between structural factors, in terms of how, for example **economic segregation**, through unemployment and low pay, for example, leads to:

- **Social segregation**, in terms of the idea the poor and non-poor lead different types of life, have different cultural lifestyles and so forth, which, in turn leads to:

- **Physical segregation**, in terms of rich and poor living in different areas, the development of private, gated, communities and the like.

We can summarise these ideas in the following terms: **structural factors** determine the general extent of poverty/deprivation in any given society. In the UK, for example, general living standards are different to some parts of Africa and South America. In turn, these factors influence the **behavioural choices** of the rich and the non-poor, in terms of their general cultural characteristics (such as their lifestyles) which, in turn, place **cultural limitations** on the behavioural choices of the poor, effectively trapping them in poverty through their own group memberships and apparent behavioural choices.

For example, schools in poor neighbourhoods may have lower status and funding, which perpetuates lower educational achievement and contributes to a 'cultural poverty trap' that sits alongside the kinds of possible economic poverty traps we have outlined above.

In short, therefore, this theory argues structural factors *determine* the development of membership groups that, in turn, *perpetuates* the risk of poverty.

Having suggested a range of individual/structural explanations for the existence and persistence of poverty, the next thing we can usefully do is look at how different perspectives and theories have produced different *solutions* to poverty.

Solutions to poverty

Introduction

This section looks at different solutions to poverty, with particular reference to the role of social policy, and we can combine the organisational structure of the previous two sections as a way of providing a general continuity to our exploration and understanding of poverty. This section, therefore, is generally organised around the two basic approaches to poverty outlined in the previous section (individual and structural approaches). Within each general category we can locate the various perspectives on poverty we encountered when examining explanations for the distribution of poverty (which, to refresh your memory, were: New Right, social democratic, Marxist and feminist perspectives).

WARM UP: SOLVING POVERTY?

As a class, use the following table as a template for suggesting possible 'solutions to the problem of poverty' in our society. For each solution, identify possible problems it might create.

Solving poverty?	
Possible solution	Possible problems?
Minimum wage	What level should the minimum be set?
Abolish all welfare	Will this create social problems?
Further examples	

We can begin this section by looking firstly (for no particular reason) at possible **cultural solutions** to poverty which, for our purposes, involve examining New Right and social democratic perspectives.

New right solutions

⚠ Preparing the ground

From this perspective, 'solutions to the problem of poverty' are constructed around three general areas.

Economic liberalism

For the New Right, the crucial variable in any fight against poverty is the creation of wealth and, from this perspective, economic inequality is the means towards securing the best possible standard of living for the largest number of people.

Although *inequality* may, at first sight, seem an unlikely means towards securing this general aim, we need to remember New Right perspectives generally subscribe to an absolute definition of poverty. Thus, although there will always (necessarily) be inequality, how poverty is defined is crucial to its solution.

A simple way to illustrate this idea is to think in terms of the total amount of wealth in a society as being like a cake (an *economic cake*, if you will – see p. 342).

As I trust this example has shown, the important idea here is neither 'who owns what amount' of the total wealth in any society, nor their relative share of total wealth. Rather, the most important idea is the greater the amount of wealth created and owned by a society the wealthier will be its individual members (that, at least, is the theory according to New Right perspectives).

We can, in passing, note a number of ideas related to the general principle of economic liberalism.

- **Wealth creation**: Given the key to solving poverty is to create wealth, individuals must be allowed free reign (within certain limits defined by fair competition) to make money. This, as you might expect, involves competition within the economic market-place.

- **Legal safeguards**: For wealth creation to occur successfully, certain preconditions need to be in place. These, for example,

relate to things like how wealth may be legally acquired and kept (privately, since you ask). The role of government is seen to be that of enforcing rules of fair competition, safeguarding the rights of property-owners and the like. Any society that allows unproductive individuals (or criminals as they're sometimes known) to steal from wealth producers is effectively creating a huge disincentive to wealth creation – an idea that leads into:

- **Low taxation**: The activities of criminals are not the only disincentive to wealth creation; the more a government takes from people in taxation, the greater is the disincentive to create wealth. For the New Right, no personal taxation would be the ideal, but some form of taxation is

---

The Economic Cake

In the first illustration imagine the share of total wealth (including, for the sake of argument, income) owned by the poorest 50% of the population is represented by the missing slice. In this instance, let's further imagine the poor do not have a large enough share of total wealth to keep them out of absolute poverty.

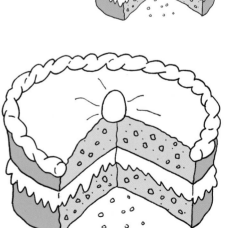

In the second illustration, the cake has increased in size and, although the *relative shares* are the same (assuming, once again, the missing slice is the share of wealth owned by the poorest 50% of the population), those at the bottom of society now have enough wealth to keep them out of absolute poverty.

required to maintain the second general idea, namely a:

- **Minimal state**: **Thomas Sowell** (*A Conflict of Visions*, 2002) notes how the New Right sees the main role of government as ensuring the operation of free economic markets, in terms of setting and maintaining basic 'rules of social order' (as I have noted, free markets are only seen to operate efficiently and successfully under conditions of personal security). The state, however, does not have a role to play in providing:

- **Welfare systems** for the poor. This is because welfare is seen to; shield people from the consequences of their behaviour (an inability to compete in the market place because they have failed to gain the qualifications they need, for example); distort the workings of markets by providing a safety net for failure (the New Right, as I hope you have discovered, don't mince their words in this respect); create disincentives for those in work because a proportion of their income goes to support those who exist within a dependency culture (namely, the underclass).

Poverty

In terms of the above, New Right solutions to poverty are based around two major policy areas.

- **Free markets**: Business should be privately owned and subject only to very light regulation by the state (minimum wage levels, for example, shouldn't be set by law). Private businesses represent the means to 'expand the wealth of the nation', thereby ensuring everyone is kept out of absolute poverty.

- **Anti-welfarism**: The existence of welfare systems is seen as part of the 'problem of poverty' and part of any solution must be to remove the poor from dependence on the state by eliminating most forms of state-sponsored welfare.

Social policy

In terms of social policy, therefore, the *Market Liberal* approach outlined above – characteristic of New Right writers such as **David Marsland** (*Welfare or Welfare State?*, 1996) – involves a number of specific ideas for resolving the twin problems of an underclass and a dependency culture.

- **Universal welfare provision** is *harmful* to society because it limits personal freedom of choice and responsibility. It should be abolished. It fails to help those who most need help (which reflects the distinction between the deserving and undeserving poor we noted in a previous section).

- **Private insurance systems** should be encouraged to allow individuals to choose their personal levels of insurance. This encourages personal and family responsibility.

- **Family groups** (by which is generally meant dual-parent, heterosexual families) should be encouraged and aided by the state since it is this group, governed by ideas of love, trust and affection, that forms the cornerstone of personal and social responsibility. In other words, where people require help they should look first to their family, not the state.

- **Charitable and voluntary groups** should be encouraged to support and supplement the basic welfare provision provided within the family.

Growing it yourself: removing the safety net?

In small groups, use the following table as a template to evaluate New Right ideas about welfare systems provided by the state by identifying possible arguments for and against state provision.

Welfare Provision	
Arguments for private provision	Arguments for state provision
People should be free to choose how to spend their income.	Ensures those who fall into poverty are helped.
	Provision for those unable to care for themselves (the sick and elderly)
Further arguments	

 Digging deeper

When thinking about New Right explanations for – and solutions to – poverty, they assume 'the poor' are a *socially* homogeneous, relatively stable and easily identifiable group. Although the evidence for this is, at best, inconclusive, the general uncertainty around this idea is magnified when we note some problems with **underclass theories** – the first of which is the is the major one of **definition**. As **Chris Jencks** (1989) notes, underclass theory

'focuses attention on the basement of the ... social system (those who are "under" the rest of us), without specifying what the inhabitants of this dark region have in common'. He notes, for example, 'a dozen different definitions' of the underclass, each one providing a different estimate of its composition, size and social significance.

Buckingham ('The Underclass', 1996), for example, wants to define the underclass in terms of 'dependency on the state', a general category that includes those in receipt of state benefits and council house tenants. Writers such as **Murray** are more specific when they include single mothers, the long-term unemployed, various types of petty (and not-so-petty criminal) and so forth. A casual sweep through the British popular press revels a long list of potential – if not necessarily actual – members of the underclass: joy riders, ram-raiders (remember them?), meths drinkers, single mothers, the unemployed, the long-term unemployed, black youths, benefit claimants, 'Chavs' and hunt saboteurs to name but a few.

Ruth Lister (1996) suggests the problem of definition is largely resolved by those who advocate the existence of an underclass, through thinking in moral, rather than material, terms. The underclass, in this respect, includes any group who are considered, for whatever reason, 'morally undesirable'. As **Jencks** (1989) notes 'The term underclass, with its echoes of the underworld, conjures up sin, or at least unorthodox behaviour. Low income may be a necessary condition for membership in such a class, but it is not sufficient'.

This lack of definitional precision – let alone concrete evidence of its existence – has led to the suggestion the underclass is **mythical** – both in the sense of the term being used to stigmatise the behaviour of the poor and in the sense it's used by writers such as **Robert Moore** ('The Underclass', 2001) when he observes: 'The underclass is invisible because it doesn't exist ...' (at least, not in the way writers such as Murray have used the term). **Paul Spicker** (*Poverty and the Welfare State*, 2002) also argues underclass theories are both too vague and, not to put too fine a point on it, wrong: 'Poverty' he argues, 'is a risk which affects everyone not just an excluded minority'.

Finally, therefore, in terms of **evidence** for underclass theories, **Nick Buck** ('Labour Market Inactivity and Polarisation', 1992) argues the economic evidence for an underclass in Britain is actually very thin. In particular, he notes unemployment varies with economic cycles, which means people may experience periods of semi-regular employment/unemployment, but *not* the permanent unemployment predicted by underclass theories. Buck characterises people who experience this type of employment pattern as: 'Unstable members of the working class, not stable members of an underclass'.

Similarly, **Anthony Heath** ('The Attitudes of the Underclass', 1992) found little or no evidence of a permanently excluded group of people who could constitute an underclass. Among the supposed 'underclass', he found such people were actually more likely to want work, less fussy about the types of jobs they took and no less active in the political process than other groups.

A major problem with underclass theory is a general failure to establish 'socially excluded

Discussion point: labelling the underclass

In small groups read the *Daily Mail* extract on 'Chav Culture', then discuss the following questions.

- What are the beliefs and values of 'mainstream society'?
- What are the similarities/differences between 'Chav culture' and mainstream society?
- Is there such a thing as 'Chav culture' or is it simply an example of media labelling?

As a class discuss your answers to the previous questions.

Apply the same line of reasoning to the question: 'Does an identifiable underclass exist in Britain – or are labels such as "Chav" simply expressions of moral distaste for people with different lifestyles?'

The year of the Chav: *Daily Mail*, 22/10/04

Chav was a word coined to describe the spread of the ill-mannered underclass which loves shellsuits, bling-bling jewellery and designer wear, especially the ubiquitous Burberry baseball cap. Queens of Chav include glamour model Jordan while its king is rock star Liam Gallagher and its prince the footballer Wayne Rooney.

Chav is just one of the many new classist labels which have exploded this year. The word is almost certainly from the old Romany word for a child, chavi. But it was reborn last year to describe certain natives of Chatham in Kent. The concept has been popularised by several websites, one of which bills itself as a guide to 'Britain's burgeoning peasant underclass'.

groups' are detached from the beliefs and values of mainstream society (whatever, in practice, these may actually be – as you will have seen in the previous exercise, it is by no means a simple identification exercise). The available evidence – drawn from both the behaviour of the poor and studies of the beliefs and values of those in poverty – suggests this is simply not the case.

Although those in poverty are, to some extent, economically detached (that is, they are poorer than other sections of society) there is little or no evidence for a persistent and wilful cultural detachment supposedly characteristic of an underclass. This observation, as you might expect, leads us to cast doubt on a further feature of underclass theory, namely the concept of a **dependency culture**. A few points are worth noting here, relating to:

- **Evidence**: **Dean** and **Taylor-Gooby** (*Dependency Culture*, 1992) found no evidence of a dependency culture among welfare claimants. What they did find was a desire to work, frustrated by problems in finding it and the low levels of wages on offer. Rather than a dependency culture they found evidence of a poverty trap.

- **Heterogeneity**: Surprising as it may seem, Dean and Taylor-Gooby also found claimants to be a very mixed group of people, living in very different situations and circumstances. Their diversity extended to the fact a proportion of the claimants they questioned had punitive attitudes towards claimants in general.

- **Meaning**: The concept of a dependency culture is an example of the way ideas can mean different things in different contexts. For example, we could characterise all social life as involving some form of culture

of dependency since any society requires its members to form dependent relationships (over such things as care for the sick, the old and the very young). We wouldn't, for example, think about characterising (and implicitly stigmatising) young children in terms of a culture of dependency surrounding their care and nurture.

Le Grand and **Winter** ('The Middle Classes and the Welfare State', 1987) have also noted how *all* social classes, to greater or lesser extents, are involved in some form of dependency culture. A range of tax credits and benefits are enjoyed by the very *rich*, for example, and the 'middle class welfare state' effectively provides cheap health care and education for those who, in reality, need it the least.

- **Independence**: From a Feminist perspective, **Mary McIntosh** ('Dependency Culture?', 1998) has argued the benefit system is:

'. . . an exercise in control, in which workers and claimants are powerless and trapped. And yet surveys have shown most claimants would rather be in employment . . . In the myth of dependency culture, some forms of dependence – wage labour, family relationships, investments, rents and pensions – are seen as normal and legitimate, so much so that they are counted as independence. Receiving state welfare, however, is delegitimized by classing it as 'welfare dependency'.

Social Democratic solutions

⚠ Preparing the ground

From this perspective, solutions to the problem of poverty are constructed around two general areas.

Economic regulation

Although social democratic societies are essentially capitalist in their economic outlook (in Britain, for example, people are encouraged to accumulate and keep wealth in private hands), the role of government is theorised rather differently to the way it is theorised by New Right perspectives. For example, in Britain since the Second World War we've experienced an economy that has mixed both privately owned companies and industries with state owned and controlled industries (such as coal mining, telephones and telecommunications, transport and so forth). Having said this, during the 1980s, the Thatcher Conservative Government introduced a policy of:

- **Privatisation** that saw most state-owned companies and industries being sold to private shareholders (the supply of gas and telephone services, for example, were sold in this way). The state still has some direct ownership and control (the Post Office, for example), but by and large it is general economic role is now one of:
- **Regulation**: That is, rather than playing a direct ownership role, governments 'set the rules' for economic behaviour, in a variety of ways; through the taxation of individuals and companies, the setting of things such as a minimum wage, the creation and policing of Health and Safety regulations and so forth.

The welfare state

Although we will examine the concept of a welfare state (and the role of *voluntary* and *informal groups*) in more detail in the final section of this chapter, Social Democratic perspectives, unlike their New Right counterparts, generally see an important role for government in the provision of welfare services for their citizens, for a number of reasons and in a number of ways.

- **Economic**: Social democratic thinking in this respect extends into two main areas.

  Firstly, some groups in society (such as the elderly, the sick and the differently-abled) are unable to compete for jobs and, consequently, find themselves at risk of poverty. For such people, a state-sponsored welfare system represents a **safety net** to prevent them falling into absolute poverty.

  Secondly, economic and political changes (the influence of globalisation, for example) frequently result in some groups (as the coal mining example (p. 348) suggests) no longer having the skills, training and qualifications needed in the workplace. Where such people become unemployed, the welfare system provides for a period of readjustment (where they retrain, develop required skills and qualifications or simply find work in a different area of the economy).

  Again, State support for such people is seen as easing the strains of economic adjustments.

Sad day for Selby as pit closes early
Sophie Hazan: *West Riding Post*:
19/07/02

Coal miners were in shock today at ... the closure of the country's biggest colliery complex. Selby miners are relatively young, with an average age of 45, and less likely to retire from the labour market following their dismissal. Most miners have worked in the mines, a well-paid manual job, since they left school. It will be very difficult for them to find alternative sources of work.

The Selby Task Force ... with representatives from the Selby District Council, UK Coal and Yorkshire Forward, must now consider the retraining of the thousands of men and their reintroduction into the economy. UK Coal and the government's £43 million redundancy package is expected to payout an average of £27,000 per miner.

• **Political**: If large numbers of the poor, living in conditions of destitution, exist in society with little or no means to support themselves (either through work or welfare) this becomes a political *problem* for governments – not least because such people are likely to turn to illegal means of money-making (crime, prostitution, drug-dealing and so forth). A welfare system, by alleviating the worst effects of poverty, not only has general economic benefits for society (allowing people to retrain, for example), it also has general political benefits in terms of preventing social unrest, the

spread of disease and the like. However, a further political consideration is the:

• **Moral** dimension to welfare. This has a couple of important aspects. Firstly, in a wealthy society such as our own, is it morally right for some people to exist in conditions of poverty while others have far more money than they need? Secondly, welfare systems represent an expression of *social solidarity*; that is, they recognise the bonds that exist between people and reflect the idea society is not simply a 'collection of individuals living in families' (as some on the New Right like to suggest) but rather, a *social collective* in which those who are rich and successful, for example, give something back to society by helping to support those who exist in – and on the margins of – poverty.

The above describes a relatively traditional view of social democratic thinking, reflected perhaps in the post-war development of the welfare state. Recent thinking, however, has turned towards the idea poverty doesn't simply have an economic dimension (not having enough money ...), it also has dimensions related to participation/non-participation in social life – which is where ideas about social inclusion and exclusion come into the picture.

The **Third Way** expresses the idea of a different role for the state – one that rejects both the *market individualism* of the New Right and the traditional 'Welfarism' of successive post-war governments in the UK (the idea, for example, all the poor require is money in the form of government benefits to keep them out of poverty). The Third Way, therefore, focuses on the idea of an **enabling** state, by which is meant the role of government is one that encourages people – through a variety of social policies – to play as full and active part in society as possible. By effectively redefining poverty (as 'exclusion') the role of various agencies – informal, voluntary, private and governmental – becomes that of preventing poverty by intervening at different points to break the cycle/chain of events that both cause poverty and prevent people escaping its clutches. These social policy interventions are currently coordinated in the UK through the Social Exclusion Unit (a government department linked to various welfare agencies) and include a range of policies designed to promote social inclusion in a number of areas.

- **Children and young people**: Policies here reflect concerns about the level of teenage pregnancy (something that links into a desire to prevent some forms of single-parent family developing), how to prevent disaffection, truancy and exclusion from school and the involvement of young people in criminal behaviour.

Specific policies in this area include action to prevent criminals re-offending, problems associated with children in care caused by parental imprisonment and the like. In addition, schemes to promote youth involvement in sport and

the arts are also seen as a way of 'lowering long-term unemployment' through community involvement as well as 'helping to develop the individual pride and capacity for responsibility that enable communities to run regeneration programmes themselves'.

- **Crime**: A range of polices have been developed to prevent adult re-offending and to punish 'anti-social behaviour' – Anti-social Behaviour Orders (ASBOs), for example, can be issued against juveniles to control their behaviour (the punishment for breaking such an order can be imprisonment).

Parenting orders have also been developed to make parents responsible (and punishable) for the behaviour of their children.

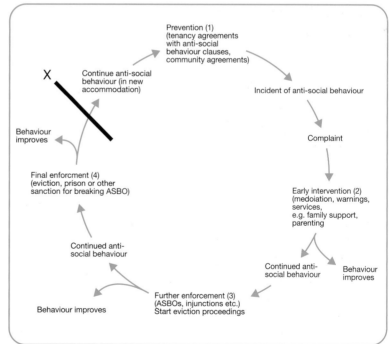

Source: 'PAT 8: Anti-social Behaviour': Social Exclusion Unit, 2000

These policies are based on the concept of a 'Cycle of Repeated Anti-social Behaviour' (pictured) which, the more alert amongst you will notice, has a strong similarity to the *cycle of deprivation* theory.

- **Employment** polices are seen as the key to resolving problems of social exclusion, since unemployment is seen to lie at its heart – those who are *economically excluded* are, proportionately, more likely to suffer *social exclusion*. A range of employment-related polices (from offering advice about returning to work – as well as tax credits for childcare – to single parents, to a range of training schemes) are employed (pun intended) in this respect. Policy in this area also involves regional regeneration initiatives (encouraging employers to relocate to areas of high unemployment, for example) as well as advice on debt management for the short-term unemployed.

- **Education**: Qualifications, training and skills – especially those relating to new technologies (computing and information services, for example) are considered a further way to prevent social exclusion by equipping people with the skills needed for work (the connection is frequently made by social democratic writers between low educational achievement, low-paid work or unemployment and social exclusion). The introduction of *Educational Maintenance Allowances* across the UK in 2004, for example, pays post-16 students up to £30 a week if they stay in full-time education.

- **Neighbourhood regeneration**: Part of the overall solution to poverty involves developing neighbourhood-based communities, which in turn involves policies to regenerate depressed neighbourhoods and create 'sustainable communities'. This is to be achieved, according to the Social Exclusion Unit, by: 'Providing homes for key workers, regenerating towns and cities, providing parks for families and children. Above all it is about helping people to live ... with pride in their community'.

Digging deeper

As I have suggested, the concept of poverty has been widened in recent years to encompass a broad range of ideas – from social inclusion and exclusion to cycles of deprivation – that suggest 'poverty' is something more than the simple lack of money. Whether or not this is actually the case is a debateable point – and whether the Third Way idea of 'tackling social exclusion' is the same as offering a solution to poverty is also something that's up for discussion. However, we can dig a little deeper into social democratic solutions by questioning two of its basic principles, namely: does social exclusion actually exist and how valid is the concept of a cycle of deprivation? We can start, therefore, by looking at **social exclusion**. Many of the problems we've noted with the concepts of an underclass and culture of dependency apply to this idea, so I don't propose to rake over this ground. However, it is worth noting the following.

Since social exclusion can't be directly observed, we have to use *indicators* of exclusion in order to measure it. The problem, however, is a lack of consensus about which indicators to use. **Le Grand** et al ('Social Exclusion in Britain', 1999), for example, used five indicators of social exclusion:

- active engagement in consumption
- savings
- productive paid work
- political attachment/involvement
- social interaction.

They found 'Less than 1% had been excluded on all five dimensions for at least five years'. However, when considering exclusion in terms of **life chances** – both positive (earning a living wage, enjoying good health and so forth) and negative (the chances of being unemployed, going to prison and the like) – **Howarth** et al (1998), used '*Forty-six* indicators to show the numbers of people facing difficulties at various points in their lives'. The indicators were grouped in terms of life stages (children, the elderly and so forth) to reflect 'the importance of multiple disadvantage to individuals'.

Cycle of Deprivation: In recent years at least, this theory has taken on an almost *axiomatic status* (the notion that something is self-evidently true) but **Townsend** ('The Cycle of Deprivation', 1974) has termed this idea a 'confused thesis', in terms of **continuity**. For **Alan Walker** ('Blaming the Victims', 1996) 'The central idea was poverty persists because social problems reproduce themselves from one generation to the next'. He notes, however, a massive UK research programme in the 1970s into a possible cycle of deprivation found '... no simple continuity of social problems between generations'. In addition, the evidence suggests no simple **patterns of disadvantage** between generations. **Rutter** and **Madge** (*Cycles of Disadvantage*, 1976) found 'at least half' of children born into a disadvantaged home didn't display the same levels of deprivation once they reached adulthood – which suggests poverty is not necessarily generational but that forms of disadvantage develop anew with each generation.

In addition, **Brown** and **Madge** (*Despite the Welfare State*, 1982) found no 'inevitable continuity of deprivation' in relation to poverty and the poor.

The basic logic of cycle of deprivation theories is also questionable since, if they exist, effects would have to be **cumulative** – we would expect, even over a couple of generations, to see an expansion of poverty (think in terms of one set of parents producing three children who, in turn produce three children ...). This simply hasn't happened – which either suggests government interventions to break the cycle of deprivation have been successful or, as both the figures for those in poverty and the available research suggests, such a cycle does not actually exist in any significant form.

Having examined individual/cultural examples of solutions to poverty, we can move-on to explore a couple of **structural solutions** that, for our purposes, involve examining Marxist and feminist perspectives.

Marxist solutions

⚠ Preparing the ground

For Marxists there is not so much a 'problem of poverty' in our society as, to paraphrase **R.H. Tawney**, a 'problem of wealth'; that is, they view the unequal distribution of wealth as a prime reason for the existence of poverty – whether you define it in absolute or relative terms. In this respect, Marxist analyses of 'the problem' focus on:

- **Economic inequality**: Capitalist societies are, by definition, unequal societies and the inequality that lies at the heart of this economic system is, as I have just noted, the primary cause of poverty. As we've seen in earlier sections, even in a society as wealthy as the UK, massive inequalities of income and wealth exist – such that a relatively small number of the very wealthy live in great comfort and luxury while those at the other end of the class scale exist on relatively little.

  Economic inequality, for Marxists, is rooted in the relationship between capital, on the one hand, and labour on the other – or, to put this another way, the relationship between those who own the means of production (capitalists) and those who do not. This relationship is fundamentally unequal not simply because owners are able to make profits – by effectively charging more for goods and services than they cost to produce (a production process involving things like wages, raw materials, machine costs and

so forth), but because these profits are kept in private hands, rather than being owned by those who make the goods and provide the services – the working class.

- **Welfarism**: State-sponsored welfare is seen as an attempt to limit the worst excesses of social and economic inequality by giving those at the bottom of society 'just enough' to keep them from destitution. Welfare, from this perspective, operates on both an economic level (payments to people who have been ignored or discarded by employers) and a political level – to prevent social unrest and upheaval.

  As **Tod Sloan** ('Globalization, Poverty and Social Justice', 2003) puts it:

  > The raw effects of capitalist relations in class society have been softened to some extent by the effectiveness of ... state welfare systems ... as 'safety nets' to ensure the basic health and housing of the unemployed ... and the unemployable, particularly when the capitalist economic system is undergoing one of its occasional recessions or depressions.

Welfare, therefore, is another form of **social control**, in a couple of ways. Firstly, it is a means of 'buying-off' discontent with a capitalist system that condemns large numbers of people to poverty and, secondly, it allows the behaviour of the poor to be policed by the state in the form of social workers ('soft policing', as it's sometimes called).

⚠ Digging deeper

In general terms, the solution to poverty is the replacement of a capitalist economic system by **communism** – a political and economic system in which the private ownership of property is abolished; everything is held 'in common' (owned 'by everyone'). The organisation of the workplace along communist principles effectively removes the relationships (owner–worker, employer–employee) that create economic and social inequality.

In other words, Marxists see capitalist societies as incapable of reform (in terms of either reducing levels of inequality or solving problems of poverty). On the contrary, inequality is built into the economic system and poverty has its social and economic uses for a ruling class (providing, as we have noted, a reserve army of labour, for example).

Given the above, it makes it difficult to link Marxist perspectives to any particular social policies related to poverty – save, of the course, the most ambitious policy of all – the replacement of one form of society (capitalism) with another (communism).

Feminist solutions

⚠ Preparing the ground

In a global context, women experience different levels of poverty to men, in a number of ways. **Caroline Sweetman** ('How Does Poverty Relate to Gender Inequality?', 1998) for example, notes that women around the world:

- have less food and suffer greater levels of malnutrition
- are less likely to have paid work
- suffer greater ill-health

- lack access to education
- experience greater levels of homelessness
- suffer greater levels of social exclusion.

In a national context, it would be useful to understand how ideas about poverty relate to female experiences in the UK, where we know, for example, women:

- have equal access to education – and out-perform men at just about every level
- live longer, on average
- are only slightly less likely to have a job than a man
- are no more likely to be malnourished or homeless than men.

Rather than talk about the *feminisation of poverty*, therefore, should we not be examining how poverty is *masculinised*? The answer (as you probably, deep down, suspected) is 'no' – which, given the ideas I've just noted, may seem surprising until you recognise that despite these apparent female advantages (or, at the very least, rough equalities with their male counterparts) women in the UK are far more likely to experience high levels of poverty than men.

This happens for a number of reasons, not the least of which, according to **Julie Mellor** ('Are men the new victims of discrimination?', 2000) relate to the idea 'Women are paying huge prices for being carers as well as breadwinners – lower pay, worse promotion prospects and ultimately poverty in old age because they make less contribution towards pensions'. If women in general are more likely to experience poverty than men, therefore, we need to briefly note how and why this situation occurs.

Economic factors

As discussed in previous sections, female participation in the workplace is conditioned by a number of important factors, including:

- **Horizontal and vertical segregation** that generally means women occupy lower-paid, lower-status, positions within the workplace – as **Lucy Ward** ('Gender Pay Gap', The Guardian, 26/10/04) has suggested in the following terms:

  The entrenched split between traditionally 'male' and 'female' careers is just as glaring among today's teenagers as among their older workmates . . . even those entering the workplace at 16 are choosing occupations along traditional gender lines.

  The continuing trend means "deep-rooted inequalities" in pay and employment prospects are mapped out for young people from the very first day of their working lives . . . Even among teenagers in their first jobs, young women earn 16% less than their male counterparts – blowing apart the myth that the effect on women's careers of having children is the sole cause of pay inequality.

- **Primary** and **secondary labour markets**, where women are over-represented in secondary markets that involve, for example, insecure forms of part-time work. According to the Office for National Statistics (2004), the gender pay gap for full-time workers is 19.5% (female average hourly earnings are approximately 80% of male average hourly earnings) and 40% for part-time workers.

Family life

Just as men and women experience family life and relationships differently, family

arrangements affect the likelihood of greater female poverty in a number of ways.

- **Single-parenthood**: Where women are more likely to be single-parents, this increases their chances of experiencing poverty because of the problems involved in juggling childcare responsibilities and paid work. One consequence of this is involvement in **homeworking**. Both Oxfam ('Made at Home', 2003) and the Equal Opportunities Commission ('EOC calls for an end to poverty pay for homeworkers', 2003) note, for example:

  British women homeworkers are paid, on average, £2.53 per hour, receive no sick, holiday, or maternity pay, are made redundant without notice or compensation, are not subject to adequate health and safety checks [and] lose their jobs if they dare to claim the rights enjoyed by others.

- **Retirement/widowhood**: One consequence of women living longer, coupled with inequalities in welfare and pension arrangements, is the greater likelihood of poverty in old age.

Welfare

The benefits system in the UK is both complicated and extensive, involving as it does a mix of:

- **universal** payments (such as Child Benefit – paid to all families who qualify as a right)

- **means-tested** payments (such as Housing Benefit), paid to claimants on a *sliding scale* related to income and savings – the higher these are, the less benefit you receive

- **insurance-based** payments (such as the Job Seeker's Allowance – pre-1996 this was called Unemployment Benefit), receipt of which is based on the individual having paid National Insurance contributions for a specific qualifying period.

This situation creates problems for women, in particular, because of the impact of their **dual role** as both unpaid domestic workers and paid employees; in basic terms, female qualification for *insurance-based* payments is reduced, according to **Bradshaw** et al ('Gender and poverty in Britain', 2003) through: 'A broken employment history because of child rearing and high rates of part-time work'.

Where benefits are *means-tested* (and assuming both a male and female in the household) Bradshaw et al note how:

> Women's poverty can be hidden by unequal income distribution within the household. When resources are tight, women are more likely than men to go without. Women tend to manage money when it is in short supply and there is debt, carrying the stressful burden of budgeting.

A further aspect of poverty here is how it 'restricts social activity, causes stress in relationships and becomes a dominant feature of everyday life.' As **Bradshaw et al** argue: 'There is some evidence that social isolation and depression are felt especially by young women, and that women and men may experience poverty in different ways'.

Female poverty in old age (roughly 60% of pensioners are women) is also related to many of the above factors; a broken work record, for example, coupled with child care responsibilities makes it harder for women to make sufficient employment-related pension payments to receive a full pension – on average, female pensioners have only 50% of male retirement income.

⚠ Digging deeper

In terms of social policy, we can note a number of possible solutions to female poverty, in four main areas.

Work

In 'Beating the gender poverty trap' (Trades Union Congress Women's Conference Report, 2003), suggestions for policy changes to benefit women included:

- raising the national minimum wage
- setting government-backed and enforced targets for raising female incomes.

    As **Mellor** argues:

    > The Equal Pay Act has not brought about equal pay . . . If you take any of the lowest paid work – cleaning, catering, home care – you will find jobs done mainly by women. You will find women who juggle two or three of these jobs at a time, because one alone wouldn't pay enough to live on. You will find women scraping together a living for themselves and their families.

- Setting targets for closing the gender pay gap (for both full time and part time workers).
- The provision of affordable childcare and an increased level of childcare tax credits.

The Equal Opportunities Commission ('Pensions – why do women face poverty in old age?', 2003) has argued policy work needs to be done to prevent women falling into poverty in old age by recognising different male and female working patterns. In particular:

- **employer pension schemes** need to include part-time workers

- **flexible part-time working** needs to be made available 'as retirement approaches without jeopardising retirement benefits'
- **pension entitlement** should be extended to more working women.

Family life

Policies to reduce or solve female poverty suggested by the TUC Women's Conference Report (2003) include:

- Child Support payment increases (from non-resident parents)
- paid carer leave from work
- earnings-related maternity pay
- increased Carer's Allowance
- more government funding for local authority care services
- tax and pension credits 'for those out of paid employment for parenting or family care reasons'.

Education

As we have seen, men and women still tend to choose different work and career paths in our society which, in some respects, may be related to gender stereotyping in schools (when, given the choice, males and females study different subjects and are encouraged, through careers services for example to pursue – or not as the case may be – different occupational paths and strategies). Social policy in this area, therefore, should be directed at ending this type of gendered curriculum.

Welfare

A range of policies could be implemented to significantly reduce disadvantages faced by women. As we have noted, extending and increasing state pension payments and linking increases to average earnings (rather than average price increases – the latter tend to rise more slowly than the former) would be one way of raising many women (and men, come to that) out of old age poverty. In addition, work-related state benefits need to reflect more closely the reality of male and female working lives.

In this section we've made frequent reference to areas such as the welfare state and the provision of welfare benefits. Although discussion has, by and large, focused on government action (or inaction), 'welfare' is not just a quality of governments. A range of organisations (some formal, some informal), exist in our society for the purpose of welfare provision and, in the final section we need to examine the nature and role of welfare providers in more detail.

Welfare provision

Introduction

When we think about the provision of welfare services in our society (as most of us probably do in those idle moments when there's nothing on the TV), we tend to think about the welfare state and the range of services it provides – from doctors and hospitals, through education to pensions. Welfare provision, however, is not simply a matter of government services – it is, as you will no doubt be disappointed to learn, a little more complicated than that – which is why in this section we are going to look at the nature and role of public, private, voluntary and informal welfare provision.

Before we begin in earnest, however, we need to clarify a few ideas.

The concept of 'welfare' considered in terms of its widest definition, simply involves the idea of help being given to someone who needs it. If I'm 'looking out for your welfare', it means I care about you, am considerate of your needs and will help you to overcome problems in your life (I'm not, by the way – this is just an example that makes me look good). We need to keep this definition in mind, since it means the concept of welfare provision potentially has many forms, the most obvious of which, perhaps, is **public welfare** that, for our purposes at least, refers to services and benefits provided by the state and generally funded through some form of direct or indirect taxation. Although the provision of public welfare – in some shape or form – has a relatively long history in Britain (the 'Ordinance of Labourers' in *1349*, for example, was designed to stop people giving relief to 'able-bodied beggars', the idea being to make them work for a living – some ideas, it seems, never change), our main focus will be on the creation and development of the Welfare State, post-1945.

Private welfare generally refers to the role of private companies in the provision of a range of personal and public services. This includes both companies who expressly exist to provide such services and also companies who provide welfare benefits to their workforce (such as a pension scheme) as part of their employment contract.

Voluntary provision, on the other hand, relates to services provided by a range of groups and individuals (charities and self-help groups, for example) independently of state provision – although, as we will see, the activities of such groups may be *regulated* and *coordinated*, on a local and national level, by the government. As you might expect, voluntary provision of welfare by charitable and religious groups has a long history in our society.

Informal welfare is the final form of welfare, whose significance should not be overlooked or underestimated. This is welfare provided by people such as family and friends – a potentially important source of care throughout peoples' lives. This type of provision is informal because there is no guarantee it will be offered when needed.

WARM UP: WELFARE PROVISION

It's a 'strange-but-true' fact that you already know a reasonable amount about these different types of welfare provision. As a class, or in small groups, therefore, use the following table as a template to identify as many examples as you can of the different types of welfare provision provided by the four agencies identified.

Forms of Welfare			
Individuals	Charities	Private Companies	Government
Babysitting	Soup kitchens	BUPA (health care)	National Health Service
Child care	Gambler's Anonymous	Occupational pensions	11–16 Education
Further examples			

Public welfare

⚠ Preparing the ground

The concept of a welfare state in Britain is something we tend to associate with developments during and immediately after the Second World War; while these are clearly very important (they formed the basis for state welfare provision that's still going strong 50 years later) some forms of state-sponsored welfare provision existed prior to this. In the early part of the last century, for example, old age pensions were introduced (however, given it was paid at age 70 – when average life expectancy for working class men was around 45 years – this didn't greatly benefit the poor); a rudimentary health service and unemployment benefit system also existed at this time.

The above notwithstanding, the focus here is on post-war developments, mainly because this period represents the most coherent attempt to develop a universal system of state welfare.

In many ways, the nature, purpose and role of public welfare has changed over the past 50 years, reflecting a movement away from a simple government concern with the *relief of poverty* and the improvement of general living standards to thinking about how some, relatively poor, groups in society are *socially excluded* (and, by extension, how government action can lead to their social inclusion). We need, therefore, to understand welfare changes in:

- **ideological** terms – how ideas about the nature and purpose of public welfare have changed, as well as:

- **political** terms – how different political groups, for example, have attempted to stamp their ideas on welfare provision and, of course,

- **economic** terms – since, in many ways, questions of cost and affordability have influenced the nature, extent and type of public provision available.

We can track this sense of change in the nature of welfare provision (and, as we will see, the role of government) by thinking, initially, about the nature and purpose of the **welfare state**, which developed in a social context very different to our present-day society. The ideas forming the basis for the welfare state (brought together in the 1942 Beveridge Report – officially known as the 'Social Insurance and Allied Services Report') developed against a background of war and environmental destruction as well as severe social and economic privation (hardship).

The nature of welfare provision, in such a situation, focused on what Beveridge considered to be '5 Giants' that needed to be conquered:

The '5 Giants' of Welfare Reform	
Giant	Example Legislation
Ignorance	Butler Education Act (1944)
Want	Family Allowance Act (1945)
Idleness	National Insurance Act (1946)
Disease	National Health Act (1948)
Squalor	The building of good-quality, low-rent, public ('Council') housing

The idea of '5 Giants' tells us something important about both the thinking behind the creation of a welfare state and the nature of the welfare it was designed to provide – this was a society in which major social problems existed and, as such, required major, state-led, changes to the way welfare was provided.

The welfare state reflected an important social democratic consensus about the desirability of both a national system of welfare provision (based on the principle of *need* rather than the ability to pay) and the way it should be funded – through a general taxation system which meant services were 'free at the point of contact'.

One of the interesting features of the post-war welfare consensus was the ambitious nature of the overall project – it aimed to provide a comprehensive system of:

- **Health care**, through a National Health Service integrating General Practitioners (neighbourhood doctor's surgeries) with hospital services.
- **Housing**, through a system of Local Authority ('Council') housing designed to provide relatively cheap – but good quality – rented accommodation for those most in need.
- **Education**: Compulsory and free education was introduced for all children between the ages of 5 and 15, via a 'Tripartite system' of grammar, secondary modern and technical schools (a system explained in more detail in the Education chapter).
- **Insurance**: A number of different forms of (compulsory) social insurance were introduced for groups such as the unemployed and the elderly, funded through a National Insurance levy on

wages. Other forms of benefits were also made available for those without the required employment history to qualify for insurance payments.

With the exception of public housing, these general forms of state welfare provision have remained in place to the present day; however, there have been a number of changes in the way state-based welfare has been provided – and related debates about how it can and should be funded.

In the 1980s, for example, a radical shift in thinking about public welfare provision developed around three main factors.

- **Ideology**: The rise of New Right ideas (initially in the USA and more gradually in the UK) prompted a reassessment of the nature and role of welfare provision. From a libertarian, New Right perspective, for example **Nigel Ashford** ('Dismantling the Welfare State', 1993) identified six reasons for arguing against public welfare.

  - **Immorality** – income is 'forcibly redistributed from taxpayers to those who are believed to deserve it by politicians'.
  - **Freedom of choice**: Free, universal, provision makes it more difficult for other alternatives (such as private health care) to compete with state provision.
  - **Welfare dependency** – the creation of 'a class ... permanently dependent on the state for all their major decisions' (an idea we've examined in some detail in relation to New Right concepts of an underclass and dependency culture).
  - **Ineffective** – State welfare systems rarely achieve the goals they are set

and rarely benefit those most in need. 'The middle classes', for example, 'are the disproportionate beneficiaries of the nationalised health system'.

- **Producer capture** involves the consumer lacking choice over welfare provision. 'In a monopoly situation the service is provided in the interests of the producer' and, consequently, provides no consumer checks-and-balances on the quality of the service provided – you can't, for example, easily change your doctor if you don't like the service they provide.

- **Inefficient** – private welfare provision, selectively targeted at those in most need, can provide welfare services more cheaply and more responsively to the needs of the consumer.

- **Politics**: Between 1979 and 1997, successive Conservative governments (under first Margaret Thatcher and then John Major) introduced a number of general changes to public welfare provision based, in part, on the general ideological principles just outlined. In particular, a system of:

  - **Internal markets**, designed to 'promote competition and increase effectiveness and efficiency' within the welfare state was developed. The National Health Service, for example, saw competition between different hospitals and departments for the treatment of patients.

  - **Privatisation** policies were also pursued, whereby state-owned assets (such as British Gas and British Telecom) were sold to private shareholders. Privatisation extended directly into the welfare sphere

through council house tenants being given the 'Right To Buy' their home at a market discount depending on a range of qualifying factors (such as having lived in the house for at least two years).

A further aspect of privatisation involved explicit government encouragement of *private pensions* (through media advertising, for example); the basic idea behind this was that people should save for their retirement throughout their working lifetime. Increased income in old age, it was believed, would lead to lower levels of elderly poverty.

However, a major problem with this idea was the *misselling* of private pensions.

Royal & Sun Alliance fined £1.35m

Lisa Bachelor: 27/08/02

Royal & Sun Alliance, one of the UK's largest insurance groups, has been fined £1.35m for failing to provide compensation to over 13,000 of its customers who were mis-sold [private] pensions.

Source: http://money.guardian.co.uk/

- **Economics**: A third factor, as **Wrigley** (*Welfare State*, 2004) notes, was the 'escalating cost' of:

  - **Unemployment-related benefits** – the early 1980s saw a massive rise in the number of unemployed.

  - The **National Health Service**, partly caused by an ageing population – a combination of a decline in the birth rate and an increase in life expectancy. The elderly, for example, tend to make greater use of GP and hospital services than other age groups.

The influence of these ideas has, it could be argued, led to a change in the nature of welfare provision and a reassessment of the role played by government. We can see this most noticeably in the changes introduced by **New Labour** governments (from 1997 onward). They continued the reform of public welfare provision begun under previous governments, partly, as **Wrigley** argues, because of a commitment to keep to previous financial spending targets and partly because of an *ideological change* in perceptions of the nature and role of public welfare. **Carey Oppenheim** ('The Post Conservative Welfare State', 1998), for example, argues the key elements of the New Labour approach to public welfare were:

- **Reciprocity** – the idea welfare provision should be based on a system of 'rights and responsibilities'. Many original aspects of the welfare state were based on this idea (individuals make national insurance contributions, for example, in order to receive benefits if and when they are needed). New Labour took this idea further, however, in a couple of ways.

- **Policies** – such as the Child Support Agency (originally created by the Conservative government in 1993 and substantially reformed by New Labour), designed to promote 'individual responsibility' for family welfare. The Child Support Agency targeted single-parent families by requiring an 'absent parent' (one living apart from their partner) to contribute to the financial upkeep of their children.

- **Participation**: One aspect of the changing role of welfare provision (over the past five or so years) has been a desire to move away from a rigid, bureaucratic, professionally administered system to one where the *consumers* of welfare (or 'clients' as they're sometimes called) have greater involvement in the *delivery* of welfare (rather than simply being recipients of state aid). This has resulted in the development of a number of initiatives for delivering welfare and, by extension, a change in the relationship between public, private, voluntary and informal welfare providers.

Although we will explore this idea in more detail in the following section, we can note for the moment how the state has developed a **coordination role** in the delivery of welfare. In other words, although government is still involved in welfare as a primary provider, its role has been modified to accommodate, sponsor and coordinate the activities of a variety of private, voluntary and informal groups. **Craig** et al (*Developing local compacts*, 1999), for example, studied the development of 'national compacts' involving 'joint working between government and the voluntary and community sectors' in areas such as:

- **Health Action Zones** – partnerships between the NHS, local authorities, community groups and the voluntary and business sectors.

- The **New Deal for Communities** – partnerships to tackle the problems of 'poor job prospects; high levels of crime; educational under-achievement; poor health and problems with housing and the physical environment'.

- **Sure Start** – designed to deliver programmes related to 'early education, childcare, health and family support'.

Welfare to work: A key element in the New Labour welfare strategy is to make a distinction between *poverty* (in the sense of economic hardship) and *social exclusion* (in the sense of social – but not necessarily economic – inequality). The original focus of the welfare state was the former; the new *focus* of welfare is the latter – and one way to promote social inclusion is through work (at least it is from a New Labour, social democratic, perspective).

To this end, various programmes have been developed with the aim of getting people (from the unemployed, through single-parents to the differently-abled) into some form of work (such as job creation schemes, the introduction of flexible working rules and so forth). An example of this type of thinking about the nature and role of welfare was the introduction of a **minimum wage**, designed to increase the income differential between those in work and those out of work. This may, at first site, seem an odd way of tackling poverty, until you realise it's designed to tackle exclusion – a subtle, but important, difference. The thinking here, therefore, was that by increasing the income differential (by forcing all employers to pay a minimum level of wages) the option of work would become more attractive to those living on welfare payments. They would, therefore, be taken out of a 'culture of dependency' (an idea, you will remember – or not as the case may be – that's central to both New Right and social democratic views on poverty and

exclusion) and *reintegrated* into mainstream society.

We will look in more detail in a moment at what all this means for the (changing) role of welfare provision in our society.

Private welfare

As the name suggests, this involves profit-making individuals and companies providing welfare services. This may involve things like:

- **fees** – money paid directly to a company for a specific service (such as buying a place at an independent (public) school, a private consultation with a doctor, a hospital operation and so forth) and

- **insurance** – which involves things like paying money regularly into a fund (such as a private pension, for example) or buying a particular policy to cover a possible eventuality (such as the risk of falling ill and being unable to work). It is, of course, possible to take out insurance that, eventually, will be used to pay something like school fees.

There is, however, a further development we could note here, namely the increasing involvement of private companies in the **welfare infrastructure**. That is, although private companies may not be directly involved in the provision of services (such as hospital treatment) they may have built (and technically own) the hospital in which the treatment takes place – which they then *lease* to the government. Private developers, according to the **University of Ulster Centre for Property and Planning** ('Accessing private finance', 1998), are also extensively involved in 'urban regeneration' schemes on a similar basis.

As **Tania Burchardt** ('Boundaries between public and private welfare', 1999) points out, 'Welfare has never been the exclusive preserve of the state'. This was as true before the development of the welfare state (most doctors, for example, charged fees for consultations) as it is today – you can, for example, buy private medical treatment and care if you can afford it. The main question here, however, is not so much the nature of private welfare provision (as indicated above), but more the changing role of private providers and, as a consequence, the changing role of public providers.

Although, as we will see, the public – private welfare provision relationship is becoming increasingly complex, we also need to consider a further aspect of this relationship.

Voluntary organisations

In general terms, we can characterise this type of welfare provider as:

- **Non-profit-making**.
- **Voluntary**: An obvious point to make, perhaps, but the activities of many of these organisations are highly dependent on volunteer help – whether in terms of things like collecting money for charity or working in a community with disadvantaged individuals and groups.

  Filiz Niyazi ('A Route to Opportunity', 1996) has noted how the 'image and culture of volunteering … perceived as a predominantly white, middle-class activity' meant groups such as the young, the elderly, the unemployed, the disabled and some ethnic minorities were likely to be underrepresented amongst volunteers.

- **Independent** of government (although some groups work closely with – and may be funded by – local and national government departments).
- **Structured** – usually, but not necessarily, along similar lines to private providers (in terms of having a skilled, professional workforce, a distinctive managerial organisation and so forth).
- **Regulated** by government: charities (such as Oxfam) are subject to rules governing how they may or may not use their funds, for example.

Having said this, one notable feature of voluntary organisations in the UK is their **diversity**. Voluntary organisations actually take a number of different forms, ranging in size from large, national (and international) organisations (charities such as Oxfam, with an income of £188 million in 2002), to smaller, locally-based, *community groups* (Cardiff Action for Single Homeless, for example, with an income of £1.1 million in 2003) or even small *voluntary associations* based at neighbourhood level.

Although, traditionally, voluntary organisations have worked independently of government, this situation is increasingly changing as they become further integrated into the changing nature of welfare provision in the UK. This, in turn, perhaps, indicates something of a changing role for such groups – especially where they are funded – but not directly controlled – by the state and where their basic organisation and composition is regulated through government departments. The process of integration has not, however, necessarily been simple or smooth.

Kumar and **Nunan** (*A Lighter Touch: an Evaluation of the Governance Project*, 2002) have suggested the integration of community-based groups, for example, into the overall welfare system has been hindered by '... confusion and contradictions over their support arrangements and the way they are governed' – especially in terms of 'unsuitable legal frameworks and poor, inappropriate constitutions'.

Despite problems of integration, voluntary organisations have an important role to play in a welfare system that, although largely *centrally funded* and directed, is increasingly *localised* in terms of where and how some forms of welfare are delivered – especially those that focus on policies for social inclusion.

In some respects, the distinction between voluntary groups and informal types of care (see below) is becoming increasingly blurred 'at the margins'; for example, the development of 'self-help' groups (characterised by **Judy Wilson** ('Two Worlds', 1994) as 'groups run by and for people who share a common problem or experience') involves a relatively informal system of help and care within communities, neighbourhoods and even families.

Informal welfare provision

This type of care has, traditionally, been provided by and within family and friendship groups (mainly, it needs to be noted, by women). General features of this type of provision include the idea it is:

- **unstructured** (in the sense of not being formally organised)
- **free** (provided at little or no cost to the government)
- **affective** – people provide care for the elderly, sick, differently-abled and so forth because they feel love, affection

and responsibility for their welfare. **Bryony Beresford** ('Positively Parents: Caring for a Severely Disabled Child', 1994), for example, noted:

The pleasure and satisfaction gained through the relationship with the disabled child was the fundamental reason why parents felt able to continue to care for their child ... [even though] the stresses associated with the care of their disabled child to be wide-ranging, unrelenting and sometimes overwhelming.

Although, as I have suggested, informal types of care are both traditional and, probably, the oldest form of welfare provision in our society, the recently developed welfare focus on inclusion and exclusion has tended to draw some forms of informal care into the general welfare net, leading to a distinct change in the role – if not necessarily the nature – of such care. For example, we can note the concept of **Care in the Community** – the idea that, rather than incarcerate (lock up) the mentally ill in large, impersonal, institutions, their welfare would, it was argued, be increased if they were cared for within the community – which, in effect, meant within the family group. The *Community Care Act* (1990), for example, created a system of patient assessment, community care and progress reviews for mentally ill individuals who were professionally assessed as posing little or no risk to the community.

In some respects, therefore, informal types of care have become part of the general, formalised, system of welfare in the UK – whether this involves family members receiving government allowances as 'carers' or the integration of a variety of self-help groups into community regeneration projects. However, although informal caring has certain **advantages**, which include things like:

- **local** delivery
- **responsiveness** to individual needs
- **personal** experiences of carers of the problems they are helping to resolve,

it also has some significant **disadvantages**, such as:

- **Patriarchy**: Feminists have generally pointed to the patriarchal assumptions underlying the establishment of the welfare state (men as the breadwinners and women the homemakers – assumptions, as we have seen, that have resulted in women being in a weaker position to claim insurance-based benefits in the past); increasingly this criticism has been applied to government involvement in informal care where, as I've noted, family care (a type of emotional, as well as physical, labour) very often means 'care by women'.

- **Resources**: Delivery of informal care is frequently provided 'by the poor, for the poor' – in effect, some aspects of the burden of welfare are shifted from government responsibility to family responsibility without a consequent redistribution of resources.

Digging deeper

In the previous section we have looked at both the changing nature of welfare provision in our society and, to a slightly lesser degree, the changing role of welfare providers. In this respect, when we think about the provision of welfare benefits and services in twenty-first century Britain, they involve a complex interplay of two main areas.

- **Between** different types of provider (public and private, voluntary and informal).

- **Within** different types of provision: government, for example, is not simply a provider of benefits and services, but also a purchaser of services from private, voluntary and informal providers. The table on p. 366 identifies some characteristics of the range of welfare interconnections in our society.

 Growing it yourself: informal caring

Using the following table as a guide, identify some advantages and disadvantages, for both governments and individuals, of informal caring:

Informal care			
Individuals		Government	
Advantages	Disadvantages	Advantages	Disadvantages
Individualised, personal, caring	Lack of resources	Cheap	Provision not targeted on those who need it most
Further examples			

Provider	Example provision
Publicly funded and administered	Unemployment benefit
Publicly funded privately administered	Some operations on the NHS are carried out in private hospitals.
Publicly funded and administered by voluntary groups	**Taylor** et al ('Independent organisations in community care', 1994) note the way responsibility for community care has been increasingly transferred to both private and voluntary organisations
Privately funded and publicly administered	Some aspects of the welfare infrastructure – such as school and hospital building – are privately funded but managed within the state system
Privately funded and privately administered	Private hospitals

To put the idea of welfare provision into some sort of overall context, therefore, we can note it involves the idea of **welfare pluralism** – that is, welfare provided by a number of different groups and institutions. Pluralism is, of course, not a new idea; as we've seen, even before the creation of the welfare state a variety of different formal and informal welfare providers existed. However, **Burchardt** (1999) suggests, welfare pluralism can be theorised in a number of different ways, in terms of, for example:

- A **one-dimensional model**, where 'welfare can be divided into a dominant and monolithic state sector with a residual 'private' category including anything that is not directly provided by the state or is not tax-funded'.

- A **two-dimensional model** which 'allows for state purchases of private services, and private purchases of public services, as well as the more traditional all-public and all-private sectors'.

She also, however, notes a possible *third dimension* to the public–private relationship, namely **decision making** on the part of consumers. This involves the idea publicly

funded welfare is provided by a range of private producers from which the consumer then chooses. Although this type of decision-making relationship has rarely been explored in the UK, one example was the introduction of a **voucher system** for the purchase of nursery care. Introduced in 1996/97 (by the then Conservative Government – it was subsequently scrapped by New Labour), government funds, in the form of a voucher, could be used by parents to purchase childcare from private providers.

Within the context of welfare pluralism, we can also note the changing nature of welfare delivery. In terms of **public welfare**, for example, we can identify three basic modes of delivery for services and benefits.

- **Universal** forms of delivery are based on the idea everyone in a given population has access to welfare benefits – whether they need them or not at any given time. Within this category we could note such things as the National Health Service as being 'universally delivered'. In terms of economic benefits, however, there are few forms of universal provision – child benefit (paid to parents with children, regardless of their income level) being a notable exception.

- **Selective** forms of delivery, on the other hand, can be considered in terms of their *targeting* at specific groups, rather than the whole population. The selection process to decide eligibility is usually based on *means testing*; for example, if your income is below a certain specified level you receive the benefit or service (Higher Education tuition fees, for example, are based around a means test of eligibility).

- **Insurance-based** benefits and services are based around the idea certain forms of risk (such as unemployment or old age) are effectively pooled, in the sense people pay a proportion of their income to the government (through National Insurance contributions, for example) and receive benefits as and when (or if) they need them.

Discussion point: feeling the benefit?

In small groups, identify and discuss the possible advantages and disadvantages of the three basic types of service and benefit delivery models identified above.

As a class, combine your ideas to evaluate the strengths and weaknesses of each type of delivery model.

Which model do you feel is the most effective way of delivering welfare services and benefits?

Depending on the precise relationship between these different types of delivery model, we can characterise the role of welfare

systems (and, by extension, the role of welfare providers) as relating to what **Neville Harris** ('The Welfare State, Social Security and Social Citizenship Rights', 1998) identifies as the 'Two chief models of welfare systems'. In idealised terms, these involve:

- **Residual models**, based on ideas relating to:
  - **Absolute poverty**: Welfare provision is aimed at those who live beneath a specified poverty line, usually – but not necessarily – defined in terms of minimal biological and cultural needs.
  - **Selectivity**: Help, where it is provided by the state, for example, is targeted specifically at those considered to be in absolute poverty.
  - **Safety net**: Welfare is seen to provide a way of ensuring the very poorest in society do not fall below a minimum standard of living for the society in which they live.
  - **Objectives**: The main objective of welfare is to help people to eventually provide for themselves and their families through, for example, work.
  - **Providers**: Although, within this type of model, the state has some role to play in welfare provision, the main providers are normally voluntary organisations (such as charities) and private welfare agencies (which means individual welfare provision tends to be largely insurance-based; individuals buy private insurance against illness, unemployment and so forth).
- **Institutional models**, based around ideas such as:
  - **Relative poverty**: Welfare provision is aimed at those who live below an

average level of living standards. These people, depending on the society in which they live, may not be considered destitute; rather, they are probably best viewed as being relatively deprived when compared to 'normal and expected' standards of living in their society.

- **Universality**: The focus of welfare provision is less on individual cases, as such, and more on the desire to ensure general levels of living standards for the majority of a population. Welfare, in this respect, is viewed in terms of social, rather than specifically individual, needs. A National Health Service, for example, has general social benefits because it prevents the spread of disease by ensuring those who are ill receive treatment, regardless of their ability to pay for it.

- **Redistributive**: Universal forms of provision are normally funded through general taxation, progressively levied on the individual's ability to pay. In the UK, for example, the greater your income, the more income tax you pay (at least in theory – the rich tend to develop ways of minimising the amount of tax they actually pay as, in some instances, do the very poor when they work 'cash-in-hand' for example).

- **Objectives** for this type of system vary. In the UK in the twenty-first century, for example, the state is faced with markedly different problems to solve than those faced at the end of the Second World War – then, the problems were ones of economic and environmental reconstruction, the relief of absolute poverty and so forth.

Now, problems are essentially two-pronged.

Firstly, although poverty relief is still important, living standards have risen; this has tended to change the welfare focus to that of social inequality – as poverty has declined, for example, inequality has increased.

Secondly, problems of social inclusion and integration are increasingly significant now (when they weren't in 1950s). The impact of economic globalisation, the problem of fragmenting social relationships, a greater sense of individual identities and needs, combined with the rise of New Right welfare ideologies and so forth have created problems of social inclusion and exclusion that, arguably, have to be solved by the state.

- **Providers**: In general, the state is seen as the one institution in society with the power and capability to both provide universal forms of welfare and to coordinate the welfare efforts of a variety of different providers.

Growing it yourself: residual and universal?

The welfare system in our society arguably combines elements of both the residual and universal models. Using the following table as a template, identify elements of welfare provision that reflect:

Residual models	Universal models
Housing benefit	National Health Service Child benefit
Further examples	

As you may recall from the Introductory chapter, one of the key ways of distinguishing sociological knowledge from 'everyday' or common sense knowledge is that sociologists try – not always successfully it has to be admitted – to test their ideas (or 'theories') about how and why people behave as they do. This being the case, it follows that to test their ideas sociologists have to do research and, as luck would have it, in this chapter we're going to examine two aspects of sociological research:

- **methods** – the various ways sociologists collect data and
- **methodology** – the different ways sociologists justify their use of different methods.

This distinction between *methods* (*what* you do) and *methodology* (*why* you do it) raises a couple of interesting possibilities in terms of the AS course because, on the one hand, it allows us to get involved in *doing sociology* (either in terms of AS Coursework or by completing the exercises embedded in this chapter) and, on the other, it allows us to stretch ourselves, academically, by reflecting on some of the less practical, more theoretical, areas surrounding such things as our *choice of research method* and *ethical questions* about who we study and how we study them.

Before we start to consider the range of research methods available to sociologists, we need to be clear about 'the distinctions between primary and secondary data,and between quantitative and qualitative data'. In addition, it would be useful to briefly explain some *methodological concepts* relating to data, namely: *reliability*, *validity*, *representativeness* and *generalisability*.

Sociological methods

⚠ Preparing the ground

- **Primary data** involves information collected *personally* by a sociologist – who, therefore, knows exactly how the data was collected, by whom and for what purpose (you don't, for example, have to trust that other people collected their data accurately). As we will see, sociologists use a range of research methods (such as questionnaires, interviews and observational studies) as *sources* of primary data.

- **Secondary data** involves information *not personally* collected by the researcher, but used by them in their research. Sources of secondary data include newspaper articles, books, magazines, personal documents (such as letters and diaries), official documents (such as government reports and statistics) and even the research of other sociologists.

Both these sources can be either of two types:

Quantitative data represents an attempt to *quantify* behaviour – to express it *statistically* or *numerically*. For example, we could count the number of people in the UK who wear glasses (if we had nothing else better to do) or the number of people who commit crimes each year. Quantitative data is usually expressed in one of three main ways. As a:

- **number**, for example, the number of people who live in poverty

- **percentage** (the number of people per 100 in a population), for example, 30% of voters in Britain regularly vote Conservative

- **rate** (the number of people per 1000 in a population), for example, if the birth rate in Britain was 2, this means for every 1000 people in a population, two babies are born each year.

Data is often expressed as a rate or percentage because it allows **comparisons** between and within societies. For example, when comparing levels of unemployment between Britain and the USA, expressing unemployment as a simple (or *raw* as it is sometimes called) number wouldn't tell us very much, since the population of America is roughly five times that of Britain. Expressing unemployment as a percentage or rate allows us to compare 'like with like', in the sense we are taking into account the fact one society has substantially more

Growing it yourself: who studies what?

For each of your A-level subjects, count the number of male and female students. Express this as a percentage for each subject.

Once you've done this, combine your data with the information collected by other students in your class to arrive at an overall picture of 'who studies what' at A-level in your school or college. In which subjects are:

- females in the majority?

- males in the majority?

- neither in the majority?

(The idea of a gendered curriculum is discussed in more detail in the education chapter).

people than the other (so we might expect the larger society to, *numerically*, have more people unemployed – even though their unemployment *rates* might be broadly similar).

Qualitative data tries to capture the *quality* of people's behaviour (what they *feel*, for example, about a sociologist asking them if they wear glasses). Qualitative data, therefore, says something about the way people *experience* the social world. It's also used to understand the *meanings* people give to both their own behaviour and that of others.

For example, **Boyle** (*A Sense of Freedom*, 1977) studied the behaviour of a juvenile gang from the viewpoint of its members. **Goffman** (*Asylums*, 1968) on the other hand, tried to understand the experiences of patients in a US mental institution. Both, in their different ways, were trying to capture and express the *qualities* of people's behaviour in different situations.

As I have suggested, research methods don't simply involve thinking about data types (qualitative and quantitative) and sources (primary and secondary); we also

need to think about our reasons for choosing particular types and sources in our research – something that involves considering **methodological concepts**. Including:

- **Data reliability** relates to the 'nuts-and-bolts' of actually doing research; in other words, it mainly refers to the methods of data collection we use (such as interviews) and, more specifically, to the *consistency* of the data we collect. Data reliability is important because it suggests we can check the data we get from our research by repeating that research (or something very similar) to see if we get the same results.

Thus, data is reliable if similar results are gained by different researchers (or the same researcher at different times) asking the same questions to similar people. For example, a researcher may try to *cross-check* the reliability of a response within a questionnaire by asking the same question in a different way:

- How old are you?
- When were you born?

If they get two different answers, it is likely the data is *unreliable*.

- **Data validity** refers to the extent to which data gives a true measurement or accurate description of 'reality' (what is *really happening* in a situation). Data, it could be argued, is only useful if it actually *measures* or *describes* what it claims to be measuring or describing.

For example, if we were interested in the extent of crime in our society, we could use official crime statistics (a *secondary*

Discussion point: your influences

Think about the subjects you are doing at A-level. Who or what influenced your decision to choose these subjects to study?

Discuss the different influences you've identified with the rest of the class – who or what seems to be the most influential factor in A-level choice for this class?

quantitative data source published by the government). We would need to be aware, however, the validity of these statistics may be limited since they only record *reported* crimes – and people may not report they have been a victim (for many possible reasons – such as a fear of reprisal from the criminal or the belief the police will not be able to trace the perpetrator, to name but two).

Synoptic link: The validity of crime statistics links to theories of crime and deviance.

This example also raises questions relating to **representativeness**. Whatever type of data we use (primary or secondary, quantitative or qualitative), an important question to always consider is the extent to which the data accurately *represents* what it claims to represent (or what we believe it represents) – something we can think about in two basic ways.

- **Data representativeness** refers to the idea that any information we collect through our research is sufficiently comprehensive to accurately represent something. Using the crime statistics example introduced above, it can be argued these statistics are *unrepresentative* of all crimes committed – anything we say about 'crime' in our society needs to be qualified by the idea that some types of criminal behaviour may not be fully represented in the statistics.

- **Group representativeness** refers to the use of *samples* (explained in more detail below) in our research. In basic terms, if we are researching a small group (of students, for example) and, on the

basis of this research, want to be able to say something about *all students*, we need to ensure the characteristics of the group we study exactly match those of the larger group; in other words, we can use one, small, group to *represent* a much larger group – an idea that leads to the related concept of:

- **Generalisability**: If data can be *generalised* it means information we collect about a small group can be applied to larger groups who share the same general characteristics of the smaller group. In other words, if the small (sample) group is representative of the larger group anything we discover about the one can be generalised to the other. The usefulness of these two concepts – representativeness and generalisability – will become clearer in a moment when we consider them in more detail in the context of *sampling techniques*.

Digging deeper

The different data types we have just identified each have their different uses and limitations, which we can briefly consider in terms of their respective *advantages* and *disadvantages*.

Primary data has a number of *advantages*:

- **Data control**: Because the researcher is responsible for collecting data they have complete control over how much data is collected, how it is collected and from whom it's collected.

- **Reliability**, **validity** and **representativeness**: Simply because you can exercise some measure of control over how data is collected doesn't, of course, guarantee its reliability, validity or representativeness (a badly designed piece of research can be none of these), but it is much easier for the researcher to consider these concepts when they design and carry out the research themselves.

This type of data also has a few potential *disadvantages*:

- **Resources**: Primary data collection can be:
  - **Time consuming** – to design, construct and carry out, for example. If the group you are researching is large and you're interviewing them individually, this is going to take a great deal of time and resources.
  - **Expensive** – as in the above example, the cost of a researcher's time may be a factor in the design of the research, as will:
  - **Access** problems: Having designed a piece of primary research, you need access to the people you want to study – your plan to interview the 10 richest people in the UK, for example, comes to nothing when they refuse to be interviewed.

NO ENTRY

Not everyone welcomes being studied by sociologists.

- **Availability**: Sometimes it is *impossible* to collect primary data. In the above example, it is impossible because the people you want to research do not make themselves available for such research. In another (admittedly more extreme)

example, if you wanted to research the reasons why people commit suicide this would be difficult because your potential subjects are dead. In this instance, one way around the problem of availability may be the use of secondary data. **Emil Durkheim** (*Suicide: A Study In Sociology*, 1897), for example, used official statistics to test whether suicide rates varied within and between societies. By so doing, he was able to argue social factors, such as religious belief, were significant in the explanation of why people took their own life.

Secondary data *advantages* has the following:

- **Resources**: Because secondary data already exists (someone else has done the work of collecting it) there are advantages in terms of *time* and *money* – collecting primary data on national crime or unemployment statistics, for example, would be a daunting task. In some instances, *access* to data is much easier, although the researcher does rely on the availability/existence of such data.
- **Reliability**: Some (but not all) forms of secondary data are highly reliable – official statistics (those produced by the UK government, for example) are a good case in point.
- **Validity**: Again, while it is difficult to make generalisations, some forms of secondary data (biographies and personal documents such as diaries for example) provide highly valid data because they give detailed insights into people's behaviour.
- **Representativeness**: Where data is produced on a national level, by the

government for example, there is normally a high level of representativeness.

In terms of *disadvantages*, however, we can note:

- **Data control**: This may be difficult because secondary data is not always produced with the needs of sociologists in mind. The data's creator will have their own reasons for producing it and these may not coincide with sociological concerns, interests and agendas. The way governments, for example, measure social class may be different to sociological ways of measuring class.

- **Reliability, validity and representativeness**: An important consideration with secondary data is whether it's simply one individual's view or it's representative of a range of views. Newspaper articles, for example, can be the personal, unsupported and unrepresentative, view of a single journalist. Similarly, historical documents may reflect the views of particular social classes (mainly because it was the upper classes who recorded their views).

Conversely, the only surviving record of an event provides a (valid) insight into that event, but without supporting evidence (a question of *reliability*) we can't be certain of its *representativeness*. In addition, the *authenticity* (has the data been faked?) and *credibility* (who produced it and for what reasons?) of secondary data may be difficult to check.

 Growing it yourself: faking it?

With the development of the Internet, questions about the *authenticity* and *credibility* of secondary data have become increasingly important, for three main reasons:

- the volume of data involved

- relatively easy access to data (through search engines such as Google: www.google.co.uk) and

- the difficulty of checking the source of this data.

As a case in point, have a look at the following photograph – widely distributed on the Internet in 2004 – which shows US Presidential candidate John Kerry pictured at an anti-Vietnam War demonstration (the 1971 Register for Peace Rally). This picture was potentially damaging to Kerry's campaign because it associates him with the actress Jane Fonda, whose anti-war activities were considered by many (especially in the media) to be 'unpatriotic' and 'anti-American'.

However, the picture was actually a *fake* – source unknown – created by combining two separate – unrelated – pictures.

What steps could we take to check the authenticity and credibility of secondary data we collect from sources such as the Internet?

In small groups, identify the sort of checks we could make to ensure – to the best of our ability – secondary data is authentic and credible.

For example, we could identify and check the *source* of the data (in the above example, how credible is an *anonymous* source?)

This photograph was widely distributed during the 2004 US Presidential election.

Ken Light photographed Kerry preparing to give a speech at the Register for Peace Rally, 1971.

Owen Franken photographed Fonda speaking in Miami, 1972.

Quantitative data has a number of *advantages*:

- **Quantification**: The ability to express relationships statistically can be advantageous if, in your research, you don't need to explore the *reasons* for people's behaviour (for example, if you simply need to know the number of murders committed each year).

- **Examination of trends/changes over time**: Following from the above, quantitative data gives us an easy, manageable, way of tracking social changes over time. For example, statistics on educational achievement over the past 25 years can show us changes in relative levels of achievement between boys and girls.

Module link: Changes in the relative levels of male and female educational achievement are explored in the Education chapter.

- **Comparisons**: Similarly, if we want to compare differences between two or more things, (such as middle class and working class family size within our society), quantitative data makes this relatively easy. Alternatively, *cross-cultural* comparisons (crime rates in different countries, for example) are similarly made possible through the use of quantitative data. Similarly '**before**' and '**after**' studies are a further type of comparison we can make using quantitative data. For example, we could examine, using statistical data, the effect changes in the law have had on patterns of divorce in our society by noting the number of divorces *before* a legal change and the number *after* the change.

Module link: The relationship between divorce and legal change is explored in more-detail in the Family chapter.

- **Reliability**: Quantitative data tends to be more reliable than qualitative data because it's easier to *replicate* (repeat) the collection of such data. This is because *standardised questions* (questions that don't change) can be asked to different groups (or the same group at different times).

Some *disadvantages* of quantitative data might be:

- **Validity**: Quantitative data can't be easily used to explore issues in any great depth (as I have suggested, knowing the number of thefts in our society doesn't tell us anything about *why* people commit this crime).

- **Meanings**: Related to the above, quantitative data isn't designed to tell sociologists much – if anything – about how people *interpret* and *understand* social behaviour.

  For example while it might be possible to quantify 'the fear of crime' (counting the percentage of people who fear being a victim, for example), this type of data tells us nothing about *why* people may fear becoming a victim.

Qualitative data: In terms of *advantages* we can note:

- **Validity**: Because this type of data encourages *depth* and *detail* (in an interview, for example, people may be encouraged to talk at great length about themselves and their beliefs) we are more likely to gain a complete, true-to-life picture of whatever we are researching.

- **Meanings**: Qualitative data allows sociologists to explore the meanings people give to events and behaviour. While we can represent divorce statistically, for example, qualitative data allows us to explore how people feel and react to this situation.

- **Imposition**: If your research objective is to understand the meaning of people's behaviour, it follows you must allow people the scope to talk freely about that behaviour. If a researcher imposes their interpretation on a situation (by asking

Qualitative data came tell us something about the meaning of people's behaviour.

direct, quantifiable, questions for example) then data *validity* will be affected because you are restricting people's ability to talk at length and in depth about what they believe.

Qualitative data may avoid this type of problem (although it may create a different kind of *imposition problem* which we'll examine in more detail when we consider different research methods).

Some *disadvantages* of qualitative data we can note are:

- **Reliability**: Qualitative research is difficult (if not impossible) to exactly repeat (think, for example, about how difficult it would it be to exactly repeat even a very recent conversation you've had with somebody). In addition, with something like historical data we may have no reliable way of knowing if our data source is representative of anything more than the views of a single individual.

- **Data overload**: Qualitative research tends to produce masses of data, much of which will be irrelevant in terms of achieving the research objective. With something like an interview, the problem of how to interpret or represent the data may also occur. Do you as a researcher report everything someone says or do you edit the data (and risk imposing your interpretation on the information)?

- **Comparisons**: Qualitative data makes measuring and comparing behaviour very difficult, mainly because the data can't be easily standardised.

To complete this section, we can look briefly at the concepts of reliability and validity.

Data reliability is an important research consideration since, if data is unreliable, any conclusions we draw from it are going to be fairly limited (if not useless). For example, if I attempt to draw conclusions about the state of education in Britain on the basis of a couple of interviews I conducted 'down the pub' with whoever happened to be present at the time, it's probable such data will be unreliable as a guide to what is really happening in the educational system.

In general terms, therefore, data reliability is affected by such things as:

- **Bias**: Are there opportunities for the researcher (consciously or unconsciously) to distort the data collection process?

- **Standardisation**: Is everyone in the group you are researching asked the same questions in the same way? If they are not, how easy would it be to check data reliability by repeating this research?

- **Consistency**: Will, for example, the same question asked of the same person in similar circumstances, produce the same answer?

- **Replication**: For example, if another sociologist attempted to repeat my 'down the pub' research, would similar results be achieved? If not, then my research would not be very reliable …

Data validity is a useful concept because it reminds us to think about the *accuracy* – or otherwise – of different data types (primary, secondary, qualitative and quantitative). While some forms of data (such as official statistics) may be reliable, their validity may be questionable for two reasons.

- **Representativeness**: They may not apply to everyone in a particular group. In the UK, for example, we need to be aware 'unemployment statistics' only represent those who are registered for unemployment benefit with the government – not everyone who doesn't have a job.

- **Depth**: They may lack the depth and detail required to accurately represent the views of a particular individual or group.

Discussion point: questionable validity?

If we wanted to compare changes in the level of unemployment in our society over the past 30 years, could we validly use government statistics for this purpose?

You might like to consider the following when researching/discussing this question.

- Have definitions of 'unemployment' changed over time? Are we comparing like with like?
- Does the definition of 'unemployment' involve counting everyone who wants to find a job, but can't?
- Are there ways governments can 'hide' unemployment (by, for example, defining someone as 'unfit for work'). If so, can you identify what some of these ways might be?

In this opening section we have introduced a range of concepts relating to sociological methods and methodology that you need to understand, by way of familiarising yourself with this particular area of the course. In the following sections we can start to locate and apply these ideas as part of our overview and investigation of the research process.

The research process

Introduction

In this section – and the following two sections (Sampling and Research Methods respectively) – we're going to focus on the idea of social research as a *process*; that is, as something *planned* and *organised*. This opening section, therefore, looks at how the research process can be *systematically organised*.

Sociological research

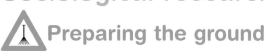 **Preparing the ground**

In the main we are concerned here with outlining the research process (or at one version of it), but before we look at this process in detail, we need to be clear about a number of research concepts:

- **Hypothesis**: This is the starting point for some forms of research and, although there are various types of hypothesis we could use, it is easiest to think of a hypothesis as a question or statement we want to answer. In this respect, a hypothesis has one very important characteristic, namely, we should be able to *test* it (to discover if it is true or false). A hypothesis, therefore, involves testing a possible relationship between two or more things.

For example, imagine we are interested in researching 'why people steal'. As it stands, this question would be difficult to answer because it doesn't specify a relationship between 'people' and 'stealing' that can be tested. What we need to do, therefore, is create a hypothesis – along the lines of 'Poverty makes people steal' – that can be tested.

- **Research question**: Not all sociologists want to test their ideas using a hypothesis. Some researchers begin with a research question – something the sociologist wants to answer by collecting evidence. Although not directly tested, a research question can be supported (or not as the case may be) through research.

An example of a (not very useful it has to be admitted) research question might be: 'What are people's attitudes to stealing?'. All we are trying to do, using this type of research question, is gather evidence on the views of people about a particular form of behaviour.

- **Operationalisation**: Whether research starts with a hypothesis or a research question, the researcher will have to *define, test* or *measure* the various elements involved in their hypothesis/question – and this is where the concept of *operationalisation* comes into the equation.

If you think about the 'poverty' hypothesis I have just outlined, to test it the researcher would have to be clear about such questions as:

- How is 'poverty' defined?
- How is 'stealing' defined?

- How are 'people' defined (not literally, in this case, but in terms of different groups, perhaps)?

- How can we test or measure the relationship between poverty and stealing (in other words, what *indicators* can we use to test this relationship)?

Our answers to these – and similar – questions will determine how we plan and organise our actual research.

 Digging deeper

So far we have outlined some important ideas relating to sociological research and we can take this further by looking at how we can organise the research process as a whole. We can do this by focusing on the way hypothesis-based research can be organised, for no better reason than this is the way you are expected to think about the organisation of any coursework (AS and/or A2) you may do as part of this course. In this respect, a classic example of how to organise social research is one suggested by **Karl Popper** ('The Logic of Scientific Discovery', 1959) which he called the **Hypothetico-Deductive Model** of scientific research, the basis of which we can generally explain in the following terms.

- **'Hypothetico'** means 'starting with a hypothesis'. For Popper, the research process revolves around the ability to develop and clearly state *testable* hypotheses.

- **Deduction** (or to give it its proper name, *deductive logic*) is a way of making authoritative statements (proofs) about what is *not known* by a thorough analysis of what *is known*. The ability to make *deductive statements* is a powerful tool because it is the basis for drawing logical conclusions about *specific events* from *general events*.

To simplify this idea, think about a fictional detective such as Inspector Morse. He solved crimes by *systematically* investigating a case, collecting and analysing facts and, on the basis of these facts, identifying the guilty party. This is an example of *deduction* because he proves something specific that was not initially known (the identity of a murderer) on the basis of general observations about things that were initially known (the facts of the case, the clues identified and so forth).

- A **model** is a small-scale *representation* of something (such as, in this instance, a research process) that helps clarify the relationship between the things involved by describing them in simplified terms. In this case, **Popper's** model suggests the various steps to follow in order to 'do research' and, as such, helps us to organise the actual research process.

Have a look at the diagram opposite that describes Popper's research process model.

We can briefly explain each of these 'steps in the research process' in the following way.

- **Phenomena**: All research starts somewhere – usually with the researcher choosing something to study (which, this being sociology, can be just about anything – we can use the example of 'crime' for the moment). However, in order to actually do research we have to narrow our initial ideas down to something more specific.

- **Observation and the generation of ideas**: The researcher starts to focus their initial interest onto something manageable. For

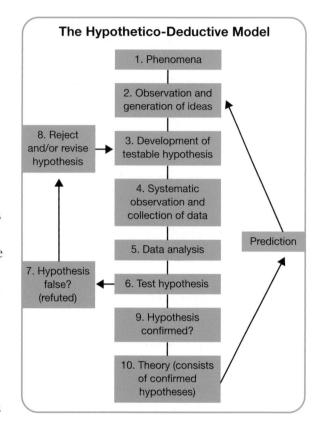

The Hypothetico-Deductive Model

1. Phenomena
2. Observation and generation of ideas
3. Development of testable hypothesis
4. Systematic observation and collection of data
5. Data analysis
6. Test hypothesis
7. Hypothesis false? (refuted)
8. Reject and/or revise hypothesis
9. Hypothesis confirmed?
10. Theory (consists of confirmed hypotheses)

Prediction

example, as we think about researching 'crime' we might read previous research and decide on a specific topic to research – the fear of crime, perhaps?

- **Development of testable hypothesis**: At this stage we are ready to develop a hypothesis to test. This provides both a focus for research and a clearly defined objective for data collection. For example, our hypothesis might be something like 'Do women have a greater fear of crime than men?'

As we noted earlier, at this stage the researcher needs to think about how to *operationalise* the various concepts in the hypothesis that require definition, testing or measurement. In the social world, of course, many of the things we want to research don't physically exist ('fear', for example). We need, therefore, to think about *indicators* of their existence that *can* be physically measured (in this example we might use indicators such as the *precautions* people take to avoid becoming a victim).

- **Systematic observation and data collection**: The researcher starts to think about who they are going to research (their *sample*) and the research method(s) they will use (both of which we'll consider in more detail later).

- **Data analysis**: Once data have been collected they have to be analysed. This may take a couple of forms:

  - **technical**

    - checking to ensure sufficient data have been collected

    - checking the sample used has remained representative

    - making decisions about whether to include or discard irrelevant data

- **interpretive**, which involves making decisions about the meaning of data collected.

- **Testing the hypothesis**: This involves deciding – on the basis of our data analysis – whether or not the tested hypothesis has either been:

  - **Falsified**: If the hypothesis is false (step 7), a decision has to be made (step 8) about whether it should be totally rejected or whether it can be revised and re-tested (a return to step 3).

  - **Confirmed**. If the hypothesis is confirmed (step 9) it contributes to the final stage in the research process, namely:

- **Theory development**: In everyday language, a *theory* normally means something that has not been tested ('It works in theory, but not in practice', for example). Sociologically, however, a theory consists of tested and confirmed

 Growing it yourself: hypotheses and operationalising concepts

Working individually or in small groups, look at the following list of potential research areas and select one (if none of the these appeal, think of an area of social behaviour you could research). For your chosen area:

1. identify a testable hypothesis

2. identify the concepts to operationalise in order to test the hypothesis.

Domestic labour	Childhood	Parental socialisation
The school curriculum	Equal opportunity laws	Male/female work roles
Deviance in the classroom	Religious beliefs	The media and drug use
Attitudes to HIV/AIDS	People's political attitudes	Defining poverty

hypotheses used to predict the behaviour originally observed (step 1).

Sampling

Having outlined an example of research design and the general processes it involves, we can begin to focus our attention on some specific aspects of research design, beginning with the concept of *sampling*.

⚠ Preparing the ground

The first thing we need to do is identify and explain a few sampling related ideas.

- **Target (or general) population**: When starting a piece of research, we always have in mind a group to study – these people are our *target* or *general population* – in other words, they're everyone in the group we're going to research. Examples of target populations might be:

1. A **small** group

   Perhaps 10 or 12 people in all, who meet regularly in your local park.

2. A **large** group

   The 70,000 fans who attend Manchester United's home games.

   With the first group, their behaviour might be relatively easy to research because the target population is small. Whether this research involves observing the group, asking them questions or participating in their behaviour, the *size* of the group makes it relatively easy to manage the research.

   With the second group, however, things might be more difficult, since its size is going to make it hard to observe or

question everyone personally. This, therefore, is where the concept of sampling comes into its own and we need to outline a few basic ideas relating to this concept:

- A **sample** is a relatively small proportion of the people who belong to the target population. For example, in the case of football fans, the researcher might choose 1000 Manchester United fans to research and, by studying their behaviour, try to say something about the characteristics or behaviour of all fans in the target population.

- **Sample size**: Rather than think in terms of size (is a 90% sample too large or a 10% sample too small?) a more significant question is 'how *representative* is the sample?'

- **Representativeness**: This idea is more important than the size of your sample because it relates to the question of whether or not the characteristics of the people selected for the sample accurately reflect the characteristics of the target population. If the sample group is representative then anything discovered about them can also be applied to the target population – regardless of how many – or how few – people are in the sample.

- **Generalisation**: This concept describes the idea the things we discover about the people in our sample can also be applied to the people in our target population. If our sample is *representative*, therefore, we can generalise the behaviour of this group to our target population. In other words, we can make statements about a group we *haven't* studied (our target population) based on the behaviour of a group we *have* studied.

Having identified some general sampling concepts, we can move on to an examination of the *sampling process* (and, more specifically *sampling techniques*) by looking at a couple of useful ideas.

- **Sampling frame**: To construct a representative sample researchers will normally need some way of identifying everyone in their target population so an accurate sample can be drawn (this is not always the case, however, for reasons we'll examine in a moment). A sampling frame (such as a list of names and addresses), therefore, is used to uniquely identify everyone in our target population. Examples of sampling frames might be:

  - **electoral register**: a list of everyone eligible to vote
  - **school registers**: lists of children attending school
  - **professional membership lists**: organisations such as the British Medical Association (BMA) keep a register of all doctors in Britain
  - **company payroll**: a list of all employees in a company.

For many types of sampling (there are important exceptions) a sampling frame is required because:

- if a researcher can't identify everyone in their target population their sample may not be representative of that population
- for a researcher to contact people in their sample, they will need to know who they are.

However, just because a sampling frame exists, it doesn't mean a researcher will automatically have access to it. It is possible access may be denied for:

- **Legal reasons**: A school, for example, may not give a researcher access to their registers.
- **Confidentiality**: A business organisation may not give a researcher access to their payroll records.
- **Secrecy**: Religious groups, political parties and criminal gangs may not want to be studied.

 # Digging deeper

As a general rule of thumb, researchers try to make their sample representative of the target population. However, there are times when they might deliberately choose *not* to draw a representative sample.

Non-representative samples: For some types of research the sociologist might *not* want to make generalisations about a very large group based only on a sample of that group. They might, for example, simply be interested in the behaviour of the group itself, rather than what they may or may not represent. Examples of this type of sampling include:

- **Case studies**: The objective here is to study, in great detail, the characteristics of a particular group (or case, as you might not be too surprised to hear it called).

Although a case study is, technically, an example of a research method (see below), we can use it to illustrate how a non-representative sample might work.

For example, a case study might involve joining a gang of young women, living among a group of monks or studying the prescribing practices of doctors in a particular part of the country. The researcher is *not* particularly concerned about whether the group being studied is representative of all other, similar, groups. In effect, therefore, the sample in this type of research *is* the target population. This is a perfectly acceptable form of research – just as long as the researcher doesn't try to generalise their findings.

- **Opportunity samples**: This type of non-representative sample has two main sub-divisions.

  - **Best opportunity** samples involve deliberately choosing a sample to provide the *best possible opportunity* to show whatever you are testing is true. If your research shows the hypothesis you're testing to be false for this group, there's a high probability it will be false for any other related groups.

    Goldthorpe, Lockwood et al's study *The Affluent Worker In The Class Structure* (1965) used this technique to test whether or not the working classes were 'becoming middle class'. Their best opportunity sample consisted of highly paid car assembly workers who they chose to study on the basis that if any working-class group was likely to show lifestyles indistinguishable from their middle-class peers it would be this group of 'affluent workers'.

  - **Snowball samples**: So called because, just as a snowball rolling downhill gets larger and larger as it picks up more snow, a snowball sample picks up more and more people to be in the sample over time. A basic example of the technique for this type of sample might be as follows.

    The researcher identifies someone in the target population who's willing to

be part of their research. This person then suggests another two or three people (perhaps more) who are also willing to participate in the research. These people, in turn, suggest further possible participants until the researcher has a sample they can use for their research. Clearly, this technique isn't going to produce a representative sample, but it may be the best that can be achieved in certain situations.

Growing it yourself: sampling frames

Identify an appropriate sampling frame for the following and briefly comment on how easy/difficult/impossible it would be to access the sampling frame.

- The voting intentions of people in Dorset
- Families with new-born babies in your home town
- Registered drug addicts in Newcastle
- Students in your school/college
- British Members of Parliament

Types of sampling

Preparing the ground

In this section we can examine some different types of sampling techniques available to sociological researchers, beginning with simple random sampling.

Simple random sampling

One of the most basic (simple) forms of sampling, is based on the probability the random selection of names from a sampling frame will produce a sample representative of a target population. One important characteristic of this type of sampling is that, for it to be truly random, everyone in the target population must have an equal chance of being chosen for the sample.

A simple random sample, therefore, is similar to a lottery:

- everyone in the target population is identified on a sampling frame
- the sample is selected by randomly choosing names from the frame until the sample is complete.

For example, a 20% sample of a target population of 100 people would involve the random selection of 20 people.

A lottery is a type of simple random sample . . .

Growing It yourself: a simple random sample

Take the name of every student in your class from the register, write all the names on separate pieces of paper and put them in a box. If you then draw out a percentage of names at random you will have constructed your simple random sample.

How representative of your class was the sample you created (for example, does it accurately reflect the relative percentages of males and females in the class)?

Systematic sampling

A variation on the above – normally used when the target population is very large – is to select names for your sample *systematically*, by taking the sample directly from a sampling frame. For a 25% sample of a target population containing 100 names, a systematic sample would involve choosing every fourth name from your sampling frame.

Growing it yourself: a systematic sample

Using your class register as a sampling frame, construct a 25% sample by selecting every fourth name.

How similar/different is this sample from your simple random sample?

Stratified random sampling

If you have done the two previous exercises you will probably have identified a potential problem with samples created using these techniques – if the target population is *not homogeneous* (that is, it doesn't consist of people who are roughly the same in terms of the characteristics important to your research) a *biased* sample can easily occur. This can happen if your target population consists of a range of smaller groups, the views of which are all important to you. Stratified random sampling, therefore, is designed to avoid problems of possible under-representation, while retaining the idea of selection based on chance.

The technique here is to divide (or *stratify*) your target population into groups who's characteristics are known to you – for example, males and females – and treat *each* group as a random sample in its own right.

For example, imagine our target population consists of 100 people, 80

females and 20 males and we need a 10% sample. To exactly represent the gender balance of the target population we would need a sample of eight females and two males, which we might get by chance – but it's easier to give chance a helping hand by splitting our target population into two groups – the 80 females and the 20 males – and then selecting 10% of each (eight females from the 'female only group' and two males from the 'male only' group). If we then combine the two samples we get a fully representative final sample.

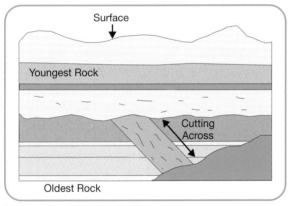

Example of rock strata

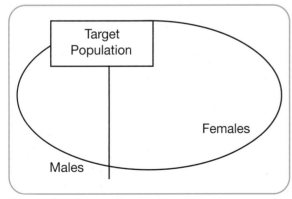

Example of sample strata

 Growing it yourself: stratified sampling

Choose a group (such as your class) and identify known characteristics important to your research (gender, for example). Construct a 20% stratified random sample based on the above example.

Compare the results from your stratified sample with those gained from your simple random and systematic samples. Which type of sample gave the most representative outcome?

Stratified quota sampling

The basic principles of this type of sampling are the same as for stratified random sampling (the division of the main sample into smaller samples on the basis of some known characteristics, such as age or gender). The main difference, using the previous example, is that when you actually select 'eight females from the "female only" group and two males from the "male only" group' these represent your 'quota'. Once you've filled your quota of females – by asking (rather than randomly selecting) each female in turn if they would be willing to help with your research – then no more can be selected. The technique is non-random (but probably random enough for sampling purposes) because not everyone in the target population has an equal chance of being selected for your sample.

Growing it yourself: quota sampling

As in the previous exercise, instead of selecting people randomly you will simply ask them if they will be in your sample. One difference you should note, therefore, is that any absent students cannot be selected for your sample (unlike with the stratified random version).

Opportunity ('snowball') sampling

We looked earlier at the idea of non-representative sampling and mentioned briefly the idea of opportunity or snowball sampling. As we noted, it is not always possible for a researcher to get hold of a sampling frame for a target population and they may know nothing about the characteristics of their target population (which rules out stratified sampling).

Therefore, the researcher may need to resort to unrepresentative means to construct a sample. This technique, as I have previously noted, is not ideal but it may represent the only way a researcher can construct a sample for their research. For example research into 'secretive' organisations that refuse to disclose details of their membership to 'outsiders' would make it impossible to construct a representative sample.

Thus, when **Roy Wallis** wanted to study a religious group called The Church of Scientology ('Scientologists'), the Church leaders refused to cooperate with his requests for information about membership. In order to carry out his research, Wallis was forced to find ex-members who could put him in touch with current members and, in this way, he was able to build up a (non-representative) sample of Church members to study. **Charlton**, **Panting** and **Hannah** ('Mobile Phone Usage and Abusage', 2001) on the other hand, simply used an opportunity sample of schoolchildren in the absence of any available sampling frame.

Growing it yourself: opportunity sampling

In small groups, identify situations in which a researcher may be forced to use opportunity sampling (for example, I've already noted how it might not be possible to research an organisation that refuses to disclose its membership in any other way – are there examples of other types of organisation that might not disclose their membership to a researcher?).

As a class, combine, discuss and record the examples identified in your groups.

Cluster sampling

This type of sampling is usually done when a target population is spread over a wide geographic area. For example, an opinion poll on voting behaviour may involve a sample of 1000 people representing the 35 (or so) million people eligible to vote in a General Election. If a simple random sample were taken the researcher might have to question 10 people in Newcastle, 15 people in Cardiff and so forth. It would be a time-consuming and very expensive process and the results from the poll would probably be out of date before it could be finished.

To avoid these problems, a researcher uses cluster samples that firstly, divide the country into smaller sampling units (in this example, electoral constituencies) and then into small units within constituencies (for example, local boroughs).

Individual local boroughs could then be selected which, based on past research, show a representative cross-section of voters and a sample of electors could be taken from a relatively small number of boroughs across the country. Thus, sampling units (electoral constituencies) have same the same basic characteristics (population size, for example), but each cluster is a small scale version of the target population.

 Digging deeper

Having outlined some of the basic features of different types of sampling we can briefly evaluate each type in terms of its general advantages and disadvantages.

Simple random and **systematic sampling** have certain *advantages* for the researcher.

- **Time**: Both are relatively quick and easy ways of selecting samples.

- **Random**: They produce random or near-random samples, based on chance (the sample cannot be accidentally biased by the researcher).

- **Expense**: Both are reasonably inexpensive to create using a sampling frame accurate for the target population.

- **Information**: Other than some way of identifying people in the target population (a name for example), the

researcher doesn't require any other knowledge about this population.

However, a couple of *disadvantages* might be:

- **Sampling frame**: These techniques *always* need a sampling frame – and one may not be available.

- **Unrepresentative**: Sampling based on chance may not produce a representative sample.

Stratified random and **stratified quota sampling** have a number of important *advantages*.

- **Known differences** in the target population will be accurately reflected in the sample. We can, therefore, be sure our sample will be broadly representative.

- **Focus**: The researcher can focus their sample on relevant distinctions in the target population (age, gender, class, ethnicity, etc.) and ignore irrelevant factors.

- **Size**: Stratified samples can be relatively small, since it's possible to make certain we have accurately reflected our target population.

- **Resources**: Quota samples are usually relatively cheap and quick to construct accurately.

They can, however, have *disadvantages*.

- **Accurate information** about the target population isn't always available.

- **Out-of-date** information: Even in situations where accurate information is available, this information may be outdated by the time the research is actually done. This is especially true where the sample is large and complex or where the composition of the target

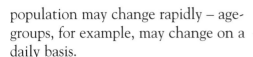

population may change rapidly – age-groups, for example, may change on a daily basis.

- **Uncertainty**: When using a team of researchers to construct a *quota sample* you can't be certain they have correctly placed everyone in the right quota category. If, for example, your research assistant cannot find '100 men over the age of 65' to fill their quota, there may be a temptation to fill it using men under that age.

- **Unrepresentative**: *Stratified quota sample* selection is not truly random; it may be unrepresentative of a target population.

Opportunity sampling has couple of distinct *advantages*.

- **Availability**: It allows a researcher to construct a sample in situations that would be impossible using any other sampling technique.

- **Resources**: It can be a relatively cheap and quick method of sampling.

It also has some serious *disadvantages*.

- **Unrepresentative**: It is very, very, unlikely the sample will be truly representative.

- **Reliability**: There is no way of checking whether your sample is representative.

- A **self-selected sample** (see below) is likely to occur.

Although not very widely used in sociological research, some **cluster sampling** *advantages* are:

- **Resources**: This type of sample saves the researcher time and money because relatively small samples can represent very large target populations.

- **Replication**: Once a reliable sample has been established, the researcher can use the same (or very similar) sample repeatedly (as with political opinion polling, for example).

There are, however, important *disadvantages*.

- **Representativeness**: Unless great care is taken, the cluster samples will be unrepresentative of the target population.

- **Resources**: Although it is a relatively cheap form of sampling, this is not necessarily the case. A sample that seeks to represent the whole of Britain, for example, is still going to be too expensive for many researchers.

Sampling errors

Although any type of sampling is generally a risky business (getting a representative sample is not always as easy as it sounds), we can identify a couple of basic sampling errors that can produce *biased samples* (samples which are unrepresentative of a target population).

- **Self-selected samples** involve creating a sample that effectively 'picks itself' rather

🌷 Growing it yourself: self-selection

A newspaper that asks its readers to respond to the question, 'Should people convicted of murder be given the death penalty?' will always produce an unrepresentative, sample.

What reasons can you identify for this?

If you don't want any help with answering this question, look away now because the following provides a range of possible reasons.

than being selected by the researcher. For example, the type of opinion polls that appear in newspapers and magazines almost invariably involve a self-selected – and hence *unrepresentative* – sample.

Reasons for this lack of representativeness are not hard to find.

- Only a minority of the population buy the newspaper on the day the poll appears and such people have, unwittingly, selected themselves for the sample.

- An unknown number of readers will not notice the poll (and so don't vote in it). Those who notice the question, therefore, have again potentially selected themselves for the sample.

- Only a proportion of readers will respond to the question. This proportion is made even smaller if the *respondent* (the name given to anyone asked to respond in some way to a piece of research) has to pay to vote (by making a telephone call, at their own expense, to a telephone number set up to record their vote, for example).

- People who do respond to such polls are likely to be those who have very strong views either way on the question (in this example, people who are strongly pro- or anti-capital punishment) – and these are unlikely to be representative of the population of Britain.

A classic example of a self-selected sample is *The Hite Report* (**Shere Hite**, 1976), an investigation into male and female sexuality in America.

🕸 **For more information on this research, go to:**
www.sociology.org.uk/as4aqa.htm

- **Statistically inadequate samples**: At the beginning of this section I suggested the question of sample size is not as important as that of how *representative* it is. This is true up to a point, but a sample that is too small to accurately represent a target population is going to be inadequate for research purposes (asking your mate what they think about the education system is probably not going to be an adequate sample).

As a general rule, therefore, the larger your sample as a proportion of your target population the greater the probability it will be statistically adequate. This may improve the chances of your sample being representative of the target population; however, a large sample is no guarantee of a representative sample.

Having covered the concept of sampling as a consideration in the research process (you need, after all, to be able to identify the people on whom you plan to do your research) we can turn next to thinking about how to collect data about such people – and this involves identifying and exploring the range of research methods available to the sociologist.

Research methods

Introduction

As we have seen, one part of the research process involves thinking about how to construct a sample on which to base your research; a second, related, aspect is to actually collect data about people's behaviour and to understand how sociologists go about this, we need to examine 'the different quantitative and qualitative methods and sources of data, including questionnaires, interviews, observation techniques and experiments, and documents and official statistics'. We can also take the opportunity here to look at 'the nature of social facts and the advantages and limitations of different sources of data and methods of research'.

Primary quantitative research methods: social surveys

 Preparing the ground

A **survey**, according to **Lawson** and **Garrod** ('Complete A-Z Sociology Handbook', 2003) is: 'The systematic collection of information about a given population' which could, of course, involve using any number of different research methods.

However, for our purposes, we can think of surveys as involving the collection of data using a **questionnaire**. This, in basic terms, is a list of written questions normally completed in one of two ways.

- **Privately** (with the researcher not present): This is normally called a '**postal questionnaire**' (even though it may not necessarily be posted – how confusing is that?). In this instance, respondents give their answers to the questionnaire without any verbal guidance from the researcher.

- **Publicly** (in the presence of the researcher): This is normally called a **structured interview** and, in this instance, respondents normally answer a researcher's questions verbally.

In this respect, the same set of questions could serve equally as a postal questionnaire or a structured interview – the main difference between the two techniques, therefore, is how they are *administered*. This being the case, we can look, firstly, at some of the shared aspects of this method, before considering some different advantages and disadvantages.

Questionnaires can be used to ask two basic types of question.

- **Closed-ended** (sometimes called *closed* or *pre-coded questions*). This type of question involves the researcher providing a set of answers from which the respondent is asked to choose one (or sometimes more) that best represents their situation, feelings, beliefs and so forth (hence the idea of questions being *pre-coded* – the researcher limits, to a greater or lesser extent, the responses that can be given).

A (very) simple example of a closed question is one that asks the respondent to choose between two options:

Do you drink coffee? Yes/No

(When using this type of question it is useful to add a third option – 'Don't Know' – just to catch those respondents who have no opinion either way).

Variations on this basic theme can be a bit more adventurous. For example, the respondent could be allowed the (limited) opportunity to fill in an answer.

Which soap powder do you regularly use?

Bold
Persil
Other? (please specify)

The inclusion of an 'other' option is often useful because it avoids the need for very long lists – and it also means the respondent can add something the researcher may not have considered.

Alternatively, a researcher could measure *attitudes* towards something, as in the following example:

There are further variations on the *closed question* theme (but I'm sure you get the picture); however, their defining characteristic is they allow respondents little, if any, scope to develop an answer beyond the categories selected by the researcher. Such questions, therefore, are used extensively to collect *quantitative data*.

Open-ended (or simply 'open') questions are different in that the researcher doesn't provide a set answer from which to choose. Rather, the respondent is given the scope to answer 'in their own words'. A simple example of an open question might be something like

'What do you like about coffee that you don't like about tea?'

This type of question, therefore, can probe a little deeper into a respondent's opinions and produces a (limited) form of *qualitative data* (although the main objective with open questions in a questionnaire is usually still to *quantify* responses in some way).

As you need to be aware, questionnaires can, of course, happily contain a mix of open and closed questions.

We can think about some of the general characteristics of questionnaires/structured interviews in the following terms:

- **Coding and quantification**: The use of pre-coded questions makes it much easier to quantify data, since the options available are already known, limited in number and (relatively) easy to count.

  Although closed questions are relatively easy to codify, this is not necessarily the case with open questions. The researcher may receive a variety of responses, each of which has to be categorised, coded and quantified. In the previous 'tea/coffee' example, answers mentioning things like 'taste' and 'flavour' might be categorised and coded in one way, whereas answers mentioning 'cost', 'value for money' and the like, might be categorised and coded differently. In this way, similar types of answer can be coded appropriately and quantified accordingly ('32% of respondents buy coffee because they like its flavour', for example).

- **Depth and scope**: One problem with closed questions, as I have suggested, is the limitation they place on the detail, depth and type of answers a respondent

'How strongly do you agree/disagree with the statement 'Nucuppa is the best-tasting coffee on the market'?				
Agree very strongly	Agree strongly	Neither agree nor disagree	Disagree strongly	Disagree very strongly

can give – it would sometimes be useful to know *why* people believe one thing as opposed to another. Open questions go some way to solving this problem, although questionnaires/structured interviews rarely – if ever – go into as much depth as other types of survey method (such as interviews – a method we will consider in more detail in a moment).

- **Ease of completion**: Open-ended questionnaires take more time and there is the danger (from the researcher's viewpoint) that respondents will:
  - write-down the first thing that comes into their head in order to complete the questionnaire quickly (something that affects the validity of the research)
  - not bother to complete the questionnaire at all, because it takes too much time and effort.
- **Response rate**: There are wide disparities between the response rate of postal questionnaires (you may be lucky to get 25% of those you send out returned) and structured interviews (where the response will always be around 100%). You need, as a researcher, therefore, to be aware of the extent to which a poor response rate may affect the *representativeness* of your sample (by creating, in some way, a biased response).

Questionnaires

Digging deeper

Thinking a little more about questionnaires, we can note the following *advantages*.

- **Sampling**: Postal questionnaires are a useful survey method when the researcher

Growing it yourself: asking questions

Asking people questions and discovering things about them can be interesting – but it's even more interesting if you can make connections between the things you discover.

As a class, test whether or not there is a connection between family and education in the following way. Write a few questions to discover:

- What qualifications each member of your class has achieved.
- The birthday of each class member.
- How many siblings (brothers and sisters) each person has.
- Their position in relation to their siblings (are they the oldest or youngest?).
- What connections (if any) can you make for the class as a whole between family life and educational achievement?

needs to contact large numbers of people quickly, easily and efficiently. The respondents, in effect, do most of the time consuming work by actually completing the questionnaire.

- **Analysis**: Where quantitative questions are asked, postal questionnaires are relatively quick and easy to code and interpret (in some instances, 'interpretation' simply involves counting responses).
- **Reliability**: A questionnaire is easy to standardise, which increases potential reliability because everyone answers exactly the same questions.

- **Interview/interviewer effect**: In basic terms, this type of effect occurs when, for various reasons (discussed in a bit more detail below in relation to *structured interviews*), the relationship between the researcher and the respondent creates a situation that biases the responses the researcher receives. Postal questionnaires – because they involve no personal (face-to-face) contacts or social interaction between researcher and respondent – may avoid this potential source of bias.

- **Validity**: Although questionnaires rarely have much depth, one area in which they may have greater validity than some alternative methods is in terms of *anonymity*. Because respondents never meet the researcher, postal questionnaires can explore potentially embarrassing areas (such as sexuality or criminality) more easily than other methods. If people can anonymously admit to crimes they have committed, for example, they may be encouraged to answer questions honestly.

In terms of potential *disadvantages* we can note:

- **Anonymity**: This feature of questionnaires can work both ways – it may encourage honesty, but if someone other than the intended respondent completes the questionnaire then research validity and representativeness will be affected (although this will depend on the size of the sample to some extent – the smaller the sample, the more significant these factors may be).

- **Reliability**: Because the researcher is not present, it's impossible to know if a respondent has understood a question properly. The researcher also has to trust the questions asked mean the same thing to all respondents – if they don't, reliability will be affected.

This problem can – to some extent – be avoided by conducting a *pilot study* prior to the real survey – this involves the researcher trialling their questions to eliminate possible sources of bias (for example, the questionnaire may be completed by a selection of respondents to check for misunderstood questions and so forth. The data collected from a pilot study would not be included in the full survey).

- **Response rates**: These, as I have noted, are notoriously low for postal questionnaires, which may mean a carefully designed sample becomes unrepresentative of a target population. Research validity may also be affected by a low response rate because it increases the chances of a self-selected sample.

- **Validity**: The questionnaire format makes it difficult to examine complex issues and opinions – even when open-ended questions are used, the depth of respondent answers tends to be more limited than with almost any other method.

Structured interviews

 Digging deeper

As I have previously suggested, the main difference between a postal questionnaire and a structured interview is how they are administered so, keeping this in mind, we can note a couple of ways structured interviews differ in terms of their advantages to the researcher.

- **Reliability**: Because structured interviews involve the researcher and respondent in personal, face-to-face contact, any issues surrounding the research can be discussed. The interviewer can, for example, explain the objectives of the research and resolve any problems with understanding/answering questions. If a respondent is unable or unwilling to provide an answer, the researcher will be aware of the reasons for this and may be able to resolve them.

- **Representativeness**: Structured interviews potentially avoid unrepresentative research caused by low response rates or self-selected samples.

This method has a few additional *disadvantages* not shared by postal questionnaires.

- **Interview effect**: This potential disadvantage comes from the idea the interview may limit the validity of a respondent's answers if they misinterpret (consciously or unconsciously) their role; for example, the respondent may view their role as one of trying to please or encourage the researcher and, by so doing, they may not answer questions honestly or accurately.

  This may not be done deliberately on the part of the respondent (although with this type of research method dishonesty and inaccuracy are ever-present possibilities); rather, it may involve something like the *halo effect* – a situation **Stephen Draper** ('The Hawthorne effect and other expectancy effects', 2004) describes as: 'uncontrolled novelty'. In other words, the novelty of being interviewed – and a desire to reward the interviewer for giving the respondent the chance to experience it – may result in unintentionally dishonest answers.

- **Interviewer effect**: This idea is related to the interview effect (and a slightly different type of halo effect may operate here, whereby the respondent feels they want to personally please the interviewer), but is subtly different in that it refers to ways the relationship between researcher and respondent may bias responses and lead to invalid data. For example, on one level, an aggressive interviewer may intimidate a respondent into giving answers that don't really reflect the latter's beliefs. On another level, status considerations (based on factors such as gender, age, class and ethnicity) may come into play, such as in a situation where a female respondent may feel embarrassed about answering questions about her sexuality if they are asked by a male researcher.

- **Imposition**: This limitation is common to both postal questionnaires and structured interviews and revolves around the idea that, by designing a 'list of questions', a researcher has effectively decided (before collecting any data) what they consider important (and, of course, unimportant). The researcher, therefore, has imposed their definition of these things in advance of the interview.

  For example, if I was researching 'Attitudes to the European Community', the questions I *fail* to ask may be as (if not more) important to a respondent than the questions I *actually* ask – such as failing to ask if the respondent is 'pro' or 'anti' the European Community. Although a daft example perhaps (although you are probably getting used to that by now), the basic principle involved is significant since the objective is to collect valid data based on the beliefs of respondents. If a researcher places artificial limits on any possible responses (by not asking certain questions, for example) this may seriously affect research validity.

Experiments

 Preparing the ground

Experimentation is another example of a primary research method – although, it needs to be initially noted, not one that is particularly widely used in sociology for reasons that will become clear. However, we can begin by noting experiments can be categorised in terms of two basic types.

- A **laboratory experiment** is a general name for an experiment where the researcher controls the *environment* in which the research takes place. The ability to do this is a feature of what are called *closed systems* – situations, such as in a laboratory, where the research conditions can be exactly monitored and controlled.

- A **natural** (or **field**) **experiment** is not carried out under controlled conditions. This type is sometimes called *opportunity experimentation* since the researcher takes advantage of a *naturally occurring opportunity* to conduct the experiment (although, having said this, it is possible to deliberately construct a natural experiment). Such experiments are normally used in *open systems* (such as the social world) where the environment cannot be closely monitored or easily controlled.

We can build on the above by identifying some of the basic features of the experimental method, neatly encapsulated by **Giddens** ('Sociology', 1989): 'An experiment can ... be defined as an attempt, within artificial conditions established by an investigator, to test the influence of one or more variables upon others'.

Aside from what we've just noted about the ability (or otherwise) of a researcher to control the environment (or conditions) under which an experiment takes place, the key idea here is that of *variables* (in basic terms, something that may change – or vary – under different conditions). The purpose (or *rationale* if you want to show off) of experimentation is fairly simple to describe (but much harder to actually do). For example, in an imaginary (and oversimplified) experiment we have two *variables*. The first we call 'Variable C' and the second we call 'Variable E'. All we want to test is: if we change Variable C in some way, what change (if any) will we see in Variable E?

If this is a bit confusing, consider this: in our laboratory we have a plant and a means of controlling the heat. The plant is Variable E and the heat control is Variable C. What we want to know, by experimenting with changes in the level of heating, is how will the plant change? For example, if we deprive it of heat what will happen?

This example highlights the importance of a *controlled environment* within a closed system. If we record changes in plant behaviour we need to be certain they were caused by changing the heating level. If we allow some other variable into the equation (such as changing the amount of light the plant receives) we can't be sure any recorded changes were due to changes in heat level. In a roundabout way, therefore, we have encountered some important ideas relating to experimentation that we need to briefly clarify.

- **Variables**: In the above we've identified two types. The first we call:
  - **Dependent variables** and these, in any experiment, are the *effect* we want to measure. Changes in the behaviour of Variable E (otherwise known as a plant) were what we wanted to measure; hence, plant behaviour would, in this instance, be the dependent variable because any changes in behaviour depend on – or are caused by – something else. The second we call:
  - **Independent variables** – the things we, as researchers, *change* in various ways in order to measure their possible *effect* on the dependent variable.
- **Causality**: This can be expressed in terms of the idea two or more things (for example, heat and plant growth) are so closely related that when one changes the other also changes. If this happens *every time* we repeat our experiment we can claim to have established a *causal relationship* – a very powerful statement, mainly because it allows us to make *predictions* about future behaviour. As an aside, a causal relationship is, by definition, highly *reliable*.
- **Correlation**: This is an observation two or more things occur at the same time (for example, if we deprive a plant of heat it dies). This is a *weaker statement* than a causal statement because we can't be certain one thing *caused* another to happen – they may have happened at the same time by *accident* or through *chance*.

We can illustrate the difference between causality and correlation using the following example, in 1989, the First-Class Cricket Averages for batting and bowling in England were as follows:

- The **top ten batsmen** all had names that were no longer than one syllable (Smith, Lamb, Jones …).
- The **top ten bowlers**, on the other hand, all had names that were two or more syllables long (Ambrose, Dilley, Foster…).

This is an example of a correlation for two reasons. Firstly, there is no *logical relationship* between the ability to bat or bowl successfully and a person's name (would changing your name, for example, make you a better or worse batsman or bowler)?

Secondly, since it is not always easy or possible to prove or disprove something logically, a better way would be to use some sort of test – in this instance, we could examine the averages for previous years. If the relationship is *not* repeated (or replicated) we would know it was the product of chance (a correlation in other words). If it *was* repeated every year, this would suggest a causal relationship (and in case you are wondering, it was a correlation – simply a chance occurrence).

Although laboratory experiments are a powerful method used extensively in the natural sciences they're not, as I've noted, used much in sociological research (for reasons we'll examine in a moment). However, **natural experiments** are used occasionally and, for convenience, we can sub-divide this category into two types.

- **Field experiments** are conducted outside the confines of a closed, controlled, environment. They take place, therefore, 'in the field' (not literally 'in a field' of course) where respondents are studied in their natural environment. The basic principles of field experiments are very similar to lab-type experiments (the objective being, as you will recall, to identify dependent and independent behavioural variables and manipulate (or change) them in some way to measure possible effects).

- **Comparative experiments** involve comparing two or more naturally occurring situations to examine their similarities and differences. For example, two identical twins separated at birth and raised in different families (perhaps, if you're very lucky, even different societies) would provide an opportunity for a comparative experiment since it would be possible to identify similarities and differences in the twins' behaviour.

🕸 **If you're interested in exploring experimentation further, examples of laboratory, field and comparative experiments can be found at:**
www.sociology.org.uk/as4aqa.htm

 Digging deeper

As I have suggested, sociologists tend not to use experiments (especially the laboratory type) in their research, mainly because of the following *disadvantages*.

- **Experimental control**: A major methodological problem with both laboratory and field experiments is the difficulty involved in identifying and controlling all the possible influences on people's behaviour.

- **Awareness**: Because people are conscious of what is happening around them, this introduces an uncontrolled independent variable into any experiment – how, for example, the fact of knowing they are part of an experiment may change someone's behaviour. This is frequently referred to as the **Hawthorne Effect**, named after the studies by **Elton Mayo** (*The human problems of an industrial civilization*, 1933) at the Hawthorne factory in Chicago. **Draper** (2004) describes this possible effect as being noted when:

  A series of studies on the productivity of workers manipulated various conditions (pay, light levels, rest breaks etc.), but each change resulted, on average and over time, in productivity rising . . . This was true of each of the individual workers as well as of the group [as a whole]. Clearly the variables the experimenters manipulated were not the only . . . causes of productivity. One interpretation . . . was that the important effect here was the feeling of being studied.

  This possible change in people's behaviour as the result of 'a feeling of being studied' leads us to note the possible effect of an:

- **Artificial environment**: A controlled experiment is, by definition, an unusual situation for people – does this mean they behave differently inside a laboratory to how they behave in society generally?

  In addition, we can note a couple of further considerations.

- **Ethical**: Do sociologists have the right to experiment on people, who may be unwitting (and unwilling) victims, in the name of 'research'?

- **Practical**: It is often the case that the kind of experiments sociologists would like to conduct (such as separating identical twins at birth, placing them in different social environments and observing their development) are *impractical* (and probably *unethical*, come to that).

Despite such problems, experiments do have a number of *advantages*.

- **Reliability**: Laboratory experiments can be highly reliable; if the experimental conditions can be controlled and standardised the experiment can be easily repeated.

- **Validity**: Experiments can be used to create powerful, highly valid, statements about people's behaviour under certain conditions. Through experimental methods, for example, it may be possible to establish *cause-and-effect* relationships in people's behaviour.

- **Assumptions**: Field experiments can be used to manipulate situations 'in the real world' to understand the *assumptions* (norms and values for example) on which people base their everyday behaviour.

Primary qualitative research methods

This general type of data collection is sometimes called *ethnography* – the detailed study of any small group. Ethnographic forms of research try to see and understand the world from the point of view of the subject or participant in that world and we can outline a range of different primary qualitative methods used by this type of research.

Growing it yourself: experimentation

A variety of simple 'classroom' experiments can be constructed (although you should always be aware of the *ethical considerations* that apply when doing this kind of research).

For example, in our society *personal space* is considered to be an area around our bodies we each own. It usually extends for 1–2 feet and we find it uncomfortable if people 'invade' our space without permission. Using a relatively closed environment such as your school or college library.

- Observe and record the responses of students whose personal space you deliberately invade (for example, by standing too close to someone looking for a book on the library shelves). Check to see how people of the same and opposite sex react to your behaviour.

- Observe and record examples of the ways people try to protect their personal space in this environment. For example, do they surround themselves with things like books and bags that seek to stop uninvited people sitting next to them?

- Place a bag on an empty chair at a desk in the library and observe and record how people respond (this is best done when the room is relatively crowded).

Focused interviews

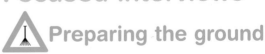

Preparing the ground

This involves the researcher setting up a situation (the interview) that allows the respondent to talk at length and in depth about a particular subject. The focus (or general topic) of the interview is decided by the researcher and there may also be particular areas they are interested in exploring – which is why this type of interview is sometimes called a *semi-structured* technique. It has a 'structure' (in the sense of things the interviewer wants the respondent to focus on), but one that's not as rigid as a structured interview – there is no list of questions to be asked and answered and different respondents may be asked different questions on the same topic, depending on how the interview develops.

The objective here is to *understand* things from the respondent's viewpoint, rather than make generalisations about people's behaviour (although this may be possible in certain circumstances). *Open-ended questions* are frequently (if sparingly) used, some of which are created in advance of the interview and some of which arise naturally from whatever the respondent talks about.

We can note a number of factors that can affect the conduct (and validity) of focused interviews.

- **Personal demeanour**: This method requires certain *skills* of the researcher – for example, when to prompt and when to listen. Although such interviews are similar to conversations, they are not arguments – people are unlikely to open up to a rude and aggressive interviewer. Similarly, how researchers present themselves (how they dress, how they talk, whether they appear interested or bored and so forth) may be important factors in the interview process.

- **Setting**: Interviews take time and the respondent should be comfortable with both their surroundings and the interviewer. To get people to talk openly it's important to build a *rapport* with the

respondent – they should feel comfortable with both the researcher, the interview and their surroundings; unlike a structured interview which can be conducted almost anywhere, focused interviews can't be easily conducted on street corners or in a noisy classroom.

- **Trust**: Interviews may deal with matters of personal importance to respondents – one reason for using this technique is, after all, the desire to explore 'what people really believe' – and it is important respondents feel they are being taken seriously (whatever they may say or do) and that the information will be confidential. Building trust between the researcher and the respondent may also, of course, help to increase the reliability and validity of the data gained using this method.

- **Interview schedule**: In essence, a schedule is a plan, developed by the researcher, used to specify and track the progress of the interview. For focused interviews, such a schedule may start with the *major topic* (or focus) and an initial, open-ended, question (for example, 'Can you tell me about . . .') designed to get the respondent talking about the general topic. The schedule may also include some subsidiary questions or topics the researcher wants to explore and these may or may not be asked, depending on how the interview develops. If they are asked, they may not be asked in the original order they appeared on the schedule. Finally, the schedule can be updated with questions that arose during the interview (which, again, may or may not be used in subsequent focused interviews with different respondents)

One further thing we can note in this context is a general development around the basic theme of the focused interview, namely **hierarchical focusing** – a technique advocated by **Tomlinson** ('Having it both ways', 1989), whereby the researcher constructs an interview schedule that starts with the most general question and develops with more specific questions, gradually introduced as the interview progresses. General questions are used to encourage respondents to talk and specific questions are used as and when required to refocus the interview.

Digging deeper

We can look at some *advantages* of focused interviews in the following terms.

- **Pre-judgement**: The problem we noted, in relation to questionnaires, of the researcher *pre-determining* what will or will not be discussed is largely (although not totally) avoided, since there are few 'pre-set questions' or topics.

- **Prior knowledge**: Since the interview allows the respondent to talk about the things that interest or concern them, it's possible for the interviewer to pick up ideas and information that had either not occurred to them or of which they had no prior knowledge or understanding (and this new knowledge can, of course, be used to inform subsequent interviews with different respondents).

- **Validity**: By allowing respondents to develop their opinions, the researcher may be able to get at what someone 'really means or believes'. By focusing on things the respondent sees as important and interesting, the researcher is likely to

receive a much greater depth of information.

- **Help and guidance**: Within limits, the face-to-face interaction of a focused interview allows the researcher to help and guide respondents – to explain or rephrase a question, for example – which may improve the overall validity of the responses.

Focused interviews, for all their undoubted uses, also have certain *disadvantages*.

- **Information overload**: Large amounts of data are produced (which needs to be interpreted by the researcher – always an important consideration in this type of research), much of which may not be directly relevant to the research hypothesis or question.

- **Focus**: Because the respondent largely dictates the direction of the interview they may go in directions that are of little or no relevance to the research (although the ever-present problem with this type of method is the researcher may not know – or be aware during the interview – whether the information being given is relevant or irrelevant in the greater scheme of their research). The researcher usually, however, has to make (skilled) decisions about when to ask questions that refocus the interview.

- **Generalisations**: Where the same questions are not necessarily put to different respondents, the result is a lack of standardisation; this, in turn, makes it difficult to generalise the results from a set of focused interviews.

- **Skills**: This relates to both the skills required of a researcher (the ability to ask the right questions, to put respondents at ease and to think quickly about relevant question opportunities as they arise during the interview) and a respondent – an *inarticulate respondent*, for example, will lack the skills to talk openly and in detail about the research topic.

- **Validity**: Although research validity may be high because of the depth and detail involved, any interview is, essentially, a *reconstruction*. Respondents are required to remember and recount events that happened in the past and this creates validity problems for both researcher and respondent.

  A researcher, for example, has no way of knowing if a respondent is lying; a more subtle problem may be *imperfect recall*. If you were asked to remember things that happened days, weeks or months ago, it is possible you would remember very little about what actually may have happened.

  An interview can also be a 'second chance' to do something; in other words, given the time to reflect, the respondent 'makes sense' of their behaviour by rationalising their actions. They are not consciously lying here, but their explanation for their behaviour, with hindsight, may be very different from what they actually felt or did at the time.

- **Recording information**: This is not necessarily a limitation (unless the researcher is trying to manually record everything – which may disrupt the flow of the interview) but electronic recording (such as a tape or video recorder) needs to be unobtrusive; if the respondent is too aware of being recorded it may make them nervous, uncooperative or self-conscious.

Unstructured interviews

 ## Preparing the ground

Unstructured (or non-focused as they are sometimes called) interviews involve the researcher entering the interview with only a general idea or topic they want the respondent to 'talk about'. The main objective, as with focused interviews, is to record a respondent's views about a particular topic and a researcher does this by encouraging the respondent to talk. The researcher's contribution to the interview is, however, minimal; they may provide *non-verbal cues* (nodding, smiling and so forth) to encourage respondents to talk about the topic, but the researcher's role is mainly to observe and record rather than to contribute.

The *non-participation* of the researcher is part of the technique, not just because they want to avoid influencing what's said (the objective, after all, is to discover the things the respondent feels are important), but also because *conversation norms* in our culture do not tolerate silence (think about how embarrassing it is when you are having a conversation and neither of you can think of anything to say). The silence of the researcher encourages – in theory at least – the respondent to talk.

 ## Digging deeper

Unstructured interviews, although similar to their focused counterparts, have a couple of distinct *advantages*.

- **Validity**: The minimal intervention of the researcher – the respondent leads and the researcher follows – means the data

Conversation norms in our society tell us silence is embarrassing.

collected reflects the interests of the respondent and, consequently, is more likely to be a true expression of their beliefs.

- **No pre-judgements**: The main objective of this method is to describe reality as the respondent sees it so they, rather than the researcher, decides what is and what is not significant information.

The drawbacks of this technique are again similar to those for focused interviews but we can note a couple of additional *disadvantages*.

- **Skills**: Unfocused interviews require researcher patience and skill, since the temptation may be to try to converse with the respondent when the objective is simply to listen and record. The respondent must also be articulate (able to express themselves clearly and understandably) and forthcoming since, if they aren't, it's difficult to use this method to produce data.

- **Focus**: By intention, the researcher has no control over the direction of the interview. The respondent may choose to talk about things of little or no immediate interest to the researcher; they may, for example, wander into areas of no relevance to the research topic. In addition, large amounts of information are generated and will involve some form of selection and interpretation process on the part of the researcher when the data is finally analysed.

- **Reliability**: This tends, as you might expect, to be relatively low. The unstandardised format makes it impossible to exactly repeat the interview (even with the same respondent). Unintentional bias can occur if a respondent is inarticulate or unwilling to open up; there may be a temptation to 'lead the respondent' ('So what you mean is . . .'). In addition, the respondent may feel pressurised into 'talking for the sake of talking' when the interviewer fails to respond. Respondents say things they don't particularly believe, simply to 'fill the silence'.

Before we leave interviews (in all their different shapes and sizes) and as a prelude to discussing *observational methods*, we can identify and examine a couple of general problems of bias.

- **Unintentional bias** involves a variety of things a careful researcher can avoid doing. Focused and unstructured interviews, for example, place demands on the skills and expertise of the researcher and an unskilful interviewer can easily bias the interview process (thereby producing invalid data). Unintentional bias can range from things like tone of voice and general demeanour (does the interviewer appear interested?) to the ability (or otherwise) to organise the interview – to ensure recording devices are not intrusive and distracting, for example.

- **Inherent bias**, on the other hand, involve things critics of interviews say cannot be avoided. Thus, the potential problems of bias we've noted so far have been basically *technical* (problems the researcher can resolve), but an idea that suggests interviews are fundamentally flawed is called the **interview effect**. Any interaction process (for example, the doctor–patient or teacher–student relationship) represents a situation in which status considerations apply. In other words, when I, as a teacher, interact with my students, certain unstated status rules exist between us. For example, when I take the register, I expect them to respond. These rules, therefore, involve people knowing and accepting their relative status positions.

Interviews, as an interaction process, are subject to such rules. **Cohen** and **Taylor** ('Talking About Prison Blues', 1977), for example, have argued one form of interview effect happens when, through the act of questioning people, a series of subtle and not-so-subtle *status manipulations* come into play, the outcome of which is respondents effectively tell the researcher what they believe the researcher would like to hear. Status differences come into play because the respondent considers the researcher to be 'in charge' (just as a patient expects the same of their doctor) and, consequently, is looking to both defer to the researcher and, in some senses, please them through their cooperation.

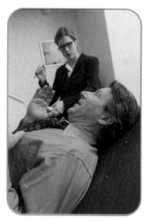

Do status differences between researcher and respondent mean interviews are inherently biased?

Interviews, so the argument goes, cannot get at 'the truth' because, like any other form of social interaction, they involve a process of what **Erving Goffman** (*The Presentation of Self in Everyday Life*) has called:

- **Negotiation** – a respondent makes decisions about how much or how little to reveal in the interview.

- **Impression management** – the way each participant in the interview attempts to manage the impression they give of themselves to each other.

- **Manipulation** – the interviewer attempting to push the respondent into a position where they feel able to reveal 'the truth' about themselves.

If we agree with the logic of the interview effect, we must seek another method that allows sociologists to collect data in as natural a way as possible – we need, therefore, to observe people and their behaviour.

Observation

Preparing the ground

The research methods we have considered so far all have one major thing in common, namely that the researcher is collecting data on the basis of what people *say* they believe or *say* they do. These methods, in their different ways, rely on people telling or remembering the truth about their behaviour – which does, of course, raise questions about their general validity. What is missing here is the ability to observe people going about their everyday lives – watching them in their 'natural setting'. This section, therefore, focuses on a couple of different types of observational method.

- **Non-participant observation** involves observing behaviour *from a distance*. The researcher doesn't become personally involved in what they are studying since, if they are not involved, their presence can't influence the behaviour of the people being watched. The technical term for this 'social distance' is *objectivity* – the ability to remain detached, aloof or personally separate from the people you're researching. There are a couple of important dimensions to objectivity (namely, personal and methodological) but for the moment we can consider it as not interacting with the people we are researching.

An experiment might be an example of *non-participant observation* since researcher involvement is limited to setting up and then observing the experiment. Alternatively, a sociologist interested in the social psychology of crowd behaviour might simply observe and record

behaviour witnessed at a football match or a pop concert. By observing people (without them knowing) we get an insight into the way they actually behave. **Yule** ('Why are parents so tough on children?', 1986) used this technique when she observed how mothers treated their children in public places.

Growing it yourself: take a walk . . .

A simple – and relaxing – way to do some sociological observation is a take a short walk around the area where you live or work. As you walk, make a note of the things you observe.

You can note things like who's around 'on the streets' and what they're doing; you can note the buildings, record graffiti etc.

If you're doing this as a class, make sure you compare notes at the end of your walk because it's probable different people will consider different things significant . . .

What sort of sociological picture of your area have you observed?

Alternatively, if you have access to a digital camera (and, more importantly, you know how to use it), take pictures of the interesting things you observe while walking.

- **Participant observation**: This type of research stresses the need for the researcher to involve themselves in the behaviour they are observing and we normally identify two main types:

  - **Covert** observation involves participating in and observing behaviour secretly; the research subject is unaware they're being observed. For example, a researcher joins and studies a group without informing them they are being studied and, as far as the group are aware, the researcher has simply joined (or been admitted) to participate in the usual activities of that group.

This method has certain advantages and disadvantages for the researcher, since they will have to balance the roles of researcher and participant while keeping the former role secret from other group members. By fully participating in a group, the sociologist may, of course, potentially become involved in various forms of unethical, personally distasteful or criminal behaviour.

- **Overt observation** involves participating in and observing the behaviour of people who know they are being studied. The researcher joins the group *openly*, telling its members about the research being undertaken (its purpose, scope, etc.) and they carry out research with the permission and co-operation of the group.

Participant observation is sometimes referred to as *subjective sociology* because the researcher aims to understand the social world from the subject's viewpoint – it involves 'getting to know' the people being studied by entering their world and participating in that world. It involves the researcher putting themselves 'in the shoes' of the respondent in an attempt to experience events in a way they are experienced by the people being studied. The technical term for this – suggested by the German sociologist **Max Weber** – is *verstehen* (literally, 'to understand'). Another way

of expressing this is to use **G. H. Mead**'s (*Mind, Self and Society*, 1933) idea the researcher should exploit the ability to *take the part of the other* in order to understand how people experience the social world.

As **Parker** (*A View from the Boys*, 1974) argues, the reason for doing this is that: 'by visiting the deviants in prison, borstal and other "human zoos" or by cornering them in classrooms to answer questionnaires, the sociologist misses meeting them as people in their normal society'.

Digging deeper

Considered as a general research method, participant observation has a number of *advantages*.

- **Flexibility**: The researcher, because they're not pre-judging issues (in terms of what they consider to be important/ unimportant) can react to events, follow leads, and develop research avenues that may not have occurred to them before becoming involved with a group.

- **Validity**: This method, because of the depth of involvement with people's behaviour, has the potential to produce highly valid data.

- **Understanding (empathy)**: By their participation and experience in the group, the researcher can understand, first-hand, the influences on behaviour.

In terms of *disadvantages*, however, we can note things like:

- **Skill** and commitment is required from the researcher – the ability to fit into the

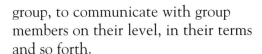

group, to communicate with group members on their level, in their terms and so forth.

- **Generalisation**: Participant observation is normally restricted to small-scale, intensive, studies carried out over a long period and the group being studied is unlikely to be representative of any other group. It would be difficult (probably) for a researcher to generalise their findings from one group to the next.

- **Reliability**: Two general reliability issues are, firstly, the research can never be replicated. It would be possible to revisit a group, but the research could never be accurately repeated. Secondly, we have, of course, to take it on *trust* the researcher saw and did the things they claimed to see and do.

Although these are advantages and disadvantages relating to the general method, its two basic forms are sufficiently different to warrant separate consideration.
Overt participant observation, for example, has some distinctive *advantages*.

- **Recording data** is relatively easy because the group knows and understands the role of the researcher. The researcher can ask questions, take notes, etc. with the permission of the people involved.

- **Access** to all levels is important if research is being done on a group that has a hierarchical structure (a large company, for example, where the researcher would have access to both the 'shop floor' and the boardroom).

- **Going native**: Overt participant observation makes it easier to separate the roles of participant and observer and reduces the chance of the researcher

becoming so involved in a group they stop observing and simply become a participant (in other words, they 'go native').

A couple of significant *disadvantages* to this method need, however, to be noted.

- **The observer effect**: A major criticism here is the observer's presence changes group behaviour in some unknown way – do people who know they are being studied change (consciously or subconsciously) the way they normally behave?

- **Superficial involvement**: If the researcher doesn't fully participate in the group, their 'involvement' may not be deep enough to fully experience the world from the viewpoint of the people being studied. Depth of involvement may also, of course, be limited by ethical considerations – not participating in the crimes committed by a criminal gang, for example.

Covert participant observation, on the other hand, also has its *advantages*.

- **Access**: This type of observational method may be the only way to study people who would not normally allow themselves to be studied (their behaviour is illegal, deviant or secretive, for example). **John Ray** in his study of groups of Australian environmentalists ('A Participant Observation Study of Social Class Among Environmentalists', 1987) argued: 'The study was covert to minimize defensiveness on the part of those studied and to avoid breakdowns in co-operation'. Similarly, **Lofland** and **Stark** ('Becoming a world-saver', 1965) used a covert approach to study the behaviour of a secretive religious sect.

- **Level of participation** is, of course, very high – the researcher may live with the people they are (secretly) studying and, in consequence, this method produces massively detailed and insightful data (observed and personally experienced) about a group's behaviour.

- **Validity**: Personal experience means the researcher understands the meanings and motivations within a group that explain why people behave in certain ways (even when such people themselves may not understand the reasons for their behaviour). In addition, when we look at behaviour 'from the outside, looking in' it can be difficult to explain why people would want to behave in ways we may find distasteful, disgusting or perverse – covert observation goes some way to resolving this problem by allowing the researcher to understand the meaning behind people's actions.

- **The observer effect** problem is avoided because people are not aware they are being observed – their behaviour is, consequently, unaffected by the researcher's observations.

The potential *disadvantages* of covert observation should, however, not be ignored.

- **Problems**: **Goffman**'s classic covert study of an American mental institution (*Asylums*, 1961) noted three major problems for the covert participant observer.

  - **Getting in**: It may be difficult for the researcher to enter a group.

  - **Staying in**: What happens if the researcher fails to either participate properly or is exposed as a 'spy'?

  - **Getting out**: In many groups it may not be particularly easy to simply 'stop participating'.

We can develop these (and some additional) ideas as follows.

- **Entrance and access**: If the researcher's characteristics (age, for example) don't match those of the group then, not to put too fine a point on it, the researcher can't enter the group (a man, for example, would find it difficult to covertly study a group of nuns). In addition, some groups (Freemasons, for example) only allow people to join by invitation, while professional occupations (such as accountancy) require particular qualifications. If a group has a hierarchical structure the researcher won't have access to all levels. Doing covert observation in a school under the guise of 'being a student' won't give you access to the staffroom.

- **Level of participation**: A researcher has to learn the culture of a group if they are to participate fully and not be exposed as a 'spy'. This may not be easy.

- **Going native**: Separating the role of participant from that of observer can be difficult to maintain when you are acting undercover.

- **Reliability** issues abound with covert research – it can't be replicated, we have to trust the researcher's observations (there's nothing to back them up) and recording data is frequently difficult (the researcher can't take notes or record conversations openly, because to do so would risk exposure).

Goffman (1961), used a *field diary* to write up his observations at the end of every working day – although this does, of course, mean the researcher must remember things accurately and make decisions about what events were significant. Having said this, it's possible to use modern technology (miniature cameras and voice recorders etc.) to ensure data is accurately captured and recorded – although these raise questions of:

- **Ethics**: These range from the effect of leaving a group who may have grown to trust and depend on the researcher, to questions about whether covert observation exploits people (does a researcher have the right to spy on people or, in **Parker's** terms, pretend to be 'one of them'?).

Visual (creative) research methods

 Preparing the ground

All of the methods we have looked at so far rely, to varying degrees, on spoken language – either in terms of people recounting their thoughts and experiences in words or through descriptive observational analyses by sociologists. However, a different approach to data generation and collection is one that focuses on visual methods, pioneered by academics such as **David Gauntlett** (examples of whose research work you can find on-line at the Centre for Creative Media Research's *Artlab* project (http://www.artlab.org.uk) run by the Bournemouth Media School).

The basic technique here is deceptively simple; respondents are required to visualise behaviour, through the use of drawings, videos and the like. Instead of asking people questions or observing them, the researcher

Growing it yourself: observing in a chatroom

A relatively simple way to get a feel for both non-participant and participant observation is to join an internet chatroom (although if you're going to do this you should check things out first with your teacher, parents and friends – some chatrooms should not be used in this way – and never give out personal information, for more advice see www.chat.danger.com). You can record the social interaction you witness (you should think about how you can do this) as both an observer and, if you wish, as a participant.

The Sixth Form Forum (http://www.sixthform.info/forum) has a chatroom you can use for this type of research (you will need to register first, but it's free – all that's required is a valid email address). It is moderated by college lecturers and students and is a relatively safe environment to use for this purpose.

Alternatively, try doing a day's covert observation of a group of which you're already a member. If you do this as a class – all 'secretly' observing each other – compare your observations at the end of the exercise. This will give you an insight into some of the practical and theoretical problems involved.

asks the respondent to 'do or create something' – the analysis of which (by both the researcher and the respondent) gives an insight into people's ideas, interests, perspectives and concerns. For example, a respondent may be asked to visualise their relationship to their physical environment through drawings, digital photographs or video recordings.

The rationale for this method is that, according to **Gauntlett**, putting feelings, emotions and beliefs into words is often difficult for people; visualisations, on the other hand, make it easier for both respondent and researcher because a drawing, serious of photographs or a video is something concrete on which to base further analysis (which may involve using more traditional research techniques such as questionnaires or interviews).

Growing it yourself: picturing reality

The best way to understand this idea is to actually do something.

Draw a picture of a celebrity you admire or would like to be. Artistic skill is not important – just include anything you think represents that person (and, by extension, you). Once you've drawn your picture:

List three words that both describe the person you've drawn and how you would like people to think of you.

In pairs, exchange drawings. Each of you should make brief notes (without showing them to your partner) identifying:

1. what you think your drawing says about you

2. what you think your partner's drawing says about them.

Compare notes – look for points of convergence (where you agree) and divergence (where you disagree) – and discuss what this exercise says about the relationship between how we see ourselves and how others see us.

Digging deeper

If you have tried the previous exercise (you should, it is great fun) I trust you'll agree this is a different – and dare I say it, interesting? – research method. We can examine some of its *advantages* in the following terms.

- **Involvement**: The respondent is an active participant (rather than just a passive audience) in the research process. This method – unlike many others – involves the researcher and the researched working (creatively) together to produce data.

- **Agenda-setting**: Visual methods, whether they be drawing, creating videos or whatever, allow respondents to set their own agenda, in the sense respondents create whatever they want to create – whatever they believe best represents their ideas.

- **Process**: Creating research data in this way gives researchers first-hand experience of the process by which people make sense of their lives – in terms, for example, of how they see themselves (their identity) and their relationship to others.

- **Reflective**: These methods encourage (demand?) respondents reflect on the 'questions' they are being asked. In other words, they avoid the problem – prevalent in methods like questionnaires or interviews – of respondents having to *reconstruct* answers to questions.

All good things, however, have their *disadvantages*.

- **Organisation**: Visual methods require a great deal of organisation – and time – on the part of the researcher and the researched. The creation of a video record/presentation, for example, is a time-intensive process that also requires access to hardware (cameras...), software (editing suites ...) and skills (how do you splice two images?).

- **Interpretation**: The meaning of data may be difficult to interpret, although respondents may be asked to explain the meaning of their work. However, a sociological context is still required from the researcher and this may mean reading things into the data that were never considered by the respondent.

Secondary sources

Introduction

This type of source – using data that already exists – is extensively used by sociologists for a couple of reasons.

- **Practical**: Secondary sources represent a substantial saving of time, money and effort for the researcher. It may be unnecessary or impractical to create some forms of data (using primary methods) when such data already exists. In Britain, for example, the government collects and freely distributes a huge amount of statistical data each year. For the price of a book, a visit to a public library or a few key presses on the Internet, the researcher has immediate access to data that would cost an enormous amount of money, time and effort to collect personally.

- **Methodological**: Secondary source data may be a necessity if historical and/or

comparative research is being carried out. **Philip Aries** (*Centuries of Childhood*, 1962), for example, used historical evidence (paintings and documents) to support his idea that childhood was a relatively recent invention. **Emile Durkheim** (1897) on the other hand used *comparative* data (suicide statistics from different countries) to test his idea that suicide had social, as opposed to psychological, causes.

In this section, therefore, we are going to outline and evaluate secondary sources under two broad categories, namely:

- **content analysis** as a way of analysing secondary data sources (such as historical and contemporary documents)

- **official statistics** as a secondary data source.

Content analysis

This involves the study of *texts* (which for our purpose refers to data sources such as television, written documents and the like – a text is just a general term referring to data and is not restricted to written material) and in this section we can examine, in turn, examples of quantitative and qualitative content analysis.

Quantative analysis

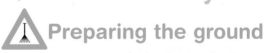 Preparing the ground

Content analysis is a popular method of quantitatively analysing media texts, using statistical techniques to categorise people's behaviour.

Some simple forms of content analysis might be:

- **Television programmes**: Analysing a programme such as *EastEnders* might involve the researcher creating two basic categories (men and women) and then counting the number of minutes each gender appears on screen. A more complex analysis might involve the use of categories like location (where each character is seen – for example, in the pub as a customer or an employee; in their own home, etc.) or activity (what each character does – for example, are they always pictured 'at work' or 'at home' and so forth?). Such analyses build up a picture of the patterns of behaviour that underlie (and are usually hidden from view) the social interaction portrayed on screen.

- **Newspapers**: This might involve counting the number of column inches given to activities that focus on men as opposed to women – or counting the number of times men and women are pictured. A more complex analysis might involve analysing data in terms of the prominence given to different stories featuring men and women.

Quantitative content analysis is mainly concerned with categorising behaviour and its main 'tool of the trade' is a **content analysis grid** – a chart developed and used to collect data systematically when an analysis is being carried out. A very simple content analysis grid designed to analyse the behaviour of characters in a television programme might look something like the table below.

An analysis of this type can tell us something about the behaviour of a character (Jo Banks, for example, has two main roles – mother and employee). Although this is a simple example, content analysis can be complex and wide-ranging. **Meehan**'s study of US daytime television for example, (*Ladies of the Evening*, 1983), used just such a complex form of content analysis to identify and analyse the stereotypical roles played by female characters.

 Digging deeper

This type of content analysis has a number of *advantages*.

- **Themes** and **patterns** to behaviour that may not be apparent to a reader, viewer or general consumer can be uncovered through relatively simple quantification. *Recurrent themes* (such as women being associated with housework) in complex forms of social interaction can also be

Character	Male/Female	Age	Place and purpose	How long on screen
Jo Banks	F	37	Pub (employee)	15 seconds
Tom Ward	M	56	Pub (customer)	43 seconds
Jo Banks	F	37	Shop (customer)	84 seconds

identified using this method. **Hogenraad** ('The Words that Predict the Outbreak of Wars', 2003), for example, developed a computer-based content analysis program to search historical accounts of war to identify key recurring themes that signify the lead up to conflict.

Similarly, **Miller** and **Riechert** ('Identifying Themes via Concept Mapping: A New Method of Content Analysis', 1994) developed the idea of *concept mapping*, which involves using computer technology to identify and describe 'themes or categories of content in large bodies of text'.

- **Reliability**: The use of *standardised frameworks* (the grid) means data can be replicated and checked fairly easily (although there are limits – see below – to the reliability of this technique).

We can note a couple of *disadvantages*, however.

- **Identification**: Although content analysis can uncover themes and patterns, it doesn't tell us very much about *how* audiences receive, understand or ignore such themes (in technical terms, this is called media *decoding*). If patterns of behaviour aren't just a product of the classification system the researcher used, we need some other way of making sense of their significance, both in terms of academic research and, perhaps more importantly, their possible effects on an audience.

- **Reliability**: Content analysis involves making judgements about the categorisation of behaviour. The researcher, for example, decides what categories will be used for analysis. In

addition, the researcher must judge which forms of behaviour fit which categories – can all observed behaviour be put neatly into a particular category (or does behaviour that cuts across different categories merit a category of its own?) In other words, would different researchers, studying the same behaviour, categorise it in the same way?

Growing it yourself: positive and negative images

This simple exercise involves reading magazines, cutting out pictures that show 'positive' and 'negative' images of something and comparing your ideas (why you think it's a positive image) and choices with others in the class.

You can choose anything you want, but make sure, as a class, you all choose the same thing (to make comparisons easier). Some possible ideas might be:

- sexuality (male/female, heterosexual/homosexual)
- men
- women
- celebrities.

Using your chosen topic (sexuality for the sake of argument), create two piles of images cut from your chosen magazines (positive images and negative images). Once you've done this you are required to justify your decisions to the rest of the class (you have to explain why something represents a positive or negative image).

Qualitative analysis

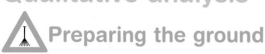 Preparing the ground

Content analysis can also be used in a more qualitative way.

- **Conceptual** (or **thematic**) analysis focuses on the concepts or themes that underlie television programmes, news reports, magazine articles, newspaper reports and the like. In this respect, such analysis can be considered an extension of the quantitative form of content analysis. **Philo** and **Berry**'s *Bad News from Israel* (2004), for example, identifies a number of recurring themes in news reports of the Israeli–Palestinian conflict, such as language differences when referring to similar forms of behaviour (Palestinians were frequently classed as 'terrorists' while Israeli settlers were called 'extremists' or 'vigilantes').

- **Relational** (or **textual**) analysis examines the way texts encourage the reader to see something in a particular way by relating one idea to something different. Media sociologists sometimes refer to this as a *preferred reading* of a text – the way text is constructed (how language, pictures and illustrations are used, for example) 'tells' the audience how to interpret the information presented (without appearing to do so). An example here might be the way sport is presented in British popular newspapers. A brief glance through the sports pages, for example, might lead you to think sport is mainly a male activity.

Module link: The concept of 'preferred reading' is analysed in more detail in the chapter on the media.

Growing it yourself: hollywood themes

A simple way of doing a bit of content analysis is to watch films (or think about films you've seen recently) and to identify common themes and patterns of behaviour.

Many action films, for example, contain fairly basic main themes (Good versus Evil, for example) and more subtle minor themes – the revenge motive, for example, which involves 'The Good' taking personal revenge on 'The Bad' (invariably by killing them in as violent, painful and personally-humiliating fashion as possible). This suggests (to me at least) 'problems' can be solved through violence of an extreme and personal kind rather than the way people normally try to solve problems (through discussion, the police, etc.).

To do this, as a group:

1. Identify a genre (that is, a group of films that have the same basic format – westerns, romantic comedies, action films and the like).

2. Discuss the common themes or behaviour patterns you think are characteristic of the genre.

Keeping the above in mind, therefore, we can move towards looking at **documents** as sources of secondary data. In our society there is a wide range of documentary evidence available to sociologists and classifying them in any meaningful way is difficult. However, for our purposes, we can think about documentary evidence as shown in the table on the following page.

In the table, we have identified a number of different documentary *types* and *sources* and also suggested documents can be both

Type	Official	Organisational	Individual
Possible sources	Government agencies and departments	Private companies and organisations	Personal documents created by individuals
Historical Current	Official Reports, Court Reports	Newspapers (local/national), film, magazines, books, Church records	Letters, autobiography diaries, biography, oral histories

historical and *current* (or contemporary) – again, this is just for convenience in terms of outlining different document *advantages* and *disadvantages*.

 Digging deeper

Documentary sources have a number of distinct *advantages*.

- **Comparison**: Historical documents can be used for comparative purposes – contrasting how people lived in the past with how we live now is useful for tracking and understanding social change. Historical analysis is also useful for demonstrating the diversity of people's behaviour – things we now take for granted may have been seen differently in the past (and vice versa).

- **Availability**: Documents can provide secondary data in situations where it's not possible to collect primary data (about things that happened in the past, for example). Documents about family life, education, crime and so forth may be the only available evidence.

  The media, on the other hand, can be a useful source of contemporary data. Some newspapers carry reports, analysis and comment on relatively up-to-date social research. The Internet is also an increasingly useful source of secondary data, through the development of search engines such as Google (www.google.com).

- **Cost**: The researcher gets access to data that would cost an enormous amount of money, time and effort to collect personally.

- **Validity**: There are a couple of aspects of validity we can note here.

  Firstly, documentary evidence may provide qualitative data of great depth and detail. Diaries, for example, (such as those of Samuel Pepys – who recorded life in England during the 1660s – or Anne Frank, who recorded her life in hiding from the Nazis during the Second World War) provide extensive details about people and their daily lives.

  Secondly, we can sometimes compare accounts across time to test the validity of current accounts of social behaviour.

- **Meaning**: Documents can, for our purpose, have two levels of meaning – a *literal* meaning (what they actually say) and a *metaphorical* meaning (what they tell us about the hopes, fears, beliefs and so forth of whoever produced the document).

Discussion point: comparing family life

Read the following accounts of family life.

Save our Children from the Collapse of Family Life: M. Benns

Family life is collapsing and responsible parents can no longer afford children' ... And lack of parental control and guidance lies behind many of today's pressing social problems, said ... Sir Keith Joseph. Part of the background to crime, to drug addiction, to low motivation at school, to poor job prospects and to the transmission of all these problems to the next generation comes from inadequate parenting ... the way to destroy a society is to destroy its children'.

An Inquiry into the Extent and Causes of Juvenile Depravity: T. Beggs

The withdrawal of women from the care of her offspring and domestic duties is an unnatural arrangement and a stain on society. Young children are left at home with inadequate parental control – to play at will and to commit all kinds of criminal act. Ignorant of cooking and sewing, unacquainted with the things needed to promote the comfort and welfare of a home ... sexually promiscuous and ignorant ... social evils are aggravated by the independence of the young of both sexes.

What kind of picture of family life do we get from reading these accounts?

Does the picture change (and in what ways) if we add the first extract was written in 1990 and the second (which I've edited slightly to bring the language a little more up-to-date) in 1849?

The extracts you have just discussed, I would suggest, are more important for what they tell us about the writers and how they saw social problems than for what they actually say about family life.

Despite their uses, documents have *disadvantages* we need to understand.

- **Reliability**: Aside from the usual points about our ability to replicate qualitative data, documents have reliability problems in that they may be incomplete, inaccurate or partial (biased towards one viewpoint – as we have just seen in the Family Life exercise).

- **Representativeness**: When using documentary sources we need to know, for example, if they are simply one individual's view (such as a diary) or whether they are representative of a range of views.

- **Authenticity**: With secondary documentary data there may be uncertainty over its source. Paper documents can be forged and we need to know whether they are originals or copies (which may have been changed by other authors). With electronic documents from the Internet, similar considerations apply (as we have previously seen with the John Kerry photograph).

- **Credibility**: We don't always know who created a document or why they created it. In other words, we can't always be certain the document is a credible source – for example, did the author have first-hand experience of the things they describe or are they simply repeating something 'second or third hand'?

- **Data control**: Finally, we need to consider how each of the above ideas connects to (and affects) the others when evaluating secondary sources. When considering data *authenticity* we would have to consider its *credibility* as a source, how *representative* it is and the *purpose* for which it was originally produced. With primary sources the researcher has control over these things. When dealing with secondary sources, however, it is not always so easy to ensure the data is reliable, authentic or representative.

Official statistics

⚠ Preparing the ground

We can complete this section by looking briefly at this major source of secondary *quantitative* data. It is useful, by the way, to note the ideas relating to official statistics in this section can also be applied to other forms of statistical data.

In Britain, the two main sources of official statistical data are government departments (such as the Department for Education and Skills) and agencies (such as the police). Governments produce *demographic data* (information about the behaviour of individuals and groups) for a couple of reasons: to inform policy making (how many teachers we will need in 10 years time, for example) and for information/ accountability purposes (for example how much is spent on defence or schooling each year).

In Britain, major sources of official statistical data are 'Social Trends', 'Regional Trends' and 'The Annual Abstract of Statistics' (all published by HMSO and available on the Internet through the Office of National Statistics (www.statistics.gov.uk).

⚠ Digging deeper

Statistics have a number of significant *advantages* for sociologists.

- **Availability**: Official statistics may be the only available source in a particular sociological area. This is especially true where the researcher is carrying out historical or cross-cultural analyses (see, for example, **Oliver Bakewell**'s 'Can we ever rely on refugee statistics?', 1999).

- **Cost**: The researcher does not have to spend money (and time) collecting data because it already exists.

- **Trends**: Using statistical data drawn from different years it's possible to see how something has changed. For example, statistics on educational achievement can show changes in relative levels of achievement between boys and girls. Similarly, statistics can be used in 'Before and After' studies, to track possible changes in behaviour. A recent example here might be the 'Year 2000 problem' relating to fears computers would not be able to cope with date changes associated with the new millennium (see, for example, **Mueller**: 'Twelve Propositions Concerning the Year 2000 Problem', 1999).

- **Comparisons**: Statistics can be used for *inter-group* comparisons (for example, the examination of differences in middle-class and working-class family size), as well as *cross-cultural* comparisons (for example, a study of crime rates in different countries). This kind of information may be too expensive and time consuming for the sociologist to collect personally.

Despite their undoubted uses, uncritical use of official statistics may involve a number of *disadvantages*.

- **Definitions**: We have noted elsewhere how definitions used by the creators of official statistics may not be the same as those used by the sociologist, but it is also important to note governments may change the definition of something (what counts as 'car crime', for example) over time. This may, therefore, create a *reliability* problem.

- **Validity**: Official statistics, apart from not providing any great depth or detail, may have validity problems associated with what governments include (or exclude) from their published data. Crime statistics are an obvious case in point (many crimes go unreported) but official unemployment statistics also illustrate this idea. According to the Office for National Statistics, in 1992, unemployment was 2.6 million people. In 2004, unemployment stood at 892,000. However, we can't simply conclude from this that 1.7 million people have now found employment.

If we look at other official statistics, we can note the number of people claiming sickness benefit (and thus not appearing in the unemployment statistics) increased from 350,000 in 1992 to 650,000 in 2004. The question to ask here, therefore, is has the health of the nation seriously declined – or are the unemployed increasingly being defined as 'sick'?

In this respect, a validity problem is that official statistics may only give us a partial picture of reality – the researcher may have to work hard to complete the whole picture.

- **Interpretation**: Although quantitative data is normally seen as more objective than qualitative data, as we have just seen, the significance of any data has to be interpreted by the researcher – the researcher has to decide what the data *means*. In the above example, you need to decide how significant (or not as the case may be) is the rise in official sickness levels in the UK over the past 10 years.

In this section we have looked at a variety of methods available to sociologists and discussed them in terms of their general advantages and disadvantages for sociological research. In the next section we are going to look at why different sociologists prefer to use some research methods but not others and, in order to do this, we need to explore the idea of sociological methodologies.

Sociological methodologies

Introduction

Thus far we have looked at the general research process in terms of the practical mechanics of doing research (although we have referred to methodological beliefs when discussing questions of reliability and validity). However, in this section we're going to develop these ideas by examining sociological methodologies – beliefs about how sociologists *should* go about collecting data and, by extension, the methods they *should* use to do this – in the context of 'the relationship between Positivism, Interpretivism and sociological research methods'.

In this respect, we're going to examine two types of methodology – *Positivism* and *Interpretivism* (which you'll sometimes see called 'social constructionism' for reasons that will become clear in a moment); there are a number of other methodologies we could examine (*realist*, *feminist* and *postmodernist*, for example) but the main purpose here is not simply to categorise sociologists in terms of their methodology; rather, it is to illustrate debates within sociology over the general direction sociological research should take. In other words, we will be looking at debates within sociology over how knowledge about the social world can be reliably and validly generated.

WARM UP: ARE YOU MAD?

To get you into the swing of what's to come (it could be a bumpy ride), pair up with your neighbour (the person sitting next to you, not the person who lives next door).

Your task is to spend five minutes convincing them you are *not* insane.

Their task, after you've had your go, is to explain why they believe you *are* insane.

What does your frank exchange of views tell you about the nature of the social world?

Positivism

Preparing the ground

The word *positivism* means *scientific* and this tells us something about the kinds of basic ideas found within this general methodology – positivists argue that it is possible (and perhaps desirable) to study social behaviour in ways similar to those used by natural scientists (physicists, for example) to study behaviour in the natural world. We can identify some elements of positivist thinking in the following way.

- **Social systems**: For positivists, a basic principle is that these consist of structures (which, as we have seen in chapter 1, can be considered in terms of rules). These structures exist independently of individuals because they represent behaviour at the institutional or large group level of society. As individuals, we experience social structures as forces bearing down on us, pushing us to behave in certain ways and, in effect, shaping our individual behavioural choices.

  An example of the way an institutional structure works is to think of communication – in order to be part of our society we need to communicate with others and we do this by using language, both verbal (words) and non-verbal (gestures). Thus, if we want to communicate we are forced to use language (in the case of this textbook, English – although, admittedly, it might not always seem as if this language is being used). As a conscious, thinking, individual I have some measure of *choice* in this matter – I could, if I wanted, speak German to people (in theory at least. In reality my knowledge of this language extends to the word for 'potato' – not very useful in the context of buying this item, less than useful when trying to fill my car with petrol). However, my freedom of choice is actually limited for two reasons: firstly, if I want to 'fit in' to social groups (such as when I teach) there would be little point speaking German to students – they barely understand when I speak English, so using another language would be a recipe for total confusion.

Secondly, even if I do choose to speak German, this is still a language – it has a structure of rules (grammar) that have to be obeyed if we are to understand each other.

- **Actions**: If people's behaviour (social action) is shaped by structural forces, it makes sense to study these *causes* rather than their *effects* (in this case, the different choices people make) – which is what positivists aim to do. If you accept social systems work in this way, it follows structures are real and *objective*; that is, they act on us whether we want them to or not – in crude terms, if you want to communicate, you have to use language; if societies are to survive, people have to work. Although these forces can't be seen, we can observe their effect on people (just as, in the natural world, gravity is an unseen force whose effect we can observe).

- **Reality**: If the forces shaping social behaviour really exist, it follows they can be discovered (in the same way natural scientists have gradually uncovered the forces shaping physical behaviour). This can be done using similar methods to those used so successfully in sciences such as physics – systematic observations that create highly reliable knowledge, organised and tested using something like Popper's Hypothetico-Deductive model of research we outlined earlier.

- **Facts**: For positivists, knowledge consists of identifying facts about how and why people behave as they do and, eventually, making connections between different facts to produce theories that explain our behaviour.

- **Methods**: Quantitative methods are generally favoured (because they allow for the collection of factual data), with due prominence being given to:

  - **Objectivity**: It doesn't involve the researcher influencing the people they are researching (so, non-participant observation is okay, but participant observation is more doubtful).

  - **Reliability**: Methods such as questionnaires/structured interviews, experiments, comparative and observational studies are perfectly acceptable in this respect because they offer higher potential levels of reliability than qualitative methods.

Digging deeper

If we examine positivist ideas a little more closely, we can identify and develop a number of significant ideas about this methodology.

- **Society**: For positivism, the social world is similar to the natural world in terms of the way it can be studied. This is because human behaviour is, in a sense, determined by rules developed within social groups. For example, the need to survive leads people to develop work groups and the need to socialise children leads people to develop family groups.

- **Structure**: Because societies are viewed as social systems – the requirements of which push people to behave in certain ways – it follows we experience the social world as a force that exists over and above our individual ability to change or influence it. Just as I cannot, for example, escape the fact of gravity (even while flying in a plane, gravity still exerts a force), positivists argue we cannot escape social forces (such as roles or norms).

- **Science**: The task of (social) science is to isolate, analyse and understand the causes of human behaviour – and to understand how social forces shape behaviour we need to (systematically) study social groups rather than individuals.

- **Evidence**: To reliably and validly study behaviour, sociologists should use *empirical* methods; that is, methods involving the use of our senses (sight, for example). Evidence about social behaviour, in other words, can only be considered reliable and valid if it is capable of being observed and tested. Anything not directly observable (such as people's thoughts) cannot be considered valid knowledge.

- **Objectivity**: Since this version of science is concerned only with what *is* – rather than what we might want something to be – scientists must be *personally objective* in their work (that is, you don't involve yourself in the behaviour being studied; this avoids biasing or influencing the data collection process). The methods used should *not* depend on the *subjective interpretations* of a researcher and research should be capable of exact *replication*. If the social world has an *objective existence* – over and above human beliefs about it – reliable and valid knowledge can be discovered in the same way natural scientists discover knowledge.

Interpretivism

Preparing the ground

In many ways we can think of Interpretivist methodology as being the mirror image of positivism, which should help us come to terms with its basic principles.

- **Social actions**: For interpretivists, a basic principle is human beings have:

  - **Consciousness** – we are aware of both ourselves (as unique individuals) and our relationship to others. This gives us the ability to:

  - **Act** – to make, in other words, conscious, deliberate, choices about how to behave in different situations. This idea is crucial for Interpretivists because it makes us – and the world in which we live:

  - **Unpredictable** – and if we are unpredictable then it means we can't study behaviour in the way Positivists want to study it.

We can understand these ideas a little more clearly in the following way.

If you slap me in the face, you have no way of knowing, in advance, how I am going to act; I might cry (because you hurt me), but then again I might not (because my friends are watching and everyone knows big boys don't cry); I may laugh at you (ha-ha); I might run away; I might tell my dad who will go round your house and beat your dad up (for no better reason than the fact he can – my dad's a bit unpredictable); I might slap you back – in short, I might do any one of a hundred different things. But the point here, of course, is that *how* I react will depend on a potentially massive range of factors.

- **Social systems**: Part of the reason for this, as I've sort of suggested above, is that for Interpretivists the social world consists of *meanings*. Society doesn't exist in an objective, observable, form; rather, it is experienced subjectively because we give it meaning by the way we behave. In other words, we create and recreate a 'sense of the social system' on a daily basis, minute by minute, piece by piece.

Every time you go to school, you help to recreate the structure of education; every time you say 'mum' or 'dad' you help to recreate a sense of family; every time you pinch something from Woolworths you help to recreate the criminal justice system (and you thought you were just showing off to your friends).

- **Reality**: In this respect, the social world is very different to the natural world, just as people (well, some people anyway) are very different to rocks. One might struggle, scream and beg if you try to throw it over a cliff while the other won't (I'll leave you to decide which is which). When we talk or think about society as *real* – as something *forcing* us do things like go to school or work – what we are actually doing, according to Interpretivist thinking, is creating a convenient fictional scapegoat for our own behaviour – 'society' doesn't make anyone do anything; only people can do that.

- **Facts**: For interpretivists, 'facts' about behaviour can be established, but these facts are always *context-bound*; that is, they will not apply to all people, at all times, in all situations. For example, if I steal something from Woolworths and get caught, it is a fact that I will be labelled 'a criminal'; if I don't get caught then it is a fact that I am seen as just another law-abiding citizen. The only difference here is not what I did, but how others *react* to what I did.

- **Methods**: Interpretivist methodology argues that, when studying behaviour, the best we can do is describe and explain it from the point of view of those involved. As the warm up exercise was designed to demonstrate, your account of behaviour is just as reliable and valid as anyone else's (as Interpretivists might say, knowledge is always *relative*). This being the case, interpretivist methodology leans towards the collection of qualitative data and uses methods (such as unstructured interviews and participant observation) that allow for the collection of this type of data.

Digging deeper

If we outline interpretivist ideas a little more thoroughly, we can identify and develop a number of significant ideas about this methodology. These include the following.

- **Society**: The social world is produced and reproduced on a daily basis by people going about their lives. Things that hold true for now (this minute, today, next week …) in our society may not hold true in the future or in another society. In this respect, the social world has no objective features (or social structures) in the way these ideas are understood by Positivists. 'Society' is simply experienced 'as if' our behaviour were constrained by forces external to us as individuals – in effect social structures are considered to be little more than *elaborate fictions* we use to explain and justify our behaviour to both ourselves and others.

- **Action**: On the basis of the above, the fact people actively (if not always consciously or deliberately) create their world means any attempt to establish cause and effect relationships is misguided (both in theory and in practice). If people's behaviour is conditioned by the

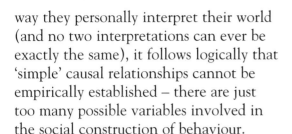

way they personally interpret their world (and no two interpretations can ever be exactly the same), it follows logically that 'simple' causal relationships cannot be empirically established – there are just too many possible variables involved in the social construction of behaviour.

- **Meanings**: The social world is understood ('interpreted') by different people in different situations in different ways (something you interpret as a 'problem', for example, may not be a problem to me). Everything in the social world, therefore, is relative to everything else; nothing can ever be wholly true and nothing can ever be wholly false; the best we can do is describe reality from the viewpoint of those who define it – people.

Understanding social behaviour, therefore, involves understanding how people (individually and collectively) experience and interpret their situation (the meanings people give to things, the beliefs they hold and so forth). Thus, the methods employed by a researcher (observation and interpretation) have to reflect the fact people consciously and unconsciously construct their own sense of social reality.

Thus far we have seen the research process involves a mix of things like methodology (whether you lean, as a researcher, towards Positivism, Interpretivism or some other form of sociological methodology such as realism or feminism), research methods and sampling techniques. In the final section we can bring these things together by thinking about a range of practical and theoretical research considerations that may, at times, influence the overall research process in a variety of possible ways.

Research considerations

Introduction

Whatever your personal perspective on the prospect of 'doing sociological research', it involves something more than simply choosing a topic, selecting a research method and wading into your chosen hypothesis or research question. Sociological research – whether it's a large-scale, government-funded project lasting many years or a small-scale, personally-funded piece of sociology coursework – is always surrounded by a range of research considerations. This section, therefore, is designed to outline and understand 'the theoretical, practical and ethical considerations influencing the choice of topic, choice of method(s) and the conduct of research'.

Practical research considerations

 Preparing the ground

Sociological research involves confronting and resolving a range of practical factors (the 'nuts and bolts' of 'doing research', as it were) relating to choice of topic and research method. We can consider these in the following way.

Choice of topic is influenced by:

- **The interests of the researcher**: Sociologists, like anyone else, have their interests, concerns and specialisms and these potentially affect their choice of research topic. The Glasgow Media

Group ('Really Bad News', 1982: 'War and Peace News', 1985), for example, have specialised (for over 20 years) in the study of bias in the media. Similarly, **Peter Townsend** had an abiding interest in the study of poverty (see, for example, *Poverty in the UK*, 1979).

- **Current debates** and **intellectual fashions**: Surprising as it may seem, research topics go in and out of fashion and sociologists – being fashionable people with their fingers on the pulse of what's hot and what's not – reflect these trends (although factors like research funding (see below) always exert some form of influence here).

  The 1960s, for example, produced a range of research into possible changes in the class structure – for example, **Goldthorpe, Lockwood** et al's 'The Affluent Worker in the Class Structure', 1965 (which tested the then fashionable *Embourgeoisement Thesis* put forward by **Zweig** (*The Worker in an Affluent Society*, 1959), who argued, in simple terms, most people had become 'middle class').

  Currently, 'media sociology' seems to be in fashion (although, by the time this gets to print it will probably be considered last year's thing). However, some sociologists just decide to 'do their own thing' – see, if you dare, **Southerton** et al's tremendously exciting: 'Home from home?: a research note on Recreational Caravanning', 1998).

- **Funding**: Research (especially large-scale research over a lengthy period of time) costs money and those who commission and pay for it, not unreasonably, want some say over choice of topic. In addition, in the UK and USA – where

government agencies or departments fund large amounts of social research – the historical trend has been to fund research designed primarily to help policymakers make decisions – so if your research doesn't, it is unlikely to be funded by the government.

- **Time** can affect choice of topic in terms of such things as the depth and scope of the research. For example, although a researcher may be interested in studying the behaviour of football supporters at major international tournaments (if anyone's willing to provide the funds, I could probably find the time), time and money considerations may restrict them to studying such behaviour on a much smaller scale.

- **Access** and **cooperation**: To research a topic, you need access to people and (usually) their cooperation (things closely related to ethical considerations – see below). This is one reason why a lot of sociological research has focused on the activities of the powerless (who lack the ability to resist) rather than the powerful (who most certainly can – and do – resist).

Choice of method(s): In a similar way to choice of topic, choice of research method is affected by a number of factors. These include:

- **Time**: Some methods are more time-intensive than others. Participant observation, for example, may involve years of research – **William Whyte** (*Street Corner Society*, 1943) spent around four years on his study of a gang in the USA. Between 1937 and 1940 he gathered extensive information about the behaviour of one gang in a small area of the country (Boston, in case you were wondering).

- **Topic**: Some topics (or aspects of them) may lend themselves more easily to one type of method than another. In general, quantitative methods tend to be used when the researcher wants reliable data to establish statistical relationships (such as **Kessler**'s really very interesting 'Sponsorship, Self-Perception and Small-Business Performance', 2000) where his main objective was to establish whether or not 'those who are sponsored are more successful than non-sponsored individuals' (as I say, heady stuff).

Alternatively, with studies such as **Diken** and **Laustsen**'s analysis of tourist behaviour in Ibiza and Faliraki ('Sea, Sun, Sex ... and Biopolitics', 2004) which *is* as interesting as it sounds (although, speaking personally, the 'bio-politics' bit I can take or leave), a qualitative approach is more appropriate, given the descriptive nature of the research.

A mix of methods (triangulation) is frequently used to satisfy different types of research question within the same topic . For example, if I am interested in understanding the possible 'Effects of marriage break-up' or 'Why people fear crime', I will probably use a method that provides in-depth, qualitative data (such as a focused interview). However, before doing my interview-based research I might need to do a small *establishing study* (so called because it is used to establish some basic information: for example, to identify people who have experienced divorce or to establish if people fear crime) using a simple (quantitative) questionnaire.

- **Funding**: In a perfect world, money would always be available for social research into any topic, using any method – but it's not a perfect world and the amount of money you have to spend will directly influence the methods used (questionnaires are generally cheaper than in-depth interviews, interviews are generally cheaper than participant observation). Money will also influence the size of any research team.

- **Who (or what) you are studying**: The size and composition of the group being studied may be a factor in choice of method(s). Social surveys and questionnaires lend themselves easily to the study of large, widely dispersed, groups. Participant observation, on the other hand, may be more appropriate for the study of small, geographically-localised groups.

Digging deeper

Returning, briefly, to the introduction to this section, in terms of the work you've just done, you could be forgiven for *now* thinking sociological research involves choosing an *appropriate* topic, selecting an *appropriate* method and *then* wading into your chosen hypothesis or research question ...

However, as we dig deeper we need to reconsider the idea that 'doing research' involves searching in the cupboard (or shed) for your 'Sociological Toolbox' (the one containing various research methods) and selecting the 'right tool for the job'. If only it was that simple.

Ackroyd and **Hughes** (*Data Collection in Context*, 1981) argue it is a mistake to view research methods as a set of 'theoretical tools' to be picked up and discarded depending on how appropriate they are for the task at hand because, unlike tools in a toolbox, sociological methods do not have a clear, single and straightforward, purpose.

For example, if we are faced with fixing a picture to a wall with a nail, we go to our toolbox and select the most appropriate tool for the job (in this instance, a hammer). A hammer is specifically designed for just such a purpose and it performs its task well. If we had selected a screwdriver, we would probably find this tool didn't do the job as efficiently.

Unfortunately, no such certainty applies to a method such as a questionnaire. Not only do we have to consider practical problems in adopting particular methods, but also our theoretical perspective may lead us to believe questionnaires are not a valid way of studying the social world. At least two major methodological considerations are involved here.

- **Validity** relates to our belief about whether a research method allows us to discover something about human behaviour 'as it really is' (whatever this may actually mean).

- **Theoretical considerations**: When collecting data we have to decide:
  - What counts as data (does it have to be quantitative or qualitative)?
  - Should the data be statistical or descriptive?
  - Do we try to test a hypothesis or simply report what respondents say?

These ideas, therefore, lead us inexorably towards theoretical research considerations.

Theoretical research considerations

Preparing the ground

Research involves confronting and resolving a range of theoretical questions – which we can express as the *how?* and the *why?* of choice of topic and research method.

Choice of topic involves a couple of major considerations.

- **Audiences** may dictate topic choice in terms of who you're trying to reach with your research. To an academic audience, something like **Jessop**'s 'Governance and meta-governance. On Reflexivity, Requisite Variety, and Requisite Irony' (2003) is a perfectly acceptable topic; to a non-academic audience, however, it probably wouldn't prove so alluring (even if we allow for the requisite irony of this statement).

- **Purpose** can be influential in terms of what the researcher is aiming to do – if testing a hypothesis, for example, the topic is likely to be much narrower in scope than if the objective is to provide a descriptive account of something.

- **Focus**: Research often evolves, in the sense of changing to meet new interests and concerns; while it's rare for a central topic to change during the research (if you begin by researching family life, you're not likely to end by researching education), aspects of the topic may well change. As research develops, changes may be made to quantitative questions or new areas of interest may open up in the light of respondent comments or researcher observations.

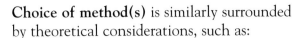

Choice of method(s) is similarly surrounded by theoretical considerations, such as:

- **Theoretical perspective**: Although this influence is by no means as strong as *some* texts might suggest (no-names, no law-suits), Interactionist researchers tend to avoid using statistical methods, mainly because their objective is to allow respondents to talk about their experiences, rather than to establish causality. Structuralists, in the main, tend to take the reverse view, mainly (but not necessarily) because they're not particularly interested in descriptive accounts of behaviour.

- **Reliability** and **validity** are *always* significant theoretical (or methodological) research concerns since beliefs about the reliability/validity of particular methods will affect decisions about whether or not to use them.

- **Values**: Researchers have values too and these are reflected in ethical beliefs about how something should (or should not) be studied. If, like **Polsky** (*Hustlers, Beats and Others*, 1971) you believe covert participation is unethical and methodologically invalid you're not likely to choose this research method.

⚠ Digging deeper

If we think about the general relationship between theory and method in sociological research we can combine Positivist and Interpretivist approaches outlined in the previous section with the material covered in this section. Questions concerning the relationship between theory and methods, therefore, boil down to four related ideas, which we can outline and apply in the following terms.

- **Ontology**: This idea poses the question 'What do we believe exists?'. In relation to sociology, an *ontological question* is one that considers what we believe the subject matter of sociology to be. For example, is it:
  - The attempt to find solutions to social problems?
  - To answer questions such as 'why are we here?'?
  - To elaborate the fundamental laws of social development?
  - To understand the nature of social interaction?

  The significance of ontological questions is our answers will condition how we view the purpose and subject matter of Sociology, how we conduct research and, of course, how we see it as appropriate to study social behaviour (especially in terms of our choice of topic and method). In the example we've used here, most sociologists' ontological belief is that social behaviour is learned, not based on instinct.

- **Epistemology**: The next question to ask is 'How we know what we claim to know' about the social world. This, in short, relates to the kinds of *proof* we will accept to justify our answer to ontological questions. For example, we may believe that:
  - 'seeing is believing' or
  - 'experiencing something is enough to prove it exists'.

  Alternatively, we may accept something on *trust*, or because we have *faith* (a characteristic, incidentally, of religious proof).

Epistemological questions, therefore, relate to the evidence we will accept to justify our belief something is true. For example, if I suspect you of stealing my pen, what sort of proof will I accept in order to convince me you didn't take it?

- Your word?
- The word of someone you were with at the time of the alleged theft (an alibi)?
- A thorough search of your belongings?

This idea is important, sociologically, because our beliefs about evidence influence our choice of research method – if you don't, for example, believe questionnaires produce valid data, you're not likely to use them in your research.

- **Methodology**: This idea is concerned with beliefs about how to produce reliable and *valid* knowledge. We have come across this type of question before, in relation to two ideas.

  - **The interview effect**: If you believe interviews are a manipulative process whereby the respondent presents a picture to you that accords with the picture they would like you to have, you are unlikely to see interview data as valid.

  - **The observer effect**: If you believe a researcher's presence affects the behaviour of those being observed, you would not see overt participant observation as a valid way of collecting data.

- **Methods**: This refers to specific techniques of data collection and our ideas about their appropriateness (or otherwise) to our research (ideas which will be conditioned by our *ontological, epistemological* and (deep breath) *methodological* beliefs).

To complete this section, we need to finally consider ethical questions relating to the research process.

Ethics refers to the *morality* of doing something and ethical questions relating to sociological research involve beliefs about what you should or should not do. As a matter of course, this will also include consideration of both *legal* and *safety* issues (for the researcher, those being researched and any subsequent researchers). We can consider some examples of ethical questions in terms of:

- **Rights** and **well-being**: The researcher needs to safeguard the interests, rights and general well-being (both physical and psychological) of respondents. Examples here might be respecting respondent privacy or minimising anxiety/distress that may be caused by the research.

- **Research consequences**: Research data can be used in many different ways (and not necessarily in terms of the way the researcher intended – through media reports of the research, for example) and participants should be aware of any possible consequences of their participation. In addition, if respondents feel they have been mistreated (physically or verbally, for example) or misled, this may have legal consequences for the researcher and create problems for any subsequent research.

- **Legal considerations**: In the UK, the collection, storage and retrieval of data are governed by things such as the *Data Protection Act*, the *Human Rights Act*, copyright laws and the laws of libel. In addition, if research involves criminal or deviant activities, the researcher may have to consider the ethical question of participation in such behaviour or their

Growing it yourself: statements of intent

The objective of this exercise is to relate the ideas we've just considered to the work you did earlier on **positivist** and **interpretivist** approaches.

Look at each dimension listed below, think about the example statement associated with it, and then select which of the statements in the positivist and interpretivist categories are most characteristic of each research methodology.

To avoid damaging this valuable textbook, you have my permission to photocopy the table and delete each statement marked * where applicable.

Dimension	Positivism	Interpretivism
Ontological Society exists . . .	Objectively* Subjectively*	Objectively* Subjectively*
Epistemological We know it exists because . . .	Behaviour is patterned, relatively stable and orderly. Therefore, something about 'society' must cause this to occur.* People behave in their day to day lives 'as if' it exists (that is, because it is a convenient fiction)*	Behaviour is patterned, relatively stable and orderly. Therefore, something about 'society' must cause this to occur.* People behave in their day to day lives 'as if' it exists (that is, because it is a convenient fiction)*
Methodological We can validate what we know using . . .	Objective methods to collect data about people's behaviour* Subjective methods in order to understand the meanings and interpretations involved in people's behaviour*	Objective methods to collect data about people's behaviour* Subjective methods in order to understand the meanings and interpretations involved in people's behaviour*
Method The objective is . . .	The collection and analysis of quantitative data* The collection/interpretation of qualitative data*	The collection and analysis of quantitative data* The collection/interpretation of qualitative data*

responsibilities to both the perpetrators and their possible victims.

- **Involvement**: Some types of research involve methods that create high levels of involvement with those being researched. Where close personal and/or intimate relationships between the researcher and respondent(s) exist, care needs to be taken to ensure that, once the research is completed and contact diminishes, distress is not caused to potentially vulnerable people. For example, if your research involves visiting the elderly on a regular basis, it would be unethical to simply stop your visits once the research is completed.

- **Power**: It would be unethical to bully or blackmail (emotionally or physically) people into participating in your research. In addition – especially when researching people who are relatively powerless – relationships need to be based on trust and personal integrity on the part of the researcher. For example, if the researcher promises anonymity as a way of researching people involved in criminal or deviant activities, disclosing respondent identities to the authorities would be unethical.

- **Consent**: Related to some of the previous categories, where possible, the researcher should always gain the consent of those being researched.

- **Safety**: Care always needs to be taken to ensure the physical and psychological safety of both the researcher and the respondent.

In the preceding sections we have covered a range of ideas relating to research methods and methodology; although many students reading this will be using the information we've covered for exam purposes, a substantial number will be putting at least some of the ideas covered into action through sociology coursework for this involves creating a research proposal for a possible piece of sociological research (which you might want to use as the basis for an actual piece of research, if you intend to take the coursework option in your A2 year). This being the case, the final section in this chapter offers advice on how to complete the AS Research Proposal.

AS Coursework: Research Proposal

⚠ Preparing the ground

If you choose the coursework option, rather than the research methods exam, you have to complete a 'Research Proposal' by Easter in the year of your AS exams. Apart from being worth 30% of the final AS grade (15% of your

Section	Maximum mark	Maximum word length
1. Hypothesis/Aims	8	100
2. Context and Concepts	20	400
3. Main Research Method and Reasons	20	400
4. Potential Problems	12	300

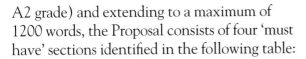

A2 grade) and extending to a maximum of 1200 words, the Proposal consists of four 'must have' sections identified in the following table:

Before starting your Coursework you need to understand both what the work involves and the required content of each section.

The Proposal: The first thing to remember is your coursework is simply a *proposal* for a piece of research – you are *not* required to carry out any actual research.

When starting your coursework, the key idea is **CARE** – your Proposal should be:

- Clear and concise in terms of what you propose to do.
- Appropriate in its choice of research method.
- Realistic in terms of it's aim/hypothesis
- Evaluative in terms of the possible problems involved.

Getting started: Your Proposal begins with a decision about what you want to research and consists of explaining, clearly and concisely, how you plan to go about doing the research.

Choice of topic is very important here because it's the focus for all subsequent work. When choosing a topic, therefore, think about:

- Something simple and straightforward – choosing something ambitious and doing it badly will not score highly.
- A question/hypothesis from an area you are studying.
- A topic well covered in textbooks – you have to easily identify and explain relevant research and sociological concepts.

The Four Sections of your proposal involve the following:

- **Hypothesis/aim**: Don't be tempted to rush the development of your

hypothesis/aim, because if you get it wrong, it is time-consuming to put things right in the other sections of the Proposal. As a general rule of thumb, if you choose a hypothesis it should:

- state a testable relationship
- not be too ambitious in what it plans to achieve
- not include ideas impossible to measure or test.

If you use an aim, make sure it is:

- not too ambitious
- clearly and precisely worded
- clear about what it's designed to achieve.

Once you have chosen an aim or hypothesis, you need to *justify* your choice with one or two clear and concise reasons related to your chosen topic.

- **Context and concepts**: 'Context' is another way of saying *supporting material* and you need to identify and summarise *two* pieces of sociological research relevant to your hypothesis/aim.

In addition, you must identify and define *two* concepts relevant to your research. You can include more, but it makes sense to stick to the minimum required. The tight word limit reinforces the importance of choosing your topic carefully. Before you begin, ask yourself:

- Can I find two pieces of relevant research?
- Can I easily identify and apply two relevant concepts to the research?

- **Main research method and reasons**: A brief description of your chosen research method is required here – one that demonstrates your understanding of how and why you would use the method to test your hypothesis/achieve your aim. You need to identify and explain clear reasons for choosing the method – make these reasons specific and relevant to your topic/hypothesis/aim. You won't score highly by just listing some general 'advantages' of your chosen method.

- **Potential problems**: This section requires brief explanations of any problems you foresee with your proposed research. Relate your ideas (gaining access to people, ethical considerations, response rates etc.) clearly to your topic/ hypothesis/aim and use your understanding of problems to explain how and why they might be problems in your research.

⚠ Digging deeper

If you know – and understand – what the examiner is looking for in each section it makes it easier for you to give them exactly what they want. The following, therefore, indicates what's required to get in to the *top mark band*.

Hypothesis/aim

- **Clarity**: Will the examiner understand exactly what you propose to test?
- **Precision**: Is your hypothesis testable or your aim achievable?
- **Appropriateness**: Is your hypothesis/aim realistic (a six-month participant observation study of Ibizan nightclubs would be nice, but it isn't going to happen, is it?)

The reasons you give for the hypothesis/aim should be relevant and appropriate for your study.

Context and concepts

Identify *two* pieces of relevant sociological research.

- **Describe** each piece accurately and concisely.
- **Explain** clearly how the research is relevant to your proposal.
- **Clearly link** the chosen research to *your* research (for example, is your research going to *replicate* (repeat) an existing study?).

Identify at least *two* concepts relevant to an understanding of your chosen topic.

- **Define** each of your concepts carefully.
- **Explain clearly** how each concept is relevant to your study (for example, do you plan to apply/test these concepts in your study?)

Main research method and reasons

- **Identify** three or four practical and/or theoretical reasons for your chosen research method.
- For each reason, explain *how* and *why* it is appropriate for your study. Be specific and relate any advantages of the method clearly to your research. For example, if you identify one advantage of the method as being the collection of quantitative data, you need to explain why such data is appropriate for the testing of your aim/hypothesis.

Problems

- **Identify** potential problems (practical, theoretical or ethical). Practical problems might include things like access to

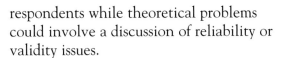

respondents while theoretical problems could involve a discussion of reliability or validity issues.

- **Explain** clearly and concisely why these are potential problems (and how you could resolve them).

- **Link** problems clearly to your hypothesis/aim (how, for example, they might potentially affect the testing of the hypothesis).

And finally: constructing your coursework

This section is designed to be an overview of what's involved in a Proposal and is based around a *worked example* that indicates the kind of material required for a finished piece of coursework. It is based on a *hypothesis*, but you could use an *aim* instead if you wish (for example: 'To discover if and how pupil behaviour in the classroom differs according to gender'). Each section illustrates some of the ways the Proposal could develop around this hypothesis – but there are, of course, many other ways to develop such a Proposal.

Hypothesis/aim

The first section will look something like:

The hypothesis for this Proposal is: "Pupil behaviour in the classroom differs according to gender".

Because it is a pilot study, I will initially research a group of 16 year old pupils in their last year at school. The main reason for choosing to do this study is to discover whether or not there are behavioural differences between males and females in our education system. Once I have

answered this question the main focus of my study is whether or not any behavioural differences reflect traditional gender stereotypes about male and female behaviour. (93 words)

Context and concepts

Most textbooks (such as … err … this one) have sections on writers whose research would be relevant to this hypothesis (Spender, Stanworth, Nash, etc.). If your research is not covered in textbooks, a decent Internet search engine such as Google (www.google.co.uk) should provide relevant material.

You need to *define* and *explain* the relevance of two significant concepts to your research. For example:

- **Gender socialisation** – are males and females socialised differently?

- **Gender stereotyping** – do teachers and pupils have different expectations about male/female behaviour?

- **Gender identities** – do males and females have different ideas about what it means to be male and female?

Methods and reasons

You have a range of choices here, depending on whether you want quantitative or qualitative data. If the former, a simple questionnaire could be used; if the latter, focused interviews (either with individual students or with the whole group – a 'focus group interview') could be used. Alternatively, if you could fit easily into the class being studied, participant observation is an option.

Whichever method you choose, you need to give reasons for your choice.

For a focused interview, for example, some reasons – clearly related and explained in terms of your research – might include discussion of:

- why qualitative data about behavioural differences was important
- data reliability issues
- data validity issues
- practical and or ethical reasons.

Problems

You could, for example, discuss:

- A practical problem in studies of this kind is *access* to a school. If you do not have easy access (through friends, your own attendance at the school …) how would you gain access to do this research?
- Some teachers will demand 'editorial control' over your work. How would you respond to demands they see (and approve) your questions?
- Is there an ethical problem involved in identifying/not identifying the school and your respondents.
- Do you (and your respondents) have the necessary skills to use this method successfully?

Finally: Keep in mind the following bits of advice (trust me, I've been there and have the torn T-shirt to prove it).

- Keep to the **word limit** for each section.

- **Plan** your time effectively – don't leave everything to the last minute.
- Set clear **targets** (and keep to them) for the completion of each section.
- Before you begin, choose a topic and do some background reading about it to generate ideas for a research hypothesis/aim. Use the following web site to help generate some ideas if you are stuck: www.sociology.org.uk/projects.htm
- Think carefully about your hypothesis/aim and the concepts it involves – how easy/difficult will it be to measure these concepts?
- Ask your **teacher** for **help** and **advice** when necessary – it is not cheating, it is their job.
- Ask your teacher to **comment** on each section you produce.

And (really this time) **finally**, remember that doing a Proposal of this type is actually a very good way to think about the *sociological research process* – what it involves, the problems you would face and – of course – the sense of achievement you will get from successfully completing this work.

As I said at the start of this section, the Proposal you produce here can be put into practice during your A2 year if you choose the coursework option; complete a good Proposal now and it will stand you in good stead for your A2 coursework – trust me, I know about these things.

References

Chapter 1: Introduction

Adams, Douglas, 1979, *The Hitchhiker's Guide to the Galaxy*: Ballantine Books

Althusser, Louis, 1968, *Lenin and Philosophy*: François Maspero

Anderson, Benedict, 1983, *Imagined Communities: Reflections on the Origin and Spread of Nationalism*: Verso

Barrett, Michelle and McIntosh, Mary, 1982, *The Anti-Social Family*: Verso

Beck, Ulrich, 1992, *The Risk Society: Towards a New Modernity*: Sage (originally published 1986)

Berger, Peter, 1963, *An Invitation to Sociology*: Doubleday

Bowles, Herbert and Gintis, Samuel, 1976, 'Schooling in Capitalist America: Basic Books

Butler, Judith, 1990, *Gender Trouble*: Routledge

Clegg, Stewart, 1989, *Frameworks of Power*: Sage

Coppick, Vicki, 1995, *The Illusions of 'Post-Feminism': New Women, Old Myths'*: Taylor and Francis

Draper, Stephen, 2004, 'The Hawthorne effect and other expectancy effects', http://www.psy.gla.ac.uk/~steve/hawth.html

Glasgow Media Group, 1982, *Really Bad News*: Pluto

Jones, Philip, 1985, *Theory and Method in Sociology*: Bell and Hyman.

Lawson, Tony and Garrod, Joan, 2003, *Complete A–Z Sociology Handbook*, 3rd edn: Hodder and Stoughton

Layder, Derek, 1987, 'Key issues in Structuration Theory: Some critical remarks', *Current Perspectives in Social Theory*.

Lyotard, Jean-Francois, 1984, *The Postmodern Condition*: University of Manchester Press

Mayo, Elton, 1933, *The human problems of an industrial civilization*: Macmillan

Mead, George Herbert, 1934, 'Mind, Self and Society': University of Chicago Press

Meighan, Roland, 1981, *A Sociology of Education*: Holt, Rinehart and Winston

Merton, Robert, 1957, *Social Theory and Social Structure*: Free Press

Parsons, Talcott, 1951, *The Social System*: RKP

    1937, *The Structure of Social Action*: McGraw Hill

Rich, Adrienne, 1980, 'Compulsory Heterosexuality and Lesbian Existence', *Signs: Journal of Women in Culture and Society*, 5.

Ritzer, George, 1979, *Sociology: Experiencing a Changing Society*: Allyn and Bacon

Sociology Review, Vol. 8, No. 2, November 1998, Philip Allan Publishers

Sugarman, Barry, 1968, *Sociology*: Heinemann

Thio, Alex, 1991, *Sociology: A Brief Introduction*: HarperCollins

Weber, Max, 1978, *Economy and Society*: University of California Press (first published 1922)

Wright Mills, C., 1959, *The Sociological Imagination*: OUP

Chapter 2: Family

Abercrombie, Nick and Warde, Alan, 1992, *Contemporary British Society*: Polity

Allan, Graham and Crow, Graham (eds) 1989, *Home and Family: Creating the Domestic Space*: Macmillan

Anderson, M., Tunaley, J. and Walker, J., 1999, 'Relatively Speaking: Communication in families', BT Forum

Anderson, Michael, 1980, *Approaches to the History of the Western Family*: Cambridge University Press (revised 1995)

Archard, David, 1993, *Children: Rights and Childhood*: Routledge

Aries, Philip, 1962, *Centuries of Childhood*: Vintage Books

Beattie, 1981, 'Who Was That Lady?', *New Society*, 08/01/81

Beck, Ulrich, 1992, *The Risk Society: Towards a New Modernity*: Sage (originally published 1986)

Bengston, Vern, 2001, 'Beyond the nuclear family: The increasing importance of multi-generational bonds', *Journal of Marriage and the Family*

Berrington, Ann and Diamond, Ian, 2000, 'Marriage or Cohabitation: a competing risks analysis of first-partnership formation among the 1958 British birth cohort', *Journal of the Royal Statistical Society: Series A (Statistics in Society)*, Vol. 163, Issue 2

Berthoud, Richard, 2004, 'Family formation in multi-cultural Britain', Institute for Social and Economic Research, 2004

Bonke, Jens, 1999, 'Children's household work: is there a difference between girls and boys?', IATUR Conference Paper, University of Essex

Brannen, Julia, 2003, 'The age of beanpole families', *Sociology Review*, 13

Callaghan, Gill, 1998, 'The Interaction of Gender, Class and Place in Women's Experience', Sociological Research Online, http://www.socresonline.org.uk/3/3/8.html

Callan, Samantha, 2002, 'A Brief History of Marriage', http://www.2-in-2-1.co.uk/articles/brhistory

Calvert, Susan and Calvert, Peter, 1992, *Sociology Today*: Harvester Wheatsheaf

Carlin, Norah, 2002, 'Family, Society and Popular Culture in Western Europe c. 1500–1700': Middlesex University http://www.mdx.ac.uk/www.hcs_history/mh3200.doc

Chester, Robert, 1985, *The Rise of the Neo-conventional Family*: New Society

Coverman, Shelley, 1989, 'Women's Work Is Never Done: The Division of Domestic Labor (sic)', in J. Freeman (ed) 1989, *Women: A Feminist Perspective* (pp. 356–367): Mayfield

Crozier, Gill, Reay, Diane, Vincent, Carol, (eds), 2004, *Activating Participation: Parents and Teachers Working Towards Partnership*: Trentham Books

Dench, Geoff, 1996, 'The place of men in changing family cultures': Institute of Community Studies

Dodd, Tricia, Nicholas, Sian, Povey, David and Walker, Alison, 2004, 'Crime in England and Wales 2003/2004': *Home Office Statistical Bulletin*

Duncombe, Jean and Marsden, Dennis, 1993, Love and intimacy: The Gender Division of Emotion and 'Emotion Work', *Sociology*, Vol. 27

Edgell, Stephen, 1980, *Middle-Class Couples: a study of segregation, domination and inequality in marriage*: Allen and Unwin

Elkind, David, 1992, 'Waaah, Why Kids Have a Lot to Cry About', *Psychology Today*, May 1992

Elston, M., 1980, 'Medicine: half our future doctors', in Silverstone, Rosalie and Ward, Audrey (eds) 1980, *Careers of Professional Women*: Croom Helm

Ermisch, John and Francesconi, Marco, 2000, 'Patterns of household and family formation', in Berthoud, Richard and Gershuny, Jon, (eds), *Seven years in the lives of British families: evidence on the dynamics of social change from the British Household Panel Survey*: Policy Press

Farson, Richard, 1974, *Birthrights*: McMillan

Ferri, Elsa, Bynner, John and Wadwsorth, Michael (eds), 2003, *Changing Britain, Changing Lives: three generations at the turn of the century*: Institute of Education

Fletcher, Ronald, 1966, *The Family and Marriage in Britain*: Penguin

Fortier, Anne-Marie, 2003, 'Making home: queer migrations and motions of attachment': Department of Sociology, Lancaster University, http://www.comp.lancs.ac.uk/sociology/papers/Fortier-Making-Home.pdf

Giddens, Anthony, 1993, *Sociology*: Polity

Gillis, John, 1985, *For Better, For Worse: British Marriages, 1600 to the Present*: Oxford University Press

Goldthorpe, John, 1987, *Family Life in Western Societies*: Cambridge University Press

Goldthorpe, John, Lockwood, David, Bechhofer, Frank and Platt, Jennifer, 1968, *The Affluent Worker in the Class Structure*: Cambridge University Press

Gomm, Roger, 1989, *The Uses of Kinship*: NEC

Goode, William, 1963, *World Revolution and Family Patterns*: Free Press

Gordon, Michael, 1972, *The Nuclear Family in Crisis: The Search for an Alternative*: Harper & Row

Green, Anne and Canny, Angela, 2003, *Geographical mobility: family impacts*: Policy Press

Hall, G. Stanley, 1904, *Adolescence*: Appleton

Hardill, Irene, 2003, 'A tale of two nations? Juggling work and home in the new economy': LSE http://www.lse.ac.uk/collections/worklife/Hardillpaper.pdf

Harris, Christopher, 1983, 'The Family and Industrial Society', *Studies in Sociology*, No. 13

Hartmann, Heidi, 1981, 'The Family as the Locus of Gender, Class, and Political Struggle: The example of Housework', *Signs*, Spring 1981

Haskey, John, 1995, 'Trends in marriage and cohabitation: The decline in marriage and the changing pattern of living in partnerships', *Population Trends*, Vol. 80

Haskey, John, 2002, 'Cohabitation in Great Britain', in *National Statistics Population Trends*, 103: The Stationery Office

Hendrick, Henry, 1990, 'Constructions and Reconstructions of British Childhood', in James, A. and Prout, A. (eds) 1990, *Constructing and reconstructing childhood: Contemporary issues in the sociological study of childhood*: Falmer

Hilary Abrahams Domestic Violence Research Group, University of Bristol

Hine, Thomas, 2002, *The Rise And Fall of the American Teenager*: HarperCollins

Hogg, Michael and Vaughan, Graham, 2002, *Social Psychology* (3rd edn): Prentice-Hall

Holt, John, 1984, *Escape From Childhood*: Dutton

Home Office Crime Reduction Service, 2004, Domestic Violence, www.crimereduction.gov.uk

Humphreys, Cathy and Thiara, Ravi, 2002, 'Routes to Safety: Protection issues facing abused women and children and the role of outreach services': Women's Aid Federation of England

Jagger, Gill and Wright, Caroline, 1999, 'End of Century, End of Family? Shifting Discourses of Family Crisis', in Jagger and Wright (eds), *Changing Family Values*: Routledge

James, Alison, 1998, 'Imaging Children "At Home", "In the Family" and "at School": Movement Between the Spatial and the Temporal Markers of Childhood Identity in Britain', in N. Rapport and A. Dawson (eds) 1998 *Migrants of Identity. Perceptions of Home in a World of Movement*: Berg

Jayatilaka, Geethika and Rake, Katherine, 2002, 'Home Truths: An analysis of financial decision making within the home': Fawcett Society Report

Jenks, Chris, 1996, *Childhood*: Routledge

Kan, Man-yee, 2001, 'Gender Asymmetry in the Division of Domestic Labour', British Household Panel Survey Research Conference, Institute for Social and Economic Research

Kirkwood, Catherine, 1993, *Leaving Abusive Partners*: Sage

Laslett, Peter, 1965, *The World we have Lost*: Methuen

Laslett, Peter and Wall, Richard, 1972, eds, *Household and Family in Past Time*, Cambridge: Cambridge University Press

Leach, Penelope, 1994, *Children First*: Vintage

Lewis, Charlie, Papacosta, Amalia and Warin, Jo, 2002, 'Cohabitation, separation and fatherhood': Joseph Rowntree Foundation

Lukes, Stephen (ed) 1990, *Power*: New York University Press

Luscher, K., 2000, 'Ambivalence: A key concept for the study of intergenerational relations', in Trnka, S., *Family Issues between gender and generations*: European Observatory on Family Matters

Macintosh, Mary, 1978, 'The State Oppression of Women', in Kuhn, A. and Wolpe, A. (eds) 1978, *Feminism and Materialism*: Routledge and Kogan Paul

McAllister, Fiona with Clarke, Lynda, 1998, 'Choosing childlessness': Family Policy Studies Centre

McDowell, Linda, 2001, 'Young men leaving school: White working class masculinity': Joseph Rowntree Foundation

McGoldrick, Monica and Gerson, Randy, 1985, *Genograms in Family Assessment*: Norton

Middleton, Sue, Ashworth, Karl and Braithwaite, Ian, 2002, 'Small Fortunes: Spending on children, childhood poverty and parental sacrifice': Joseph Rowntree Foundation

Mintel Housework Survey, 2004

Morgan, Patricia, 2000, *Marriage-Lite*: Civitas

Morris, Susannah, 2004, *Social Policy: From the Victorians to the Present Day*: LSE

Murdock, George, Peter, 1949, *Social Structure*: Macmillan Co

National Commission of Inquiry into the Prevention of Child Abuse, 1996

National Statistics, 2004, *Social Trends 34*, London: The Stationery Office

National Statistics, 2004, 'Living in Britain: Results from the 2002 General Household Survey': The Stationery Office

Neale, Bren, 2002, 'Theorising Family, Kinship and Social Change', University of Leeds, http://www.leeds.ac.uk/cava/papers/wsp6.pdf

Npower Home Running Costs Survey, 2002

O'Day, Rosemary, 2000, *Women in Early Modern Britain*: Longman

O'Donnell, Mike, 1997, *Introduction to Sociology*: Nelson

Oswald, Andrew, 2002, 'Homes, Sex and the Asymmetry Hypothesis': University of Warwick, http://www.2.warwick.ac.uk/fac/soc/economics/staff/faculty/Oswald

Pahl, Jan with Vogler, C., 1994, 'Money, power and inequality within marriage', *Sociological Review*

Parsons, Talcott, 1959, 'The Social Structure of the Family', in Anshen, R. (ed) *The Family: Its Functions and Destiny*: Harper

Pleck, Joseph, 1985, *Working Wives. Working Husbands*: Sage

Pollack, Linda, 1983, *Forgotten Children: Parent–Child Relations from 1500 to 1900*: Cambridge University Press

Postman, Neil, 1985, *The Disappearance of Childhood*, W.H. Allen

Pregnancy & Birth magazine, March 2001

Radford, Lorraine and Sayer, Sarah, 1999, 'Unreasonable fears? Child Contact in the Context of Domestic Violence: A Survey of Mother's Perceptions of Harm': Women's Aid Federation of England

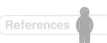

Ramos, Xavi, 1998, 'Domestic Work Time and Gender Differentials in Great Britain 1992–1998', British Household Panel Survey Conference, Institute for Social and Economic Research

Rappoport, R., Rappoport, R. and Fogarty, M., 1982, (eds), *Families in Britain*: Routledge and Kegan Paul

Rodgers, Bryan and Pryor, Jan, 1998, 'Divorce and separation: the outcomes for children': Joseph Rowntree Foundation

Shipman, Martin, 1973, *The Limitations of Social Research*: Longman

Smart, Carole and Neale, Bren, 1997, 'Good enough morality? Divorce and Postmodernity', *Critical Social Policy*, 17

Smart, Carol and Stevens, Pippa, 2000, 'Cohabitation breakdown': Family Policy Studies Centre

Social Trends 30–34: The Stationery Office, 1999–2004

Speakman, Susan and Marchington, Mick, 1999, 'Ambivalent patriarchs, shiftworkers, "breadwinners" and housework, *Work, Employment and Society*, Vol 13. No. 1, Sage Publications

Stacey, Judith, 1998, *Brave New Families: stories of domestic upheaval in late twentieth century America*: Basic Books

Stacey, Judith, 2002, 'Fellow Families? Genres of Gay Male Intimacy and Kinship in a Global Metropolis': CAVA International Seminar, University of Leeds, 2002

Stoller, Robert, 1968, *Sex and Gender: on the Development of Masculinity and Femininity*: Hogarth Press

Suematsu, Dyske, 2004, 'Postmodern Family', http://www.dyske.com

The Family Expenditure Survey, 2000: Office for National Statistics

Weber, Max, 1958, *The Protestant Ethic and Spirit of Capitalism*: Charles Scribner and Sons (first published 1904/05)

Wegge, Simone, 1999, 'To Part or Not to Part: Emigration and Inheritance Institutions in Mid-19th Century Germany', *Explorations in Economic History*, 36 (1)

Weiss, Heather, 1998, 'Family support and education programs…', in Weiss & Jacobs (eds) 1998, *Evaluating Family Programs*: Aldine De Gruyter

Willmott, Michael, 2000, *Complicated Lives: Sophisticated Consumers, Intricate Lifestyles, Simple Solutions*: William Nelson

Willmott, Peter and Young, Michael, 1973, *The Symmetrical Family*: Routledge

Willmott, Peter, 1988, 'Urban Kinship Past and Present', *Social Studies Review*

Zeitlin, Marian, Megawangi, Ratna, Kramer, Ellen, Colletta, Nancy, Babatunde, E.D. and Garman, David, 1998, 'Strengthening the Family : Implications for International Development', UNU Press Books http://www.unu.edu/unupress/unupbooks/uu13se/uu13se00.html

Zero Tolerance Charitable Trust report, 1998

Chapter 3: Media

Anderson, Craig, L. Rowell Huesmann Leonard Berkowitz, Donnerstein, Edward, Johnson, James, Linz, Daniel, Malmuth, Neil and Wartella, Ellen, 2003, 'The Influence of Media Violence on Youth': Psychological Science

Bandura, Albert, Ross, Dorothea and Ross, Sheila, 1961, 'Transmission of aggression through imitation of aggressive models', *Journal of Abnormal and Social Psychology*, 63

Barnes, Colin, 1992, *Disabling Imagery and the Media: An Exploration of the Principles for Media Representations*: The Disability Press

Barnes, Colin and Mercer, Geoffrey (eds) 1996, *Exploring the Divide: Illness and Disability*: The Disability Press

Barrat, David, 1992, *Media Sociology*: Tavistock

Baudrillard, Jean and Patton, Paul, 1995, *The Gulf War Did Not Take Place*: Open University Press

BBC News, 'Watchdog bites back', http://news.bbc.co.uk, 10/03/99

Belson, William, 1978, *Television Violence and the Adolescent Boy*: Saxon House

Berelson, Bernard, Lazerfeld, Paul and Gaudet, Hazel, 1944, *The People's Choice*: Duell, Sloan and Pearce

Bernard, Alix and McDermott, Patricia, 2002, *Media Ownership Rules*: Bird & Bird http://twobirds.com

Blake, Trevor, 2004, 'What is Systematic Ideology?', www.gwiep.net/site/whatissi.html

Boardman, Terry, 1998, 'Patten and Murdoch Quarrel – David and Goliath Again?', *East West Issues*, http://www.monju.pwp.blueyonder.co.uk/indexEW4htm

Bordo, Susan, 1993, *Unbearable Weight: Feminism, Western Culture and the Body*: University of California Press

Browne, Anthony, 2003, 'Age bar to curb forced marriages', *The Times*, 14 May 2003

Buckingham, David, 1996, *Moving Images: Understanding Children's Emotional Responses to Television*: Manchester University Press

Buckingham, David, Davies, Hannah, Jones, Ken and Kelley, Peter, 2004, 'Public Service Goes To Market: British Children's Television in Transition', Economic and Social Research Council

Bulsara, Ashwin, 2001, 'Depictions of people with disabilities in the British media': Media Diversity Institute, http://www.media-diversity.org

Burnham, James, 1941, *The Managerial Revolution*

Campaign for Press and Broadcasting Freedom, 1997, 'Britain's Media: How They Are Related'

Carrington, Ben, 2002, ' "Race", Representation and the Sporting Body', *new formations*, 45

Castells, Manual, 1996, *The Information Age: Economy, Society and Culture Vol. I: The Rise of the Network Society*: Blackwell

Caudwell, Jayne, 2004, 'Tipping the Velvet: Straight [forward] voyeurism? Problematising the viewing of lesbian bodies and lesbian pleasure', in Kennedy, Eileen and Thornton, Andrew (eds) 2004, *Leisure, Media and Visual Culture: Representations and Contestations*: LSA Publications

Chandler, Daniel, 1995, 'Cultivation Theory', http://www.aber.ac.uk/media/Documents/short/cultiv.html

Chandler, Daniel, 2001, 'Media Representation', http://www.aber.ac.uk/media/Modules/MC30820/represent.html

Chibnall, Steve, 1977, *Law-and-Order News: An analysis of crime-reporting in the British Press*: Tavistock

Chomsky, Noam, 1989, *Necessary Illusions: Thought Control in Democratic Societies*: South End Press

Cohen, Stan, 1972, *Folk Devils and Moral Panics*: McGibbon and Kee

Collins, Richard, 2002, 'Comments on the Consultation on Media Ownership Rules': The Open University, http://open.ac.uk/socialsciences/staff/rcollins/media_ownership.pdf

Compaine, Benjamin, 2000, 'Mergers, Divestitures and the Internet: Is Ownership of the Media Industry Becoming too Concentrated?', Lawrence Erlbaum Associates, http://users.primushost.com/~bcompain/articles/alliances_innovacion_WAP.pdf

Compaine, Benjamin, 2001, 'The myths of encroaching global media ownership', http://www.compaine.com

Connor, Gerry, 2001, 'Representation and Youth', http://mediaed.org.uk/posted_documents/repsyouth.html

Corner, John, 1983, 'Textuality, Communication and Power', in Davis, Howard and Walton, Paul (eds) 1983, *Language, Image, Media*: Basil Blackwell

Crosbie, Vin, 2002, 'What Is New Media?': Digital Deliverance, http://www.digitaldeliverance.com

Cudney, Milton, 1993, *Self-Defeating Behaviors (sic): Free Yourself from the Habits, Compulsions, Feelings, and Attitudes That Hold You Back*: HarperCollins

Cumberbatch, Guy, 1994, 'Legislating mythology: Video violence and children', *Journal of Mental Health*

Cumberbatch, Guy, 2003, Office of Film and Literature Classification Conference

Curran, James, 2000, 'Global media concentration: shifting the argument', Open Democracy, http://www.opendemocracy.net

Curren, James, 2002, *Media and Power*: Routledge

Darke, Paul, 2003, 'Introductory Essay on Normality Theory', *Outside Centre*, http://www.darke.info

Davis, Caroline, 2000, 'The Culture of Publishing Website': Oxford Brookes University, http://www.brookes.ac.uk/schools/apm/publishing/culture/conglom/congint.htm

DeFleur, Melvin and Ball-Rokeach, Sandra, 1989, *Theories of Mass Communication*, 5th edn: Longman

Destutt de Tracy, Antoine, 1801–1815, *Eléments d'idéologie*, Paris: Courcier

Djankov, Simeon, McLiesh, Caralee, Nenova, Tatiana and Shleifer, Andrei, 2001, 'Who Owns the Media?': National Bureau of Economic Research

Dutton, Brian, O'Sullivan, Tim and Rayne, Phillip, 1998, *Studying the Media*: Arnold

Enciso, Nuria, 1995, 'Turning the Gaze Around and *Orlando*': *Mediatribe*, 5(1), http://collection.nlc-bnc.ca/100/202/300.mediatribe/mtribe95/orlando.html

Evening Standard, 'War on minicab sex attackers', 27/11/03

Fawbert, Jack, 2003, 'Social class, replica football shirts and televisual communication: towards a more social semiotic understanding', Leeds Metropolitan University

Festinger, Leon, 1957, *A Theory of Cognitive Dissonance*: Stanford University Press

Fiske, John, 1987, *Television Culture: popular pleasures and politics*: Methuen

Fiske, John, 1995, 'Popular Culture', in Lentricchia, Frank and McLaughlin, Thomas (eds) 1995, *Critical Terms for Literary Study*, 2nd edn: University of Chicago

Frewer, Lynn, Miles, Susan and Marsh, Roy, 2002, 'The media and genetically modified foods: evidence in support of social amplification of risk', Institute of Food Research

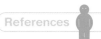

Galtung, Johan and Holmboe Ruge, Mari, 1973, 'Structuring and Selecting News', in Cohen and Young (eds) 1973, *The Manufacture of News*: Constable

Gauntlett, David, 1995, *Moving Experiences: Understanding Television's Influences and Effects*: John Libbey

Gauntlett, David, 1998, '10 Things Wrong with the "Effects Model"' in Dickinson, Harindranath and Linné (eds) 1998, *Approaches to Audiences – A Reader*: Arnold http://www.theory.org.uk

Gauntlett, David, 2002, *Media, Gender and Identity: An Introduction*: Routledge, www.theoryhead.com/gender

Gerbner, George, 1973, 'Communications Technology and Social Policy: Understanding the New "Cultural Revolution"': Interscience Publication

Gerbner, George, 1994, 'Reclaiming Our Cultural Mythology: *IN CONTEXT #38*, Context Institute, http://www.context/org/ICLIB/IC38/Gerbner.htm

Gerbner, Gross, Morgan and Signorielli, 1986, 'Living with Television: The Dynamics of the Cultivation Process', in Bryant and Zilmann (eds) 1986, *Perspectives on Media Effects*: Lawrence Erlbaum Associates

Gill, Ros, 2003, 'From sexual objectification to sexual subjectification: The resexualisation of women's bodies in the media', *Feminist Media Studies*

Gilroy, Paul, 1990, 'One Nation under a Groove: The Cultural Politics of "Race" and Racism in Britain', in Eley, Geoff and Suny, Ronald (eds) 1996, *Becoming National: A Reader*: Oxford University Press

Glasgow Media Group, 1976, *Bad News*; 1980, *More Bad News*; 1982, *Really Bad News*; 2004, *Bad News from Israel*: Pluto Press

Goffman, Erving, 1969, *The Presentation of Self in Everyday Life*: Penguin

Gray, Andrew, 2003, *Embedding Gave War Reporters Access – and Anxiety*: Reuters

Hagell, Ann and Newburn, Tim, 1994, *Young Offenders and the Media: Viewing Habits and Preferences*: Policy Studies Institute

Hall, Stuart, 'Encoding/decoding', in the Centre for Contemporary Cultural Studies (ed) 1973/1980, *Culture, Media, Language: Working Papers in Cultural Studies*: Hutchinson

Hall, Stuart, 1995, 'The Whites of Their Eyes: Racist Ideologies and the Media', in Dines, Gail and Humez, Jean (eds) 1995, *Gender, Race and Class in Media*: Sage

Hall, Stuart (ed) 1997, *Cultural Representations and Signifying Practices*: Open University Press

Hall, Stuart, Crichter, Chas, Jefferson, Tony, Clarke, John and Roberts, Brian, 1978, *Policing the Crisis: Mugging, the State and Law and Order*: Macmillan

Hargreaves, Ian and Thomas, James, 2002, 'New News, Old News', Broadcasting Standards Commission

Harrison, Lisa, 2002, 'Media Representations of Young People in the 2001 British General Election', Political Studies Association, http://www.psa.ac.uk/cps/2002/harrison.pdf

Harrison, Martin, 1985, 'Television News: Whose Bias?', *Policy Journals Publication*

Heider, Don, 2004, *Class and News*: Rowman & Littlefield

Heller, Joseph, 1974, *Something Happened*: Knopf

Henderson, Penny, 1981, 'A-Level Sociology: NEC

Hussain, Mustafa, 2002, 'Mapping Minorities and their Media: The National Context – Denmark', LSE, http://www.lse.ac.uk/collections/EMTEL/Minorities/papers.denmarkreport.pdf

Information Centre about Asylum and Refugees (ICAR), 2004, Media image, community impact

Jacobsson, Eva-Maria, 1999, *A Female Gaze?*, Sweden: Royal Institute of Technology

Joseph, Martin, 1990, *Sociology For Everyone*: Polity

Katz, Elihu and Lazarsfeld, Paul, 1955, *Personal Influence*: The Free Press

Klapper, Joseph, 1960, *The Effects of Mass Communication*: The Free Press

Klimkiewicz, Beata, 1999, 'Participation of ethnic minorities in the public sphere', Poland: Institute of Political Sciences, Jagiellonian University, http://www.policy.hu/klimkiewicz/interim.html

Lang, Gladys and Kurt, 1983, *The Battle for Public Opinion: The President, The Press, and the Polls During Watergate*: Columbia University Press

Lanson, Gerald and Stephens, Mitchell, 2003, *Writing and Reporting The News* OUP

Lee, Martin and Solomon, Norman, 1990, *Unreliable Sources: A Guide to Detecting Bias in News Media*: Carol Publishing Group

Lusted, David, 1991, *The Media Studies Book*: Routledge

Macdonald, Helen, 2003, 'Magazine advertising and gender', *MediaEd*, http://www.mediaed.org.uk/posted_documents/MagazineAdverts.html

McChesney, Robert, 2000, *Rich Media, Poor Democracy: Communication Politics in Dubious Times*: New Press

McCombs, Maxwell and Estrada, George, 1997, 'The news media and the pictures in our heads', in Iyengar, Shanto and Reeves, Richard (eds) 1997, *Do the media govern? Politicians, voters, and reporters in America*: Sage

McCombs, Maxwell and Shaw, Donald, 1972, 'The agenda-setting function of mass media', *Public Opinion Quarterly*, 36

McLean, Gareth, 2002, 'It's a male thing', *The Guardian*, 25 March 2002

McLuhan, Marshall and Powers, Bruce, 1989, *The Global Village: Transformations in World Life and Media in the 21st Century*: Oxford University Press

McQuail, Dennis, 1994, *Mass Communication Theory: An Introduction*: Sage

McQuail, Dennis, Blumler, Jay and Brown, J.R., 1972, 'The television audience: a revised perspective', in McQuail (ed) 1972, *Sociology of Mass Communication*: Longman

McRobbie, Angela, 1999, *In the Culture Society: Art, Fashion and Popular Music*: Routledge

Medhurst, Andy, 2004, 'Tracing Desires: Sexuality in Media Texts', in Briggs, Adam and Cobley, Paul, 2004, *The Media: An Introduction*: Longman

Meyer Sir Christopher, chair of Press Complaints Commission, 2003, Speech to the Newspaper Society

Meyrowitz, Joshua, 1994, 'Medium Theory', in Crowley, David and Mitchell, David (eds) 1994, *Communication Theory Today*: Stanford University Press

Milliband, Ralph, 1969, *The State In Capitalist Society*: Weidenfeld and Nicolson

Mitchell, W.J. Thomas, 1994, *Picture Theory*: University of Chicago Press

Mobbs, Paul, 2002, 'Media Regulation and Convergence: The impact of the new digital media on society', Civil Society Internet Rights Project

Moores, Shaun, 1993, *Interpreting Audiences: The Ethnography of Media Consumption*: Sage

Morris, Jenny, 1997, 'A Feminist Perspective', in Pointon, A. and Davies, C. (eds) 1997, *Framed: Interrogating disability in the media*: BFI Publishing

Morris, Rachel, 2000, 'Gypsies, Travellers and the Media: Press regulation and racism in the UK', *Communications Law*, Vol. 5, No. 6

Muir, Hugh, 2002, 'Sometimes a mugger's race does matter', *Evening Standard*, 6 February 2002

Mulvey, Laura, 1975, 'Visual Pleasure and Narrative Cinema'. *Screen 16*

Murdock, Graham and Golding, Peter, 1977 'Capitalism, Communication and Class Relations', in Curran, James, Gurevitch, Michael and Woollacott, Janet (eds), 1977, *Mass Communication and Society*: Arnold

Myers, Kathy, 1983, 'Understanding Advertisers', in Davis, Howard and Walton, Paul (eds) 1983, *Language, Image, Media*: Basil Blackwell

Neil, Andrew, 2004, 'Murdoch's Sun still shines on the PM ... for now', *The Scotsman*, 22/04/04

Newbold, Christopher, 1995, 'Approaches to Cultural Hegemony within Cultural Studies', in Boyd-Barrett and Newbold (eds) 1995, *Approaches to Media, A Reader*: Arnold

Ohlin Wright, Eric, 1985, *Classes*: Verso

Orwell, George, 1949, *1984*: Signet

Pearson, Geoffrey, 1983, *Hooligan: A History of Respectable Fears*: Macmillan

Peters, Bettina, 2001, 'Corporate Media Trends in Europe': CPBF

Pidgeon, Nick, Kasperson, Roger and Slovic, Paul (eds) 2003, *The Social Amplification of Risk*: Cambridge

Roper, Lynne, 2003, 'Disability in Media', *The Media Education Journal*, 2003

Ross, Kristina, 1995, 'Mass Culture', http://www.mediahistory.umn.edu/masscult.html

Scott, 1991, 'National Patterns of Corporate Power'

Severin, Werner and Tankard, James, 2001, 'Uses of Mass Media', in Severin, Werner and Tankard, James, (eds) 2001, *Communication Theories*, 5th edn: Longman

Shannon, Claude and Weaver, Warren, 1949, *The mathematical theory of communication*: University of Illinois Press

Simon, Adam and Xenos, Michael, 2000, 'Media Framing and Effective Public Deliberation', Communicating Civic Engagement conference paper

Sreberny, Annabelle, 1999, 'Include Me In: Rethinking Ethnicity on Television: Audience and Production Perspectives', Report for the Broadcasting Standards Commission in conjunction with the Independent Television Commission, December 1999

Staiger, Janet, 2000, *Perverse Spectators: The Practices of Film Reception*: New York University Press

Stam, Rob, 2000, *Film Theory*: Blackwell

The Henley Centre, http://www.henleycentre.com/

The Sun, 'Swan Bake: Asylum seekers steal the Queen's birds for barbecues', July 2003

Thomas, Graham, 2004, 'Political Communication: The Media and Politics', University of Reading, http://www.rdg.ac.uk/AcaDepts/lp/PolIR/Part1lectures/Part 1PDFs/Pt1BgovtLect8.pdf

Thompson, John, 1995, *The Media and Modernity*: Polity Press

Trowler, Paul, 1988, *Investigating the Media*: Collins Educational

Tuomi, Ilkka, 2002, 'The Blog and the Public Sphere: Future Media and Emerging Research Topics', European Joint Research Centre, http://www.jrc.es/~tuomiil/articles/TheBlogAndThePublicSphere.pdf

Wilkins, Leslie, 1963, *Social Deviance*: Tavistock

Willis, John, 1999, 'Over 50 and overlooked', *The Guardian*, 5 July 1999

Wren-Lewis, Justin, 1983, 'The Encoding/Decoding Model: Criticisms and Redevelopments for Research on Decoding', *Media Culture & Society*, 5

Yarde, Rosalind, 2001, 'Demons of the day', *The Guardian*, 12 November 2001

Chapter 4: Education

Abbot, Pamela and Wallace, Claire, 1996, *Feminist Perspectives*: Routledge

Abbs, Peter, 1994, *The Educational Imperative: a defence of Socratic and Aesthetic Learning*: Falmer Press

Althusser, Louis, 1971, 'Ideology and Ideological State Apparatuses', in Althusser, Louis, *Lenin and Philosophy*: Monthly Review

Aymer, Cathy and Okitikpi, Toyin, 2001, 'Young Black men and the Connexions Service', DfES

Ball, Stephen, 1981, *Beachside Comprehensive*: Cambridge University Press

Ball, Stephen, 1995, 'Education, Majorism and the "Curriculum of the Dead"', in Murphy, P., Selinger, M., Bourne, J. and Briggs, M. (eds) 1995, *Subject Learning in the Primary Curriculum*: Routledge

Bamford, Caroline, 1989, 'Gender and Education in Scotland: A Review of Research', *Research in Education*, No. 42

Barber, Michael, 1994, 'Young People and Their Attitudes to School', Centre for Successful Schools. Keele University

Barrett, R., 1999, 'Middle schooling: A challenge for policy and curriculum', *Education Horizons*, 5(3)

Bates, Inge, Clarke, John, Cohen, P., Finn, Dan, Moore, Robert and Willis, Paul, 1984, *Schooling for the Dole*: Macmillan

Bates, Inge and Riseborough, George (eds), 1993, *Youth and Inequality*: Open University Press

Bell, Colin, Howieson, Cathy, King, Kenneth and Raffe, David, 1988, 'TVEI and the Education–Industry Relationship', *Research in Education*, No. 40

Bell, David, 2004, 'Change and continuity: reflections on the Butler Act', Speech to commemorate the 60th anniversary of the 1944 Education Act, House of Commons, April 2004, http://www.ofsted.gov.uk/publications/index.cfm?fuseaction=pubs.displayfile&id=3615&type=doc

Bennett, Andy, 1999, 'Subcultures or Neo-tribes?', *Sociology*, Vol. 33, No. 3 (BSA Publications Ltd)

Bernstein, Basil, 1971, 'On the Classification and Framing of Educational Knowledge', in Young, M.F.D. (ed), 1971, *Knowledge and Control*: Collier-Macmillan

Beron, Kurt and Farkas, George, 2001, 'Family Linguistic Culture and Social Reproduction: Verbal skill from parent to child in the preschool and school', Population Association of America conference paper

Best, Lesley, 1992, 'Analysis of sex-roles in pre-school books', *Sociology Review*

Burn, Elizabeth, 2001, 'Do Boys need Male Primary Teachers as Positive Role Models?', British Educational Research Association Annual Conference

Bhattacharyya, Gargi, Ison, Liz and Blair, Maud, 2003, 'Minority Ethnic attainment and Participation in Education and Training', DfES Research Paper

Bourdieu, Pierre, 1986, 'The Forms of Capital', in Richardson, John (ed) 1986, *Handbook of Theory and Research for the Sociology of Education*, Greenwood Press

Cabinet Office Performance and Innovation Unit, 2002

Cano-Garcia, Francisco and Hughes, Elaine, 2000, 'Learning and thinking styles: An analysis of their interrelationship and influence on academic achievement', *Educational Psychology*, 20

Carter, Rebecca and Wojtkiewicz, Roger, 2000, 'Parental involvement with adolescents' education: Do daughters or sons get more help?', *Adolescence*, 35(137)

2001 Census, HMSO, published 2003

Cohen, Albert, 1955, *Delinquent Boys: The Culture of the Gang*: The Free Press

Cohen, Michele, 1998, 'A Habit of Healthy Idleness: Boys' underachievement in historical perspective', in Epstein, D., et al. (eds) 1998, *Failing Boys? Issues in Gender and Achievement*: Open University Press

Collins, Clinton, 1993, *Truth as a communicative virtue in a postmodern age: From Dewey to Rorty*: Philosophy of Education Society

Cooper, M. and McDonald, G., 2001, 'Why Science: Why Stirling? Variety in Chemistry Teaching', Lancaster University

Coward, Rosalind, 1999, *Sacred Cows: Is Feminism Relevant to the New Millennium?*: HarperCollins

Crespi, Isabella, 2003, 'Gender socialization within the family: a study on adolescents and their parents in Great Britain', Centre of Studies and Research on Family

Croxford, Linda, 2000, 'Inequality in Attainment at Age 16: A "Home International" Comparison', Economic and Social Research Council

Davies, Peter and Adnett, Nick, 1999, 'Market Forces and School Curriculum', Staffordshire University, Business School Working Paper, No. 991

Davis, Kingsley and Moore, Wilbert, 1945, 'Some Principles of Stratification', *American Sociological Review*, Vol 10, No. 2

Deem, Rosemary, 1980, *Schooling for Women's Work*: Routledge & Kogan Paul

Delamont, Sara, 1999, 'Gender and the Discourse of Derision', in Wragg, Ted (ed) 1999, *Research Papers in Education Policy and Practice 14*, Routledge

Demack, Sean, Drew, David and Grimsley, Mike, 1998, 'Myths about underachievement: Gender, Ethnic and Social Class. Differences in GCSE results 1988–93', British Educational Research Association Annual Conference paper

Desforges, Charles, 2003, 'The impact of parental involvement, parental support and family education on pupil achievement and adjustment: A literature Review', DfES Research Report 433

Dewey, John, 1916, *Democracy and Education*: The Macmillan Company

DfES Education and Training Statistics in the United Kingdom, 2002 Edition

Eichler, Margrit, 1980, *The Double Standard*: Croom Helm

Elkind, David, 1998, *Schooling the Post-Modern Child*: Waldorf Education Research Institute

Epstein, Debbie, Elwood, Jannette, Hey, Valerie and Maw, Janet (eds), 1998, 'Failing Boys? Issues in gender and achievement': OUP

Fielding, Michael, 2001, 'Students as Radical Agents of Change', *Journal of Educational Change*, vol. 2, no. 3

Figueroa, Peter, 1991, *Education and the Social Construction of Race*: Routledge

Finn, Dan, 1988, 'Education for Jobs: The route to YTS', *Sociology Review*, Vol. 4.1: Philip Allan Publishers

Foster, Peter, Gomm, Roger and Hammersley, Martyn, 1996, *Constructing Educational Inequality*: Falmer Press

Foucault, Michel, 1971, *L'order du discourse*: Gallimard

  1977, *Discipline and Punish*: Penguin

Francis, Becky, 2000, *Boys, girls and Achievement: Addressing the Classroom Issues*: Routledge

Gardner, Howard, 1993, *Frames of Mind: The theory of multiple intelligences*: Fontana

Gardner, Howard, 2003, *Multiple Intelligences after Twenty Years*: American Educational Research Association

Gewirtz, Sharon, 1998, 'Can All Schools Be Successful? An Exploration of the Determinants of School "Success"': *Oxford Review of Education*, 24(4)

Gillborn, David, 1992, 'Citizenship, "Race" and the Hidden Curriculum', *International Studies in Sociology of Education*, Vol. 2 No. 1

Gillborn, David and Gipps, Caroline, 1996, 'Recent Research on the Achievements of Ethnic Minority Pupils', HMSO: Office for Standards in Education

Gillborn, David, 2002, *Education and Institutional Racism*: Institute of Education

Giroux, Henry, 1994, *Slacking Off: Border Youth and Postmodern Education*: Routledge

Goodwin, Robin, 1997, 'Social Support and Marital Well-being in an Asian Community', Joseph Rowntree Foundation

Gorard, Stephen, Rees, Gareth and Salisbury, Jane, 2001, 'Investigating the patterns of differential attainment of boys and girls at school', *British Educational Research Journal*, 27

Gordon, Tuula, 1996, 'Citizenship, difference and marginality in schools – spatial and embodied aspects of gender construction', in Murphy and Gipps (eds) 1996, *Equity in the Classroom: towards effective pedagogy for girls and boys*: Falmer Press

Gramsci, Antonio, 1971, *Selections from the Prison Notebooks*, edited and translated by Quintin Hoare & Goffrey Nowell Smith: Lawrence and Wishart

Griffin, Christine, 1986, 'It's different for girls: the use of qualitative methods in a study of young women's lives', in Beloff, H. (ed) 1986, *Getting into Life*: Methuen

Hallam, Sue, Ireson, Judy and Hurley, Clare, 2001, *Ability Grouping in the Secondary School: Practices and Consequences*: Institute of Education

Hanafin, Joan and Lynch, Anne, 2002, 'Peripheral Voices: parental involvement, social class, and educational disadvantage', *British Journal of sociology of Education*, Vol. 23, No. 1

Hanafin, Joan, Shevlin, Michael and Flynn, Marie, 2002, 'Responding to Student Diversity: lessons from the margin', *Pedagogy, Culture & Society*, 2002, vol. 10, no. 3

Harlen, Wynne and Malcolm, Heather, 1999, 'Setting and Streaming: A Research Review', Scottish Council for Research in Education, http://www.scre.ac.uk/pdf/setting.pdf

Hattersley and French, 2004, 'Wrong Division', *The Guardian*, 3 February 2004

Heath, Sue, 1997, *Preparation for Life? Vocationalism and the Equal Opportunities Challenge*: Ashgate

Hill, Dave and Cole, Mike (eds) 2001, *Schooling and Equality: Fact, Concept and Policy*: Kogan Page

Hinsliff, Gaby, 2002, '"Scared" white teachers fail black students', *The Observer*, 6 January 2002

Howe, Neil and Strauss, William, 2000, *Millennials Rising*: Vintage

Jackson, Brian and Marsden, Dennis, 1970, *Education and the Working Class*: Penguin

Jackson, Phillip, 1968, *Life In Classrooms*: Holt, Rinehart and Winston

Johnson, Martin, 1999, *Failing School, Failing City: The Reality of Inner City Education*: Jon Carpenter Publishing

Jones, Susan and Myhill, Debra, 2003, 'Seeing things differently: Teachers' constructions of underachievement

Keddie, Nell, 1971, 'Classroom Knowledge', in Young, M.F.D. (ed) 1971, *Knowledge and Control*: Collier-Macmillan

Kerr, David, Lines, Anne, Blenkinshop, Sarah and Schagen, Ian, 2002, 'England's results from the IEA International Citizenship Education Study: What citizenship and education mean to 14 year olds', DfES

Lacey, Colin, 1985, 'Professionalism or Bureaucracy?', in *The Quality Controllers: Bedford Way Papers*, No. 22, 1985

Lea, John, 2001, 'Post-compulsory education in context' in John Lea, Dennis Hayes, Andy Armitage, Laurie Lomas and Sharon Markless, 2003, *Working in post-compulsory education*: Open University Press

Lees, Sue, 1993, *Sugar and Spice: Sexuality and Adolescent Girls*: Harmondsworth

Lupton, Ruth, 2003, *Do poor neighbourhoods mean poor schools*: LSE

Lydon, N., 1996, 'Man Trouble', *The Guardian*, 14 May

Mac an Ghaill, Mairtin, 1991, 'Black voluntary schools: the invisible private sector', in Walford, G., 1994, *Choice and Equity in Education*: Cassell

Mac an Ghaill, Mairtin, 1994, *The Making of Men*: Open University Press

Mac an Ghaill, Mairtin, 1996, 'What about the Boys? Schooling, Class and Crisis Masculinity', *Sociological Review*, 44(3)

MacBeth, John, Kirwan, Tony, Myers, Kate, McCall, Jim, Smith, Iain and McKay, Euan, with Sharp, Caroline, Bhabra, Sunita, Weindling, Dick and Pocklington, Keith, 2001, 'The Impact of Study Support', DfES

MacBeth, John, Kirwan, Tony, Myers, Kate, McCall, Jim, Smith, Iain and McKay, Euan, 2001, 'The Impact of Study Support', Department for Education and Skills Research Report no 273, http://www.gtce.org.uk/pdfs/supportstudy.pdf

MacDonald, Robert and Marsh, Jane, 2003, 'Disconnected Youth? Young People, the 'Underclass' and Social Exclusion', http://www.tsa.uk.com/YCSC/RB/TSA_RB_06.pdf, in MacDonald, Robert, 2005, *Disconnected Youth? Growing Up In Poor Britain*: Palgrave Macmillan

MacDonald, Robert and Marsh, Jane, 2005, 'Disconnected Youth? Young People, the 'Underclass' and Social Exclusion', http://www.tsa.uk.com/YCSC/RB/TSA_RB_06.pdf, in MacDonald, Robert, 2005, *Disconnected Youth? Growing Up In Poor Britain*: Palgrave Macmillan

Mackenzie, Jeannie, 1997, 'It's a Man's Job … Class and Gender in School Work-Experience Programmes', Scottish Council for Research in Education

Malcolm, Heather, Wilson, Valerie, Davidson, Julia and Kirk, Susan, 2003, 'Absence from School: A study of its causes and effects in seven LEAs', The SCRE Centre, University of Glasgow

McCulloch, Gary, 1988, 'The Norwood Report and the secondary school curriculum', *History of Education Review*, 17(2)

Merton, Robert K., 1938, 'Social Structure and Anomie', *American Sociological Review*, 3

Mirza, Heidi, 1992, *Young, Female and Black*: Routledge

Mirza, Heidi, 2001, 'Black supplementary schools: Spaces of radical blackness', in Majors, R. (ed), 2001, *Educating our Black Children: New directions and radical approaches*: Routledge

Mortimore, Peter, 1998, *The Road to Improvement: Reflections on School Effectiveness*: Swets and Zeitlinger

Mortimore, Peter, Sammons, Pam, Stoll, Louise, Lewis, David and Ecob, Russell, 1988, *School Matters: The Junior Years*: Open Books

Moser, Sir Claus (chairman), 1999, 'Improving Literacy and Numeracy: A Fresh Start, The Report of the Working Group', Department for Education and Employment

Murphy, Patricia and Elwood, Jannette, 1998, 'Gendered experiences, Choices and Achievement – Exploring the links', *International Journal of Inclusive Education*, Vol. 1, No. 2

Murray, Charles and Phillips, Melanie, 2001, *The British Underclass 1990–2000*: Institute for the Study of Civil Society

Murray, Lee, 2002, 'How far did the 1998 Education Act usher a radically new direction in British Education?'

Nash, Robin, 1972, *Keeping In With Teacher*

National Literacy Trust, 2004, 'The structure of the literacy hour', http://www.literacytrust.org.uk/Database/Primary/lithour.html#structure

Nehaul, Kamala, 1999, 'Parenting, Schooling and Caribbean Heritage Pupils', *International Studies in Sociology of Education*, Vol. 9, No. 1

Norman, Fiona, Turner, Sue, Granados Johnson, Jackie, Schwarcz, Helen, Green, Helen and Harris, Jill, (Anti-Sexist Working Party), 1988, 'Look, Jane, Look, in Woodhead, Martin and McGrath, Andrea (eds) 1988, *Family, School and Society*: OUP

Northern Ireland Department of Education's Research Briefing, 1997, A review of research evidence on the apparent underachievement of boys

Padfield, Pauline, 1997, '"Skivers", "saddos" and "swots": pupils' perceptions of the process of labelling those "in trouble" at school', Scottish Educational Research Association Annual Conference paper

Paechter, Carrie, 1999, *Issues in the study of curriculum in the context of lifelong learning*: Open University Press

Parsons, Talcott, 1959, 'The School Class as a Social System', *Harvard Educational Review*

Pateman, Trevor, 1993, 'Education and Social Theory', in Outhwaite, W. and Bottomore, T. (eds), 1993, *The Blackwell Dictionary of Twentieth-Century Social Thought*: Blackwell

Platten, Jon, 1999, 'Raising boys' achievement', *Curriculum*, 20(1)

Poulantzas, Nicos, 1975, *Classes in Contemporary Capitalism*: New Left Books

Power, Sally, Edwards, Tony, Whitty, Geoff and Wigfall, Valerie, 1996, *Education and the Middle Class*, Open University Press

Provenzo, Eugene, 2002, *Teaching, Learning, and Schooling: A 21st Century Perspective*: Allyn and Bacon

Queensland Department of Education and the Arts, 2002, 'Boys Gender and Schooling'

Qureshi, Tarek, Berridge, David and Wenman, Helen, 2000, 'Where to turn? Family support for South Asian communities', Joseph Rowntree Foundation

Reay, Diane, 2000, 'A useful extension of Bourdieu's conceptual framework?: Emotional capital as a way of understanding mothers' involvement in children's schooling', *Sociological Review*, Vol. 48, No. 4

Reay, Diane, 2001, '"Spice Girls", "Nice Girls", "Girlies", and "Tomboys": discourses, girls' cultures and femininities in the primary classroom', *Gender and Education*, Vol. 13, No. 2

Reiss, Michael, 2001, *Representing Science*: Institute of Education

Robinson, Peter, 1998, *Literacy, Numeracy and Economic Performance*: London School of Economics

Roger, Angela and Duffield, Jill, 2000, 'Factors Underlying Persistent Gendered Option Choices in School Science and Technology in Scotland': *Gender and Education*, 12(3)

Royal Society for the Arts, 1998, 'Opening Minds'

Runnymeade Briefing Paper, 2003, 'Black and Minority Ethnic issues in teaching and learning'

Rutherford, Jonathan, 2003, *Education as a Frontier Market*: Institute of Education

Sammons, Pam, Smees, Rebecca, Taggart Brenda, Sylva, Kathy, Melhuish, Edward, Siraj-Blatchford, Iram and Elliot, Karen, 2002, 'Special educational needs across the pre-school period', Institute of Education

Scottish Executive National Statistics, 2004

Seaton, Andrew, 2002, 'Reforming the hidden curriculum: The Key Abilities Model and four curricular forms', *Curriculum Perspectives*

Sharpe, Sue, 1976, *Just Like a Girl: how girls learn to be women*: Penguin

Shields, Rob (ed), 1992, *Lifestyle Shopping: the Subject of Consumption*: Routledge

Sizer, Theodore, 1984, *Horace's Compromise: The Dilemma of the American High School*: Houghton Mifflin

Skelton, Alan, 1997, 'Studying hidden curricula: developing a perspective in the light of postmodern insights', *Curriculum Studies*, 5

Smith, Emma, 2003, 'Failing Boys and Moral Panics: Perspectives on the Underachievement Debate', *British Journal of Educational Studies*, vol. 51, no. 3

Spender, Dale, 1982, *Invisible Women*: Writers and Readers

Spendlove, David, 2001, 'Sometimes it's hard to be a boy', *TES*, 8 June 2001

Stanworth, Michelle, 1981, *Gender and Schooling*: Hutchinson, 1981

Strand, Steve, 2002, 'Pupil Mobility, Attainment and Progress During Key Stage 1: a study in cautious interpretation', *British Educational Research Journal*, vol. 28, no. 1

Summerfield, Carol and Babb, Penny (eds) 2004, *Social Trends* 34

Swann, Joan, 1992, *Girls, Boys, and Language*: Blackwell

Taylor, Mark, 2004, 'Generation Next Comes to College: Meeting the Postmodern Student', Arkansas State University, www.lib.wayne.edu/org/accreditation/examples/documents/generationnext/pdf

Taylor, Paul, Walton, Ian and Young, Jock, 1973, *The New Criminology*: Routledge

The Runnymeade Trust, 1997, 'Black and Ethnic Minority Young People and Educational Disadvantage'

Thomas, Sally and Mortimore, Peter, 1996, 'Comparisons of value added models for secondary school effectiveness', *Research Papers in Education*, 11(1)

Treneman, Anne, 1998, 'Will the boys who can't read still end up as the men on top?', *The Independent*, 5 January 1998

Troyna, Barry and Hatcher, Richard, 1992, *Racism in children's lives: a study of mainly-white primary schools*: Routledge

Urry, John, Abercrombie, Nick and Turner, Bryan, 1975, *The Dominant Ideology Thesis*: Routledge

Walker, Barbara, 1996, 'Understanding boys' sexual health education and its implications for attitude change', Economic and Social Research Council

Ward, Lucy, 2004, 'Pupils at good schools "gain 18 months"', *The Guardian*, 9 August 2004

Warrington, Molly and Younger, Michael, 2000, 'The Other Side of the Gender Gap', *Gender and Education*, Vol. 12, No. 4

White, John, 2003, *Rethinking the School Curriculum*, Institute of Education

White, John and Bramall, Steve (eds) 2000, *Why Learn Maths?*: Institute of Education

Wilkin, Anne, Kinder, Kay, White, Richard, Atkinson, Mary and Doherty, Paul, 2002, 'Towards the development of extended schools', National Foundation for Educational Research

Wilkinson, Helen, 1994, *No Turning Back: Generations and the Genderquake*: Demos

Williamson, Judith, 2003, 'Going Private', *The Guardian*, 17 October 2003

Willis, Paul, 1977, *Learning To Labour: How Working class kids get working class jobs*: Saxon House

Willis, Phil, 2003, 'Social class "defines school achievement"', *The Guardian*, 23 April 2003

Woods, Pete, 1976, 'The myth of subject choice', *British Journal of Sociology*, 27

Wright, Cecile, 1992, *Race Relations in the Primary School*: David Fulton Publishers

Yang, Shen-Keng, 2002, 'Educational research for the dialectic process of globalization and localization', European Conference on Educational Research paper, http://www.leeds.ac.uk/educol/documents/00002276/htm

Yeomans, David, 1996, 'Constructing vocational education: from TVEI to GNVQ'

Young, M.F.D. (ed) 1971, *Knowledge and Control*: Collier-Macmillan

Young, Michael, 1999, 'Knowledge, learning and the curriculum of the future', *British Educational Research Journal*, 25

Chapter 5: Wealth and Poverty

Ashford, Nigel, 1993, 'Dismantling the Welfare State: Why and How', *Libertarian Alliance, Political Notes*, No. 86

Atkinson, John, 1987, 'Flexibility or fragmentation? The United Kingdom labour market in the eighties': *Labour and Society*, Vol. 12, No. 1

Atkinson, Rowland and Flint, John, 2004, 'The Fortress UK? Gated Communities, The Spaital Revolt of the Elites and Time-Space Trajectories of Segregation', CNR Paper 17

Bane, Mary Jo and Ellwood, David, 1994, *Welfare Realities: From Rhetoric to Reform*: Harvard University Press

Bardasi, Elena and Jenkins, Stephen P., 2002, *Income in later life: Work history matters*: Policy Press

Bennett, Fran with Roberts, Moraene, 2004, 'From input to influence: Participatory approaches to research and inquiry into poverty', Joseph Rowntree Foundation

Bennett, Katy, Beynon, Huw and Hudson, Ray, 2000, *Dealing with the consequences of industrial decline*: Policy Press

Berthoud, Richard, 1998, 'Incomes of Ethnic Minorities', Institute for Social and Economic Research

Beresford, Bryony, 1994, 'Positively Parents: Caring for a Severely Disabled Child', Social Policy Research Unit

Beresford, Peter, Green, David, Lister, Ruth and Woodard, Kirsty, 1999, 'Poverty First Hand: Poor people speak for themselves', Child Poverty Action Group

Berthoud, Richard, 1998, 'Incomes of Ethnic Minorities', Institute for Social and Economic Research

Bhattacharyya, Dilip, 1999, 'On the Economic Rationale of Estimating the Hidden Economy', Economic Journal

Bolender, Ron, 2004, 'Robert King Merton', www.bolender.com

Bradshaw, Jonathan, Finch, Naomi, Kemp, Peter, Mayhew, Emese and Williams, Julie, 2003, 'Gender and poverty in Britain', EOC Briefing Paper

Brown, Murial and Madge, Nicola, 1982, *Despite the Welfare State*: Heinemann

Bruegal, Irene, 1979, 'Women as a Reserve Army of Labour: A Note on Recent British Experience', *Feminist Review*, no. 3

Buck, Nick, 1992, 'Labour market inactivity and polarisation'; Heath, Anthony, 1992, 'The attitudes of the underclass', in Smith, David (ed), 1992, *Understanding the Underclass: PSI*

Buckingham, Alan, 1996, 'The Underclass: A Statistical Update'; Walker, Alan, 1996, 'Blaming the Victims', in Lister, Ruther (ed) 1996, *Charles Murray and the Underclass: The Developing Debate*', Institute of Economic Affairs

Burchardt, Tania, 1999, 'Boundaries between public and private welfare: a typology and map of services', Centre for Analysis of Social Exclusion

Burchardt, Tania, Le Grand, Julian and Piachaud, David, 1999, 'Social Exclusion in Britain 1991–1995', *Social Policy and Administration*, Vol. 33, No. 3

Chambers, Robert,, 1995, 'Poverty and livelihoods: whose reality counts?', *Environment and Urbanization*, Vol. 7, No. 1

Craig, Gary, Taylor, Marilyn, Szanto, Clare and Wilkinson, Mick, 1999, 'Developing local compacts: Relationships between local public sector bodes and the voluntary and community sectors', York Publishing Services

Datamonitor, 2004, http://www.datamonitor.com

Davies, Rick, 1997, 'Beyond Wealth Ranking: The Democratic Definition and Measurement of Poverty', Overseas Development Institute

Dean, Hartley and Taylor-Gooby, Peter, 1992, *Dependency Culture: The explosion of a myth*: Harvester Wheatsheaf

Denny, Charlotte, 2003, 'Profits of loss', *The Guardian*, 25 November 2003

Department for Work and Pensions, 1999, 'Opportunity for All. Tackling Poverty and Social Exclusion'

Department for Work and Pensions, 2002, 'Low Income Dynamics'

Department for Work and Pensions, 2002, 'Households Below Average Income 1994/95 to 2000/01', Corporate Document Services

Department for Work and Pensions, 2004, 'Opportunity for All'

Department of Social Security', 2001, 'Households Below Average Income 1994/95 to 1999/2000', Corporate Document Services

Dolado, Juan, Felgueroso, Florentino and Jimeno, Juan, 2003, 'Where Do Women Work?: Analysing Patterns in Occupational Segregation by Gender', *Annales d'Economie et de Statistique*

Drever, Frances, Fisher, Katie, Brown, Joanna and Clark, Jenny, 2000, 'Social Inequalities', Office for National Statistics

Duffy, Katherine, 1995, 'Social Exclusion and Human Dignity in Europe', Office for Public Management, http://www.opm.co.uk/download/papers/Soc-ex3.pdf

Durlauf, Steven, 2002, 'Groups, Social Influences and Inequality: A Memberships Theory Perspective on Poverty Traps', Santa Fe Institute Working Paper

Edwards, Christine and Robinson, Olive, 2003, 'A "New" Business Case For Flexible Working?: The Case of Part-Time Qualified Nurses in the UK National Health Service', UK Government Women and Equality Unit, http://www.womenandequalityunit.gov.uk/research/gender_research_forum/8_nov_02.htm

Equal Opportunities Commission, 2003, 'Pensions – why do women face poverty in old age?'

Equal Opportunities Commission, 2004, 'Response to the Low Pay Commission's Consultation on Extending the National Minimum Wage to 16 and 17 year olds'

Evans, Martin and Noble, Michael with Wright, Gemma, Smith, George, Lloyd, Myfanwy and Dibben, Chris, 2002, *Geographic patterns of change of Income Support and income-based Jobseeker's Allowance claimants in England between 1995 and 2000*: Policy Press

Evans, Terry, 2002, 'Part-time Research Students: The "Reserve Army" of Research Students for Universities', in Kiley, M. and Mullins, G. (eds) *Quality in Postgraduate Research: Integrating perspectives*: University of Canberra

Falkingham, Jane, 2000, 'A Profile of Poverty in Tajikistan', Centre for Analysis of Social Exclusion

Field, Frank, 1995, *Making Welfare Work*

    1989, *Losing Out: the Emergence of Britain's Underclass*: Blackwell

Gans, Herbert, 1971, 'The Uses of Poverty: The Poor Pay All', *Social Policy*, July/August 1971

Giddens, Anthony, 1998, *The Third Way: The Renewal of Social Democracy*: Polity

Giddens, Anthony, 2000, *The Third Way and its Critics*: Polity

Glendinning, Caroline and Millar, Jane, 1999, 'Poverty: the forgotten Englishwoman', in MacLean, M. and Groves, D. (eds) 1999, *Women's Issues in Social Policy* Routledge

Goode, William, 1964, *The Family*: Prentice-Hall

Gordon, Dave, Nandy, Shailen, Pantazis, Christina, Pemberton, Simon and Townsend, Peter, 2003, *Child Poverty in the Developing World*: Policy Press

Green, Anne, 1994, 'The Geography of Poverty and Wealth', Institute for Employment Research

Gregg, Paul, Harkness, Susan and Machin, Stephen, 1999, 'Child development and family income', Joseph Rowntree Foundation

Guo, Guang and Harris, Kathleen, 2000, 'The mechanisms mediating the effects of poverty on children's intellectual development: Demography

Hakim, Catherine, 1981, 'Job segregation: trends in the 1970s', *Employment Gazette*

Harris, Neville, 1998, 'The Welfare State, Social Security and Social Citizenship Rights', in Harris, Neville (ed) 2000, *Social Security Law in Context*: OUP

Hills, John, 1998, 'Income and Wealth: the latest evidence', Joseph Rowntree Foundation

Horowitz, Carl, 1995, 'On the Dole in United Kingdom', *Investor's Business Daily*, 30 August 1995

Howard, Marilyn and Garnham, Alison, 2001, 'Poverty: the Facts', Child Poverty Action Group

Howarth, Catherine, Kenway, Peter, Palmer, Guy and Street, Cathy, 1998, 'Monitoring poverty and social exclusion: Labour's inheritance', Joseph Rowntree Foundation

Hunter, Laurie, McGregor, Allan, MacInnes, John and Sproull, Allan, 1993, 'The "flexible firm": strategy and segmentation', *British Journal of Industrial Relations*, Vol. 31, No. 3

Institute of Development Studies, 2001, 'Briefing paper on the "Feminisation of Poverty"'

Institute of Fiscal Studies, 2000, 'Inequality, income distribution and living standards'

Jarvis, Sarah and Jenkins, Stephen, 1997, 'Changing places: income mobility and poverty dynamics', Working Paper 96–19

1997, 'Low income dynamics in 1990s Britain', *Fiscal Studies*, vol. 81(2)

1998, 'How much income mobility is there in Britain?', *Economic Journal*

Jencks, Chris, 1989, 'What is the Underclass – and is it Growing?', *Focus*, Vol. 12, No. 1

Jenkins, Stephen, 1990, 'The Distribution of Wealth: Measurement and Models', *Journal of Economic Surveys*, Vol. 4 No. 4

Kumar, Sarabajaya and Nunan, Kevin, 2002, *A lighter touch: an Evaluation of the Governance Project*, York Publishing Services

Le Grand, Julian and Winter, David, 1987, 'The Middle Classes and the Welfare State', *Journal of Public Policy*, 6:4

Levitas, Ruth, 1999, 'Defining and Measuring Social Exclusion: A Critical Overview of Current Proposals', *Radical Statistics*, 71, http://www.radstats.org.uk/no071/article2.htm

Lewis, Oscar, 1959, *Five Families: Mexican case studies in the culture of poverty*: Basic Books

1961, *The Children of Sanchez: The autobiography of a Mexican family* Random House

1968, 'The Culture of Poverty', in Moynihan, Daniel, (ed) 1968, *On Understanding Poverty*: Basic Books

Lister, Ruth, 1996, 'In Search of the "Underclass"' in Ruth Lister (ed), 1996, *Charles Murray and the Underclass: The Developing Debate*: Institute of Economic Affairs

Lister, Ruth, 2000, 'To Rio via the Third Way: New Labour's 'welfare' reform agenda', Political Economy Research Centre paper, University of Sheffield

Lunn, Simon, 2003, 'Low-Income Dynamics 1991–2001', Department for Work and Pensions

Mack, Joanna and Lansley, Stewart, 1984, *Poor Britain*: Allen and Unwin

Marquand, David, 1998, *The Blair Paradox*: Prospect

Marshall, Mike, 1999, 'Flexibility and Part-Time Work: An Assessment', University of East London

Marsland, David, 1996, *Welfare or Welfare State? Contradiction and dilemmas in social policy*: Macmillan

Maxwell, Simon, 1999, 'The Meaning and Measurement of Poverty', Overseas Development Institute

McClements, L., 1977, 'Equivalence Scales for Children', *Journal of Public Economics*, Vol. 8

McIntosh, Mary, 1998, 'Dependency Culture? Welfare, Woman and Work', Radical Philosophy

McLennan, David, 2004, English Indices of Deprivation', Social Disadvantage Research Centre, University of Oxford

Mellor, Julie, 2000, 'Are men the new victims of discrimination?', EOC

2003, 'EOC calls for an end to poverty pay for homeworkers', EOC

Moore, Karen, 2001, 'Frameworks for understanding the intergenerational transmission of poverty and well-being in developing countries', Chronic Poverty Research Centre, Working Paper 8, http://www.chronicpoverty.org/pdfs/igt.pdf

Moore, Robert, 2001, 'The Underclass', in Burgess, R. and Murcott, A. (eds) 2001, *Developments in Sociology*: Prentice Hall

Murray, Charles, 1984, *Losing ground: American social policy, 1950–1980*: Basic Books

Murray, Charles, 1999, *The Underclass Revisited*: AEI Press

Niyazi, Filiz, 1996, 'A Route to Opportunity – Younger People; Older People; Unemployed People; Black People and Disabled People', National Centre for Volunteering

O'Brien, Mike and Briar, Celia (eds) 1997, 'Beyond Poverty: Citizenship, Welfare and Well-Being in the 21st Century', Conference Proceedings, Peoples Centre, Auckland 1997

Office for National Statistics Composition, *Social Trends 31*, 2001

Oppenheim, Carey, 1998, 'The Post Conservative Welfare State: a framework for the decade ahead', Institute of Public Policy Research

Oxfam, 2003, 'The facts about poverty in the UK', http://www.oxfamgb.org/ukpp/index.htm

Oxfam Briefing Paper (with the National Group on Homeworking and the TUC), 2003, 'Made at Home'

Palmer, Guy, North, Jenny, Carr, Jane and Kenway, Peter, 2003, 'Monitoring poverty and social exclusion', Joseph Rowntree Foundation

Platt, Lucinda and Noble, Michael, 1999, 'Race, place and poverty: Ethnic groups and low income distributions', Joseph Rowntree Foundation

Ramsay, Maureen, 1994, 'Political Theory and Feminist Research', Centre for Interdisciplinary Gender Studies, University of Leeds, e-paper 8

Rigg, John and Sefton, Tom, 2004, 'Income Dynamics and the Life Cycle', Centre for Analysis of Social Exclusion

Rownlinson, Karen, Whyley, Claire and Warren, Tracey, 1999, 'Wealth in Britain: A lifecycle perspective', Policy Studies Institute for the Joseph Rowntree Foundation

Rowntree, Seebohm, 1901, *Poverty, A Study of Town Life*: Macmillan

Ruggeri Laderchi Caterina, Saith, Ruhi and Stewart, Frances, 2003, 'Everyone agrees we need poverty reduction, but not what this means: does this matter?: id21, http://www.id21.org/society/s5bcl1g1.html

Ruspini, Elisabetta, 2000, 'Engendering poverty research. How to go beyond the feminization of poverty', *Radical Statistics*, 75

Rutter, Michael and Madge, Nicola, 1976, *Cycles of Disadvantage*: Heinemann

Saunders, Peter, 1990, *Social Class and Stratification*: Routledge and Kagan Paul

Sen, Amartya, 1999, *Development as Freedom*: Oxford University Press

Shephard, Andrew, 2004, 'Poverty and Inequality in Great Britain', Institute for Fiscal Studies

Shropshire, Jules and Middleton, Sue, 1999, 'Small expectations: Learning to be poor', Joseph Rowntree Foundation

Sikka, Prem, 2003, 'Socialism in reverse', *The Guardian*, 15 April 2003

Sloan, Tod, 2003, 'Globalization, Poverty and Social Justice', in Nelson, G. and Prilleltensky, I. (eds) 2003, *Community psychology: In pursuit of well-being and liberation*: Macmillan

Sommerlad, Hilary and Sanderson, Peter, 1997, 'The Legal Labour Market and the Training Needs of Women Returners in the United Kingdom', *Journal of Vocational Education and Training*, Vol. 49, No. 1

Sowell, Thomas, 2002, *A Conflict of Visions: Ideological Origins of Political Struggles*: Basic Books

Spicker, Paul, 2002, 'Poverty and the Welfare State: Dispelling the myths', Catalyst

Startup, Tom, 2002, 'Poor Measures', Social Market Foundation

Sunday Times Rich List, 2004, http://www.timesonline.co.uk/section/0,,2108,00.html

Sweetman, Caroline, 1998, 'How Does Poverty Relate to Gender Inequality?': Oxfam

Szreter, Simon, 2002, 'A New Political Economy for New Labour: the Importance of Social Capital', Political Economy Research Centre Paper 15, University of Sheffield

Taylor, Marilyn, Langan, Joan and Hoggett, Paul, 1994, 'Independent organisations in community care', School for Policy Studies, University of Bristol

Tony Blair, 1999, Speech to the Institute for Public Policy Research, London, 14 January 1999

Townsend, Ian, 2004, 'Income, Wealth & Inequality', UK Government Research Paper 04/70

Townsend, Peter, 1954, 'Measuring Poverty', *British Journal of Sociology*

Townsend, Peter and Abel-Smith, Brian, 1965, *The Poor and the Poorest: A New Analysis of the Ministry of Labour's Family Expenditure Surveys of 1953–4 and 1960*: Bell

Townsend, Peter, 1974, 'The Cycle of Deprivation: the History of a Confused Thesis', National study conference paper, University of Manchester

Townsend, Peter, 1979, *Poverty in the UK*: Allen Lane and Penguin

Trujillo, Monica, Ordóñez, Amado and Hernández, Carlos, 1997, 'Risk-Mapping and Local Capacities: Lessons from Mexico and Central America', Oxfam working papers online, http://www.oxfam.org.uk/what_we_do/resources/wp_mexca_risk.htm

TUC Women's Conference Report, 2003, 'Beating the gender poverty trap'

Ulster Centre for Property and Planning, 1998, 'Accessing private finance: the availability and effectiveness of private finance in urban regeneration'

Veenhoven, Ruut, 1992, Social Equality and State-Welfare-Effort, 'Towards the Good Society: Applying the Social Sciences' Conference Paper, Rotterdam, http://www.2.eur.nl/fsw/research/veenhoven/Pub1990s/92a-full.pdf

Walters, Sally, 2002, 'Female Part-time Workers' Attitudes to Trade Unions in Britain', *British Journal of Industrial Relations*, 40

Welshman, John, 2002, 'The cycle of deprivation and the concept of the underclass', *Benefits*, vol. 10, no. 3

Wilson, Judy, 1994, *Two Worlds: self help groups and professionals*: Venture Press

Wise, Sarah, 2004, 'Multiple Segregation in Nursing Careers: Causes and Consequences', Employment Research Institute, http://www.napier.ac.uk/depts/eri/Downloads/EdinburghConf04.pdf

Wrigley, Christopher, 2004, *Welfare State*

Chapter 6: Methods

Ackroyd, Stephen and Hughes, John, 1992, *Data Collection in Context*, 2nd edn, Longman (1st published 1981)

Aries, Philip, 1962, *Centuries of Childhood*: Vintage Books

Bakewell, Oliver, 1999, 'Can we ever rely on refugee statistics?', *Radical Statistics*, 72

Boyle, Jimmy, 1977, *A Sense of Freedom*: Pan Books

Charlton, Tony, Panting, Charlotte and Hannan, Andrew, 2002, 'Mobile Phone Usage and Abusage By Year 6 Pupils in Gloucestershire Primary Schools', *Emotional & Behavioural Difficulties Online*, Vol. 7, No. 3

Cohen, Stan and Taylor, Laurie, 1977, 'Talking About Prison Blues', in Bell, Colin and Newby, Howard, (eds) 1977, *Doing Sociological Research*: George Allen and Unwin

Diken, Bülent and Bagge Laustsen, Carsten, 2004, 'Sea, Sun, Sex ... and Biopolitics', Department of Sociology, Lancaster University, http://www.comp.lancs.ac.uk/sociology/papers/diken-laustsen-sea-sun-sex-biopolitics.pdf

Durkheim, Emile, 1897, *Suicide: A Study In Sociology*: Routledge & Kagan Paul

Glasgow Media Group, 1982, *Really Bad News*: Writers and Readers

1985, *War ad Peace News*: OUP

Goffman, Erving, 1959, *The Presentation of Self in Everyday Life*: Doubleday

Goffman, Erving, 1968, *Asylums*: Penguin (first published 1961, Doubleday Anchor)

Goldthorpe, John, Lockwood, David, Bechhofer, Frank and Platt, Jennifer, 1968, *The Affluent Worker in the Class Structure*: Cambridge University Press

Hogenraad, Robert, 2003, 'The Words that Predict the Outbreak of Wars', *Empirical Studies of the Arts*, 21

Jessop, Bob, 2003, 'Governance and meta-governance. On Reflexivity, Requisite Variety, and Requisite Irony', Department of Sociology, Lancaster University, http://www.comp.lancs.ac.uk/sociology/papers/jessop-governance-and-metagovernance/pdf

Kessler, Matthew, 2000, 'Sponsorship, Self-Perception and Small-business Performance', *American Association of Behavioral and Social Sciences*, Volume 3

Lofland and Stark, 1965, 'Becoming a world-saver: A theory of conversion to a deviant perspective', *American Sociological Review*, 30

Mead, George Herbert, 1934, *Mind, Self and Society*: University of Chicago Press

Meehan, Diana, 1983, *Ladies of the Evening: Women Characters of Prime-Time Television*, Metuchen, NJ: Scarecrow

Miller, Mark and Riechert, Bonnie, 1994, 'Identifying Themes via Concept Mapping: A New Method of Content Analysis', Association for Education in Journalism and Mass Communication Annual Meeting, 1994

Mueller, Karl, 1999, 'Twelve Propositions Concerning the Year 2000 Problem', Institute for Advanced Studies

Parker, Howard, 1974, *View from the Boys: Sociology of Downtown Adolescents*: David and C

Philo, Greg and Berry, Mike, 2004, *Bad New from Israel*: Pluto Press

Polsky, Ned, 1971, *Hustlers, Beats and Others*: Harmondsworth

Ray, John, 1987, 'A Participant Observation Study of Social Class Among Environmentalists', *Journal of Social Psychology*

Southerton, Dale, Deem, Rosemary, Shove, Elizabeth and Warde, Alan, 1998, 'Home from home?: a research note on Recreational Caravanning', Department of Sociology, Lancaster University, http://www.comp.lancs.ac.uk/sociology/papers/southerton-et-al-home-from-home.pdf

Tomlinson, Peter, 1989, 'Having it both ways: hierarchical focusing as research interview method', *British Educational Research Journal*, Vol. 15, No. 2

Townsend, Peter, 1979, *Poverty in the United Kingdom*: Allen Lane and Penguin

Whyte, William, 1943, *Street Corner Society*: University of Chicago

Yule, C., 1986, 'Why are parents so tough on children?', *New Society*, September 1986

Zweig, Ferdynand, 1961, *The Worker in an Affluent Society*: Heinemann

Name Index

Subject Index